The Psychology of Prosocial Behavior

Group Processes, Intergroup Relations, and Helping

Edited by
Stefan Stürmer and Mark Snyder

**Library Commons
Georgian College
One Georgian Drive
Barrie, ON
L4M 3X9**

A John Wiley & Sons, Ltd., Publication

This edition first published 2010
© 2010 Blackwell Publishing Ltd.

Blackwell Publishing was acquired by John Wiley & Sons in February 2007. Blackwell's publishing program has been merged with Wiley's global Scientific, Technical, and Medical business to form Wiley-Blackwell.

Registered Office
John Wiley & Sons Ltd, The Atrium, Southern Gate, Chichester, West Sussex, PO19 8SQ, United Kingdom

Editorial Offices
350 Main Street, Malden, MA 02148-5020, USA
9600 Garsington Road, Oxford, OX4 2DQ, UK
The Atrium, Southern Gate, Chichester, West Sussex, PO19 8SQ, UK

For details of our global editorial offices, for customer services, and for information about how to apply for permission to reuse the copyright material in this book please see our website at www.wiley.com/wiley-blackwell.

The right of Stefan Stürmer and Mark Snyder to be identified as the author of the editorial material in this work has been asserted in accordance with the Copyright, Designs and Patents Act 1988.

All rights reserved. No part of this publication may be reproduced, stored in a retrieval system, or transmitted, in any form or by any means, electronic, mechanical, photocopying, recording or otherwise, except as permitted by the UK Copyright, Designs and Patents Act 1988, without the prior permission of the publisher.

Wiley also publishes its books in a variety of electronic formats. Some content that appears in print may not be available in electronic books.

Designations used by companies to distinguish their products are often claimed as trademarks. All brand names and product names used in this book are trade names, service marks, trademarks or registered trademarks of their respective owners. The publisher is not associated with any product or vendor mentioned in this book. This publication is designed to provide accurate and authoritative information in regard to the subject matter covered. It is sold on the understanding that the publisher is not engaged in rendering professional services. If professional advice or other expert assistance is required, the services of a competent professional should be sought.

Library of Congress Cataloging-in-Publication Data

The psychology of prosocial behavior : group processes, intergroup relations, and helping / edited by Stefan Stürmer and Mark Snyder.
    p. cm.
  Includes bibliographical references and index.
  ISBN 978-1-4051-7881-5 (hardcover : alk. paper) — ISBN 978-1-4051-7880-8 (pbk. : alk. paper) 1. Social groups. 2. Social psychology. 3. Interpersonal relations. 4. Helping behavior. I. Stürmer, Stefan. II. Snyder, Mark.
  HM716
  155.2'32—dc22
                                                                           2009012049

A catalogue record for this book is available from the British Library.

Set in 10.5/12.5pt Galliard by Graphicraft Limited, Hong Kong
Printed and bound in Malaysia by Vivar Printing Sdn Bhd

1 2010

Contents

List of Contributors ix
Acknowledgments xi

Introduction

The Psychological Study of Group Processes and Intergroup Relations in Prosocial Behavior: Past, Present, Future 3
Stefan Stürmer and Mark Snyder

Part I: Motivations for Helping In-Group and Out-Group Members

1 The Tribal Instinct Hypothesis: Evolution and the Social Psychology of Intergroup Relations 13
  Mark van Vugt and Justin H. Park

2 Helping "Us" versus "Them": Towards a Group-Level Theory of Helping and Altruism Within and Across Group Boundaries 33
  Stefan Stürmer and Mark Snyder

3 Stigmas and Prosocial Behavior: Are People Reluctant to Help Stigmatized Persons? 59
  John B. Pryor, Glenn D. Reeder, Andrew E. Monroe, and Arati Patel

4 The Strategic Side of Out-Group Helping 81
  Esther van Leeuwen and Susanne Täuber

Part II: Consequences of Giving or Receiving Help in the Context of Groups

5 Discrimination Against Out-Group Members in Helping Situations   103
Donald A. Saucier, Jessica L. McManus, and Sara J. Smith

6 Receiving Help: Consequences for the Recipient   121
Samer Halabi and Arie Nadler

7 Turning to Others in Times of Change: Social Identity and Coping with Stress   139
Jolanda Jetten, S. Alexander Haslam, Aarti Iyer, and Catherine Haslam

8 Volunteering Across the Life Span: Doing Well by Doing Good   157
Jane Allyn Piliavin

Part III: Intervention Strategies: Targeting Individuals, Groups, and Organizations

9 Perspective Taking and Intergroup Helping   175
Mark H. Davis and Angela T. Maitner

10 Recategorization and Prosocial Behavior: Common In-Group Identity and a Dual Identity   191
John F. Dovidio, Samuel L. Gaertner, Nurit Shnabel, Tamar Saguy, and James Johnson

11 Groups, Identities, and Bystander Behavior: How Group Processes Can Be Used to Promote Helping   209
Mark Levine and Clare Cassidy

12 Influences of Psychological Sense of Community on Voluntary Helping and Prosocial Action   223
Allen M. Omoto and Mark Snyder

13 Empowering the Volunteer Organization: What Volunteer Organizations Can Do to Recruit, Content, and Retain Volunteers   245
Naomi Ellemers and Edwin J. Boezeman

Part IV: The Broader Picture: Political and Societal Implications

14 Interpersonal and Intergroup Helping Relations as
   Power Relations: Implications for Real-World Helping   269
   Arie Nadler

15 Beyond Help: A Social Psychology of Collective
   Solidarity and Social Cohesion   289
   Stephen Reicher and S. Alexander Haslam

16 Cross-Group Helping: Perspectives on Why and
   Why Not   311
   Stephen C. Wright and Norann T. Richard

17 Helping Disadvantaged Out-Groups Challenge Unjust
   Inequality: The Role of Group-Based Emotions   337
   Aarti Iyer and Colin Wayne Leach

Bibliography   355
Author Index   417
Subject Index   434

Contributors

Edwin J. Boezeman
Leiden University, eboezeman@fsw.leidenuniv.nl
Clare Cassidy (deceased)
formerly University of St. Andrews
Mark H. Davis
Eckerd College, davismh@eckerd.edu
John F. Dovidio
Yale University, john.dovidio@yale.edu
Naomi Ellemers
Leiden University, ellemers@FSW.leidenuniv.nl
Samuel L. Gaertner
University of Delaware, gaertner@udel.edu
Samer Halabi
Zefat Academic College, samerh@zefat.ac.il
Catherine Haslam
University of Exeter, c.haslam@exeter.ac.uk
S. Alexander Haslam
University of Exeter, a.haslam@exeter.ac.uk
Aarti Iyer
University of Queensland, a.iyer@uq.edu.au
Jolanda Jetten
University of Queensland/University of Exeter, j.jetten@psy.uq.edu.au
James Johnson
University of North Carolina – Wilmington, johnsonj@uncw.edu
Colin Wayne Leach
University of Connecticut, colin.leach@uconn.edu
Mark Levine
Lancaster University, m.levine@lancaster.ac.uk
Jessica L. McManus
Kansas State University, jlm7@ksu.edu

Angela T. Maitner
University of Kent, a.maitner@kent.ac.uk
Andrew E. Monroe
University of Oregon, amonroe1@uoregon.edu
Arie Nadler
Tel Aviv University, arie@freud.tau.ac.il
Allen M. Omoto
Claremont Graduate University, allen.omoto@cgu.edu
Justin H. Park
University of Groningen, The Netherlands, j.h.park@rug.nl
Arati Patel
Illinois State University, ampatel@ilstu.edu
Jane Allyn Piliavin
Professor Emerita, University of Wisconsin-Madison, jpiliavi@ssc.wisc.edu
John B. Pryor
Illinois State University, pryor@ilstu.edu
Glenn D. Reeder
Illinois State University, gdreeder@ilstu.edu
Stephen Reicher
University of St. Andrews, s.reicher@st-and.ac.uk
Norann T. Richard
Simon Fraser University, nrichard@sfu.ca
Tamar Saguy
University of Connecticut, tamar.saguy@uconn.edu
Donald A. Saucier
Kansas State University, saucier@ksu.edu
Nurit Shnabel
Yale University, nurit.shnabel@yale.edu
Sara J. Smith
Kansas State University, sjs6655@ksu.edu
Mark Snyder
University of Minnesota, msnyder@umn.edu
Stefan Stürmer
FernUniversität Hagen, stefan.stuermer@FernUni-Hagen.de
Susanne Täuber
Friedrich-Schiller-University Jena, susanne.taeuber@uni-jena.de
Esther van Leeuwen
Free University Amsterdam, eac.van.leeuwen@psy.vu.nl
Mark van Vugt
University of Kent at Canterbury, m.van-Vugt@kent.ac.uk
Stephen C. Wright
Simon Fraser University, scwright@sfu.ca

Acknowledgments

The idea for this book project was formed during a European Association of Experimental Social Psychology (EAESP) small group meeting on "Group-level perspectives on giving and receiving help," held in October of 2006 in Mühbrook, Germany (with funding by the EAESP and the Deutsche Forschungsgemeinschaft [DFG]). The meeting not only provided several of the contributors to this volume, it also offered opportunities to meet and discuss key issues examined in this book and to explore the relations between and among their theoretical perspectives and programs of empirical research.

Resource support for this project came from several sources. Grants from the DFG to Stefan Stürmer supported the collaborative research with Mark Snyder that is reported in this book, as well as work on this volume. Mark Snyder's research (including work on this book) was supported by grants from the National Institute of Mental Health and the National Science Foundation.

We also want to acknowledge the support of the people at Wiley-Blackwell. Specifically, we thank Chris Cardone, who commissioned the book, as well as Kelly Basner and Constance Adler, who were admirably enthusiastic and supportive. Last but not least, we would like to acknowledge the help of the people involved in multiple ways in the editorial work. Therefore we thank: Birgit Awizio, Markus Barth, Alexander N. Bodansky, Jana Schneider, and Nicole Voß at the Social Psychology Department of the FernUniversität in Hagen and Stefan Stürmer's partner, Markus Lang. Our gratitude extends to all who served in different ways to make this book become reality.

Clare Cassidy, the co-author of Chapter 11, died unexpectedly before publication of this book. We will miss her as a distinguished colleague and friend.

Introduction

The Psychological Study of Group Processes and Intergroup Relations in Prosocial Behavior
Past, Present, Future

Stefan Stürmer and Mark Snyder

The scientific study of prosocial behavior – including phenomena such as altruism, helping, and social solidarity – has a long and rich history in theorizing and research on human sociality. For many scholars, this topic has been particularly fascinating because it ultimately engages fundamental questions about human nature, questions that have been the subject of intense philosophical debate for centuries (Are humans good or bad? Are they selfless or selfish by nature? Are they capable of pure altruism or is their motivation always egoistic?). Another enduring source of fascination has been its immediate linkage to practical social goals and societal problems. If we better understand the determinants of prosocial actions (when and why it occurs, and does not occur), then, ideally, we might be able to devise interventions to foster a wide range of beneficial behaviors that are vital for the well-being of individuals and society at large.

The contributions to this volume represent current directions in psychological theorizing and research on prosocial behavior, with a particular emphasis on helping in the context of social groups and larger organizations. The focus on the role of group processes in prosocial behavior reflects relatively recent developments in the social and behavioral sciences. This volume, therefore, presents a new and distinctive perspective that differs in many respects from that found in contemporary treatments of prosocial behavior. Historically, theory and research on prosocial behavior, on the one hand, and research on group processes and intergroup relations, on the other, have developed in relative isolation from each other. This state of affairs has been particularly true for social psychological research on helping behavior. Starting in the mid-1960s, with investigations of helping (and the lack thereof) in emergency situations, the traditional focus of social psychological research has been on *interpersonal* contexts of helping (i.e., contexts in which people perceive and react to one another as individuals rather than as members of groups). Thus, in this tradition, explanations of why people help one another and why they fail to help one another typically have revolved around the role of *individual* dispositions (e.g., Davis, 1983a), *individual* decision-making processes (e.g., Piliavin, Piliavin, & Rodin, 1975), *individual* emotions (e.g., Batson, Duncan, Ackerman, Buckley, & Birch, 1981), and the norms that govern the interpersonal relationship between *individual* helpers and *individual* recipients of help (e.g., Clark, Mills, & Corcoran, 1989). In fact, only recently have researchers started to systematically investigate how such individual-level processes are affected through processes at the *group* level by such factors as salient in-group/out-group distinctions and the nature of the intergroup relations (for notable "early" exceptions, see Hornstein, 1976; Dovidio, Piliavin, Gaertner, Schroeder, & Clark, 1991; also Turner, Hogg, Oakes, Reicher, & Wetherell, 1987, especially pp. 50–51 and 65).

Research on group processes and intergroup relations, on the other hand, has traditionally focused on behaviors classified as negative or even antisocial (e.g., intergroup discrimination, conflict, and aggression), while the role of group processes in forms of prosocial behavior, specifically helping, has been relatively neglected (see, for instance, Hogg & Abrams, 2001). Within this tradition, when helping behavior has been studied in the domain of intergroup research, it typically has been in the context of intergroup discrimination, with helping behavior serving simply as an outcome variable to demonstrate the negative effects of in-group/out-group categorizations on social behavior (i.e., discrimination against out-group members in helping). Thus, critically important phenomena of helping across group boundaries or solidarity between groups have been largely ignored.

In recent years, however, several factors have led these two social psychological research traditions to "talk" to each other, to build bridges between their perspectives, and to generate integrated perspectives on helping and prosocial action. A particularly relevant contributor to this integration, we suggest, has been provided by an increasing interest in the study of volunteerism as a form of prosocial behavior. Although, from the mid-1960s to the 1980s, research focused on studying spontaneous or short-term acts of helping (e.g., giving aid to a victim of an accident), in the 1980s and 1990s researchers moved on to investigating more planned and sustained forms of helping behavior, such as volunteerism and related behaviors (e.g., volunteering to serve as a "buddy" or companion for a person affected by HIV/AIDS). Volunteerism represents a distinct form of planned helping, involving people devoting substantial amounts of time and energy to helping others, others with whom they have no bonds or connections that would obligate them to help (e.g., marital bond or blood relationship), and doing so on a sustained and ongoing basis. One intriguing feature of volunteerism is that it can be conceived, at one and the same time, as an *individual* as well as a *collective* phenomenon, because it involves the activities of individual volunteers *and* the collective context in which these efforts occur. Much volunteerism occurs in the context of formal organizations involving cooperation among volunteers in order to realize desired personal and collective goals. Further, and from a more structural perspective, volunteerism is often embedded in social and political contexts structured by social group memberships (e.g., volunteerism in the context of social movements aiming to improve the situations of marginalized or stigmatized social groups). Volunteerism thus offered not only an intriguing opportunity to study the role of group and intergroup processes in helping, but it also provided a meaningful context to link the study of helping to the more general issue of the study of collective behavior – a traditional topic of the intergroup literature – thereby facilitating theoretical and empirical integration (e.g., van Vugt, Snyder, Tyler & Biel, 2000; Simon, 2004).

Meanwhile, a growing body of theoretical and empirical work has emerged, using theories of intragroup and intergroup behavior to explain prosocial behavior in the contexts of groups or large organizations. This development offers several important promises, we believe. First, it has the potential for linking research on prosocial behavior at different levels of social scientific inquiry, specifically, the "macro" (or social structural) level and the "micro" (or individual) level. As one example to illustrate this potential, from a social structural or macro-level perspective, the emergence of community-based volunteerism in the US and Western European countries as a response to the AIDS crisis in the early 1980s has been traced back to the failure of the traditional health care system to adequately deal with a lethal and sexually transmitted virus infection affecting primarily members of stigmatized and marginalized social groups and communities (e.g., Rosenbrock & Wright, 2000). However, to understand how such social structural, political, or epidemiological factors translate into concrete experiences, motives, and actions at the individual level (empathy, solidarity, volunteerism and the like), analyses at the "meso" (or group) level are also required. Structural factors or events hardly ever affect individuals' reactions directly or unfiltered. Instead they derive their subjective meaning through social and political framing processes in the context of the groups or communities to which individuals belong (e.g., Gamson, 1992). Hence, to understand who engages in AIDS volunteerism and why (and who does not and why they do not), we need to take individuals' group memberships into account, and examine how AIDS and related structural issues are framed in the in-groups or community relevant to individuals in a given context (e.g., as a common threat to the in-group requiring intragroup solidarity or as a deserved punishment for sexually deviant out-groupers). More generally, many researchers have also acknowledged that the study of prosocial behavior may significantly benefit from a multi-level perspective and increased interdisciplinary exchange (e.g., Penner, Dovidio, Piliavin, & Schroeder, 2005). We thus strongly believe that the articulations and elaborations of group-level perspectives presented by the contributors to this volume have the potential to make a significant contribution to this effort.

Another relevant contribution of the study of group processes in prosocial behavior, we believe, is of an even more general nature. The current and dominant view in the social and human sciences (including psychology) is that hostile competition is a main driving force in intergroup behavior. Therefore, acts of prosocial behavior or helping across group boundaries have commonly been conceived as rather exotic exceptions. Meanwhile, however, there is increasing evidence – some of which is reviewed in this volume – suggesting that people do, in fact, help out-group members much more often than this perspective would lead one to expect. Allport (1954a) has proposed that even though humans may be thought of as "tribal" – and there do seem to be plenty of reasons to assume that they are – their preferential attachment to the in-group does not necessarily imply negativity or hostility toward out-groups, but rather a general concern for the in-group's well-being (see also Brewer, 1999). In fact, it seems reasonable to argue that the long-term well-being of groups significantly and substantially depends on successful cooperation with other groups and mutual support (rather than conflict or discrimination). Research on intergroup prosocial behavior may thus prove fertile ground for a more general reconsideration of the forces governing intergroup relations, acknowledging that intergroup competition is but one of many means to foster the in-group's well-being, with intergroup helping and reciprocal cooperation being potent other ones. At a more general level, then, one important potential future outcome of this research, we suspect, could be a more nuanced picture of "our" social nature, specifically human sociality in the context of groups.

The major objective of this edited collection is to provide examinations of representative lines of theory and research on prosocial behavior as it occurs in the context of social groups. Specifically, we have sought to bring together contributions that focus on different levels of analyses (e.g., psychological processes versus intergroup relations), address the role of group memberships from different perspectives (the helper's versus the recipient's perspective), and study different forms of helping (e.g., helping in emergency situations versus volunteering). Moreover, since the study of group processes in prosocial behavior has both theoretical and practical potential, we have been especially keen to include not only contributions stimulating further theoretical development but also ones that deal explicitly with interventions designed to foster helping in the context of groups (and to improve its quality) in real-world settings.

We have organized the volume into four parts. The four chapters in Part I focus primarily on theoretical and empirical analyses addressing differences in the motivational foundations of helping in-group and out-group members. In the introductory chapter to this part, Mark van Vugt and Justin H. Park (Chapter 1) outline an evolutionary perspective on helping in the context of groups. A main hypothesis put forward by these authors is that evolution may have shaped a tendency in humans to preferentially help in-group over out-group members. Stefan Stürmer and Mark Snyder (Chapter 2) base their theoretical account on a theoretical and empirical integration of pertinent social psychological research on the effects of perceived (group-based) self-other similarity on people's motivation to help. Like Park and van Vugt, they conclude that there exist significant differences in helping "us" versus "them." Still, their analysis suggests that people help in-group members not necessarily more than they help out-group members; rather, it is the motivation for helping "us" versus helping "them" that is often of a fundamentally different nature. In Chapter 3, John B. Pryor, Glenn D. Reeder, Andrew E. Monroe, and Arati Patel offer a fine-grained analysis of the psychological and motivational processes potentially implicated in helping out-group members, specifically members of stigmatized out-groups. Their dual-process model of reactions to stigma assumes a temporal pattern of reactions to the stigmatized, such that stigma, at first, evokes a spontaneous and avoidance reaction, which may be eventually overridden through subsequent deliberate adjustments – providing the necessary preconditions for approach and prosocial action. While the preceding chapters focus primarily on the effects of in-group/out-group distinctions on individual-level processes (cognition, motivations, and potential evolutionary roots), the emphasis of Esther van Leeuwen and Susanne Täuber's contribution (Chapter 4) is on the in-group serving functions of out-group helping. A key hypothesis in their analysis is that in intergroup contexts of helping, it is no longer the individual's needs but the group's needs that motivate people to help, and they review the relevant lines of research supporting this contention.

The four chapters in Part II revolve more closely around the consequences of giving or receiving in the context of social groups and large organizations. The chapter by Donald A. Saucier, Jessica L. McManus, and Sara J. Smith (Chapter 5) focuses on the issue that has been in the forefront of much of the early research on the role of group memberships in helping: discrimination against out-group members in the interracial context of helping. A particular emphasis of their analysis is on the situational factors of the helping situations rendering interracial discrimination in helping more (or less) likely. Samer Halabi and Arie Nadler (Chapter 6) present a review of research on their model of intergroup helping as status relations, which makes specific predictions for low- and high-status group members concerning seeking, providing, and responding to intergroup help. A particularly unique contribution of their analysis is its focus on the recipients' perspectives and the psychological implications of receiving help from an out-group. Jolanda Jetten, S. Alexander Haslam, Aarti Iyer, and Catherine Haslam's contribution (Chapter 7) also focuses on the perspective of the person needing and seeking help. Specifically, it examines the role that in-group affiliations and social identity processes play in coping with stress in facilitating seeking, receiving, and accepting help from others, specifically fellow in-group members. Jane Allyn Piliavin's contribution (Chapter 8), finally, completes Part II by offering a theoretical and empirical analysis of the beneficial effects of continuous involvement in community-oriented volunteer activities for the actor. Her analysis suggests that volunteering across the life span improves psychological well-being because it leads people to develop other-oriented values, motives, and a sense of the self that lead them to believe that they matter to others in the social world.

The five chapters of Part III consider strategies to promote prosocial behavior by targeting the concerns of individuals, groups, or organizations. The contribution by Mark H. Davis and Angela T. Maitner (Chapter 9) is concerned with the prospects of perspective taking – one of the most prominent and potent strategies in promoting helping in interpersonal contexts – in facilitating helping in intergroup contexts. One particularly relevant contribution of their analysis with regard to designing practical interventions concerns the identification of potential pitfalls and boundaries in the application of perspective-taking interventions in intergroup settings. The contribution by John F. Dovidio, Samuel L. Gaertner, Nurit Shnabel, Tamar Saguy, and James Johnson (Chapter 10) elaborates on the strategy of recategorization – an intervention by which members of different groups are induced to conceive of themselves as a single superordinate group, rather than two separate groups. While this strategy has originally been developed as a means to reduce intergroup bias, there is increasing evidence that this strategy (and innovative variants) can also be effectively used to promote helping. The two subsequent contributions further elaborate on the role that the sense of common group memberships plays in promoting prosocial action. Mark Levine and Clare Cassidy's contribution (Chapter 11) examines the role of perceived shared group memberships in promoting helping in emergency situations. One particularly beautiful aspect of their analysis is that it revisits an issue providing the starting point for much of the social psychological research on helping (bystander intervention) and puts it in perspective with recent developments of the role of group processes in helping. Although bystander intervention concerns short-tem and single acts of helping, Allen M. Omoto and Mark Snyder's contribution (Chapter 12) is concerned with promoting sustained helping in terms of volunteerism. Specifically, building on a review of research on their model of the processes of volunteerism, these authors first investigate the influences of psychological sense of community on voluntary helping, then they outline promising strategies as to how helping can be promoted through bolstering people's sense of community. The chapter by Naomi Ellemers and Edwin J. Boezeman (Chapter 13) completes the third part by providing a unique theoretical and empirical analysis linking social psychological analyses of volunteerism to the organizational context in which volunteerism occurs. Their conceptual framework proposes that both status evaluations concerning the volunteer organization (pride) and evaluations concerning their own position within the organization (respect) contribute to psychological engagement and cooperation of individual volunteers. A particular strength of their framework is that it offers a number of scientifically informed suggestions as to what volunteer organizations can do to recruit, content, and retain volunteers.

The four chapters in the concluding part, Part IV, put the study of helping into a broader picture by linking it to more social structural or macro-level perspectives. One particularly unique contribution of this part is that it shows that helping and prosocial action are not only affected by macro-level or social structural factors, but that collective prosocial action also has the potential to feed back on social structure and contributing to societal change. A particular focus of the chapter by Arie Nadler (Chapter 14) is on the connection between intergroup helping, power relations, and social change. According to his analysis, and illustrated by several real-world examples, linking the study of helping to the structural dynamics characterizing intergroup relations is key for understanding both what types of help groups offer to other groups and the recipient group's reactions to these offers. The specific concern of Stephen Reicher and S. Alexander Haslam's contribution (Chapter 15) is with in-group helping (or more generally social solidarity). Their analysis suggests that helping (and social solidarity more generally) may best be understood as a crucial link in a cycle of processes that shape the creation and social cohesion of social groups in our society. The remaining two contributions both focus on helping and supporting disadvantaged out-groups challenging injust inequalities. A particularly fascinating and novel aspect of Stephen C. Wright and Norann T. Richard's contribution (Chapter 16) is their analysis of how and why specific social structural conditions, particularly tokenism, undermine advantaged group members' support for disadvantaged out-groups. Aarti Iyers and Colin Wayne Leach's contribution (Chapter 17) completes this section by linking the study of helping to research on collective action on behalf of disadvantaged out-groups. While many frameworks of participation in collective action fighting social injustice have focused on the processes motivating members of the disadvantaged groups, a specific and unique contribution of their analysis is that it provides intriguing insights as to when members of the advantaged groups will support members of disadvantaged groups.

Our main objective in this volume is to advance the emerging group-level perspective on prosocial behavior. The ultimate success of this effort will, of course, only become apparent with the passage of time. But, with that passage of time, we hope that the future will bring further investigations along the lines represented by the contributions to this volume (as well as in new and novel directions), and that these investigations will add further weight and substance to this endeavor. If they do, and we are both hopeful and optimistic that they will, then they will have the potential to contribute meaningfully to understanding the role of prosocial action in understanding human sociality.

Part I

Motivations for Helping In-Group and Out-Group Members

1

The Tribal Instinct Hypothesis
Evolution and the Social Psychology of Intergroup Relations

Mark van Vugt and Justin H. Park

Introduction

If a team of alien biologists were to collect data about different life forms on Planet Earth, what observations would they make about us humans? They would witness the cities, churches, schools, and hospitals that we have built and note that we are very good at helping fellow humans in sometimes very large groups. But they would also see evidence of our darker side: All around the world, they would witness incidents of violence and warfare between armies, militias, religious groups, and street gangs. Upon their return, the alien research team would likely conclude that humans are a tribal species, capable of both extreme benevolence toward members of in-groups and extreme hostility toward members of out-groups. On that basis, they would presumably put us in the same category as some colonial insect species – such as ants, bees, and termites – that also engage in tribal warfare (Wilson, 1975).

Luckily, we do not have to wait for invading aliens to make such astute observations about humans. Almost 150 years ago, Charles Darwin (1871), the father of the theory of evolution by natural selection, made the following statement in his book *Descent of Man*:

> A tribe including many members who, from possessing in a high degree the spirit of patriotism, fidelity, obedience, courage, and sympathy, were always ready to aid one another, and to sacrifice themselves for the common good, would be victorious over most other tribes; and this would be natural selection. (p. 132)

Darwin's observation had little impact on the social sciences for over a century. But this is changing. In this chapter, we analyze human intergroup psychology from an evolutionary perspective by conceptually integrating existing data and by offering several novel hypotheses.

Evolutionary Perspective on Intergroup Psychology

In recent years, an increasing number of scholars have adopted an evolutionary approach to integrate existing theories of human group psychology and deduce novel hypotheses (Buss, 2005; van Vugt & Schaller, 2008). This approach is based on the simple premise that the human mind – and its behavioral outcomes – has been shaped by biological evolution, just as human physiology has been shaped by evolution, and just as all other animal species have been shaped by evolution. Evolutionary social psychology, an interdisciplinary branch of evolutionary psychology, proposes that because other people constituted a prominent feature of human environments, the human mind has evolved to be a highly social mind, comprising many functional psychological adaptations specifically designed to solve problems associated with group life (Buss, 2005; Cosmides & Tooby, 1992).

Although sociality conferred considerable benefits to humans – leading to the evolution of a diverse array of psychological mechanisms that make cooperative group living possible – it also generated a large number of problems, both within and between groups. Different problems call for different, functionally specialized solutions, and several research programs have made significant strides by focusing on those functionally specialized adaptations (Schaller, Park, & Kenrick, 2007). Suggested instances of such adaptations include theory of mind, social intelligence, language, sex-specific mating tactics, altruism and aggression, and specific strategies for managing intergroup relations (Kenrick, Li, & Butner, 2003; Kurzban & Neuberg, 2005; van Vugt & Schaller, 2008). Individuals (or groups) with such capacities would have been better equipped to extract reproductive benefits from group living, allowing these psychological mechanisms to spread. As we emphasize in this chapter, many of these adaptations pertain to unique problems that emerged in intergroup contexts.

In the search for specific social adaptations, it is useful to make a distinction between *proximate* and *ultimate* explanations. Upon observation of some instance of intragroup or intergroup helping, one could ask at least two distinct kinds of questions. First, one could inquire into the specific aspects of individuals or contexts that lead people to display such tendencies; this is the strategy adopted by the vast majority of social psychologists – see, for instance, Batson's (e.g., Batson et al., 1997) and Cialdini's studies (Cialdini, Brown, Lewis, Luce, & Neuberg, 1997) regarding the relationship between empathy and helping, or research into the costs and benefits of different helping acts (Dovidio, Piliavin, Schroeder, & Penner, 2006). Second, one could inquire into the ultimate, evolutionary functions of such acts, by asking questions such as: In what ways did the capacity for empathy or helping increase the reproductive fitness of ancestral humans and groups? Or, what specific problems associated with survival and reproduction were solved by tendencies to empathize with and preferentially help in-group members over out-group members?

A related question concerns the *phylogenetic* origins of such tendencies – when did empathy and helping emerge in our species, and are there perhaps homologues in other species? Addressing such different kinds of questions is likely to produce a more complete picture of the phenomenon; however, it is important not to confuse these distinct levels of explanation (Buss, 2005; van Vugt & van Lange, 2006). For instance, explanations invoking evolutionary function do not imply that people are actually motivated – consciously or unconsciously – to behave in a manner that maximizes their reproductive fitness. The actual contents of people's motivations are empirical matters, to be illuminated by psychological research.

Below, we proceed by discussing some key findings from the literature on intergroup relations that lend credence to the idea that humans may have a specific tribal psychology. We then offer three possible evolutionary scenarios for the emergence of the peculiar tendencies that are suggested by the literature. The most likely scenario, in our view, is that intergroup psychology emerged as a specific adaptation to deal with the pressures of complex group life in ancestral environments, which were marked by coalitional conflict and cooperation – we refer to this as the *tribal instinct hypothesis*. We review pieces of evidence consistent with this hypothesis. This hypothesis further suggests that there may be sex differences in particular aspects of our evolved intergroup psychology, due to the differential selection pressures on men and women in ancestral environments – we refer to this as the *male warrior hypothesis*. We describe evidence for a specific male warrior psychology. Finally, we discuss implications of the tribal instinct hypothesis for managing intergroup relations in contemporary society.

Key Findings on Intergroup Relations

The social science literature on intergroup relations is substantial and diverse (Abrams & Hogg, 1990; Brewer & Brown, 1998; Hewstone, Rubin, & Willis, 2002). Amidst the mountain of data, there are several consistent empirical findings that paint a clear picture about human intergroup psychology. Here we present a non-exhaustive list of eight key findings than can be distilled from this literature.

First, humans make spontaneous in-group–out-group categorizations and preferentially help in-group members over out-group members. People sometimes perform quite costly helping acts on behalf of ethnic groups, religious groups, businesses, or states (van Vugt et al., 2000). In life-and-death situations, people are more likely to help kin than non-kin (Burnstein, Crandall, & Kitayama, 1994). Intergroup discrimination also occurs under minimal group conditions. Many experiments have shown that people preferentially give money or points to in-group rather than out-group members even when people are divided into groups based on a trivial criterion, such as preference for a particular painter (Brewer, 1979; Tajfel & Turner, 1986).

Second, humans appear to be unique in their capacity to form deep emotional attachments to large, anonymous groups that are merely symbolic in many ways. Once people identify with a particular group, such as a sports team, they feel good when it does well and suffer when it does poorly (Branscombe & Wann, 1991). Empathy, an emotional experience that often moves people to behave altruistically, does not move us as much when the potential recipients are members of out-groups (Stürmer, Snyder, Kropp, & Siem, 2006; Stürmer, Snyder, & Omoto, 2005). Humans also display loyalty to symbolic groups, sticking with them despite being better off by allying themselves with other groups (Abrams, Ando, & Hinkle, 1998; van Vugt & Hart, 2004; Zdaniuk & Levine, 2001).

Third, humans dislike group members who are disloyal. In opinion groups, members who hold different opinions than the majority are disliked and ignored – the *black sheep effect* (Marques, Yzerbyt, & Leyens, 1988). Members of task groups who are not pulling their weight for the group – the "bad apples" – are subject to scorn, exclusion, or punishment (Fehr & Gächter, 2002). One recent study found that group members spend a substantial portion of their experimental earnings (25 percent) to altruistically punish disloyal in-group members (van Vugt & Chang, 2008).

Fourth, humans have a tendency to derogate or even actively harm out-group members. For instance, people tend to think that out-group members are less moral and trustworthy than members of the in-group (Judd & Park, 1988). People denigrate members of out-groups when they get an opportunity and feel Schadenfreude when a rival group loses status (Leach, Spears, Branscombe, & Doosje, 2003); they even deny typical human emotions to out-groups (i.e., *infrahumanization*;

Leyens et al., 2001). Finally, people find it easy to morally justify aggressive actions against members of out-groups (Brewer & Brown, 1998).

Fifth, intergroup contexts are often automatically perceived as competitive and hostile. When individuals play prisoner's dilemma games against other individuals, they tend to make cooperative decisions; yet, when individuals form groups and play the same game against other groups – or play as leaders on behalf of their groups (Johnson et al., 2006) – they tend to make competitive decisions (a phenomenon known as the *group discontinuity effect*; e.g., Insko et al., 1994). Fear and distrust of out-groups seem to underlie the discontinuity effect (Insko, Schopler, Hoyle, Dardis, & Graetz, 1990). When groups (rather than individuals) work together, people almost automatically expect the other party to cheat, which then serves as justification for a pre-emptive strike (Johnson et al., 2006; cf. Snyder, 1984).

Sixth, intergroup helping sometimes happens. When individual members of in-groups and out-groups form a friendship or cooperative partnership, this can serve as a catalyst for reducing intergroup prejudice and hostility. A successful example is the jigsaw classroom in which schoolchildren of different ethnic groups are encouraged to work together on cooperative tasks, and, under the right conditions, these activities promote positive intergroup relations (Aronson, Blaney, Stephan, Sikes, & Snapp, 1978). Furthermore, high-status groups sometimes offer help to low-status groups to affirm their superior status – an example of *competitive altruism* (Hardy & van Vugt, 2006). However, as Nadler and Halabi (2006) have recently shown in the context of relations between Israeli Arabs and Israeli Jews, low-status group members (Arabs) might refuse help from high-status group members (Jews) if they believe that the status relations between the groups are either unstable or illegitimate.

Seventh, findings from the anthropological and sociological literatures indicate that managing intergroup relations is primarily a male activity. In most societies, intergroup aggression and warfare occur almost exclusively between coalitions of men in the form of armies, militias, street gangs, and hooligans (Goldstein, 2003); and most victims of intergroup conflict are men (Daly & Wilson, 1988; Keeley, 1996). However, men are also the primary peacemakers between groups (De Waal, 2006). Men (but not women) even suffer vicariously from intergroup competition. Dutch scientists observed a higher number of cardiovascular deaths among Dutch male soccer fans on the day that their national football team was eliminated on penalties from a major tournament (Witte, Bots, Hoes, & Grobbee, 2000).

Eighth, and finally, humans share some aspects of their tribal psychology with other species such as ants, termites, bees, and – our closest living genetic relatives – chimpanzees. Wild chimpanzees form coalitions to defend their territory against neighboring troops and are known to attack and kill "foreign" chimps, which is also limited to males (Goodall, 1986; Wrangham & Peterson, 1996). Furthermore, female chimps can safely migrate between communities, whereas male chimps are often injured or killed.

In sum, the social psychological literature suggests that humans have a pronounced tribal psychology, comprising tendencies to (a) quickly distinguish in-group from out-group members and prefer in-group members, (b) form deep affections toward in-groups, (c) dislike disloyal in-group members, (d) actively discriminate against out-group members, and (e) engage in competition with out-groups. Related literatures suggest that (f) acts of intergroup helping sometimes occur, (g) managing intergroup relations in the real world is primarily a male activity, and (h) some aspects of tribal psychology are observed in other social species, including non-human primates and social insects, suggesting a degree of continuity across species.

Evolutionary Origins of Tribal Instincts

Where does this tribal psychology come from? More to the point, were there adaptive problems that might have been solved, at least partly, by this tribal psychology? Evolutionary explanations fall into three broad categories (see also Kurzban & Neuberg, 2005).

The first explanation interprets our tribal psychology as a by-product of a domain-general capability for stimulus categorization. The influential social identity and self-categorization theories of intergroup relations are based on this assumption (Tajfel & Turner, 1986; Turner et al., 1987). Essentially, the argument is that intergroup processes result from our cognitive tendency to make sense of the world around us. Just as we distinguish between, say, plants and animals to categorize our physical world, we categorize people as belonging to the same versus different groups to make sense of our social world.

From an evolutionary perspective, it is quite unlikely that intergroup psychology is merely the product of a general cognitive categorization capacity, because different categories of people (e.g., in-group–out-group, male–female, kin–non-kin) pose specific adaptive threats and opportunities that are simply not encountered in other, non-social categorization contexts. Upon encountering a group of strangers, it would have been crucial for our ancestors to know – and know quickly – whether they were members of the same or a different clan, which would then elicit different adaptive responses (e.g., fight-or-flight). Inappropriate responses could have been lethal. Although domain-general cognitive processes – such as memory and recognition – no doubt play a role in shaping tribal psychology, such processes, by themselves, cannot produce the functional content of adaptive responses, including specific cognitions and emotions pertaining to the social category in question, and the specific behavioral response that is most likely to be adaptive.

The second explanation views our tribal psychology as a side effect of the extreme sociality of our species. The argument is that the innate tendency to help in-group members sometimes unintentionally produces conflict with other groups (Brewer, 1979; Brewer & Caporael, 2006). For instance, it would have made sense for ancestral humans to share food with members of the same band because of the likelihood of reciprocation (Trivers, 1971). Thus, a request for food coming from members of a different band should be met with some suspicion. Perhaps a problem with this second hypothesis is that it cannot explain why humans are sometimes openly hostile against members of out-groups rather than just mildly distrusting. One possibility, suggested by realistic group conflict theory (Campbell, 1965), is that intergroup contact is a relatively modern phenomenon. In ancestral environments, population densities would have been much lower and thus competition among groups might have been rare. In modern environments, resource competition between groups is more intense and so a certain suspicion against out-groups could easily turn into intergroup hostility. Indeed, intergroup discrimination is often stronger when there is resource competition (Brewer & Campbell, 1976). However, it is well documented that intergroup prejudice occurs in the absence of direct resource interdependence (Turner et al., 1987), suggesting that it is perhaps a more deeply ingrained response. Thus, it seems unlikely that our tribal psychology is a byproduct of a deep in-group commitment.

The third explanation is that humans have evolved specific adaptations for managing intergroup relations – specifically, evolved tendencies to form coalitional alliances in order to exploit and dominate other individuals or groups (Kurzban & Leary, 2001; Sidanius & Pratto, 1999; van Vugt, De Cremer, & Janssen, 2007). Indeed, intergroup conflict appears to have been quite common in ancestral environments (Alexander, 1987; Tooby & Cosmides, 1988). Fossil evidence of warfare dates back at least 200,000 years, and it is estimated that 20–30 percent of ancestral men died as a result of intergroup violence, constituting a strong selection pressure (Keeley, 1996). Comparable percentage is obtained in an anthropological study of the Yanomamo, a modern hunter-gatherer tribe in the Amazon basin (Chagnon, 1988). Alexander (1987) has argued that the biggest threat for early humans came from other groups, which instigated an evolutionary arms race to form ever larger coalitions, ultimately resulting in the constitution of modern states and nations. As Kurzban and Leary (2001) noted, "membership in a potentially cooperative group should activate a psychology of conflict and exploitation of out-group members – a feature that distinguishes adaptations for coalitional psychology from other cognitive systems" (p. 195).

We refer to this idea as the *tribal instinct hypothesis*. It assumes that our tribal psychology is the result of a long history of intense intergroup rivalry and competition, a history that shaped the way we think and behave in intergroup contexts.

According to the tribal instinct hypothesis, not all intergroup contexts are equal. Notwithstanding the fact that people spontaneously form in-group-out-group categories and favor in-groups in minimal group settings, powerful attachments to the in-group and malicious hostility toward out-groups are observed in only a limited subset of all possible in-group–out-group contexts. (Imagine all the possible in-group–out-group categories, such as male–female, old–young, rich–poor, tall–short, blonde–brunette, righty–lefty, innie–outie, ad infinitum.) Specifically, only out-groups that conform to a sort of "tribal out-group" status are targets of the various functional psychological and behavioral responses associated with the tribal instinct (Schaller, Park, & Faulkner, 2003). Because not all "groups" matter from a tribal perspective, humans should have evolved coalition-alliance detection mechanisms that are responsive to various indicators of tribal alliances – for example, "patterns of coordinated action, cooperation, and competition" (Kurzban, Tooby, & Cosmides, 2001). In modern environments, heuristic cues such as skin color, speech patterns, and linguistic labels – regardless of whether they actually signal tribal alliances – may activate these mechanisms (Kurzban et al., 2001; Schaller, Park, & Faulkner, 2003).

Specific Groups, Specific Responses

One implication of the tribal instinct hypothesis is that the contents of psychological responses to groups that fit a "tribal template" (ethnic groups, nations, sports teams) should be distinct from contents of psychological responses to other kinds of groups (genders, age groups, innies or outies). Because of the potential threat posed by tribal out-groups to one's well-being, humans likely evolved functional responses associated with the perception of such out-groups. What are these functional responses? "One answer is obvious: The construction of overly simplistic stereotypes and prejudicial beliefs describing out-group members as hostile, untrustworthy, and dangerous" (Schaller, 2003, p. 224). Moreover, evolutionary cost-benefit analysis suggests that walking around cloaked in constant fear and distrust is likely to have imposed substantial costs in addition to conferring benefits – thus, such responses are likely to have evolved to be functionally flexible, being activated when additional information (from the environment or from within) suggests heightened danger or probability of intergroup contact (Schaller, Park, & Faulkner, 2003).

One piece of information indicating heightened danger is the onset of darkness. A series of studies has examined the effects of ambient darkness on functionally specific psychological responses. In one study, Schaller, Park, and Faulkner (2003) asked Canadian students to rate the in-group (Canadians) and an out-group (Iraqis) on four trait dimensions, two of which were danger relevant (hostile, trustworthy) and two of which were not (ignorant, open-minded). The ratings were made in either a dark room or a well-lit room. By reverse-scoring the negative items and by subtracting ratings of the out-group from ratings of the in-group, a measure of in-group favoritism was created. The results showed that, for the traits unrelated to danger, in-group favoritism was identical across the dark and light conditions; however, for traits connoting danger, in-group favoritism was higher in the dark. Schaller, Park, and Mueller (2003) conducted similar studies employing computer-based reaction-time methodology. They found that students placed in a dark room were more likely to implicitly associate members of an out-group (Africans) with danger-relevant stereotypes (but not with danger-irrelevant negative stereo-types); moreover, these effects were specific to participants with chronically heightened beliefs about danger.

Another cue suggesting heightened threat posed by out-group members is being a member of a numerical minority. Schaller and Abeysinghe (2006) observed that there often are "double minority" situations in which all members of conflicting groups perceive themselves to be in the minority. For instance, Sinhalese outnumber Tamils within Sri Lanka but, within southern Asia more broadly, Tamils outnumber Sinhalese. In a study conducted in Sri Lanka, Schaller and Abeysinghe (2006) asked Sinhalese students to first complete a geography task that temporarily made salient either just the island nation of Sri Lanka (within which Sinhalese outnumber Tamils), or a broader region of south Asia (within which Sinhalese are outnumbered by Tamils), and then to complete measures of stereotypes and conflict-relevant attitudes. Results revealed that when participants focused on the broader geographical region (and thus perceived the in-group as the minority), they were more likely to ascribe danger-relevant stereotypes to Tamils.

More broadly, this sort of evolutionary functional approach has greatly aided inquiry into mental events by facilitating the articulation of more textured and fine-grained hypotheses (Schaller et al., 2007). Research has found, for instance, that it is not simply a general feeling of negativity that underlies all forms of prejudice; rather, different emotional-motivational states, activated within specific people and under specific circumstances, compel specific kinds of aversive reactions that underlie phenomena categorized as "prejudice" (Cottrell & Neuberg, 2005; Neuberg & Cottrell, 2006).

Sex Differences: The Male Warrior Hypothesis

Another implication of the tribal instinct hypothesis is that intergroup relations may have affected the evolved psychologies of men and women differently because of different selection pressures on the sexes throughout evolution. Due to differences in parental uncertainty and investment, men and women are likely to have evolved different mating strategies (Buss & Schmitt, 1993). Intergroup relations have historically involved males more than females (Keegan, 1994), which is true for humans as well as chimpanzees (Chagnon, 1988; De Waal, 2006; Goodall, 1986). As a consequence, not only are males more likely to be perceived as harmful out-group members, the functional psychological mechanisms that are activated in response to out-group threat may also be especially sensitized among males (Schaller & Neuberg, 2008). Furthermore, under some conditions, it could have been advantageous for ancestral men to participate in coalitional aggression and peacemaking afterwards as a means to increase their mating opportunities. For ancestral women, this strategy would have been less profitable given the risks to themselves and their potential offspring (Taylor, Klein, Lewis, & Gruenewald, 2000).

Although we describe the sex difference in greater detail below, it is worth noting some previous findings. In general, intergroup biases (racism, ethnocentrism) are more strongly held among men than women (e.g., Gerard & Hoyt, 1974; Sidanius & Pratto, 1999). The notorious Stanford Prison Experiment (Zimbardo, 1971), a demonstration of intergroup humiliation, sadism, and aggression, was conducted entirely with a male sample. In addition, in several of the studies reviewed above, men revealed greater sensitivity to the presence of vulnerability cues. For instance, in one study reported by Schaller, Park, and Mueller (2003), men showed a stronger interactive effect of chronic vulnerability and ambient darkness on the activation of danger-relevant stereotypes. There was a similar sex difference in the study that examined Canadians' beliefs about Iraqi untrustworthiness (Schaller, Park, & Faulkner, 2003).

In sum, we deem it rather unlikely that the rich and complex social psychology of intergroup relationships is just an accidental byproduct of a need for categorization or a desire for in-group sharing. In light of the historical and recent empirical evidence, it seems much more plausible that humans have evolved a specific psychology to deal with intergroup relations. We argue that this tribal instinct is perhaps more extreme among men than among women, with implications for present-day intergroup war and peace relations.

The Male Warrior Hypothesis

How and why did men evolve this pronounced tribal psychology? There are various selection models available to explain what we refer to as the *male warrior hypothesis* (van Vugt, De Cremer, & Janssen, 2007). We must draw a distinction between individual- and group-selection models. Tooby and Cosmides's (1988) risk contract theory of warfare is an example of the first. It posits that it may have been advantageous for men to participate in coalitional aggression, as it enabled them to increase access to reproductive resources such as new mates and territories. This propensity could only have evolved – like any physical or psychological trait – if the cumulative reproductive benefits outweighed the cumulative reproductive costs. Tooby and Cosmides (1988) specify a number of conditions that would favor selection of traits associated with intergroup aggression. First, members of coalitions must believe that their group will be victorious (cf. Johnson et al., 2006). Second, people who go into battle must be cloaked in what they referred to as a "veil of ignorance" about who will live or die. Third, the risk that each member takes and the importance of each member's contribution to the success must translate into corresponding benefits.

The latter condition is crucial. Participating in coalitional aggression is essentially a cooperative activity among several individuals. Like any form of cooperation, it is vulnerable to the free-rider problem. In order for this trait to spread, there must be mechanisms in place to reward heroism and bravery in intergroup conflict and punish cowardice. Such mechanisms were arguably in place in ancestral warfare and continue to be observed today (Keegan, 1994). For instance, war heroes receive compensating benefits for the risks they incurred on behalf of their group, such as a greater share of the loot or prestige in the form of honors and medals. These benefits are not available to those who stay home or desert — deserters often receive harsh punishment.

Whether or not this tribal psychology paid in terms of reproductive success — the currency in evolution — still remains to be seen, but there is supportive evidence. Brave male warriors in traditional hunter-gatherer tribes such as the Yanomamo have more wives and more children (Chagnon, 1988). In modern society, a study of male street gangs in the US suggested that their members had more sexual liaisons than controls (Palmer & Tilley, 1995). In some societies, military men also seem to have greater sex appeal (Schreiber & van Vugt, 2008). Thus, there may be reputational benefits associated with "warrior" behavior, which could make it a profitable strategy for men in particular (cf. competitive altruism; Hardy & van Vugt, 2006; van Vugt, Roberts, & Hardy, 2007).

Even without compensating individual benefits, a male tribal psychology could have evolved via group selection. Multi-level selection theory holds that if there is substantial variance in the reproductive success among groups, then group selection becomes a genuine possibility (Wilson, van Vugt & O'Gorman, 2008). As Darwin himself had noted (see his earlier quote), groups in which self-sacrifice is more common will fare better, especially if there is competition between groups. Although participating in intergroup competition may be personally risky because of the risk of death or injury, genes underlying propensity to serve the group can be propagated if group-serving acts contribute to group survival.

One condition conducive to group-level selection occurs when the genetic interests of group members are aligned, such as in kin groups. In kin-bonded groups, individuals benefit not just from their own reproductive success, but also from the success of their family members (inclusive fitness; Hamilton, 1964). Interestingly, ancestral human groups appear to have been based around male kin, with females moving between groups to avoid inbreeding (so-called patrilocal groups; De Waal, 2006). This could offer another explanation for why men rather than women would have been more concerned about intergroup conflict (i.e., intergroup conflict would have consequences for their inclusive fitness). The same patrilocal structure is incidentally found in chimpanzees. The males of these groups also engage in coalitional aggression (Goodall, 1986; Wrangham & Peterson, 1996).

These evolutionary models do not preclude the possibility that cultural processes may be at work that could exacerbate or undermine these stronger male tribal instincts (Richerson & Boyd, 2005). In fact, many of the evolved propensities are likely to be translated into actual psychological and behavioral tendencies by socialization practices and cultural norms. Thus, it is entirely possible that, in certain environments, it could be advantageous for societies to turn females into warriors. A modern-day example is Israel, a country at war with surrounding nations. To increase the size of its military, Israel has actively recruited female soldiers, and it currently has the most liberal rules regarding the participation of females in wars (Goldstein, 2003). We would expect the socialization practices among Israeli girls to match those of boys, potentially overriding any evolved psychological sex differences.

Evidence for Male Warrior Psychology

The tribal instinct hypothesis makes numerous predictions regarding the evolved psychological mechanisms underlying intergroup behavior in humans. These can be tested using the extant social psychological literature on intergroup relations. Some of these evolved psychological mechanisms will apply to both men and women to the same degree. In addition, the male warrior hypothesis implies specific sex differences in intergroup psychology. We focus on these in the remainder of this chapter. We review six domains of evidence, representing different aspects of warrior psychology in which we expect to find sex differences: (1) intergroup cognition and behavior, (2) ingroup helping, (3) attitudes toward bravery and heroism in intergroup encounters, (4) preference for between-group hierarchies, (5) social identity, and (6) development.

Intergroup Cognition and Behavior

Warfare, the pinnacle of human intergroup conflict, is an almost exclusively male activity (Keegan, 1994), and when we look elsewhere, most forms of organized violence occur between male coalitions. Does this extend to less violent encounters between groups, such as in competitive sports? Yes. In an international web-based survey (602 participants, 388 women, 214 men), we asked people to recall all the meaningful social interactions they had had in the past month; these were then categorized as person–person encounters (e.g., an argument with a friend), person–group encounters (e.g., ganging up on someone), or group–group encounters (e.g., a hockey match). They were then asked to rate how competitive these interactions were. As expected, men rated their group–group interactions as more competitive than women (3.10 versus 2.29 on a 1–7 scale). These results are consistent with the results reported by Pemberton, Insko, and Schopler (1996). A quantitative review of the aforementioned discontinuity effect suggested that this effect was stronger among men than among women (Wildschut, Pinter, Vevea, Insko, & Schopler, 2003). Interestingly, in summarizing their results on the discontinuity effect, Pemberton et al. (1996) noted that although both sexes showed the effect, "with women, the effect may have related more to cooperative interactions with individuals, whereas with men, the effect may have related more to competitive interactions with groups" (p. 964).

What about affective reactions toward intergroup conflict? The same web survey asked the sample to rate warfare on a number of affective scales, such as exciting (1) versus boring (7), useful (1) versus useless (7), and pleasant (1) versus unpleasant (7). As expected, men found warfare to be more exciting (3.06 versus 3.83), more useful (4.00 versus 4.71), and less unpleasant (6.35 versus 6.61) than women.

There also appears to be a consistent sex difference in the support for warfare in opinion polls. We inspected the poll data of an ICM/Guardian survey measuring the support for the war in Afghanistan conducted among the British public in the autumn of 2001 (image.guardian.co.uk/sys-files/Politics/documents/2001/11/19/guard-war.xls). On the question "Do you approve or disapprove of the military action by the United States and Britain against Afghanistan," 76 percent of men and 56 percent of women approved.

Given that intergroup conflict is primarily a male activity, any adaptive cognitive and emotional responses (i.e., attributions of hostile intent, prejudicial reactions) concerning out-group members should be specific to *male* out-group members. One set of studies tested this hypothesis using an intriguing methodology. Termed *functional projection*, Maner and colleagues (2005) proposed that people may tend to perceive anger in the faces of out-group members (especially male out-group members), even if those people are holding neutral expressions. In two studies, Maner et al. (2005) found that experimentally heightened self-protective motive (which involved showing participants scenes from the movie *Silence of the Lambs*) increased the tendency among White American participants to perceive anger in the faces of Black men and Arab men (but not in the faces of White men or women). In real-world contexts, not only are out-group females not feared or avoided, they are often treated by men as spoils of intergroup conflict. There are all too many examples of women being abducted and raped during war.

In-Group Helping and Sacrifice

The male warrior hypothesis also predicts a difference in reactions to out-group threats. More specifically, it predicts that men (more than women) ought to be relatively more willing to help their in-group during intergroup competition. To test this prediction, van Vugt et al. (2007) conducted a series of public good experiments in which individuals could contribute to a group fund and, depending on how much each member contributed, receive a return from their investment. Contributing in these games is essentially an altruistic act, because it is not certain whether one gets a return from the group fund (De Cremer & van Vugt, 1999). Van Vugt et al. (2007) created two game conditions. In the interpersonal condition, participants played the normal public good game; in the intergroup condition, participants ostensibly played the game against groups from other universities. As predicted, more men contributed their endowment to the group in the intergroup than interpersonal condition (92 percent versus 57 percent); women appeared not to be affected by this manipulation (53 percent versus 51 percent).

Attitudes toward Bravery and Heroism

Buss (1999) reported a study in which students were asked the extent to which they valued various traits in others – such as physical bravery, heroism, risk taking, pain tolerance – that could be seen as proxies of warrior characteristics. His findings suggest that these attributes are valued in men more than in women. Another study found striking differences in the frequency with which male and female students test their fighting prowess, by, for instance, arm wrestling or throwing objects at targets (Fox, 1997; reported in Buss, 1999). Almost 30 percent of men in this sample indicated that they tested their fighting abilities daily, compared with only 5 percent of women. In addition, a review of differences in helping behavior between men and women found that men were more likely to engage in more heroic, risky, and physically demanding forms of helping (Becker & Eagly, 2004) – in other words, the kind of helping associated with bravery in intergroup conflict.

Between-Group Hierarchies

Another prediction from the male warrior hypothesis is that men should have a relatively stronger preference for between-group hierarchies, the outcome of intergroup competition. According to *social dominance theory* (Sidanius & Pratto, 1999), groups in society compete for scarce resources, and as some groups are more successful than others, a social status hierarchy emerges in which some groups have greater access to resources than others. This is analogous to the individual dominance hierarchy that we find within other species such as the lion, wolf, or gorilla. Sidanius, Pratto, and their colleagues created a *social dominance orientation* (SDO) scale, which measures people's dispositional preferences for between-group hierarchies. Sample items from this questionnaire are, "To get ahead in life, it is sometimes necessary to step on other groups," "Inferior groups should stay in their place," "Group equality should be an ideal," and "We should do what we can to equalize conditions for different groups" (the latter two items are reverse scored). We administered the SDO scale (1 = low dominance, 7 = high dominance) to our Internet sample and found that men scored significantly higher on social dominance than women (2.56 versus 2.28; for a similar result see Pratto, Sidanius, Stallworth, & Malle, 1994).

Social Identity

If the male warrior hypothesis is valid, it suggests that there may be differences in the way social identities are formed among men and women. In particular, one would expect that men's social identities are relatively more intergroup based (i.e., based on favorable comparisons with out-groups). The male warrior experimental data by van Vugt et al. (2007) suggest that this might be the case. In the intergroup condition, the rise in group contributions among men was mirrored by an increase in group identification (intergroup versus interpersonal conditions: 6.56 versus 4.27; group identification was measured on a 9-point scale). This was not true for women as their group identification remained relatively stable across the intergroup and interpersonal (5.06 versus 4.80).

Along similar lines, Baumeister and Sommer (1997) suggested that men's need to belong is satisfied more by the broader social structure – specifically, "the male quest for belongingness may emphasize hierarchies of status and power" (p. 39). On the other hand, women's need to belong is satisfied more through interpersonal dyadic bonds (see also Gabriel & Gardner, 1999).

Another preliminary finding that might give us some insight into men and women's social identity is an experiment we conducted recently on preference for colors. We asked a convenience sample of 24 men and 30 women to pick their favorite color and tell us why this was their favorite color. A significantly higher proportion of men than women (42 percent versus 17 percent) chose a color associated with a tribal in-group – such as their favorite sports team, flag of country, brand color of university.

Developmental Sex Differences

A final set of findings pertaining to the male warrior psychology has to do with differences between boys and girls in their social play activities. Research conducted in schools and playgrounds in the 1970s found that boys were more likely to engage in competitive, complex team games involving larger numbers of children and different groups (Lever, 1976). This difference is paralleled by sex differences in friendships. Whereas girls tend to have stable and exclusive friendships with other girls, boys' friendships are more fleeting and less exclusive (Eder & Hallinan, 1978), which is useful for building coalitional alliances for the purpose of intergroup competition.

Alternative Theories, Implications, and Concluding Thoughts

We began this chapter by noting that humans are a tribal species. We put forward different evolutionary hypotheses to explain our distinctive in-group–out-group psychology. The tribal instinct hypothesis proposes that humans have evolved a specific intergroup psychology, which is the product of an evolutionary history of managing intergroup relations. This hypothesis is superior, we believe, to alternative explanations that see our intergroup psychology as a byproduct of some other evolved capacity (e.g., stimulus categorization, sharing with in-group members). The tribal instinct hypothesis uniquely predicts differences between the sexes in intergroup psychology as a function of different selection pressures operating on men and women. The behavioral and attitudinal data that we presented on the male warrior effect are consistent with this hypothesis: Men are more prone to respond to intergroup threats, for example, by preferentially helping in-groups.

Alternative Theories

Nevertheless, we should consider alternative explanations for these findings, such as theories that focus on gender roles (e.g., Eagly & Wood, 1999). Essentially, gender-role theories suggest that because of anatomical differences between the sexes (e.g., men having more upper-body strength, women having to bear children), women and men have historically filled different roles, leading to socialization practices that shape boys and girls to develop different psychological characteristics. In a nutshell, the male warrior hypothesis points to natural selection as the origin of psychological differences between women and men; gender-role theories point to socialization.

From a logical standpoint, it seems extremely unlikely that evolution would shape such distinct and highly specialized male and female anatomies while leaving the psychologies untouched. This sort of Cartesian mind–body dualism is no longer tenable. Evolutionary biology and psychology have convincingly shown that selection operates on all aspects of an organism's phenotype – including their physique, brains, and behavior – and there is a wealth of data to support this (Alcock, 2004; Dawkins, 1976). The simple fact is that there have been different patterns of selection pressure on males and females, not only during human evolution, but long before the emergence of hominids. And the consequences of such different selection pressures can be observed across the animal kingdom today, in sex-differentiated patterns of behavior in species that simply cannot be said to have "gender roles." It is thus a major conceptual leap to suggest that human sex differences are unique in the animal kingdom, being dependent entirely on socialization.

Practical Implications for Real Intergroup Settings

The tribal instinct hypothesis and the male warrior hypothesis have several implications for understanding real-world intergroup conflict and for devising interventions to promote more harmonious intergroup relations. As illustrated by the recent empirical findings, these hypotheses provide us with new insights into why certain kinds of intergroup settings arouse especially strong responses among people, and why those responses so often involve fear, danger-relevant stereotypic beliefs, and desire to avoid out-group members if at all possible. Although intervention methods based on the notion of social identity show promise (e.g., Fiske, 2002; Gaertner & Dovidio, 2000), the tribal instinct hypothesis explains why actual prejudice reduction in the real world is often easier said than done. In modern life, many kinds of out-groups (ethnic out-groups, national out-groups, religious out-groups) likely tap into the psychology of tribal alliances, and thus, prejudice against such out-groups is, not surprisingly, highly resistant to intervention.

Of course, our hypotheses do not imply that reducing intergroup conflict is hopeless. In fact, our hypotheses offer some specific directions regarding the kinds of efforts that are most likely to pay off. Most obviously, to the extent that resources are limited, efforts toward reducing intergroup conflict should be focused on men more than women, and on male out-group targets more than female out-group targets. And because certain groups are more strongly associated with danger-relevant stereotypes (e.g., Muslim men), interventions might focus on people's perceptions of those groups.

Furthermore, one way automatic bias might be reduced is by removing the heuristic perception that certain cues signal coalitional alliances. The research by Kurzban et al. (2001) is illustrative. It has been observed that people have a tendency to automatically categorize others on the basis of race. According to Kurzban et al., this is not because of any evolutionary relevance of "race," but because race-related features are perceived (often incorrectly) as cues for coalitional alliances. Kurzban et al. demonstrated that by providing other, more valid cues of coalitions, people's tendency to automatically categorize according to race could be eliminated. An interesting implication is that one way to reduce intergroup conflict is by reducing people's over-perceptions of coalitional alliances in their social world.

The concept of functional flexibility also offers some insights. To the extent that information connoting danger enhances negative reactions toward out-groups (e.g., Schaller, Park, & Faulkner, 2003), it might be useful to cut down the prevalence of such information in our environments, especially when such information unnecessarily heightens people's fears. Indeed, there is evidence of a link between exposure to crime news and fear of violence (Smolej & Kivivuori, 2006).

Similarly, to the extent that individual differences in beliefs about danger are associated with negative reactions, it might be useful to exercise prudence when teaching children about all the dangerous people in the world.

Finally, evolution teaches us that intergroup relations in humans are never static (unlike in many other species): Your enemy today can be your friend tomorrow, and vice versa (Keegan, 1994). To cope with these uncertainties, humans have likely evolved a flexible tribal psychology that enables them to form coalitions to compete as well as cooperate with other groups, depending upon the assessment of costs and benefits. For instance, in the face of a formidable enemy, it would make sense for minority groups to forge alliances with others despite previous hostilities. Similarly, dominant groups are sometimes better off helping a subordinate group to assert their dominance rather than starting a potentially costly conflict. This requires psychological mechanisms for peacemaking and peacekeeping between groups, which humans abundantly possess. For instance, acts of helping and reconciliation – such as exchanging gifts and making apologies – are common in relations between human groups (Hardy & van Vugt, 2006; Nadler & Halabi, 2006; van Leeuwen, 2007). Furthermore, humans have the capacity to form cross-group reciprocal arrangements, via friendships or intermarriage, which can be another powerful tool for peacemaking.

Thus, although humans have a dark side, history teaches us that progress is possible, if sometimes slow. One might be able to temporarily disregard our darker side by denying our evolutionary history. But having a clear idea of what we are up against is indispensable, if we are serious about improving the human condition.

2

Helping "Us" versus "Them"
Towards a Group-Level Theory of Helping and Altruism Within and Across Group Boundaries

Stefan Stürmer and Mark Snyder

Introduction

The main objective of this chapter is to present an outline of a social psychological theory of helping and altruism in the context of social groups and to review empirical evidence in support of its key assumptions. Historically, theory and research on prosocial behavior, on the one hand, and research on group processes and intergroup relations, on the other, have developed in relative isolation from each other. In recent years, however, several factors have led these two social psychological research traditions to "talk" to each other, one result of which is the possibility of an integrative perspective on helping and altruism in the contexts of groups (see Introduction to this volume).

At first glance, given the literature on in-group bias and intergroup discrimination (e.g., Brewer, 1979; Brown & Gaertner, 2001), shouldn't one simply expect that people help members of their own group more than they help members of an out-group? Indeed, most of the early research on the role of group memberships in helping started precisely from this assumption. Findings revealed, however, that the effects of in-group/out-group categorizations on helping were often more complex. For example, although some investigation showed that research participants helped out-group members less than in-group members (e.g., Benson, Karabenick, & Lerner, 1976; Gaertner & Bickman, 1971), other researchers have found no association between in-group/out-group status of the recipients of help and the amount of help provided (e.g., Bickman & Kamzan, 1973; Wispé & Freshley, 1971). Still, other researchers have found that out-group members were helped even more than in-group members – a phenomenon labeled "reverse discrimination" in helping (e.g., Dovidio & Gaertner, 1981; Dutton & Lake, 1973). In fact, a recent quantitative meta-analysis including 48 hypothesis tests investigating Whites' discrimination in helping against Blacks in the context of interracial relationships in the US did not reveal evidence for universal discrimination in helping against Blacks (Saucier, Miller, & Doucet, 2005).

A prominent explanation for the apparent "failure" to discover consistent evidence for discrimination against out-group members in helping revolves around the idea that, due to prevalent egalitarian norms and moral beliefs in modern societies, the expression of discrimination against out-groupers has generally become more subtle. Accordingly, overt discrimination is particularly likely to occur under conditions when the individual's behavior can not be interpreted as discriminatory (e.g., racist or sexist) by others and/or when the situation is ambiguous enough for the individual to justify the behavior with plausible alternative rationalization (Dovidio & Gaertner, 2004; Gaertner & Dovidio, 1986; see also Saucier et al., 2005). Still, this explanation has its limits. To be sure, throughout the history of humanity, there exist devastating examples of out-group discrimination in helping; and, in societies worldwide, the withholding or refusal of help and support pose grave social problems for members of stigmatized groups. Nevertheless, there are also striking counterexamples – help and support provided to refugees and asylum seekers, assistance offered to members of stigmatized out-groups affected by HIV/AIDS, transnational aid in the wake of natural catastrophes such as the tsunami in 2004 – just to mention a few examples. In fact, the raison d'être of countless social and political organizations precisely consists in providing support to members of stigmatized or underprivileged outgroups. It thus seems that, at least under some specific conditions, people do not just help to avoid the normative or moral costs of discriminating against "out-groupers." Rather, they seem to deliberately and actively seek out the opportunity to help members of groups to which they do not belong – sometimes also collectively, as a joint effort with fellow in-group members, but sometimes individually and even against the will and the norms of their in-group or community.

Understanding the phenomenon of helping in the contexts of groups, specifically helping across group boundaries, thus requires a perspective that goes beyond the prediction of out-group discrimination, one that takes the goals and motives that lead people to help into account. The issue of the motivational "pathways" leading people to help lies at the heart of the present chapter. Specifically, we will consider whether and how the in-group/out-group relationship between a helper and the recipient of help ("helpee") affects the motivational processes leading people to help. Building on this analysis, we will then return to the issue of discrimination and discuss when discrimination in helping, specifically discrimination against out-group members, is likely, and when, by contrast, it becomes more likely that people will be motivated to engage in out-group helping or forms of intergroup solidarity.

Helping "Us" versus "Them": A Motivational Analysis

We will begin our analysis with a capsule overview of theory and research on motives for helping in interpersonal contexts. Next, we will derive a series of theoretical propositions that specify more precisely why and how salient in-group/out-group distinctions may affect these motivational processes. Then, we will present empirical evidence from a research program designed to test some of the key assumptions of this perspective.

Individual Motivations for Helping

A prominent distinction in the helping literature – which will provide a point of departure for the discussion to follow – concerns the difference between egoistic (or self-focused) motivation and altruistic (or other-focused) motivation (e.g., Batson, 1991; Batson & Shaw, 1991; Penner, Dovidio, Piliavin, & Schroeder, 2005). While egoistic motivation is functionally related to the goal to preserve, maintain, or enhance one's own welfare, altruistic motivation is functionally related to the goal to preserve, maintain, or enhance the welfare of another being. The question of whether altruistic motivation falls in the range of human functioning – or if not all forms of human behavior, including helping, are motivated by egoistic concerns – has been a subject of philosophical debates for centuries. Following the theorizing of philosophers such as Adam Smith (1759/1976) and early psychologists including William McDougall (1908), many researchers have subjected this question to systematic empirical testing (e.g., Batson, 1991; Hoffman, 1981; Krebs, 1975; Stotland, 1969). Their work suggests that, even though, in many social situations, including those involving helping, the pursuit of egoistic goals may be a motivational "default," at least under some specific conditions, people may also at times be motivated principally, and perhaps even solely, by altruistic motivation.

Turning to the proximal psychological processes implicated in helping motivations, with regard to egoistic motivation, research suggests two broad classes of motives (see Batson & Shaw, 1991; Dovidio, Piliavin, Schroeder, & Penner, 2006, for reviews). First, as a result of their learning histories, people may perceive helping as an opportunity to gain material, social, and/or self-administered rewards through helping behavior (either immediately or in the future), to avoid costs associated with not helping or both. Accordingly, people may actively seek to help a person in need because they may expect to receive financial compensation or social recognition, because they may expect that the person will help them in the future, because they may expect to feel good about themselves because they have acted on their inner values, or because they may seek to avoid public sanctions or inner feelings of guilt or shame which would ensue if they decided not to help. Second, people may also be motivated to help out of a desire to reduce aversive arousal resulting from seeing another person suffering. Seeing another person in distress typically elicits a vicarious physiological response in the observer including negative feelings such as distress, anxiety, or uneasiness (e.g., Eisenberg & Fabes, 1991; Hoffman, 1981). People may have learned that terminating the other's distress is efficient to reduce these unpleasant feelings. Accordingly, unless other and less costly behavioral alternatives are available, they may help the other person in order to feel better (Dovidio, Piliavin, Gaertner, Schroeder, & Clark, 1991). Reward seeking and punishment avoidance, on the one hand, and the desire to reduce aversive arousal, on the other hand, are distinct psychological motives. What both processes have in common is that they produce egoistic motivation: the helper's ultimate goal is to improve (restore or preserve) his or her own welfare while improving the other's welfare serves primarily as an instrumental means to do so.

The psychological understanding of altruistic motivation, on the other hand, has been significantly advanced through investigations on the role of empathy in helping. The most prominent and easily the most influential empathy-based perspective is offered by the empathy–altruism hypotheses of Batson and associates (Batson, 1991). According to this perspective, perception of another person's need in conjunction with a special interpersonal relationship to that person (based on, for instance, perceived self–other similarity, friendship, closeness) evokes empathy, which is an other-oriented emotional reaction including feelings of compassion, sympathy, and concern. Empathy, in turn, is sought to amplify altruistic motivation. In line with this perspective, there have been many empirical demonstrations that feeling empathy for an individual in need increases helping even in situations in which helping is relatively demanding or even self-sacrificing (e.g., Batson, 1991; Davis, 1994; Dovidio et al., 1991). Moreover, the empathy–altruism hypothesis has been repeatedly confirmed in response to challenges from a variety of egoistically based and alternative explanations for the observed empathy-helping relationship such as negative self-focused emotions (e.g., distress, sadness, or guilt) or feelings of interpersonal oneness (e.g., Cialdini, Brown, Lewis, Luce, & Neuberg, 1997). There also exists evidence suggesting that empathically motivated persons are more sensitive to the long-term consequences of their intervention for the recipients of their help – a further important piece of evidence in support of the idea that empathy produces helping that is oriented to the needs of the recipients and not to one's personal or individual needs (Sibicky, Schroeder, & Dovidio, 1995). In sum, then, there is much evidence that empathic emotion increases the motivation to relieve the need for which empathy is felt, and, what is even more important, that this motivation is altruistic in nature (i.e., directed toward the ultimate goal of relieving the other's need and not toward some self-benefit).

Social Cognitive Factors in Helping Motivations: Perceived Self–Other Similarities

The group-level perspective on helping motivations presented here has been informed in important ways by theorizing and research in the domains of social and evolutionary psychology on the social cognitive underpinnings of empathy and human altruism. According to this perspective, one important cognitive factor facilitating empathy and helping is the perception of the similarities between the helper and the target (e.g., Batson et al., 1981; Batson, Turk, Shaw, & Klein, 1995; Hornstein, 1976; Krebs, 1975; Stotland, 1969; see also Burnstein et al., 1994; Park & Schaller, 2005). For purposes of the analysis presented here, the role of perceived self–other similarities in empathy and altruism is particularly interesting, because salient in-group/out-group categories play an important role in influencing perceptions of self–other (dis)similarities among people. One of the perhaps most prominent demonstrations of the role of self–other similarity in instigating altruistic motivation is provided by an experiment on the empathy–altruism hypothesis (Batson et al., 1981, experiment 1). In this experiment, research participants (female undergraduates) observed a young woman named Elaine (actually a confederate), whom they believed was receiving highly uncomfortable electric shocks in the context of an investigation on task performance under stressful conditions. To manipulate feelings of empathy, participants in one experimental condition were led to believe that Elaine was highly similar to themselves with regard to her attitudes, traits, and interests, while in another experimental condition, participants were led to believe that Elaine was highly dissimilar to them. Half of the participants in each similarity condition believed that they were free to quit the experiment after having observed only a limited number of Elaine's trials on solving the task ("easy escape" = low costs for not helping); half believed that they had to observe the total number of Elaine's trials ("difficult escape" = high costs for not helping). In line with the self–other similarity manipulation, when provided with an unexpected opportunity to relieve Elaine's suffering by volunteering to take the shocks in her stead, participants in the high self–other similarity condition (= high empathy) were more likely to help Elaine than participants in the low self–other similarity condition (= low empathy), and this even under the condition in which it would have been easy for them to quit the experiment without helping.

Interestingly, related research suggests not only that perceptions of interpersonal self–other similarities strengthen the role of empathy in helping, but that compared to helping similar others, motivations for helping dissimilar others may be of a rather different nature. For instance, in an experiment simulating helping under conditions of common threat (Batson, Pate, Lawless, Sparkman, Lambert, & Worman, 1979), participants were given the opportunity to help either a similar or dissimilar confederate with whom they shared a threatening experience. Half of the participants in each similarity condition believed that they were still vulnerable to threat (i.e., a "natural disaster") when confronted with the opportunity to help; half believed that they were no longer vulnerable. Results revealed that, when perceived self–other dissimilarity was high, helping was less frequent in the threat-past condition than in the threat-present condition, suggesting that one important factor motivating helping a dissimilar other was the desire to ensure reciprocity in case one might require help oneself from the other in the future. When perceived self–other similarity was high, however, participants helped independent of whether they were still vulnerable to threat. Apparently, the sense of psychological connectedness induced through perceptions of self–other similarities overrode the more strategic reciprocity considerations fostering helping a dissimilar other, suggesting that, when the other was perceived as similar to the self, participants helped out of an increased concern for the other's welfare. Consistent with this reasoning, more recent experimental work by Batson and colleagues showed that perceived interpersonal self–other similarities led to increased valuing of another person's welfare, which, in turn, increased empathy and helping when this person was in need (Batson et al., 1995, experiments 1 and 2).

Some researchers have contended that the role of perceived self–other (dis)similarities in the empathy-helping relationship may have evolutionary roots (e.g., Cialdini et al., 1997; Krebs, 1987; Park & Schaller, 2005; see also Burnstein et al., 1994). Evolutionary accounts distinguish between two different mechanisms for steering helping and altruism within one species. One mechanism is *kin selection* – a genetic tendency to help (or share resources with) genetically related others in order to ensure the survival of one's genes (located in one's genetic relatives; Hamilton, 1964). Another mechanism is *reciprocal altruism* – a genetic tendency for helping (or sharing resources with) non-kin in the context of relationships ensuring a high likelihood of receiving future aid in reward (which, in turn, increases the likelihood of individual survival and reproductive success; Trivers, 1971). Several pieces of evidence suggest that among humans (but potentially also among non-human primates) kinship altruism and reciprocal altruism are brought about by different motivational systems: Specifically, although helping kin seems to involve a strong emotional component (e.g., Krebs, 1987; Maner & Gailliot, 2007), helping among non-kin seems to involve a careful processing of the individual transaction costs for helping, including systematic considerations of whether the other will reciprocate one's help in the future (Cosmides & Tooby, 1992; also Stone, Cosmides, Tooby, Kroll, & Knight, 2002; for evidence on non-human primates, see Dugatkin, 1997). The conceptual linkage between social psychological findings on the role of self–other (dis)similarity in helping and evolutionary perspectives is as follows: According to the evolutionary literature, humans have to rely on visible cues to detect their degree of genetic overlap with one another (e.g., Cunningham, 1986). Because in the evolutionary past self–other similarity may have been reliably correlated with actual kinship, people may still unconsciously associate self–other similarity with genetic relatedness (e.g., Krebs, 1987; Park & Schaller, 2005). To the extent that people recognize similarities between themselves and others (in a biological sense, in terms of common genes, see Cunningham, 1986; in a more abstract psychological sense, in terms of a common essence or makeup, see Keller, 2005; Medin & Ortony, 1989; Rothbart & Taylor, 1992), the other's welfare should thus become increasingly valued (there is something of the self implicated in the other). This, in turn, should promote kin-like responses, specifically empathy and altruism, even to genetically unrelated individuals. Self–other dissimilarity, by contrast, may function as a cue for non-relatedness. Accordingly, helping dissimilar others may be guided by psychological principles commonly attributed to helping among non-kin such as expectations of reciprocity and/or, more generally, patterns of social exchange. Interesting support for this perspective comes from an experimental study using a reaction-time methodology to assess cognitive associations between self–other (dis)similarity based on individual attitudes and kinship cognitions (Park & Schaller, 2005). Analyses confirmed that relative to targets with dissimilar attitudes, attitudinally similar targets were automatically associated with kinship cognitions. Moreover, and of particular relevance for our analysis, additional analyses also provided evidence that the activation of kinship cognitions was significantly correlated with perceivers' willingness to help similar others.

The Impact of In-Group/Out-Group Categorizations on Helping Motivations

The impact of perceived self–other (dis)similarity on helping motivations observed in interpersonal contexts of helping directly points to a possible role of in-group/out-group categorization processes in moderating the nature of the motivations underlying helping in the context of groups. According to the literature on intergroup relations, especially that generated by the social identity and self-categorization approaches (Turner et al., 1987), salient in-group/out-group categories play a key role in regulating the perception of self–other similarities. When a specific group membership is salient, people's perceptual focus is on the self-aspects that they share with members of the in-group but not with members of the out-group (e.g., cultural background, ethnicity). As a consequence, people come to perceive in-group members (including the self) as similar to each other whereas out-group members are perceived as *dis*similar and different from the in-group and the self (e.g., Wilder, 1986). The research literature documents a variety of effects ensuing from the increased perception of group-based similarities between self and in-group members (and dissimilarities between the self and out-group members) that are immediately relevant to helping. For instance, people tend to think of members of their own group in more positive terms compared to members of other groups (e.g., Brewer, 1979), they feel more secure in interacting with in-group members (e.g., Stephan & Stephan, 1985), they tend to trust members of their in-group more than out-group members (e.g.,

Kramer, 1999), and they are more generous in their allocation of resources to them (e.g., Tajfel, Billig, Bundy, & Flament, 1971). Further, and of particular relevance for the focus of this chapter, people also tend to attribute more human essence to members of their in-group than to out-group members – and do so even in the absence of intergroup conflict (e.g., Leyens et al., 2001).

Turning to the proximal motivational processes leading people to help, and building on the foregoing analysis, one can assume that the motivational differences brought about by salient in-group/out-group distinctions parallel the motivational differences observed in interpersonal contexts of helping among similar versus helping among dissimilar others. Still, as in intergroup contexts, the perception of self–other (dis)similarities is particularly accentuated (e.g., Wilder, 1986), and one might expect that social categorizations lead to even stronger motivational differences. An integration of theory and research in the domains of social and evolutionary psychology with theory and research on the effects of social categorization processes thus leads to the following assumptions. First, one can expect that similar group membership between the helper and the person in need amplifies the impact of empathy in helping while, at the same time, it may attenuate the impact of potential individual costs for helping. Group-level similarity signals to the perceiver that the self and the other are "of the same kind" (in a biological sense, defined by common genes, see Cunningham, 1986; and in a more abstract psychological sense, defined by an attributed common essence or makeup, see Keller, 2005; Medin & Ortony, 1989; Rothbart & Taylor, 1992). To the extent that people recognize aspects of themselves (of their genes, of their essence) in the other, the other's welfare becomes increasingly valued (not as a means toward some end, but, like one's own welfare, as an end in and of itself). This, in turn, should increase the likelihood that, as people experience empathy because the other's welfare is threatened, they follow this emotional signal and help. Moreover, as people's focus of attention is on promoting or preserving the other's welfare (rather than their own welfare), they may pay less attention to the costs ensuing from this behavior for themselves.

Dissimilar group membership between the helper and the person in need, in contrast, should make empathy-motivated helping less likely. First, people may experience less or little empathy for a dissimilar other, specifically in intergroup contexts marked by animosity and conflict, in which the out-group is devalued or even dehumanized. Second, even if people experience some empathy for an out-group member – for instance, as a spontaneous reaction to the severity of the other's need – a variety of processes may undermine the influence of this emotional impulse on their decision to help. When in-group/out-group differences are salient, perceived self–other dissimilarities may function as a warning signal (i.e., a cue of stigma or deviance) which is likely to evoke negative emotions, such as feelings of anxiety, insecurity, or threat (e.g., Dijker, 1987; Jackson & Sullivan, 1989; Stephan & Stephan, 1985). Such processes, in turn, are likely to direct people's attention away from the needs of the other and toward the need to maintain or preserve their own welfare. Accordingly, it seems likely that even if people experience empathy for an out-group member, this impulse may eventually be overridden or ignored by more pressing self-centered concerns (for a similar reasoning, see Batson, 1991, p. 216).

Initial empirical evidence for this proposed differential role of empathy in helping comes from a panel study by Penner and Finkelstein (1998) on the role of dispositional empathy in AIDS volunteerism in the US. AIDS volunteerism provides a particularly interesting context for studying the impact of in-group/out-group categories on helping motivations, because in Western countries, based on sexual orientation, the majority of recipients of AIDS volunteerism are in-group members for some volunteers (i.e., homosexual volunteers working with homosexual clients) but out-group members for others (i.e., heterosexual volunteers working with homosexual clients). Interestingly, analyses revealed that dispositional empathy was only a reliable predictor of AIDS volunteerism in the sub-sample of predominantly homosexual male volunteers, whereas empathy did not significantly predict helping among the sub-sample of predominantly heterosexual female volunteers – and this even though participants in both sub-samples did not significantly differ in their disposition to feel empathy. Although this finding was not predicted *a priori* by the authors, it falls clearly in line with our analysis, as outlined above. From our perspective, similar group membership based on sexual orientation may have facilitated the translation of dispositional empathy into actual helping behavior, whereas different group membership between volunteers and beneficiaries of help impeded this effect.

Another proposition that can be derived from integrating the interpersonal helping literature and theorizing and research on group processes and intergroup relations revolves around the idea that when people contemplate offering help to an out-group member, they may do so in a more systematic and controlled mode of information processing by carefully considering the potential costs and benefits related to helping (i.e., their "transaction costs"), including assessments of the prospects of future reciprocity. Group-level dissimilarity signals the perceiver that the self and the other are "of a different kind." Accordingly, by contrast to situations in which the target is an in-group member, the focus of people's attention is likely to remain on the goal of maintaining or even preserving their own welfare (or, depending on the social context, the welfare of their in-group as a whole).

Moreover, in intergroup encounters, a variety of processes may operate that further enhance self-focused motivation. For instance, factors such as negative intergroup emotions, feelings of distrust, or negative prejudice may signal high costs for helping out-group members. In addition, compared to helping in-group members, helping may also appear riskier, as the reactions of out-group members to one's efforts may seem less predictable (e.g., Kurzban & Leary, 2001). In contexts marked by intergroup conflict or animosity, people may also fear being punished by fellow in-group members for providing assistance to "them" (e.g., Snyder, Omoto, & Crain, 1999), or they may feel that helping "them" might ultimately harm their own group. Still, even though people may perceive helping out-group members as a result of such factors as a more costly endeavor than helping fellow in-group members, this is not to say that people may help out-group members necessarily less than they help in-group members. In fact, in many contexts, specifically, when intergroup relations are relatively benign, people may not only expect negative consequences from helping out-group members, they might also expect that this behavior brings about distinct benefits. For instance, due to their learning histories and socialization experiences, people might conceive helping out-group members as a unique opportunity to satisfy important individual needs or functions, such as increasing self-esteem, gaining knowledge and understanding, or expressing general humanitarian values that they share with other members of their community or in-group (e.g., Omoto & Snyder, 1995; see also Simon, Stürmer, & Steffens, 2000).

People may also come to help out-group members because in some contexts intergroup helping may bring about specific collective benefits (i.e., positive outcomes improving the situation of the in-group as a whole). For instance, in some contexts, out-group helping may serve as an effective means to contradict one's in-group's negative reputation (e.g., Hopkins, Reicher, Harrison, Cassidy, Bull, & Levine, 2007). In others, helping out-group members may also serve as a strategic means to maintain the power difference between the in-group and the out-group by furthering the out-group's dependence upon the in-group's resources (e.g., Nadler & Halabi, 2006). In sum, then, despite the costs that people may associate with out-group helping, there exists also a whole range of potential benefits ensuing from helping out-group members. From a cost–reward analysis of helping, one can thus assume that, paralleling helping dissimilar others in interpersonal contexts of helping, people will help out-group members as the anticipated individual and/or collective benefits exceed the anticipated costs.

One more specific prediction that directly follows from this analysis is that, as in intergroup contexts of helping people may be particularly attuned to the costs and benefits of helping, they may also be especially sensitive to cues allowing them to predict their "transaction costs." There is good theoretical and empirical reason to believe that one particularly informative class of cues consists in the individual characteristics of the person in need (his or her physical appearance, traits, interests, and so on). On the one hand, attractive features of the target may boost expectations of positive interaction outcomes (e.g., getting to know an interesting or excitingly "exotic" person). On the other hand, discovering personal characteristics of an out-group member that one finds attractive may also lead to a modification of the initial stereotype-based impression of that person (e.g., Fiske, Lin, & Neuberg, 1999). Thus, instead of perceiving the person as a "typical" out-group member, he or she is seen as a member of a specific sub-group (e.g., Brewer, Dull, & Lui, 1981) or as an unusual or atypical out-group member (e.g., Manis, Nelson, & Shedler, 1988); in short, the person is seen as *less* prototypical and less threatening. As a result of these processes, if the out-group member in need happens to possess individual characteristics that the potential helper finds attractive, he or she should be more likely to help.

To summarize, an integration of the helping literature with that on intergroup processes suggests that, depending on the in-group/out-group relationship between the helper and the recipient of assistance, people are led to help by different processes and motivations. When a common group membership with a person in need is salient, people come to value the other's welfare as an end in itself. Accordingly, if they feel empathy because the welfare of the other is being threatened, they are likely to follow this emotional signal and help, and this relatively irrespective of the costs ensuing from this behavior for themselves. When the person in need belongs to a different group, by contrast, empathy may be rather inefficient as a motivational source. Under this condition, helping is thus more likely to occur as a function of the perceived cost and benefits for helping and/or in the presence of relationship cues signaling a rewarding cross-group interaction.

Empirical Research Program

Even though, in recent years, the role of group processes in helping has received increasing attention, few attempts have been made to systematically compare the motivational processes underlying in-group and out-group helping (for notable exceptions see Simon et al., 2000; also Dovidio, Gaertner, Validzic, Matoka, Johnson, & Frazier, 1997). The main objective of the research program that we will now present has been to fill this gap.

The overarching aim of our empirical investigations has been to systematically examine some key assumptions of the group-level perspective on helping motivations outlined above. For this purpose, we (together with our colleagues) have conducted a series of six studies designed to investigate the impact of in-group/out-group categorizations on helping in various different intergroup contexts. Consistent with the analyses that we have outlined in this chapter, our main prediction was *not* that people would help in-group members necessarily more than they help out-group members. Rather, we expected that, depending on the in-group/out-group relationship, people would be led to help by different motivational processes.

In our initial studies, we focused on two specific hypotheses that we derived from our group-level perspective. Specifically, and drawing directly from our group-level perspective on the role of empathy, we predicted that effect of empathy on helping should be stronger when the target is an in-group member ("same kind") than when the target is an out-group member ("different kind"). In addition, and drawing directly on our group-level analyses of the role of the target's perceived attractiveness, we predicted that the effect of the target's perceived attractiveness on helping is stronger when the target is an out-group member ("different kind") than when the target is an in-group member ("same kind"). The overarching objective of the subsequent studies was to replicate and to further extend these findings. In addition, each study pursued additional goals which we will outline when we report on our research in more detail.

Studies 1 and 2: Does the In-Group/Out-Group Relationship between Helper and Helpee Moderate the Roles of Empathy and Attraction in Helping?

The overarching goal of our first two studies (reported by Stürmer et al., 2005) was to provide an initial test of our group-level perspective on the role of empathy and attraction in helping. The data used in the first study were collected as part of a large-scale longitudinal project on the social and psychological aspects of volunteerism in which individuals who were serving as volunteers with community-based AIDS service organizations were followed over the course of their service as volunteers (Omoto & Snyder, 1995). The sample used to test our specific predictions consisted of homosexual and heterosexual volunteers who were providing companionship and/or help with day-to-day living to a homosexual male client with HIV/AIDS.

As derived from our group-level perspective on empathy and attraction in the specific context of AIDS volunteerism, we tested the following two hypotheses. First, we predicted that the effect of empathy on volunteering would be stronger for homosexual AIDS volunteers ("in-group helping") than for heterosexual AIDS volunteers. Second, we predicted that the effect of attraction on helping would be stronger for heterosexual AIDS volunteers ("out-group helping") than for homosexual AIDS volunteers. Moderated regression analysis on the longitudinal data yielded clear support for the predicted role of sexual orientation (as an indicator of the in-group or out-group relationship between volunteer and client) in strengthening (or attenuating) the effects of empathy and attraction on helping. As expected, and replicating findings by Penner and Finkelstein (1998) reported earlier, empathy was a stronger predictor of helping for homosexual AIDS volunteers (for whom the client was an in-group member) than for heterosexual volunteers (for whom the client was an out-group member) – among heterosexual volunteers, in fact, empathy did not significantly predict helping. Conversely, but also as expected, attraction was a stronger predictor of helping for heterosexual volunteers (for whom the client was an out-group member) than for homosexual volunteers (for whom the client was an in-group member) – among homosexual volunteers, attraction did not significantly predict helping. It is particularly noteworthy that this pattern was obtained not only on an overall measure of helping but also on three individual criterion measures of helping (i.e., time spent with the client, practical help provided to the client, duration of service in the organization). Moreover, the differential predictive power of empathy and attraction for homosexual and heterosexual volunteers also held up when we controlled for alternative determinants of AIDS volunteerism such as the perceived personal risk for AIDS and perceived personal outcomes of volunteerism (e.g., Omoto & Snyder, 1995).

The main objective of Study 2 was to strengthen the validity and generalizability of the findings of Study 1 by replicating the specific moderation hypotheses in a similar helping context, but in the more controlled conditions provided by the psychological laboratory. For this purpose, we conducted a laboratory experiment in which we assigned heterosexual college students to either an in-group helping or an out-group helping condition (i.e., helping either a fellow heterosexual student or a homosexual student). Participants were led to believe that they would communicate with one other participant in the session via instant messaging. In the course of the experiment, participants received a (pre-programmed) message allegedly sent from their communication partner explaining that he/she was feeling down and scared after having learned that his/her dating partner was infected with hepatitis. To manipulate the in-group/out-group relationship between participants and their ostensible partner, for participants randomly assigned to the *in-group condition*, the communication partner's message stated that the partner was dating a person of the opposite sex. For the remaining participants, assigned to the *out-group condition*, this message stated that the partner was dating a person of the same sex.

The main criterion outcome of interest in this study was participants' spontaneous willingness to provide support for this other student. Results generally replicated the findings of the field investigation in Study 1. As in Study 1, empathy was a stronger predictor of helping intentions when the helpee was an in-group member than when the helpee was an out-group member – when the helpee was an out-group member the effect of empathy was non-significant. Conversely, interpersonal attraction was a significant predictor of helping intentions when the helpee was an out-group member but not when the helpee was an in-group member – when the helpee was an in-group member the effect of attraction was non-significant. Importantly, the observer pattern of relationships between empathy/attraction and helping intentions held up when we controlled for additional predictors, namely perceived oneness, and feelings of distress and sadness (variables that have been suggested as alternative explanations of the empathy–helping relationship, see Cialdini et al., 1997). Taken together, the converging evidence from longitudinal field and laboratory experimental data thus provided encouraging support for the validity of our group-level perspective.

Studies 3, 4, and 5: The Impact of In-Group/Out-Group Distinctions on the Empathy–Helping Relationship – Underlying Psychological Mechanisms

The overarching goal of our next two experimental studies (reported by Stürmer et al., 2006) was to further explore the motivational differences in in-group and out-group helping. Specifically, we focused in these studies on the differing role that empathy plays as a motivator for helping. Our studies conducted in the context of helping people with sexually transmitted diseases provided encouraging evidence for our perspective. Still, one cannot rule out that specific and context-dependent factors (e.g., specific anti-gay stereotypes) may have contributed to the in-group/out-group differences in the role of empathy observed in the two studies reported above. The main objective of Study 3 was thus to replicate and extend the critical empathy by group membership moderation effect in a different intergroup context of helping. Toward this end, German and Muslim participants were randomly assigned to either an in-group helping or an out-group helping condition (i.e., helping either a student of the same or of a different cultural background). The study was introduced to participants as one concerned with solving personal problems via Internet discussions.

To manipulate the in-group/out-group relationship, participants received a (pre-programmed) message allegedly sent from their partner indicating his cultural background. Specifically, depending on the experimental condition (i.e., in-group or out-group helping), and the participant's own cultural background, the partner introduced himself either with a German or a Muslim first name ("Markus" or "Mohammed"). The latter participants in both conditions received another bogus message from their communication partner explaining that he was new to town and urgently looking for new accommodation.

The main outcome variable of interest in this study was participants' spontaneous intention to provide support for the other student. Replicating our previous findings, moderated regression analyses clearly confirmed that empathy had a stronger impact on helping intentions when the target was categorized as an in-group member (similar cultural background) than when the target was an out-group member (different cultural background). Importantly, separate regression analyses replicated the predicted pattern for both sub-samples of participants in this experiment (i.e., German and Muslim participants), even when we controlled for additional predictors such as interpersonal oneness and feelings of sadness or distress. This replication was particularly important in light of the finding that both German and Muslim participants tended to report higher levels of empathy for the Muslim student, possibly because they felt that, due to negative stereotypes of Germans against Muslims, it was more difficult for a Muslim student than for a German student to find accommodation. Still, in line with our group-level perspective on empathy-motivated helping, only for Muslim participants for whom the target was an in-group member was empathy actually translated into helping intentions. For German participants, for whom the Muslim student was an out-group member, empathy was ineffective as a predictor of helping intentions.

The results of Study 3 speak convincingly for the generalizability of our group-level perspective on empathy across different intergroup contexts of helping, and perhaps even across different cultures. However, we could not yet rule out that factors typically confounded with in-group/out-group categorizations in natural intergroup settings (e.g., relationship history, conflict of interests, stereotypes) were responsible for the observed moderation effects. In Study 4, we therefore opted for a more "radical" approach. Specifically, we sought to replicate the critical in-group/out-group difference in empathy-motivated helping in a modified minimal group paradigm using artificial groups created in the laboratory (Tajfel et al., 1971).

Study 4, which contrasted an in-group helping with an out-group helping condition, was presented to participants as one concerned with factors affecting money investment. Participants were informed that they would receive a specific amount of real money ($5) that they could invest using different strategies. Participants further learned that the study examined two different factors influencing money investment: first, communication – they would be able to communicate with one other participant via email (their communication partner); and second, the way that people perceive and process information. To create an in-group/out-group distinction, participants were informed that research allegedly distinguishes between two groups of people, *detailed* and *global* perceivers, characterized by different modes of information processing. To assess their mode of perceiving, they then completed a bogus test on the computer (a dot estimation task). All participants were provided with feedback on their scores indicating that they were "detailed perceivers." In the course of the experiment, participants received a message allegedly sent from another detailed perceiver (an in-group member) or a global perceiver (an out-group member), explaining that he/she recently suffered a financial loss.

The critical helping measure used in this experiment consisted of the total amount of their own money participants donated to this person in order to benefit him or her. Results of this experiment demonstrated that even a seemingly trivial in-group/out-group categorization can be sufficient to evoke in-group/out-group differences in the role of empathy in helping. In line with our predictions, empathy was a stronger predictor of helping when the helpee was an in-group member (i.e., a detailed perceiver) than when he or she was an out-group member (i.e., a global perceiver) – then, in fact, empathy did not predict helping.

At this point it is important to note that Study 4 not only replicated the differing role of empathy, but also provided direct empirical evidence for the hypothesized cognitive mechanism underlying the empathy (in-group) helping relationship. Our group-level perspective suggests that, as common in-group membership is salient, people come to perceive in-group members (including the self) as similar to each other ("We are all alike"). This similarity, in turn, should increase the likelihood that people act on feelings of empathy and help (i.e., invest their personal resources). To test this specific hypothesis, we also included a measure of perceived *intra*group similarities in Study 4 and used this measure as a moderator of the empathy in-group helping relationship. Analyses confirmed that the effect of empathy on helping was indeed significantly stronger when participants perceived a high degree of intragroup similarities (i.e., when participants perceived in-group members, including the self and the target, as all alike), whereas this effect was weaker (and in fact non-significant) when people perceive only few similarities between the members of the in-group (including the self and the target).

We successfully replicated the critical analyses in the context of an independent laboratory experiment (Study 5) using a similar research paradigm, as well as in the sample created by collapsing participants of the critical in-group conditions across the two experiments. Taken together, these analyses clearly support the proposition that when common group membership is salient, the perception of group-based self-other similarities regulates the empathy-helping relationship.

Study 6: The Moderating Role of Intercultural (Dis)similarities

The research that we have reported suggests that, due to the effects of salient in-group/out-group categories on perceived self-other (dis)similarities, when in-group/out-group distinctions are salient, empathy-motivated helping is typically restricted to "us" whereas empathy-motivated helping across group boundaries to "them" is less likely. Still, people do not perceive all out-groups as equally (dis)similar to their in-group. Instead, depending on historical, ideological, and specific social contextual factors (e.g., the salient frame of reference, see Haslam & Turner, 1992), people may perceive some out-groups as more similar to their in-group than others. For instance, in a comparison context involving only Germans and Turks, Germans are likely to perceive Turks as relatively dissimilar to Germans on the basis of predominant cultural values, habits, and so on. However, in a comparison context involving multiple other cultural or national groups, such as, for instance, Chinese or Zulu, Germans may come to perceive Turks as culturally rather similar to themselves – by contrast to Chinese or Zulu, Germans and Turks both use the Latin alphabet and Arabic numbers, the predominant religions in both countries have common historical roots, and so on. From our group-level perspective, one could thus argue that in contexts involving multiple comparison out-groups, the likelihood that people are motivated through empathy to help an out-group member should increase as they perceive the target's group as relatively similar to their in-group. This should be so because perceptions of *inter*group similarities should facilitate the attribution of a common essence shared by members of both the in-group and the out-group (and consequently empathy-motivated helping). Likewise, and following a similar logic, one should also expect that, in contexts involving multiple comparison out-groups, the impact of processes such as considering the target's attractiveness should be more pronounced when helping members of out-groups perceived as dissimilar to one's in-group (i.e., when detection of a common essence is more difficult) than when the out-group is perceived as relatively similar.

To test these predictions, and to further examine our perspective on the role of perceived group-based self-other (dis)similarities in helping motivations, Siem and Stürmer (2008, Study 1; see also Siem, 2008) conducted a study in the context of a student volunteer program (the "study-buddy program") in which German student volunteers provide forms of direct and practical assistance to incoming international students (their buddy) on a one-on-one basis. This program provided a particularly intriguing context to test the hypothesized role of perceived intergroup (dis)similarities in multicultural contexts because some volunteers are matched with buddies from countries whose cultures appear, from a German perspective, rather similar to the German culture (e.g., German students matched with international students from Sweden or the UK), while others are matched with buddies from countries whose cultures appear rather dissimilar to the German culture (e.g., German students matched with international students from Cameroon or China). As derived from our group-level perspective, we expected that the perceived intercultural (dis)similarity between Germany and the international student's home country would moderate the motivations leading the German students to help. Specifically, we predicted that perceived intercultural (dis)similarities would strengthen (or attenuate) the role of empathy and attraction in helping international students.

The study combined controlled laboratory experimentation with a longitudinal field research design with three points of measurement over a six-month period. At Time 1, prior to meeting their buddy, student volunteers participated in a laboratory experiment in which we manipulated the intercultural (dis)similarity between the volunteer and a fictitious international student using a scenario modeling a first contact situation. At Time 2 (after 3 months of service), we distributed questionnaires among student volunteers including measures tapping volunteers' feelings of empathy for their buddy (a stranger in a new country) and the buddy's perceived attractiveness as well as a measure of the time the volunteers spent in a typical week on activities supporting their buddy. With an additional follow-up at Time 3 (after 3 months of service), we gathered information whether (yes or no) the volunteer–buddy relationship was still ongoing.

Although the main purpose of the experiment at Time 1 was to provide an initial test of our predictions under controlled conditions, the field data collected at Time 2 and Time 3 also constitute a replication of our findings in the context of the actual volunteer-buddy relationships. Analyses using either the experimental data or the longitudinal field data provided converging support for our predictions. Specifically, moderated regression analyses confirmed that empathy was a stronger predictor of helping (or helping intentions) among volunteers matched with a culturally similar student (i.e., German students matched with, for instance, international students from France or Greece) than among volunteers matched with a culturally dissimilar student (i.e., German students matched with, for instance, international students from Africa or East Asia); in fact, among volunteers matched with culturally dissimilar student, empathy did not predict helping (or helping intentions). Conversely, but also as expected, among volunteers matched with culturally dissimilar students, attraction was a stronger predictor of helping (or helping intentions) than among volunteers matched with culturally similar students.

At this point, it is worth noting that this study not only confirmed our specific predictions about the role of intercultural (dis)similarities in moderating helping motivations, but it also extended our perspective in several important ways. First, our data also provided evidence for the hypothesized psychological mechanisms underlying the role of attraction in helping out-group members, specifically members of out-groups perceived as culturally dissimilar to one's own group. Our theoretical analysis suggests that detecting attractive characteristics in an out-group member increases the likelihood of helping because such features signal a more rewarding (or more satisfying) interaction. To test this "attraction signal" mechanism, we also included measures of the perceived (or anticipated) relationship satisfaction at Time 1 and Time 2 in our research design and used these measures as mediators of the effect of attraction on helping (or helping intentions) in a set of meditational analyses (Baron & Kenny, 1986). In line with our expectation, we found that the attraction effect was mediated completely by perceived (or anticipated) relationship satisfaction. To the extent that German volunteers perceived the international student as attractive, they perceived (or anticipated) a greater satisfaction with the outcomes resulting from the relationship to this particular person; this, in turn, strengthened their motivation to support the student. In addition, our study also provided further support for the hypothesized role of cost-benefit calculation processes implicated in the decision in helping out-group members, specifically members of out-groups perceived as dissimilar to one's in-group. Our theoretical analysis suggests that when contemplating helping an out-group member, they pay particular attention to what they "get out of it." The Time 2 questionnaires also included items measuring participants' satisfaction with the outcomes of their voluntary work related to various different areas (e.g., getting social recognition from friends, acting upon humanitarian values; see Clary et al., 1998). Analyses revealed that volunteers' satisfaction with the outcomes of their volunteer work was only a significant predictor of time spent with the buddy among volunteers matched with culturally dissimilar students, but not among volunteers matched with culturally similar students. In fact, comparing the total amount of the proportion of variance explained in time spent with the buddy reported at Time 2 through variables pertaining to individual cost-benefit calculation processes (attraction, relationship satisfaction, outcome satisfaction) showed that among volunteers matched with culturally dissimilar students, these variables explained nearly four times as much of the criterion's variance as they did among volunteers matched with culturally similar students after controlling for volunteers' socio-demographic characteristics and their feelings of empathy. Taken together, these additional findings provide strong evidence that when perceived intergroup dissimilarity is high, people base their decision to help on more systematic and controlled processing of the potential costs and benefits resulting from helping for the self.

Summary of the Empirical Investigations

The overarching aim of our empirical investigations has been to systematically examine theoretical propositions about helping in the context of social groups that we derived from an integration of the literature on helping and the literature on group processes and intergroup relations. Our studies employed a variety of research methodologies (field research and controlled experimentation) and focused on different intergroup contexts (artificial groups and natural groups), different samples of research participants (community volunteers and students, Westerners and Muslims), and different forms of helping situations (volunteering or spontaneous helping); nevertheless, the overall pattern of effects across studies was remarkably consistent. In line with predictions, as perceived group-based self–other similarity (including perceived *inter*group similarity) increased, empathy became a significant motivator for helping (or helping intentions), while processes pertaining to the calculation of the individual costs and benefits of helping were relatively unimportant or irrelevant in people's decision to help. Conversely, but also as predicted, as perceived group-based self–other dissimilarities (including perceived *inter*group dissimilarity) increased, the opposite pattern of effects emerged – empathy became less important (or even irrelevant) as a motivating force, while the decision to help was significantly influenced through the target's individual characteristics – signaling a rewarding or satisfying interaction – or perceived individual benefits resulting from the act of helping itself. It is important to note at this point that across studies we did not observe significant in-group/out-group differences in the amount of help provided or the intentions to do so. Thus, people helped out-group members to a similar extent that they helped in-group members. Still, as our analyses of the underlying motivational processes revealed, the motivations for helping "us" versus "them" were of a fundamentally different nature. Taken together, the converging support from longitudinal field and laboratory experimental data presented here thus provides strong support for the validity and generalizability of our group-level perspective suggesting that, depending on group-based self-other (dis)similarities, people are led to help by different motivations (other-oriented empathy versus self-directed cost–benefit calculations).

Discussion

We began our analysis with the observation that much of the early research on the role of group processes in helping has focused on the negative influences of salient in-group/out-group categories. Specifically, it has been assumed that salient in-group/out-group distinctions would more or less inevitably lead to tendencies to discriminate against out-group members in helping – even though, under some circumstances, the overt expression of these tendencies might be subtlety disguised (Dovidio & Gaertner, 2004; Gaertner & Dovidio, 1986). The theoretical and empirical analyses presented here, in which we systematically compared people's motivations to help in-group versus out-group members, offer a more differentiated picture.

First, our analysis suggests that the focus on out-group discrimination presents an overly negative depiction of the role of group processes in helping as it neglects the amazing potential of common group membership to foster the expansion of empathy and helping to people one has never seen before or who are geographically distant but to whom one feels psychologically connected through perceptions of similarities on the basis of a common "we" (e.g., victims of a deadly epidemic, a natural catastrophe, or a terrorist attack in a different country). Emphasizing commonalities among groups may thus offer promising prospects for designing social and educational programs to promote empathy and altruism even across group lines (e.g., through fostering, for instance, the salience of superordinate groups or communities that include both the in-group and the out-group; see, for instance, Dovidio et al., 1997; also Chapters 10 and 12 in this volume).

Second, our analysis suggests that the focus on out-group discrimination is also overly narrow as it neglects the fact that, in many situations, people do help out-group members – and do so not only to avoid appearing prejudiced and/or to escape social sanctions for not helping. Our theoretical perspective highlights the role of anticipated benefits in motivating people to help out-group members. From this perspective, rather than being an exceptional or exotic phenomenon, out-group helping seems rather mundane: People are likely to help out-group members as long as they feel they get something out of it (in terms of individual benefits such as in the contexts of "one-on-one" helping in which we examined our hypotheses, or in terms of collective outcomes benefiting the in-group as a whole, such as, for instance, in contexts in which group identity is insecure or threatened; e.g., Hopkins et al., 2007; Nadler & Halabi, 2006; van Leeuwen, 2007). In this regard, helping out-group members bears many similarities with helping strangers in interpersonal contexts governed by social exchange and social reciprocity (e.g., Clark, Mills, & Corcoran, 1989; also Trivers, 1971).

The conceptualization of out-group helping as social exchange is reminiscent of the old idea that group members' behavior toward other groups is not by nature negative or hostile (Allport, 1954a). Rather, it is *functional* with regard to realizing the group's goals and interests (Sherif, 1966; see also Blau & Schwartz, 1984). In fact, it seems reasonable to argue that the long-term well-being of groups significantly and substantially depends on successful cooperation with other groups and mutual support rather than on conflict or discrimination. Further elaborations on the role of social exchange and reciprocity principles in out-group helping, and on the multiple functions this behavior may fulfill for groups and their members (resource supply, coalition formation, etc.) may thus prove fertile ground for a more general reconsideration of the forces governing intergroup relations, acknowledging that hostile intergroup competition or discrimination is but one of many means to foster the in-groups' well-being, with intergroup helping and reciprocal cooperation being potent other ones.

However, our propositions for a "new look" on people's motivations to help out-group members should not lead us to overlook important differences in in-group and out-group helping. Perhaps the most striking motivational difference in helping in-group versus helping out-group members concerns the lack of empathy in out-group helping. Our empirical data suggest that, even in benign intergroup encounters such as those in which we tested our hypotheses (i.e., the volunteer context, "chatting" with a fellow student in a research laboratory), empathy is "deactivated" as a significant motivator of helping out-group members, specifically helping members of out-groups perceived as dissimilar to the in-group (see Stürmer et al., 2005; Stürmer et al., 2006; see also Penner & Finkelstein, 1998). To receive help, members of (dissimilar) out-groups have thus either to possess specific individual attributes, gifts, or properties that a potential helper perceives as attractive (and which signal a rewarding interaction), or the act of helping has to be instrumental for the helper for other reasons, for instance, because it serves to achieve specific individual and/or collective benefits.

The implications of our analysis and the distinctions that it draws are, we believe, considerable. First, one may conclude that in comparison to in-group helping, out-group helping is rather "fragile." For instance, one should assume that, as out-group helping is more contingent upon perceived costs and rewards by contrast to helping in-group members, helping out-group members becomes increasingly less likely in situations involving high costs for helping – a conclusion which is largely in line with findings documented in the literature suggesting that, as costs for helping increase (for instance in emergency situations), people tend to help out-group members less than they help in-group members (see, for instance, Saucier et al., 2005). Second, one may conclude that helping out-group members is also more "selective" than helping in-group members. As suggested by our empirical findings on the role of perceived attractiveness in out-group helping, people are particularly likely to help out-group members who possess attractive qualities, gifts, or properties suitable to compensate their costs. As a result, out-group members perceived as unattractive or poor may often have a considerably lower chance of receiving help – even though, in all likelihood, they may be precisely the ones who need help most. Third, and finally, one may also conclude that due to the differing role of empathy, even though in-group and out-group helping may often not differ with regard to the amount of help provided, it may still differ with regard to the quality of help. Following the empathy literature, when people are motivated through feelings of empathy, they are more likely to provide help that matches the specific needs of the recipient than when they are motivated through more self-focused concerns (e.g., Batson, 1991; Sibicky et al., 1995). One can thus expect that people may perceive the help offered from fellow in-group members as more beneficial than help offered from out-group members. In fact, findings of a recent study in which data from both volunteer helpers and recipients of help were collected in a cross-cultural context of helping provide tentative evidence for this assumption (Siem & Stürmer, 2008, Study 2). Thus, even though people may help out-group members and in-group members to a similar extent, the motivational differences between in-group helping and out-group helping may nevertheless matter in that they provide the ground for differential in-group/out-group treatment and eventually discrimination against out-group members in helping.

Conclusion

Allport (1954a) has proposed that even though humans may be thought of as "tribal" – and there do seem to be plenty of reasons to assume that they are – their preferential attachment to the in-group does not necessarily imply negativity or hostility toward out-groups, but rather a general concern for the in-group's well-being (see also Brewer, 1999). The group-level perspective presented here supports this view by suggesting that people do not necessarily discriminate against out-group members in helping. Rather, it is the motivation for helping "us" versus "them" that is often of a fundamentally different nature. While in-group helping can be conceived as (empathy-based) in-group altruism, out-group helping, on the other hand, can be understood as helping as social exchange.

3

Stigmas and Prosocial Behavior
Are People Reluctant to Help Stigmatized Persons?

John B. Pryor, Glenn D. Reeder,
Andrew E. Monroe, and Arati Patel

Introduction

The focus of this chapter is upon the relationship between stigma and prosocial behavior. According to Crocker, Major, and Steele (1998), "a person who is stigmatized is a person whose social identity, or membership in some social category calls into question his or her full humanity – the person is devalued, spoiled or flawed in the eyes of others" (p. 504). In his pioneering treatise, Goffman (1963) identified three general types of stigma: *abominations of the body* (e.g., physical deformities, disease afflictions), *moral character stigmas* (e.g., a criminal record, addiction to drugs), and *tribal stigmas* (i.e., membership in a discredited social group). *Prosocial behaviors* may be generally defined as actions that benefit others. In this chapter, we argue that people display an inherent aversion to stigmatized persons and that this aversion represents a psychological barrier that must be overcome for prosocial behavior to take place. The aversion to stigmatized persons is found in both immediate affective responses and stereotypic beliefs about the potential hazards related to coming into contact with stigmatized persons. Below we will scrutinize evidence for these two types of aversion to stigmatized persons and will then examine the roles of attributions as potential contributors to and moderators of stigma aversion. Finally, we will describe a dual-process model of reactions to stigmatized persons that casts these psychological reactions into a framework of reflexive and deliberative processes. The relevance of reflexive and deliberative processes for prosocial behaviors toward stigmatized persons will be examined.

Aversion to Stigmatized Persons

I had a lot of friends and until I got older, it stayed that way. I guess what changed that was the fact that a lot of people didn't want to be around my Daddy or when they would find out that he had schizophrenia they would stop coming around. (Quote from Living with Stigma, April 7, 2008)

Implicit Reactions to Stigma

A growing body of research suggests that people often have automatic affective reactions to stigmas. Though individual differences exist in the strength and valence of these *affective* reactions, they are typically negative. When compared to non-stigmatized persons, stigmatized persons are more likely to evoke negative affect. While people may be aware of these feelings, they are not necessarily based upon conscious beliefs about stigmas. Such spontaneous reactions to stigmas have been assessed through various methodologies used to measure implicit attitudes (e.g., the Implicit Associations Test [IAT], the Affective Misattribution Procedure, evaluative priming techniques; Fazio & Olson, 2003; Payne, Cheng, Govorun, & Stewart, 2005). In the domain of Goffman's *abominations of the body*, research has shown that people have negative implicit attitudes toward persons with disabilities (Pruett & Chan, 2006), people with AIDS (Neumann, Hulsenbeck, & Seibt, 2004), obese persons (Bessenoff & Sherman, 2000; Teachman, Gapinski, Brownell, Rawlins, & Jeyaram, 2003; Wang, Brownell, & Wadden, 2004), and people with facial dermatitis (Grandfield, Thomson, & Turpin, 2005). In the domain of what Goffman termed *moral character flaws*, research has shown that people have implicit negative attitudes toward persons with mental illness (Teachman, Wilson, & Komarovskaya, 2006), drug abusers (Brener, von Hippel, & Kippax, 2007), homosexuals (Jellison, McConnell, & Gabriel, 2004), and people who smoke (Pryor, 2007). In the domain of what Goffman termed *tribal stigmas*, research has shown that White Americans have negative implicit attitudes toward Black Americans (Kawakami, Phills, Steele, & Dovidio, 2007; Payne et al., 2005), Japanese have negative implicit attitudes toward Koreans and vice versa (Greenwald, McGhee, & Schwartz, 1998), Christians have negative implicit attitudes toward Muslims (Park, Felix, & Lee, 2007), and Hispanics have negative implicit attitudes toward other Hispanics who have a darker skin color (Uhlmann,

Dasgupta, Elgueta, Greenwald, & Swanson, 2002). These are just a few examples.

In some studies, dissociations have been found between explicit and implicit attitudes toward persons with stigmas. Those who profess positive attitudes toward stigmatized persons may or may not have positive implicit attitudes. A number of factors have been found to moderate the relationships between measures of implicit and explicit attitudes toward stigmatized persons (Hofmann, Gschwendner, Nosek, & Schmitt, 2005; Nosek, 2007), including political correctness concerns plus attitude strength and elaboration. People are often reluctant to admit to unfavorable attitudes toward many stigmatized groups, particularly those who are not blamed for their conditions (e.g., blind people). Such self-presentation concerns can skew explicit attitudes and create potential dissociations between explicit and implicit attitude measures. Also, explicit attitude measures can deviate from implicit measures when people have little experience with a particular stigma. With repeated experience, attitudes gain in strength and explicit and implicit measures tend to converge.

Recent research has examined the roles of specific behavioral information and stigma in forming impressions about strangers (McConnell, Rydell, Strain, & Mackie, 2008). While the valence and consistency of behavioral information about a stranger importantly determined people's explicit attitudes, their implicit attitudes (as measured by an IAT) were more strongly connected to the presence or absence of a stigma. For example, participants formed more positive explicit attitudes about a stranger named Bob when his initial and subsequent behaviors were positive than when they were negative or became negative over time. Whether or not Bob was obese or African American made no difference in explicit attitude ratings. However, participants' implicit attitudes were more negative toward Bob if he was obese or African American. When Bob possessed one of these stigmas, variations in his behavior failed to improve implicit attitudes.

Stereotypes about Stigma

In addition to the spontaneous aversion that people feel about stigmatized persons, people often hold conscious beliefs about why interacting with stigmatized persons is aversive. For example, the stereotypes that people hold about many illness-related stigmas often include an exaggerated sense of dangerousness. A modern case in point is HIV disease. In a 1999 national US survey, more than 40 percent of respondents indicated that they believed it possible to transmit HIV through public toilet seats (Herek, Capitanio, & Widaman, 2002). Twenty-six percent said that they were uncomfortable using a restaurant drinking glass once used by someone with HIV. In a 2008 national US survey, 59 percent said they would be only somewhat comfortable or not at all comfortable with an HIV-positive woman serving as their childcare provider (amfAR, 2008). Despite public education campaigns regarding the actual routes of HIV transmission, many are still leery of transmission through casual contact.

Dangerousness is also part of the stereotype that people hold about many mental illnesses. For example, results from a national survey found that 61 percent of Americans believed that adults who have schizophrenia are likely to act violently (Link, Phelan, Bresnahan, Stueve, & Pescosolido, 1999). This same survey found that the perceived link between violence and mental illness is weaker for some mental illnesses than others. By comparison, only 33 percent indicated some likelihood of violence from a person who had major depression. Still, the expectation of violence from a depressed person was much higher than that from a *troubled person*. Only 17 percent expected a troubled person to be likely to exhibit violence. Substance abuse showed even stronger links to expectations of violence: 71 percent of the participants rated someone with alcohol dependence and 87 percent rated someone with cocaine dependence as prone to violence. In all cases, perceiving someone with these stigmas as more dangerous was related to a greater desire for social distance from them. The stereotype that persons with mental illnesses are prone to violence also extends to children and adolescents. Results from a recent national survey found that both 8-year-olds and 14-year-olds were believed to be more likely to be dangerous (i.e., more likely to be violent to others and to the self) if they had attention deficit hyperactivity disorder (ADHD) or depression than children and adolescents who had "normal troubles." As with adults, the tendency to endorse these dangerousness stereotypes of mental illness was related to greater desires for social distance from these children and adolescents (Martin, Pescosolido, Olafsdottir, & Mcleod, 2007).

Research has documented a sense of dangerousness evoked by many other stigmas as well. For example, gay men are sometimes stereotyped as dangerous to children because they are assumed to be potential child molesters (Herek, 1991). Though recent public opinion polls show that most people in the US no longer openly endorse the view that homosexuals are likely child molesters (Herek, 2002), a majority still opposes adoption by gay parents (Pew Research Center, 2006). Also, more than one out of four people polled in the US feel that school boards ought to have the right to fire teachers known to be homosexuals (Pew Research Center, 2007) and more than two out of five feel that homosexuals should not be hired as elementary school teachers (Gallup, 2009). So, many people still seem leery about children coming into contact with homosexuals. People who have moral character stigmas are sometimes perceived to be dangerous because they are believed to corrupt others (Jones et al., 1984). In the case of openly gay and lesbian soldiers in the US military, it has been argued by Pentagon officials that their presence represents a threat to morale and group cohesion, a contention not borne out in foreign militaries where gay and lesbian soldiers serve openly (Gade, Segal, & Johnson, 1996).

Origins of Stigma Aversion

Stigma aversion tendencies could potentially stem from several sources. Evolutionary psychologists have theorized that stigma represents an evolved mechanism for reducing the risk of contracting contagious pathogens (Kurzban & Leary, 2001; Schaller & Duncan, 2007). From this perspective, stigmas might instinctually evoke fear or a sense of dangerousness. Another possible evolutionary angle on the origins of stigma aversion is that humans might have evolved to avoid people who are incapable of reciprocal altruism. For example, people who are disabled might not be able to return prosocial behaviors directed toward them in kind. A third possible evolutionary origin of stigma aversion stems from humans' desire to belong to groups (Baumeister & Leary, 1995). In-group membership is partially defined or at least accentuated by the presence of out-groups. One potential evolutionary advantage of forming coalitions or in-groups was the systematic exclusion and exploitation of other social groups (Kurzban & Leary, 2001). So, the aversion to people marked with tribal stigmas could derive from the sense that these groups seek to exclude and exploit you as a member of a rival group (Sidanius, Pratto, & Bobo, 1996).

In general, it might be argued that the evolutionary account of stigma aversion as an instinctual reaction seems consistent with the prevailing negative implicit reaction to stigma documented in the implicit attitude research described above. Spontaneous stigma aversion appears instinctual and universal, requiring no conscious deliberation and perhaps no specific prior learning experiences. On the other hand, implicit affective reactions to stigma also could be the products of evaluative conditioning (Walther, Nagengast, & Trasselli, 2005), a process that might account for the initial acquisition of a stigma as well as stigma-by-association, the transmission of stigma to related persons.

Rozin and his colleagues have theorized that stigma aversion might stem from the perceived danger of contamination from stigmas (Rozin, Markwith, & McCauley, 1994). The fear of contamination is a superstitious sense that mere contact with a stigmatized person is sufficient to transmit all sorts of properties, including personal characteristics and moral standing. In Rozin's research, people were found to be reluctant to come into contact even with objects somehow associated with stigmatized persons. For example, people were hesitant to wear a sweater once owned, but not even worn by, a person with HIV. Rozin, Millman, and Nemeroff (1986) suggested that such reactions to potential contamination from mere contact suggest that people implicitly follow laws of sympathetic magic such as *once in contact, always in contact*. Recent research on perceived evaluative contagion (Olson, Dunham, Dweck, Spelke, & Banaji, 2008) found that older and younger children (ages 4–12 years) believed that siblings of unlucky children were more likely to commit intentional bad acts (e.g., cheating on a test) than siblings of lucky children. So, even random events seem to have the power to transmit some favorable or unfavorable essence through social associations.

Regardless of whether someone personally endorses the magical power of a stigma to contaminate others, the expectation that others will look down upon people associated with stigmatized persons seems like a rational concern. Many studies have documented interpersonal stigma-by-association effects, the spreading of stigma from a "marked" person to people who are somehow associated with this person in the minds of others (Neuberg, Smith, Hoffman, & Russell, 1994; Ostman & Kjellin, 2002). While one of the most common routes for stigma-by-association seems to be through family ties (e.g., Corrigan, Watson, & Miller, 2006), even incidental associations have been found to be sufficient to transmit stigma from one person to another. For example, simply being seen in the proximity of an obese woman was found to result in the devaluation of a man interviewing for a job (Hebl & Mannix, 2003). Thus, stigma aversion sometimes could represent a conscious concern about sharing the stigma (Mehta & Farina, 1988).

In summary, aversions toward stigmas are in evidence in both the implicit affective reactions to stigma and in the stereotypic beliefs that people have about stigmas. While the stigma aversion may have evolved as an instinctual human reaction to many forms of deviance, modern people often incorporate reasons to avoid stigmatized persons into their stereotypes about stigmas. Also, people may be consciously leery about the potential costs of interacting with stigmatized persons. For all of these reasons, people are often reluctant to help stigmatized persons in need.

Attribution and Stigma

Given the pervasive aversions that people feel toward stigma, it might seem unlikely that stigmatized persons would ever be the recipients of prosocial behaviors. This impression is far from true. For example, a field study of helping in 23 cities across the world found that 70 percent of pedestrians willingly helped a blind person cross a busy street and 64 percent offered to help a person with an obvious leg brace pick up some dropped magazines (Levine, Norenzayan, & Philbrick, 2001). It seems as though people often somehow manage to overcome their aversions to some stigmas.

The aversion to stigmatized persons can be ameliorated by a number of factors. Among the most widely studied are attributions of personal responsibility for the onset of the stigmatizing condition. When a stigma is perceived to have been due to factors beyond the control of the stigmatized person, negative reactions may be reduced. For example, Crandall and Moriarty (1995) examined the social acceptance/rejection of people with 66 different types of physical illnesses. College students rated their preferred social distance to stigmatized people described in case histories that included symptoms, disease vectors, treatments, and prognoses. Participants were less likely to socially reject those whose illnesses were perceived as less severe and less behaviorally caused. In multiple regression analyses, behavioral causality was the strongest predictor of social distance. Similarly, Feldman and Crandall (2007) examined factors that predicted college students' social acceptance/rejection of people with 40 different mental illnesses. Descriptions of mental illnesses were based upon symptoms and diagnostic labels from the DSM-IV-TR. Once again, the degree of perceived personal responsibility for a mental illness was the strongest predictor of social acceptance/rejection followed by dangerousness and rarity.

Variations in perceived behavioral control are importantly related to reactions to many non-illness stigmas as well. For example, heterosexuals who believe homosexuality to be something over which people have no control (e.g., it is caused by biological factors) are less likely to express negative attitudes toward homosexuals than those who believe it is a behavioral choice (Herek & Capitanio,

1995). Perceived behavioral control has also been linked to stigmatizing reactions to obese persons (Crandall, 1994). Crandall and his colleagues suggest that an ideology of blame derived from traditional American values of self-determination and individualism provides a psychological foundation for anti-fat attitudes. In a cross-cultural study of anti-fat prejudice in six countries, Crandall, D'Anello, Sakalli, Lazarus, Wieczorkowska, and Feather (2001) found that attributions of controllability and a negative cultural value toward fatness separately predicted anti-fat prejudice.

Helping and Attribution

One theoretical account that ties attributions of blame and responsibility for stigmas to emotions and prosocial behavior was offered by Weiner (Weiner, 1995; Weiner, Perry, & Magnussen, 1988). Weiner's attribution-emotion-action theory postulates that people have an initial, typically negative affective reaction to a stigma followed by an assessment of the degree to which the onset of the stigma was controllable – was the stigma the foreseeable result of actions taken by the stigmatized person? When the onset of a stigma is perceived to have been brought on by factors beyond the control of the stigmatized person, then this person is unlikely to be blamed for his/her condition. The resulting emotional reactions are increased sympathy and less anger or feelings of irritation toward the stigmatized person. Feelings of sympathy subsequently predict a desire to help the stigmatized person. On the other hand, perceived onset controllability leads to blame, anger or irritation, and less desire to help.

In support of this model, Weiner et al. (1988) found, through participants' reports, that many physical illness stigmas such as blindness and paraplegia were perceived as onset uncontrollable and that people who had these conditions were not blamed for them. Such uncontrollable stigmas tended to elicit pity and no anger, and produced a willingness to help. On the other hand, many "mental-behavioral" stigmas such as drug abuse and obesity were perceived as onset controllable, elicited little pity and more anger, and produced an unwillingness to help. Weiner and his colleagues also showed that additional information can sometimes alter perceptions of onset controllability for a specific stigma and result in changes in emotions and willingness to help. For example, a person with AIDS was perceived as less responsible, elicited more pity and less anger, and more willingness to help if the person was described as having contracted HIV from a blood transfusion than from leading a promiscuous sex life.

Numerous subsequent studies examining various stigmas have found support for Weiner's model (e.g., Corrigan, Markowitz, Watson, Rowan, & Kubiak, 2003). Research also supports the notion that factors besides just onset control can influence attributions of responsibility for a stigmatizing condition. For example, people are more likely to be blamed if a stigmatizing condition was caused by a criminal act than by an altruistic act (Dijker & Koomen, 2003) or if the person already had an otherwise stigmatized status. For example, people blame homosexuals more for sexually contracting HIV than heterosexuals (Seacat, Hirschman, & Mickelson, 2007). There also seem to be individual differences in the degree to which people blame stigmatized persons for their conditions. For example, Des Jarlais, Galea, Tracy, Tross, and Vlahov (2006) found that people who blame persons with HIV/AIDS (e.g., they "got what they deserved") are also more likely to blame persons with SARS for their disease even though the means of contracting these two diseases are very different. The tendency to blame persons with HIV/AIDS for their illness has been associated with more general beliefs in a just world – a world where people get what they deserve and deserve what they get (Connors & Heaven, 1990). Lerner (Lerner & Miller, 1978) suggested that some people might blame and derogate victims as a way of preserving their beliefs in a just world. In essence, the notion that bad things could happen to good people may be threatening to people's beliefs in a just world.

Some researchers have suggested that one avenue to reduce stigma might be to devise interventions that reduce the degree to which people perceive a stigma to be onset controllable. Thereby, blame would be reduced and sympathy plus a willingness to help would be increased. For example, educational programs that characterize mental illness as a "brain disease" might reduce public stigma by emphasizing the uncontrollable onset of mental illness (Corrigan & Watson, 2004). Those wishing to design anti-stigma interventions with such goals in mind should be cautious because the notion that mental illness is a "brain disease" could actually enhance public stigma by emphasizing the stability of the condition over time. People who have a "brain disease" may be perceived as unlikely to benefit from treatment or to get better over time. Consistent with this later notion, Dietrich, Beck, Bujantugs, Kenzine, Matschinger, and Angermeyer (2004) found that believing that mental illness has biological causes is actually associated with increased tendencies to avoid mentally ill persons. In other studies, attempts to reduce obesity-related stigma by interventions that emphasize the biological causes of obesity have found mixed results (DeJong, 1993; Teachman et al., 2003).

Alternatives to Weiner's Theory

In Weiner's model, affect (or emotion) comes into play at two junctures. First, people have immediate affective reactions to stigmas assumed to be related to factors like the severity of the stigma. Second, people have emotions that are derived from attributions based upon perceived onset control. More blame leads to less pity or sympathy and more anger or irritation. Prosocial behaviors toward the person are directly linked to the emotional reaction of pity or sympathy. An alternative explanation of the relationship between attributions and reactions to stigma is found in the justification-suppression model (JSM) of prejudice (Crandall & Eshleman, 2003). According to the JSM, some people have immediate negative emotional reactions to a target based upon a label or perceived group membership – called *genuine prejudice*. This emotional reaction may be based upon early learning experiences akin to evaluative conditioning. For some targets of prejudice, people have learned that it is socially unacceptable to experience or express negative reactions (Crandall, Eshleman, & O'Brien, 2002). In such cases, people attempt to suppress their negative feelings and refrain from acting upon them. For example, treating blind people in a negative way is considered by most people to be socially unacceptable. For other targets, most people feel it is socially acceptable to be prejudiced and to express that prejudice. For example, many people in the US feel that it is okay to be prejudiced against drug abusers. In the JSM, when people feel that their prejudices are justified, they express them in the form of discrimination against the targets of those prejudices. In contrast to Weiner's model, the JSM does not portray emotions as derivative of attributions. In this model, attributions of blame based upon normative beliefs can provide just-ification for prejudicial emotions and thereby promote their expression in behavior. For example, following the JSM reasoning people might have negative emotional reactions to drug abusers and because social norms sanction blaming drug abusers for their stigmatized conditions, people feel justified in discriminating against them or not helping them.

Another possibility is that emotions actually determine attributional cognitions instead of being derived from them or moderating their expression (Haidt, 2001). In this view, when we have sympathy for a stigmatized person, we seek to justify it by formulating attributions absolving the person from blame. On the other hand, when we feel angry or irritated with a stigmatized person, we might be predisposed to blame the person for the stigma – blaming the victim in many cases. So, in this view, the emotional tail can wag the cognitive dog of rationalization.

Inducing Sympathy

People know how to feel sympathy and apparently can feel this emotion for stigmatized persons when instructed to do so. For example, instructing people to try to feel empathy (or sympathy) for a drug addict can result in their reporting more empathy (or sympathy), demonstrating more willingness to help drug addicts as a social group (through financial donations), and having more positive attitudes toward the group as a whole (Batson, Chang, Orr, & Rowland, 2002). Such empathy induction techniques seemed to work both when the stigmatized person was perceived as responsible for his/her condition, as in the case of someone with HIV from unprotected sex, and when the stigmatized person was not perceived as responsible, as in the case of someone with HIV from a blood transfusion (Batson, Polycarpou et al., 1997). However, induced empathy did have less impact when the stigmatized person was perceived as responsible than when he was perceived as not responsible.

Summary

Are the emotional reactions to stigmas relevant to prosocial behavior the products of cognitive processes such as attributions about blame and responsibility? Or do stigmatizing feelings come first, which are then expressed or suppressed depending upon normative beliefs about whether or not they are justified? Or are stigma attributions driven by immediate emotional reactions and simply the epiphenomenal products of people justifying their feelings? At this point, it seems likely that the cognitive and emotional reactions to stigmas can be related in all of these ways. From Weiner's early work, it seems clear that empathy and anger concerning a specific stigma (e.g., HIV) can be altered by manipulations that affect attributions of blame. At the same time, people are quite capable of blaming disliked groups more for their stigmatized conditions than liked groups (e.g., homosexuals versus heterosexuals for HIV) independent of the perceived onset controllability of the stigma. Furthermore, empathy for a stigmatized person can be altered by empathy induction manipulations even when the stigma is one for which the person is blamed. People seem capable of feeling some empathy even for those they blame. So, while related to attribution, empathic feelings are not tied in a lock-step manner to attributions of responsibility.

A Dual-Process Model

Katz (1981) suggested that affective reactions to stigmatized persons are often characterized by ambivalence. People might have both positive and negative reactions to stigmatized persons simultaneously. For example, the early work of Kleck and his associates (Kleck, 1969; Kleck, Ono, & Hastorf, 1966) indicated that people manifested both positive and negative reactions to people with physical disabilities. When asked to teach origami to someone in a wheelchair, able-bodied individuals displayed two distinct patterns of behavior: Verbal reports of their impressions of the physically disabled person were very positive, whereas non-verbal behaviors indicated anxiety and avoidance. Hebl and Kleck (2000) suggested that the verbal reports were the products of controlled processes and reflected people's conscious efforts to conform to a norm of being "kind" to disabled people. Non-verbal behaviors, on the other hand, may have been more "automatic" and may have reflected "an underlying negative affective disposition toward physically disabled individuals" (p. 423). These studies imply that dual processes are involved in reactions to perceived stigma.

Social psychologists have formulated "dual-process" models of the psychological processes involved in a vast array of social cognitive phenomena (Chaiken & Trope, 1999). For example, dual processes have been found to be important in understanding racial attitudes (Devine, Plant, Amodio, Harmon-Jones, & Vance, 2002; Fazio, Jackson, Dunton, & Williams, 1995). Drawing on this research, Pryor and his colleagues (Pryor, Reeder, & Landau, 1999; Pryor, Reeder, Yeadon, & Hesson-McInnis, 2004; Reeder & Pryor, 2000) developed a dual-process model of psychological reactions to perceived stigmas. This model suggests that two psychological systems may be jointly involved in reactions to stigmas across a variety of social contexts. One system is primarily reflexive or impulsive, whereas the other is deliberative or rule-based (Gawronski & Bodenhausen, 2006; Lieberman, Gaunt, Gilbert, & Trope, 2002; Sloman, 1996; Smith & DeCoster, 2000; Strack & Deutsch, 2004).

Reflexive Processes

Reflexive reactions are fast. The reflexive system concerns instinctive reactions (Kurzban & Leary, 2001) or else spontaneous reactions that have developed through evaluative conditioning (Walther et al., 2005). For example, people may have instinctive avoidance reactions to individuals perceived to be incapable of reciprocal altruism, to individuals perceived to be members of out-groups, or to individuals with signs of disease (Schaller & Duncan, 2007). A stigma label, like a stereotype label, may also evoke conditioned emotional reactions developed through learning (Biernat & Dovidio, 2000). People learn consensual, culturally held associations to a label or mark. For example, the sense of peril that people often associate with the label *mental illness* may have been learned from the frequent associations between dangerousness or violence and mental illness that are encountered in the media (Corrigan, Watson, Garcia, Slopen, Rasinski, & Hall, 2005). Research on implicit associations suggests that stigma associations can be very general or specific to the type of stigma. For example, while people implicitly associate obesity with general negative affect, they also associate obesity specifically with *laziness* (Teachman & Brownell, 2001).

Several specific emotions might be reflexively evoked by stigmas. For example, Rozin, Lowery, and Ebert (1994) suggest that *disgust* is a common emotion evoked by many stigmas ranging from abominations of the body such as physical deformity to moral character stigmas such as people who commit incest. Rozin and his colleagues conceptualize disgust as a defensive emotion: It conveys a rejection from the self. Things that elicit disgust are perceived as having the potential to physically or socially contaminate the self. A sense of disgust may lead to an immediate desire to avoid stigmatized persons.

Blascovich, Mendes, Hunter, Lickel, and Kowai-Bell (2001) found that people reflexively manifest cardiovascular reactivity patterns consistent with the experience of *threat* when interacting with stigmatized others. When participants interacted with either a person who had a facial disfigurement or an African American person, cardiovascular reactivity patterns indicated threat experiences. Interestingly, post-interaction self-reports of participants' subjective states did not show any impact of stigma upon admissions of threat experiences, a finding that Blascovich and his colleagues attributed to social desirability demands. Also of interest, participants who reported greater intergroup contact experiences with African Americans (participants were all White) did not manifest threat reactions related to race.

Strack and Deutsch (2004) also theorized that the reflexive (or impulsive) system may be directly associated with motor schemata that may elicit overt behavior. Approach and avoidance motor tendencies, such as pulling something or someone toward one's body versus pushing the object or person away, can be automatically evoked by positive or negative attitudes toward the object or person. For example, Neumann et al. (2004) demonstrated that participants' implicit attitudes toward people with AIDS, as measured by the IAT (Greenwald et al., 1998), were significantly correlated with avoidance behaviors as indexed by the speed with which a subject pushed a computer mouse away from him- or herself when presented with a photograph of a person with AIDS. Recent research by Kawakami et al. (2007) found that inducing people to simulate approach to stigmatized groups can result in a reduction of implicit negative attitudes. Specifically, participants who were instructed to pull a joystick toward them every time they saw photographs of African Americans projected on a computer screen came to evidence less negative implicit attitudes toward African Americans as measured by the IAT.

Deliberative Processes

The deliberative or *rule-based* system, in contrast to the reflexive system, involves thoughtful reactions (Sloman, 1996). People may reflect upon the appropriateness of their spontaneous emotional reactions as well as their overt behavioral responses to a stigmatized person. Deliberative processes feel volitional, controllable, and effortful to the person who is engaged in them (Lieberman et al., 2002). While reflexive processes are continuously engaged during consciousness, deliberative processes may be turned on and off. Even in circumstances where perceivers have a negative reflexive reaction to someone with a stigma, if perceivers have enough time, motivation, and cognitive resources, they may adjust or suppress their initial reactions. Devine, Fazio, and their colleagues found that individual differences in European Americans' motivations to control racial prejudice are related to more positive reactions to African Americans. Similarly, research by Pryor et al. (1999) found that individual differences in motivations to control stigma-related prejudice were linked to more positive reactions to persons with HIV stigma as well as other stigmas.

Not all emotional reactions to stigmas need to be considered reflexive. Deliberative processes may also lead to emotional reactions to stigma. Weiner's attribution-emotion-action model of stigmatization (Weiner, 1995; Weiner et al., 1988) suggests that the emotional reactions of pity and anger may be derived from an attributional consideration of stigma. Pryor et al. (1999) theorized that such attributional considerations – whether a stigma is perceived to have a controllable or uncontrollable onset – often take time to entertain.

Rule-based reflections upon the uncontrollable origins of a stigma may provide a rationale for formulating positive feelings. Thus, Pryor and his colleagues predicted that people would show more positive reactions to a person with an uncontrollable stigma when given time to consider their responses than when they were asked for immediate responses. Consistent with these predictions, the prospect of having lunch in the company of a little girl with AIDS (an uncontrollable stigma) was rated more positively by people who delayed their responses (by 15 seconds) than by people who responded immediately. For a controllable stigma (drug addiction), delay made no difference.

Testing the Dual-Process Model of Reactions to Stigma

This dual-process model of stigma reactions is outlined in Table 3.1. Theoretically, reflexive reactions may be characterized as faster than deliberative reactions. Reflexive processes are particularly important when a stigmatized person is first encountered. Rule-based or deliberative processes are slower to come on line. In essence, deliberative processes may represent people thinking about their reactions to stigmatized persons. *Am I justified in my immediate reactions to this person? Are my immediate reactions consistent with how I think I should act according to my personal values? Are my reactions socially appropriate?* These are the types of thoughts that may occur when people have the time, opportunity, and cognitive resources to engage in deliberative processes. These two systems are assumed to interact dynamically over time to produce not only subjective states in the perceiver (such as emotional experiences), but also overt behaviors. While the emotional and behavioral responses to stigma may be very complex, a basic underlying dimension of both emotions and behaviors is one of approach and avoidance (Bargh, 1997; Cacioppo, Gardner, & Berntson, 1999; Neumann & Strack, 2000). Thus, stigma approach/avoidance behaviors can be driven theoretically by both reflexive and deliberative processes.

In an empirical test of this dual-process model of stigma, Pryor et al. (2004) asked college students to consider how comfortable they might feel in interacting with individuals who had a variety of stigmatizing conditions. The cover story of this study asked participants to imagine interactions with patients in a hospital setting where participants had a job that involved helping patients in and out of wheelchairs during discharge. Photographs of patients were presented on a computer screen along with a label of their conditions (i.e., a stigma label). Participants were asked to move a cursor toward

Table 3.1 A dual-process model of stigma reactions

	Reflexive processes	*Deliberative processes*
Onset	Spontaneous when stigma is encountered	Requires time, motivation, and cognitive resources
Role of emotion	Emotions are evoked by the stigma	Emotions are the products of cognitive processes
	Emotions are often negative (e.g., disgust, fear, uneasiness)	Emotions may be positive (e.g., sympathy) or negative (e.g., irritation)
Role of cognition	Cognitions (e.g., labels) trigger emotions and motor responses	Attributional cognitions moderate reflexive reactions
		Consideration of personal values and social appropriateness
Characteristic behavior	Avoidance	Approach or avoidance
		Prosocial behavior or social exclusion
Theoretical origins	Associative learning or evolved instincts	Socialization

or away from the photos to indicate their comfort levels. They were asked to move the cursor quickly in the direction of their immediate feelings (closer for more comfort and further for less comfort) when the patient photo first appeared and then to adjust the cursor/photo distance to "fine tune" the approximation of their feelings as they thought about them. They were given 10 seconds to adjust the cursor/photo distance for each stigma. Reflexive processes were hypothesized to influence initial approach/avoidance behaviors as evidenced by cursor movements. Deliberative processes were hypothesized to be more influential in cursor movements as time passed. Several variables related to reflexive and deliberative processes were examined in connection to the cursor distance to the photos over time. Consistent with the notion that emotions might be reflexively evoked by stigmas, individual differences in *disgust sensitivity* (Rozin, Haidt, McCauley, Dunlop, & Ashmore, 1999) were correlated with early movements of the cursor (within the first 3 seconds). Participants who had more disgust sensitivity kept the cursor farther from the stigma photos than those with less disgust sensitivity – thus indicating more initial stigma avoidance for people who readily experienced disgust. The correlations between cursor/photo distance and disgust sensitivity dissipated over time.

In contrast, deliberative processing showed a different pattern. Consistent with the notion that deliberative processes might be more likely to come into play after sufficient time had passed, the correlations between cursor/photo distance and individual differences in participants' motivations to control stigma prejudice slowly grew over time and then leveled off, reaching an asymptote around 6–7 seconds. Participants who were more strongly motivated to control stigma prejudice moved the cursor more closely to the stigma photos – thus indicating more stigma approach for people who tried to control their prejudicial reactions to stigmas.

This study also provided evidence that attributional considerations about stigmas represent deliberative or rule-based processes that require time to unfold. The 15 stigmas that were used in this study were selected on the basis of pre-testing to represent three levels of perceived onset controllability: controllable (e.g., addicted to drugs), neutral (e.g., depressed), and uncontrollable (e.g., legally blind). Analyses of cursor movements over time revealed that participants kept more distance from controllable onset stigmas than either neutral or uncontrollable. This difference in avoidance tendencies increased over time. Participants ultimately moved the cursor closer to uncontrollable than to neutral stigmas, but this differentiation only happened after about 5 seconds. Such a pattern suggests that participants needed time to consider the adjustments they made when the stigmatized persons were not to blame for their conditions.

Dual Processes in Ongoing Interaction

The study just described was unique in that reflexive and rule-based processes were found to influence the same behavior over time. More commonly, reflexive and deliberative processes might influence different aspects of ongoing behavioral interactions with stigmatized persons. For example, Dovidio, Kawakami, Johnson, Johnson, and Howard (1997) found that implicit racial attitudes were important predictors of White students' non-verbal behaviors in a group discussion with a Black student, while explicit racial attitudes were better predictors of self-reports of how much they enjoyed the interaction. Thus, measures of reflexive processes such as implicit attitudes seemed better predictors of more automatic behaviors, whereas measures of deliberative processes such as explicit attitudes were better predictors of more controlled behaviors.

A similar set of findings emerged in a recent study that examined game-playing behaviors in an online computer game of catch (called Cyberball). Pryor, Reeder, Wesselmann, Williams, and Wirth (2007) found that implicit anti-fat attitudes were important predictors of hesitancy (a latency measure) in throwing the virtual ball to an obese woman, while explicit anti-fat attitudes were important predictors of choosing to delay her inclusion in the game. Both of these relationships only emerged when two other players excluded the obese woman from play. As in the study by Dovidio and his colleagues, measures of reflexive processes were better predictors of more automatic behaviors, whereas measures of deliberative processes were better predictors of more controlled behaviors. Additionally, this study points to the contributing role of social influence in mistreatment of a stigmatized person.

Stigma's Impact on Prosocial Behavior

In a recent review of the research on prosocial behavior, Penner and his colleagues suggested three levels of analysis of prosocial behavior: a micro level that focuses upon the origins of prosocial behavior and psychological processes that give rise to prosocial behavior, a "meso" level that focuses upon prosocial behavior in the context of interpersonal interaction, and a macro level that focuses upon prosocial behavior in the context of groups or large organizations (Penner, Dovidio, Piliavin, & Schroeder, 2005). At a micro level of analysis, the core behavioral response to stigmas seems to be social avoidance or exclusion. This core response seems likely to be most important when contact is involved in interpersonal interactions – the meso level of prosocial behavior. At the macro level, sometimes basic avoidance tendencies are translated into support for policies that are harmful to stigmatized persons or deny them human treatment.

The dual-process model outlined above provides a useful account of how basic reflexive processes can initiate stigma avoidance behaviors as well as how rule-based processes can either serve as countervailing forces to reflexive avoidance reactions or else perpetuate them through blame and justification. The Cyberball study (Pryor et al., 2007) described above showed how reflexive and rule-based processes can be interwoven in the subtle and overt social exclusion of stigmatized persons that takes place in ongoing interpersonal interactions.

Macro-Level Processes

While it is beyond the scope of this chapter to scrutinize at length a macro-level analysis of the relationship of stigma to prosocial behavior, the concept of *institutional stigma* provides some useful insights into how stigma affects prosocial behavior at a macro level. Institutional stigma is the legitimatization and perpetuation of a stigmatized status by society's institutions and ideological systems (Herek, 2009). For example, the stigma of HIV disease is perpetuated by US policies that discriminate against persons with HIV such as the US government ban on individuals with HIV from entering the United States as tourists, workers, or immigrants. Another example is the US Foreign Services ban on hiring applicants with HIV (Lambda Legal HIV Project, 2007). Both of these policies convey the idea that it is acceptable to discriminate against persons with HIV under some circumstances.

Self-Stigma

Stigmas have an impact not only upon the potential performance of prosocial behavior, but also upon people's willingness to seek help. Seeking help related to a stigmatizing condition sometimes entails disclosing an otherwise concealable stigma to others – an enterprise often seen as risky by people who possess a stigma (Pachankis, 2007). For example, people who are at risk for HIV infection are often reluctant to be tested for HIV or to seek treatment because of concerns about being stigmatized (Brown, Macintyre, & Trujillo, 2003). The very act of admitting that one needs help also can be stigmatizing. For example, combat veterans who suffer mental health problems are often reluctant to seek psychiatric treatment because of concerns about being stigmatized (Hoge, Castro, Messer, McGurk, Cotting, & Koffman, 2004). These concerns include being viewed by others as weak, a person who is incapable of handling his or her problems without the assistance of others. Among college students, anticipated self-stigma is a significant determinant of attitudes toward seeking counseling for psychological problems (Vogel, Wade, & Hackler, 2007). Students who believe that they would suffer a loss of self-esteem or that others would look down upon them for seeing a mental health professional are reluctant to do so.

Self-stigma involves the internalization of societal reactions to a stigma. In self-stigma, those with stigmatizing attributes come to base their sense of self upon the reflected appraisals of others (Link, Cullen, Struening, Shrout, & Dohrenwend, 1989). The dual-process model outlined above may have relevance for understanding self-stigma as well as the stigmatizing reactions that people have to others. From the perspective of deliberative processes, self-stigma entails an awareness of the societal reactions to a stigma, believing that those reactions are to some extent justified, applying the stigma to the self, and a resulting diminished sense of self-esteem or self-efficacy (Corrigan, Watson, & Barr, 2006). Research has also shown that the implicit valence associations that people have to social groups (as measured by the IAT) combined with their implicit associations of their self-concepts to those groups predict their senses of implicit self-esteem (Greenwald, Banaji, Rudman, Farnham, Nosek, & Mellott, 2002). Implicit self-esteem represents the degree to which people implicitly associate themselves with positive versus negative valence. Greenwald and his colleagues found that people seem more strongly prone to achieve a balance among the implicit associations relevant for self-esteem than parallel explicit evaluations and beliefs. How reflexive and rule-based processes jointly influence a sense of self-stigma represents a promising avenue for future research.

Conclusions

Stigmas seem to evoke spontaneous aversion responses. In addition, people often hold stereotypes that interacting with stigmatized persons can be perilous. For these reasons, people seem to be predisposed to socially avoid stigmatized persons. Avoidance tendencies can be exacerbated when stigmatized persons are blamed for their conditions. Conscious deliberations about one's reactions to stigmas potentially function as *double-edge swords*. Deliberation can reduce stigma blame and create conditions for increased empathy and prosocial behavior when a stigma's onset seems to have been uncontrollable. It can also entail mustering prejudice control processes for those who are motivated to control their negative reactions to stigmatized persons. On the other hand, deliberative processes do not represent a panacea for stigma amelioration. Sometimes increased thinking about a stigma seems to result in coming up with reasons that initial negative reactions seem justified.

Stigma may be rooted in naturally selected predilections that helped our ancestors survive, but it is defined proximally in modern social contexts and involves a series of higher-order reasoning processes as well as some that seem more instinctual. One paramount reason to further study how stigma relates to prosocial behavior is that stigmatized persons are often those who are in the most need of help from others. The study of stigma is often the study of factors that cause people to turn their backs on people who are in need of help.

Some future directions for the study of stigma and prosocial behavior might include the study of how people react to stigmas in combination with other social information. Recent work by Stürmer and his colleagues (Stürmer, Snyder, Kropp, & Siem, 2006; Stürmer, Snyder, & Omoto, 2005) found that the degree to which people felt empathy for a stigmatized person (e.g., a person with AIDS) was more predictive of prosocial behaviors when the person was an in-group member (e.g., someone of the same sexual orientation) than when the person was an out-group member. For out-group members, variations in attractiveness were more strongly predictive of prosocial behavior. Dijker and Koomen (2007) have suggested that in addition to an instinctive aversion reaction to stigmas, people also might react instinctively with empathy and care, especially when the stigmatized person is kin or a member of one's in-group. While Stürmer and his colleagues did not find that people felt more empathy for stigmatized in-group than out-group members, they did find that differences in empathy were more likely to moderate prosocial behaviors when the stigmatized person was an in-group member. The strength of this empathy-helping relationship among in-group members systematically varied as a function of the degree to which people saw the in-group member as similar to themselves. Future studies might examine whether the emotional reactions that people have to in-group members are indeed, as Dijker and Koomen speculated, the products of reflexive processes. Are people reflexively empathic to some stigmatized persons and reflexively threatened by others? Do people sometimes experience both of these reactions in parallel, creating ambivalence as Katz theorized? Recent research by De Liver, van der Pligt, & Wigboldus (2007) has found that people can have both strong implicit positive and negative associations to some stigmatized groups such as immigrants. So, ambivalence can exist on an entirely implicit level, not just in dissociations of implicit and explicit reactions as depicted by the dual-process model.

4

The Strategic Side of Out-Group Helping

Esther van Leeuwen and Susanne Täuber

The Strategic Side of Out-Group Helping

The act of helping is a way of sharing information and expertise, a means of redistributing wealth, and the primary tool by which people take care of less fortunate others. We often do this, as a society, out of genuine empathic concern for others (Batson, 1994), sometimes augmented by reciprocity beliefs (Eisenberger, Armeli, Rexwinkel, Lynch, & Rhoades, 2001; Hardy & van Vugt, 2006). Recently researchers have begun to recognize the importance of group membership in the study of helping behaviors (e.g., Hopkins, Reicher, Harrison, Cassidy, Bull, & Levine, 2007; Levine, Prosser, Evans, & Reicher, 2005; Nadler & Halabi, 2006; Stürmer, Snyder, Kropp, & Siem, 2006; Stürmer, Snyder, & Omoto, 2005). A growing body of evidence is showing that people are not necessarily less willing to help members of other groups (thus there is no clear evidence pointing in the direction of an in-group bias in helping; Saucier, Miller, & Doucet, 2005); however, the *reasons* for helping out-group members as opposed to in-group members do differ substantially (Stürmer et al., 2006). Some of the motives for out-group helping can be labeled "prosocial," for example when they are rooted in the belief that we share a common bond with the out-group (e.g., Levine et al., 2005). However, oftentimes out-group helping is beneficial only to the in-group and to the self as a member of that group, potentially even at the expense of the out-group who is the recipient of help. These in-group-serving motives for out-group helping are the central focus of the current chapter.

The argument that helping may be advantageous to the provider of help as well as to the recipient of help is not new. For example, Gil Clary, Mark Snyder, and their colleagues have already argued that many acts of volunteerism occur because volunteer behavior provides several benefits to the individual (Clary & Snyder, 2002; Clary et al., 1998; Snyder, Clary, & Stukas, 2000). These functions of volunteerism include new learning experiences and career-related benefits, the opportunity to engage in activities that are valued by important others, the reduction of guilt about being more fortunate than others, and the opportunity for self-esteem enhancement. Clary et al. (1998) state that planned helpfulness "engages processes that encourage individuals to look inward to their own dispositions, motivations, and other personal attributes for guidance in deciding whether to get involved in helping, in the selection of a helping opportunity, and in the maintenance of helping over an extended course of involvement" (p. 1529). The decision to engage in a helping relationship, and to remain involved in that relationship, is thus determined in part by the extent to which this helping relationship meets the helper's needs.

When the helping context is transformed from an interindividual to an intergroup context, it is no longer the individual's needs but the group's needs that are most salient. In a salient intergroup context, the decision to help a member of another group is determined by the extent one's needs *as an in-group member* are met. Since groups exist by virtue of their distinctiveness from other groups, group members are often concerned with the need to differentiate their group from other groups – that is, to stress their group's distinctiveness and portray their group as better than relevant comparison groups. Positive distinctiveness contributes to collective self-esteem and strengthens members' ties with their group (cf. social identity theory or SIT; Tajfel & Turner, 1979). However, groups – like individuals – do not exist in social isolation. Smaller groups are nested within larger groups, such as departments within an organization, or states within a nation. Groups also form alliances and agree to cooperate with other groups in order to strengthen their position. The need for positive distinctiveness, which is often achieved through intergroup competition, thus needs to be met within the overarching framework of interdependence and intergroup cooperation. This mutual dependency requires members from different groups to collaborate – for example by sharing information and exchanging help when necessary. However, these acts of cooperation may be driven, in part, by more strategic or in-group-serving motives, which stem from the need for independence and positive distinctiveness.

Helping relations are complicated. On the surface, they can be viewed (and intended) as prosocial behavior. Below the surface, the exchange of help can serve to challenge or maintain social dominance relations.

Nadler and Halabi (2006) have argued that helping relations are inherently unequal social relations. This is because helping is typically associated with power, dependence, and with valued commodities such as the possession of resources, knowledge, and skills. The act of helping serves to underline an existing inequality. That is, by providing help, the helper can (re)affirm his or her position as independent and high status, and the helpee is portrayed as dependent and low status. This is particularly the case when the type of help concerns dependency-oriented help. *Dependency-oriented help* provides a full solution to the problem, is less concerned with the recipient's autonomy, and reflects the helper's view that the needy cannot help themselves. In contrast, *autonomy-oriented help* is partial and temporary, it is aimed at empowering the helpee, and assumes that, given the appropriate tools, recipients can help themselves (Nadler & Halabi, 2006). When an intergroup status difference is perceived as stable and legitimate, members of high-status groups are willing to provide dependency-oriented help to members of low-status groups, and the latter are also quite willing to seek this type of help from the former. However, when the status difference is unstable and illegitimate, members of high-status groups become even more motivated to provide dependency help to members of low-status groups, whereas the latter are far less willing to seek or accept this type of help (Nadler, 2002). The struggle for social dominance thus becomes particularly prominent when status relations are subject to change, and is expressed most clearly through an increased willingness to provide, and a decreased willingness to seek dependency-oriented help.

The In-Group-Serving Functions of Out-Group Helping

Group superiority through helping can be demonstrated in a number of ways. Ultimately, all these in-group-serving functions of out-group helping serve to achieve and maintain positive distinctiveness. However, at a more specific level, they do this by tapping into different (albeit related) needs. Based on an overview of existing literature, we propose to distinguish between three types of strategic motives. *Power and autonomy* refers to the motivation to exert power over another group through helping, and the motivation to remain autonomous by rejecting such attempts from other groups. *Meaning and existence* refers to the notion that, through the provision of help, groups can restore the meaningfulness of a threatened group identity. Finally, *impression formation* involves the motivation to use helping in order to create a positive impression of the in-group, either as a kind and generous group (*warmth*) or as a capable group (*competence*).

Power and Autonomy

First, the act of helping in and of itself is associated with power differentials and is often threatening to the helpee's need for autonomy (cf. Nadler's model of intergroup helping, 2002). Power is the experience of social influence (Hexmoor, 2002). Autonomy refers to a person's self-governance (Ryan & Deci, 2006) and thus the opportunity to reject social influence if so desired. Helping relationships are often characterized by power inequalities, as the helpee's dependency upon the helper assigns more power to the latter. This is particularly the case with respect to dependency-oriented helping, which has relatively little educational value and implies continued dependency upon the helper. Nadler and Harpaz-Gorodeisky (2006) have argued that an out-group's dependence on the in-group constitutes a behavioral demonstration of the in-group's greater worth. They showed that high-identifying group members can attempt to cope with a threat to their group identity by helping the source of this threat, i.e., the out-group. In doing so, they can regain power and reduce threat.

Probably the ultimate demonstration of helping as an attempt to influence another is captured by the term "overhelping" (Gilbert & Silvera, 1999). Overhelping occurs when people go so far as to deliberately provide unsolicited help to the degree that others perceive the helpee as less qualified than she really is, thus influencing the helpee's public image, against her will, in a negative direction. Providing someone with unsolicited support reflects the helper's view that she is qualified to provide help and that the helpee is lacking an important competence. Receiving unsolicited support has been reported to result in a number of negative consequences. For example, Deelstra, Peeters, Schaufeli, Stroebe, Zijlstra, and van Doornen (2003) found that receiving unsolicited support was even more stressful than being faced with an unsolvable problem. Unsolicited support elicited negative reactions among recipients, which at best turned to "neutral" but not positive when the problem was unsolvable and thus support was unavoidable. In a study among Black and White students, Schneider, Major, Luhtanen, and Crocker (1996) found that Black students who received unsolicited support from a White peer had lower competence-based self-esteem than Black students not receiving this type of help. Interestingly, receiving unsolicited support from a White peer resulted in more depressed self-esteem among black students than among White students. This finding suggests that it matters not only what type of help is given and under what conditions, but also by whom: an in-group member or a member of the out-group.

The provision of unsolicited support is a clear example of a situation where the reception of help is a threat to the need for autonomy. Although linked, autonomy is not equivalent to independence. That is, receiving help in and of itself need not undermine autonomy – for example, Deci, La Guardia, Moller, Scheiner, and Ryan (2006) showed that receiving autonomy-oriented support from a close friend was positively related to the experience of relationship quality and psychological health. What is crucial to autonomy is the individual's freedom to choose – thus, a person choosing to depend on another may still keep her autonomy. As autonomy is undermined by forces experienced as alien or pressuring, the experience of a need for help could undermine autonomy when the person in need feels she has little choice in matters such as whether she seeks help, who she seeks help from, and what type of help she may receive. The costs of a reduced sense of autonomy are well documented and include reduced performance on tasks that require complicated or creative capabilities (Utman, 1997), ego-depletion (Moller, Deci, & Ryan, 2006), less satisfaction of intrinsic needs (Baard, Deci, & Ryan, 2004), and the experience of poor relationship quality (Deci et al., 2006).

Across a series of studies that tested their model of intergroup helping, Nadler and Halabi (2006) found that, when status relations were unstable, members of low-status groups were least receptive to help from members of high-status groups when the help was dependency oriented. Interestingly, in the short term, dependency-oriented help (defined as providing the recipient with a full solution to the problem) tends to be more instrumental than autonomy-oriented help, which is often operationalized as help in the form of a hint (e.g., Nadler & Halabi, 2006). The denial of dependency-oriented help would indicate the prevalence of the psychological need for autonomy over the instrumental value of (dependency-oriented) help.

We tested this notion in two experiments (van Leeuwen, Täuber, & Sassenberg, 2006). Participants in both studies were university students who were led to believe that they were part of a three- or four-person team that was about to participate in a knowledge quiz. The goal of this knowledge quiz was to assess the team's overall level of general knowledge (a relevant performance dimension for university students). Participants would be presented individually with a set of difficult quiz questions. The number of correct answers of all team members combined would constitute the team's performance, which would subsequently be compared to that of another team currently present in the research laboratory (Study 1) or a team from a rivaling university situated in the same city (Study 2). However, it was also explained that an additional goal of the study was to compare both team's joint performance to that of other paired teams in the study (Study 1) or to that of paired teams from different university cities (Study 2). The task therefore was characterized by a mixed motive structure (Komorita & Parks, 1995), containing both a competitive element (outperforming the other team) and a cooperative element (collectively outperforming other team pairs). Cooperation was enabled through the computerized opportunity to seek help from the other team – which, ostensibly for technical reasons, meant that during the knowledge quiz participants could send requests for help to the other team but not receive requests for help from the other team until a future round of the knowledge quiz. In seeking help, participants could opt between requesting a hint (i.e., autonomy-oriented help) or requesting the complete answer (i.e., dependency-oriented help).

We expected that under conditions of social competition, where the other team had ostensibly challenged the participants' team by describing it as incompetent, participants would be (1) less willing to seek help in general and (2) less willing to seek dependency-oriented help in particular. This is because requesting dependency-oriented help from an out-group that views the in-group as inferior would violate the help seeker's need for autonomy. Help-seeking behavior was compared to a realistic competition condition, where a monetary reward was promised to the best performing team (which should prompt people to seek help when necessary, particularly dependency-oriented help, which has the highest short-term instrumental value). Results from both studies confirmed our hypotheses. In Study 1, participants in the social competition condition indeed sought less help from the other team in general, and less dependency-oriented help in particular, than participants in a realistic competition condition. In Study 2, participants in the social competition condition sought less dependency-oriented help not only compared to participants in the realistic competition condition but also compared to participants in a control condition.

These results attest to the importance of the need for autonomy in the process of help seeking. People may not necessarily object to depending on others for support, but it appears that a number of preconditions need to be met so that the exchange can occur on a basis of mutual respect and without the suspicion of ulterior motives that seem to come into play in more competitive settings. For example, Worchel, Wong, and Scheltema (1989) found that an offer of help from another group following an intergroup competition reduced attraction for the aid giver, whereas the same offer of help increased attraction when it followed independent group work. As we will discuss in more detail, further in this chapter, the provision of help can be a tool through which individuals and groups can compete in asserting superiority.

Meaning and Existence

A second function of out-group helping refers to its ability to render the provider of help a sense of meaningfulness and purpose. Being able to provide help implies that one is valued and needed. Strong dependency relations often shape our identity to the point where part of who we are is defined by the fact that others depend on us – for example, in the case of parents or nurses. As helping implies a dependency relationship between the aid-recipient and the aid-giver, helping can serve as a tool to provide meaning to one's existence. It follows from this that when the meaningfulness of one's identity is threatened, helping can be used to restore it.

Research on the "Scrooge effect" (Jonas, Schimel, Greenberg, & Pyszczynski, 2002) provides evidence from the interpersonal domain to support the notion that helping can ward off an existential threat. After confronting participants with their own mortality, Jonas et al. (2002) found that participants had more positive attitudes toward important charities and contributed more to a charity supporting an in-group cause.

The question arises whether a threat to the existence of an important in-group will result in a tendency to restore that in-group identity through out-group helping. This question was investigated in two studies that were conducted shortly after the December 2004 tsunami that affected wide areas of Southeast Asia (van Leeuwen, 2007). The hypothesis was tested that a threat to the national identity of the Dutch participants would result in an increased belief that the Dutch government should help the countries victimized by the tsunami. However, given that this tragedy triggered a huge international effort to provide help, a general type of aid such as donating funds would do little to restore the positive distinctiveness of one's national identity if it were overshadowed by similar efforts from other nations. It was therefore expected that the increased desire to help would be limited to domains that were positively and uniquely related to the threatened national identity. One such domain which is relevant in this context is that of water management, which participants themselves viewed as an internationally acknowledged expertise of the Dutch.

Participants in both studies were first presented with a bogus newspaper article describing the position of the Netherlands within the European Union (EU). Half of the participants read that this position was secure and that the Netherlands was a well-respected member of the EU (low identity threat). The other half of the participants, however, read that this position was under threat, and that it would only be a matter of time before the Netherlands was assimilated within the larger context of the EU and disappeared (high identity threat). Participants were subsequently introduced to a second, ostensibly unrelated study in which their beliefs about Dutch aid to the victims of the tsunami were assessed.

Results from both studies showed that participants in the high threat conditions were more strongly in support of help in the domain of water management (e.g., providing help with building storm surge barriers and flood protection systems) than participants in the low threat conditions. Moreover, their endorsement of water management help was related to a reduction in perceived identity threat in the high threat condition, indicating that expressing the desire to provide water management help to the areas affected by the tsunami served to restore the threatened national identity.

Impression Management

A third in-group-serving function of out-group helping refers to the fact that helping can create a favorable group impression. When groups strive to portray themselves as different from and better than other groups, acts of helping can be a subtle yet very effective tool to this end. In fact, when competitive and cooperative motives operate simultaneously, helping is arguably a very effective impression management tool, where under the guise of prosocial intentions groups can demonstrate their superior competence through helping.

In the stereotype content model, *warmth* and *competence* are described as the primary dimensions underlying stereotypes (Fiske, Cuddy, Glick, & Xu, 2002). People who are perceived as warm and competent elicit uniformly positive emotions and behavior (Fiske, Cuddy, & Glick, 2006). Interestingly, the act of helping can score high on both dimensions, demonstrating warmth as well as competence. This is because helping is typically viewed as an act of kindness, as morally valued behavior. At the same time, helping can serve to demonstrate a group's competence, for example with respect to specific knowledge or skills. There are many ways in which helping can serve to create a positive impression. In the following, we will distinguish between the motivation to portray the in-group as warm, kind, or generous and the motivation to emphasize group competence by demonstrating knowledge or skills.

Demonstrating warmth
A central assumption of SIT is that favorable comparisons with relevant out-groups contribute to a positive social identity (Tajfel & Turner, 1979; Turner, Hogg, Oakes, Reicher, & Wetherell, 1987). Positive in-group stereotypes help to positively differentiate the in-group from other groups. *Meta-stereotypes* are beliefs regarding the stereotype that out-group members hold about the in-group (Vorauer, Main, & O'Connell, 1998). When confronted with others' negative impression of the in-group, people are motivated to employ persuasive strategies in order to modify this meta-stereotype (Klein & Azzi, 2001).

Hopkins and colleagues (Hopkins et al., 2007) proposed that helping would be particularly effective in disconfirming stereotypes that portray the in-group as having specific antisocial characteristics. In other words, helping can be an act of communication through which people can demonstrate their generosity to doubting others. They tested this notion in three studies conducted among Scottish participants. First, they showed that Scots believe they are perceived as mean by the English, and think that helping may be a good way to refute this stereotype. In a second study, Scots described themselves as more generous in terms of charitable giving in response to a salient English meta-stereotype of Scots as mean. In the third study of this paper they subsequently demonstrated that this effect is not limited to descriptions of the in-group and behavioral intentions, but translates into actual helping behavior as well. When the mean stereotype was salient, participants expressed higher levels of helping (operationalized as giving to charity) toward out-group members, but not toward in-group members. This latter finding is consistent with the argument that helping is an act of communication: Through helping out-group members, people attempt to modify their view of the in-group stereotype. Helping the in-group is only weakly diagnostic of such qualities (such behavior is to be expected from any group; Hopkins et al., 2007).

In the research conducted by Hopkins et al. (2007), participants were confronted with a specific stereotype content – that is, their Scottish in-group was described as mean by the English out-group. Their behavior in response was aimed at refuting this stereotype by demonstrating acts of generosity, or describing the in-group in those behavioral terms. Importantly, these acts of generosity were not directed at the out-group holding the negative meta-stereotype (the English), but either at foreigners in general (Study 1), at no group in particular (i.e., donating to charity, Study 2), or at members of another out-group (the Welsh, Study 3). This is of course not surprising as learning of another group's negative view of the in-group likely evokes some feelings of hostility, thus suppressing the inclination to favor that out-group through acts of generosity, despite the desire to portray the in-group as such. As described earlier in this chapter, we (van Leeuwen et al., 2006) also found that group members were unlikely to seek (dependency-oriented) help from an out-group that had previously described the in-group in unfavorable terms.

In a field study, we tested the notion that helping could also occur in response to a more general belief that the in-group is evaluated by a relevant out-group (van Leeuwen & Oostenbrink, 2005). That is, in line with research on meta-stereotypes (Vorauer, Hunter, Main, & Roy, 2000), we reasoned that the *potential for evaluation* in and of itself is a sufficient condition for group members to be motivated to portray their in-group in a favorable manner. Moreover, because group members are not confronted with an out-group's negative view of the in-group, there would be no reason why their helping should not be directed at the out-group that is evaluating them. In fact, in line with Hopkins et al.'s (2007) argument that helping is a form of communication, it could be argued that it is most effective in creating a positive group impression or refuting a negative impression when it is directed at the out-group that is forming (or reforming) that impression.

The study was conducted on the campus grounds of the two universities in Amsterdam: the University of Amsterdam (UvA) and the VU University Amsterdam (VU). Students from both universities were approached at either a busy or a quiet location on their own university campus by a male experimenter. The experimenter briefly introduced himself as a student of the participant's own university (thus as an *in-group* member) or as a student from the other Amsterdam university (an *out-group* member). He then explained that he was writing a thesis on how students from the other university view students from the participant's university (i.e., *activation of out-group evaluation potential*), or that he was writing a thesis on computer facilities at universities (*control* condition). He then indicated that he was looking for directions to the university's information center. As dependent variable, we assessed participants' willingness to provide the experimenter with directions. This measure was created as follows. A total of 170 participants were approached with an initial request for directions. Participants who complied with this request were subsequently given another request, i.e., to draw a map with directions. Those who drew a map were then asked to walk the experimenter to the exit of the current building and point him in the right direction. After doing so, a small sample of participants even spontaneously offered to accompany the experimenter to his intended location. For each time a help request was granted (or help spontaneously given), participants scored 1 point. The resulting measure is thus a variable running from 0 to 3, with 0 indicating no help and 3 indicating a maximum amount of help given in response to the experimenter's request(s).

The results demonstrate the importance of evaluation potential in helping. As expected, the potential for out-group evaluation yielded higher levels of helping compared to the control condition only when the helpee presented himself as an out-group member but not when he presented himself as an in-group member. This effect was most pronounced when the helping interaction occurred on relatively quiet locations (perhaps the presence of an audience diffuses responsibility for creating a positive group impression, cf. bystander research, Levine et al., 2005). Together, these data lend support to the notion that the potential for evaluation by another group can cause group members to behave in a more helpful manner. The fact that this behavior was specifically targeted at an out-group member (but not, or to a lesser extent, at an in-group member) is in line with our reasoning that, through helping, people can communicate to relevant out-groups an impression of their in-group as warm and helpful.

Demonstrating competence
In the previous section we presented research in which helping, due to its positive moral connotations, served to convey to other groups an image of the in-group as warm and generous. In this section we will focus on another communicative aspect of helping: a demonstration of competence. In their strive toward positive distinctiveness, groups can achieve positive comparisons through the display of important group qualities. A particularly suitable manner to achieve this is through out-group helping. Through helping, the helper can demonstrate important knowledge or skills that the helpee is currently lacking and is in need of. The act of helping underlines this difference and assigns higher status to the helper (Nadler, 2002). This is particularly the case with dependency-oriented help, where the recipient is provided with a solution to the current problem but not empowered to solve similar future problems. In contrast, autonomy-oriented help empowers the

helpee and ultimately serves to improve the helpee's qualifications in dealing with similar problems in the future. If the aim is to demonstrate the in-group's superior competence, the provision of dependency-oriented help would suit this goal best (cf. van Leeuwen et al., 2006).

In two experiments (van Leeuwen & Täuber, in prep.), we tested the notion that members of low-status groups who experience their current low-status position as subject to change will be motivated to demonstrate their competence through helping in an attempt to change the status quo. The paradigm we used in these studies is similar to that described earlier in this chapter (see also van Leeuwen et al., 2006). That is, participants believed that they were member of a small team consisting of three or four students from their own university, and that they were competing with other universities in a knowledge quiz. After the first part of the quiz, they received feedback about their team's performance in comparison to a team from a rival university in the same town. Participants learned either that their team had outperformed the other team (high in-group status) or that it had performed worse than the other team (low in-group status). They then entered the second round of the knowledge quiz, consisting again of a number of difficult quiz questions. Because an additional goal of the study was to compare the teams' joint performance to that of other paired teams from different university cities (ostensibly), an opportunity for cooperation was created by enabling participants to help the other team by sharing one or more of their answers to the quiz questions. The situation that was thus created contained both competitive and cooperative motives.

To the extent that helping is used to demonstrate existing knowledge, there should be a difference between providing answers that reflect participants' real knowledge (i.e., their own answers to the quiz questions) and providing answers that do not reflect that knowledge but that are nonetheless helpful (i.e., sending answers that come from a file on the experimenter's computer). Moreover, if the motive is to demonstrate existing knowledge, more help should be given to the extent that this knowledge is actually present. That is, participants performing poorly in the knowledge quiz are unlikely to share their own answers with the other team as these answers may be incorrect and thus not a good demonstration of knowledge (on the contrary). The results from this study confirm these expectations. Participants' own knowledge level was only significantly and positively related to the amount of help given to the other team among members of low-status groups who could help by sharing their own answers. No such association was found among members of high-status groups, nor among participants from low-status groups who could help only by sharing the experimenter's answers. Moreover, in the low group status condition, team identification and team-based collective self-esteem were higher among participants who could share their own answers than among participants who could only share the experimenter's answers. This finding speaks against an individual mobility strategy in which participants may want to distance themselves from their low-status in-group by demonstrating how they deviate (in a positive manner) from that group. It is on the other hand consistent with a social change strategy which assumes that effort on behalf of the group is required to change the status quo – as indicated by raised levels of identification and self-esteem (Ellemers, van Knippenberg, & Wilke, 1990).

In a follow-up study, we replicated the finding of a positive relationship between own knowledge and sharing own answers among members of low-status groups. We also included a condition where group members were given the opportunity to offer help to the other team, instead of responding to a request for help. Offering help is a more proactive form of helping, and is arguably associated with feelings of confidence in one's own competence and/or the perception of incompetence of the help recipient. Only in the high group status condition was participants' own knowledge found to be positively related to the amount of help they offered to the other team. No such association was found in the low group status condition. Put differently, to the extent that the helpers were qualified, members of low-status groups were more likely to respond to a request for help, whereas members of high-status groups were more likely to offer their help. Moreover, offering help was predicted by the perceived recipient's need for help in the high status condition but not in the low status condition. This finding is interesting as it suggests that an offer of help is motivated by different factors than the provision of help in response to a direct request. Offering help to someone is potentially a very kind and useful strategy as it saves the helpee the (sometimes humiliating) step of having to ask for help. However, whether the consequences are intended or not, in its most extreme form, the offering of unsolicited help can make the recipient feel incompetent (Schneider et al., 1996) and appear incompetent in the eyes of others (Gilbert & Silvera, 1999).

Whereas the provision of help can demonstrate a group's competence, the search for help can threaten the group's image as it sends a signal that the group is lacking this competence. In the remainder of this section, we will describe three studies in which we investigated how groups juggle the competing motives of a strong need for help on the one hand, and the psychological threat associated with seeking help on the other hand (see Täuber & van Leeuwen, 2007).

In the first of these studies, we tested the notion that publicly seeking help can be experienced as a threat to the reputation of a high-status group. For this purpose, German research participants were asked whether and to what extent German industrial organizations should seek support from and cooperate more with Chinese enterprises. We also assessed the extent to which they believed that such help seeking was visible to members of the out-group, and their feelings of threat regarding Germany's reputation as a higher-status group (based on economic standards). Findings confirmed that perceived reputation threat was positively associated with perceived visibility. Moreover, as perceived reputation threat increased, the reported need to demonstrate independence vis-à-vis the out-group increased, which, in turn, strongly suppressed the willingness to seek help. Thus, acting publicly was perceived as threatening by members of a high-status group. In line with expectations, reputation threat indirectly suppressed help seeking via an increased need to demonstrate the in-group's independence vis-à-vis the low-status out-group.

The previous study showed how members of existing high-status groups can feel threatened by the prospect of having to request help in public. We further explored this notion in two laboratory experiments, using the knowledge quiz paradigm described earlier. We hypothesized that being in need of help is particularly threatening for high-status groups. This is because, when status relations are subject to change, members of high-status groups are under pressure to keep up their high performance level in order to reaffirm their group's competence. Thus, being unable to perform without help creates a dilemma, as requesting help can damage their reputation perhaps as much as delivering a lower performance without help. In situations such as these, members of high-status groups typically suffer the burden of their good reputation, putting them under constant pressure to perform without help. Of course, members of low status also suffer psychological losses when seeking help (cf. Nadler, 2002), but their expected performance level is lower and they risk "only" the affirmation of their low-status position whereas members of high-status groups risk losing their advantaged position.

To disentangle the competing needs for the instrumental value of help and the threat associated with seeking help, we manipulated the extent to which a request for help would be visible to the helper. That is, participants (from either low- or high-status groups) could either send requests for answers on the quiz questions to the other team (i.e., help is visible), or they could obtain the other team's answers without their knowledge (i.e., spying on the other team). Results showed that this visibility manipulation had a stronger effect on help-seeking behavior by members of high-status groups compared to members of low-status groups. That is, most answers were sought by members of high-status groups who could spy on the other team. This level of help seeking dropped significantly when members of high-status groups could only publicly request answers. The difference between requesting and spying answers was much smaller in the low group status condition. Moreover, seeking help under visible conditions was associated with higher levels of threat in the high status condition but not in the low status condition.

In a follow-up study, we included a manipulation of legitimacy of the status difference to test the assumption that it is indeed the prospect of change that is driving these effects. Help-seeking behavior (i.e., requesting an answer or spying) was manipulated within subjects in this study, thus allowing participants the choice whether to seek help and, if so, whether to send a public request or to spy. The results were in line with expectations and revealed that members of high-status groups spy more than members of low-status groups when the status difference is illegitimate but not when it is legitimate. Together, these results suggest that members of high-status groups who are in need of help experience a particularly strong dilemma between the desire to uphold their high performance level (which requires them to seek help) and the fear of damaging their reputation through seeking help.

Discussion

Intergroup relations are often characterized by an element of competition, in which groups strive to positively distinguish themselves from other groups. The result is a tendency to favor in-group members over out-group members in various domains. Combined with the frequently held belief that "groups should take care of their own," it is easy to imagine why researchers and laypeople alike would expect to find in-group favoritism in helping. Indeed, negative attitudes toward out-groups are often accompanied by reduced tendencies to help (e.g., Dovidio, Gaertner, Validzic, Matoka, Johnson, & Frazier, 1997; Gaertner, Dovidio, & Johnson, 1982; Jackson & Esses, 1997; Levine, Cassidy, Brazier, & Reicher, 2002; Levine et al., 2005). Recently, however, researchers have begun to argue for a more nuanced view of intergroup helping (e.g., Stürmer et al., 2005, 2006). People do not necessarily help in-group members more than out-group members – rather, what differs is the underlying motivation to help out-group members as opposed to in-group members. By acquiring a better insight into the motives for helping members of different groups, we can further our understanding of the conditions underlying positive intergroup behavior.

This chapter presents an overview of strategic motives for out-group helping. The need for power and independence, the need to affirm the meaningfulness of a group identity, and the need to create a positive group impression are a set of (interrelated) motives with a few characteristics that require further attention in the remainder of this chapter. First, the proposed classification into three motives should be viewed neither as exclusive, nor as all-encompassing. We acknowledge that there is a certain degree of overlap between these motives, and that there will be situations in which it is difficult to distinguish between them. For example, the quest for a meaningful identity is served to some degree by exerting power over another group and assuring its dependency upon the in-group. There may be also other strategic motives for helping that are not included in the framework outlined above. In addition, it is important to note that these motives may not be chronically present or active, but that they can be triggered under specific conditions, for example when an intergroup status inequality is considered unstable and illegitimate (Nadler & Halabi, 2006). The proposed framework should not be treated as a rigid model in which all in-group-serving motives for out-group helping can be neatly classified into one category or another; rather, it is proposed here to help researchers and practitioners to recognize and interpret various motives which contribute to those forms of out-group helping that can be viewed to be in the in-group's interest.

Another important characteristic of the strategic motives listed in this chapter is the fact that they are all, by definition, located at the level of the in-group. This notion has important consequences with respect to potential interventions aimed at promoting intergroup tolerance. Researchers operating in the domain of problematic intergroup relations have often suggested that one way to promote positive intergroup attitudes and behavior is by inducing a perception of the aggregate as one common in-group instead of two clearly distinct groups (e.g., Gaertner et al., 1999; Levine et al., 2002; Levine et al., 2005). Indeed, to the extent that a reluctance to help out-group members originates from negative out-group attitudes or a mere tendency to favor the in-group, it could be very effective if group members were made aware of the fact that, at a higher level, they all belong to the same inclusive group. As a nice illustration of this point, Levine et al. (2005, Study 2) showed that Manchester United supporters who were induced to think of themselves in terms of a higher-order inclusive category (soccer fans) were equally likely to offer help to Liverpool fans as to Manchester United fans in an emergency, whereas both were helped significantly more than strangers who could not be identified as soccer fans. By contrast, when their perceptual focus was on their membership as Manchester United fans, they were less likely to offer help to Liverpool fans compared to Manchester fans (Study 1).

In Levine's research, a salient in-group–out-group distinction resulted in the tendency to favor in-group members over out-group members with respect to offering help in an emergency. By recategorizing to a higher level of inclusiveness (soccer fans in general), in-group favoritism was eliminated (or rather, diverted to a higher level). However, when helping an out-group is viewed to directly benefit the in-group, as is the case with the strategic motives for out-group helping listed in this chapter, the situation changes. In the case of strategic motives for out-group helping, diverting attention away from the in-group–out-group categorization to a more inclusive common identity should reduce the extent to which helping serves to fulfill any of these motives. As a consequence, recategorizing to a more inclusive level could reduce, rather than increase, out-group helping. For example, in the research by Hopkins et al. (2007) described earlier in this chapter, Scottish participants were more inclined to help the Welsh in an attempt to counteract the English stereotype of the Scots as mean. The helping behavior thus served to communicate a more positive image of the Scots. To serve this strategic purpose, it appears crucial that Scottish–English categorization is salient, for only then can the behavior be perceived as descriptive of the Scots (and not the English, or British citizens in general). When the motive for helping out-group members is located at the in-group level, out-group helping should be promoted by enhancing the salience of this in-group–out-group categorization, while recategorizing to the level of a common in-group should reduce the willingness to help (former) out-group members. Future research might focus on empirical tests of this line of reasoning.

Another characteristic of the strategic motives listed in this chapter is the fact that they all imply that helping out-group members is beneficial to the in-group. However, there are differences in the extent to which this in-group benefit is accompanied by out-group harm, which ultimately has important consequences for the extent to which it is desirable to promote these motives for helping. In the tsunami study, for example (van Leeuwen, 2007), participants wanted their government to help the victimized countries particularly in those domains that were uniquely and positively associated with their threatened national identity. To the extent that this type of help is useful for the recipient it can be considered as a win/win situation – the out-group receives instrumental help, and the benefits for the in-group (in reaffirming a threatened national identity) are not at the expense of the out-group. Other situations with a win/win potential are those where helping is used to create an impression of the in-group as warm and prosocial. For example, helping visiting students from another university find their way to an information center (van Leeuwen & Oostenbrink, 2005) is beneficial both to the visiting student and to the helper in terms of generating a positive impression of the in-group. Although it is certainly possible for groups to compete over which one is the most warm and kind, occasions where helping as a demonstration of such warmth is experienced by the recipient as damaging and hostile are probably rare (in fact, we can think of no examples). More specifically, portraying the in-group as warm and kind by helping another group does not automatically suggest that the recipient group is cold or unkind.

The situation is different when the competition is not about which group is the most kind, but about which group is the most competent. This is because helping another group with the aim of demonstrating the in-group's competence can simultaneously communicate that the recipient of help lacks this particular competence (at least in the eyes of the helper). For the helper, this only further serves their cause, as the in-group, by comparison, is viewed as more competent. The helpee, on the other hand, is facing a dilemma in which accepting help may be beneficial in instrumental terms, but it will also be at the expense of their group's image. Probably the most detrimental motive for out-group helping occurs when help is used to gain power or control over the out-group. Receiving unsolicited support causes stress (Deelstra et al., 2003) and lowers competence-based self-esteem (Schneider et al., 1996).

It seems rather clear that under normal circumstances help should not be offered or provided when it is psychologically harmful to the recipient, to the point where the help is rejected if possible or other (feasible) forms of help are greatly preferred. However, it is nonetheless worthwhile to consider the potential merits of those forms of strategic out-group help that have the potential of benefiting both the provider and the recipient of help. When caution is taken to respect the recipient's needs – both at the instrumental level and at the psychological level – there is great potential in simultaneously acknowledging the added value of helping for the helper's needs. This is because acts of help that reflect genuine altruism are difficult to accomplish and even harder to sustain – perhaps even more so at the intergroup level where behavior tends to be more competitive in nature (Wolf, Insko, Kirchner, & Wildschut, 2008). Moreover, there are limits to the effectiveness of other tools that may promote out-group helping. Decategorizing, defined as viewing out-group members as separate individuals in order to overcome in-group bias, is difficult to accomplish with large out-groups or when help cannot easily be targeted at separate individuals. Along similar lines, recategorizing or emphasizing common identities whilst downplaying subgroup identities is not always possible, and often undesirable. For example, departments within an organization can have different and sometimes conflicting goals, such as production and sales. Downplaying the different departments' needs in favor of a shared cooperative goal not only distracts people from accomplishing these (functional) goals, it often backfires and promotes intergroup conflict in a collective attempt to (re)establish a distinctive group identity (Eggins, Haslam, & Reynolds, 2002). It is therefore important that we further our study of the conditions under which people are motivated to help out-group members – not because they are viewed as separate individuals, not because they are viewed as fellow in-group members at a higher level of inclusiveness, but exactly because they are seen for what they are: out-group members.

Part II

Consequences of Giving or Receiving Help in the Context of Groups

5

Discrimination Against Out-Group Members in Helping Situations

Donald A. Saucier, Jessica L. McManus, and Sara J. Smith

Introduction

The factors that influence an individual's decision to help or not to help another individual in an emergency situation have long been studied by social psychologists. One factor that appears influential in the potential helper's decision to help or not to help is the relative group status of the individual who needs help. Several theories have attempted to describe the situations in which discrimination is and is not likely to emerge in helping, including aversive racism theory (Gaertner & Dovidio, 1986), the justification–suppression model for the expression and experience of prejudice (Crandall & Eshleman, 2003), and the arousal: cost–reward model of helping (Piliavin, Dovidio, Gaertner, & Clark, 1981). This chapter will discuss these theories, and will discuss the specific factors that have emerged from the intergroup helping literature that affect preferences to help members of one's own social group more than members of other groups in the same situations. Further, that body of work is extended by studies we will describe that examine how perceptions of targets and situational characteristics affect perceptions of helping responses (e.g., in the aftermath of Hurricane Katrina). Finally, we will discuss directions for future research that could further illuminate the process of out-group discrimination in helping decisions.

The Evolution of Racial Prejudice

Racial prejudice has become more covert over the past several decades. While old-fashioned prejudice consisted of blatant expressions of negativity that were clearly motivated by prejudice, contemporary forms of prejudice consist of more subtle behaviors that are more ambiguously motivated. These behaviors could be motivated by prejudice, but often can be plausibly attributed to some other non-prejudiced motivation. Several social psychologists have offered models reflecting this evolution of prejudice that specify the routes by which prejudice will emerge and/or the situations that may prompt its expression. For example, these include regressive racism (Rogers & Prentice-Dunn, 1981), symbolic racism (Sears, 1988), modern racism (McConahay, 1986), ambivalent racism (Katz & Hass, 1988), dual racism (Czopp & Monteith, 2006), subtle versus blatant prejudice (Pettigrew & Meertens, 1995), the dissociation model of prejudice (Devine, 1989), aversive racism (Gaertner & Dovidio, 1986), and the justification–suppression model of prejudice (Crandall & Eshleman, 2003).

While the expression of racism has changed, it is important to note that racism has not disappeared; it has only become less visible. While studies using obvious survey-type measures have suggested that racism has decreased substantially (e.g., Dovidio & Gaertner, 1991), other studies have suggested that racism remains at robust levels (e.g., Fazio, Jackson, Dunton, & Williams, 1995). For example, Jones (1997) reported that discrimination still exists in the employment domain, with Blacks having higher rates of unemployment and lower levels of compensation when employed than similarly qualified Whites. One clever study showed that racial discrimination only emerged when the behavior could be rationalized with a non-prejudiced explanation (Dovidio & Gaertner, 2000). Having to evaluate candidates for a peer counseling position, White participants rated White and Black candidates similarly when the candidates were blatantly strong or when the candidates were blatantly weak. However, when the candidates' qualifications were ambiguous, the participants discriminated; the ambiguous qualifications were perceived to be stronger for the White candidates and weaker for the Black candidates. These results were replicated in samples taken in both 1989 and 1999, even though the latter sample self-reported lower levels of prejudice against Blacks. The expression of prejudice occurred only when it was not obviously prejudice.

This change in the expression of prejudice may be explained by social norms in contemporary society that generally prohibit overt expressions of prejudice (Crandall, Eshleman, & O'Brien, 2002; Monteith, Deneen, & Tooman, 1996). It is possible that individuals would face some form of social punishment or sanction if they behaved in prejudiced ways. Further, individuals may have internalized these social norms and consequently would feel guilty if they perceived themselves to behave prejudicially (Fazio & Hilden, 2001; Monteith, 1993). Two different conceptualizations have been offered to explain and measure how these motivations to inhibit expressions of prejudice exist within individuals. One conceptualization asserts that individuals have separate internal and external motivations to respond without prejudice. The internal motivation arises from one's personal belief that prejudice is wrong while the external motivation arises from one's recognition of social pressure that compels adherence to social norms (Plant & Devine, 1998). The other conceptualization asserts that individuals have two aspects within their motivation to control prejudiced responding. The first aspect consists of the individuals' concern that they will appear prejudiced to themselves or to others. The second aspect consists of their use of restraint to avoid dispute and social conflict (Dunton & Fazio, 1997). These conceptualizations combine to illustrate that individuals' social behavior will be produced not only by their underlying attitudes toward others, but also by their own evaluation of the norms of the situation and how their behavioral choice may be perceived in those situations.

Manifestations in Helping Behavior

To identify and measure expressions of contemporary forms of prejudice, researchers have employed paradigms in which participants react to a target individual of a different social group (e.g., based on race) in some situation. These reactions are compared to the reactions given when the target individual is of the same social group as the participants. These highly creative paradigms have used a variety of behaviors as the dependent measure, such as aggression (e.g., Beal, O'Neal, Ong, & Ruscher, 2000; see Crosby, Bromley, & Saxe, 1980, for a review), non-verbal behaviors (see Crosby et al., 1980, for a review), decisions about guilt or sentencing in mock court decisions (e.g., Marcus-Newhall, Blake, & Bauman, 2002; Saucier, Hockett, & Wallenberg, 2008), ratings of job candidates and hiring decisions (e.g., Dovidio & Gaertner, 2000), and customer service behaviors (e.g., Hebl, Foster, Mannix, & Dovidio, 2002; LaPiere, 1934). One measure of particular interest is helping behavior. In these studies, participants are given the opportunity to help target individuals in some situation. The decision to help or the extent of help is recorded, and the rates of help given to members of the same race are compared to the rates of help given to members of a different race. Thus, the dependent measure is a relatively overt expression of discrimination at the behavioral rather than at the cognitive or affective level. These studies, often conducted in the field, have included such diverse situations as having people in need of help request money (e.g., Bickman & Kamzan, 1973), drop items (e.g., Lerner & Frank, 1974), appear to pass out due to illness or drunkenness (Piliavin, Rodin, & Piliavin, 1969), have car trouble on the side of the road (e.g., West, Whitney, & Schnedler, 1975), lose school applications (e.g., Benson, Karabenick, & Lerner, 1976), call wrong numbers (e.g., Gaertner & Bickman, 1971), or appear to be crushed by falling chairs (e.g., Gaertner & Dovidio, 1977).

In each of these paradigms, the behavior that individuals commit (or omit) toward in-group members is compared to the behavior that individuals commit (or omit) toward out-group members. The extent of this difference is the measure of discrimination. However, the motivation for the discrimination is often difficult to identify. Brewer (1999) argues that discrimination (i.e., the differential treatment of in-group and out-group members) is often produced by increases in positive behaviors (or decreases in negative behaviors) toward in-group members, not by decreases in positive behaviors (or increases in negative behaviors) toward out-group behaviors. Thus, the motivation for discrimination would be positivity related to in-group identification rather than negativity related to out-group derogation. Unfortunately, much of the fieldwork examining behavioral expressions of discrimination, including the vast majority of research using helping behavior, does not allow for the motivations for the differences in behavioral expressions to be assessed and evaluated.

The decisions by many researchers to use helping behavior as the dependent measure and differential rates of helping as evidence of discrimination stem from the intriguing nature of helping behavior in general. Helping is usually perceived as positive behavior; this is specified in its definition as "prosocial." However, much research has explored the various self-centered, rather than other-centered, motivations that inspire individuals' decisions to help others (see Dovidio, Piliavin, Schroeder, & Penner, 2006). These motivations could include expectations of tangible or social rewards (Moss & Page, 1972), expectations of increased mood (e.g., Manucia, Baumann, & Cialdini, 1984; Williamson & Clark, 1989), adherence to reciprocity norms (e.g., Regan, 1971; Whatley, Webster, Smith, & Rhodes, 1999), avoidance of expected social punishment (e.g., Archer, Diaz-Loving, Gollwitzer, Davis, & Foushee, 1981; Moss & Page, 1972), or avoidance of negative feelings that are produced by the situation itself or expected to be produced if one did not help (e.g., Cialdini, Kenrick, & Baumann,

1982; Schaller & Cialdini, 1988). While it is certain that some helping is selfishly motivated, some researchers have asserted further that selfless helping, or altruism, does not exist at all (or at least that its existence has not yet been confirmed by research; Cialdini, Schaller, Houlihan, Arps, Fultz, & Beaman, 1987; Maner, Luce, Neuberg, Cialdini, Brown, & Sagarin, 2002). Thus, helping is a behavior that one may use as self-presentational (Gustavo, Eisenberg, Troyer, Switzer, & Speer, 1991) because others perceive the behavior positively.

In the case of helping someone of a different race, the decision to help could be a way for individuals to show others how unprejudiced they are. However, it may not be true evidence that one is unprejudiced. Interestingly, arguments can be made that helping in an interracial context may be an expression of one's superiority, a paternalistic statement of how a minority group must rely on a majority group for its own well-being. Studies have shown that majority group members may be more willing to help minority group members who appear to be subordinate or submissive than those who appear more equal or assertive (Clark, 1974; Katz, Cohen, & Glass, 1975). Consistent with the implications of these findings, our own work has shown that White participants may perceive Blacks more negatively when the participants help Black organizations at the request of a Black experimenter in a forced compliance paradigm (Saucier & Miller, 2001). Further, when majority group members help minority group members in stereotype-relevant domains, the consequences of that help may not be completely beneficial. One study (Schneider, Major, Luhtanen, & Crocker, 1996) has demonstrated that assumptive help (i.e., help that was not requested) given by majority group members to minority group members on a difficult cognitive task was perceived positively by the minority group members, who were thankful for the help and liked the helpers. However, the minority group members suffered decrements in their competence-based self-esteem and more depressed affect as a result. Thus, helping may not be entirely prosocial in all cases, and a majority group member's decision to help a minority group member may not always be an indication that the majority group member is unprejudiced.

Further, a majority group member's decision not to help a minority group member may not always be an indication that the majority group member is prejudiced. In order for an individual to decide to help someone else, a process of several steps must be completed. These steps include noticing the situation, interpreting the situation as requiring help, taking responsibility for providing the help, planning the specific helping response, and implementing the helping response (Latané & Darley, 1970). An interruption of this process at any step will result in no help being given. If the individual does not help, it is difficult to isolate why. When the individual fails to help someone of another race, it is possible that this act of omission is a manifestation of racial discrimination. However, it is possible that the lack of help was due to the individual not noticing the situation, interpreting it correctly, or taking personal responsibility to help. Even if these were not the reasons for the lack of help, they provide possible "safe" (i.e., non-prejudiced) rationales that the individual may employ to explain the decision not to help.

It is our contention that the respective races of the potential helpers and the target individuals who need help are factors in the decisions to help or not. However, we do not believe that individuals will always discriminate against members of other races in helping situations. Rather, we predict that discrimination will occur when situations offer individuals the opportunity to attribute a decision not to help to a motivation other than prejudice. We believe it is then that individuals will show reliable differences in their decisions to help: They will help members of their own race more than members of a different race. This prediction is based on the justification-suppression model of prejudice (Crandall & Eshleman, 2003). According to this model, the extent of an individual's actual level of negativity toward another social group, called "genuine prejudice," is affected by both justification and suppression factors before expression. The final form of the "expressed prejudice" may bear little resemblance to the actual level of genuine prejudice. This model asserts that virtually all theories of contemporary prejudice state that individuals possess prejudice toward other groups, but that this prejudice is often inhibited as a function of social norms and internalized standards of non-prejudiced behavior. Therefore, prejudice is suppressed unless it is justified in its expression. Factors that contribute to the suppression of prejudice and reduce expressed prejudice include social norms, self-presentational concerns, egalitarian values, and other personal moral standards. Factors that contribute to the justification of prejudice and increase the levels of expressed prejudice include beliefs in social hierarchies, system justification, the Protestant ethic, attributions of blame to individuals for their own plights and stigmas, scapegoating, and "covering" the behavior with a plausible alternative motivation. By examining the presence and levels of various suppression and justification factors in helping situations, we expect to be better able to identify those situations in which expressed prejudice would emerge.

Synthesizing the Literature Examining Racial Discrimination in Helping Situations

The literature examining the extent to which individuals do and do not help members of the same or different races has primarily employed situations in which majority group members (i.e., Whites) are given the opportunity to help target individuals who either are also majority group members (i.e., Whites) or are minority group members (i.e., Blacks). For that reason, we will confine our discussion to these studies. We are not the first to examine the patterns of discrimination reported in the helping literature in terms of how often or how much discrimination is shown and what situational factors affect the patterns of discrimination. Crosby et al. (1980) reviewed studies that investigated these effects. Overall, their review showed that racial discrimination did not emerge in the form of differential helping rates in the majority of the studies. Only 44 percent of the studies demonstrated that potential helpers helped members of their own racial group more than they helped members of a different racial group in the same helping situations.

Crosby et al. (1980) also examined how the type of helping required by the situation would affect the rates of discrimination by categorizing studies according to the characteristics of the helping situations. The first category consisted of studies in which helping would require face-to-face contact between the potential helper and the person who needed help. The second category, which they described as "remote," consisted of studies in which helping would not require face-to-face contact between the helper and the person who needed help. Crosby et al. (1980) showed that discrimination was much more likely to occur in remote helping situations than in face-to-face situations. They attributed this difference to Whites' tendencies to inhibit prejudice in the face-to-face situations so that they would avoid negative social penalties. They reasoned that Whites would be less motivated to inhibit prejudice in remote situations when the likelihood of the same social penalties was lower, and they could get away with choosing not to help more easily.

The Crosby et al. (1980) literature review demonstrated that situational factors, specifically the nature of the interpersonal contact between the potential helper and the person who needed help, were important in determining when discrimination against minority group members would occur in helping situations. We used their contribution as the foundation for our own meta-analytic synthesis of the literature examining discrimination in helping situations, but expanded the scope of the situational factors that we assessed (Saucier, Miller, & Doucet, 2005). We used the theory of aversive racism (Gaertner & Dovidio, 1986) and the justification–suppression model of prejudice (Crandall & Eshleman, 2003) to help isolate various situational elements that could provide individuals with defensible reasons to decide not to help someone in a helping situation.

Aversive racism refers to the aversive feelings, such as fear, disgust, and uneasiness, that members of one group may feel in the presence of members of another group. Rather than an overt display of hostility, these feelings may produce less obvious expressions of discrimination, such as avoidance (Gaertner & Dovidio, 1986) or, we reasoned, decisions not to help members of other groups. Both aversive racism theory and the justification-suppression model of prejudice support predictions that individuals will express prejudice when it is not obvious that they are doing so. This prejudice may be more likely to occur when it would result in a defensible withdrawal from potential social interactions, such as those that would occur in helping situations. We believed the factors contributing to the ability to attribute decisions not to help to some plausible alternative (i.e., non-prejudiced) rationale included the time it would take to help; the risk, effort, difficulty, and financial cost involved; the distance between the potential helper and the person needing help; the level of emergency; and the ambiguity of the helping situation (i.e., how clear it was that the person needed help). In any situation, it seemed plausible that individuals could more reasonably decline to help another person of any social group without fear of being accused of being prejudiced if the type of help needed was objectively higher in its time cost, risk effort, difficulty, and financial cost, if the person needing help was further away, if the level of emergency was lower, and if the level of ambiguity was higher. We predicted that when these reasons were more readily available, individuals who were majority group members (i.e., White) would use them more to rationalize decisions not to help when the person needing help was a minority group member (i.e., Black) than when the person needing help was another majority group member (i.e., White) (Saucier et al., 2005).

Further, we used the arousal: cost–reward model of helping (Piliavin et al., 1981) as the basis for assessing other elements of the helping situations that could contribute to understanding when discrimination is likely to occur in helping situations (Saucier et al., 2005). This model states that helping situations create feelings of arousal in potential helpers who then feel compelled to alleviate that arousal. Their choice of action for alleviating that arousal depends on their assessment of the relative costs of helping and costs of not helping in that situation. The costs of helping would include many of the factors we described above, such as the time, risk, and effort involved in helping. The costs of not helping would include the level of emergency for the person needing help and the negative feelings that the potential helpers would feel if they chose not to help, such as guilt and regret.

We retrieved all of the published studies that examined the rates of help given by White potential helpers to both White and Black individuals who needed help in the same situations. Independent coders rated the levels of the situational factors inspired by aversive racism theory, the justification–suppression model of prejudice, and the arousal: cost–reward model of helping that existed in the helping situations. We assessed the levels of discrimination shown in the rates of help given to Whites compared to Blacks in the same situations. We then assessed how these rates related to the situational factors of the helping situations (Saucier et al., 2005).

Our results showed that, overall, discrimination was not shown universally. The rates and extent of help given to White and Black targets were not significantly different, and the effect size actually demonstrated a very small tendency for more help to have been given to Blacks than to Whites. More importantly, the levels of discrimination were found to depend on the situational factors of the various helping situations. Specifically, in support of aversive racism theory, discrimination against Blacks relative to Whites increased as the help in the given situations required more time, risk, difficulty, and effort, and as the distance between the potential helper and the person needing help increased. Thus, when there was more opportunity for non-prejudiced rationales to explain decisions not to help, less help was given to Blacks than to Whites. These results also supported the justification–suppression model of prejudice: when more justification for not helping existed, prejudice was suppressed less in helping situations (Saucier et al., 2005).

Not all of the results supported the predictions made by aversive racism theory, however. Higher levels of ambiguity and financial cost were not associated with higher levels of discrimination. Further, the levels of emergency in the situation were significantly related to levels of discrimination, but not in the predicted direction. We hypothesized that higher levels of emergency would make the decision not to help less justifiable, and would therefore be associated with lower levels of discrimination. Contrary to that hypothesis, our results indicated that higher levels of emergency were associated with higher levels of discrimination; that is, when the levels of emergency increased, Blacks received less help than did Whites in the same situations (Saucier et al., 2005).

Our results regarding the arousal: cost–reward model of helping indicated that higher levels of discrimination were associated with higher costs of helping and with higher costs of not helping. The first finding was consistent with our predictions. When helping required greater levels of overall investment, less help was given to Blacks than to Whites in the same situations. Rather than invest resources to help Blacks, the potential helpers were more likely to conserve their resources and choose not to help. The second finding did not support our hypotheses as nicely. This finding indicated that as the costs of not helping increased, such as the level of emergency in the situation and how bad or regretful helpers would feel if they did not help, discrimination against Blacks also increased. It is important to note that the independent coders in our research laboratory who rated the costs of helping and not helping in the various situations did so based solely on the factors related to the actual helping situation without considering the race of the person needing help. What this finding may indicate is that the potential helpers in those situations perceived the costs of not helping to be higher when the person needing help was White than when the person needing help was Black. That is, the potential helpers may have seen less emergency in the situations in which Blacks needed help, and may have felt less bad and less regret when not helping Blacks (compared to Whites). Thus, while increases in the costs of not helping may increase helping, the discrimination we found may indicate that the perception of the costs of not helping may depend on the perceptions of, and possibly prejudice toward, the individuals who need the help (Saucier et al., 2005).

Our finding that discrimination against Blacks was higher in situations in which the emergency level was higher deserves further comment. We originally predicted that discrimination would be negatively associated, or not associated, with the level of emergency in helping situations. We reasoned that as the level of emergency increased, the ability for White individuals to justify not helping Blacks with non-prejudiced rationales would be lower, and the levels of help the Blacks received in those situations would either exceed or be similar to the levels of help that Whites received in the same situations. Further consideration of these situations, however, led us to believe that we may have been incorrect in our thinking. Emergency situations are stressful. The potential helpers in those situations are likely experiencing greater levels of stress and increased levels of cognitive load. This stress and cognitive load may make them less able to consciously suppress or inhibit the expression of prejudice through avoidance or withdrawal behaviors. Indeed, this finding appears consistent with Devine's (1989) conceptualization of prejudice as a combination of automatic and controlled processes (see also Fazio et al., 1995; Greenwald & Banaji, 1995; Smith & DeCoster, 2000; Wilson, Lindsey, & Schooler, 2000). Attempts to suppress prejudice are not always successful (Bargh, Chen, & Burrows, 1996; Monteith, Sherman, & Devine, 1998), and this failure may be related to limits in cognitive capacity (Gilbert & Hixon, 1991) and efforts to conserve cognitive resources (Macrae, Milne, & Bodenhausen, 1994). Thus, the increased expression of discrimination when the emergency level was higher may be due to inabilities to inhibit the automatic negativity often possessed by Whites toward Blacks because of interruptions in these control processes. It is a sobering conclusion that prejudice may be especially uninhibited and produce more discrimination in helping situations when the consequences of not receiving help are most dire.

The Possibility of Discrimination in the Helping Response to Hurricane Katrina

Shortly after we published our meta-analysis (Saucier et al., 2005), we had the opportunity to use our conclusions in a retrospective attempt to understand a real-world catastrophe in which the consequences for not receiving help were especially dire. On the morning of August 29, 2005, Hurricane Katrina made landfall on the Louisiana coast, devastating the area. Thousands of people, many of whom were Black and/or poor, were left without the resources to meet even their most basic needs. While it appeared obvious that the level of emergency required an enormous helping response from the federal government, that response was initially far from adequate. For instance, Louisiana Governor Kathleen Blanco's calls to President Bush to plead for assistance were not answered or were rerouted (Thomas, 2005). Personnel for the Federal Emergency Management Agency (FEMA) did not receive orders to help the region until more than a day later and the National Guard did not receive their orders to assist until two days later. Further, New Mexico Governor Bill Richardson was not allowed to send his state's National Guard to assist until two days after his initial request (O'Brien & Bender, 2005). In addition, the USS *Bataan*, a naval vessel, was not initially deployed to provide assistance, despite being in the area (Hedges, 2005).

The federal government's slow and inadequate response was quickly accused of being at least somewhat attributable to prejudice against the many Black and poor victims. These accusations came from New Orleans City Councilman Oliver Thomas, members of the Congressional Black Caucus, and the Reverend Jesse Jackson (CBS/Associated Press, 2005). Probably the most famous accusation was made by rapper Kanye West during a live television event aired to raise funds to assist the victims of Hurricane Katrina. West asserted that the helping efforts were lacking because "George Bush doesn't care about Black people" (Associated Press, 2005). Was the federal government expressing prejudice based on the race and/or socioeconomic status of the victims of Hurricane Katrina by not exerting more strenuous efforts to help them?

The Hurricane Katrina situation presented a potential real-world manifestation of the ways in which discrimination may emerge in helping behavior. However, this type of discussion is rightfully limited. The psychological literature has examined individuals' helping decisions that generally benefit one other individual. In this situation, one large group (the federal government) was presented with the situation to help another large group (the victims of Hurricane Katrina). Further, the Hurricane Katrina situation was not a controlled study designed and conducted to test *a priori* hypotheses. Instead, we are left to retrospectively apply theoretical perspectives in an attempt to explain what happened. While this was speculative and not truly explanatory, we believed there was value in doing so.

Other researchers have similarly examined the Hurricane Katrina situation through the retrospective theoretical lens of prejudice and discrimination theories. Avdeyeva, Burgetova, and Welch (2006) discussed the possibility that helping following Hurricane Katrina may have been slow and inadequate due to contextual factors, including the dissimilarity between the potential helpers and the victims of Hurricane Katrina, the levels of intergroup contact, intraracial norms regarding the appropriateness of requesting help, and the situational factors of the actual helping situation, such as the ambiguity of the situation. Napier and colleagues discussed the Hurricane Katrina situation in terms of system justification, arguing that the situation compelled many people to blame the Hurricane Katrina victims for their own plight so that the status quo and perceptions of the system as fair would remain intact (Napier, Mandisodza, Andersen, & Jost, 2006). Henkel, Dovidio, and Gaertner (2006) argued that institutional racism may have contributed to the slow helping response.

Our own examination of the Hurricane Katrina situation (Saucier, Smith, & McManus, 2007) concluded that the situation appeared to exhibit the situational factors that we had previously shown to be associated with expressions of racial discrimination in helping situations (Saucier et al., 2005). There were several available reasons other than the race and/or socioeconomic status of the people needing help to explain why the helping response may have been less substantial than the situation warranted. These included that the helping response would require a great deal of time, effort, difficulty, risk, and financial cost. Each of these situational characteristics was associated with racial discrimination in our earlier meta-analysis, with the exception of financial cost. As these factors increased, the ability to explain decisions not to help with non-prejudiced explanations increased, and overall helping decreased. Further, the emergency level of the Hurricane Katrina situation was undeniably high, which we found to be associated with the expression of discrimination. Finally, paralleling our results from the arousal: cost-reward model of helping in which we showed that discrimination was associated with higher costs of helping and higher costs of not helping, the Hurricane Katrina situation was one in which the costs of both helping and not helping were very high. We concluded that, while we can not definitively determine the extent to which racial and/or class discrimination was expressed in the federal government's slow and weak initial helping response for the Hurricane Katrina victims, the helping situation did share many of the situational factors that have been associated with racial discrimination across the social psychological literature (Saucier, Smith, & McManus, in prep.).

Perceptions of the Victims of Hurricane Katrina and of the Helping Response

We designed a study to explore the relationships among perceptions of the victims affected by Hurricane Katrina, perceptions of the situational characteristics, and perceptions of the adequacy of the helping response provided to those victims (Saucier et al., in prep.). We created questionnaires in which we measured participants' perceptions of the victims of Hurricane Katrina, of the situational factors of the helping response, of the costs of helping and not helping in the Hurricane Katrina situation, and of the adequacy of the federal helping response. Further, we included individual difference measures to assess participants' levels of conservatism, empathy (Davis, 1983a), belief in a just world (Rubin & Peplau, 1975), social dominance orientation

(Pratto, Sidanius, Stallworth, & Malle, 1994), values related to the Protestant ethic and humanitarianism/egalitarianism (Katz & Hass, 1988), and racism (i.e., the Racial Argument Scale; Saucier & Miller, 2003).

Participants generally reported that they perceived the majority of the victims of Hurricane Katrina to be members of minority groups ($M = 61$ percent) and of lower socioeconomic status ($M = 56$ percent), and these perceptions did not vary as a function of any of the individual difference measures. To assess how the individual difference variables related to the participants' perceptions of the victims of Hurricane Katrina, the situational factors, and the federal helping response, we included the participants' scores on each of the individual difference factors in regression models to predict those perceptions. Negative perceptions of the victims and blaming the victims for staying in the path of Hurricane Katrina were generally uniquely associated with higher levels of racism and social dominance orientation, $\beta s > .10$, $ps < .018$, and with lower levels of empathy, $\beta s > |-.14|$, $ps < .007$. Perceptions that the federal helping response was inadequate were uniquely associated with higher levels of empathy, $\beta = .11$, $p = .049$ and lower levels of conservatism, $\beta = -.12$, $p = .020$. Perceptions that the inadequacy of the helping response was due to prejudice against the victims of Hurricane Katrina were uniquely associated with lower levels of racism, $\beta = -.14$, $p = .003$, and conservatism, $\beta = -.14$, $p = .005$. These results suggest that perceptions of the victims and the situation of Hurricane Katrina did depend on the participants' individual differences, including their levels of racism.

Further, the perceptions of the federal helping response for the Hurricane Katrina victims depended on the participants' perceptions of the Hurricane Katrina victims and of the situational factors associated with the helping situation overall. We controlled for the participants' sex, their scores on each of the individual difference measures, and their ratings of the percentages of how many Hurricane Katrina victims were minority group members and how many were of lower socioeconomic status. We then assessed the extent to which the participants' perceptions of the victims and their perceptions of the costs of helping and the costs of not helping predicted their perceptions of the federal helping response. We found that negative perceptions and blaming of the victims of Hurricane Katrina were generally uniquely associated with the participants' perceptions that the situation was less of an emergency and that the victims needed less help, $\beta s > |.13|$, $ps < .022$. Participants' perceptions that the costs of helping were higher were, in general, uniquely associated with perceptions that the victims of Hurricane Katrina needed more help, β = .14, p = .004, that the situation was a greater emergency, β = .24, p < .001, but that the lack of help was less due to prejudice, β = −.18, p = .001. This finding confirms our general prediction that higher costs of helping provided defensible non-prejudiced rationales for not helping. Participants' perceptions that the costs of not helping were higher were generally uniquely associated with perceptions that the Hurricane Katrina victims needed more help, β = .09, p = .046, that the help they received was inadequate, β = .18, p < .001, that the situation was a greater emergency, β = .32, p < .001, and that the lack of help was more due to prejudice, β = .12, p = .011.

Overall, this study showed that individuals' perceptions of victims in helping situations and their perceptions of the adequacy of the helping response were related to their levels of racism and other individual difference variables. While we may not be able to definitively conclude that racism was (or was not) a factor in the adequacy of the federal helping response to assist the victims of Hurricane Katrina, this study suggests that individuals' levels of racism may be associated with their perceptions of the situational factors of the helping situation, the victims themselves, and the helping response received by those victims. Given the magnitude of the Hurricane Katrina catastrophe, it is important to explore how prejudice can affect the perceptions of what objectively appeared to be an undeniably large emergency in which thousands of people did not receive, and have not received, the help they needed.

Financial Cost as a Factor Affecting Discrimination in Helping Situations?

The financial cost required in helping situations was not associated with the levels of discrimination found in our meta-analysis. However, we wondered if that conclusion was a product of those studies including only helping situations that required relatively low levels of financial cost. The studies that we retrieved for the meta-analysis that required a financial investment by the potential helpers either asked for a specific amount of money or asked for a donation or handout of some unspecified amount. In each of these cases, the amount of actual financial cost was objectively low. The amount requested specifically and the average donation received when the amount was unspecified was generally less than $2. Even considering that several of these studies were conducted several decades ago, it appears that the levels of financial cost that have been employed in the past do not provide information about how helping requiring objectively high levels of financial cost relate to discrimination. Given the results of the Hurricane Katrina helping response questionnaire study, we still expected that financial cost would be a factor that would provide the type of defensible non-prejudiced rationalization that would allow majority group individuals to not help members of minority groups without fearing social penalties for discriminating or arousing their own feelings of compunction. To test this, we designed a study in which we manipulated the level of financial cost that would be required by the helping situation to levels that exceeded those employed by the earlier research (McManus & Saucier, in prep.).

Because we did not expect that participants would realistically be able or willing to pay objectively high costs at the time of the study, we did not design the study to collect actual money from our participants in the helping situation. Instead, we structured the request in the helping situation as a proposal to raise scholarship money that participants, who were White, would pay through raises in the tuition amounts that they already pay to their university. In these proposals, we varied who the scholarships would benefit: Black students or students whose race was not specified. Further, we varied the amount that the participants' tuition payments would be raised to provide the funds for the scholarships from relatively low levels (e.g., $2 per semester) to relatively high levels (e.g., $240 per semester). We also measured the participants' levels of racism toward Blacks using the Racial Argument Scale (Saucier & Miller, 2003). Our dependent measure was the level of support that the participants reported for the scholarship proposals.

Our results showed that participants supported scholarship proposals with higher costs less than scholarship proposals with lower costs regardless of whether the scholarships would benefit Black students or students whose race was not specified. This was unsurprising, and supported our prediction that higher levels of financial cost would provide a defensible rationale for deciding not to help. More importantly, the participants' levels of racism, whether the advantaged group's race was Black or not specified, and the level of financial cost interacted to predict the participants' levels of support for the scholarship proposals, R^2 change = .035, $F(5, 341) = 2.69$, $p = .021$. Interestingly, the results did not neatly support our hypothesis that more discrimination would be shown at higher levels of financial cost, with greater levels of discrimination shown by participants higher in racism. We calculated the relationships between racism and support for the scholarship proposals for each combination of the advantaged group's race (Black or unspecified) and financial cost level (six levels that increased in a non-linear fashion from $2 to $240 per semester). Participants' racism levels predicted their support for the scholarship proposals for three of the combinations. At the highest level of financial cost, the participants' racism scores were negatively associated with the support for the scholarships when the advantaged group's race was not specified, $\beta = -.36$, $p = .041$. At the lowest levels of financial cost, the participants' racism scores were positively associated with support for the scholarships when the advantaged group's race was not specified, $\beta = .43$, $p = .006$, but were negatively associated with support for the scholarships when the advantaged group was Black, $\beta = -.36$, $p = .059$. It appears that when the costs of helping are lower, lower prejudice levels in Whites are associated with more helping of Blacks, possibly as attempts to appear non-prejudiced. This finding is consistent with previous research that has shown efforts by people lower in prejudice to "bend over backwards" to show positivity biases toward out-group members (Harber, 1998; Saucier & Miller, 2003; von Hippel, Sekaquaptewa, & Vargas, 1997). Future work is needed to better understand the relationship between helping and discrimination when the financial costs of helping are both high and low.

Directions for Future Research

Research on how discrimination manifests in helping situations has yielded fascinating results that have improved our understanding of how and why discrimination is expressed. However, it has also identified a number of interesting, but unanswered, questions. Future research is needed to explore how the perceptions of the characteristics of helping situations may be affected by potential helpers' perceptions of and prejudice toward the individuals who need help in those situations. It is possible that the altered perceptions of the characteristics of the helping situation provide the justification for not helping. For instance, perhaps Whites higher in prejudice would perceive Black targets to be in less danger than White targets in the same situations, or that helping Black targets would be more difficult, risky, or aversive than helping White targets, and therefore would choose to help the Black targets less often without being consciously aware that their decisions were affected by the targets' race. These perceptions may mediate the relationship between group membership and discrimination in helping situations. Further examination is also warranted of how (potentially conscious) retrospective explanations for not helping make use of justification strategies and capitalize on higher costs of helping, allowing individuals to express prejudice at lower risks that they will be perceived as prejudiced by others or by themselves. It is also important that research on discrimination in helping situations extend beyond race. Much of the work to date has focused on the discrimination shown by the racial majority (i.e., Whites) toward a racial minority (i.e., Blacks) in helping situations. Further investigation of these processes among other social groups is necessary, with particular emphasis on group memberships that may be less visible or even mistakenly assumed, such as sexual orientation, or may vary within rather than between common conceptions of social groups (e.g., rival sports fans; Levine et al., 2005). Our understanding of discrimination in helping situations may be enhanced further by exploring the interaction of individual difference variables (e.g., empathy; Stürmer et al., 2006) with levels of prejudice to produce individuals' decisions to help or to not help. Finally, it is important to better understand how the relatively independent motives of behaving positively toward in-group members and negatively toward out-group members (Brewer, 1999) uniquely contribute to behavioral expressions of discrimination in helping situations.

Conclusion

Our research shows that individuals are more likely to discriminate against members of other social groups in helping situations that have characteristics that would make a decision not to help justifiable. These results are consistent with many of the predictions made by aversive racism theory, the justification-suppression model of prejudice, and the arousal: cost-reward model of helping. Further, we have shown that discrimination may be more likely when the levels of emergency are higher, and that the perceptions of the characteristics of helping situations may depend on the potential helpers' levels of prejudice. Further research on the processes that contribute to the "justifiable" discrimination shown in helping situations is needed to produce a more egalitarian and helpful society.

6

Receiving Help
Consequences for the Recipient

Samer Halabi and Arie Nadler

Introduction

Following the 1993 Oslo agreement between Israelis and Palestinians, the Israeli government attempted to assist Palestinians in various spheres based on an assumption that they needed help. Such efforts were often opposed by Palestinians on the grounds that they would perpetuate Palestinians' economic, academic, or cultural dependence on Israelis (Nadler & Saguy, 2004), and the assistance ultimately did not further conciliatory aims as was initially hoped. Not only in this instance but almost by definition, helping occurs between unequals: A person who has superior resources directs those resources to another person in need. Past research on interpersonal helping has shown that helping can convey caring and generosity on the part of the helper, but at the same time can signify that the recipient is dependent on the helper, threatening the recipient's self-esteem and leading to resistance and the rejection of help (Nadler & Fisher, 1986). Although this interpersonal perspective on helping relations has considered the dynamics of power relations on helping (Worchel, 1984), only recently has this aspect been examined at the intergroup level. We seek to present a model of intergroup helping relations that accounts for the power dynamics attention to the role these dynamics play on the receiving side.

The implications of helping others or being helped by others on the relative status of helpers and recipients has been considered in classical writings in social sciences. Sahlins (1972) argued that the social divide between donors and recipients is usually greater in unreciprocated giving, in which recipients are not obligated to give back in return. For example, for various reasons states sometimes act with the intention to benefit other states without expecting them to reciprocate in kind. Nevertheless, oftentimes this help is perceived as a threat and as promoting hierarchical differentiation (Nishi, 2004). In this respect, Sahlins stated that recipients of unreciprocated giving are not likely to be the social equals of donors or to ever become donors, themselves, to a new generation of recipients. The inability to reciprocate a gift thus affirms the existing hierarchy between donor and recipient.

According to Bourdieu (1990), it is via helping that the donor achieves *symbolic domination*; giving gifts that recipients cannot reciprocate emphasizes that the donor is more competent and worthy of status. Bourdieu writes: "In such a universe, there are two ways of getting and keeping a lasting hold over someone: debts and gifts" (p. 126). The desire of a high-status group to be perceived as just and benevolent and yet to dominate a low-status group reinforces giving as an expression of dominance over recipients. By giving un-reciprocated gifts, the donor's status is transformed from "dominant" to "generous" while the donor still asserts dominance in practice (Bourdieu, 1990).

This dual meaning of helping – expressing care for the other while asserting status – has been considered in previous research in social psychology (Fisher, Nadler, & Whitcher-Alagna, 1983; Nadler & Fisher, 1986), albeit traditionally from an *interpersonal* perspective. For example, such research has focused on how situational or individual characteristics influence whether help is perceived to threaten or enhance the recipient's self-esteem (Fisher et al., 1983; Nadler & Fisher, 1986). More recently, we have shown in parallel to these studies that receiving help from an out-group member can threaten recipients' *collective* self-esteem and thus produce negative personal, collective, and intergroup responses (Halabi, Nadler, & Dovidio, 2008; Nadler & Halabi, 2006). Consequently, we have suggested that intergroup helping may manifest social mechanisms though which groups challenge or preserve existing social hierarchies.

In the present chapter we examine helping as intergroup phenomena, using a framework that incorporates findings and concepts from social identity and helping behavior research. Specifically, we will consider the intersection of the intergroup and interpersonal processes that describe intergroup helping relations as status relations (Nadler, 2002). We will begin by presenting the Intergroup Helping as Status Relations model (IHSR; Nadler, 2002; Nadler & Halabi, 2006), which integrates between key tenets of the social identity perspective (Turner & Reynolds, 2001) and helping relations research (e.g., Dovidio, Piliavin, Schroeder, & Penner, 2006; Nadler & Fisher, 1986). We then present empirical data that support this model, and describe the implications of this approach for a better understanding of interpersonal and intergroup helping relations.

Theoretical Background: The Intergroup Helping as Status Relations Model

Social identity theory (Tajfel & Turner, 1979) has examined the effects of power inequality between groups and its divergent consequences for high- and low-power groups' construal of their social reality (Brown, 2000). These different perspectives on social reality form the basis for the different perceptions, motivations, and behaviors expressed by low- and high-power group members in intergroup interactions. Social identity theory proposes that high-power groups strive to maintain their existing advantage, whereas low-power groups strive to change the status quo and achieve equality.

In parallel, self-categorization theory (Turner, Hogg, Oakes, Reicher, & Wetherell, 1987) has centered on the idea that identity fluctuates between the individual and social levels, depending on the person's frame of reference in the social context. Specifically, when group membership is salient people are likely to think of themselves and others more as group members than as individuals. This tendency is stronger when group members experience a high threat to their social identity, for example if the in-group is portrayed as less successful than a relevant out-group (Branscombe, Ellemers, Spears, & Doosje, 1999).

Negative information about the self threatens personal self-esteem, and studies have shown that in helping contexts recipients sometimes experience decreased self-worth and negative affect (Nadler & Fisher, 1986). Specifically, Nadler and Fisher (1986) argued that receiving assistance is threatening to the extent that it is perceived as challenging one's sense of efficacy. Being dependent on the goodwill of others may constitute a threat to self-esteem because it emphasizes the power discrepancies between the helper and the recipient, between the "independent" party that provides assistance and the "dependent" party that receives it. This inherent inequality in helping interactions makes the receipt of help potentially self-threatening. When this is the case, receiving help can elicit a cluster of negative or defensive reactions from recipients such that they may be unwilling to seek help, refuse offers of help, report negative personal affect, and provide negative evaluations of the helper (Fisher et al., 1983).

Building on an integration between the social identity perspective and research on interpersonal helping relations, Nadler (2002) proposed the Intergroup Helping as Status Relations (IHSR) model. The model proposes that intergroup helping relations can be a mechanism for groups to assert or challenge their status relative to a relevant out-group, and that offers of assistance, especially for low-status groups, can lead to negative personal, collective, and intergroup responses by threatening low-status group members' collective self-esteem. For example, Schneider, Major, Luhtanen, and Crocker (1996) found that Black participants who received assumptive help (i.e., unsolicited help given in the absence of evidence of personal need) from a White experimenter experienced negative affect and decreased self-worth, but that this was not the case when the helper was Black. In a similar study, Halabi, Nadler, and Dovidio (2008) found that Arab Israelis who received assumptive help from a Jewish Israeli (i.e., low- versus high-status groups in Israel, respectively) suffered a decrease in perceptions of self-worth and collective self-esteem, whereas those who received assumptive help from an Arab Israeli did not. These effects were particularly pronounced for participants who were induced to perceive that their need for help was high as opposed to low.

The IHSR model proposes a systematic account of the way in which intergroup helping relations serve as a vehicle for high-status groups to preserve their social advantage and for low-status groups to challenge their disadvantaged position in the hierarchy. It makes specific predictions for the low- and high-status group members in terms of seeking, providing, and responding to help and argues that intergroup helping relations between them are influenced by the characteristics of three elements of the helping situation: the structure of the *social hierarchy* (i.e., the security of status relations), the *type of help* offered (i.e., autonomy- versus dependency-oriented help), and the *individual group member* (e.g., degree of in-group commitment and social dominance orientation).

The Intergroup Helping as Status Relations Model: Basic Determinants

Structural Characteristics: The Security of Status Relations

Tajfel and Turner (1979) proposed that the perceived *security of existing status relations* is the main determinant of group members' reactions to existing inequality. When a status hierarchy is perceived as secure (i.e., stable and legitimate), high- and low-status groups are less motivated to engage in collective action aimed at changing power relations, since the possibility to create social change is low. However, when the status hierarchy is perceived as insecure (i.e., unstable

```
                        Intergroup status relations
                         ↙              ↘
        Low perceived legitimacy          High perceived legitimacy
           and stability of                   and stability of
           status relations                    status relations
            ↙        ↘                        ↙        ↘
```

High-status group	Low-status group	High-status group	Low-status group
High motivation to reassert power and diffuse threat to social dominance	High motivation of low-status group to challenge existing hierarchy	Medium to low motivation of the high-status group to assert power	Dependency on the high-status group is relatively non-threatening to social identity
↓	↓	↓	↓
Increased effort to provide dependency-oriented help to low status out-group	• No help seeking from high status out-group • Unwillingness to receive assumptive help from high status out-group • Greater willingness to seek and receive autonomy-oriented help	High level of giving dependency-oriented help to low status out-group	• High level of seeking dependency-oriented help from high status out-group • Willingness to receive dependency-oriented help from high status out-group

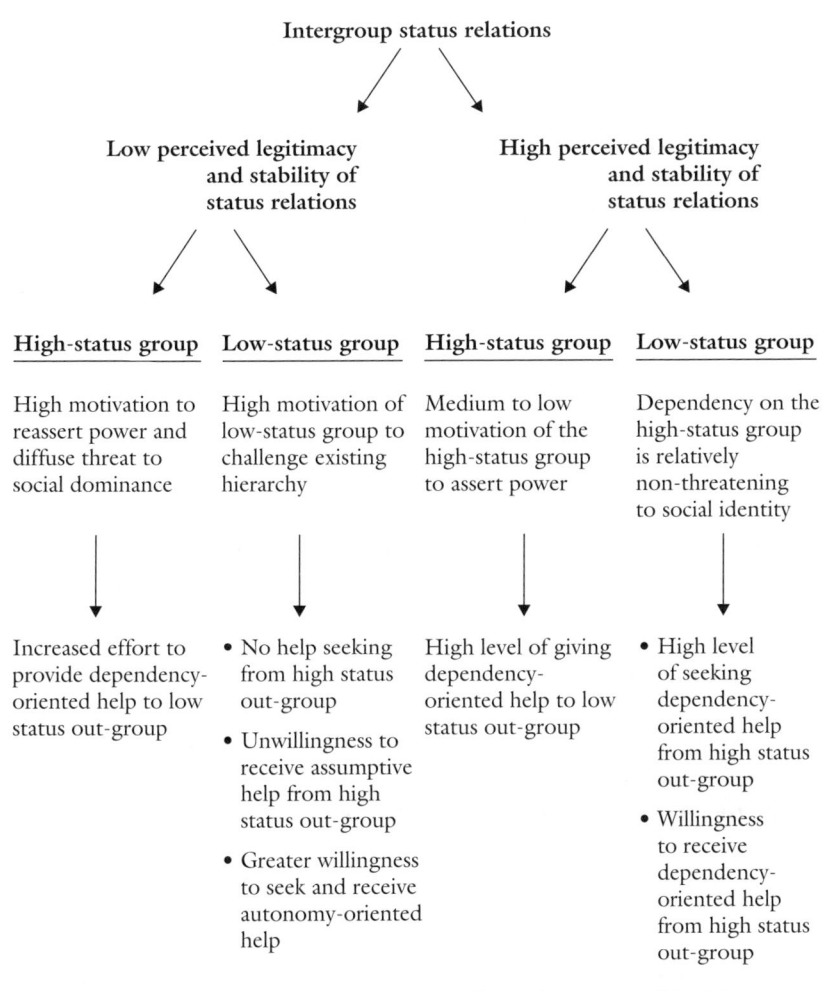

Figure 6.1 Intergroup helping relations as affected by perceived legitimacy and stability of status relations between groups.

and illegitimate), high-status members are motivated to defend their advantaged position by asserting their group's positive distinctiveness. Under these conditions, low-status group members view their group's disadvantaged position as changeable and are therefore expected to act collectively to change the status quo and attain equality with the high-status group (Tajfel & Turner, 1986; Turner & Brown, 1978; see also Ellemers, Wilke, & van Knippenberg, 1993).

Using this distinction between secure versus insecure status relations, the IHSR model posits that when status relations are perceived to be insecure, members of low-status groups will be particularly unwilling to be dependent on the high-status group, and hence unwilling to receive or seek help from its members. Moreover, members of low-status groups are likely to interpret help offered by members of the high-status group as intended to maintain the helping group's relative dominance. This inconsistency between dependency on the high-status group and the motivation for greater equality will lead members of low-status groups to reject offers of help when status relations are perceived as insecure. If help is indeed received under these circumstances, it will elicit a cluster of responses intended to restore low-status members' positive social identity and minimize the degree of threat to social identity.

Characteristics of Help: Autonomy-Oriented versus Dependency-Oriented

In dependency-oriented help the helper gives the recipient the full solution to a problem; although this kind of help fulfills recipients' immediate needs, it does very little to help them become self-sufficient over time. In autonomy-oriented help, on the other hand, the helper gives the recipient partial or temporary help that allows them to obtain the full solution to the problem at hand. This type of help provides recipients with the tools to attain self-reliance. It meets recipients' immediate needs and also imparts the knowledge that enables recipients to fend for themselves in the long run (Nadler, 1997, 1998).

In the IHSR model the distinction between autonomy- and dependency-oriented help is assumed to affect whether dependence on a more privileged out-group will threaten recipients' personal and social identity. Members of high-status groups who are motivated to maintain their in-group's advantage will offer dependency-oriented help to the low-status group. By withholding knowledge that will allow recipients to gain future self-reliance, the helping group maintains its advantage over the receiving group. This motivation of the high-status group to maintain its advantage will be particularly high when the status hierarchy is perceived as insecure. Under these conditions of perceived status insecurity, members of low-status groups will view the status hierarchy as changeable and will be especially reluctant to accept or seek dependency-oriented help, which implies long-term dependency on the advantaged group. When status differences are viewed as secure, members of low-status groups accept their relative inferiority and their dependence on the high-status group's help, and thus are likely to be receptive to dependency-oriented help from the high-status group.

Characteristics of the Individual Group Member: Degree of In-Group Commitment and Social Dominance Orientation

The IHSR model also posits that characteristics of individual group members affect intergroup helping dynamics. The intensity of the threat to social identity and resultant defensive behaviors (e.g., in-group favoritism, out-group devaluation) are affected by how strongly the individual identifies with his or her in-group (Branscombe et al., 1999; Ellemers, Spears, & Doosje, 1999). For example, when their group's ethics were questioned, high identifiers expressed stronger identification with their in-group and employed behaviors that increased positive distinctiveness (Doosje, Ellemers, & Spears, 1995). Low identifiers, on the other hand, tended to decrease their attachment to the group (Branscombe et al., 1999). Applied to the present context of intergroup helping, this suggests that the reactions of low-status group members to the threat induced by dependency on the high-status out-group depend on their in-group identification. Under conditions of status insecurity, high identifiers will be more threatened by help from the high-status out-group than low identifiers and will show more defensive reactions (e.g., increased commitment to the in-group, greater discrimination against the out-group, and out-group devaluation). In the same vein, members of high-status groups who are high identifiers will respond more intensely to a perceived threat to their group's identity than low identifiers, and will provide more dependency-oriented help to the source of this threat.

The Intergroup Helping as Status Relations Model: Empirical Support

In the following sections we present data that support our main argument that intergroup helping embodies social mechanisms through which groups maintain or challenge existing power relations. First, we shall describe research, conducted in both real and minimal group settings, that has tested the influence of the perceived security of status relations on reactions to receiving help from high-status members. This research supports the key distinction made by the IHSR model between intergroup helping relations when the status hierarchy is perceived to be secure as opposed to insecure (cf. Figure 6.1). After considering the structural characteristics of status, we shall proceed to describe research that has investigated the roles of characteristics of help and characteristics of recipients in the IHSR model.

Structural Characteristics: The Security of Status Relations

In a series of studies we examined the willingness of low-status group members to receive help from a high-status out-group, while manipulating and assessing different levels of status stability and legitimacy. In one study designed as a minimal group experiment (Nadler & Halabi, 2006, Study 1), we created ad hoc groups using the over-/under-estimators procedure (Jetten, Spears, & Manstead, 1996; Tajfel & Turner, 1986). We manipulated group status by informing participants that the out-group had greater scholastic abilities. Half of the participants were then told that this status difference was expected to remain constant (stable status relations condition), while the other half was informed that measures of scholastic ability are subject to change and therefore that there was a good chance that their group would exceed the out-group in the future (unstable condition). Within each condition, half of the participants were given help from an ostensible out-group member in solving an anagram task and the other half worked on the task without help. Consistent with our predictions, participants in the unstable status condition who received help expressed more negative and homogeneous perceptions of the out-group and exhibited more discrimination than participants in the other three experimental cells. These results show that, as predicted, receiving help from the high-status group when status relations are insecure poses a threat to the social identity of low-status group members, who respond in turn with a cluster of defensive reactions (Ellemers, Spears, & Doosje, 1997).

Consistent with the importance that is assigned to the demonstration of basic intergroup phenomena with both minimal and real groups (Jetten et al., 1996), the second study set out to assess the role of perceived status stability (stable or unstable) on a low-status group's reactions to help from a high-status out-group in a real-group setting. Israeli Arab participants (i.e., members of the low-status group) received help from either a Jewish or an Arab helper on an ego-relevant task (Nadler & Halabi, 2006, Study 2). In the unstable condition participants were told that the achievement gap between Arabs and Jews (e.g., scores on aptitude tests) was constantly narrowing, whereas in the stable condition participants were informed that these differences have remained stable over the years and that there was little chance that the situation would change in the future. Following this the experimenter, who presented himself as either an Israeli Arab or an Israeli Jew, gave help to participants on an experimental task.

In line with our predictions and with the findings of the previously described minimal group experiment, the participants, who were all Israeli Arabs, exhibited defensive reactions when they received help from the high-status out-group *and* status relations had been presented as unstable. Participants in this experimental cell exhibited the highest level of out-group discrimination in a resource allocation task, perceived out-group members most negatively, and had the lowest affect scores compared to participants in the other experimental conditions.

The findings described above affirm that receiving help from high-status group members can pose a threat to the social identity of low-status group members because it may be seen by the low-status group as an attempt by the dominant group to maintain existing power relations. Our findings indicate that this occurs when status relations between the groups are perceived as insecure. Under these conditions receiving help from the out-group is inconsistent with the group members' quest for equality and social change. Therefore, help is a source of threat to low-status groups' social identity, elicits defensive perceptions and behaviors (Ellemers et al., 1999), and contributes directly to negative attitudes toward the help-giving out-group. These findings are consistent with previous research that explored the relationship between threat to social identity and negative attitudes toward the out-group (Riek, Mania, & Gaertner, 2006).

Characteristics of Help: Autonomy-Oriented versus Dependency-Oriented

The IHSR model maintains that only the receipt of dependency-oriented help implies dominance by the high-status group. Consequently, under conditions of status insecurity, members of the low-status group are expected to reject assistance from the high-status group if such assistance is dependency-oriented, but not if it is autonomy-oriented. To test this hypothesis we conducted an experiment in a real-group setting that sought to examine the relationship between the perceived instability of the existing social hierarchy and the autonomy- versus dependency-oriented nature of the help given (Nadler & Halabi, 2006, Study 4). In this experiment Israeli high school students were told that the gap in scholastic achievement between their school and another, more prestigious, high school was either steadily narrowing (unstable status condition) or had remained constant over the last five years (stable status condition). In addition, half of the participants were induced to identify with their high school and the other half was not. Specifically, in the high in-group identification condition participants read a short article, said to have been taken from a local newspaper, which recounted the history of their high school, praising the school and emphasizing the strong school commitment of its students and graduates. In the control condition participants read an article of similar length, which focused on environmental issues. Following these manipulations, participants were asked to work on three insoluble math problems; they were given the opportunity to seek either the full solution to the problem (dependency-oriented help) or hints (autonomy-oriented help) from a member of the high-status out-group. When status relations were perceived as unstable, high identifiers were unwilling to seek dependency-oriented help from the high-status out-group. This was not the case when status relations were perceived as stable, in-group identification was low, or when help was autonomy-oriented. The findings of this experiment support the model's assertion that intergroup helping relations are determined by an interaction between the structural characteristics of the status hierarchy (i.e., the security of status relations), the type of help that is made available (i.e., dependency- or autonomy-oriented help), and characteristics of the individual group member (e.g., in-group identification).

In further support for the role of type of help, we recently explored the relationship between dependency- or autonomy-oriented help seeking and the perceived security of status relations in the context of gender relations (Shlomniuk, Nadler, & Halabi, 2008). In this study, female participants were led to believe that the differences between males' and females' mathematical achievements reflected either a secure or insecure status difference. In the secure status relations condition, participants were told that the relative superiority of males over females in mathematics was biologically determined from birth, while in the insecure condition they were told that this difference was socially determined. This manipulation contains an element of perceived status stability (i.e., if these differences are socially determined they can change, whereas if they are biological they cannot). Compared to the manipulations in the previous experiments described, which consisted of information about the stability of status relations, we view this manipulation as closer in meaning to differences in the perceived *legitimacy* of status differences, since differences based on biological fact cannot be expected to change, no matter how inequitable their consequences. Following this, participants worked on a difficult math problem and could seek dependency- or autonomy-oriented help from a male participant. Consistent with our predictions, when status relations were perceived as insecure rather than as secure (i.e., differences in mathematical abilities were said to be socially determined rather than biological), female participants sought more autonomy-oriented help. Under conditions of status security participants preferred dependency-oriented rather than autonomy-oriented help.

Characteristics of the Individual Group Member: Degree of In-Group Commitment and Social Dominance Orientation

The interaction between the structural characteristics of the status hierarchy (i.e., security of status relations) and the characteristics of help (i.e., dependency- or autonomy-oriented help) is also affected by the characteristics of the individual group member. In this section we examine the role of two such characteristics: in-group identification and social dominance orientation (Sidanius & Pratto, 1999).

In-group identification
We found that high identifiers experienced a greater threat to social identity and were less willing to seek help than low identifiers when the out-group offered dependency-oriented help and status relations were insecure (Nadler & Halabi, 2006, Study 4). Further, we found that low-status group members respond defensively to the receipt of help from the high-status out-group only if they are first induced to identify with their in-group (Nadler & Halabi, 2006, Study 3). In this latter experiment, members of a low-status group (i.e., Israeli Arabs) who had been induced to identify with their group displayed more defensive behaviors than low identifiers following the receipt of help from a member of the high-status group (i.e., an Israeli Jew). They tended to display greater discrimination and devaluation of the out-group and experienced a decrease in their collective self-esteem. No such differences were observed between high- and low-identifiers when help was not given.

Social dominance orientation

The IHSR model holds that high-status group members will be motivated to protect their group's advantaged status by giving dependency-oriented help to the low-status group. Such help, which aims to maintain the existing status quo, should be highest when the low-status group poses a threat to the high-status group's social identity. Recent theorizing on the role of personal dispositions in intergroup processes has suggested that people vary in their support for stratified social systems and that these variations can be assessed by a relatively stable disposition termed social dominance orientation (SDO; Sidanius & Pratto, 1999). People who are high in SDO are likely to endorse attitudes that maintain the unequal status quo. When the existing social order is threatened, members of the high-status group who are high in SDO are expected to work harder to maintain the social hierarchy than low-SDO individuals, who tend to endorse attitudes and policies that promote social equality (Pratto & Shih, 2000).

Applied to the present context of intergroup helping as status relations, this suggests that high-SDO members of a high-status group will respond to a threat to their group's status by providing more dependency-oriented help than low-SDO members to the threatening out-group. To assess this hypothesis we examined the willingness of Israeli Jews to provide assistance to Israeli Arabs (i.e., a high- versus low-status group, respectively) when status relations had been described as stable or unstable (Halabi, Dovidio, & Nadler, 2008). In line with our prediction we found that high-SDO Israeli Jews offered less help to out-group members, and when they did offer help they were more likely to offer dependency-oriented assistance than were those lower in SDO. Further, we found that threat to group's status produced less help offered to Arab students for Jewish students high in SDO but not for those low in SDO. Overall, we have found converging evidence for the effects of in-group identification on the reactions of low-status members to help from a high-status out-group. Specifically, receiving help from a high-status out-group precipitates a greater threat to social identity for high as opposed to low in-group identifiers when the social hierarchy is unstable. Thus, as expected and as consistent with previous research (Branscombe & Wann, 1994; Spears, Doosje, & Ellemers, 1997), high identifiers exhibit more group-based behaviors that can contribute to combating the threat to their social identity. Regarding members of the high-status group, our research indicates that when the dominant group's advantaged position is threatened, group members provide more dependency-oriented help to members of the low-status group than autonomy-oriented help (cf.

also Nadler, Harpaz-Gorodeisky, & Ben-David, 2008). This type of help, which serves to defend the in-group's advantaged status, is especially characteristic of high-SDO group members.

Different Perspectives on the Same Phenomenon: Intergroup Help as a Source of Social Tensions

In our ongoing research we have attempted to specify how intergroup helping dynamics affect the tensions that exist between differentially powerful groups. Intergroup relations, even among groups that have no previous history of conflict, are often tense, competitive, and conflictual (Insko & Schopler, 1998; Sherif, Harvey, White, Hood, & Sherif, 1961; Tajfel & Turner, 1979). Thus, even ostensibly prosocial actions, such as intergroup assistance, may be interpreted in ways that escalate intergroup tensions.

Our emphasis on the role of status security suggests that this is especially likely during times of social change, when the high-status group is motivated to maintain its social advantage as part of the status quo and the low-status group is motivated to change the status quo and attain equality. Because of the ambivalent nature of helping, high- and low-status groups may perceive the same behavior as expressing different motives and advancing different ends. Consistent with this reasoning, we recently explored the effects of the perceived security of the social hierarchy on how high- and low-status group members interpret the help that is offered by the high-status group (Halabi, Nadler, & Saguy, 2008). In this study we assessed Israeli participants' perceptions of the stability and legitimacy of status differences between Israeli Arabs and Israeli Jews. Next we asked participants to evaluate help that was offered by Jewish to Arab individuals. Arab participants, who perceived status relations as insecure, considered help from the high-status out-group as a means of control, as an assertion of dominance, and as egoistically motivated. Jewish participants perceived the same behavior as showing goodwill and as providing a way to build bridges between the two groups. Further, we found preliminarily evidence that trust plays a crucial role on how this help is interpreted by the low-status group. Specifically, we found that trust can contribute positively to overcoming misunderstandings generated by intergroup assistance. When Arabs had a higher basic trust in the Jewish out-group, they expressed more positive interpretations of help from the out-group and perceived such help as a means to improve existing relations between the two groups.

Summary and Implications

The empirical evidence presented in this section supports and extends the assertion of the IHSR model. Intergroup helping relations are determined by an interaction between characteristics of the social structure (i.e., the security of status relations), of the help that is offered (autonomy- or dependency-oriented help), and of the group members themselves (in-group identification and SDO). When status relations are insecure, high identifiers in the low-status group resent dependency on the high-status group. They react defensively to receiving help and avoid seeking it. High-status group members respond to threats to their group's advantaged position by giving comparatively more dependency-oriented help to the low-status group, who embody the source of this threat. Here again, these relationships are moderated by characteristics of the individual group members. In the research program presented we demonstrated the role of SDO in this context, and in other related research we found evidence that the tendency to maintain status through the extension of dependency-oriented help characterizes members of high-status groups who are high identifiers (Nadler et al., 2008). Finally, our research on the different prisms through which high- and low-status groups view assistance from the high-status group suggests that these different perspectives on intergroup helping may intensify rather than quell intergroup tensions. Chapter 14 in the present volume expands on these dangers and discusses ways to circumvent them.

Our analysis of intergroup helping relations focuses on the behaviors, feelings, and perceptions of individual group members. It does not bear on collective and strategic concerns that may be produced by group-level helping relations. For example, although as individuals group members of the low-status group may be reluctant to rely on the high-status out-group because of the associated threat to social identity, the group may adopt a diametrically opposite strategy on the collective level. The low-status group may act to exploit the high-status group by getting whatever it can from that group even though individual group members experience such dependency as threatening to their social identity. In this case the long-term strategic concerns of the group in receiving outweigh the psychological costs to its members, which emanate from the injury to social identity that such dependency implies. Because our theoretical model is couched within social identity and self-categorization theories it has not analyzed the collective-level strategic concerns that may dominate intergroup helping relations. Yet, we should be cognizant of their potential role in shaping intergroup helping.

Beyond the support that our research has provided for the IHSR model's assertions, the different experimental contexts in which the findings were achieved bear on the generalizability of these effects. Status was manipulated within a minimal group paradigm and in three types of real groups: a national group (i.e., Israeli Jews and Israeli Arabs), a high school, and a gender group. The empirical consistency across these different operationalizations is an important source of support for the robustness and generalizability of these effects.

The empirical consistency across the different manipulations of "status security" reinforces our confidence that this perceived security of status relations is the conceptual variable that is responsible for the effects that we reported in this chapter.

Finally, most of the studies reported here have manipulated status security through variations in the perceived stability of status relations. Yet, the fact that we found similar empirical patterns when manipulating the legitimacy of gender differences (Shlomniuk et al., 2008) suggests that, in accordance with social identity theorists, the concept of the security of status relations is parsimonious, accounting for variations in perceived stability and perceived legitimacy (Turner & Brown, 1978).

The IHSR model suggests that the responses of low-status group members to intergroup helping are determined largely by the consistency between group members' dependency on more powerful out-group(s) and their motivation for social change. The studies described focused on the case of inconsistency between the reality of dependence and the motivation for social equality. But what can be learned about the opposite case, when dependency is consistent with group members' motivation to maintain the existing status quo, and receiving help does not threaten social identity? Under these circumstances recipients are expected to welcome dependency on the out-group's help and to express gratitude toward the helper. Such gratitude can take overt form or may be expressed implicitly, such as through acceptance of the helping out-group's privileged status. Under such conditions intergroup helping relations serve as the behavioral solidification of an unequal social order. In this sense receptivity to dependency-oriented help is a behavioral manifestation of a high level of system justification beliefs (Jost, Banaji, & Nosek, 2004). By being receptive to such help, members of low-status groups convey their approval of the existing unequal status quo and their place in it.

Almost two centuries ago Alexis de Tocqueville observed that elites maintain their dominance over unprivileged classes by providing them with assistance, which "would be like the authority of a parent... but contrary to the behavior of the 'good parent' it does not seek to let people gain independence but keep them in perpetual childhood." The recipients of such assistance display "servitude of the regular, quiet and gentle kind" (Tocqueville, 1853/1956, pp. 303–304). This is a clear and eloquent statement of the way in which the *continual downward flow of dependency-oriented help* from the more to the less dominant group stabilizes an existing system of social inequality.

The present approach and empirical findings have focused on intergroup relations but they are equally applicable to interpersonal helping relations. Although the concept of security of status relations was developed by social identity theorists in the quest for a better understanding of intergroup relations, it also describes social reality between individuals. Thus, for example, certain employees may perceive their lower status in an organization as stable and legitimate and therefore unchangeable. Under these circumstances our model suggests that they will be willing to receive their supervisors' dependency-oriented help and will reciprocate by endorsing the unequal status hierarchy and their place in it. If, however, they view their subordinate position in the group as either unstable (e.g., they expect to be promoted soon) or illegitimate (e.g., their supervisor was promoted because of a personal friendship with the CEO), they are likely to resist being dependent on that supervisor's help or counsel. The supervisor is likely to respond to this threat through excessively demonstrative behavior. She may "force" her help or counsel on the lower-status person even when it is clear that the help is not needed.

Such interpersonal processes of trying to subdue others by helping them have been discussed by scholars of paternalism (Jackman, 1994). Jackman aptly labeled paternalism the "velvet glove" by which a high-status person or group (e.g., males) asserts its dominance indirectly and in ways which seem benevolent to observers. In the same line, Pratto and Walker (2001) argued that oppression can be justified behind a guise of care and protection while preserving structural inequality. While the dominant group might consider a specific behavior as showing concern and empathy, the dominated group may interpret these same actions as restrictive or authoritarian. In the same vein, the present context suggests that a disadvantaged group's refusal to accept help from an advantaged group may signify a challenge to the status quo, while accepting help may signify acceptance of social inequality and may possibly reinforce it. Indeed, and as we mentioned earlier, our findings confirm this logic. Help from the out-group was interpreted by recipients from the low-status group as a means through which the high-status group maintains its dominance (Halabi et al., 2008).

Understanding the different orientations of the in-group and out-group to a certain behavior is essential to improving intergroup relations. This is especially true with behavior such as helping, a highly valued behavior in most of human societies, which may be determined both by empathy for the out-group and by ulterior motivations to preserve in-group advantage. Keeping in mind that most real group relationships exist between groups of unequal power and status (Sachdev & Bourhis, 1984), offering help to a low-status group can likewise represent a subtle means of asserting existing power relations between the two interacting groups, and receptivity to such help can be a behavioral affirmation of the receiving party's lower status. Because of these different perspectives of low- and high-status groups on offering and receiving assistance, intergroup helping is a complex phenomenon that needs to be further explored using traditional intergroup concepts such as power relations, in-group favoritism, and discrimination.

Our approach suggests that groups maintain power relations not only through direct and explicit means as social identity theory posits (e.g., discrimination or devaluation), but also through implicit and seemingly benevolent means such as offering dependency-oriented assistance to an out-group. By doing so, high-status groups may create a climate in which low-status out-groups are chronically dependent on a more powerful benefactor (Nadler, Halabi, & Harpaz-Gorodeisky, 2008). For example, countries sometimes offer help to one another in order to gain political influence. By creating a uni-directional relationship, high-status countries can use their power to intervene in processes that further their own agenda. From the low-status perspective this climate of dependency can evoke feelings of threat and status anxiety. An interesting real-life example that is consistent with our logic is the sense of inadequacy and fear expressed by Greek citizens during the process of European integration, who perceived the European Union's financial aid to Greece as promoting dependency on wealthier European nations and as preserving existing status differences between European Union countries (Chryssochoou, 2000).

In conclusion, we propose viewing intergroup helping as a constellation of subtle phenomena whereby groups either challenge or institutionalize existing power relations between them. We suggest that groups arrange power and status relations not only through negative behaviors such as discrimination and hostility, but also through benign forms of social behavior such as helping. In times of social change, when existing status relationships become insecure, low-status groups are particularly reluctant to become dependent on the high-status group. Refusing the high-status group's help rather than initiating open and active opposition may be a safer way for the low-status group to signal its desire for social change. The real-world implications of this approach to improving relations between groups within societies and between societies are many. They are discussed at greater length in Chapter 14 in the present volume.

7

Turning to Others in Times of Change
Social Identity and Coping with Stress

Jolanda Jetten, S. Alexander Haslam,
Aarti Iyer, and Catherine Haslam

> *One cannot discover new lands unless one has the courage to leave sight of the shore. (André Gide)*

Introduction

Regardless of the excitement that is associated with life changes such as changing jobs, becoming a parent, or emigrating, any change brings with it the danger of having to break with that what we know best. The difficulty of such change is captured well in the above quote by Gide. The shore not only represents the familiar, it also very literally represents the ground upon which we stand. When we embark on a search for new territory, we risk losing that ground and this fear of loss can be a major source of stress.

In this chapter we argue that an important component of the ground on which we stand is the social groups to which we belong (Lewin, 1948; Tajfel & Turner, 1979). Leaving these identities behind can be difficult because these groups provide us with stability, security, reassurance, social support, and – most of all – a sense of identity. A second source of stress in times of change is that the future is uncertain: people often do not know what awaits them beyond the horizon. At such times, stress is likely to be enhanced because no relationship is yet formed with the new identity and the individual perceives, at least temporarily, that there is no identity to fall back on.

The question we address in this chapter is how the negative effects of identity change on well-being can be minimized. In the past, researchers have advocated a number of strategies to help individuals deal with important life transitions. For example, because transitions undermine perceived control, researchers have argued that helping individuals to regain control can help minimize stress (Cooper, 1990). Other suggestions involve (a) encouraging individuals to cognitively reappraise stressful transitions (Brammer, 1992), (b) helping individuals restructure their lifestyle in order to minimize stress (Friedman & Rosenman, 1974), (c) training individuals to relax in times of change so that they can better manage the demands associated with their changed circumstances (see Cooper, 1990), or (d) working with individuals to foster a sense of optimism rather than pessimism (Brissette, Scheier, & Carver, 2002). For example, in the context of expatriates who suffer from culture shock, it has been suggested both that stress can be reduced and that adaptation to the new context can be facilitated by providing information about the new culture, offering programs to heighten cultural sensitization, or by taking part in intercultural social skills training (for a critical evaluation, see Furnham, 1990).

Despite the fact that these suggestions may all have some capacity to alleviate stress and promote well-being, in this chapter we argue that these approaches may not be best suited to the task of minimizing stress in times of change. The reason for this is that there is likely to be a mismatch between these solutions and the core problems associated with identity loss. In particular, starting from the assumption that identity loss affects both the *personal* and the *social* self, we argue that such strategies can provide neither an optimal nor a complete approach because they focus on individual actions as a means of combating the stress associated with change and thereby fail to appreciate the group-based dimensions of *social* identity loss. As a result, they do not help individuals (a) to retain contact with their *social* "shore" (and may indeed disconnect them further from it), or (b) to establish themselves on "new land." As a result, we argue that such approaches can effectively cut people off from the best potential resource they have for coping with major life-changes: fellow group members – either on the shore, in the same boat, or waiting for them in the new land.

Social Identity, Stress, and Coping

Despite a recognition that groups play an important role in providing individuals with social support in times of change, limited consideration has been given to when and how individuals draw upon the group to protect the self and what the consequences are of seeking out help from other group members. In this chapter, we provide a social identity analysis of stress, arguing that identification with a social group plays a key role in determining whether people give and receive support as well as their reactions to that support and to identity related stressors. In this context, we will outline the recently developed Integrated Social Identity model of Stress (ISIS; Haslam, O'Brien, Jetten, Vormedal, & Penna, 2005; Haslam & Reicher, 2006b; see also Haslam, Jetten, O'Brien, & Jacobs, 2004) and attempt to develop it to enhance our understanding of the role of stress during identity change.

The ISIS model focuses on the idea that social identity affects both primary and secondary stress appraisal (Lazarus, 1966; Lazarus & Folkman, 1984). That is, on the one hand, it is a basis for perceiving a given stressor as threatening (or not) to the self, and, on the other, it is a basis for receiving and benefiting from social support that can help individuals to cope with, and effectively resist, the negative impact of those stressors (Haslam & Reicher, 2006b). In contexts where people are confronted with major life changes, a person's broad identity network can thus determine whether the life-transition or identity change is perceived to be a positive or negative event (eustressing rather than distressing; Suedfeld, 1997), and whether old or new social identities provide a basis for the receipt of effective support that makes the change a more positive experience. In particular, drawing effectively on the resources that the new identity offers may buffer individuals from stress associated with change and thereby protect their long-term well-being. As we will discuss, though, willingness and ability to take a new identity on board itself depends on the relationship between new and old identities and on the broader context within which change occurs.

Before proceeding, it is helpful to precede our analysis with definitions of some key concepts. We define stress as the strain imposed on a person by stressors in the environment that are perceived to be threatening to the individual's well-being (see Folkman, Chesney, McKusick, Ironson, Johnson, & Coates, 1991; Haslam, 2004; Lazarus, 1966). Social identity is defined as that part of an individual's sense of self that is derived from his or her membership in a social group (Tajfel & Turner, 1979). It is important to emphasize that even though social identity and social support are closely related constructs, the two are not identical. Instead, the relationship between the two is one where social identity makes social support possible and effective.

Although we acknowledge that social identities are always in flux and changing (Condor, 1996; Turner, Oakes, Haslam, & McGarty, 1994), the present analysis focuses on radical changes that are perceived by the individual as involving substantial upheaval and as requiring significant adjustment due to the marked discontinuity between old and new contexts (see Jetten, O'Brien, & Trindall, 2002). Such identity change is encountered in a broad range of circumstances and relates to life events that can be either (a) anticipated (e.g., progressing from secondary school to university, moving house, starting a new job) or unanticipated (e.g., change that results from sudden illness, retrenchment, or organizational restructuring), (b) positive (i.e., sought out or welcomed) or negative, and (c) associated with (some mix of) group membership loss (e.g., unemployment), gain (e.g., starting university), or transmutation (e.g., emigration). To encompass this broad range of events, our model is examined in a correspondingly broad range of social, organizational, and clinical contexts.

Social Identity is a Determinant of Stress Appraisal

Following the classic studies of Lazarus and Folkman (1984; see also Lazarus, 1966) which demonstrate how perceptions of the degree to which a given stressor is threatening can vary as a function of appraisal conditions, there is now a wealth of empirical work showing that group membership can play a significant role in the appraisal of stressors (Levine & Reicher, 1996). In line with self-categorization theory (Turner, Hogg, Oakes, Reicher, & Wetherell, 1987; Turner, 1991), two interrelated processes are particularly important here: social identity salience and social influence.

Illustrative of the first process, work by Levine and colleagues has shown that a given stressor will be perceived as more stressful to the extent that it threatens a group membership that defines a person's sense of self in the context of judgment. So, for example, when the sporting identity of female sports scientists was made salient, the threat of a knee injury was rated as more stressful than the threat of a facial scar (Levine & Reicher, 1996; see also Levine, 1999). However, this pattern was reversed when participants' gender identity was salient.

Speaking to processes of social influence, it is argued that when appraising stressors perceivers are more likely to accept social influence from in-group than from out-group members because the former are perceived to be more qualified to inform them about social reality. Perceivers should therefore be more persuaded by in-group members who inform them that a situation or task is (or is not) stressful than when out-group members express similar views. Evidence of this effect emerged from a study by Haslam et al. (2004) in which participants were brought to the laboratory and told that they were required to complete a series of mental arithmetic tasks. Before doing the tasks, they were asked to watch one of two videos in which a female actor either described the tasks as stressful (e.g., "the testing experience was very stressful. My heart was pounding and I couldn't concentrate. I got more and more stressed") or as challenging (e.g., "It was a positive experience, nothing bad about it. In fact, I found the tests challenging and enjoyable"). Critically, though, in different conditions, this person was described either as a first-year psychology student (an in-group member) or as a stress-disorder sufferer (an out-group member). After they had performed the tasks themselves, results showed that participants experienced them to have been more stressful when (someone who was understood to be) an in-group member had described them as stressful rather than challenging (i.e., a standard information effect, akin to that observed by Lazarus and Folkman, 1984). However, participants who were told by an out-group member that the tasks were challenging or stressful did not differ in the extent to which they perceived the task as stressful. In this way, the appraisal of a situation as stressful can be seen to depend on *who says* it is stressful. In-group members, because they share social identity with the perceiver (and hence are seen to be part of the same *social self*), are perceived as valid sources of information (Turner, 1991) and their assessment of the situation therefore has a significant bearing on the nature of appraisal (for a similar point in the context of evaluating group-directed criticism, see Hornsey, 2005).

Further support for the idea that stress appraisals are socially mediated and dependent on group membership was obtained in a follow-up study (Jetten & Haslam, 2005). In this, before taking part in an exercise to assess their IQ, female students were told that the test was either "stressful and that the experience was pretty nerve-wracking" or that the experience was "neither demanding nor stressful." This feedback was provided either by a female experimenter or by a male experimenter and manipulation checks indicated that participants identified more with the former than the latter (i.e., the female experimenter was more of an in-group member than the male). After taking the test, participants were asked how stressful they had felt while answering the questions. Replicating Haslam et al.'s (2004) findings, when the female experimenter had said that the task was stressful, female participants experienced the task as more stressful and reported having felt more tense than when she had said it was easy. Ratings were unaffected though by the views expressed by the male experimenter (see Figure 7.1).

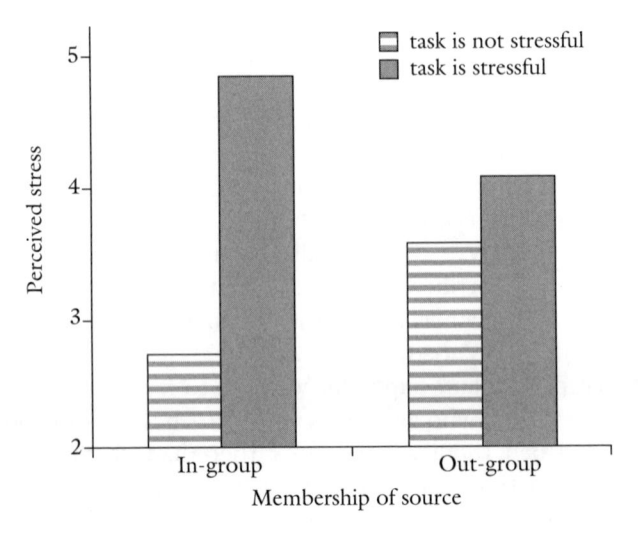

Figure 7.1 Perceived stress as a function of group membership of the source and communication by the source about task difficulty.

Moreover, we would argue not only that social identity affects the appraisal of stressors, but also that identity-led appraisal can change the relationship between the individual and the group. Indeed, in a separate study, we found evidence that communicating about stress and evaluating the stressfulness of events in the context of salient identity affected identification with other group members (Jetten & Haslam, 2006). In this, care workers were asked to rate the stressfulness of different life-changing events and occupations (after Cooper, 1995; Holmes & Rahe, 1967; see S. A. Haslam, 2004, pp. 187–188). However, they did this in the context of feedback about these same ratings provided by the Bureau of Statistics, by other care workers, or in a control condition where no feedback about others' ratings was provided.

Even though there was no evidence that care workers' stress ratings were more in line with the ratings of in-group members (i.e., other care workers) than those of the out-group (the Bureau of Statistics), there was evidence that identification with the care profession varied across the three conditions. Specifically, relative to the other two conditions, professional identification was higher when respondents provided their ratings in the context of other care workers' views. This suggests that when thinking about stressful events, validation of one's views by other in-group members itself contributes to enhanced social identification. In other words, a sense that one shares one's perceptions of stressors with other in-group members can itself be an important affirmation of that shared identity – reinforcing a sense that you are "in the same boat." In this way, we can see not only that social identification structures stress appraisal, but also that stress appraisal structures social identification.

Social Identity is a Resource in Times of Stress

We noted above that group membership not only impacts upon the appraisal of stress, but also that it can determine whether people feel they are able to cope effectively with any stress to which they are exposed (i.e., secondary appraisal; see Lazarus, 1966). In this regard we noted too that social identities have the capacity to buffer individuals against the negative effects of stress because they provide a basis for both receiving and benefiting from *social support* (Haslam, 2004; Jetten, Branscombe, Schmitt, & Spears, 2001; Miller & Kaiser, 2001; see also Levine, 1999; Levine & Reicher, 1996).

Evidence for this has been obtained in a range of contexts in which individuals respond to different types of social stressors. For example, Haslam et al. (2005) found that higher social identification was associated with lower reported stress among both (a) patients recovering from heart surgery and (b) professionals thinking about stress associated with their work (as bar staff and bomb disposal officers). Moreover, in both samples, perceived social support was found to mediate this relationship – consistent with the argument that support derived from shared group membership can minimize the negative impact of stress on well-being.

Along similar lines, group-based support has also been found to protect individuals from the negative consequences for their well-being of being targeted by group-based discrimination (Jetten et al., 2001). In other words, in-group support can counteract the negative impact of threats to the value of an in-group. Evidence of this emerged from a study conducted by Jetten, Schmitt, Branscombe, and McKimmie (2005) in which Queenslanders were told that their state was not valued (or was valued) by other states in Australia. Provision of this unwelcome information enhanced the extent to which Queenslanders saw themselves as being respected by other Queenslanders while simultaneously enhancing perceptions that their situation was one of "Us versus Them" (as indicated by agreement with statements such as "We Queenslanders are different from those in other Australian states"). Importantly for the present argument, there was also a positive relationship between perceived in-group respect and group identification. That is, individuals' emphasis of the respect they received from other in-group members was a means by which they could suppress the negative effects of a given stressor (i.e., threats to the value of a social identity) on group identification. Indeed, this reasoning is similar to that of recent self-verification research which suggests that group identity can be an important resource when the integrity of the group is threatened. For example, Sherman, Kinias, Major, Kim, and Prenovost (2007) found that group-serving biases were eliminated after an opportunity for group affirmation was provided – presumably because resources provided by the group were able to restore threatened identity without the need for this to be achieved by other means.

It is important to note that the positive effect of group identification is not necessarily the result of the extent to which the group provides *actual* social support. At times, the mere expectation that the group is there if one needs it to fall back on may be enough to bring about the positive effects of social support. We predict that features of the group become more important when actual support is sought out. However, even though some groups will be better suited to provide social support than others, it is also clear that there are no golden rules in what embodies a "good support group" (for a review of the role of cohesion of support groups, see Hornsey, Dwyer, & Oei, 2007).

A Social Identity Model of Adjustment to Identity Change

Life changes are often associated with stress. This, of course, is not surprising when one thinks about some of the negative events that many people experience in their lives (e.g., the death of a spouse, being fired from work). However, the fact that positive changes can be just as stressful is perhaps more difficult to explain. As the English novelist Arnold Bennett noted, "Any change, even a change for the better, is always accompanied by drawbacks and discomforts."

At first blush, it may strike one as rather strange that positive life changes such as getting married, getting a promotion at work, or gaining a new family member (e.g., through birth, adoption) appear at all on inventories of stressful life events (e.g., Holmes & Rahe, 1967). After all, aren't such events not only desired, but also highly sought after? What is more, in the abstract, positive life changes do not appear to be less stressful than negative life changes. What this suggests is that change itself requires adjustment and that the extent to which transitions affect self-definition matters more than whether the change is for the better or for the worse (Iyer, Jetten, & Tsivrikos, 2008; Jetten et al., 2002).

In this chapter we attempt to further develop the ISIS model in the context of reflecting on the stress that results from identity change. In line with the ISIS model and the principles outlined above, we argue that, given its central role in self-definition, social identification with old and new groups both (a) affects the appraisal of how stressful identity change is, and (b) is an important source of coping with changes and challenges to one's identity.

The main assumption underlying our reasoning is that stress resulting from identity loss can be countered when people are willing (and able) to take on a new identity (to replace the lost identity). This is because taking on a new identity not only provides grounding and a new sense of belonging, it also forms the basis for receiving and benefiting from new sources of social support. Indeed, if people can take on a new identity this indicates that they are able to respond and become involved in the new environment, and hence will be better able to deal with its demands. On the other hand, if people are unable or unwilling to take on a new identity, they will be inclined to withdraw from the new challenges they face, and to run the danger of "living in the past" and not being able to engage with the new groups around them. This puts them at risk of poor adjustment.

Several processes affect adjustment in the process of losing an old identity and taking on a new identity. First, we argue that "unfreezing" (Lewin, 1948) or moving away from an old identity is a necessary in order to establish new identifications. However, this is not easy because people are often unwilling to give up identities that have served as a source of social support in the past. Underlining this point, work by Ellemers (2003) with different organizational samples (teachers, employees of a child protection agency, police) has shown that resistance to change (e.g., following an organizational restructuring) is higher among those who identify strongly with a given organizational group prior to that change than among those whose commitment to the group is lower (see also Jetten et al., 2002).

Yet even if people are willing to relinquish an old identity, or are able to integrate an old identity in a new context, adjustment also depends on ability and willingness to identify with the new group. Features of the new identity are again important here. For instance, research on mergers has shown that a merged identity is adopted more quickly if the new identity is of higher status. Among other things, this is because, for members of a low-status group, the merger between a low-status and high-status group may hold the promise of status improvement (Terry, Callan, & Sartori, 1996). However, research also shows that such effects are not necessarily straightforward. Members of low-status groups may, for example, perceive the merger with a high-status group as an opportunity at first, but if promises of status improvement do not materialize, they may become frustrated and, as a result, identification with the new merged identity may decline. Here too leaders of the new merged group may come to be viewed with renewed suspicion (Jetten, Duck, Terry, & O'Brien, 2002). Moreover, acquiring a new high-status identity may challenge an individual in new ways. For example, being promoted at work may be associated with rewards (e.g., higher salary, increased respect and status), but it may also bring with it an increased workload and greater responsibilities – factors that themselves are likely to constitute new sources of stress.

What predicts whether people are willing to relinquish old identities and adopt new ones? As intimated above, we argue that key predictors here are (a) features of the identity that is left behind in interaction with (b) features of (possible) future identities. Equally important, however, are features of the broader social context within which change occurs. This is because identity change does not occur in isolation, but in the context of a broader network of identities. As Figure 7.2 indicates, when comparing the identity network before and after change, important life changes affect (a) the *centrality* of identities to self-definition relative to other identities and (b) the relationships between identities.

For illustrative purposes this figure presents data from a case study of a 52-year-old woman's life change after a stroke (Haslam, Jetten, Haslam, & Yates, 2007). It shows that for this stroke sufferer, her extended family (i.e., husband, children, cousins, and her siblings) became a more central identity (relative to other identities) after the stroke and this identity replaced her immediate family (i.e., husband and children) as a primary group membership. Here, the extent to which identities are totalizing is also important; prior to stroke her work group identity was the main identity in addition to family and friends, but after the stroke more identities were acquired in the process of coping with life change. Relationships between identities also changed because the most central identity after stroke (the extended family) was compatible with, and became linked to, a number of other identities (e.g., choirs and different work groups), whereas her network of identities had been less extensive and more exclusive before. Importantly too, the new central identity affected the nature of the new identities that were sought after the stroke – so that the groups

7 | *Turning to Others in Times of Change* 149

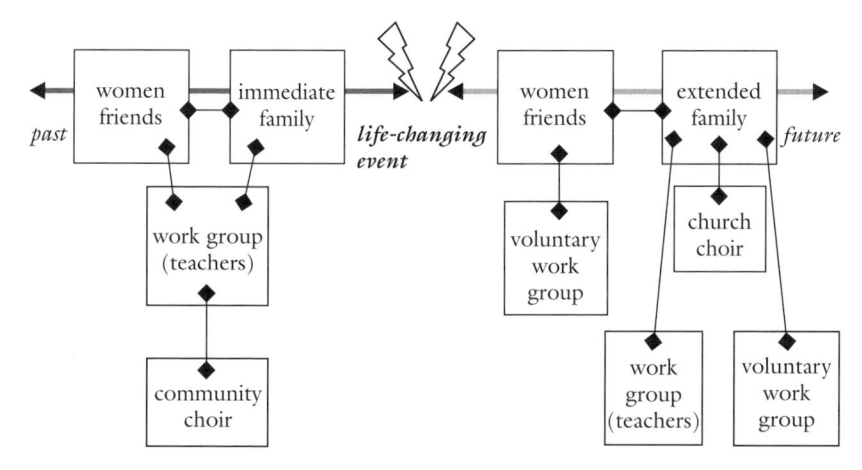

Figure 7.2 A schematic representation of identity change following stroke.
Note: At any point in time, and across points in time, social identities differ in the degree to which they are (a) *central* (self-defining, valued; indicated by size of square), and *exclusive* (totalizing vs. multiple; indicated by number of squares), and (b) mutually *compatible* (indicated by thickness of lines joining squares). Data are drawn from a case study of an individual stroke sufferer (Haslam et al., 2007). The procedure used was based on Eggins and colleagues' method for Ascertaining Identity Resources – AIRing (for details, see Eggins, O'Brien, Reynolds, Haslam, & Crocker, 2008).

she joined were compatible with her new central social identity (e.g., voluntary groups that her spouse encouraged her to join).

From this example it can be seen that (a) the centrality relative to other identities, (b) the totalizing nature, and (c) the compatibility of the changed identity with other identities interactively impact upon the primary appraisal of any given stressor and also the individual's ability to draw on social support in order to combat it (thereby affecting secondary appraisal too). Along the lines of cognitive models of complexity (Linville, 1987; for an overview, see Rafaeli-Mor & Steinberg, 2002), we distinguish between two factors that are particularly important when considering the degree to which any given social identity forms the basis for both primary and secondary appraisal (Iyer, Jetten, Tsivrikos, Postmes, & Haslam, in press). The first is the *differentiation* within the network in terms of the number of distinct non-overlapping identities it contains. Here we predict that the larger individuals' networks of social identities are (as indicated at times by the extent to which the central identity is not totalizing), the greater their potential to buffer them against the negative consequences of identity change. Second, we argue that adjustment to change is also determined by the degree of (potential) *integration* between pre- and post-change identities – in particular, their coherence, unity and compatibility.

Before discussing both factors in more detail below, it is important briefly to point out how our model is different from self-complexity models or models highlighting individual identity in coping with change. In contrast to these models that assume that differentiation and integration resides within the individual (e.g., roles, traits), we propose that it is the broader social network and combination of group memberships that is crucial to understand adjustment to change. In other words, social identities form the starting point of network differentiation and network integration and these processes shape individual identity. This not only shows the close connection between social and individual identity, it also underscores our assumption that coping with change cannot be understood without knowledge of the individual's broader social identity network because the individual self is defined by the groups to which the individual belongs (for a similar argument, see Kampmeier & Simon, 2001).

Factors that Facilitate and Hinder Coping with Change

Multiple Identities

There is a growing recognition that most people are simultaneously members of multiple social groups (e.g., Ashforth, 2001). Moreover, although at any given point in time these alternative identities may not be salient, they may still affect our identification with any one particular identity. Illustrative of this point, Roccas (2003) showed that people's identification with a group was not simply affected by the status of that particular social identity, but also by the status of other groups that they belonged to. Across three studies (using both naturally occurring and experimentally created groups) she found that membership in another group that had low status (rather than high status) led participants to emphasize the relatively high status of the group that was salient and to report enhanced identification with it.

When individuals have many identities, membership of alternative groups can be a source of support in times of change. Support for this hypothesis is provided by a study that examined the reactions of employees to the disbanding of their work-teams after an organizational restructure (Jetten et al., 2002). Here the negative consequences associated with loss of work-team (subgroup) identity were buffered by the resilience of superordinate identity. We argued that identification with a superordinate identity affected the appraisal of the restructure at the subgroup level because the more employees identified with the organization as a whole, the more likely they were to take the organizational perspective. We also argued that organizational identification buffered against stress (Ashforth & Mael, 1989; Begley & Czajka, 1993) because it determined the extent to which team members felt they could draw on support from the organization (and its members) while undergoing change. This in turn contributed to openness to change and had positive impact on job satisfaction (Allen, 1996).

Along similar lines, across a range of social, clinical, and organizational settings we have observed that having multiple social groups before change can protect people from any negative consequences of that change and that taking on a new identity proves less traumatic when individuals can fall back on other group memberships. As argued above, a fundamental reason for this is that multiple group memberships provide those who are exposed to stressors with many more sources for potential social support. What this also means is that people who have access to many identities may not perceive change itself to be so dramatic when one of those identities is changing. In contrast, when people have few identities, change to one of those identities is not only more noticeable, it is also likely to affect the individual in a more profound way (Thoits, 2003). In other words, multiple group memberships heighten a person's sense of self-continuity across time and place and this sense of continuity in itself can buffer against the negative consequences of change (Sani, 2008).

Support for this analysis was found in a study looking at predictors of recovery among patients who had recently suffered from a stroke (Haslam, Holme, Haslam, Iyer, Jetten, & Williams, 2008; see Figure 7.3). Here those who reported having belonged to more social groups before their stroke reported higher well-being and life satisfaction after the stroke. Importantly too, this effect was mediated by patients' ability to maintain their membership of those social groups after the stroke. In other words, these data are consistent with the argument that if people have many identities before a significant (and potentially life-threatening) change, they are more likely to maintain some of these group memberships after that change, and it is this that protects their long-term well-being.

One further interesting feature of this study was that it also examined participants' perceptions of the everyday cognitive failures they experienced after their illness. Unsurprisingly, these failures (e.g.,

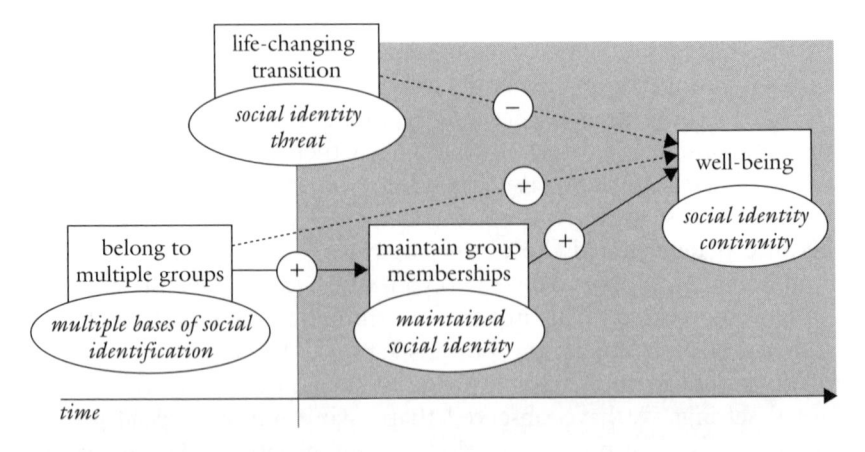

Figure 7.3 A schematic representation of key elements of a social identity model of adjustment to identity change (from Haslam et al., 2008). Reproduced with permission.

problems with directions, forgetting names, trouble making up one's mind; see Broadbent, Cooper, FitzGerald, & Parkes, 1982) were associated with reduced quality of life. However, mediational analysis suggested that the negative impact of these cognitive failures could at least partly be attributed to the fact that they compromised the stroke sufferers' ability to maintain valued group memberships. In other words, it was not cognitive impairment per se that was the problem but rather the fact that such impairment restricted the patients' access to ongoing group life and the support that this afforded them.

These broad conclusions are also supported by a longitudinal study with a very different sample – students entering a British university (Iyer et al., in press). As with the clinical population, it was apparent that having multiple identities before the move to university predicted students' adjustment and well-being after having been away from home for a couple of months. In the study participants completed questionnaires one month before starting university (Time 1) and after three months at university (Time 2). At a gross level the transition had a detrimental effect on well-being, but identification as a university student improved well-being. However, we also found that having had multiple group memberships before the transition increased identification with the university once students had been there for three months. Moreover, this relationship remained reliable when controlling for other factors relevant to the transition (e.g., uncertainty, support, academic obstacles). Again, then, it appears that group identification can help assuage the negative consequences of change and that multiple group memberships are an important resource that facilitates the process of taking on new identities.

In sum, it would appear that other identities (past and present) that are not directly affected by identity change can nevertheless be a basis for social support in times of change. The more compatible those other identities are with the new identity the more they facilitate this adjustment process and the more identities there are to fall back on, the more likely it is that individuals will adjust well to change. These conclusions are perhaps not surprising in so far as they accord with the conventional wisdom that it is better not to have "all one's eggs in the same basket" (Linville, 1985) because there is nothing to fall back on in the event that misfortune befalls that one basket. This relationship between multiple group membership and mental health has been observed across many social contexts and clearly has profound consequences for minimizing the negative consequences of change. This is clearly articulated by Putnam (2000) on the basis of his review of research into the relationship between social networks and health:

> As a rough rule of thumb, if you belong to no group but decide to join one, you cut your risk of dying over the next year *in half*. If you smoke and belong to no groups, it's a toss-up statistically whether you should stop smoking or start joining. These findings are in some ways heartening: it's easier to join a group than to lose weight, exercise regularly, or quit smoking. (p. 331)

Compatibility of Old and New Identities

Yet going beyond previous formulations, we argue that adjustment to change is not simply a question of the number of identities available to a person, but also of the relationships between them. In particular, this is because change can place a strain on relationships (and social support systems) if either (a) old and new identities are incompatible, (b) the social network before the change is incompatible with the new identity, or (c) the social network associated with the new identity is incompatible with the old identity. Among other things, this is because if there is incompatibility of this form it is likely that there will be tensions between the social networks that are needed to support the individual through the adjustment process. Here identities will no longer be able to serve the buffering and resource function that is necessary for individuals to achieve a sense of self-continuity over time. In other words, when identities are incompatible, an inability to reconcile one's present and former self – and the associated social worlds – poses a threat to self-continuity which is likely to inhibit adjustment and compromise well-being.

Processes of just this form are described by Reay (2005) in an analysis of the stress and anxiety experienced by those for whom university education is incompatible with their class background. She quotes from a working-class student who describes the process of applying at a high-status university in Britain:

> I was put off [named university], the interview there was really, really stressful. It was like what I'd imagined to be a conversation round a dinner table in a really upper-class, middle-class family and I was like "Oh my God, I'm not ready for this. This is not for me." It was awful. (p. 922)

This quote captures quite painfully the process by which means perceptions of the incompatibility between old and (potential) new identities impact upon the experience of stress. In this instance, identity change is appraised as stressful because (a) entering a high-status university is perceived to be incompatible with one's social background, and this incompatibility enhances both (b) the perceived need for social support but also (c) the perceived ineffectiveness of the support that one's old identities are able to provide in the new context.

Empirical evidence for these processes was also obtained from our longitudinal study that tracked first-year students over time. Here we found that adjustment to university life was less successful (e.g., led to greater self-reported depression) among students who perceived that their working-class background was incompatible with the status of the university they attended (Iyer et al., 2008). Moreover, identification as a university student mediated this relationship. That is, perceived incompatibility of identities increased students' unwillingness to identify with other university students, and this lack of identification accounted for the negative impact of the transition on long-term well-being. Incompatibility between old and new identities thus cuts individuals off from the best resource for social support: their past social identities. Again, then, we see that when individuals undergo change, adjustment is not simply a matter of how many groups they can draw support from, but also of the ease with which past, present, and future identities can be successfully reconciled, so that they can coexist – psychologically and interactively – within the new context.

Against suggestions that such issues are either trivial or short lived, it is apparent too that the negative consequences of such incompatibility can be long lasting. Indeed, within this longitudinal dataset it was apparent not only that students from lower-class backgrounds were less likely to take on the new student identity within three months after entering university, but that social class and perceptions that university attendance is incompatible with one's social background also predicted identification after having been at university for eight months. Moreover, we found that these students were *less* likely to believe (compared to others who identified more strongly with the university) that higher education is a useful individual mobility strategy (Jetten, Iyer, Tsivrikos, & Young, 2008). Indeed, this dynamic contributes to one of the fundamental ironies of social mobility – that it is most problematic for those to whom it is marketed as being most useful.

Concluding Remarks

To date, research into coping with identity change has been informed by approaches that tend to focus very much on the abilities and capacities of individuals *qua* individuals. Such approaches have explored the role of (a) individual differences (e.g., suggesting that personality traits such as "hardiness," "resilience," and "extroversion" can help to buffer people against instability in the environment), (b) personal cognitions (e.g., attributional styles), or (c) interpersonal support (Underwood, 2000) in seeking to explain variation in people's ability to cope with life transitions and associated identity change. In the present chapter we have argued that although such approaches may be able to explain some aspects of the adjustment process, they are limited by the fact that they present individualistic analyses of what are primarily *group*-based processes grounded in the dynamics of social identity. And by taking issues of identity change out of their social context, they leave the collective dimensions of these processes unexamined.

In this chapter, we developed the recently proposed ISIS model to explore processes of identity change, and thereby pointed to ways in which social identities (present and past) are implicated in the primary appraisal of stress (i.e., perceived threat to self), and how the social support that is associated with those social identities also affects secondary appraisal (i.e., perceived ability to cope). In this regard, we suggest that groups can protect, buffer, and sometimes even reverse the negative effects of stressors when individuals are able to effectively draw upon them as a basis for self-definition and social support in times of change.

In mapping the path that leads from life transition to enhanced well-being we pointed to the importance of two key factors: (a) the number of group memberships that provide an individual with a sense of social identity, and (b) the compatibility of pre- and post-change identities. In short, the more groups a person is a member of, and the more their pre-existing group memberships are compatible with their post-change identities, the more likely it is that they will adjust positively to the change. The key reason for this is that group memberships and the sense of shared social identity they provide is a critical basis for receiving and responding positively to social support (Haslam et al., 2005). Having multiple potential sources of support increases the chances that some of those sources will be preserved across the transition, and having sources whose support is compatible over time reduces the likelihood of psychological and social conflict. The combination of these elements in turn makes it more likely that the individual will have a sense of identity continuity despite the change.

Indeed, put together, this means that identity change may be most effective when it is not experienced as change at all, but rather as a natural development and extension of one's social self. If, as Pericles observed, "what you leave behind is not what is engraved in stone monuments, but what is woven into the lives of others," then so too it is only the strong social fabric of our lives that enables us to leave the certainties of the past behind and explore uncertain new futures with confidence and purpose. Moreover, it is only this fabric – and its internalization into our sense of self – that allows us to appreciate change as the affirmation of life rather than its disruption.

8

Volunteering Across the Life Span
Doing Well by Doing Good

Jane Allyn Piliavin

Introduction

In the volunteering supplement to the Current Population Survey of 2007, roughly 27 percent of a sample of 60,000 Americans age 16 and older reported volunteering at some time in 2006. The survey done by the Gallup Organization on behalf of Independent Sector in 2001 found that 44 percent of adults did some volunteering in the previous year. These differences are due not to a change in volunteering – each survey has found relative stability over the past ten years – but to different definitions of the population and of how to define volunteering. Regardless of whether it is one quarter or 40 percent of the US population that volunteers, it is still a very large number of people. Independent Sector also found that (1) adults who say they began volunteering in youth are twice as likely to volunteer as those who say they did not volunteer when they were younger; (2) in every income and age group, those who volunteered as youth give and volunteer more than those who did not; (3) those who volunteered as youth and whose parents volunteered became the most generous adults in giving time.

These data are cross-sectional and are based on self-reports in 2001 of what respondents did both as teenagers and in the previous year. We know that reports of behavior in the distant past are not reliable. Thus, one of the aims of the research to be reported here is to check, with a longitudinal sample, whether actual participation as a youth in community activities leads to greater participation as adults. Other questions to be explored here are (1) How and why do people become volunteers? (2) What are the long-term benefits of volunteering? (3) Are there optimum amounts of volunteering for obtaining benefits? (4) Are certain kinds of people benefitted more than others?

(5) Why should we expect these long-term benefits? That is, what is the process by which they come about?

Review of Past Research and Theory on These Five Questions

1. How Do People Get Into Volunteering?

We will begin with the question of how people get into volunteering. One could, of course, ask, "How do people get into sports participation? Why do individuals participate in hobbies, music groups, gardening, or politics?" The habits of a lifetime generally begin in adolescence, although of course one can begin activities at any stage of life. There is clearly some selection of certain people into certain activities based on family background, personality, and opportunity (for an excellent summary of research and theory on volunteering, see Wilson, 2000). We will briefly look at some data that can help to answer this question regarding volunteering.

2. What Are the Long-Term Benefits of Volunteering for the Volunteer?

Adolescents
There is considerable evidence for positive effects on adolescents, in terms of steering them away from "bad" activities, as well as some evidence for positive effects on self-esteem (e.g., Uggen & Janikula, 1999). There is also some longitudinal evidence that both participation in high school extra-curricular activities and volunteering in the community develop habits that carry over into adulthood (e.g., Astin & Sax, 1998). That is, teenagers who participate in their communities – in their schools, churches, or the community at large – grow up to be adults who do the same. It is also possible that participation in activities in high school leads to obtaining more education, and having higher socioeconomic status later in life. To the extent that health and well-being are improved both by such lifelong participation and by higher socioeconomic status (SES), there are benefits for the individual as well.

Older adults
Numerous studies reveal protective effects of volunteering on mental and physical health. Newman, Vasudev, and Onawola (1985) interviewed

180 older adults (55 to 85) volunteering in three school programs in New York, Los Angeles, and Pittsburgh. Sixty-five percent reported improved life satisfaction, 76 percent better feelings about themselves, and 32 percent improved mental health. Young and Glasgow (1998) found that self-reported health status increased as instrumental social participation increased for both men and women, using a longitudinal sample of 629 non-metropolitan elderly.

Longitudinal research has provided an even stronger case for the benefits of time spent volunteering. Moen, Dempster-McClain, and Williams (1989), who followed a sample of women who were between the ages of 25 and 50 when first interviewed in 1956, found that participation in clubs and volunteer activities had a significant protective effect on mortality in 1986. The analysis controlled for many other relevant factors, including the number of other roles and health in 1956, and the article makes clear that the activities were indeed largely community oriented (e.g., Parent Teacher Associations [PTA], scouting, book drives, etc.). In a second, more complex analysis based on interviews done in 1986 with the 313 surviving women, Moen, Dempster-McClain, and Williams (1992) found effects on three measures of health: self-appraised health, time to serious illness, and functional ability. Oman, Thoresen, and McMahon (1999) also examined volunteering and mortality in a 1990–1 prospective study of 2,025 community dwelling elderly aged 55 and older in Marin County, California. Mortality was assessed through November 1995. Controlling for health habits, physical functioning, religious attendance, social support, and many other factors, high volunteers (two organizations) had 44 percent lower mortality rate than non-volunteers.

A number of excellent studies have employed the Americans' Changing Lives dataset (House, 1995). Thoits and Hewitt (2001) discover that both the number of volunteer hours in 1986, and the change in volunteer hours from then to 1989, show significant effects on six measures of well-being: happiness, life satisfaction, self-esteem, mastery, depression, and physical health at time two. Controls for demographic factors as well as for other forms of community participation (and change in participation), such as church attendance and participation in other organizations, do not eliminate these effects.

3. Are There Optimum Amounts of Volunteering for Obtaining Benefits?

Friedland et al. (2001) found that people who engaged in more different kinds of activities in mid-life were less likely to have Alzheimer's disease in their seventies. Both Musick, Herzog, and House (1999) and Luoh and Herzog (2002) found that moderate volunteering led to decreased mortality, but that there appeared to be a ceiling effect – 40 hours a year in the first study, 100 hours in the second. Using three waves of the Americans' Changing Lives study, Musick and Wilson (2003) found an effect – especially for the elderly – of consistency over time. The more consistently individuals volunteered over time the greater the decrease in depression.

4. Do Certain People Benefit More than Others?

A number of researchers have found that volunteering has greater positive mental and physical health effects on the elderly than on younger people (for a review, see Oman et al., 1999). Musick, Herzog, and House (1999) found that the protective effect of volunteering on mortality was found only among those with low informal social interaction.

5. Why Should We Expect to Find These Positive Long-Term Effects of Prosocial Behavior?

There are a number of theoretical approaches that have been taken to explain why one might expect to find positive outcomes for individuals who engage in prosocial behavior such as volunteering, community activism, and informal helping of friends and neighbors. We will briefly sketch those that have received the most support and that we have been able to test with our data.

Alienation vs. social integration
Sociologists have proposed for many years that there are benefits of social participation. In the nineteenth century, Durkheim (1898/1951) argued for the importance of group ties, norms, and social expectations in protecting individuals from suicide. Van Willigen (2000) states, "Beginning with Durkheim (1951) . . . sociologists have argued that some positions in society foster a subjective sense of alienation . . . while others promote a sense of attachment or integration (Mirowsky & Ross, 1986; Seeman, 1959)." Referring to Seeman's five types of alienation (powerlessness, isolation, self-estrangement, meaninglessness, and normlessness), she goes on to suggest that "the extent to which individuals feel they control the outcomes of their lives, believe they are part of a supportive community, find their daily work rewarding, have a sense of purpose to their lives, and expect that

rewards can be achieved through socially normative means affects their psychological well-being" (p. 2). Volunteering, she suggests, can facilitate the development of these "psychosocial resources" and thus lead to positive effects on well-being.

This approach is consistent with a long tradition of research on social roles – the actions we engage in by virtue of a position we hold, such as mother, worker, or – in the case we are discussing – volunteer. The "role accumulation" approach (Marks, 1977; Sieber, 1974; Thoits, 1986) assumes that social roles provide status, role-related privileges, and ego-gratification, as well as identities that provide meaning and purpose. In general, the literature provides support for it: more is usually better in terms of roles. Thoits (1992, 1995), however, suggests that voluntary roles, such as friend or group member, may be more responsible for the positive effects of multiple roles than are obligatory roles such as parent or spouse. Keyes (1995) tested this suggestion and found that, indeed, voluntary social roles predicted higher levels of social and psychological well-being. The relevance of these results for our concerns here is that half of the voluntary roles he asked about are clearly helping roles: community activist, blood donor, volunteer, and caregiver.

Identity theory, social identity theory, volunteer motives, and mattering
How does engaging in helping roles translate into positive health and well-being outcomes? Identity theory (McCall & Simmons, 1978; Stryker, 1980) suggests that our *self* is made up of a hierarchy of identities tied to such social roles, based on how much time we spend in them and the number of our relationships that depend upon carrying out those roles. Social identity theory (Tajfel, 1970; Tajfel & Turner, 1986) suggests that we obtain some of our sense of self – our self-esteem – from the groups and organizations to which we belong. It is not much of a leap to think that we may also obtain self-esteem from engaging in participatory roles in society. To the extent that one's identities are visible and held in high esteem in society – as is the case for volunteering – individuals holding such identities may come to feel that they *matter* in society – that people notice them, respect them, and can rely on them (Elliott, Kao, & Grant, 2004; Rosenberg & McCullogh, 1981). Thus, this sense of mattering may mediate between volunteering and the psychological benefits that appear to flow from it.

A distinction between "eudaimonic" and "hedonic" well-being is useful in this context (Ryan & Deci, 2001). Measures of life satisfaction and happiness are indicators of hedonic well-being – feeling good about one's situation in life. Eudaimonic well-being, on the other hand, is defined in terms of meaning and self-realization. This involves not only feeling good, but also feeling *good about oneself*. We propose that this is the power of volunteering and similar other-oriented activities (e.g., political activism). When engaging in social activities or hobbies, one experiences hedonic well-being, a sense of enjoyment. But in other-oriented activity such as volunteering, one can enjoy the activity itself but also feel a sense of satisfaction that one is living up to one's values by helping others and society. It is our contention that it is this focus outside oneself that provides the greatest benefit to mental health, perhaps in part through enhancing self-esteem and the sense of mattering. This sense of mattering can help combat alienation and anomie and lead to psychological well-being. Elliot, Colangelo, and Gelles (2005) have also found that, as a consequence, mattering is protective against suicide.

Psychologists have usually used approaches that emphasize individuals' motives and values rather than their connection to the community through the performance of roles. For example, volunteers have a variety of motives for engaging in their unpaid activities (e.g., Clary et al., 1998). Two of these in particular – value expression and esteem enhancement – should, when satisfied, lead individuals to feel better about themselves. Thus, although all freely chosen activity should increase psychological well-being and have the potential to increase physical health, volunteering should give one that extra boost.

Methodology

Sample and Variables

We have explored these issues in a longitudinal study that has followed a large sample of individuals from high school graduation through retirement. The Wisconsin Longitudinal Study (WLS) began with a 1/3 random sample ($N = 10,317$) of women and men who graduated from Wisconsin high schools in 1957. The next two waves of survey data were collected from the graduates' parents in 1964 and from the graduates in 1975 and 1992, and again in 2004. The last two waves involved extensive telephone and mail surveys. Major strengths of the dataset are that retention has been excellent and a great deal of information has been obtained. A major weakness is that the sample reflects the Wisconsin of the late 1950s, in that very few minority group individuals are included, and, because the sample members are all high school graduates, the level of education, occupational status, and income are above average (see Sewell, Hauser, Springer, & Hauser, 2004). In the interest of letting the chapter flow more easily, details of all measures are omitted. These can be obtained from the author or from Piliavin & Siegl (2007).

Briefly, social participation variables include a measure of high school extra-curricular activities as well as diversity (number of activities) and consistency (duration over time) of adult volunteering from 1975 through 2004. The measure of adult volunteering – which excludes religious volunteering – is the sum of participation in five kinds of "other-oriented" activities (PTA, youth groups, charity and welfare organizations, community centers, and neighborhood organizations). Dependent variables include psychological well-being (Ryff, 1989) in 1992 and 2004, and self-reported health in the same years. Intervening variables – obtained only in 2004 – include volunteer motives (Clary et al., 1998), volunteer identity (Grube & Piliavin, 2000), and mattering (Elliot et al., 2004). The most important control variable, social participation in 1975, is a measure of participation in more self-oriented activities (veterans' organizations, fraternal organizations, organizations of the same nationality, sports teams, and country clubs), in contrast to "other-oriented" volunteering. Other controls for social involvement in 1975 include participation in church-related groups and church attendance. The number of children aged 6–12 in 1975 is included, because some volunteering is related to having children. Perceived social support, marital status, and work status are included as other measures of social integration in 1975. Three dummy variables are used as proxies for psychological well-being in high school: interest and disinterest in school, and certainty with regard to the future. A fourth variable, perceived support, is based on two items concerning the encouragement of significant others – parents and teachers – for college studies. Many other variables that predict volunteering, psychological well-being, or physical health are included as controls.

Findings

Predicting Participation

The first question we ask is "How/why do people become volunteers?" We found what other researchers have typically found. In terms of extra-curricular activities in high school, students who are female, who are planning on college, have better-off parents, have higher IQs, are more interested in school, and get better grades participate more. Environment also plays a part. Students in smaller schools participate more: that is, the fewer people there are to participate in the activities, the more activities each person participates in. This is true even given that there are more things to do in larger schools. This is consistent with Barker's "under-manning" theory, based on his observations in schools in the 1940s and 1950s (Barker & Gump, 1964). He argued that a certain minimum number of people are needed for each activity; for example, to have a football team, you need probably a minimum of 30 boys. People who would never get to play in a big high school will be pressured into getting involved so that those who want the activity can participate in it. (Very small high schools have sometimes gone to 8-man football in order to be able to have the sport.) Thus, in smaller schools, you get to do more because the activities need to be "manned." In our multiple regression analysis, about one third of the variation in participation in activities is predictable, and by far the most important predictor is school size.

We also examined whether we can predict participation in community service later on in life, again based on factors in the person and the situation. The literature suggests that both personal factors and organizational factors are important in getting people involved, and that being female and having high socioeconomic status (personal factors) and being involved in church activities (organizational factor) are particularly strong predictors of volunteering. In our analysis of volunteering in 1975, when the respondents were in their middle thirties, we indeed find that women volunteer more, and that both father's social status in 1957 and the respondent's own status in 1975 are predictors of volunteering, as are being married, having children, and church attendance. Controlling for all of these factors, however, participation in high school extra-curricular activities still has a significant effect. That is, we have evidence that participation in high school began a habit of community participation that carried over to adulthood, even taking into account the personal characteristics that were related to both high school and later participation.

Volunteering in 1975 is, in turn, the strongest predictor of volunteering in 1992, and 1992 volunteering is the strongest predictor of volunteering in 2004. Personal characteristics such as gender, education, earnings, and occupation continue to predict volunteering. In addition, scores on the social activity index (the more "self-oriented" participation) and specifically involvement with church-related groups also predict secular volunteering. Sociologists stress that there is a recruitment function to participation, and this often takes place in other kinds of groups. In other words, the more you do, the more you are likely to do – of a variety of activities.

Why does early participation lead to later volunteering? Clearly, certain kinds of people are more likely to initially engage in community service. But what leads those who do – including those who might not have done so based on personal characteristics – to continue? We propose that as one participates in these activities, one develops a set of motivations and a self-concept that is consistent with this participation. We believe that it is the volunteer identity and motives that sustain the volunteering activity across the life span. We are what we do, and we engage in activities that reinforce whom we believe ourselves to be. There is a positive correlation of .163 between having a volunteer identity in 2004 – at about age 65 – and our measure of high school extra-curricular participation taken in 1957, when the participants were 18. The correlations for volunteering in 1975, 1992, and 2004 with volunteer identity were .200, .266, and .386, respectively. There are similar correlations between participation and measures of volunteer values. All correlations are positive and significant and increase over time as the year of participation in the activities gets closer to the measure of the values.

Aside from developing attitudes and a self-concept that are supportive of continued community participation, what are some other consequences of participation? First, does participation in high school activities lead to success in later life, controlling for the factors that predict participation? The answer appears to be yes. The impact of engaging in extra-curricular activities in high school is particularly strong for educational attainment. There are smaller positive effects on whether the person is working in 1975 and for the occupational status level of the job held (both controlling for education), and on family income in 1974 (controlling for both education and occupational status).

Health and Well-Being Consequences of Participation: Hypotheses

Our final set of questions, on which we will spend the most time, are the last four we asked in the introduction, having to do with the effects of volunteering on mental and physical health in later life: (1) Are there long-term benefits of volunteering? (2) If so, how much volunteering is best for obtaining benefits? (3) Are certain people benefitted more than others? (4) Why are there these benefits? What are the mechanisms?

With regard to these four questions we have stated four specific hypotheses. First, we expected that volunteering will positively affect psychological well-being and self-reported health. (Only about 10 percent of the original sample has died, so we can't test for mortality effects. We have a healthy, relatively young group of seniors, who for the most part exercise, do not smoke, and are not as overweight as the average 65-year-old American.) Second, we hypothesized that volunteering for more organizations, and more continuous involvement in those organizations, will lead to more positive effects, at least up to some point. There will not be a point at which more volunteering will become bad for one's health, but there may be a ceiling effect. Third, we assumed that the relationship of volunteering to psychological well-being will be moderated by level of social integration: those who are less well integrated will benefit the most. In other words, those who are single, do not interact much with friends or relatives, and live in rural areas will benefit most from volunteering. Our fourth hypothesis was that the relationship of volunteering to psychological well-being will be mediated by volunteer identity, volunteer motives, and the sense of mattering. That is, volunteering improves psychological well-being because it leads people to develop other-oriented values, motives, and a sense of self that lead them to believe that they matter to others in the world.

The initial analyses of hypotheses 1 and 2 – shown in Table 8.1 – are based on the measures of well-being taken in 1992, when the respondents were in their early fifties. The remaining analyses use the 2004 wave, when respondents were in their mid-sixties, because mattering, identity, and motives were measured only in that wave. Whether one uses the 1992 or 2004 data the answers to questions 1, 2, and 3 are essentially the same.

Health and Well-Being Consequences of Participation: Results

(1) Are there effects?

Based on simple first-order correlations, the first hypothesis – that there will indeed be positive effects of volunteering on health and well-being – is strongly confirmed (not shown). It is clear that in this dataset, as well as in the other studies cited earlier, volunteering has positive effects for the volunteer. Analyses to be presented later will show that the relationship remains when stringent controls are applied, and can be shown to be *causal*.

Table 8.1 Well-being as a function of diversity and consistency of volunteering

	Measured 1992		
	Psychological well-being	Depression	Self-reported health
Diversity: 1975 Volunteering			
No volunteering	127.49***	16.96*	4.12***
1 Organization	129.67	16.45	4.17
2+ Organizations	132.37	15.71	4.21
Consistency: 1975–1992			
No waves	125.77***	17.74***	4.07***
One wave	129.00	16.76	4.17
Two waves	132.71	15.34	4.21

*$p < .05$. **$p < .01$. ***$p < .001$.

(2) How much?
To test hypothesis 2 – "How much volunteering is best?" – Table 8.1 shows relationships between two measures of the extent of volunteering – diversity and consistency – and three measures of well-being: psychological well-being, depression, and self-reported health. The figures in the table are the averages of respondents' scores on each of the three scales as a function of how many organizations they serve and how consistently they have volunteered over time.

Note that both diversity and consistency of volunteering have effects: as the number of organizations the respondent worked with in 1975 increases, the measure of well-being in 1992 also improves. Note that the impact of diversity on depression, both statistically (.05 level) and in terms of the score, is minimal. In both 1992 and 2004 the impact of diversity (number of organizations) tends to level off after two (not shown). The longer and more consistently the person has participated in volunteering, the higher the level of well-being. In the 2004 analyses (not shown) participation in all three waves leads to even higher well-being than participation in one or two.

(3) For whom?
Hypothesis 3 states that those who are otherwise less integrated into society will benefit more by volunteering. In testing this hypothesis and hypothesis 4 we focus on the dependent variable of psychological

Table 8.2 Hierarchical regression analysis predicting psychological well-being in 2004

	Variable	Standardized coefficients
Step 1	Diversity/consistency of volunteering 1975–1992 (VOL)	.309***
	Integration 1992	.221***
	Integration X VOL	−.299***
	Volunteering 2004	.082***
Step 2	VOL	.291**
	Integration 1992	.217***
	Integration X VOL	−.285**
	Volunteering 2004	.065***
	Volunteer identity 2004	.053**
Step 3	VOL	.220**
	Integration 1992	.157***
	Integration X VOL	−.233**
	Volunteering 2004	.033*
	Volunteer identity 2004	.028
	Mattering 2004	.426***
Step 4	VOL	.111
	Integration 1992	.060**
	Integration X VOL	−.145*
	Volunteering 2004	.032*
	Volunteer identity 2004	.010
	Mattering 2004	.289***
	Psychological well-being 1992	.483***

Note: Controls that were significant when added at $p < .05$: gender, IQ in high school (HS), HS certainty of plans, HS support, years of education, frequency of church attendance, married 1975, visits with friends, 1975, the index of self-oriented involvement, 1975, family earnings, 1974. Other controls (n.s.): measure of family SES, 1957, and Working, number of kids 6–12, and involvement in church-connected groups, all measured in 1975.
*$p < .05$. ** $p < .01$. *** $p < .001$.

well-being, since the relationships to depression and self-reported health are less robust, and move to the analysis of the 2004 data. In Table 8.2 we present the results of a stepwise regression analysis that controls for a large number of variables, including those that predict volunteering, such as measures of SES and religiosity, early proxy measures of well-being taken from the original 1957 questionnaire, the measure of more self-oriented volunteering, and participation in specifically church-related groups. These were all included in the first step of the regression analysis. We do not include the coefficients for these variables in the table for the sake of simplicity, but they are named in the footnote to the table. The numbers in the table are standardized regression coefficients: they can be interpreted as partial correlation coefficients.

As can be seen in the first step in Table 8.2, the effect of volunteering on psychological well-being remains very strong when the controls are included in the regression model. The first measure in the table – called diversity/consistency of volunteering – is the simple sum of the volunteering indexes for 1975 and 1992. A high score can be obtained only by volunteering over both waves. Both this combined measure and the index of volunteering in 2004 have highly significant positive effects on psychological well-being in 2004. The footnote to the table indicates that the measures of more self-oriented social participation and of involvement in church-connected groups are not significant in the full equation (although the social participation measure had a significant effect on the very first regression step, not shown in the table). This provides evidence that it is *other-oriented, secular* volunteering that is most likely to lead to the kind of eudemonics well-being that is measured by Ryff's scales. Participation in a country club, or playing sports, may make you happy, but only doing for others makes you feel good *about yourself.*

The first step in Table 8.2 also provides support for hypotheses 3. We include here the measure of social integration in 1992 and the interaction of integration and volunteering – called integration X VOL in the table. What the latter term tests for is whether the impact of volunteering has more effect for those who are less integrated. Integration itself has a very strong impact on psychological well-being, as one would expect. The sociological literature back to Durkheim (1898/1951) has found that those who are less connected with their fellow human beings are more subject to depression, loneliness, hopelessness, and general unhappiness. Confirming our hypothesis, the *interaction* of social integration in 1992 with volunteering up to that point in time has a significant *negative* impact. This shows that the *less* socially integrated the respondent is otherwise – in terms of work and marital status, rural–urban residence, and visiting with friends – the *stronger* is the positive effect of volunteering. In other words, volunteering has a more positive effect on just those individuals who need social contacts – and perhaps a sense of mattering – most.

(4) Why? What is the mechanism?
In Table 8.2 we also present the results of analyses testing hypothesis 4, that the impact of volunteering on psychological well-being is mediated by volunteer identity and the sense of mattering. To test this hypothesis, we add the variable of volunteer identity on step 2 and mattering on step 3. Volunteer identity has a significant effect when it is added, and does show a small mediating effect on past volunteering and somewhat more on current 2004 volunteering. How do we know this? The size of the coefficients for these other variables decreases when the volunteer identity variable is added. This shows that a small part of the impact of volunteering is picked up by the identity variable.

When mattering is added in step 3 it is highly significant and more than doubles the overall predictability of well-being. (The adjusted overall R^2 for the regression equation increases from .111 to .276.) However, our focus here is on the sizable mediating effect of mattering on the volunteering-well-being link. The coefficient for the VOL variable drops from .291 to .220 – about 25 percent. The impact of the interaction term drops by 20 percent, and the coefficient for 2004 volunteering drops by about half. This is a classic mediation effect. It tells us that volunteering leads to eudemonics well-being *because* it makes us feel that we matter in the world. Also note the impact on 1992 social integration, again about 25 percent, indicating that being married, working, and visiting with friends also have their effects in some measure because they make people feel that they matter in their community. When mattering enters the equation, the effect of volunteer identity disappears entirely. This is a clear indication that identity has its effect through its relationship to a sense of mattering.

Is the effect of volunteering on well-being causal?
The final step in the table shows the impact of the introduction of our prior measure of psychological well-being. It is generally said that the best predictor of current performance is past performance. Thus it is not surprising that past well-being is a very strong predictor of current well-being. But adding previous well-being can answer a more important question for us: Is volunteering merely correlated with well-being – perhaps because people with higher well-being are more likely to volunteer? Or has engagement in volunteer activities, in fact, a causal impact on well-being? How will we know from this analysis? Presumably, past volunteering contributed to past well-being. So when we put past well-being into the equation, some of the impact of past volunteering should disappear. This is because the past volunteering

led to past well-being, which led to current well-being. A second expectation would be that the effect of current volunteering – in 2004 – should not be affected. This tells us that there is an impact of volunteering reported in 2004 for the preceding year on contemporaneous well-being *controlling for past well-being*.

These effects are clearly shown in Table 8.2. The effect of 1975–1992 volunteering disappears – or at least becomes statistically non-significant. The volunteering by integration interaction drops by over one third. The impact of 1992 integration also drops perceptibly. Since we have argued that 1975–1992 volunteering led to 1992 well-being, this is support for our contention. The strongest evidence for the causal argument, however, comes from the fact that the impact of *current* volunteering is not reduced at all. What this indicates is that volunteering *between* 1992 and 2004 leads to a positive change in well-being (or not volunteering leads to a negative change), because 1992 well-being can be seen as a baseline.

Conclusions and Implications

What do these findings mean for social psychology? In regard to social psychological theory, we have learned again that the factors leading to long-term social participation are rooted in the family of origin and in high school extra-curricular participation. The mechanisms that lead to continuation are related to the development of motives for volunteering, particularly value expression, and to a volunteer identity. It is not clear, however, that these motives and identities are causal with regard to continuation in volunteering. Whether altruism is natural to the species or not – and the jury is still out – helping others appears to be good for our mental as well as our physical health. One of the mechanisms by which this positive effect occurs appears to be through the processes of integration as opposed to alienation from society, as proposed long ago by Durkheim (1898/1951), and then the related subjective sense of "mattering" as suggested by Rosenberg (e.g., Rosenberg & McCullogh, 1981) and operationalized by Elliot (e.g., Elliot, Kao, & Grant, 2004).

What do the findings mean for practical issues of public policy regarding volunteering? It seems clear that the current practice of encouraging teenagers – and even pre-teenagers – to engage in multiple activities and particularly in community service is a wise one if the goal is to produce public-spirited citizens for the future. More surprisingly, however, there appears to be another value in volunteering. There is a payoff to the volunteer in terms of psychological well-being and health. The more socially marginal individual appears to benefit most. Thus, in the long run, encouraging volunteering should also be good for the society, in terms of happier citizens, and even, perhaps, reduced healthcare costs. Thus, communities should think particularly about encouraging volunteer participation on the part of the elderly, the poor, and single and childless individuals. It's good for them, and it's good for society, for them to be better integrated.

NOTE

This research was supported by grant 1R03AG21526-01 from the National Institute on Aging.

Part III

Intervention Strategies: Targeting Individuals, Groups, and Organizations

9

Perspective Taking and Intergroup Helping

Mark H. Davis and Angela T. Maitner

Introduction

Sterna antillarum, otherwise known as the least tern, creates its nest in an unusual way. Rather than constructing a familiar nest of twigs, leaves, or other organic matter, the least tern scratches out a shallow circular depression on the ground (the scrape), and the eggs are laid within this space. Interestingly, when otherwise healthy eggs for some reason come to rest outside the scrape, the adult tern becomes markedly less likely to care for them. Even when the distance from the scrape is small, the adult bird may completely ignore the egg, thus ensuring that it will not survive. The rule seems simple: care for eggs inside the scrape and ignore all others.

Research on intergroup relations suggests that *homo sapiens* are to a considerable degree like *sterna antillarum*. We tend to view members of our in-groups more positively, and to value their welfare more highly than we do the welfare of out-groups. To us, of course, the features that define in-groups and out-groups seem far less arbitrary than one's location inside or outside a rough circle on the ground, but we are in fact capable of drawing some very narrow distinctions indeed. It doesn't take much to make another ... "the other."

This volume is concerned with group perspectives on helping, and this chapter specifically considers the role that perspective taking might play in facilitating intergroup helping. Surprisingly, as it turns out, this issue has attracted almost no empirical attention. That is, almost no investigations have specifically examined the effect of perspective taking on the quality or quantity of help offered to out-group members relative to in-group members. Considerable evidence exists, however, that bears on a set of related issues, and it is possible to use this evidence to begin fashioning an answer to the question of how perspective taking may influence intergroup helping. There are two such issues to be considered in this chapter.

The first of these is the effect of perspective taking on cognitive responses to other people. Such responses include the kinds of attributional judgments we make about others, the degree to which we activate and apply stereotypical knowledge to them, and the kind of cognitive representations we form of them. The second issue is the effect of perspective taking on emotional responses to potential recipients of help. The affective underpinnings of helping behavior are powerful and varied – and perspective taking influences these affective states in important ways. In the first two sections of the chapter we will briefly consider relevant evidence bearing on both of these issues. In the final section we will attempt to use this information to answer the primary question of this chapter: how effective an intervention can perspective taking be?

Perspective Taking and Cognitive Responses to Others

One way in which perspective taking may have an effect on out-group helping lies in the impact it has on the way we think about possible recipients of help. Thus, an examination of the effect of perspective taking on cognitive responses to others is useful. At least three ways of approaching this issue have generated enough research for consideration. The first of these has to do with the effect of perspective taking on attributional judgments made about targets.

Attributions

Much of the research on the link between perspective taking and causal attributions is rooted in the long-established finding that actors and observers have differing attributional perspectives on the behaviors of the actor – actors tend to stress the situational reasons for their behavior while observers tend to stress the actors' dispositions. A number of investigations have found that inducing observers to imagine the targets' psychological perspective eliminates this difference, and leads observers to explain the behavior in a more "actor-like" fashion (e.g., Batson & Ahmad, 2001; Galper, 1976; Regan & Totten, 1975). More recently, Vescio, Sechrist, and Paolucci (2003) specifically found that inducing White observers to take the perspective of an African American target also led the observers to offer more situational explanations for the target's difficulty in adjusting to college. Importantly, situational attributions also largely mediated the effect of perspective taking on more favorable attitudes toward African Americans in general.

Another approach to the question of perspective taking and attributions has focused on the controllability dimension rather than locus (internal vs. external). Considerable evidence exists that when observers attribute a target's plight to factors under his or her control (e.g., drunkenness as opposed to illness), they become less sympathetic and willing to help. In a pair of studies, Betancourt (1990) found that having observers take the target's perspective led them to view the target's plight as less controllable; in turn, observers were more sympathetic and more willing to help. Thus, perspective taking clearly seems to influence judgments about two dimensions of causality, at least one of which has been reliably linked to helping behavior.

Representations of Self and Other

Perspective taking may also influence cognitive reactions to others by affecting our cognitive representations of self and other. A number of studies have addressed this issue in recent years, and one consistent pattern emerging from this research is that perspective taking tends to produce a cognitive "merging" of self and other.

Davis, Conklin, Smith, and Luce (1996) offered some of the first direct evidence for this pattern. In two experiments, observers watched a videotape of a same-sex target being interviewed about his or her adjustment to college. Some weeks prior to this experimental session the observers had completed an adjective checklist describing themselves, and now after viewing the videotape they completed the same checklist to describe the target. Thus, it was possible to calculate the percentage of traits – earlier rated as descriptive of the self – that were now rated as descriptive of the target. In essence, how much of the *self* is perceived in the *target*?

Prior to viewing the tape, some observers were instructed to engage in perspective taking (either by imagining how the target feels, or by imagining how they themselves would feel in the target's position), and others were given instructions designed to *inhibit* perspective taking. Compared to those observers who were instructed not to adopt the target's perspective, those receiving either perspective-taking set were more likely to ascribe self-traits to the target. Davis et al. (1996) interpreted this pattern to mean that perspective taking led observers to imagine how they *themselves* would feel. Doing so encouraged greater activation of self-knowledge, which then led to a greater ascription of self-information to that target. However, this investigation provided no direct evidence for this interpretation.

More recently, in a pair of studies Davis et al. (2004) specifically examined the effect of perspective taking on the content of observers' thoughts, and on the accessibility of self-related information. In the first study, observers watched a short videotape of a woman describing her need to undergo regular dialysis. Observers received instructions to take the perspective of the target on the tape, to imagine how they themselves would feel, or to inhibit perspective taking. After watching the tape, observers engaged in a free recall procedure in which they wrote down all the thoughts that they could recall having while watching the tape; these responses were then coded to reflect their content.

As expected, instructions to imagine the target's perspective increased the percentage of target- and (to some degree) self-related thoughts; instructions to imagine oneself in the target's position substantially increased the percentage of self-related thoughts. Interestingly, the traditional (inhibitory) control instructions were the only instructional set to increase the percentage of "distancing" thoughts – those that tended to psychologically separate the observer from the target. Thus, this study provided the first direct evidence that the thoughts reported by perspective-taking observers *do* contain more self-related content than those reported by non-perspective-taking observers.

In the second study observers watched a young woman describing her adjustment to college. The same instructional sets were used, but the dependent variable in this case was performance on a task that required the observers to complete 20 different sentences by choosing from one of four possible pronouns. As expected, relative to the control condition, perspective taking was associated with significantly greater use of first person pronouns, suggesting greater accessibility of self-related constructs.

The increased likelihood of projecting the self onto others during perspective taking has also been found by other investigators. For example, Maner, Luce, Neuberg, Cialdini, Brown, and Sagarin (2002) report data suggesting that perspective taking produces a greater overlap between concepts of self and other as measured by the Inclusion of Other in Self (IOS) scale (Aron, Aron, & Smollan, 1992). Of special interest for our purposes in this chapter, Galinsky and Moskowitz (2000; Study 2) found that having college students imagine a day in the life of an elderly adult led them to describe the entire social category "the elderly" in a way that resembled their self-conceptions.

Given such findings, it is perhaps not surprising that recent theoretical conceptions of perspective taking as a process have tended to emphasize this kind of projection (see Nickerson, 1999). Both Ames (2004) and Epley, Keysar, Van Boven, and Gilovich (2004) propose models based on the idea that a common perspective-taking strategy is to initially assume similarity between one's own internal states and those of others. In Epley et al.'s model, the projection of self-states onto others is conceived of as the initial step in perspective taking, which may then be followed by a more effortful process of evaluating and refining the initial judgment. In Ames' model, projection is conceived of as one inference strategy that can be used to infer another's internal state; another, complementary, strategy is to apply stereotype information.

Use of Stereotype Information

In fact, there is at least some evidence suggesting that perspective taking may lead observers to rely less on stereotype information when making judgments about other people. In the Galinsky and Moskowitz (2000) investigation mentioned earlier, perspective taking was consistently found to reduce the use of stereotypes in describing out-group targets (e.g., the elderly). In a similar vein, Aberson and Haig (2007) report evidence that perspective taking reduces stereotyping of an out-group (African Americans) through a specific mechanism – by reducing intergroup anxiety, which is associated with greater stereotyping.

However, perspective taking is not always found to reduce stereotyping. Three recent investigations have used instructional sets to induce White college students to take the perspective of an African American target, but found no reduction in stereotyping as a result. Vescio et al. (2003) found no effect of perspective-taking instructions on stereotyping, even though perspective taking did influence attributions regarding the target and overall attitudes toward African Americans as a class. Dovidio et al. (2004) reported a similar pattern – perspective-taking instructions reduced reported levels of prejudice, but had no effect on stereotyping. Finlay and Stephan (2000) induced perspective taking in White undergraduates but found no simple or direct effect on subsequent stereotyping of the target. Thus, while perspective taking does seem to be generally associated with having more favorable attitudes toward out-groups and out-group members (e.g., Galinsky & Ku, 2004; Vescio et al., 2003; Aberson & Haig, 2007), it does not always result in less use of stereotypes.

Application to Out-Group Helping

The general outline that emerges of perspective taking's effect on our cognitive responses to targets is clear; in a variety of ways, taking another's perspective tends to produce cognitive responses to the target that are more self-like than the responses that occur in the absence of perspective taking. The causal explanations that we offer for others more closely resemble the explanations we offer for our own behaviors; we (sometimes) become less likely to apply stereotypical information to others; and the actual mental representations that we form of other people more closely resemble our cognitive representations of self.

What are the consequences for out-group helping of "elevating" the other to a more self-like status? At the theoretical level, doing so may change our moral stance toward the other. Reed and Aquino (2003) use the felicitous term "circle of moral regard" to describe this phenomenon. They argue that under the proper circumstances the psychological boundary that defines in-group membership may be expanded to include individuals who ordinarily fall outside of it. This is important because people are more likely to show concern for the needs and welfare of those within the circle. Reed and Aquino focus on the role of moral identity in expanding the circle of moral regard, but the evidence reviewed thus far suggests that perspective taking may have the same effect.

At the empirical level, Cialdini and colleagues offer evidence that such cognitive representations actually affect helping. Cialdini, Brown, Lewis, Luce, and Neuberg (1997) carried out three studies examining the effect on willingness to help of several variables, including the feeling of "oneness" that observers experience with regard to the target. In each study participants were asked to imagine a specific target falling into one of four categories – near-stranger, acquaintance, good friend, or family member – and to further imagine that person facing a particular need situation. Participants were asked to indicate their willingness to help, along with their feelings of oneness and empathic concern. Consistently across all three studies, feelings of oneness emerged as the most powerful influence on willingness to help; in fact, empathic concern had no significant effect on such willingness after the effect of oneness was accounted for.

Although Cialdini et al. (1997) did not directly examine the role of perspective taking, Maner et al. (2002) did so in an investigation also concerned with the role of oneness in motivating helping.

Participants heard a purported radio broadcast describing the plight of Katie Banks, a young woman who had lost her parents in a car accident. Both perspective taking and oneness were manipulated, and amount of actual help offered was assessed; in addition, several possible mediating variables were measured. Although the analyses reported in this paper do not allow a direct evaluation of the link between manipulated perspective taking and the resultant experience of oneness, it appears that inducing perspective taking did tend to increase oneness, especially in the condition in which no oneness manipulation was presented. Consistent with Cialdini et al. (1997), oneness had a consistent effect on helping independent of the effect of all the other possible mediators.

Although suggestive of the role that cognitive representations of self and other may play in helping, neither of these studies actually examined helping for a target who is clearly a member of an out-group. However, Dovidio, Gaertner, Validzic, Matoka, Johnson, and Frazier (1997) carried out an interesting investigation that did so. Two subgroups were experimentally created by providing false feedback that they were either "overestimators" or "underestimators" on a task requiring them to estimate the number of dots appearing on a computer screen. Once formed, the two subgroups worked together, and then had the opportunity to offer help to a stranger from an earlier session; this person was described as being an in-group member (e.g., a "fellow underestimator") or an out-group member. Prior to this helping opportunity, the two groups were brought into the same room and treated in a way that either maintained the separate group identities that had been established, or in a way that recategorized all the participants as members of one larger group. The key finding was that when the two groups were recategorized, the usual bias of helping in-group members more than out-group members was eliminated.

Levine, Prosser, Evans, and Reicher (2005) report a similar pattern in a more naturalistic setting. Participants walking from one experimental site to another witnessed a (confederate) jogger fall and cry out in pain. When the jogger was wearing a soccer team shirt of the participant's own favorite team (in-group), almost all participants stopped to help; when the jogger was wearing a rival team's shirt or a plain shirt, helping was much less likely. In a second study, after the superordinate category of soccer fan was made salient, a different pattern emerged: those wearing either kind of team shirt were likely to receive help, and only the jogger wearing a plain shirt did not. Thus, the degree to which targets fell within the circle of moral regard had a significant impact on the help they received; importantly, the size of this circle was successfully increased following the introduction of a new superordinate identity.

Perspective Taking and Emotional Responses

Another path through which perspective taking may affect out-group helping lies in its effect on emotional responses to potential helping recipients. A considerable amount of research has been carried out over the past three decades in an attempt to identify the affective antecedents of helping. At the risk of oversimplification, it may be fair to say that two affective states have been consistently linked with greater levels of help. The first state is referred to variously as empathy (Batson, 1991), sympathy (Eisenberg & Strayer, 1987), or empathic concern (Davis, 1994), and consists of feelings of sympathy, compassion, and concern for another in distress. Considerable evidence indicates that higher levels of empathic concern are associated with greater help, even when the costs to the helper are high and escape without helping is relatively easy (see Batson, 1991).

The second affective state is characterized by unpleasant arousal and feelings of distress. This is the type of response sometimes referred to as personal distress (Batson, 1991; Davis, 1994), and roughly corresponds to the "arousal" state in the arousal: cost–reward model (Piliavin, Dovidio, Gaertner, & Clark, 1981). This state has been linked to helping, but the association is often conditioned by other factors: difficulty of escape (e.g., Batson, Duncan, Ackerman, Buckley, & Birch, 1981), or the costs associated with offering help (see Dovidio, Piliavin, Gaertner, Schroeder, & Clark, 1991).

Evidence suggests that perspective taking tends to increase the likelihood that observers will experience both of these states when exposed to distressed target (see Davis, 1994). However, the precise nature of the perspective-taking induction will influence the particular emotional state(s). The most reliable link between perspective taking and empathic concern has resulted from the use of instructions to "imagine how the target feels" (e.g., Toi & Batson, 1982). Such instructions have increased empathic concern in the vast majority of studies (see Davis, 1994), but have not had such a reliable effect on personal distress. Instead, feelings of distress seem to result more consistently when observers receive a different instructional set: to "imagine how you yourself would feel" (e.g., Batson, Early, & Salvarani, 1997).

Application to Out-Group Helping

The general outline that emerges regarding the effect of perspective taking on emotional responses to distressed targets is fairly clear. Perspective taking tends to increase the likelihood of at least two different emotional responses, perhaps especially feelings of compassion. In turn, both emotional states can lead to helping, with perhaps the strongest evidence again supporting the link between empathic concern and helping.

So, what are the implications for out-group helping? As it turns out, there are no investigations that have directly examined personal distress as a mediator of the link between perspective taking and helping of out-group members. The little evidence that does exist regarding the relationship between this emotional state and out-group helping comes from two studies by Stürmer and colleagues, and the pattern is mixed. Personal distress was found to be unrelated to out-group helping by Stürmer, Snyder, Kropp, and Siem (2006), and negatively related to such helping by Stürmer, Snyder, and Omoto (2005).

The interpretation of these results is further complicated by the fact that in an intergroup context, the meaning of "personal distress" is not altogether clear. In addition to the distress one may feel as a result of witnessing the target's plight, observers may also experience intergroup anxiety in the presence of an out-group member. Thus, it is difficult to interpret the findings to date, and future attempts to examine the role of personal distress in out-group helping will need to be sensitive to the complexities in such endeavors.

There is a greater body of evidence regarding the impact of empathic concern on out-group helping. One line of investigation has suggested that empathic concern plays a different role in eliciting helping of in-group members, kin, and close friends than strangers (Maner & Gailliot, 2007; Schlenker & Britt, 2001; Stürmer et al., 2005). For instance, recent work by Stürmer and colleagues (e.g., Stürmer et al., 2005, 2006), has examined the role of empathic concern in helping for in-group and out-group members. A series of studies found evidence for the position that empathic concern is reliably associated with helping only for in-group members, and is essentially unrelated to helping when the potential recipient is a member of an out-group. Helping for an out-group member was instead associated with such variables as liking for the recipient (Stürmer et al., 2006). Thus, it may be that out-group members do not receive any less help, but that the motivational impetus for such help is less altruistic. Likewise, Maner and Gailliot (2007) report that empathic concern is associated with helping behavior for kin, but not for strangers, while Schlenker and Britt (2001) report that dispositional empathy is related to helping friends but not strangers. Thus empathic concern may not be as potent an elicitor of helping behavior when the target of help is an out-group member.

However, research that has explicitly examined the impact of perspective taking on feelings of empathic concern and helping behavior as specifically regards out-group members has painted a more optimistic picture. Batson and colleagues, for instance, have shown that taking the perspective of an out-group member does in fact increase feelings of empathic concern for that individual (Batson, Polycarpou et al., 1997), which, in turn elicits helping of the out-group as a whole (Batson, Chang, Orr, & Rowland, 2002). Specifically, Batson et al. (2002) investigated whether taking the perspective of a jailed drug addict (who expressed a desire to stay clean) increased allocation of resources to a local drug treatment facility. Participants who were instructed to take the perspective of the drug addict reported empathic concern and allocated significantly more money to the drug treatment facility than participants instructed to remain detached. Critically, enhanced feelings of empathy mediated the link between perspective taking and helping. Thus, this study suggests that taking the perspective of out-group members can increase helping of the out-group as a whole. Likewise, Levy, Freitas, and Salovey (2002) demonstrated that to the extent that perceivers are likely to take a target's perspective, they feel more empathic concern and have a stronger desire to help even members of stigmatized groups such as the homeless or people with AIDS.

Although promising, these studies do not speak directly to the question of whether perspective taking can lead participants to provide the same level and quality of help to the out-group as they would the in-group. In fact, to our knowledge only one investigation has compared perspective-taking-induced helping of in-group and out-group members (Batson, Sager, Garst, Kang, Rubchinsky, & Dawson, 1997). In two studies, University of Kansas students read the story about Katie Banks, the female student whose parents had been killed in a car accident. Participants were given the opportunity to donate time to help Katie, who they learned was either a fellow University of Kansas student, or was a student at (rival) Kansas State. Results showed that participants felt more empathic concern for Katie when they had been instructed to take her perspective. Moreover, these participants were also more likely to help Katie, and the increased feelings of empathic concern seemed to mediate this process. Most importantly, Katie's status as an in-group or out-group member had no effect on these results. In other words, perspective-taking participants were equally likely to help Katie whether she was a member of the in-group or the out-group. Overall, then, it would appear that deliberately taking the perspective of out-group members can lead to empathic concern for and helping of out-group members in the same way it does for in-group members.

However, an important caveat must be offered. In the Batson studies, and in Levy et al. (2002), there is at least some ambiguity regarding the nature of the out-group target. In brief, it is possible that these targets were viewed as stigmatized members of an in-group rather than as members of an out-group per se. That is, the stigmatizing characteristics (drug addition; homelessness; attending a rival school) are ones that in theory could one day apply to the observers themselves – as opposed to unchanging group categories such as race or (usually) gender. Thus, the drug addict in Batson et al. (2002) or the homeless targets in Levy et al. (2002) might have been viewed as stigmatized, but nevertheless within the in-group circle.

In addition, it should be noted that most work investigating the impact of perspective taking on helping has depicted a sympathetic individual – the drug dealer in Batson et al. (2002) was reformed and wanted to make a better life for himself, while the homeless people in Levy et al. (2002) were working to find jobs. It remains less clear whether unsympathetic individuals, or members of hated out-groups, would receive the same level of compassion. This distinction may turn out to be a critically important one as researchers continue to investigate the impact of perspective taking on intergroup helping and more general intergroup relations.

How Effective an Intervention Can Perspective Taking Be?

It is now possible to address the central question of this chapter: how effective can perspective taking be as an intervention to improve out-group helping? As this brief review makes clear, there is abundant evidence documenting the generally positive effect of perspective taking on helping; what is also clear is that the potential help recipients in this research are almost never identified as out-group members. Thus, the critical issues affecting the efficacy of perspective-taking interventions will revolve around this fact.

Will Perspective Taking Work with Out-Group Targets?

A potential recipient of help can be construed in different ways: as a person, a student, a woman, a daughter, a Kansas Jayhawk, and so on. One influence on the efficacy of a perspective-taking intervention will be the nature of this construal. The most general paradigm in this literature asks participants to take the perspective of a sympathetic individual (one who just broke up with a significant other, is struggling in school, or has suffered personal tragedy). Under these circumstances, group boundaries such as school affiliation are unlikely to be the most salient feature of the target, and thus the perceiver is likely to relate to the target as an individual rather than as an out-group member. Even when the target is a member of a stigmatized group, s/he may well be perceived and evaluated as an individual (after all, it is probably the counterstereotypic, and therefore individuated, homeless person who searches for a job, or drug addict who wants to improve his life). Clearly perspective taking increases the help that is offered to such individuated targets, primarily via the mediating effects of cognitive representations and empathic concern. The question is: will similar effects be obtained when the target is viewed primarily in terms of her out-group membership?

With regard to the PT→Cognitive Representations→Out-group Helping path, there has been no research to date that directly examines this sequence. Thus, no simple answer is possible. However, research suggests that in clear intergroup situations, perceivers not only view targets in terms of their group membership, they also view themselves in this way – categorizing themselves as members of the salient in-group, taking on the traits and characteristics, goals and motives of the in-group (Mackie, Maitner, & Smith, 2009; Turner, Hogg, Oakes, Reicher, & Wetherell, 1987). Given that perspective taking leads to a projection of self-traits to an individuated target, it may well be that in intergroup settings observers will ascribe in-group traits to the out-group member. This would tend to bring the out-group member more fully into the circle of moral regard and lead to more favorable treatment, including helping.

This is the kind of logic underlying theoretical approaches such as the Common In-group Identity Model (Gaertner & Dovidio, 2000), which argue that negative attitudes and behaviors toward out-groups can be reduced to the extent that the in-group and out-group can be "recategorized" as part of one superordinate category. Considerable evidence supports this view (see Gaertner & Dovidio, 2000). Thus, there is reason to be hopeful that perspective taking may help foster recategorization and subsequently increase helping. Such hopes would be strengthened, of course, by empirical demonstrations that have thus far been lacking.

With regard to the PT→Empathic Concern→Out-group Helping path, there is a bit more relevant evidence to consider. By using instructional sets to induce perspective taking, Batson and colleagues (Batson et al., 2002) were able to produce greater empathic concern for an out-group (drug addict) target, which then led to greater help for drug addicts in general; Batson, Sager et al. (1997) found a similar pattern with regard to help for a single out-group target (rival university student); and Levy et al. (2002) found that dispositional perspective taking was associated with greater sympathy for and willingness to help a variety of out-groups. Thus, there is some empirical reason to believe that perspective taking can influence out-group helping via its effect on feelings of compassion for members of that out-group. As noted earlier, however, this conclusion should be tempered by the knowledge that the targets in these studies might not have been viewed as clearly belonging to an out-group.

Batson has proposed a three-step model to account for such findings. First, perspective taking influences empathic concern for an individual out-group member perceived to be in distress; second, such empathic concern leads to a greater valuing of that individual's welfare; third, this increased valuing then generalizes to the out-group as a whole. Of course, there are obstacles to be overcome in this multistage process. As Batson notes, empathizing with a member of a stigmatized group may be personally threatening, which might prevent an initial empathic response; in fact, exposure to any distressed target can be anxiety provoking, and can contribute to the defensive victim blaming that characterizes the Just World effect (Lerner & Simmons, 1966). Even when a sympathetic response does occur, it may not generalize to the group as a whole because of subcategorization (Batson, Sager et al., 1997).

Pitfalls and Boundaries

Although perspective taking has promise as an intervention, there are some clear boundary conditions on its likely effectiveness. One such factor is the particular nature of the out-group in question. There are out-groups . . . and then there are *out-groups*. It seems quite likely that the effect of perspective taking on helping will be more fragile when the out-group is one that is more disliked, feared, or has a long history of conflict with the in-group. A variety of out-groups have been used in the research we have been reviewing, including some based on race (Aberson & Haig, 2007; Vescio et al., 2003), sexual orientation (Stürmer et al., 2005), medical status (Davis et al., 2004; Levy et al., 2002), university or athletic affiliation (Batson, Sager et al., 1997; Levine et al., 2005), and ones based solely on laboratory manipulations (Dovidio et al., 1997). What has been largely lacking in this work are out-groups reflecting the deep-seated enmity that may be most resistant to intervention – Israelis and Palestinians, Shia and Sunnis, Serbs and Croats.

The biggest difficulty in these cases is the vast psychological distance between such highly polarized groups. In addition to the high level of negative affect associated with such hated out-groups, recent research suggests that people actually ascribe less *humanness* to members of disliked out-groups (see Leyens et al., 2000, 2003). That is, members of such groups are seen as less likely to possess characteristics and have the kind of emotional responses that characterize humans as opposed to animals (Leyens et al., 2000). Further research suggests that dispositional empathy and perspective taking may not be sufficient to overcome these biases (Haslam & Bain, 2007). Thus when facing a particularly hated out-group in a salient intergroup context, a general tendency to take other perspectives may not be sufficient to humanize out-group members, much less to elicit intergroup helping. It is less clear whether deliberate, situational perspective taking would overcome such biases, but it remains quite possible that perceiving the out-group member *as* an out-group member may undermine the positive consequences perspective taking would otherwise have for helping behavior.

A related issue is the problem of motivation. Simply put, there will often be very little inclination to take the perspective of an out-group member when there is significant intergroup conflict – even if the psychological distance is small enough to allow it. Thus, perspective-taking interventions may need to be combined with explicit efforts to increase the motivation to do so. One way to accomplish this would be to make the outcomes of in-group and out-group members more interdependent. By linking their outcomes, the motivation to understand an out-group target – and thus potentially benefit the self – may be increased. For example, programs such as the jigsaw classroom (Aronson, Blaney, Stephan, Sikes, & Snapp, 1978) are designed to make members of differing subgroups not only work together but to rely on each other for group and individual success. As a result, the stakes are high enough to produce perspective taking even for targets who are initially both dissimilar and disliked.

Another potential problem with perspective-taking interventions is somewhat ironic – the more successful such an intervention is in recategorizing two groups into a superordinate one, the less successful it may be for those who are most highly identified with the initial groups. Part of the reason people categorize the world into in-groups and out-groups is because we have a desire to be both similar to and different from others – a state known as optimal distinctiveness (Brewer, 1991). High identification with an in-group may reflect that a person is in such a state, and thus recategorization into a superordinate group may be threatening. In fact, recent research suggests that individuals who highly identify with their in-groups actually show increased prejudice and discrimination when their in-group's distinctiveness is threatened by superordinate categorization (Crisp, Stone, & Hall, 2006). Thus, making the out-group more in-group-like may actually increase prejudice and discrimination for at least some members of the group. One solution is to combine the recategorization intervention with a continued salience of the original subgroups – in essence, allowing individuals to maintain a "dual identity." Initial investigations support such a strategy (e.g., Crisp et al., 2006).

It is also possible that taking the perspective of out-groups can lead to difficulties if doing so makes salient to the perspective taker the negative stereotypes that the out-group holds regarding the in-group. A growing body of evidence indicates that when in-group members become aware of such "meta-stereotypes" it can produce evaluative concerns that interfere with normal social functioning and can lead to a defensive distancing from the out-group (Vorauer, Hunter, Main, & Roy, 2000; Vorauer & Turpie, 2004). To the degree that taking an out-group's perspective increases awareness of that out-group's unflattering stereotype about the in-group, there is a risk of an unintended negative effect of the intervention.

Finally, the nature of the perspective-taking intervention itself will be an important factor in determining its efficacy. The most common form of perspective-taking manipulation in this research has been the instructional set. This method has the advantage of being straightforward and easy to carry out; moreover, it has been effective in a number of investigations, including Batson's work on helping for an out-group target (Batson et al., 2002; Batson, Sager et al., 1997). However, as noted earlier, instructional sets have proven largely ineffective at reducing stereotype use. The research that has found such a link has tended to employ other kinds of manipulation such as having observers write an essay about a day in the life of the out-group target (Galinsky & Moskowitz, 2000).

In fact, this pattern may point to an important distinction: between relatively passive interventions such as instructional sets, and active ones that require more of the participant. Essay-writing tasks are one example of such active interventions, as are the kind of role-playing exercises that are often included in formal prejudice-reduction programs (e.g., McGregor, 1993). The jigsaw classroom technique, mentioned earlier, is one form that this can take. Conflict resolution programs often require the participants to adopt the point of view of their antagonist as part of the training. Such interventions demand noticeably more from participants than a simple instructional set. However, as Finlay and Stephan (2000) have noted, it is difficult to tell just how effective such programs are, and even more difficult to determine which components of the programs are most useful.

Conclusion

Considerable research attests to the fact that perspective taking holds great promise as an intervention for increasing out-group helping. To date it has not yet received many tests under the most stringent conditions, but we remain cautiously optimistic about its value even in those situations. Researchers may need to be innovative in finding ways to induce perspective taking without highlighting negative meta-stereotypes or threatening the distinctiveness of the out-group, but we would like to think that perspective taking, as a process, can rise to the challenge in even the most aggressive intergroup situations. For *sterna antillarum*, the treatment of "out-group" members is rather rigid and inflexible: out of scrape, out of mind. For *homo sapiens*, things are more complex. The circle of moral regard is not fixed, but may expand to bring out-group members psychologically closer to the self and thus subject to the kind of empathic processes often reserved for intimates. Perspective taking's great promise lies in its power to help us expand this circle – to alter the lines that ordinarily define the boundary between self and others.

10

Recategorization and Prosocial Behavior
Common In-Group Identity and a Dual Identity

John F. Dovidio, Samuel L. Gaertner, Nurit Shnabel, Tamar Saguy, and James Johnson

Introduction

A range of different interventions, such as appropriately structured intergroup contact (Pettigrew & Tropp, 2006) and emphasis on shared social identity (Gaertner & Dovidio, 2000), have been demonstrated to improve intergroup attitudes. However, more favorable intergroup attitudes do not always translate directly to more positive intergroup action. For example, meta-analysis has revealed that racial prejudice is only modestly correlated ($r = .32$) with discriminatory behavior of Whites toward Blacks (Dovidio, Brigham, Johnson, & Gaertner, 1996). Also, whereas intergroup contact has generally robust effects on attitudes, its impact on support for policies aimed at helping minorities is less reliable (Dixon, Durrheim, & Tredoux, 2005).

In this chapter, we review the evidence supporting the Common In-Group Identity model (Gaertner & Dovidio, 2000), which suggests that biases in prosocial behavior toward out-group members can be reduced when in-group members recategorize themselves within a superordinate group. Our empirical emphasis is on the orientations of majority group members toward minorities, because by virtue of their position in society it is the majority group members' help that is more often required. We also discuss how understanding the different perspectives of majority and minority group members can provide insight into the conditions that influence prosocial behavior.

We begin by providing a brief overview of the nature of social categorization and its relation to intergroup bias. We then summarize the Common In-Group Identity model and present evidence supporting it, first in terms of reducing intergroup bias and then with regard to helping behavior. We introduce new research on helping that investigates, in the context of race relations in the United States, how Whites respond to Blacks expressing different forms of common identity. The concluding section explores promising directions for improving understanding of intergroup helping and related phenomena.

Social Categorization and Social Bias

In general, categorization, which often occurs spontaneously on the basis of physical similarity, proximity, or shared fate (Campbell, 1958), enables people to make rapid decisions about incoming information. In this respect, people may be characterized as "cognitive misers" who tend to compromise accuracy for efficiency (Fiske & Taylor, 1991). When this tendency operates in the social domain (i.e., social categorization) it is associated with the formation and perpetuation of systematic intergroup biases.

In particular, one basic distinction associated with social categorization involves differentiation between the group containing the self, the in-group, and other groups, the out-groups – that is, between the "we's" and the "they's" (see Social Identity Theory, Tajfel, & Turner, 1979; Self-Categorization Theory, Turner, Hogg, Oakes, Reicher, & Wetherell, 1987).

Even when the basis for the categorization of people into in-groups and out-groups is quite trivial, this distinction has a profound influence on social perception, affect, cognition, and behavior. For example, people spontaneously experience more positive affect toward members of their in-group than toward members of the out-group (Otten & Moskowitz, 2000) and believe that they are more capable of expressing uniquely human emotions (Leyens et al., 2003). Furthermore, when in-group–out-group social categorizations, rather than personal identities, are salient, people tend to behave in a more greedy and less trustworthy way toward members of other groups than if they were reacting to each other as individuals (Insko et al., 2001). In terms of prosocial orientations, which are the focus of the present chapter, people are more readily disposed to be helpful toward in-group than toward out-group members (Piliavin, Dovidio, Gaertner, & Clark, 1981).

Although the functional nature of the relations between groups (e.g., actual competition over resources) can further influence the degree to which discrimination is manifested (Sherif, 1966), the process of social categorization itself provides the basis for social biases to develop and to be maintained. Social categorization is a dynamic process, however, and people possess many different group identities and are capable of focusing on different social categories. By modifying a perceiver's goals, motives, perceptions of past experiences and expectations, there is opportunity to alter the level of category inclusiveness that will be primary or most influential in a given situation. This malleability of the level at which impressions are formed is important because of its implications for altering the way people behave toward members of in-groups and out-groups and consequently, altering intergroup relations.

The Common In-Group Identity Model and Intergroup Bias

Because categorization into and identification with social groups are basic processes that are fundamental to intergroup bias, social psychologists have targeted these processes as a starting point for improving intergroup relations. A variety of different approaches have been employed successfully. For example, decategorization strategies that emphasize the individual qualities of others (Wilder, 1981) or encourage personalized interactions (Miller, 2002) have been used to reduce social biases by minimizing the salience of social identities.

The approach we have employed, the Common In-Group Identity model (Gaertner & Dovidio, 2000), draws upon the theoretical foundations of Social Identity Theory (Tajfel & Turner, 1979) and Self-Categorization Theory (Turner et al., 1987). This strategy emphasizes the process of recategorization, in which the goal is to reduce bias by systematically altering the perception of intergroup boundaries, redefining who is conceived of as an in-group member. If members of different groups are induced to conceive of themselves as a single superordinate group, rather than as two separate groups, attitudes toward former out-group members would be expected to become more positive through processes involving pro-in-group bias, thereby reducing intergroup bias (see Gaertner & Dovidio, 2000). A common in-group identity can be achieved by increasing the salience of existing common superordinate memberships (e.g., a school, a company, a nation) or by introducing factors perceived to be shared by these memberships (e.g., common goals or fate).

Within the framework of the Common In-Group Identity model, different types of cognitive representations (i.e., one group, two subgroups within one group, two groups, or separate individuals) of members of groups are hypothesized to have specific cognitive, affective, and behavioral consequences. For example, Gaertner, Mann, Murrell, and Dovidio (1989) found that, relative to a condition that maintained the boundaries between two groups, decategorizing members of the groups to produce a separate individuals representation reduced bias by decreasing the attractiveness of former in-group members; in contrast, recategorizing in-group and out-group members as belonging to the same superordinate group reduced bias by increasing the attractiveness of former out-group members.

Considerable empirical support has been obtained for the Common In-Group Identity model in laboratory and field experiments involving temporary and enduring groups (see Gaertner & Dovidio, 2000, 2007). In the next section, we examine in more detail studies directly related to intergroup prosocial behavior.

Common Identity and Prosocial Behavior

Beyond improving intergroup attitudes, interventions involving recategorization of members of two groups within a superordinate identity have been found to facilitate prosocial intergroup behavior. In one of our earlier tests of the Common In-Group Identity model (Dovidio, Gaertner, Validzic, Matoka, Johnson, & Frazier, 1997), for example, participants initially worked in two separate subgroups, supposedly representing different personality types (overestimators and underestimators). They were then induced to either develop a common superordinate representation or to maintain a two-group representation using a procedure similar to that used in our previous research on group differentiation (Gaertner et al., 1989). Next, under the conditions representing the One Group or Two Group manipulations, participants worked on a decision task.

To examine helping, participants were escorted to separate rooms and informed that they had been chosen for the one-way communication aspect of the study and that they would be listening to an audiotape of one of the previous participants in the study. The person on the tape was presented as either a member of participants' original subgroup category (e.g., an overestimator) or as a member of the other group. The person on the tape explained that she was unable to complete an important project because of illness. At the conclusion of the session, participants were given an opportunity to help the person in need by placing posters to recruit participants for the other person's project.

The results provided support for the facilitating role of recategorization in intergroup helping. As expected, in the Two Group condition that reinforced the original group memberships, participants were more helpful (i.e., agreed to place more posters for the other person) for in-group than for out-group members ($Ms = 4.83$ vs. 2.25). In the One Group condition, in contrast, there was no bias against original out-group members ($Ms = 3.08$ vs. 3.92). These findings offer direct support for the applicability of the Common In-Group Identity model for understanding and promoting intergroup helping.

Other research provides evidence that emphasizing a common in-group identity can facilitate other forms of prosocial behavior, such as cooperative and socially responsible behavior in a commons dilemma. Kramer and Brewer (1984) led participants to focus either on their different group identities (i.e., half of the participants were college students whereas the other half were not) or on a superordinate identity (i.e., participants were all residents of the same city). When resources became scarce, participants whose superordinate identity was emphasized cooperated more to conserve the resources than those who saw themselves as members of different groups. Wit and Kerr (2002) examined the choices people made in a commons dilemma when the experimenter emphasized that the person would be participating in the session as (a) one of a group of six people, (b) a member of one of two different three-person groups, or (c) one of six individuals. The results showed that participants were most generous in giving their resources to a fund benefiting the six participants collectively when they believed they shared one collective identity. Participants allocated the fewest resources to the 6-person collective account when the subgroup social identity was salient.

Additionally, evidence for the effectiveness of a common group identity for promoting prosocial responses was found outside the laboratory with naturalistically consequential groups. In particular, it was demonstrated that a salient superordinate identity can increase behavioral compliance with a request for assistance from a person of a different race. In a field experiment (Nier, Gaertner, Dovidio, Banker, Ward, & Rust 2001, Study 2) conducted at the University of Delaware football stadium prior to a game between the University of Delaware and Westchester State University, Black and White interviewers approached fans from both universities just before they entered the stadium. These fans were asked if they would be willing to be interviewed about their food preferences. The interviewers systematically varied whether they were wearing a University of Delaware or Westchester State University hat. By selecting fans who wore clothing that identified their university affiliation, we systematically varied whether the fans and our interviewers had common or different university identities in a context where these identities were particularly salient.

Although we planned to oversample Black fans, the sample was still too small to yield any informative findings. Among White fans, however, sharing common university identity with the Black interviewers significantly increased their compliance (59 percent) relative to when they did not share common identity with the Black interviewer (36 percent). When the interviewers were White, however, there was no significant difference in their levels of compliance as a function of their university identity: equivalent levels of compliance were gained when they shared common university identity with the fan (44 percent) as when they appeared to be affiliated with the rival university (37 percent). These findings together with those of the preceding study offer support for the idea that out-group members will be treated more favorably in terms of prosocial behavior when they are perceived to also share a more inclusive, common in-group affiliation.

Dual Identities

Despite the evidence that the strategy of achieving a common group identity can improve intergroup relations, its effectiveness may be limited by the difficulty of maintaining a common identity in the face of powerful social forces within naturalistic settings that emphasize group differences and reinforce separate group memberships (Hewstone, 1996). Also, because membership in particular groups satisfies many psychological and material needs, people may often resist interventions designed to make superordinate group identity primarily salient. Introducing conditions that challenge the positive distinctiveness of one's group (Tajfel & Turner, 1979), such as emphasizing similarity or overlapping boundaries between the groups (Dovidio et al., 1997; Jetten, Spears, & Manstead, 1997) or their shared identity (Hornsey & Hogg, 2000), can stimulate motivations to reaffirm the different group identities, particularly among people who strongly identify with their original group (Crisp, Walsh, & Hewstone, 2006). Consequently, when group identities and the associated cultural values are central to members' functioning, it may be undesirable for people to relinquish these identities.

These insights are reflected in the inclusion of another form of shared identity recategorization, besides a one group identity, within the Common In-Group Identity model. This form, a dual identity, involves the simultaneous activation of original subgroup identities *and* a common in-group identity. We believe that it is possible for members to conceive of two groups (for example, Blacks and Whites) as distinct units within the context of a superordinate identity (i.e., American).

However, we have also found that majority and minority group members may have different preferences for these different forms of recategorized representations. Whereas majority group members prefer a common in-group identity representation of intergroup relations, minority group members prefer a dual identity representation (Dovidio, Gaertner, & Kafati, 2000). From a broader perspective, one group and dual identity representations are parallel to assimilation and multicultural ideologies, respectively (Dovidio, Gaertner, & Saguy, 2007).

Within the acculturation literature, the ideologies of assimilation and multiculturalism have received significant attention, and they have commonly been considered oppositional (Wolsko, Park, & Judd, 2006). Assimilation requires minority group members to conform to dominant values and ideals, often requiring the abandonment of inconsistent racial or ethnic group values, to achieve full acceptance in society. Multicultural integration, in contrast, strives to be inclusive by recognizing, and often celebrating, intergroup differences and their contributions to a common society. Paralleling our results for one group and dual identity preferences, across a range of different types of groups, majority groups have been found to possess a greater preference for assimilation, whereas minority groups preferred multiculturalism (see Verkuyten, 2006).

These different perspectives and preferences for majority and minority group members are of particular importance because intergroup relations are determined by the extent to which they are taken into account and reconciled (Dovidio, Gaertner, Kawakami, & Hodson, 2002). Piontkowski, Rohmann, and Florack (2002) found that discordance in acculturation values between majority and majority groups was directly related to feelings of intergroup threat (see also Bourhis, Moïse, & Perrault, 1997). It is possible, thus, that the expression of an identity that is valued and functional for a member of one group (e.g., a dual identity for a minority group member) may pose a threat to the values and worldviews of a member of another group (e.g., a

198 John F. Dovidio et al.

one group, assimilationist value held by a majority group member). One consequence of this threat may be less positive and helpful orientations toward out-group members.

We consider this issue in the next section, focusing on both the attitudes and prosocial orientation of Whites toward Blacks.

Responses to Expressed Identity: Prejudice and Helping

In this section, we examine the possibility that even though Whites and Blacks both value connection within a superordinate collective identity, the different preferences for the form of this representation, a one group identity versus a dual identity, can elicit negative intergroup behavior. In particular, we describe two studies testing the hypothesis that Whites would respond negatively (in terms of both attitudes and pro-social behavior) to Blacks who express their preference for a dual identity representation because it deviates from Whites' ideal one group representation (which primarily reflects their racial values). Due to practical concerns, we did not examine the way Blacks respond to Whites expressing different types of identities. Whereas it is more common and acceptable for a Black person to describe himself or herself as Black, such an emphasis on race by a White person is more unusual and is likely to convey that the person advocates an extreme racial position, such as White supremacy.

In the first study in this set (Dovidio, Gaertner, & Johnson, 1999), we explored the effects of Whites' exposure to a Black person who expressed his feelings of identity with the different representations outlined in the Common In-Group Identity model (one group, different groups, dual identity, and separate individual). In this experiment, White college students from Colgate University viewed a videotape that portrayed an interview with a Black male student (actually a confederate), with whom they anticipated interacting in a subsequent session. The confederate responded to the questions posed to him using a script developed, based on pilot testing, to make a positive impression. After a series of questions intended to create this positive impression (e.g., about college activities and educational goals), the interviewer asked the confederate, "And how do you see yourself?" The response was constructed to reflect one of the four representations outlined in the Common In-Group Identity model: (a) "I see myself primarily as a Colgate student" (one group), (b) "I see myself primarily as a Black person" (different group), (c) "I see myself primarily as a Black Colgate student [or a Colgate student who is Black]" (dual identity), or (d) "I see myself primarily as a unique individual" (separate individuals).

Our main interest in this study was in how this brief, positive intergroup "contact" could influence responses toward Blacks as a group. The primary dependent measures were White participants' responses on Brigham's (1993) Attitudes toward Blacks Scale, a well-validated measure of general racial prejudice, and willingness to volunteer to help a Black student organization on campus. Thus, after the videotaped interview ended, participants responded to items assessing their impressions of the confederate and attitudes toward Blacks in general. Then, at what appeared to be the conclusion of the session, the experimenter handed each participant an envelope with the logo of a campus volunteer organization.

Inside the envelope was a letter announcing four volunteer activities for the month, with a request for students to volunteer for at least one of them. The experimenter explained that participants were under no obligation to respond to it. Participants were asked to place the envelope, whether the materials inside were completed or not, in the collection box on the way out of the laboratory. Our focus was on the number of hours participants volunteered to assist a Black student organization that was sponsoring activities for local children and adolescents. We hypothesized that Whites would respond negatively to Blacks who express an identity that deviates from Whites' ideal one group representation, even when that identity involves an essential component of common identity, that is, a dual identity.

The results for both dependent measures suggest that minorities' expression of their dual identity might have quite negative effects on majorities' responses. With respect to attitudes toward Blacks, as illustrated in the top panel of Figure 10.1, the manipulation based on a one group representation (the common university identity condition), which was most compatible with an assimilation ideology, was related to the lowest level of prejudice for White college students. Attitudes toward Blacks in general were less prejudiced when the Black student described himself solely in terms of common university identity than when the Black confederate described himself with a different racial identity (i.e., as a Black person), with a dual identity (i.e., as a Black Colgate student), or as a unique individual. The latter three conditions did not significantly differ from one another. Indeed, attitudes toward Blacks tended to be the most negative when Black confederates expressed a dual identity.

The manipulation of the Black confederate's expression of identity also systematically influenced White participants' willingness to

200 *John F. Dovidio et al.*

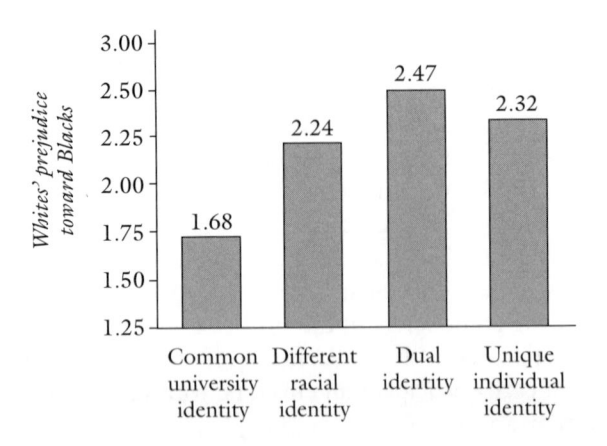

Figure 10.1 Whites' prejudice toward Blacks and time volunteered to help a Black organization as a function of the expressed social representation of a Black confederate.

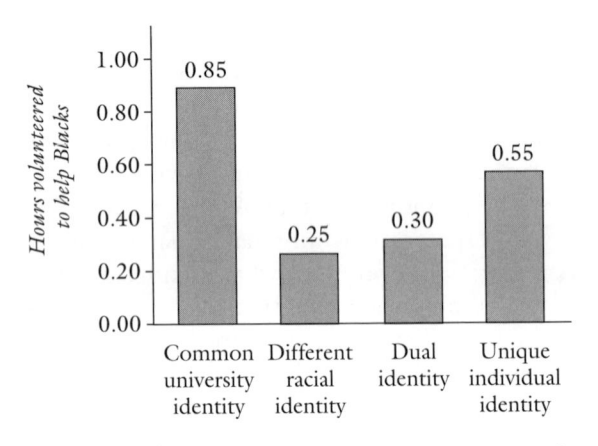

volunteer to help the Black student organization on campus. However, as depicted in the bottom panel of Figure 10.1, the pattern was somewhat different. As expected, participants volunteered the most time when the Black confederate emphasized only his common university identity. White participants helped the next most in the condition in which the confederate emphasized his unique individual identity, which also reflects an orientation compatible with an assimilation ideology (individualism being a core value in White American dominant culture). They helped the least, and equivalently so, in the conditions in which the confederate emphasized only his different racial identity (as a Black person) or a dual identity (as a Black Colgate student).

Although the results of this experiment were generally consistent with our hypotheses, the processes underlying the helping responses were not clear. Unexpectedly, the pattern of helping was not mediated by responses on the Attitudes toward Blacks Scale. In fact, the correlation between Attitudes toward Blacks and volunteering to help the Black student organization ($r = .25$) was comparable to the modest meta-analytic relationship between racial and discriminatory behavior ($r = .32$) obtained in the Dovidio et al. (1996) study. A possible reason for the failure of attitudes toward Blacks as a group to mediate volunteering to help the Black student organization is that these measures represented responses to different entities, that is, Blacks in general and the subset of Blacks in the campus organization, respectively. Indeed, considerable empirical evidence (Ajzen & Fishbein, 2005) suggests that the attitude–behavior relationship is substantially stronger when attitudes are measured in a way more directly representative of the behavior being considered. To test this possibility, in a subsequent experiment we examined how the attitudes and emotional responses to a Black person relate to Whites' willingness to help this particular person.

This study was modeled after the previous one. Again, White college students viewed a videotape of a Black confederate interviewed in a way designed to create a favorable impression of him. Once more, the interview ended with the key question, "And how do you see yourself?" This time the confederate answered in ways that reflected the three collective representations in the Common In-Group Identity model: one group (i.e., common university identity: Colgate student), dual identity (Black Colgate student), or different groups (different racial identity: Black person). Also, a segment was added in which the confederate discussed a serious illness (pneumonia) that made him get behind in his senior project, which he needed to complete for graduation. The confederate explained that he needed students to complete questionnaires to help him finish this project.

The dependent measures in this study were attitudes toward the confederate (e.g., friendly; Gaertner et al., 1989), empathic concern aroused by the person's problem (e.g., sympathetic; Batson, 1991), and helping behavior. The procedure for assessing helping was based on that used by Dovidio, Allen, and Schroeder (1990; see also Dovidio et al., 1997). After the experimental session was allegedly concluded, the experimenter casually mentioned that the professor in charge of this study asked her to handle a sealed envelope to participants. Inside the envelope was a cover letter from the professor informing participants that the envelope contains a request for help from students whose materials were used in the study, stressing that participants are *not* obligated to comply with this request. The envelope also contained a letter from the Black confederate who was interviewed in the videotape in which he asked participants to help him by distributing posters across campus. The number of posters that participants agreed to distribute in different campus buildings was our primary measure of helping.

We again hypothesized that the representations expressed by the Black confederate would systematically affect White participants' attitudes, emotional reactions, and helping behavior. Specifically, we expected that White participants would have more positive attitudes, respond with greater empathic concern, and be more helpful when the confederate expressed a one group (common university) identity than a different racial group (Black) identity (see Dovidio et al., 1997). Moreover, on the basis of our previous study showing Whites' negative reactions to a Black person's expression of a dual identity (Black Colgate student), we anticipated that participants in the dual identity condition would respond similarly to those in the different group condition.

The results of this study were generally consistent with our hypotheses. Although the difference among the common university (one group), different racial (different group) identity, and dual identity conditions was only marginally significant for the attitude measure ($p = .08$), it was significant for both empathic concern ($p = .04$) and helping ($p = .01$). Responses were much more positive in the common university identity (one group) condition than in the different racial identity (different groups) and the dual identity conditions. Attitudes toward the confederate, for example, were more positive in common university identity condition ($M = 5.00$) than in the different racial identity and dual identity conditions ($Ms = 4.33$ and 4.55). With respect to prosocial responses, White participants expressed the most empathic concern for the Black confederate when he expressed a common university identity than when he expressed a different racial identity or a dual identity (see top panel of Figure 10.2); White participants showed a corresponding pattern for the number of posters they agreed to help distribute (see bottom panel of Figure 10.2). For each of the main measures in this study – attitudes, empathic concern, and helping – there was no significant difference between the different racial identity and dual identity conditions, but the means for the

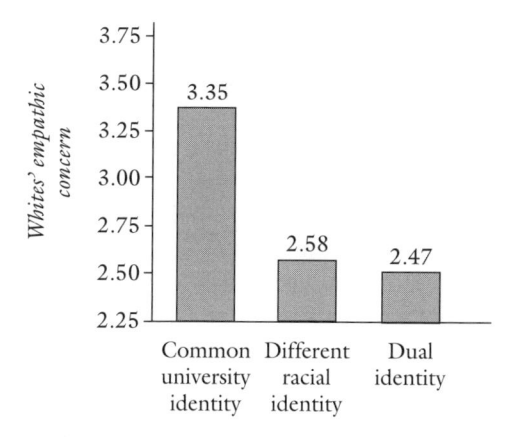

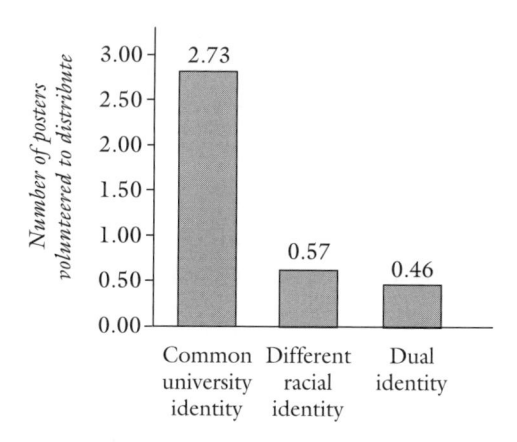

Figure 10.2 Whites' empathic concern and number of posters volunteered to help distribute for a Black confederate as a function of the confederate's expressed social representation.

one group (common university identity) condition were significantly higher ($ps < .04$) than the means for the other two conditions combined for each measure.

We next tested for mediation of the effect of the manipulation of common university identification condition versus the different racial identity and dual identity conditions combined on helping by both attitudes toward the confederate and empathic concern. Although, as described earlier, Whites had more favorable attitudes toward the Black confederate in the one group condition than in the other two conditions, attitudes toward the confederate did not mediate the differences in helping. However, not only was empathic concern greater in the one group (common university) condition than in the other two representation conditions combined, but also empathic concern partially mediated the difference in helping between the one group condition and the other conditions. When empathic concern was included with representation condition as a predictor of helping, the effect for empathic concern was significant, $\beta = .34$, $p < .01$, while the effect for representation condition was significantly reduced, from $\beta = .46$ to .35, Sobel $z = 1.99$, $p < .05$, albeit still significant ($p < .01$).

These results conceptually replicate and extend our earlier work. In the field study described earlier in this chapter (Nier, Gaertner, Dovidio, Banker, Ward, & Rust, 2001), even while their race was highly salient, Blacks were helped more by Whites when they emphasized their common group membership with college signature clothing than when they did not wear clothing indicating their common university membership. Furthermore, in the first study we described about responses to a Black person emphasizing different representations (e.g., common university identity, dual identity), we found that this identity manipulation influenced both attitudes and helping directed toward the Blacks as a whole. In that study, as well as in the second study using this manipulation, attitudes did not mediate helping. However, the findings of the second study manipulating a Black confederate's identity expression did reveal that responses of empathic concern, which were stronger when the confederate expressed a one group (common university) identity rather than a dual identity or different racial group identity, mediated helping.

Taken together, the studies described in this section reveal how even when members of two groups value some form of common identity, the concordance between the specific form of recategorization, that is, common group (assimilation) versus dual identity (multiculturalism), is a critical factor determining whether intergroup orientations will be positive and helpful. The responses of White participants in these experiments were positive and prosocial when a Black person identified himself in a way compatible with an assimilation ideology (i.e., a common university, one group representation in both studies as well as unique individual in the first study) but were relatively negative when the Black person emphasized their racial identity, either in conjunction with a common identity (i.e., a dual identity) or by itself.

As we acknowledged at the beginning of our description of these studies, we did not include an examination of Blacks' reactions to Whites who emphasized their racial identity because such behavior is highly non-normative. For example, the statement "I see myself primarily as a White person" is likely to be perceived as extremely racist, unlike its equivalent for Blacks. As a consequence, the current research, by itself, cannot disentangle whether it is discordance in representations per se that underlies the effects we observed or the particular type of expressed identity that might be interpreted as less inclusive, and therefore exclusionary. Further research is necessary to clarify this issue.

Mechanisms and Moderators

Although both involve some form of recategorization in terms of a superordinate group, the presented research demonstrates that responses to a one group or a dual identity can be substantially divergent. As mentioned, further research is necessary to fully explain the underlying mechanisms that mediate the process through which discordance between majority's and minority's preferred representations may lead to negative reactions.

One promising candidate for such mediating mechanism is social comparison and projection processes. In particular, Mummendey and Wenzel (1999) proposed that when a common, superordinate identity is salient, people tend to overestimate the extent to which their own group's standards and values are prototypical of the superordinate category relative to the standards and values of other groups. This tendency to project one's group values onto others is more pronounced among majorities than minorities (Sidanius, Feshbach, Levin, & Pratto, 1997). When the standards of one's own group are perceived to represent those of the superordinate category, the standards of other groups may be seen as more deviant and non-normative and – due to social comparison processes – as more inferior. Thus, an out-group member who stresses his or her subgroup identity is likely to be reacted to more negatively.

Another mechanism that may explain the process through which discordance in preferred representations may lead to negative reactions is identity threat. For majority group members learning that the minority adopts a dual identity representation may be threatening because it undermines the hegemony of the dominant culture. In contrast, for minority group members, knowing that the majority adopts a one group representation may be threatening because it implies a denial of the value of their subgroup's culture and traditions. These types of threats to identity may be particularly strong for members who highly identify with their subgroup.

Cultural context may be another factor that influences bias due to discordance in intergroup representations. In contrast to our findings for Blacks and Whites in the US, Rebelo, Guerra, and Monteiro (2005) reported that recategorization as one group was more effective for reducing intergroup bias for Black children in Portugal, whereas a dual identity tended to reduce bias among European Portuguese children. Guerra et al. (2007) proposed that these different patterns of findings may in part be related to the longevity and dynamics of intergroup relations in these countries. Whereas Black–White relations have been important historically in the US, much of the presence of Blacks in Portugal is the result of recent immigration from Africa. A dual identity may not be functional or desirable for second generation African (Black) Portuguese children, who may strive for assimilation and equality with European Portuguese children. However, for European Portuguese children the dual identity representation may ameliorate identity threat by offering a degree of positive differentiation from African Portuguese children, thus lowering intergroup bias more than recategorization as one common group. Although the exact processes that account for these cultural differences have yet to be identified, their implication is clear: the different values and representation preferences of the groups need to be considered to understand intergroup relations.

Conclusion

In this chapter we explored how the processes of recategorization, as outlined in the Common In-Group Identity model (Gaertner & Dovidio, 2000), can influence not only intergroup attitudes but also prosocial behavior. The work we described extends our earlier research in this area in three fundamental ways. First, whereas our initial research on recategorization and intergroup helping employed laboratory groups and considered only the one group form of recategorization, newer studies presented in this chapter reveal the importance of distinguishing between two forms of shared identity representations, that is recategorization as one group and dual identity.

A second extension is the focus on the correspondence between one group and dual identity representations and assimilation and multicultural acculturation values, respectively. Although our emphasis in this chapter was on the association between assimilation values and preference for a one group representation, it should be noted that assimilation can represent one of two forms of colorblind perspectives. One is an emphasis on common or shared identity (e.g., "we are all Americans"), reflecting a preference for a one group representation. The other represents a decategorized orientation, in which the emphasis is on the unique qualities of individuals and individual outcomes (e.g., an emphasis on meritocracy beliefs, such as the Protestant Work Ethic). This orientation may correspond to the "separate individuals" representation within the Common In-Group Identity model (Dovidio et al., 2000). In fact, some common manipulations to prime colorblindness (Wolsko, Park, & Judd, 2000) encourage people to focus on both types of perspectives. The research we have presented in this chapter suggests that it might be valuable to distinguish these two types of colorblindness.

The third extension of our previous work represented in the current chapter points to the importance of acknowledging the different perspectives of majority (high power or high status) and minority (low power or low status) group members on collective identity and intergroup relations. We suggest that discordance between these different perspectives can lead to negative intergroup reactions through processes of social comparison and projection as well as identity threat.

Finally, although we acknowledge that intergroup helping is not *necessarily* prosocial and may instead promote the dependency of minority groups (Halabi, Dovidio, & Nadler, 2008), we contend that helping is a particularly important behavior for intergroup relations. Assistance that is withheld can confirm negative intergroup expectations and generate further distrust, which in turn fuels intergroup conflict. Conversely, prosocial action typically elicits reciprocal behaviors and thus can stimulate and reinforce movement toward more harmonious intergroup relations.

11

Groups, Identities, and Bystander Behavior
How Group Processes Can Be Used to Promote Helping

Mark Levine and Clare Cassidy[†]

Introduction

The brutal rape and murder of Kitty Genovese in New York in 1964 has come to dominate the intellectual landscape of research on the psychology of emergency intervention. The story of the 38 bystanders who witnessed events from their apartment windows and did nothing to help has been the touchstone for those trying to explain the behavior of bystanders in emergencies. From the outset, research on emergency helping was absorbed by the question of why individuals sometimes fail to help. The answer seemed to be that people were adversely affected by the presence of others. A variety of psychological processes like "diffusion of responsibility," "pluralistic ignorance," and "audience inhibition" were mobilized to suggest that individual decision making could be degraded by the immersion of the individual in the social world. Concepts like "the bystander effect" (Latané & Darley, 1970; Latané & Nida, 1981) seemed to suggest that individuals were more likely to help if they were free of the potential contamination of the presence of others.

This approach paints a rather negative picture of the effects of the group on helping behavior. However, in this chapter we will propose that this tale of the inhibition of helping by the group is only half the story. While the bystander effect may indeed be one of the most robust findings in social psychology, we will suggest that it is a particular rather than a generic quality of the effect of groups on helping. We will show that, just as the presence of others can lead to inhibition, so it can also lead to the facilitation of helping. In doing so we will endorse Billig's (1987) injunction that psychological knowledge is always a balance of argumentative positions (what Billig, following the Greek philosopher Protagoras, calls the opposition of logoi and anti-logoi). Using recent advances in theories of group processes and intergroup relations we will demonstrate that the power of the group can be harnessed to promote bystander interventions in emergencies.

The "Myth" of the 38 Witnesses

In order to set the scene for this "rediscovery" of the positive contribution that group processes can make to helping behavior, we begin by returning to the seminal event on which the bystander effect literature has been built. Recent research on the Kitty Genovese murder (Manning, Levine, & Collins, 2007) shows that the story of the failure of the 38 witnesses to help is in fact a stubborn and intractable myth. Analysis of court transcripts and other material associated with the murder shows that, contrary to popular belief (and to what appears in most undergraduate psychology textbooks), there were (at best) 3 rather than 38 witnesses who saw Genovese and her murderer Winston Moseley together; none of whom witnessed the murder (which in fact took place in an enclosed stairwell), and there were several attempts by bystanders to intervene directly or to call the police. The story of the 38 inactive bystanders was something which appeared in a *New York Times* article two weeks after the murder (Rosenthal, 1964/1999). It was this inaccurate and sensationalized article which became the motivation for Latané and Darley's (1970) empirical work.

The importance of the mythologized story of the 38 witnesses is not that it invalidates the canon of bystander effect research. The elegant and inventive body of empirical studies carried out by Latané and Darley (and others) which produced the bystander effect is both robust and impressive. To be clear, the claim here is not that this literature is wrong – but rather that it provides only half the picture. We suggest that the powerful (and mythological) image of the 38 witnesses who fail to act holds such sway over the way emergency intervention is conceptualized, that it limits the kinds of questions which are asked. It populates the psychological imagination in a way that "crowds out" the potential search for ways in which groups could contribute positively to emergency intervention. Traditional approaches to bystander behavior have treated the presence of others as the source of the problem, rather than imagining ways in which the group could be the start of a solution.

Reconceptualizing the Role of the Group in Bystander Research

It is important to recognize that, even at the outset, there was a strand of bystander research which suggested that group size might not be the only important factor in emergency helping. For example, early research by Darley, Lewis, and Teger (1973) showed that if bystanders could see each other (and thus be able to communicate) then group size did not inhibit helping. Similarly, Rutkowski, Gruder, and Romer (1983) demonstrated that if bystanders were allowed to get to know each other (and build up a sense of cohesion) then groups did not inhibit helping. At the same time, studies which retained a focus on intervention in violence (Schwartz & Gottlieb, 1976; Shotland & Straw, 1976) produced evidence that increasing group size was not always an inhibiter of intervention. However, these studies were in the minority and the space they opened up for wider exploration of factors affecting emergency intervention was soon swamped by the volume of studies pointing to group size as the key variable.

Over the last few years a body of literature has begun to develop which offers a way of reconceptualizing how "the presence of others" is imagined in helping research. Rather than focusing on the question of whether others were present or not, this research explores the psychological relationships between all those present in an emergency. In doing so it draws on the central insight of the Social Identity tradition – in particular social identity theory (SIT: Tajfel, 1978a, 1982) and self-categorization theory (SCT: Turner, Hogg, Oakes, Reicher, & Wetherell, 1987), suggesting that people can define themselves in terms of their memberships of social groups and act accordingly. Unlike earlier psychological approaches to the presence of the group (which assumed that the presence of others would undermine personal identity and thus lead to anti-social behavior) (cf. Zimbardo 1969), social identity theory suggests that the presence of others provides the opportunity for people to define themselves in terms of their social identities and act in terms of the norms and values of those identities. More specifically, it proposes that there are three key dimensions that shape the way group processes can impact on helping behavior. These are the *salience* of social identities, the *boundaries* of social identities, and the *content* of social identities.

Taken together, research on these three dimensions has produced a range of evidence to show how group processes can facilitate helping.

Social Identity and Helping

One of the earliest discoveries of the Social Identity literature was the tendency of people to favor the in-group – even when that group membership was based on trivial criteria (Tajfel, Billig, Bundy, & Flament, 1971). This notion of in-group favoritism, and the related idea that people come to see themselves as functionally interchangeable with other members of their group, suggests that people are more likely to help in-group as opposed to out-group members. The salience of a social identity brings with it the conditions for people to experience the emotions and sense of responsibility or obligation that increases the likelihood of help. For example, Dovidio, Gaertner, Validzic, Matoka, Johnson, & Frazier (1997), using the minimal group paradigm, have found evidence of in-group bias in helping. Students were more likely to offer help to a student in need when she was believed to be an in-group member than an out-group member. Similarly, Hornstein (1972, 1976) and colleagues have shown that people are more likely to help others believed to be members of the same community or to share similar attitudes. In early studies using the "lost letter" paradigm (Hornstein, Masor, Sole, & Heilman, 1971; Hodgson, Hornstein, & LaKind, 1972), Hornstein found that pedestrians from a predominantly Jewish section of Brooklyn, New York, were more likely to post an apparently lost questionnaire if the questionnaire appeared to have been completed by someone with similar (pro-Israeli) than dissimilar (pro-Arab) sentiments to their own.

Of course, we should not assume that the salience of group membership means that out-group members will never be helped. As we will see later in this chapter (and elsewhere in this volume), out-group helping does occur. Take, for example, the extensive literature that uses helping as a non-reactive measure of prejudice (Saucier, Miller, & Doucet, 2005). While some studies have found in-group favoritism, others have found no differences (Bickman & Kamzan, 1973) or even "out-group favoritism" (Dutton & Lake, 1973). Saucier et al. (2005) reveal a complex picture of the likelihood of help being offered by White people to Black people. Out-group helping is most likely as a result of prejudice avoidance. This can be a consequence of an individuals' attempt to avoid internal aversive states, or to avoid public accusations of discrimination. Out-group helping is least likely when behavior can be justified on grounds other than race – or in situations of high emergency. The point here is that the social identity approach to helping does not argue that group membership always implies in-group favoritism. Rather, the argument is that when social identity is salient (and this may not always be the case – even in studies on "race" and helping), then people will act in terms of the norms and values of the group. For the most part, this means that people are more likely to be helped when they are seen as members of the group than when they are not. However, it can also lead to out-group helping as an expression of group norms and values or interactional context.

Identity Salience and the Flexibility of Group Boundaries

In our own research, we have taken this idea of the importance of group membership for helping behavior and explored some of the ways in which group processes can be used to promote helping. We focused in particular on the question of identity salience (the ways in which particular social identities come to be important in helping contexts) and category boundaries (how identities are constructed to include and exclude people from the group). Using insights from the social identity literature which show that identities are not automatically given (but rather emerge as a result of comparative context (Oakes, Haslam, & Turner, 1994) and the struggle over definition of meanings (Reicher & Hopkins, 2001), we have examined the dynamic role that identities can play in helping. In doing so, we have combined laboratory based experimentation, field experiments in non-laboratory settings, and analysis of documents and archive material relating to "real life" bystander behavior. Taken together, this research suggests not only the importance of social identity processes for bystander behavior, but also the ways in which these processes can be drawn upon to promote group-level intervention.

For example, in our laboratory experiments (Levine, Cassidy, Brazier, & Reicher, 2002), we demonstrate that group membership is important not only for bystander–victim relationships but also for bystander–bystander relationships. In these experiments, a closed-circuit television (CCTV) clip depicting a violent attack was shown to participants. We discovered that people were more likely to intervene when they believed the victim was an in-group rather than an out-group member. We also showed (in a study using confederates) that fellow bystanders are more influential when they are believed to be in-group rather than out-group members. When in-group confederates said (publicly) that they would be likely to intervene, participants (privately) indicated that they would intervene too. When in-group confederates said they would not intervene, participants were also less likely to intervene. However, when the confederates were out-group, public expressions of intention (either to intervene or not to intervene) did not influence the judgments of participants.

In short, our laboratory experiments seem to suggest that group membership is important for more than just ensuring that in-group members get help. Group membership also shapes the way the actions of fellow bystanders are perceived. This is important because traditional bystander research tends to focus simply on the numbers of others who are present. It does not look at the psychological relationships between those who might be present as bystanders to an emergency. Where traditional research suggests that increasing group size inhibits helping, our research suggests that the salience of social identities can lead to both the inhibition *and* the facilitation of helping. When bystanders share a common social identity, then behavior will be shaped by the contents of the identity. If group norms favor non-intervention, then the presence of the group will inhibit helping. However, if group norms favor intervention, then the presence of the group can facilitate intervention. In this way, a social identity based approach to bystander behavior offers the theoretical platform for using group processes to increase the likelihood of bystander intervention.

Of course, these laboratory experiments do not deal with actual helping behavior. Expressions of intention to intervene (in experimental dependent measures) may be useful for demonstrating theoretical principles, but they should not be treated as veridical acts. This is especially true in the domain of helping research where it is clear that words are not always matched by deeds. One of the major strengths of the traditional bystander literature is that it placed participants in situations where they believed they were witnessing "real life" emergencies — and then looked to see how they actually behaved. It is important therefore to demonstrate that social identity processes can shape actual helping behavior in real emergencies.

With that in mind we set out to conduct field experiments (in the spirit of the traditional research on helping) that explored the impact of social identity on people's willingness to help strangers in need. We borrowed the structure of a famous traditional experiment, Darley and Batson's (1973) "good Samaritan" study, which manipulated the cost of helping a victim in distress. In our studies, cost of helping was replaced by information about group membership. We took a sample of English football (soccer) fans and exposed them, one at a time, to a situation where a stranger has an accident. The fans were all supporters

Table 11.1 Frequencies of helping (and % help) by shirt condition for Study 1 and Study 2 in Levine et al., 2005

	Study 1			Study 2		
	Manchester United identity			Football fan identity		
	Help	No Help	% Help	Help	No Help	% Help
Manchester United	12	1	92	8	2	80
Liverpool	3	7	30	7	3	70
Plain	4	8	33	2	7	22

of Manchester United, a famous and well-supported English team. In the first study (Levine, Prosser, Evans, & Reicher, 2005: Study 1) fans were invited to the psychology department and asked to fill in questionnaires about Manchester United and to write an essay about the joys of being a Manchester United fan. Having raised the salience of the Manchester United social identity, the fans were then directed to another building (on the pretext of being directed to a screening room to watch a film about football). To get to the second building, they had to cross a car park. While they were doing so, an accident was staged in which a confederate came running down a grass bank on the side of the car park (in the eye-line of the participant) and then fell over and clutched his ankle in pain. The confederate was wearing either a Manchester United football shirt (in-group member); a Liverpool FC shirt (out-group member – Manchester United and Liverpool are traditional rivals and have an animosity that can manifest in intergroup violence); or was wearing an ordinary sports shirt which conveyed no information about group membership. Results showed that participants were significantly more likely to help the stranger when he was wearing the Manchester United shirt than either the Liverpool shirt or the ordinary unbranded sports shirt (see Table 11.1). This provides behavioral confirmation of the tendency to help in-group members over others.

However, in a second study we were able to demonstrate the consequences of one of the key implications of a social identity approach to helping – namely, the flexibility of group boundaries and the importance of category inclusiveness. In this study (Levine et al., 2005: Study 2), Manchester United fans were again invited to the psychology department. This time, however, they were asked to fill in questionnaires about being a football fan and to write an essay about the joys of being a football fan. In this way a more inclusive, football fan identity was made salient for participants. Once this had been completed, participants were again exposed to the accident in which the confederate fell in front of them – wearing either the Manchester United, Liverpool, or ordinary, unbranded sport shirt. In this study, participants were as likely to help the stranger when he was wearing the Liverpool shirt as the Manchester United shirt, but not when he was wearing the unbranded sports shirt (see Table 11.1). This is a particularly striking finding given the degree of antipathy that usually exists between Manchester United and Liverpool fans when they think about themselves in terms of their team affiliations. However, by appealing to a more inclusive and superordinate category ("all football fans") the benefits of group membership – and associated helping behavior – are extended to those who would previously have not been helped.

While this field experiment is a striking demonstration of the power of social identities, category boundaries, and category inclusiveness, it might still be objected that the importance of identity processes has yet to be demonstrated outside the confines of experimentation. To show that category constructions *can* affect helping does not demonstrate that, in situations where helping becomes a life or death matter, they *are* used in order to promote intervention.

One place to look for research which might shed light on this question is in the growing literature on the "psychology of rescue" developed by Holocaust scholars (Monroe, 1996; Oliner & Oliner, 1988). While much of this research has been concerned with explaining the motivations of individuals who carried out acts of rescue of Jews from Nazi persecution, there is also work which recognizes the differences in the way different societies responded to Nazi occupation. This more group-level focus (Hilberg, 1993; Monroe, 1996) reveals that while some countries (e.g., Netherlands, France) were complicit in rounding up Jews for deportation, others (e.g., Denmark, Bulgaria) were able to organize effective resistance such that their Jewish populations survived relatively intact.

Our research has taken one of these cases, the rescue of Bulgarian Jews (for a full history, see Bar-Zohar, 1998; Ben-Yakov, 1990; Boyadjieff, 1989; Todorov, 2001). Using transcripts of letters, speeches, and official documents from the King of Bulgaria and from political and religious leaders (see Todorov, 2001), we explored the way in which the population was asked (in these public documents) to oppose the deportation of the Jews (Reicher, Cassidy, Wolpert, Hopkins, &

Levine, 2006). More specifically, we analyzed how the population was appealed to in the texts; whether (and how) Jews were included or excluded from the in-group; and how normative behavior for the group was described.

It quickly became apparent that the population was being appealed to in national terms – as Bulgarians. In other words, attempts were made to make national identity salient – as opposed (say) to a more superordinate categorization of "all humanity." It was also clear that the Jews were placed inside the national category boundaries. Jews and Bulgarians were presented as having the same qualities, sharing the same experiences and allegiances and being part of the same Bulgarian polity. Thus, to allow the deportation of the Jews would be to allow the deportation of fellow Bulgarians. At the same time, the documents describe Bulgarian norms and values as being qualities which required the defense of the Jews. To give the Jews up would be to act against the very essence that makes people Bulgarian.

While this thumbnail sketch may seem a little self-evident or even banal, the power of these category constructions becomes apparent when contrasted with examples where they are not in place. For example, while the Jews of "old" Bulgaria were placed inside the boundaries of this national category, the same could not be said for the Jewish populations of Thrace and Macedonia. In the early years of the war (1941), treaty negotiations between Bulgaria and Germany meant that Bulgaria was given territory recently annexed by the Germans in exchange for the right to move German troops through Bulgaria. This territory included Thrace, Macedonia, and parts of eastern Serbia. For the Bulgarians, this satisfied long-held nationalist dreams of a "Greater Bulgaria." However, although the Bulgarians were now in charge of these territories, when, two years later, the Nazis applied pressure to transport all Bulgarian Jews to the concentration camps, there was no move to protect the Jewish population in these lands. While the Jews inside the "old" borders of Bulgaria were placed inside the national in-group – and thus protected – the Jews of the new territories were not. The deportation of Jews from these occupied territories went ahead between March 20 and 29, 1943. In total, 11,343 people were taken to Auschwitz and Treblinka. Twelve survived.

Helping the Out-Group

Thus far we have developed an argument, using laboratory and field experiments as well as analysis of historical documents, which shows how social identity processes can be central to helping. The salience of social identities, the content of those identities, and the boundaries of the identities are central to determining who will receive help. By making the boundaries as inclusive as possible, and by ensuring that the contents of salient social identities favor helping, we can use the principles of social identity theory to promote helping. However, despite the promise of this social identity influenced approach, it is important to avoid the temptation of seeing the creation of inclusive in-groups as the only way to promote helping.

While it is clear that being an in-group member is more likely to bring with it the protection of the group, this does not automatically imply that out-group members will be treated with indifference at best, or deliberate neglect at worst. For social identity theory, behavior can never be derived simply from the fact of group membership. Rather, one must take into account the content of the specific identity that is made salient. For some groups, there may be strong injunctions to "look after our own," while for other groups, acting prosocially and being charitable to strangers may be the dimensions along which we differentiate our group from others (Jetten, Spears, & Manstead, 1996; Reicher, Hopkins, Levine, & Rath, 2005). Analytically, then, we need to distinguish between helping based on in-group inclusion and helping based on in-group norms.

In fact, helping the out-group can sometimes be a strategic expression of in-group norms and values. In a fascinating set of studies, van Leeuwen (2007) shows how the willingness of Dutch respondents to help those who were victims of natural disasters in other parts of the world (the Asian Tsunami, Hurricane Katrina) can be shaped by respondents' beliefs about the place of the Netherlands in the world. Respondents are more likely to help when they think it will lead to appropriate group recognition, and are also more likely to offer help on dimensions on which the Dutch are perceived to have specific and unrivaled expertise (in flood defenses, for example).

Our own research has also revealed strategic aspects to out-group helping. In a study using Scottish respondents (Hopkins, Reicher, Harrison, Cassidy, Bull, & Levine, 2007), we discovered that helping the out-group can sometimes be used as a way of trying to improve the stereotype of the in-group. When Scots were told that the English viewed them as mean, they strongly resented this stereotype, were motivated to refute it, and used out-group helping as a way of doing so. In other words, they responded more favorably to requests for help from out-group members than they did to requests from in-group members. This is because helping others is a way of demonstrating that you are not mean. However, helping members of your own group could be discounted as simple self-interest – leaving the stereotype unchallenged. However, helping the out-group is more difficult to dismiss as an act of self-interest – and can thus be offered as unambiguous evidence to counteract the stereotype of the Scots as mean.

Practical Implications

In this chapter we have presented evidence for the importance of identity processes in helping both in-group and out-group members. However, the important step for any new theoretical approach is the turning of theory into practice. After all, one of the main criticisms leveled at the traditional "bystander effect" approach is that, despite being one of the most robust and reproduced findings in academic social psychology, it lacked practical utility when it came to increasing real world interventions. How then might our focus on social identity be useful in promoting helping in emergencies?

We began this chapter with the story of Kitty Genovese and the 38 witnesses. We argued that there was no evidence to support the idea that bystanders failed to act or that the presence of others had an inhibitory effect. Despite this, the 38 witnesses story still has a hold over the psychological imagination. When we think about bystander behavior in emergencies we think about a "society of strangers" who share public spaces (like city streets, public parks, shopping malls, and train carriages) but who are psychologically isolated from each other. At first sight, this seems to pose particular problems for a social identity based account of helping. These public spaces are places where people are unlikely to share a common group identity. Thus, the first issue for a social identity based account of emergency helping is whether collective identities can ever be engendered in such contexts.

In their studies of responses to disasters and emergencies (in particular the London bombings on July 7, 2005), John Drury and colleagues have shown (Drury, 2004; Drury, Cocking, & Reicher, 2006) that emergency events themselves can lead to the formation of common identities. Drury reports how survivors of the London bombings contrast the difference between the usual, atomized experience of being a commuter in a crowded train, with the feelings of solidarity and commonality they felt with fellow passengers in the aftermath of the bombs. When emergencies are viewed as a threat to collective safety, then people tend to act in cooperative rather than selfish ways. Rare selfish acts tend not to spread. In other words, contrary to the common perception that people tend to "panic" and behave irrationally or act in their own narrow interests, common threat tends to result in common identity. People behave in helpful and prosocial ways towards others who are sharing the emergency.

Clearly, these common threat emergencies are different from emergencies where there is no perceived common threat. This might include an assault by one train passenger upon another. In order to improve the likelihood that bystanders will intervene to help victims of situations such as this, the task is to find ways in which collective identification can be engendered proactively. The key is to make an attack upon one person feel like an attack upon all. This is no straightforward task. While a social identity approach can point to the importance of the salience, boundaries, and contents of identity in shaping behavior, it cannot offer a universal prescription. Each public place and each set of social relations will have a specific set of identity relations which need to be understood in their own terms. However, what Drury's work reveals is that it *is* possible for strangers in public to define themselves and act in terms of a common identity.

A social identity perspective would warn against public policy initiatives that threaten to atomize or divide the collective fabric. For example, it would warn against the policy direction encapsulated in ex-British Prime Minister Margaret Thatcher's aphorism that "there is no such thing as society. There are individual men and women, and there are families." While this was intended as the vanguard of a political attack on what Thatcher saw as the evils of a reliance on the "welfare state," it limited the boundaries of social responsibility to the confines of the family. It undermined the sense that we have a responsibility for the welfare of others – particularly when those others are strangers. Furthermore, it played into the idea of a contract of mutual indifference – if I am only looking after myself and my family, and the same can be said for everybody else, then I cannot expect anybody to help me should I be the victim of an emergency. These are the kinds of conditions which are likely to keep bystander intervention low.

By contrast, policy initiatives which create conditions whereby an injury to one can be an injury to all, are most likely to promote intervention behavior. Take, for example, the decision by the Swedish government in 1976 to outlaw corporal punishment of children. Over the last thirty years there has been radical change in attitude and practice with respect to violence towards children in Sweden. The Child Rights Information Network – run by the Commissioner for Human Rights in the Council of Europe – reports that "increased sensitivity to violence to children in Sweden has led to an increase in reporting of assaults, but there has been a declining trend in prosecutions of parents, and a substantial reduction in compulsory social work interventions and in numbers of children taken into care. Public attitudes towards hitting children have changed which has facilitated early supportive intervention in individual cases." In Sweden, people intervene if they see a child being hit by an adult in a public place. They do so because they are not inhibited by the idea that family members have the "right" to hit their children. For them, violence towards a child is not something that is covered by the "privatized" boundaries of the family. Hitting children is against the law – but it is also "not Swedish." Conditions have been created in which particular behaviors are seen to reflect badly on the Swedish public as a whole. Thus, intervention rates are high and collective support for intervention is assured.

Conclusions

In this chapter we have argued that, in traditional research on bystander behavior, there is a generally negative view of the role played by groups and group processes. We have suggested that some of this can be traced back to the "signal crime" which was the launching pad for bystander research in social psychology – the inaction of the 38 witnesses to the murder of Kitty Genovese. We have shown how this event, although not supported by the available evidence, has come to dominate the landscape of helping research. The failure of the group is seen as the crux of the research problem, and as a consequence, there has been little attempt to explore the ways in which groups and group processes could be mobilized to promote helping behavior. We have suggested that this has resulted in a body of literature which tells only half the story. While it is clear that, under some conditions, the presence of others can inhibit helping, there is little work that examines whether the presence of others can ever facilitate helping.

We have offered, as an alternative, an approach to bystander behavior based on some of the insights of a social identity theory approach to group processes. This approach suggests that people can define themselves in terms of their membership of social groups, and that when they do, they act in terms of the norms and values of that social identity. Through a series of empirical studies including laboratory experiments, field experiments, and analysis of historical documents, we have shown how social identity processes can be mobilized to promote helping. In particular, we have identified the importance of the salience of social identities, the boundaries of social identities, and the content of social identities as the key to understanding the role of the group in bystander behavior. We have shown that people are more likely to help others when they are in-group members – and that the more inclusive the identity boundaries are, the greater the range of people who will be helped. However, we also argued that identity processes do not limit helping to in-group members only. We showed that, alongside the importance of identity inclusiveness, identity contents are also important. Some group identities embody norms and values which promote helping the out-group as a way of establishing or maintaining in-group value and distinctiveness.

The importance of this group-level approach to bystander behavior lies in its potential for revitalizing an area of research which has become somewhat moribund over the last two decades. One of the great ironies of traditional work on the bystander effect was that it produced one of the most robust and reproduced findings in social psychology (Dovidio, 1984; Latané & Nida, 1981) and yet researchers were unable to use it to increase the likelihood of helping in emergencies. By highlighting the potential of the group to facilitate helping (as well as to inhibit helping), it becomes possible once again to imagine the contribution of research to practice. The approach outlined in this chapter not only offers the potential for contributions to practice, but, by drawing on the insights of a social identity approach to group processes, suggests some of the theoretical mechanisms which make for practical theory.

12

Influences of Psychological Sense of Community on Voluntary Helping and Prosocial Action

Allen M. Omoto and Mark Snyder

Introduction

In many ways, working alone and working together, people take action to help other people and in order to benefit society. Consider several examples from North America. People practice the habits of recycling and conserving energy, as well as use mass transit, in order to preserve and conserve natural resources or even to save money or to avoid the stress of driving at rush hour. They serve as volunteers and provide help to other people who have difficulty caring for themselves. They participate in programs in schools and in the workplace that provide opportunities for community service. In addition, people join neighborhood groups and organizations and, where none exist to meet the needs of their communities, take the initiative to found them and assume leadership roles in them. As well, they vote and work on political campaigns, and even run for office themselves, in order to elect political leaders who will work on behalf of causes that they value. They engage in lobbying and advocacy efforts, working for the passage of legislation of concern to them. They join and are active in social movements dedicated to causes of importance to them. Similar activities and commitments can be found throughout the world (e.g., Allik & Realo, 2004; Curtis, Grabb, & Baer, 1992; van Vugt, Snyder, Tyler, & Biel, 2000).

These activities are all instances of people seeking to address problems of society by engaging in what is often referred to as civic engagement, citizenship behaviors, or more generically, social action (e.g., Boyte & Kari, 1996; Snyder & Omoto, 2007, 2008). Promoting various forms of social action may be one way of solving many of society's problems (e.g., Omoto, 2005; Omoto & Snyder, 2002; Oskamp, 2000; Snyder & Omoto, 2000, 2001; van Vugt & Snyder, 2002), and a way to generate "social capital," or bonds of trust among citizens (Coleman, 1990; Portes, 1998; Putnam, 1993, 1995, 2000). In fact, there is a substantial body of research that examines such citizenship behaviors and the ways in which the coordinated activities of individuals help others and serve the common good (e.g., Kymlicka & Norman, 1994; Putnam, 1993, 1995; Snyder & Omoto, 2007; van Vugt, Snyder, Tyler, & Biel, 2000; Verba, Schlozman, & Brady, 1995).

Involvement in and service to a community is generally conceived of as prosocial action intended to help others or to have beneficial social impact. Most often this involvement is in local and geographically defined communities, such as a neighborhood or a city, but it can also take place in relational or interest-based communities in which members are geographically dispersed and may or may not know one another personally (e.g., work on environmental protection or on behalf of people living in poverty in other locations; see Omoto & Malsch, 2005). A specific form of social action is *volunteerism*, or when individuals willingly give time and effort for the good or welfare of others without expectations of compensation or reward. Volunteering can be informal, as when neighbors help one another, or it can be formally institutionalized in organizations and agency based programs. Every year, millions of people around the world devote substantial amounts of their time and energy to volunteering. In the United States alone, it is estimated that some 61 million people or close to 30 percent of the US adult population volunteered at least once during 2006–2007 (US Dept. of Labor, 2008). Meanwhile, a different and earlier survey estimated that nearly 45 percent of the US adult population engages in regular volunteer work, doing so for an average of 3.6 hours each week (Independent Sector, 2001).

The Volunteer Process Model

Our program of research, which has been ongoing for close to twenty years, is guided by a conceptual model, the Volunteer Process Model, that emphasizes volunteerism as a process that unfolds over time. This process involves individuals deciding to get involved, seeking out volunteer opportunities, engaging in volunteer activities, and eventually ceasing their efforts (see Omoto & Snyder, 1990, 1995, 2002; Omoto, Snyder, & Berghuis, 1993; Snyder & Omoto, 2000, 2007, 2008). The fuller model is summarized in Figure 12.1. As can be seen, the model specifies psychological and behavioral features associated with each of three sequential and interactive stages (i.e., antecedents,

	Volunteer process		
Level of analysis	Antecedents	Experiences	Consequences
Individual			
Interpersonal			
Organizational			
Societal			

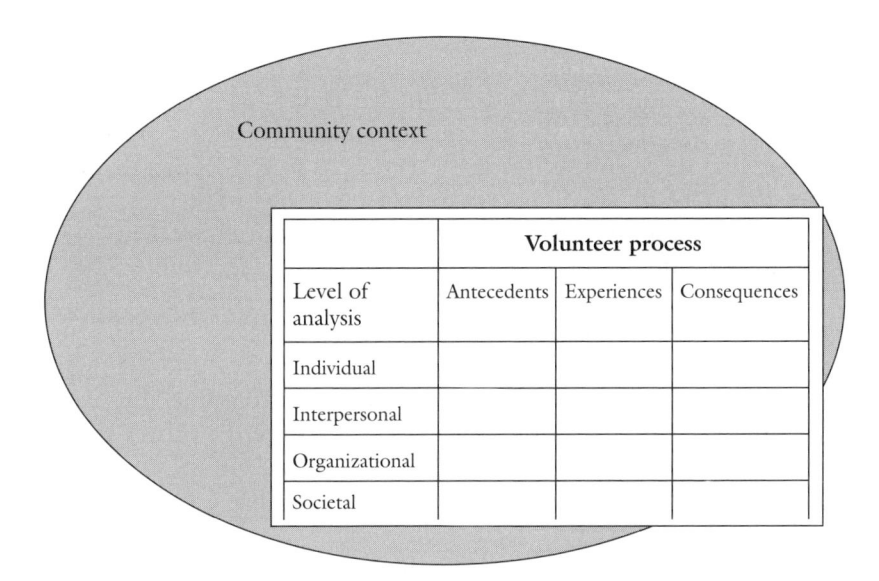

Figure 12.1 The volunteer process embedded in community context. Community as process influences stages of the volunteer process at different levels of analysis.

experiences, consequences) and speaks to activity at multiple levels of analysis (i.e., the individual, the interpersonal, the organizational, and the social system). Guided by this model, we have conducted coordinated field and laboratory studies employing longitudinal and cross-sectional methodologies and sampling from diverse populations. A good deal of our research has focused on direct, face-to-face volunteer work in which a volunteer helps another person, group of people, or cause (as opposed to less direct assistance such as making monetary donations or providing administrative services). Moreover, we have most often investigated "formal" volunteerism, or volunteer work performed through the auspices of a coordinating organization or agency.

At the *antecedents* stage, we have identified, both theoretically and empirically, personality and motivational factors, as well as characteristics of people's life circumstances that predict who becomes a volunteer and who is most effective and satisfied as a volunteer (see Omoto & Snyder, 1990, 1993, 1995; Omoto, Snyder, & Martino, 2000; Snyder & Omoto, 1992a, 1992b; Snyder, Omoto, & Smith, 2009). At the *experiences* stage, we have explored the interpersonal relationships that develop between volunteers and recipients of their services and the ways that these relationships lead to the continued service of volunteers and positive benefits to the recipients of their services (Crain, Snyder, & Omoto, 2000; Lindsay, Snyder, & Omoto, 2003; Omoto, Gunn, & Crain, 1998). We have also examined correlates of satisfaction for volunteers and recipients of service, as well as factors that may make for more pleasant and rewarding experiences (such as organizational integration) and those that detract from enjoyment (such as stigmatization by others) (Kiviniemi, Snyder, & Omoto, 2002; Snyder, Omoto, & Crain, 1999). Finally, at the *consequences* stage, we have studied the impact of volunteer service on the attitudes and behaviors of volunteers, the recipients of their services, and the members of their social networks, including such "bottom line" behaviors as continuing involvement and willingness to recruit others to the volunteer service organization (O'Brien, Crain, Omoto, & Snyder, 2000; Omoto & Snyder, 1995; Omoto, Snyder, Chang, & Lee, 2001; Snyder et al., 1999).

At the level of the *individual*, the model calls attention to the activities and psychological processes of individual volunteers and recipients of volunteer services. For example, people make decisions to help, identify service opportunities, engage in volunteer work for some period of time, and eventually quit volunteering. At the *interpersonal* level, the model expands this focus further and incorporates the dynamics of the helping relationships between volunteers and recipients of service, between members of volunteer corps, and between volunteers and paid staff in coordinating organizations. At an *organizational* level, the model focuses on the goals associated with recruiting, managing, and retaining an unpaid work force as well as associated concerns about work performance, compensation, and evaluation. In recognition of the fact that many volunteer efforts take place through or in cooperation with community based organizations or other institutions, we have incorporated aspects of organizational structure, roles, and operations into our model. Finally, at a broader *societal* level, the model considers the linkages between individuals and the social structures of their societies as well as collective and cultural dynamics.

Conceptualizing Community: Context and Process

Although the majority of our research has focused on the unfolding process of volunteerism at the individual level of analysis, we have recently begun to attend more systematically to other levels of analysis in our model, or the embeddedness of voluntary helping in broader levels of analysis such as communities. In conceptualizing community, we consider it both as *context* and *process* for volunteer efforts (see Omoto & Snyder, 2002).

To begin, we place volunteerism and social action in the broader context of the communities in which, and on behalf of which, they occur. That is, many volunteer service organizations are situated squarely in a community – they have community origins, roots, and connections that are acknowledged in their histories, mission statements, and public relations efforts. Moreover, the standards, norms, resources, and institutions of the community provide a backdrop for coordinated volunteer efforts. As such, the community provides a *context* for volunteer efforts and prosocial action. And, in reciprocal fashion, a community is often directly and indirectly changed by the activities of volunteers and the time and energy that they invest in responding to community needs. For example, in response to demands and unmet needs, volunteers mobilize and develop new programs and agencies (e.g., after-school programs, homeless shelters) or educate and encourage community members to adopt new patterns of behavior (e.g., recycling and energy conservation). Many organizations are conceived, developed, and continue to exist for purposes of community change (e.g., Hughey, Speer, & Peterson, 1999). That is, the community provides a backdrop for individuals and organizations to undertake volunteer activities that are aimed at promoting social change and that may contribute to societal cooperation and civic participation. Sometimes, the community provides only backdrop for the actions of individuals and groups, but other times the target of social action is to change the community itself.

Consistent with this perspective, many traditional definitions of community and related research refer to a specific place (Dunham, 1986) and are generally illustrative of a locational, territorial, geographical, or structural community. Hence, in such definitions of community, the focus is on (for example) a college dormitory, a village, a small town, or simply a network of individuals living in close proximity to people they know. This geographically rooted definition of community, namely the feelings about specific places or geographic entities, has been central to most of the theorizing and research on sense of community (see Hill, 1996). In addition, "community" as a descriptor or characteristic of a locality has also been examined (Sonn & Fischer, 1998). In our analysis, this emphasis is most similar to our notion of community as context.

Our second interest in community – *community as process* – has a decidedly more psychological flavor in that it emphasizes how concerns about, and connections to, community can motivate and sustain the actions of individuals. In addition, we consider some of the potential effects of belonging to communities on individuals in terms of their feelings of empowerment, efficacy, responsibility, and support, and ultimately their behaviors, including helping. In community as process, therefore, we seek to extend the concept beyond a geographically bounded place and focus instead on communities that are formed out of shared interests, characteristics, experiences, or opinions, and that are not restricted to individuals in physical proximity to each other. To identify with or to belong to psychological communities, an individual does not need to have direct knowledge or the acquaintanceship of other community members or even disclose community defining characteristics or status to others. Psychological communities are potentially quite diffuse and also changeable. We believe that the meanings, attachments, and consequences of psychological communities are important to explore, and especially for their implications for motivating and sustaining social action.

We propose that *psychological sense of community* (see also McMillan, 1996; McMillan & Chavis, 1986; Sarason, 1974) may be importantly implicated in the processes of helping and volunteerism. Consider, for example, the case of the community based organizations that emerged in the US in response to the HIV/AIDS epidemic – organizations of volunteers involved in caring for persons living with HIV and AIDS, in educating the public about HIV disease, and in raising awareness of HIV and AIDS and pushing for supportive legislation and funding mechanisms.

In the specific case of AIDS volunteerism, we suggest one potential conceptualization of community as the *broad and diverse community of people concerned with HIV*. In this sense, community includes not only people infected with HIV and at risk for it, but also the members of their social networks, as well as the volunteers and staff of organizations that provide services relevant to HIV. This broad conceptualization of community and the feelings of connection, attachment, and esteem that the individual derives from it constitute a psychological sense of community for the community affected by HIV/AIDS.

Potential Implications of Psychological Sense of Community

What, then, are the connections between psychological sense of community and the processes of helping and volunteerism? Theoretically, psychological connections to a broad and diverse community of concern may promote feelings of efficacy and support. That is, they should lead to increases in feelings of responsibility and obligation to help others, and in the confidence that the help one provides as a volunteer can and will make a difference. In addition, and as a consequence of these feelings, psychological sense of community should motivate individuals to become volunteers and also encourage them to persist longer in their service and to strive to be as effective as they can possibly be in their work. A psychological sense of community should also increase an individual's confidence that support is available to those with problems and that he or she is surrounded by a community of caring and compassionate others. This knowledge should empower individuals and make it easier for them to seek out assistance when they need it, including being receptive to the services offered by volunteers and community based organizations, and ultimately to derive greater benefit from working with volunteers and volunteer agencies.

Thus, considerations of psychological sense of community, we believe, focus attention on the processes by which community can positively affect individuals involved in volunteer efforts. In our research, we have examined this psychological sense of community in the volunteers and clients in AIDS service organizations. For example, for clients living with HIV, a bolstered sense of community may help to ease the sense of isolation and indifference that many feel. Similarly, as seen in our research (e.g., Snyder, Omoto, & Crain, 1999), some volunteers experience stigmatization that could be eased through a sense of community. Heightening and broadening sense of community may also be likely to have beneficial effects on feelings of personal efficacy and support for people living with HIV and volunteers who help them. That is, increases in sense of community should lead to increases in feelings of responsibility and comfort – in seeking assistance, in helping others, and in helping oneself by way of health maintenance behaviors. The increased confidence that comes with a greater sense of community should make individuals more optimistic in facing their problems, including problems related to physical health, caregiving, stigmatization, or social isolation. The community as an entity also possesses more and different resources to draw on for both clients and volunteers. Not only is there an expanded network of people from whom to get and offer help, but there are greater and potentially more specialized collective material and psychological resources available through community connections.

Moreover, we suggest that self-esteem is likely to increase with increases in community for several reasons. First, community is likely to provide a source of collective self-esteem (Crocker & Luhtanen, 1990) and valued social identity (e.g., Tajfel & Turner, 1986; Turner, Hogg, Oakes, Reicher, & Wetherell, 1987) for individuals as they connect and identify with it. The sense of belonging that comes with community also enhances and reaffirms an individual's worth as an individual and as a member of a valued social group. And, possessing a community identity that is valued and shared by others offers additional positive regard due to social consensus and validation. To the extent that the community is successful (particularly those organized for purposes of action; Hughey et al., 1999), then community members should enjoy increased feelings of efficacy and accomplishment. Individuals also can bask in the accomplishments of successful community members (Cialdini, Borden, Thorne, Walker, Freeman, & Sloan, 1976; Tesser, 1988), and members may experience pride in the community's ability to provide services and support for its members.

Furthermore, successful community members may become models of upward social comparison (e.g., Gibbons & Gerrard, 1989; Suls & Wills, 1990) and motivate others to strive for success and greater community contribution. Thus, social comparison processes may encourage people living with HIV to seek out and persist with their medical care and regular social activities, and may lead volunteers to serve longer and recruit others to AIDS volunteerism. Community connections and identity also are likely to provide members with consensus and support for solving problems and overcoming barriers to effective action that they face. Thus, sense of community should contribute to individual and collective action (Simon, 1998; Simon et al., 1998) as well as to communal coping processes (e.g., Lyons, Mickelson, Sullivan, & Coyne, 1998).

Finally, a broad conceptualization and sense of community should promote other forms of civic participation, including helping and being helped. Community members are likely to feel responsible for working on behalf of the community and to be good team players. Thus, they should work and volunteer to improve their own conditions and those of the community. In addition, feelings of reciprocity for past help received (and possibly for future needs) should be heightened by community connections. The increased resources, confidence, and esteem provided by a sense of community should also breed feelings of psychological empowerment (Chamberlin, 1997; Corrigan, Faber, Rashid, & Leary, 1999; Rogers, Chamberlin, Ellison, & Crean, 1997; Zimmerman & Rappaport, 1988; Zimmerman, Israel, Schulz, & Checkoway, 1992). As a consequence, attempts at effective action are likely to be enacted, whether in the sphere of volunteerism or other forms of community involvement and civic participation. In this way, then, psychological sense of community may lead individuals to act to change or participate in their surroundings and communities through volunteerism and other forms of civic participation.

Community and the Volunteer Process

Based on our analysis, then, psychological sense of community is not only relevant to, but is predicted to benefit, volunteers and clients in community based organizations. As an initial test of our theoretical notions, then, we examined data from several studies of AIDS volunteers and the people living with HIV disease with whom they were paired to work (i.e., clients). Specifically, we turned to data from several multi-site, longitudinal field studies that we conducted looking for empirical evidence relevant to the role of community in the volunteer process.

Antecedents

When it comes to individuals' decisions to become volunteers, there is clear evidence that motivations reflecting concern for community figure prominently in these decisions. That is, people have different reasons for getting involved as volunteers, and indeed, we have successfully identified a diverse set of motivations for volunteer work. We know from several data collections that one main impetus for volunteering revolves around motivations reflecting concern for community (see Omoto & Crain, 1995; Omoto & Snyder, 1993, 1995; Omoto et al., 2000). For example, when new volunteers rate their reasons for volunteering, the reasons that explicitly mention a community concern or connection (e.g., "Because of my concern and worry about communities affected by AIDS," "Because of my obligation to communities affected by AIDS," and "To get to know people in communities affected by AIDS") typically receive relatively high ratings.

In addition to volunteering out of community concern motivations, the participants in our research seem to have been drawn to volunteerism by the influences of other members of their communities. In fact, the majority of new volunteers in one longitudinal study claimed community based routes to volunteering; that is, they began their volunteer work because they were asked to volunteer by someone they knew, they already knew people who were volunteers, or because they participated in other community events (e.g., AIDS fundraising walk). In addition, over two-thirds of these new volunteers claimed that their parents had modeled some volunteer activity, and over three-quarters of them said that they knew at least one other person doing non-AIDS volunteer work (see Omoto & Snyder, 1995, 2002).

These findings are not unique to our AIDS research context. According to data from the 2007 Current Population Survey conducted by the US Department of Labor (2008), when asked how they became involved with their volunteer organization, the majority of respondents (43 percent) claimed that they were asked by someone, with the majority of these respondents having been asked by someone in the organization itself. As this evidence suggests, people's sense of community and their social networks may be important at the antecedents stage of the volunteer process – in people's decisions to become volunteers.

Experiences

Moreover, over the course of their service, volunteers become increasingly connected to other members of their communities, including communities defined by the volunteers, staff, and clients associated with their volunteer service organizations. Many AIDS service organizations have buddy programs in which volunteers are assigned to work one-on-one with a person living with HIV for purposes of providing daily living assistance, emotional support, and a general social outlet. When we looked at the extent to which volunteers introduced these clients to other members of their existing social networks and the extent to which they were introduced to members of their clients' social networks, we found that, over time, both volunteers and clients became increasingly likely to be integrated into each other's social networks. That is, they did not keep their relationship with each other separate from other aspects of their lives, but instead, worked to create a broader and more inclusive community, or at least an expanded and integrated social network. After six months of working together, fully 76 percent of volunteers had been introduced to client social network members and 52 percent of volunteers had introduced their client to members of their own social network.

Furthermore, these community connections were related to positive benefits for the recipients of volunteers' services. For example, the more volunteers were motivated by community concern and the more that they integrated their client into their (previously separate) personal communities, the better their clients' health. And, for clients, the more that they connected to broader communities and had larger social networks, the more they engaged in health maintenance behaviors, the less severe their functioning problems, and the better their mental health. Of particular interest for the community affected by HIV/AIDS, the more close friends at their AIDS service organization that clients reported, the better their own ratings of health, the higher their life satisfaction and feelings about themselves, and the less their reported problems of daily living, loneliness, and general depression and listlessness. Taken together, these correlational findings speak to the potential importance of community in understanding the experiences of volunteers as well as the experiences reported by the clients served by these volunteers.

Consequences

Taking things a step further, it appears that volunteering also builds community. For instance, our longitudinal data reveal that, as a consequence of their work, volunteers were increasingly surrounded by people connected to their volunteer service and their volunteer service organization, including people they recruited themselves to be volunteers. In fact, after only three months of service, over 80 percent of the volunteers claimed to have at least one friend at their AIDS service organization, and after six months of service, 28 percent reported having recruited at least one new volunteer to the organization. Over this same six-month period, the proportion of each volunteer's social network that was made up of other volunteers also increased by over 1.5 times. In short, as a consequence of their volunteer work, the social networks of volunteers were changed so as to have greater focus on HIV/AIDS and to have created a larger community of people affected by and working on behalf of HIV/AIDS.

Our data also suggest that, as connections to a community of shared concerns increase, so too does participation in forms of prosocial action other than volunteerism (such as giving to charitable causes, attending fundraising events, and engaging in social activism). Specifically, when we tracked the activities of AIDS volunteers over their first six months of service in our longitudinal study, we found that these individuals significantly increased the frequency with which they made donations to AIDS groups, attended AIDS fundraisers, and also involved themselves further in AIDS activism. That is, they tended to act on behalf of the community affected by HIV/AIDS in more and diverse ways.

In summary, then, research on the volunteer process has provided recurring indications that connections to community can draw people into volunteerism and sustain their involvement over time. In reciprocal fashion, moreover, involvement in volunteerism seems to strengthen and build community connections. Specifically, community concern and the influences of other community members figure prominently in the motivations of new volunteers (Omoto & Snyder, 1995; see also Stürmer & Kampmeier, 2003). Over the course of their service, volunteers also become increasingly connected with their surrounding communities, including the communities defined by the volunteers, staff, and clients associated with their volunteer service organizations (Omoto & Snyder, 2002). And, their effectiveness as volunteers seems to be enhanced by a sense of connection to a relevant community (Omoto & Snyder, 2002).

Reversing the causal order, volunteering also appears to build and foster a sense of community. For example, as a consequence of their work, volunteers are increasingly surrounded by a community of people who are somehow connected to their volunteer service, including people they have recruited to be volunteers (Omoto & Snyder, 2002). In addition, volunteering apparently contributes to the creation of bonds of social capital (e.g., Stukas, Daly, & Cowling, 2005), and even has been considered a central indicator of social capital itself (Putnam, 2000). Research also suggests that, as psychological connections to a community of shared concerns increase, participation and involvement in broader community activities and activism also increases (Malsch, 2005; Omoto & Malsch, 2005; Omoto & Snyder, 2002).

Measuring and Creating Psychological Sense of Community

In our most recent, and ongoing, field-based work, we are beginning to disentangle some of the bidirectional processes that seem to link sense of community, volunteerism, and broad prosocial action utilizing an experimental research design. Specifically, we have attempted to create and enhance psychological sense of community and harness some of its power in promoting volunteerism and other forms of prosocial action. Furthermore, we have begun to examine some of the "extended" impact of psychological sense of community, including for the mental health and health protective actions of individuals.

As an initial step, we sought to more fully develop our theoretical analysis of the construct of psychological sense of community. This analysis is anchored in the literature on sense of community and also informed by our past research. In our new and original conceptualization, we posit six key facets or dimensions of *psychological sense of community*. Moreover, we have developed a multiple-item inventory to tap each of the facets, and based on extensive psychometric work, have honed this inventory to 18 items, with three items used to tap each of the six facets. This research has been conducted in cooperation with AIDS service organizations in two different states in the United States, and we have attempted to capture a broad range of interests, roles, perspectives, and experiences of people affiliated with these AIDS service organizations. In focusing on psychological sense of community, therefore, we examine the community of people affected by HIV and AIDS.

The first facet of psychological sense of community is *knowledge*; individuals must know that there is a broad community, who its members are, and that community resources are potentially available to all members. If people do not know or are unaware that there are other individuals who share their interests, attitudes, and beliefs, they cannot have a sense of community organized around those interests, attitudes, and beliefs. In straightforward fashion, sample items from our inventory that tap knowledge include, "There is such a thing as the community affected by HIV/AIDS," and "If someone asked, I could define the community affected by HIV/AIDS."

The second facet is *conceptualization*, and it involves individuals redefining their personally relevant communities and knowing what features, attitudes, interests, or characteristics are required for entry into the community. In short, conceptualization conveys information about who can and cannot belong to the community of interest. It also stresses what people have in common with other members of the community. In our research, we have attempted to get individuals involved in AIDS service organizations to redefine and broaden their typically more narrow conceptualizations of community (e.g., people who are infected with HIV) so as to be more inclusive and encompassing (e.g., the community of people affected by HIV/AIDS). Sample items from our measure of psychological sense of community are, "All people, regardless of HIV status, are members of the community affected by HIV/AIDS," and "All members of the community affected by HIV/AIDS, even HIV-negative individuals, face similar challenges." These two items clearly indicate how conceptualization stresses membership characteristics, commonality, and broad inclusivity.

The third facet we have named *identification*, and it refers to people's affective reactions to being members of a psychological community and the importance of community membership to their self-image and identity. In our view, people who feel more positively about the community and see community membership as more central and important to their self-definition have stronger sense of community; community membership is also a source of pride and esteem. In short, people come to feel a sense of shared identity or community membership and agree with items on our inventory such as, "I identify with the community affected by HIV/AIDS," and "I feel a sense of community with people affected by HIV/AIDS."

The fourth facet of psychological sense of community is labeled *connection* and it refers to the feelings that individuals have and their affective bonds or attachments to the community. As they develop a stronger sense of community, people should become increasingly more positive about the community (and vice versa). An item on our inventory that taps these bonds is "I feel a sense of attachment and belonging to the community affected by HIV/AIDS." In addition, people who are higher in sense of community should display willingness to invest in the community and its members, and also be likely to extend a helping hand or to offer support to other (even unknown) community members. Thus, another item on our inventory is, "If someone I did not know within the community affected by HIV/AIDS had an emergency, I would be willing to help."

Success is the fifth facet of psychological sense of community. It involves belief in coordination of community members and perceptions of community efficacy. That is, people believe that communities have the ability to accomplish more when working together than individuals can accomplish by working alone. Furthermore, as community members work together and succeed, they should increasingly take greater responsibility for one another and come to feel greater and lasting efficaciousness, empowerment, and mutual concern. Personal actions are also then undertaken not only out of self-interest but on behalf of and for the benefits of the community as a whole. In our inventory, this facet is tapped by items such as, "Members of the community affected by HIV/AIDS have an obligation to work together to help other members," and "The success of the community affected by HIV/AIDS depends on members working together."

Finally, the sixth facet of psychological sense of community is future-oriented and considers the rights and responsibilities of current community members to insure an enduring, healthy, and successful community for potential future members. We have named this facet *legacy* and tapped it with items such as, "The community affected by HIV/AIDS should work to create a better future for its members," and "The actions of today's community affected by HIV/AIDS will have an impact on future community members." In this facet, therefore, community members care not only about themselves and other current members, but they look to the horizon and strive to create and preserve a shared history and future for the community. The community itself is an entity and resource worth sustaining, nurturing, and growing.

We do not expect these six facets to be tightly related to each other. In fact, we can readily imagine situations in which individuals have knowledge of a community and its membership characteristics, but do not themselves feel a strong positive bond to the community or are not necessarily motivated to sustain it. Similarly, individuals may believe in the strength and efficacy of certain communities to work together to create change or to help others, and these individuals may also engage in behaviors that help to preserve and build those communities. However, they may not themselves feel that they can be full members of the community or they may view this community membership as relatively unimportant to their own sense of self and personal identity. We also acknowledge that our six facets may be able to be grouped into three broader categories, with two of them (knowledge and conceptualization) relatively cognitive in nature, two of them (connection and identification) emphasizing affective states, and two of them (success and legacy) being future oriented and emphasizing behavioral elements. In some preliminary analyses, we have obtained evidence for precisely this hierarchical structure for our different scales, including establishing that this higher-order three-factor structure better fits the data than alternative multi-factor solutions.

Whereas different patterns or constellations of endorsement of the six facets may have implications for when help is offered, the quality and quantity of assistance provided, to whom help is proffered and by whom, our interests have focused on psychological sense of community in its fullest form, with all six facets present and at relatively high levels. Based on our conceptual analysis, we expect psychological sense of community to produce greater helping, sharing, reciprocity, and trust among community members. Individuals who have greater sense of community should be more likely to volunteer and to engage in other forms of social action that benefit community members (e.g., activism), they should take better care of themselves and other community members, and they should feel psychologically healthier and happier, at least relative to individuals whose sense of community is less fully developed.

Armed with our conceptualization, therefore, we have attempted to create psychological sense of community, taking care to be sure that each key facet was included in our mix. That is, rather than simply attempting to measure or approximate psychological sense of community, we have sought to intentionally foster it among individuals who are previously unacquainted with each other, encouraging them to generalize the principles and facets of community to other and even unknown people. Specifically, we have developed interventions designed to create community based on our six facets, interventions that we have implemented through a series of workshop sessions conducted in small groups. As well, and as noted above, we have developed a psychometrically sound, 18-item inventory to measure psychological sense of community with items written to tap each facet of community.

We have incorporated both the intervention and our measure in a field-based experiment that has been conducted with over 600 participants recruited through AIDS service organizations in two different states. In this research, participants were randomly assigned to one of three conditions. In one condition, the community building condition, participants took part in workshop sessions led by trained facilitators that included group exercises designed to teach and foster our six facets of the community affected by HIV/AIDS. The facilitators introduced all of the group-based exercises by discussing and highlighting the different facets of sense of community the exercise addressed. The facilitators also brought each exercise to a close by again stressing one or more conceptual facets of sense of community and also challenging participants to think about how the exercise and facet of community was or could be made relevant to their own life circumstances outside of the workshop sessions.

In a comparison condition, workshop sessions were of similar size and length but did not include community building activities. Instead, participants took part in educational activities designed to increase their knowledge, skills, and confidence in negotiating the AIDS service system. These participants learned about community as context – the resources potentially available and how to access them or assist in their delivery – and without engaging in discussions about and casting of exercises in terms of considerations of community as process. Finally, a third of participants were assigned to a control condition in which they did not take part in any workshops.

By way of these experimental conditions, then, we sought to assess whether our carefully planned workshops, built on our conceptual framework, would increase psychological sense of community relative to the other experimental conditions, and also we endeavored to track different effects of research involvement among our participants. To do so, all participants completed an extensive self-report battery of attitudinal, behavior, and mental health measures at baseline (enrollment in the study), again soon after they completed their workshops, and finally again several months later (control group participants completed the battery at the same points in time, but did not take part in any workshops until after they had completed the follow-up measure). Included in this battery was our measure of psychological sense of community, as well as items tapping organizational involvement, motives for participation, mental health, and civic participation.

At baseline, we found that, as expected, our individual facets of psychological sense of community were internally consistent. They were also related to each other, although they were by no means redundant with one another; the correlations between individual scales ranged from $r = .38-.67$, ps $<.01$. All but one of the individual facet measures was positively related to participation in AIDS-related activism and engaging in more HIV prevention behaviors. In addition, among participants who themselves were HIV-positive, all of the facets were significantly related to more positive feelings about their HIV status. In other words, greater sense of community was related to indicators of better mental health. Finally, when we created a composite measure of psychological sense of community by summing over the six facets (rather than examining constellations or patterns of responding across the facets), we found that overall sense of community was positively related to AIDS activism, activism in non-AIDS contexts, prevention behaviors, and positive feelings about HIV. As these cross-sectional data reveal, therefore, sense of community, whether as cause or consequence, was related to a range of prosocial actions, including activism and self- and other-focused protective behaviors (e.g., health promotion or disease prevention behaviors) as well as to better mental health.

Turning to the field-based intervention portion of this research, preliminary results indicate that our community building intervention does indeed enhance psychological sense of community. In looking at reports from baseline compared to the immediate and even the longer term follow-up measurement points among participants who took part in our community building intervention, we have detected a significant increase in overall scores on our measure of psychological sense of community. In addition, our intervention increased feelings of empowerment, as reflected in increases in reports of efficacy, feelings of responsibility, and confidence in participants' knowledge about the community and its resources. Finally, and as assessed immediately following the workshops, the community intervention also produced increases in intentions to become involved in the community through diverse forms of social action (e.g., giving money and goods to charity, joining community groups and organizations, participating in social activism) and increased intentions to help and educate others in the community, at least as compared to the no workshop control condition.

This pattern of results is exactly as we would predict. It suggests that, first and foremost, psychological sense of community can be created. Second, and owing to our experimental design, the findings demonstrate that psychological sense of community may cause people to take action that benefits themselves, others, and the broader social system. Although far from comprehensive, we offer these preliminary findings as illustrative of the potentially important role of psychological sense of community as a mechanism responsible for broad forms of helping and social action (e.g., Snyder & Omoto, 2007), and also as implicating community as process in sustaining and enhancing individual and community health.

Community and Social Action

Building on the important and potentially causal role of sense of community in facilitating prosocial behavior, let us now turn to other research that has examined the connections between community and social action of different types. Across a wide range of research approaches and settings, we find that proxy measures of sense of community are related to actions that do not clearly benefit the individual actor but do nonetheless demonstrate concern for or benefit the community at large.

For example, Oishi et al. (2007) studied differences in community stability, reasoning that when people have lived in a specific geographic location (e.g., community) for a long time, they would come to be invested in and concerned about the well-being of the community and would get involved in doing good for it. Consistent with these expectations, residents of relatively stable communities (as indexed by the proportion of residents in each research participant's zip code who lived in the same house as they did five years ago) more often purchased "critical habitat" license plates than residents of relatively mobile communities. The funds from these license plate purchases go to environmental preservation. Thus, they represent one form of pro-community or prosocial action, and in our conceptualization of psychological sense of community can be construed as a legacy related concern.

In a second study, these same authors examined home game attendance for Major League Baseball teams in different cities that varied in residential stability. Residents of relatively stable cities tended to turn out for baseball games regardless of the team's won-loss record; that is, the team received unconditional support from community members. However, baseball teams in relatively mobile cities tended to receive conditional support in that fans turned out for games when the team was winning but not when it was losing. The reliable relationship between stability and support is consistent with the notion that individuals in stable communities compared to mobile communities are more likely to feel psychologically connected to representatives of their communities, and also to more strongly identify with city symbols. In addition, they appear more likely to publicly display their support (by going to games) and also seem willing to endure costs (because attending games involves investments of time and money) to express their concern.

Finally, in a laboratory study, Oishi et al. (2007) obtained evidence that members of stable micro-communities (who worked on a series of tasks together) helped each other more than members of unstable micro-communities (who worked on tasks with different people) and that this stability effect was mediated by identification with the community. Although the causal mechanism of sense of community was not directly tested in this series of studies, the pattern of findings fits our theoretical explanation. Moreover, the work of other researchers has also linked diverse forms of helping behaviors, pro-community involvement, collective efficacy, and social action to residential stability and identification with a community (Kang & Kwak, 2003; Kasarda & Janowitz, 1974; Sampson, Raudenbush, & Earls, 1997).

Beyond residential stability, there are indications of positive associations between community and other forms of social action. Thus, for example, individuals who report a stronger psychological sense of community, as gauged by a variety of different measures, are more likely to be registered voters and to be active in their neighborhoods (Brodsky, O'Campo, & Aronson, 1999). They are also more likely to engage in neighboring behaviors, such as lending their neighbors food or tools (Kingston, Mitchell, Forin, & Stevenson, 1999), and to participate in community organizations (Chavis & Wandersman, 1990; Perkins & Long, 2002; Wandersman, 1980; Wandersman, Florin, Friedmann, & Meier, 1987) and political activities (Davidson & Cotter, 1989). Moreover, bonds of connection within communities and the social capital associated with them have been implicated in the provision of public goods (Anderson, Mellor, & Milyo, 2004), the reduction of crime within localities (Saegert, Winkel, & Swartz, 2002), and the promotion of the health of community members (Kawachi, Kennedy, & Lochner, 1997).

Taken together, the research on community and diverse forms of social action contributes to an emerging "big picture" of the mutual interplay of individuals and their contexts. It appears that some types of communities (e.g., stable ones) promote identification with the community and, in turn, helping behavior and social action. Meanwhile, individuals also act on their motivations and engage in social action that subsequently fosters stronger community connections. Thus, it appears likely that there is a cyclical process at work, one in which connections to community lead individuals to help others and engage in social action which, in turn, further builds community connections and social capital. As a result of this self-perpetuating and accretionary process, social action becomes more likely and sense of community is increased. More generally, and as our field-based experimental work suggested, it may be that social action begets social action via sense of community. As such, one of the more important consequences of social action is the creation and perpetuation of a culture of service, participation, and involvement.

Concluding Comments

To conclude, it appears that, at minimum, community concern, community connections, and psychological sense of community are clearly, consistently, and powerfully related to the many and varied ways that individuals involve and invest themselves in society and work for common good. These findings and observations are important, we believe, for what they say scientifically about the nature of community and its linkages to diverse forms of social action. They are also important for what they say practically about creating and promoting an actively engaged society, one in which citizens individually and collectively help each other and also work to solve the problems that confront society.

Our research findings lend credence to a purely psychological conceptualization of sense of community, not necessarily with reference to an identifiable area or institution, measured at an individual level. It seems reasonable, therefore, to devote future theorizing and research to understanding communities based on shared experiences and interests (e.g., the community affected by HIV/AIDS) and communities with inclusive membership that extend beyond traditional boundaries of region, ethnicity, and nationality. Indeed, with communication and technological advances (e.g., the Internet), psychologically meaningful communities that literally cut across the globe are being formed and sustained every day. Based on our results, we suggest that one way to build social capital may be by intervening to increase people's sense of community. This suggestion derives from the reciprocal relationship between sense of community and behaviors indicative of social capital (e.g., Putnam, 2000), as well as our findings that psychological sense of community predicts subsequent volunteerism and social action.

A strong tradition already exists in many cultures, including among North American countries, whereby people feel they should give back to society and engage in prosocial actions (see Curtis et al., 1992). The question does not seem to be "*Do* people believe in the value of doing social good?" but rather, "*Why* do they not act on their beliefs?" (see Snyder, Omoto, & Smith, 2009) One strategy for motivating helping might be to bolster people's psychological sense of community and to call attention to the responsibility of community members to mobilize and work on behalf of other community members. We found that, to the extent that individuals report stronger psychological sense of community, they are likely to engage in more frequent activism, feel psychologically healthier, and to intend to perform other prosocial actions in the future. In short, community involvement and volunteerism seems to lead individuals to feel more positively about and more strongly connected to the people around them and to psychological communities. In reciprocal fashion, these feelings are linked to greater willingness to engage in community affairs and to work for the reduction of social problems. In the end, knowledge gained from research on psychological sense of community, and especially interventions designed to create it, is useful not only for understanding helping behavior, but also because it can be put to use in making more effective social programs that are geared toward enhancing quality of life, ameliorating social problems, and increasing general civic participation.

13

Empowering the Volunteer Organization

What Volunteer Organizations Can Do to Recruit, Content, and Retain Volunteers

Naomi Ellemers and Edwin J. Boezeman

Introduction

Volunteer work is unpaid work, without any obligations, for the benefit of others and/or society. This unique form of helping behavior, which takes place in an organizational context (i.e., at a macro-level, see Penner, Dovidio, Piliavin, & Schroeder, 2005) implies that a deliberate choice is made to provide aid to unknown others over an extended period of time and at personal costs (Omoto & Snyder, 1995, 2002). Volunteers thus provide valuable services to society and its members that would not be available if they had to be paid (Davis, Hall, & Meyer, 2003; Fisher & Ackerman, 1998; Pearce, 1993). Due to the specific nature of this work, volunteer organizations can only address *non-material* features to recruit, content, and retain volunteers. Building on social identity theory (Tajfel & Turner, 1979) and the social identity based model of cooperation (Tyler, 1999; Tyler & Blader, 2000) we develop a conceptual framework to argue that status evaluations concerning the volunteer organization as well as one's own position within the organization contribute positively to psychological engagement and cooperation of individual volunteers. In doing this, we identify organizational features that may help engage and commit volunteers by inducing a sense of organizational and/or individual value. These insights point to concrete interventions that can empower volunteer organizations to recruit, content, and retain volunteer workers.

Volunteer Motivation as an Organizational Problem

Previous research on the organizational behavior of volunteers has addressed the motivation to volunteer from different perspectives. Pearce (1993) characterizes this research as either focusing on individual motives for volunteering (e.g., Clary et al., 1998; Cnaan & Goldberg-Glen, 1991), or as specifying demographic, socioeconomic (Wilson, 2000), or personality characteristics of (potential) volunteers (e.g., Carlo, Okun, Knight, & De Guzman, 2005). In the present contribution we take a different approach in that we consider how the motivation of individual volunteers relates to perceived characteristics of the volunteer *organization*. That is, we aim to identify specific features of the volunteer organization that are likely to elicit, enhance, and sustain motivation among (prospective) volunteers.

Previous work has addressed the recruitment, satisfaction, and retention of volunteers as separate macro-level processes which depend on different variables (Penner et al., 2005). However, it has also been suggested that these may be considered as subsequent stages of volunteer involvement (Omoto & Snyder, 2002). In line with this approach, our current aim is to develop a single parsimonious model which can help understand and predict volunteer motivation at different stages. This is not only relevant for analytical purposes but also of practical interest, as it offers a way for volunteer organizations to address recruitment, satisfaction, and retention of volunteer workers in an integral fashion.

Our approach builds on previous work in this area, in that we examine social identity processes (Tajfel & Turner, 1979) as relevant to the motivation of individual volunteers. Nevertheless, our current analysis extends previous work in that we address the way individuals perceive specific characteristics of the volunteer organization and their position within it as important determinants of such identity concerns. That is, while previous work considered how individuals relate to the *target group* they are trying to help (e.g., homosexuals vs. heterosexuals in AIDS-volunteerism, Simon, Stürmer, & Steffens, 2000, or members of the National Association to Advance Fat Acceptance, Stürmer, Simon, & Loewy, 2008), we focus on how volunteer workers relate to the *volunteer organization* in which they perform these efforts. In doing this, we extend a model that has been developed to understand how non-material concerns impact on the motivation and cooperative intent of paid employees (Tyler, 1999; Tyler & Blader,

2000). It is not self-evident that existing insights on the motivation of paid employees help understand the behavior of volunteers, as there are fundamental differences between the work conditions of these two types of workers (Cnaan & Cascio, 1999; Farmer & Fedor, 1999; Pearce, 1993). Standard control mechanisms that are used to monitor and direct the behavior of paid employees (such as financial rewards, contractual obligations, or career prospects) simply are not available in the case of volunteer workers, as compensation and incentives are symbolic instead of material (Pearce, 1993; see also Ellemers, De Gilder, & Haslam, 2004; Farmer & Fedor, 1999; Haslam, 2004). Thus, even though self-oriented as well as other-oriented concerns may be relevant to the motivation of volunteers (e.g., Clary et al., 1998; Omoto and Snyder, 1995), these refer to psychological outcomes and benefits, which have no legal or material basis.

Social Identity and Work Motivation

In view of the special nature of volunteer work as detailed above, we take a social identity approach to examine the organizational behavior of volunteers (see also Tidwell, 2005). Social identity theory (Tajfel & Turner, 1979) posits that non-material concerns, such as status evaluations and the subjective valuation of group-based identities, affect individual behavior in groups and organizations. This theory is based on the assumption that people derive (part of) their self-image from the groups and organizations they belong to – this is referred to as their social identity. As a consequence, organizational characteristics that are positively valued can contribute to a positive social identity, inducing feelings of self-esteem and self-worth. As social identity theory assumes that people prefer to feel good about themselves, the theory maintains that people generally consider it attractive to be included in groups and organizations that contribute positively to their social identity (see also Ashforth & Mael, 1989; Ellemers et al., 2004; Haslam & Ellemers, 2005; Hogg & Terry, 2000). Based on social identity theory, Tyler and Blader (Tyler, 1999; Tyler & Blader, 2000, 2001, 2002) have argued that when organizational members view their organization as having high value, this facilitates their psychological and behavioral engagement with their organization. In addition, Tyler and Blader (2000; see also Tyler, 1999) have proposed that organizational members also evaluate their individual position within their organization as a potential source of positive self-evaluation, social identity, and organizational engagement. Thus, feelings of organizational pride (the conviction that the organization has high value), and individual respect (the feeling that one is valued as a member of the organization) are seen to contribute to psychological engagement and cooperation with organizations.

This model has received empirical support from correlational studies among paid employees (Fuller, Hester, Barnett, Frey, Relyea, & Beu, 2006; Tyler, 1999; Tyler & Blader, 2000, 2001, 2002), which have demonstrated the explanatory value of pride and respect in accounting for cooperative intent above and beyond the effects of material rewards or concrete individual benefits (see also Stürmer, et al., 2008). Additionally, experimental research among various types of group members (see, for instance, Branscombe, Spears, Ellemers, & Doosje, 2002; Doosje, Spears, & Ellemers, 2002; Ellemers, Wilke, & van Knippenberg, 1993; Simon & Stürmer, 2003; Sleebos, Ellemers, & De Gilder, 2006) has further demonstrated that evaluations of pride and respect contribute to psychological engagement and cooperation with groups and organizations.

In the literature, different terms have been used to refer to similar constructs. For instance, studies examining collective identification (e.g., Stürmer et al., 2008) or role identity (e.g., Grube & Piliavin, 2000) can be seen as addressing psychological engagement. Likewise, terms such as organizational prestige (Grube & Piliavin, 2000) and collective self-esteem (Stürmer et al., 2008) are used to describe the extent to which volunteers can derive a sense of pride from their connection with the organization, while enhancement (Clary et al., 1998) or esteem (Omoto & Snyder, 1995) refer to the desire of individual volunteers to feel good about themselves. To avoid conceptual confusion, in the remainder of this chapter we will use the labels and constructs as defined by Tyler and Blader (e.g., Tyler, 1999; Tyler & Blader, 2000). Thus, we examine *pride* as referring to the extent to which people derive a sense of value from their association with the volunteer organization (e.g., "I am proud of being a member of this organization"), and *respect* as indicating the extent to which people feel valued as individual workers of the volunteer organization (e.g., "I feel respected as a volunteer by this organization"). As we will explain below, this conceptualization allows us greater precision in distinguishing for instance between organizational and interpersonal experiences as different sources of esteem that may contribute to perceived individual respect. Likewise, this enables us to compare the extent to which the public visibility of the volunteer organization and its achievements and the self-perceived importance of the volunteer work contribute to feelings of pride. In our different studies, we assess

Table 13.1 Overview of opportunities for empowering the volunteer organization

Interventions	→ Pride/Respect	→ Psychological engagement	→ Behavioral engagement
Volunteer contentment (existing volunteers)			
Importance of the volunteer work	Pride	Satisfaction with the volunteer work	Effort Performance
Organizational support	Organization respect		
Clientele appreciation/ Acceptance of help	Clientele respect		
Volunteer retention (existing volunteers)			
Importance of the volunteer work	Pride	Organizational commitment	Intention to remain a volunteer with the volunteer organization
Organizational support	Organization respect	• Normative • Affective	
Volunteer recruitment (non-volunteers)			
Organizational support	Anticipated respect as a volunteer	Attraction to the volunteer organization	Willingness to participate in the volunteer organization as a volunteer

psychological engagement with the volunteer organization by examining satisfaction, organizational commitment, and attraction to the volunteer organization, and address the willingness to participate and the intention to remain as relevant indicators of *behavioral engagement* with the volunteer organization (see also Table 13.1).

A Social Identity Model of Engagement With Volunteer Organizations

Based on the work of Tyler and Blader (Tyler, 1999; Tyler & Blader, 2000, 2001, 2002), we developed a program of research to examine

```
┌─────────────────────┐
│ Importance/         │      ┌───────┐              ┌──────────────┐
│ successfulness      │─────▶│ Pride │              │ Engagement   │
│ of volunteer work   │      └───┬───┘              │ with volunteer│
└─────────────────────┘          │                  │ organization │
                                 ▼                  └──────────────┘
                    ┌──────────────────────────┐
                    │ Psychological engagement │────▶ Recruitment
                    │ with volunteer           │
                    │ organizations            │      Satisfaction
                    └──────────────────────────┘
                                 ▲
┌─────────────────────┐      ┌─────────┐              Retention
│ Organizational      │─────▶│ Respect │
│ support             │      └─────────┘
└─────────────────────┘
```

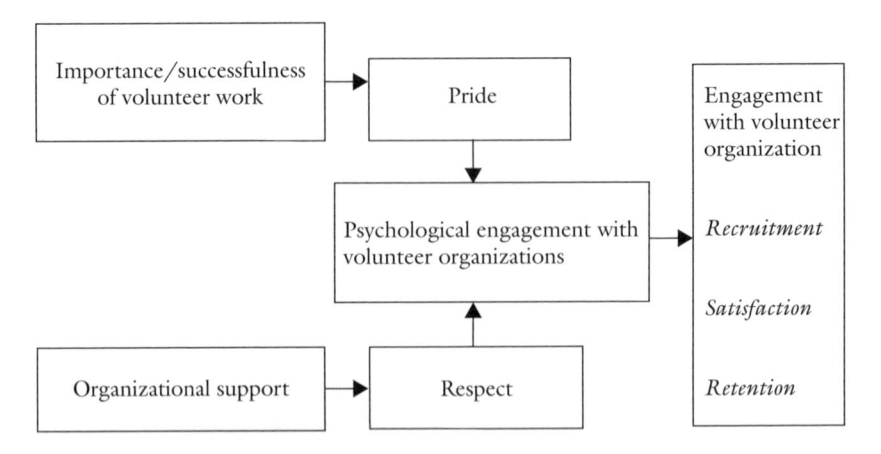

Figure 13.1 Basic research model.

whether the processes they specify also help explain the engagement and work motivation of individual volunteers within volunteer organizations (see Figure 13.1).

The primary goal of volunteer organizations is to help society and its members through their services. The fact that these services would not be available if they had to be paid for is generally considered a positive feature of volunteer organizations (e.g., Fisher & Ackerman, 1998; Harris, 2001; Pearce, 1993). Accordingly, we argue that the perceived importance and effectiveness of the volunteer work indicates the status of the volunteer organization, and can be a source of *pride* to its members. Hence, we expect individual volunteers to experience pride when they participate in a volunteer organization that they see as effective in helping its clientele. Volunteer organizations are generally expected to direct their efforts and resources to benefit their clientele – not to their volunteer workers (Handy, 1988). Under these circumstances, the provision of support to individual volunteers can be seen as communicating that they are valued by the organization, and can be an important source of perceived *respect*. This is why we predict individual volunteers to feel respected when they see their volunteer organization as investing in them through, for instance, the provision of organizational support.

We examined the validity of our reasoning (see Figure 13.1) in a preliminary study (Boezeman & Ellemers, 2008a), in which we developed measures to assess volunteer pride and respect, as well as the perceived importance of the volunteer work and perceived task and emotional support as antecedents of pride and respect. This first study was conducted among a sample of 89 fundraising volunteers from a Dutch volunteer organization whose primary mission is to find a cure for cancer by funding relevant scientific research.

First, confirmatory factor analyses indicated that pride and respect could be assessed independently from the perceived importance of volunteer work and from perceived (task and emotional) support provided by the volunteer organization. Second, as predicted, the extent to which volunteers perceived their volunteer work to be of importance to the clientele of the volunteer organization predicted their experience of pride. Likewise, the extent to which volunteers saw their volunteer organization as providing them with task and emotional support predicted their experience of respect. Third, in line with our model, the experience of pride and respect in turn predicted the extent to which individual volunteers psychologically engaged with their volunteer organization, as indicated by their organizational commitment. Finally, structural equation modeling with EQS 6.1 (Bentler & Wu, 2004) confirmed that the effects of the importance of the volunteer work and the support provided by the organization on psychological engagement with the organization were mediated by pride and respect, respectively (Boezeman & Ellemers, 2008a).

Sources of Pride and Respect, and Satisfaction With Volunteer Work

We proceeded to examine whether work satisfaction among volunteer workers might be predicted from pride and respect, and assessed in more detail which organizational features contribute to the experience of pride and respect among volunteers. Employee satisfaction is a central construct in the work motivation literature (Brief, 1998; Spector, 1996), and is seen as an important precursor of relevant work behaviors. For instance, satisfaction is seen as a predictor of emotional attachment and behavioral engagement (e.g., task performance and organizational citizenship behavior) (e.g., Ostroff, 1992) vs. distress and (motivational) withdrawal among paid workers (for overviews, see Hulin, 1991; Tett & Meyer, 1993). However, as noted by Brief (1998), in popular measures such as the Job Descriptive Index (JDI; Smith, Kendall, & Hulin, 1969) or the Minnesota Satisfaction Questionnaire (MSQ; Weiss, Dawis, Lofquist, & England, 1966), satisfaction is assessed by asking about work aspects such as pay and compensation, promotion/advancement opportunities, and security. Not only are these aspects less relevant (or even not applicable) in the case of volunteer workers, this also raises the question of whether current insights on work satisfaction that have been established among paid employees also hold in the case of volunteer work (Galindo-Kuhn & Guzley, 2001).

In the literature on the implications of group status for individual group members, a distinction is made between the private vs. public image of the group as a potential source of esteem and group pride (Crocker & Luhtanen, 1990). A relevant question therefore is whether the status of the volunteer organization and resulting feelings of pride primarily relate to the self-perceived effectiveness and importance of the volunteer work, or also depend on the external image of the volunteer organization. Indeed, among paid employees, the public visibility of the organization and its successes appear to be relevant in this respect (Fuller et al., 2006). In parallel, it may well be that the experience of pride among volunteer workers not only derives from the perceived effectiveness and importance of the volunteer work but also depends on the public visibility of the volunteer organization and its achievements. We addressed this issue in our research.

We conducted a first study to examine different sources of volunteer satisfaction (Boezeman, Ellemers, & Duijnhoven, 2007, Study 1) among 93 volunteers working in an organization whose global mission is to find a home for children that are homeless. The tasks of the volunteers participating in the preliminary survey study consisted of either monitoring one of the various projects of the volunteer organization or providing information to the people that were found willing to offer a home for a homeless child. The results of this study indicated that both pride and respect reliably predict the satisfaction of volunteer workers, in line with our model. Additionally, with structural equation modeling in EQS 6.1 (Bentler & Wu, 2004) we found that the perceived importance of volunteer work contributes to the experience of pride, and hence offers an indirect source of volunteer satisfaction. Likewise, we found that the perception of organizational support results in the experience of respect, and in this way also contributes to volunteer satisfaction.

In addition to these findings with respect to volunteer satisfaction, which parallel our initial study on psychological engagement (Boezeman & Ellemers, 2008a), this further research also offered additional insights. That is, this time the social-emotional support provided by the organization proved a more important determinant of respect and work satisfaction than organizational task support. Furthermore, even though the perceived visibility of the volunteer organization seems a relevant precursor of organizational status among paid employees (see Fuller et al., 2006), it did not emerge as a reliable source of pride and satisfaction among volunteers. Thus, we found among volunteers that only the self-perceived importance of the work of the volunteer organization determined their experience of pride, not its public visibility.

In a second study, we additionally examined whether respect from the clientele of the volunteer organization also contributes to the satisfaction of volunteer workers. Even though volunteer organizations provide help to groups in need with the best of intentions, this does not necessarily imply that those at the receiving end always accept and appreciate such help. In the literature (see Nadler, 2002), a distinction is made between help that can instill a sense of dependence and inferiority (e.g., the temporary provision of food or shelter) versus help that intends to increase autonomy by providing those who receive such help with the means to address their own problems (e.g., offering education or skills training). Furthermore, people are generally more inclined to ask and accept help when they see this as increasing their autonomy and independence (Nadler & Halabi, 2006). Based on this knowledge, we argue that when the clientele of the volunteer organization is seen to accept and appreciate the help received, this should cause volunteers to feel valued and respected by their clientele. Therefore, we examined whether the feelings of respect raised in this way contribute to the satisfaction of volunteer workers.

Social relationships with other volunteers are generally considered as a factor of importance in the motivation to volunteer (e.g., Clary et al., 1998). For people without paid employment in particular, the association with a volunteer organization indeed offers an important opportunity for social integration through relations with co-volunteers. Accordingly, previous research suggests that social integration in the volunteer organization and interpersonal relations with co-volunteers contribute to satisfaction of volunteer workers and enhance the intention to stay in the volunteer organization (e.g., Galindo-Kuhn & Guzley, 2001). However, volunteer work often is casual in nature (Pearce, 1993), and even regular volunteers only work for a few hours per week (Cnaan & Cascio, 1999), making it difficult to develop a sense of continuity and integration among one's co-workers within the volunteer organization. Therefore, it is important to assess whether the amount of contact and social integration in the volunteer organization (or the lack of it) is relevant for the degree to which one feels valued and *respected* by one's co-volunteers, and in this way contributes to (or undermines) the work satisfaction of volunteers.

The primary mission of the organization that hosted the second study (Boezeman, Ellemers, & Duijnhoven, 2007, Study 2) was to improve medical care for people with burns and to provide information about the prevention of such injuries. This organization's 238 fundraising volunteers participated in our study. The results of this study again showed that the experience of pride and respect contribute significantly to the satisfaction of volunteer workers. Additionally, we replicated the finding that among volunteers the experience of pride only relates to the perceived importance of the volunteer work, and that the public visibility of the volunteer organization and its achievements is less relevant for the experience of pride and its effects on volunteer satisfaction. When examining the antecedent conditions of respect, we again observed that the support provided by the organization is a reliable source of respect, and contributes to volunteer satisfaction through the experience of organizational respect. We also replicated the finding that social–emotional support provided by the volunteer organization is a more relevant antecedent of organizational respect and volunteer satisfaction than task support provided by the organization. Additionally, as anticipated, the degree to which the clientele of the volunteer organization accepts and appreciates the help provided, elicits the feeling of being respected by this clientele, and in this way also contributes to volunteers' satisfaction with the volunteer work. However, even though the degree of social integration in the volunteer organization leads volunteers to feel respected by their co-volunteers, social integration and co-volunteer respect are not reliable predictors of volunteer satisfaction.

In sum, our theoretical analysis and the empirical results obtained in relation to volunteer satisfaction reveal a number of interesting conclusions. First, we established that pride and respect emerge as reliable predictors of volunteer satisfaction. Second, the perceived importance of volunteer work is a reliable source of pride, and the support provided by the volunteer organization consistently emerges as a source of respect. Importantly, our results suggest that the provision of organizational support does not necessarily detract from the resources available to help the clientele of the organization, as socio-emotional support was more important than task support in this regard. Third, we established that the sense of pride that is relevant to volunteer satisfaction does not depend on the public visibility of the volunteer organization and its achievements. Rather, it is the personal conviction that the organization is effective in achieving its mission and the perceived importance of the volunteer work in accomplishing this that is crucial to the experience of pride that contributes to volunteer satisfaction. Finally, the acceptance of the help provided to the clientele of the organization and the resulting sense of being respected by those who benefit from this help also contributes to volunteer satisfaction. However, even though social integration and the availability of interpersonal relations with co-workers is often cited as an important motive in volunteer work, we found that such relations and the co-worker respect they generate do not contribute to volunteer satisfaction (beyond pride, organizational respect, and clientele respect). This finding is relevant for volunteer organizations, as it suggests that the absence of such integration – as often is the case with occasional volunteers – does not necessarily undermine volunteer satisfaction.

The Importance of Normative Commitment in Volunteer Retention

Organizational commitment is of particular interest as an aspect of work motivation among volunteers (Dailey, 1986), because it can be shaped independently of material rewards (Ellemers, Van Rijswijk, Bruins, & de Gilder, 1998; Haslam & Ellemers, 2005). Furthermore, it is relevant to volunteer retention, as organizational commitment has been found to predict intentions to remain a volunteer at the volunteer organization (see also Jenner, 1981; Miller, Powell, & Seltzer, 1990). Therefore, we examined whether pride and respect as a member of the volunteer organization predict organizational commitment and intentions to stay among volunteers.

In research on organizational commitment among paid employees, a distinction is made between three types of commitment (Allen & Meyer, 1990) that reflect different forms of psychological attachment to the organization. According to Allen and Meyer (1990), *affective* organizational commitment refers to emotional attachment to the organization (feeling "part of the family"), *continuance* commitment reflects a calculative form of attachment to the organization (e.g., due to loss of material benefits or participation in a pension plan), and *normative* organizational commitment indicates an attachment to the organization which is based on feelings of responsibility (e.g., due to the moral significance of the mission of the organization).

In research among paid employees in profit organizations, affective commitment is most strongly related to relevant indicators of work motivation, such as attendance and job performance (for an overview, see Meyer, Stanley, Herscovitch, & Topolnytsky, 2002). Continuance commitment ties the individual to the organization, but can induce negative work behaviors (e.g., slacking or absenteeism), due to its calculative nature. Normative commitment is usually less clearly associated with the behavior of paid employees. In our research, we focused on affective and normative organizational commitment, as these have been found particularly relevant to volunteers, in contrast to continuance commitment (Dawley, Stephens, & Stephens, 2005; Liao-Troth, 2001; Stephens, Dawley, & Stephens, 2004).

Even though normative commitment seems of little relevance in the work motivation of paid employees, we expect this to be of particular importance in the case of volunteer workers. In fact, normative commitment may even prove to be more important than affective commitment for volunteer retention, due to the occasional nature of much volunteer work implying that the interaction with the volunteer organization and its members tends to be infrequent or intermittent. Thus, we expect the retention of volunteers to rely heavily upon their normative commitment to the organization, as this type of commitment focuses on the perceived responsibility and morality concerns regarding the mission of the organization which are seen as central elements in the motivation of volunteer workers (Cnaan & Cascio, 1999). As a result, the degree to which individual volunteers feel morally obliged to help accomplish the mission of their organization, and are concerned with the continuity of their organization's efforts in pursuing its goals, should predict their intentions to remain a volunteer with their organization.

To examine this, we surveyed 170 fundraising volunteers working for a Dutch volunteer organization whose primary mission is to find a cure for diabetes by funding relevant research. The fundraising volunteers that we surveyed all had their own districts across the Netherlands in which they helped the volunteer organization in preparing, setting up, and managing its one-week-a-year fundraising campaign. We assessed their feelings of pride and respect as a volunteer at this organization, measured their normative and affective commitment to their volunteer organization, and recorded their intentions of remaining a volunteer with their volunteer organization (Boezeman & Ellemers, 2007, Study 1).

The results of this study supported our reasoning, in that we found that feelings of pride and respect contribute to volunteers' sense of affective and normative commitment, indicating their psychological engagement with the volunteer organization, as was the case in our preliminary study (Boezeman & Ellemers, 2008a). Additionally, however, we found that only normative commitment reliably predicted volunteers' intentions to remain with the organization. As a result, the beneficial effects of pride and respect on intentions to remain, were reliably mediated by normative commitment, but not by affective commitment. Thus, this study again reminds us that existing knowledge regarding the motivation of paid employees does not necessarily apply to the situation of volunteer workers. That is, whereas normative commitment is generally seen as a relatively unimportant factor in the work behavior of paid employees, our research suggests that normative commitment may be a central factor in the retention of volunteers.

After having established the importance of normative commitment for volunteers' intentions to stay with their volunteer organization, we conducted an additional study to cross-validate the core aspects of our model, and further identify antecedents of pride and respect that would contribute to organizational commitment (Boezeman & Ellemers, 2007, Study 2). In this study, we assessed the perceived importance of the volunteer work as an antecedent of pride, we assessed emotion and task support provided by the organization as antecedents of respect, and we examined whether the effects of these antecedents on normative and affective commitment to the volunteer organization were mediated by pride and respect, respectively.

We surveyed two separate samples of fundraising volunteers working for different types of Dutch volunteer organizations. The mission of the first volunteer organization was to help the handicapped integrate into society, for instance by providing information about relevant legal arrangements: 173 volunteers of this organization participated in our research. Some of the volunteers participate in this organization because they have family members or acquaintances who are handicapped. The second volunteer organization, from which 164 volunteers participated in our research, supports healthcare initiatives in developing countries through financial aid, the local delivery of materials and equipment, and other means of direct support. Accordingly, the volunteers in this organization are not related in any way to the clientele of the organization. These two organizations thus differ in the likelihood that volunteers might (indirectly) benefit from the activities of the organization, as well as in the type of help they provide (i.e., oriented towards autonomy vs. dependence), and offered the opportunity to examine the validity of our model across different types of volunteer organizations and organizational activities.

Confirmatory factor analyses supported the distinction between the different constructs in each of these two samples, as intended. Furthermore, in both samples structural equation modeling executed in EQS 6.1 (Bentler & Wu, 2004) confirmed that relations between these theoretical constructs were as hypothesized. Thus, the results of two separate samples of volunteers working in different types of volunteer organizations converged to suggest that when volunteers perceive that their volunteer work is of importance to the clientele of their volunteer organization, they feel proud as a volunteer at their volunteer organization, which in turn causes them to feel committed to their volunteer organization. Likewise, regardless of the type of volunteer organization our research participants worked in, perceived task and emotional organizational support provided by the organization predicted the experience of organizational respect, which also contributed to volunteer commitment to the organization. Importantly, although our previous study had shown that normative commitment is more relevant as a predictor of intentions to remain than affective commitment, the antecedents of pride and respect we examined in this follow-up study elicited both types of commitment. Thus, from these results it seems that the unique value of normative commitment for the work behavior of volunteers emerges in its *consequences* for volunteer retention, but not in the unique antecedents of this type of commitment.

Organizational Success, Anticipated Pride, and the Recruitment of Volunteers

Now that we have established that pride and respect help to understand the motivation of existing volunteers, we turn to the issue of volunteer recruitment, to see whether the *anticipation* of pride and respect relates to the willingness of non-volunteers to participate in the volunteer organization, and to examine which organizational features induce anticipated feelings of pride and respect. We tested our predictions in a series of experimental studies which systematically compared different features of a bogus volunteer organization to see how the provision of information about specific aspects of the organization and its activities might instill anticipated pride and respect in non-volunteers and hence foster their willingness to become involved with the volunteer organization.

The recruitment of volunteers involves attracting non-volunteers to the volunteer organization and interesting them in becoming a volunteer with the volunteer organization. Volunteer organizations are commonly in need for additional human resources (Farmer & Fedor, 2001; Pearce, 1993) and volunteer recruitment is a recurring issue for volunteer organizations. However, research to date has not highlighted how potential volunteers can become attracted to volunteer organizations.

In line with signaling theory (Spence, 1973), researchers (e.g., Ehrhart & Ziegert, 2005; Rynes, 1991; Turban & Cable, 2003) have suggested that non-members create an impression of what it will be like to be a member of an organization by considering the information they have about the organization as relevant signals of organizational characteristics. Barsness, Tenbrunsel, Michael, and Lawson (2002) have posited that non-members can use such information to derive expectations about the pride and respect they *anticipate* to experience as members in that organization. Accordingly, we argue that a particular organization might become attractive to non-members, through *anticipated* feelings of pride and respect they derive from the information they have about organizational membership.

In line with social identity theory, researchers (e.g., Cable & Turban, 2003; Ehrhart & Ziegert, 2005; Turban & Cable, 2003; Turban & Greening, 1996) have argued that it should be attractive for applicants to become a member of an organization to the extent that it is seen as successful, as membership in such an organization should contribute to a positive social identity. Empirical findings among paid employees are in line with this reasoning. For instance, it has been found that corporate reputation is positively correlated with organizational attractiveness (Turban & Greening, 1996), and that a company's reputation is positively associated with the number of applicants seeking employment with that organization (Turban & Cable, 2003). Additionally, expected pride from employment in a profit organization was found positively associated with applicants' job pursuit intentions and negatively associated with the minimum salary they were willing to accept (Cable & Turban, 2003).

However, in the case of volunteer organizations, communicating about the current success of the organization may also have negative side effects. The mission of charitable volunteer organizations is directed at providing services that would otherwise not be available (Fisher & Ackerman, 1998). As a result, communicating about the success of a particular organization in achieving its mission might (unwittingly) lead non-volunteers to conclude that this organization does not need additional help, and that their volunteer efforts might be better used elsewhere. Indeed, in a fundraising competition the perceived need of a fundraising group for additional volunteer help was found to be lower when the group was more successful (Fisher & Ackerman, 1998).

Thus, it may well be that providing information about the current success of the organization backfires in the case of volunteer organizations, in that it decreases the perceived need for additional volunteers of this organization, which might impact negatively upon non-volunteers' attraction to the organization. We examined this possibility in our first recruitment study, in which we experimentally manipulated the perceived success of a bogus volunteer organization (Boezeman & Ellemers, 2008b, Study 1). We assessed how this impacted upon anticipated pride and the perceived need of the volunteer organization for additional volunteers, and examined how these related to attraction to the organization among non-volunteers.

Participants in this experiment were informed that the Dutch Ministry of Social Affairs (which coordinates volunteer work in the Netherlands) planned to launch a campaign in order to inform Dutch citizens about volunteer work and recruit them for volunteer organizations. They then received leaflets providing information about a fictionalized volunteer organization, to ensure that the participants were all non-volunteers *at this organization*, and were not predisposed to the organization in any way. The organization presented allegedly was a charity whose mission was to help homeless people through services such as providing shelter, meals, clothing, and medical care, which is considered a characteristic volunteer act across cultures (Handy, Cnaan, Brudney, Ascoli, Meijs, & Ranade, 2000).

The results of this experiment revealed that providing non-volunteers with information about the success of a volunteer organization did not relate to their anticipated feelings of pride as a volunteer at that volunteer organization, nor did it increase the perceived attractiveness of the volunteer organization through anticipated pride (even though anticipated pride itself was a reliable predictor of attraction to the volunteer organization). At the same time, the information provided about the current success of the volunteer organization reduced the perceived need of the volunteer organization for additional volunteers. Thus, we found that non-volunteers are inclined to think that a volunteer organization is in less need for additional volunteers when that organization is presented as being successful, while the current success of that organization did not induce a sense of pride nor did it enhance the attractiveness of the volunteer organization as a place to work in as a result. This suggests that, contrary to what is found among those seeking paid employment in profit organizations, emphasizing the success of the volunteer organization does not contribute to the recruitment of volunteers.

Organizational Support, Anticipated Respect, and the Recruitment of Volunteers

Parallel to the reasoning with respect to anticipated pride, we hypothesized that anticipated respect as a volunteer might also be relevant to volunteer recruitment. We further argued that providing non-volunteers with information about organizational support might induce such feelings of anticipated respect and enhance organizational attractiveness. However, this time too, we explored whether such information might have negative side-effects. We reasoned that an organization that provides support to its volunteers might be seen as less efficient in using its available resources to achieve its mission, and hence may seem less attractive as an organization to volunteer for. This is why we also manipulated the information participants received about the amount of support the organization offered to its volunteers, to examine how this relates to anticipated respect, perceived organizational efficiency, and attraction to the volunteer organization.

The results of this study revealed that whereas non-volunteers indeed consider a volunteer organization less efficient when it offers support to its volunteers, this does not reduce the perceived attractiveness of that organization. At the same time, information about organizational support did induce anticipated respect, and in this way increased non-volunteers' attraction to the volunteer organization. Thus, in contrast to the information about the current success of the volunteer organization, providing information about organizational support appeared to offer more scope as a viable tool in volunteer recruitment. Hence, we conducted two additional studies to further elaborate on how information about the support provided to volunteers can help attract new volunteers to the organization.

Because the literature emphasizes social relations among volunteers as a relevant concern in volunteer motivation and retention (e.g., Clary et al., 1998; Galindo-Kuhn & Guzley, 2001), we focused in a second experiment on organizational support versus co-volunteer support and examined their impact on anticipated respect and attraction to the volunteer organization. Thus, we examined how different sources of support (i.e., the volunteer organization and co-volunteers) impacted upon specific forms of anticipated respect (from the volunteer organization as well as from prospective co-volunteers), and examined how this affected the perceived attractiveness of the volunteer organization as a place to work in. In this study we focused on emotional support as a relevant source of support for volunteer workers (see also Clary, 1987), that can be equally well provided by the volunteer organization as by individual volunteers.

The results of this second recruitment experiment (Boezeman & Ellemers, 2008b, Study 2) showed again that providing information to convey that the volunteer organization offers (emotional) support to its volunteers caused non-volunteers to anticipate respect, which in turn enhanced their attraction to that volunteer organization. However, even though informing non-volunteers about the mutual support among volunteers at this organization induced them to anticipate co-volunteer respect, this type of support and respect did not affect their attraction to the volunteer organization. Thus, it appeared that the support provided by the volunteer organization and the anticipated respect this induces is more relevant to volunteer recruitment than support and respect from one's co-volunteers.

In a third experiment, we therefore elaborated on the different types of support that can be provided to volunteers within a volunteer organization, to further examine how information about such support might play a role in volunteer recruitment through anticipated respect. Extending our previous experiments, this time we also assessed the actual willingness of non-volunteers to participate in the activities of the volunteer organization (i.e., by enlisting for an internship in the organization), in addition to asking about their perceived attractiveness of the volunteer organization. In this third experiment (Boezeman & Ellemers, 2008b, Study 3) we therefore examined both emotional support (e.g., being attentive to problems encountered by volunteers, providing encouragement) and task support (e.g., providing material goods and services to facilitate the work of individual volunteers) as potentially relevant to volunteer recruitment (see also Clary, 1987; Galindo-Kuhn & Guzley, 2001; Gidron, 1983). We assessed the impact of providing information about these different types of support on anticipated respect, attraction to the organization, and the willingness to participate among non-volunteers.

The results of this study again pointed to the importance of providing information about intra-organizational support in volunteer recruitment efforts. That is, both information about task support and information about emotional support instilled a sense of anticipated respect among non-volunteers. Furthermore, path analysis executed in EQS 6.1 (Bentler & Wu, 2004) showed that due to this information and the anticipated respect it induced, non-volunteers saw the volunteer organization as a more attractive place to work in, and as a result actually were more likely to become involved in the activities of the organization than when such support appeared to be lacking.

What Have We Learned About Volunteer Recruitment, Satisfaction, and Retention?

In this chapter our aim was to develop a parsimonious model of volunteer motivation to shed light on psychological processes relevant to the recruitment, satisfaction, and retention of volunteers. Across the board, we found converging support for our theoretical predictions in different types of volunteer organizations, for different indicators of work motivation, and using different research methodologies. Consistent findings were: (1) that the conviction that the volunteer work is of importance to the volunteer organization and its clientele contributes to a sense of pride in the volunteer organization; (2) that support provided by the volunteer organization contributes to the experience of respect; and (3) that both pride and respect induce psychological engagement with the organization, as is evident from measures of work satisfaction, commitment, and intentions to stay, as well as for the attractiveness of the organization and willingness to engage among non-volunteers. This supports the core predictions of our model (see Figure 13.1).

In addition to these converging results, we also observed some interesting differences when examining the recruitment, satisfaction, and retention of volunteer workers, which we summarize here. First, we established that the experience of pride among volunteer workers primarily relates to their *own* convictions about the importance of their volunteer work, instead of being derived from the public image of the volunteer organization. Indeed, we found that the public visibility of the volunteer organization and its achievements seems less relevant (in predicting volunteer satisfaction through pride), while the current success of the organization can even backfire (in the case of volunteer recruitment). This is different from observations that the public image and perceived success of profit organizations is an important factor in the attraction and motivation of paid employees. Second, although the experience of respect can derive from different aspects of the volunteer work, not all forms of respect are equally relevant to the work motivation of volunteers. Across different studies and indicators, we found that the support provided by the volunteer organization, and the organizational respect this induced, always mattered. Our findings with respect to the nature of organizational support were less consistent in that task support appeared to be less relevant to predict volunteer satisfaction. Nevertheless, our results converged to show that the provision of emotion-oriented support and the organizational respect this conveys always has a positive impact on the motivation and engagement of volunteers.

A third conclusion that can be drawn when comparing the results of our different studies is that social integration in the volunteer organization and relations with co-volunteers are less important for the motivation and engagement of volunteer workers than is often assumed. This is evident, for instance, from our finding that the quality and intensity of relations with co-workers and the co-worker respect this induces does not predict work satisfaction. Furthermore, affective ties within the organization and its members (affective commitment) are less relevant than normative and moral considerations in the retention of volunteers. Additionally, information about co-volunteer support and the anticipation of co-worker respect this induces do not increase the attractiveness of the volunteer organization for non-volunteers. Thus, although the common belief is that volunteers focus on the opportunity that volunteer work offers for social integration and interpersonal relations, the combined results of our research suggest that volunteer work is primarily motivated by the individual involvement with the *mission* pursued by the volunteer organization and the support the organization provides to volunteers trying to accomplish that mission. We found that people seek (in recruitment) and value (in satisfaction) support from the organization when doing their volunteer work, want their efforts to be accepted and valued by the clientele of the organization (in volunteer satisfaction), and continue their activities as long as they feel morally responsible for the accomplishment of the organization's mission (in volunteer retention), rather than seeking social integration through their volunteer work.

Thus, even though the present analysis is based on existing knowledge on the motivation of paid employees, the application to the situation of volunteer workers has yielded a number of novel insights. Some of the conclusions drawn from our work relate to the unique characteristics of volunteer work as compared to paid employment, but others also are unexpected in view of current insights on volunteer workers, attesting to the added value of our theoretical analysis and research above and beyond existing knowledge. We also think there is promise in this approach, in that it offers scope to integrate insights from theoretical models on the different functions of volunteer work (e.g., Clary et al., 1998) or the different levels of analysis at which helping behavior can be defined (Penner et al., 2005). That is, a focus on how individual volunteers perceive their interactions with the volunteer organization allows for the consideration of individual differences, fulfilment of specific needs, interpersonal interactions, and organizational features as different sources of perceived value of the volunteer experience. Future research is needed to further examine whether our current model can help in specifying the psychological processes through which these different individual, interactional, and organizational features impact on the motivation and behavior of individual volunteers.

Empowering the Volunteer Organization

Our current analysis offers a number of concrete suggestions of the types of organizational activities and policies that are most likely to contribute to the recruitment, satisfaction, and retention of individual volunteers (see Table 13.1). When considering the possibilities for volunteer organizations to influence and direct the motivated behavior of individual volunteers from a traditional point of view, the main concern seems to be that the available means to do this are quite limited. That is, as we have indicated above, material resources tend to be scarce, there often is little regular interaction with individual volunteers, and there are no legal obligations or other formal means to tie individual volunteers to the volunteer organization. However, our analysis and results suggest that these characteristics of volunteer work do not necessarily limit the organization's opportunities to engage and motivate individual volunteers.

A first recommendation that can be made is that volunteer organizations may do well to communicate clearly and explicitly about the mission of their organization, the appreciation of the organization's activities for its clientele, and the importance of the (continued) contributions of individual volunteers for the accomplishment of the organization's mission. When resources to do this are limited, the internal communication within the organization about these issues, and the information provided about the organization in the recruitment of new volunteers, should take precedence over investing in the public image of the volunteer organization, for instance by external communications about its successes.

A second recommendation is for the organization to support the activities of individual volunteers, as this helps convey the appreciation and respect of the organization for their efforts. If such support can only be provided at an emotional level, it still serves this important function. However, the addition of task support further contributes to the experience of respect. Indeed, the benefits of task support likely outweigh the potential disadvantages, as a reasonable level of task support will tend to facilitate the efforts of individual volunteers and optimize the effectiveness of the volunteer organization, even if at first sight investing in this form of support may appear to be a less efficient way to serve the mission of the organization. At the same time, it is important to note that limited resources should not be problematic in this respect, as the provision of emotional support – not task-support – is key. Regardless of the type and amount of support available, the organization should be explicit in what can and cannot be expected in this sense, and deliver on promises made. If the organization is successful in doing this the (anticipated) provision of support can be part of its psychological contract with individual volunteers, even in the absence of more formal obligations (see also Farmer & Fedor, 1999).

A final issue to be aware of is that when the organization is making progress in achieving its mission, any communications conveying this should recognize that the contributions of each volunteer are needed to accomplish the goals of the organization. Furthermore, to prevent (prospective) volunteers from thinking their efforts are better used elsewhere, the organization should emphasize that their continued involvement and effort are needed for the organization's activities to be truly beneficial for its clientele.

Part IV

The Broader Picture: Political and Societal Implications

14

Interpersonal and Intergroup Helping Relations as Power Relations

Implications for Real-World Helping

Arie Nadler

Introduction

Giving a helping hand to those in need is a central maxim in most, if not all, human societies (Batson, 1994). We are taught that we should be sensitive to the plight of others, and that failing to do so may lead others to label us immoral. The central place of helping in social life is reflected in social psychological research, which has sought to uncover the *psychological mechanisms* that propel helping, specify the *situations* under which people are more or less likely to help, and the *personality antecedents* of willingness to help others (Dovidio, Piliavin, Schroeder, & Penner, 2006). The underlying assumption of this research has been that helping others is a positive behavior that should be encouraged.

Yet, helping relations are also unequal social relations between one party, which has ample knowledge or resources to bestow, and another, which is dependent on the generosity of the former. Past research has given less attention to this aspect of helping relations and its consequences for interpersonal and intergroup relations. The present chapter focuses on this link between helping relations and power relations and its applied implications. It presents two bodies of theory and research that are united in the view that dependency on the help of others may spell weakness and lower status for the recipient, while signifying relatively more strength and higher status for the giver.

The first body of research focused on *interpersonal helping relations* and was conducted within the theoretical framework of the Threat to Self-esteem model of reactions to help (Nadler & Fisher, 1986). This research explored the conditions under which receiving help is threatening to recipients' view of themselves as worthwhile and equal social actors and their subsequent willingness to seek and receive help from others. The second body of research and theory focused on *intergroup helping relations* and was conducted within the framework of the model of Intergroup Helping as Status Relations (Nadler, 2002; Nadler & Halabi, 2006; Halabi & Nadler, Chapter 6 in the present volume), which suggests that because receiving help is associated with lower status and giving help with higher status, helping relations can create, maintain, or challenge intergroup social hierarchies. In subsequent sections we consider both of these lines of research and their applied implications. We begin with a more detailed consideration of the link between helping relations and power relations.

Helping and Social Inequality: The Basic Link

Society holds an ambivalent attitude as far as helping relations are concerned. Social norms dictate that we should help all those who need our assistance, but heeds against relying on others when we need help ourselves. This is reflected in cultures across the globe. In the Jewish prayer book in the Grace that people say after meals they ask God: "Do not makes us dependent on the gifts of flesh and blood, or their loans"; the Raja Yoga, a sacred Hindu text, states that "the mind of the man who receives a gift is acted on by the mind of the giver so the receiver is likely to become degenerate" (quoted in Kuppuswamy, 1978), and the Koran advises helpers to be sensitive to the adverse psychological consequences of dependence and to make charitable deeds appear "as a duty man owes to man, so that it conveys no idea of the superiority of the giver or the inferiority of the receiver" (2:262).

The links between help and status have also been noted by the founders of modern social science, who observed that groups and individuals maintain their position of social privilege by giving to others. Close to two centuries ago, in his book *Democracy in America*, Alexis de Tocqueville observed that members of the American ruling class exercised dominance over unprivileged classes by providing them with assistance; he described dependence on such assistance as "servitude of the regular, quiet and gentle kind" (de Tocqueville, 1853/1956, pp. 303–304). In his classic essay "The Gift" Marcel Mauss describes the custom of Potlach in the American North West, where Native American tribal leaders conferred lavish gifts on other leaders in order to ascertain their clan's superior status (Mauss, 1907/1957). Benedict (1946/1967) described the usage of the word *on*, meaning indebted or obligated, in Japan's prewar society: "A man receives *on* from a superior and the act of accepting an *on* from any man not definitely one's superior or at least one's equal gives one an uncomfortable sense of inferiority" (p. 104). More recently, on the basis of an evolutionary analysis, Boone (1998) summarizes this position by asserting that human altruism is an indicator of relative superiority; "expenditure of time or energy in altruistic behavior signals the sender's ability to bear the short term costs of cooperation or sharing" (p. 13).

Within social psychology there exists empirical evidence that supports the idea that helping increases the giver's status while dependence on help signifies the recipient's lower status and lack of ability. Research on interpersonal helping indicates that people offer help to other group members in order to gain status in the group (Hardy & Van Vugt, 2006; Van Vugt & De Cremer, 1999) and to restore feelings of self-worth. For example, in an experiment by Brown and Smart (1991), participants who had failed on a task subsequently provided more help to another person than their counterparts who had not failed. Research on reactions to receiving help indicates that when dependency implies inferiority on ego-central dimensions people react negatively to receiving help (e.g., Nadler, Fisher, & Ben-Itzhak, 1983; Worchel, Wong, & Scheltema, 1989) and prefer to endure hardship rather than seek help (Nadler, 1987). Similar phenomena have been observed in research on intergroup helping relations. Group members maintain perceptions of positive in-group distinctiveness by providing more help to an out-group that poses a threat to in-group status than to a non-threatening out-group (Nadler, Harpaz-Gorodeisky, & Ben-David, 2008), and are reluctant to seek or receive help when dependency on the out-group would imply that the in-group was inferior (Nadler & Halabi, 2006).

The Threat to Self-Esteem Model of Receiving Help

Although receiving help can be detrimental to status, it also has psychological benefits. The extension of help can make manifest the care or concern of the helper for the recipient. Help also obviously entails some instrumental profit. The Threat to Self-esteem model of receiving help proposes a systematic account for this Janus-like quality of help. It suggests that help confers a mixture of self-supporting and self-threatening psychological elements – for example, self-supporting information about the helper's sympathy alongside self-threatening information about the recipient's relative inferiority (Nadler & Fisher, 1986).

When people in need view themselves as sufficiently able to cope with a difficulty on their own, receiving help is inconsistent with this view of the self as autonomous and is therefore self-threatening. Under these conditions people may be unwilling to seek or receive help, even if this entails prolonging their hardship. When dependence on others is consistent with people's view of themselves as being unable to cope alone, receiving help constitutes a self-supporting experience, and they may seek help whenever the need arises. Such is the case when children depend on their parents or when a new employee relies on the assistance of a knowledgeable supervisor. In both cases dependency is a consensual feature of the social relationship.

The model and related research suggest that characteristics of the *helper*, the *recipient*, and the *help* that is offered will determine the degree of consistency between recipients' dependence on help and their view of themselves, and as a consequence, whether the help that is offered will be considered self-threatening or self-supporting. For example, dependency on similar others (i.e., a *helper characteristic*) who serve as frames of reference for self-judgments is inconsistent with recipients' expectations that they be as successful and independent as their potential helpers. As a consequence, when help hinges on ego-central qualities (i.e., a *characteristic of the help*), high self-esteem individuals (i.e., a *recipient characteristic*) are less willing to seek (Nadler, 1987) or receive (Nadler, 1986) help from similar than dissimilar others. Regarding long-term consequences, the model suggests that the receipt of self-threatening help will motivate recipients to invest in self-help efforts aimed at terminating their uneasy dependency, and will therefore lead to future independence. When the receipt of help is experienced as self-supporting, recipients are not motivated to end the relationship of dependency. In this case receiving help is likely to result in long-term dependency.

Autonomy-Oriented and Dependency-Oriented Help: Chronic or Transient Dependency

More recently, researchers have observed that the implications of giving or receiving help for future equality and self-reliance versus inequality and chronic dependence hinge on the autonomy or dependency orientation of the help offered (Nadler, 1997, 1998, 2002). This bears on a broader distinction between helping relations as reflecting transient or chronic dependency. These distinctions are important to consider in applying the Threat to Self-esteem model of responses to help. Dependency-oriented help consists of providing recipients with the full solution to their problem. In this kind of help, the helper solves the problem for the recipient; in the words of a well-known metaphor, the helper gives the recipient fish for a day, rather than teaching him to fish so he can eat for a lifetime. In autonomy-oriented help, the helper gives the recipient the tools with which he can solve the problem on his own, making the recipient part of the solution.

These two kinds of help convey different messages to recipients. Dependency-oriented help conveys the message that recipients are weak and unable to contribute to resolving the problem they face. Such help reinforces perceptions of lack of control and dampens the probability of future self-reliance. When such help is given to recipients who expect that they can solve their problems on their own, such help is self-threatening. If it comes against the background of expectations of dependency, such help will be self-supporting. Autonomy-oriented help conveys an opposite message. It tells recipients that they are strong and capable enough to use the tools bestowed them to solve the problem on their own. This assistance allows recipients to retain their view of themselves as independent actors (cf. also Brickman, Rabinowitz, Karuza, Coates, Cohn, & Kidder, 1982) and reinforces the expectation that they can transform dependency into self-reliance by investing in self-help efforts. Such assistance has a lower self-threat potential than dependency-oriented help.

It is not suggested that autonomy-oriented help is always the preferred option. In extreme emergencies, dependency-oriented help may be the only viable route. When people are starving they need to be given food rather than be taught how to cultivate land and grow food on their own. This can come later. Yet, in many helping interactions the autonomous or dependent nature of help shapes recipients' expectations about their ability to transform dependency into self-reliance.

Although there is no data directly supporting the contention that receiving autonomy-oriented help prompts recipients to view themselves as more able to achieve self-reliance than those receiving dependency-oriented help, recent empirical evidence on the ways in which requests for help by high- and low-status individuals are interpreted by the helper supports this rationale. In two experiments, we studied helpers' reactions to a request for help from a high- or low-status person in need. The first experiment used the minimal group paradigm to define high and low status and the second experiment used real groups with high and low status. In both experiments, findings showed that when the request for help came from a member of the high-status group, helpers attributed the request for help to the recipient's motivation for future independence and subsequently offered autonomy-oriented help. When the same request came from a member of the low-status group, the request was perceived to reflect lack of ability and led to more offers of dependency-oriented help (Chai-Tcherniak & Nadler, 2008).

Autonomy- and dependency-oriented help have implications for the broader distinction between *transient* and *chronic dependency*. Autonomy-oriented help implies transient dependency; it is limited in degree and duration to the transfer of specific tools or instructions from the helper to the recipient, who will then use this assistance to regain self-reliance within a relatively short period of time. Dependency-oriented help implies chronic dependency. It solves the problem for the recipient and does not rely on his or her skills to do so. It will therefore be given again whenever the need arises.

Two other characteristics of help are relevant to the distinction between transient and chronic dependency: The *assumptive* versus *responsive* and *discriminating* versus *non-discriminating* nature of help given. Assumptive help is given without waiting for the needy to ask for it (Schneider, Major, Luhtanen, & Crocker, 1996). It indicates the helpers' assumption that the recipients cannot overcome the problem on their own and require outside assistance to cope with the difficulty. This is consistent with viewing the recipient as *chronically* dependent on others. When recipients are viewed as sometimes able to cope individually and at other times needing to rely on others' help, we wait for them to request help before we assist them. This help is *responsive* to the recipient's request and implies that dependency is *transient*.

The third characteristic of help which implies transient or chronic dependency is whether it reflects the helper's discrimination between problems that are easily soluble and those that are difficult to solve (Nadler, Harpaz-Gorodeisky, & Ben-David, 2008). Help which is given indiscriminately on both difficult *and* easy problems implies that recipients are unable to cope on their own in most, if not all, problem situations and is therefore consistent with viewing them as chronically dependent. Giving help only on problems that are perceived as difficult is consistent with viewing recipients as transiently dependent.

In summary, help that is *dependency-oriented*, *assumptive*, and *non-discriminating* reflects the helper's view that the recipient is chronically dependent, whereas help that is *autonomy-oriented*, *responsive*, and *discriminating* reflects the helper's view that the recipient's dependency is transient.

Implications of the Threat to Self-Esteem Model of Reactions to Receiving Help and Chronic vs. Transient Dependency for Real-World Helping

Threat to recipients' self-esteem has been invoked to explain the underutilization of helping resources by people in need (Fischer, Winer, & Abramowitz, 1983). Such underutilization of needed help is likely to prolong recipients' suffering and reduce their well-being overall. Epidemiological studies repeatedly find that most adults with mental health disorders do not seek professional help to ease their sufferings (e.g., Montjabi, Olfson, & Mechanic, 2002). For example, half of the people with major depression do not consult a health professional (Henderson, Pollard, Jacobi, & Merkel, 1992). This reluctance to seek assistance for psychological problems has been attributed to the stigma that people in need associate with such help (e.g., Hoyt, Conger, Valde, & Weihs, 1997). Similarly, in educational contexts students often refrain from asking for help because seeking help is viewed as a sign of incompetence (e.g., Butler & Neuman, 1995) and in organizational contexts, employees prefer to avoid seeking help from colleagues or superiors because of concern over saving their own face (e.g., Morrison, 1993). This reluctance to depend on outside help is not without costs. For example, students' willingness to seek outside assistance in order to overcome difficulties in their class-work is viewed as an important coping skill in educational environments in individual (Nadler, Ellis, & Bar, 2003) and team performance (Geller, Ellis, & Nadler, 2008), as assessed by independent supervisors' ratings. This is positively associated with the use of adequate patterns of help seeking (i.e., seeking help when the alternative is either failure or unnecessary dependence).

The emphasis on the threat to self-esteem in receiving help and the distinction between dependency- and autonomy-oriented help suggest two central dilemmas for real-world helping. The first dilemma relates to *help seeking* and considers the over-, under-, and adequate utilization of help, and the second concerns the conditions under which *receiving help* promotes future self-reliance or chronic dependence on others.

The Pitfalls of Under- and Overutilization of Help

Feeling comfortable with dependency may entrench a pattern where recipients habitually seek dependency-oriented help, forfeiting the prospects of self-reliance too readily. This behavioral pattern reflects an *overutilization* of available help. It leads recipients to forego the psychological benefits that are associated with individual achievement. On the other hand, people who are highly sensitive to self-threat may develop a paranoid-like attitude towards being dependent on others' assistance and be unnecessarily obstinate about "doing it alone." This will result in an *underutilization* of necessary assistance. The latter scenario is more likely when help is dependency-oriented or perceived by the recipient as such. Indeed, people who are highly sensitive to the self-threatening aspects of help are more likely to view any assistance as dependency-oriented help.

Our research indicates that situational and personality variables determine the sensitivity of recipients to the self-threatening aspects of receiving help. When the receipt of help carries a high self-threat potential (e.g., the task on which help is needed is ego-relevant), individuals with high self-esteem are more sensitive to the implied threat than those having low self-esteem (Nadler, 1986, 1997, 1998). Further, the underutilization of help may eventually lead to reduced performance or well-being. In support of this, research shows that on tasks that require frequent consultation with other team members, high self-esteem individuals do less well than low self-esteem individuals (Weiss & Knight, 1980). This phenomenon, aptly titled "the utility of humility," has been attributed to the reluctance of those having high self-esteem to receive help from others.

Adequate help seeking consists of relying on others' help only when the alternative is continued hardship, but avoiding help when one can solve the difficulty on one's own. Since such a pattern of help seeking avoids the pitfalls of over- and underutilization, it is likely to be associated with better coping. Research supporting this likelihood shows a curvilinear relationship between how willing employees are to seek help on job-related problems and their overall job performance as rated by their supervisors (Nadler, Ellis, & Bar, 2003). The job performance of employees who seek an average amount of outside help is higher than that of employees who either under- or overutilize outside help. Similar findings have recently been found at the group level (Geller et al., 2008).

The distinction between autonomy- and dependency-oriented help suggests that this curvilinear relationship between help seeking and performance is limited to cases where the type of help requested is dependency-oriented. When help is perceived as autonomy-oriented, a positive relationship should be expected between the amount of help sought and performance, since autonomy-oriented help consists of giving the recipient tools which increase their ability to cope with similar future difficulties. The results of a recent study support the rationale of this hypothesis: High school students filled out a specially constructed questionnaire to assess how they typically dealt with difficulties in their studies. Each participant was scored on their tendency to: (a) Seek dependency-oriented help (i.e., solutions to problems), (b) seek autonomy-oriented help (i.e., tools to solve the problem on their own), or (c) keep on trying to solve the problem on their own. The scores were stable across time and suggest a fixed behavioral preference. The findings indicate that scores on the dependency-oriented and avoidance of help sub-scales were negatively correlated with school performance, as assessed by grade improvement over the course of the school year. This replicates the pattern found in organizational settings by Nadler et al. (2003) and Geller et al. (2008). Yet, consistent with the present suggestion, the amount of autonomy-oriented help sought was positively related with the improvement in students' grades (Harpaz-Gorodeisky, 2008).

How can the ineffective patterns of help seeking that are associated with the belief that "I can't do it on my own" or "I must do it on my own" be modified? One approach that may allow people to escape the habitual patterns of over- or under-utilization is to encourage them to assess their strengths and weaknesses before deciding to choose between dependency-oriented, autonomy-oriented, or no help. This will avert the danger of relying on others' help habitually, or of obstinately refusing to seek help. Moreover, when people with low self-esteem differentiate between situations where they have to rely on dependency-oriented help and those in which they can cope independently or use autonomy-oriented help, they learn that they might be better at coping with difficulties than they originally thought. This may allow them to break the habitual cycle of overutilizing the kinds of help that further reinforce low self-regard.

The Receiving Paradox: Help Encourages Long-Term Dependency for Those Who Need It Most

Another dilemma concerns the way in which recipients of help behave *after they have received help*. People in need of help are likely to be at a low point in their lives, missing out on many positive self-cognitions and expectations. The Threat to Self-esteem model and related research suggests that during such low points, people will welcome dependence on outside help and will not see dependency-oriented help as inconsistent with their self-perceptions. This may further reinforce their relatively negative view of their situation and contribute to the perception that their dependency is chronic and unchangeable. Areas that are central to one's self-esteem (e.g., depressive thoughts and doubts about self-worth or failure on an important and ego-relevant task) are particularly likely to spur this vicious cycle. Thus, the times of greatest need for help may be the least effective contexts for promoting future self-reliance. This phenomenon is labeled the "receiving paradox."

How can the receiving paradox be resolved? How can we transform feelings of low self-regard that make dependency seem permanent into perceptions that one is efficacious enough to transform dependency into self-reliance? One way is by giving people in an acute state of need autonomy-oriented help, which conveys the message that they can achieve self-reliance even in times of hardship. Yet, the extension of autonomy-oriented help during an acute state of need may clash with the helper's wish to do everything possible to resolve the recipient's source of pain and suffering. Thus, it is not only recipients who must avoid the habitual overutilization of help, even when they do not perceive themselves as part of the solution. Helpers must do the same and correctly assess the strengths of those who need their help, providing assistance that capitalizes on these strengths even when the state of need is compellingly high.

Intergroup Helping as Status Relations: Helping Relations, Power Relations, and Social Change

Similar to the Threat to Self-esteem model of receiving help, the Intergroup Helping as Status Relations model (IHSR) emphasizes the consistency between dependency, recipient expectations, and the transient or chronic nature of helping relations. Specifically, the IHSR model centers on the ways in which groups create, maintain, or challenge status relations through helping relations (Nadler, 2002). It is based on an integration between the basic tenets of the Threat to Self-esteem model, of reactions to help (Nadler & Fisher, 1986), with key concepts from the Social Identity perspective on intergroup relations (Turner & Reynolds, 2001). Based on Self-Categorization theory, it suggests that when the group memberships of the helper and the recipient are salient, the helping interaction is an intergroup interaction and must be analyzed by the appropriate conceptual tools. Consistent with the Threat to Self-esteem approach, it suggests that giving help to an out-group results in high status for the in-group and that dependency on the out-group's help is associated with lower status. The model and the evidence that supports it are reviewed by Halabi and Nadler in Chapter 6 in the present volume and I shall therefore limit myself to reviewing its key postulates. These are needed to consider the implications of the model for helping relations between groups in the real world.

The IHSR model suggests that the extension of dependency-oriented help to an out-group establishes the higher relative status of the in-group. The repeated willingness of the group in need to seek and receive such help is a behavioral affirmation of its relative low status and chronic dependency. Moreover, such a repeated unidirectional flow of dependency-oriented assistance from the higher to the lower status group reinforces the unequal social hierarchy. Consistent with social identity theory's emphasis on the *structural characteristic* of the *security* of the status hierarchy as a determinant of intergroup relations, the model suggests that such habitual top-down helping relations characterize secure status hierarchies (i.e., hierarchies that are perceived by interactants as stable and legitimate). As an example one may think of helping relations between men and women in a patriarchal society, where the dominance of men over women is regarded as both stable and legitimate. In this context men are expected to protect women and to take care of their material needs, and women, in turn, are expected to welcome and be appreciative of this dependence on men.

Intergroup helping relations are "stormier" when the status hierarchy is viewed as insecure (i.e., perceived as unstable and/or illegitimate). Under these conditions members of the low-status group view their inequality as changeable and are motivated to change the unequal status quo. Dependency on the high-status group is inconsistent with this motivation and members of low-status groups are expected to be unwilling to seek or receive dependency-oriented help from the high-status group; because they view their dependency as transient, they will welcome only autonomy-oriented help. The corollary to this is that insecure status hierarchies are threatening to the high-status group's social advantage. Members of the high-status group are expected to respond by trying to maintain their in-group's positive distinctiveness – by providing help which reinforces the low-status group's chronic dependency (i.e., dependency-oriented, assumptive, and undiscriminating help; cf. Nadler, Halabi, & Harpaz-Gorodeisky, 2009).

This view of helping relations, which incorporates power dynamics that are affected by the perceived legitimacy and changeability of existing inequality and the nature of the helping interaction itself (i.e., help that implies chronic or transient dependency), has important applied implications for intergroup relations. Key among these is the way in which helping relations affect and are affected by processes of social change. I shall outline these implications and illustrate their importance by using three real-world examples of intergroup helping relations during times of social change.

Implications for Real-World Helping: Social Change and Intergroup Helping

Intergroup helping relations in secure status hierarchies are mechanisms that reinforce the unequal status quo because they legitimize social inequality. When the advantaged group caters to the needs of the disadvantaged group its dominance is no longer an expression of the naked desire to maintain power and privilege. Instead, such advantage has an element of moral responsibility. Dominance becomes a tool in the service of caring and is therefore more legitimate. The disadvantaged group's receptivity towards such unidirectional helping reinforces the legitimacy of the unequal status quo. The chronic dependency of the low-status group imbues social inequality with moral justification and renders it more resistant to change. In previous centuries such a unidirectional flow of assistance has characterized relations between colonial powers and indigenous populations, men and women, and the "haves" and "have-nots" within societies.

Intergroup helping relations take on a different shape during times of social change. The unwillingness of the low-status group to receive dependency-oriented assistance may be the first sign that it views its inequality as illegitimate. The high-status group is likely to be angered when its generosity is spurned. From this perspective, times of social change are a fertile ground for social tensions around issues of intergroup helping. The advantaged group is motivated to defend its position by maintaining the low-status group's chronic dependency on its help and the disadvantaged group views such assistance as seeking to reinforce its inferiority. In a recent experiment we obtained support for the hypothesis that in the face of information indicating social change, advantaged groups will seek to maintain their dominance by giving substantial dependency-oriented help to the low-status group (Nadler, Harpaz-Gorodeisky, & Ben-David, 2008). In the chapter by Halabi and Nadler in the present volume (Chapter 6), we describe the evidence that under similar conditions low-status groups seek to break the cycle of chronic dependency by refusing to seek or receive help from the high-status group (Nadler & Halabi, 2006).

Another way in which the low-status group may respond to offers of help from the high-status group during times of change is by redefining the helping relationship to imply transient rather than chronic dependency. If the high-status group is oblivious to these motivations for social change and continues to assert its dominance through repeated efforts to give help which has the characteristics of chronic dependency, helping is likely to poison intergroup relations. Under these conditions, what the dominant group views as an expression of goodwill will be regarded by the disadvantaged group as a manipulative ploy intended to maintain the high-status group's dominance.

There are numerous real-world examples for these social dynamics of intergroup helping; I shall briefly illustrate three of them. The first are affirmative action programs that aim to expedite social equality by providing necessary opportunities to members of disadvantaged groups (e.g., women and African Americans). Although minorities tend to be in favor of such programs (Arthur, Doverspike, & Fuentes, 1992) and these programs have been successful in promoting equality in various life domains such as education and the workplace, a number of observers have noted that giving on the basis of recipients' group affiliation positions members of low-status groups as dependent and inferior (e.g., Heilman, 1996). In terms of the present analysis such giving constitutes *assumptive* help that is relatively *non-responsive to the recipient's actual need* and reinforces the view that recipients are chronically dependent on the high-status group. In the context of change towards greater equality, this is inconsistent with the motivation of the low-status group for equality and may therefore fuel suspicion about the helpers' intentions and reluctance to participate in such programs. The cost of such perceptions in terms of increased social tensions is high. A greater awareness of these aspects of giving during times of change will ameliorate some of the costs.

Another example is peace-building projects where former adversaries cooperate to achieve common goals in spheres of life that are important to both of them, such as agriculture, medicine, or transportation. Cooperation on common goals is expected to increase trust and mutual acceptance between parties (cf. Lederach, 1997; Nadler, 2002). Yet, viewed from the present perspective, such projects carried out by differentially powerful parties represent helping interactions.

The peace-building projects between Israelis and Palestinians that were initiated after the signing of the Oslo peace accords in 1993 serve as an example. It has been suggested that some of the difficulties these projects came up against were that they constituted a helping interaction between differentially powerful groups (Nadler & Saguy, 2004). In many projects in various life domains (e.g., computer technology, medical know-how) Israelis were the more advantaged party and considered themselves as generous benefactors. Palestinians viewed such generosity as a paternalistic attempt by their adversaries to assert their advantage. Their reactions were taken by Israelis as a sign that the other side did not really want to move beyond conflict to coexistence. In fact, what the more advantaged party saw as benevolent cooperation was perceived by the less advantaged party as humiliating dependency which was to be avoided (Nadler & Saguy, 2004). It is not suggested that this was the cause for the seeming failure of the Oslo accords. Yet, these dynamics demonstrate that when the power dimension of intergroup helping is not considered, efforts to build bridges of trust and cooperation may turn into sources of animosity and suspicion (cf. also Belloni, 2001 and Byrne, 2001 for discussions of similar processes in the Balkans and Northern Ireland, respectively).

A third example of giving by the powerful to the powerless during times of social change is the assistance given by the West to HIV-stricken nations in Africa. A recent analysis maintains that these efforts are seen to encourage chronic dependency and are therefore rejected or ignored by the receiving societies (Fisher, Nadler, Little, & Saguy, 2008). This assistance takes the form of dependency-oriented help. It consists of giving medicines rather than the know-how to produce them or to implement behavioral changes that will avert their need. Although these programs saved lives and were motivated by genuine caring and goodwill, they were designed in a manner that did not empower recipients, but rather encouraged a state of chronic dependency. Such programs, designed by the helper, may have done more to consider the unique cultural and social context of the recipient (Fisher, Cornman, Norton, & Fisher, 2006). Had they been better designed they could have saved more lives.

Consistent with the IHSR model's emphasis on the security of status relations, such a unidirectional downward flow of dependency-oriented help from rich Western countries to impoverished HIV-stricken nations in Africa may have been more palatable to recipients during colonial times, when the inferior status of indigenous peoples was viewed as stable and legitimate. The superior knowledge and resources of the colonial powers was taken for granted as "how things are, and ought to be." This is not true at the beginning of the 21st century. People in Africa no longer view the superiority of the West as legitimate. They aspire to destabilize the unequal hierarchy by gaining greater equality and independence. Under these conditions of relatively insecure status relations, assistance which has the ingredients of chronic dependency produces tensions which may detract from the effectiveness of help.

How to Overcome Inequality in Intergroup Helping

Negotiating helping relations

How can the implications of inequality that are associated with intergroup helping during times of social change be modified? Part of the answer is provided by distinguishing between chronic and transient dependency. Operationally, assistance that is autonomy-oriented, non-assumptive, and responsive to the real needs of recipients is empowering. Further, helping projects between groups need to be conceptualized as bilateral common projects that are designed jointly by donor and recipient rather than as unilateral helping projects that are implemented by a more powerful and knowledgeable benefactor. A relevant distinction in this respect is that between *didactic* and *negotiating* help-seeking styles (Asser, 1978). This distinction is close in meaning to the one between seeking autonomy- or dependency-oriented help but adds an important behavioral dimension: The didactic style of help seeking consists of pursuing a solution to the problem, while in the negotiating style, helping arrangements are achieved collaboratively with the helper. In a negotiating style the recipient is an equal partner rather than a dependent recipient of help. It is an empowering and equalizing experience for the party in need and is likely to result in future independence and more positive feelings of self-worth.

Common in-group identity and intergroup helping

Another way of constructing intergroup helping relations that go beyond status concerns is by highlighting the common identity between the helper and the recipient groups. Research and theory within the Common In-group Identity model suggests that status concerns and the motivation for positive in-group distinctiveness are lower when members of the in-group and out-group view themselves as sharing an overarching common identity (Gaertner & Dovidio, 2000). Under these conditions group members exhibit less devaluation of the out-group (Anastasio, Bachman, Gaertner, & Dovidio, 1997) and are more willing to provide the out-group with help (Dovidio, Gaertner, Validzic, Matoka, Johnson, & Frazier, 1997). This suggests that when helper and recipient groups are induced to share a common group identity, intergroup helping is governed less by status concerns. The high-status group does not engage in defensive helping aimed at maintaining its advantaged status (i.e., giving dependency-oriented help) and dependency on the out-group when the status hierarchy is insecure is not inconsistent with the low-status group's motivation for equality with the out-group.

A recent experiment supports this hypothesis (Nadler, Harpaz-Gorodeisky, & Ben-David, 2008). In one of the experimental conditions, members of a high-status group were given the opportunity to provide help to a low-status out-group when the status relationship between them was presented as either *stable* or *unstable*, and when either both groups' *common identity* or the *in-group's identity* was made salient. Compared to all other experimental cells, under these circumstances, members of the high-status group who had been told that the status gap with the out-group was narrowing (unstable status condition) gave the highest amount of autonomy-oriented help to the low-status group. Put differently, under the condition of common in-group identity, members of a higher status group provided the lower status group with the type of assistance (i.e., autonomy-oriented help) that encouraged future independence and the eventual closing of the status gap. When only the identity of the higher status group was made salient and when status relations were said to be unstable, members of the higher status group gave the most dependency-oriented help to the lower status out-group. Such helping is defensive in that it aims to defend against threats to group identity by reinforcing the dependency of the source of this threat (i.e., the low-status out-group).

The integration of the IHSR model with the assertions of the Common In-Group Identity model has a number of real-world implications. It suggests that in social settings where social groups are separate yet share a common identity, helping relations will be driven by a concern for the recipient's future independence and equality and not by the motivation to defend the in-group's status. Thus, for example, helping relations between two European nations will be relatively free of status concerns when the parties' common European identity is made salient. Another example is what has been labeled elsewhere "earthquake diplomacy" (Keridis, 2006). This refers to assistance given by a nation to an adversary under the conditions of a massive natural disaster. In the 1990s Greece, an adversary of Turkey, came to the aid of its historical enemy following a massive earthquake. The relations between these two adversaries have seen much improvement since that time. An interpretation derived from the present analysis is that as a consequence of a massive natural disaster both victims and bystanders share, however briefly, the common identity of human beings vulnerable to the mercy of random natural catastrophes. This perception of a common identity shifts the adversaries' perspective from a prevailing mode of competition to a mode that is more inclusive and tolerant. This changed perspective represents a window of opportunity. If seized upon, intergroup relations may undergo a relatively enduring positive change.

The discussion in the previous sections focused on intergroup helping relations. Yet, the same processes apply to interpersonal helping relations. Thus, for example, the concept of common group identity also applies in organizational contexts when two individuals with different resources and knowledge need to work together to further a team project. The logic of the preceding discussion indicates that the induction of a salient organizational identity common to both interactants will disarm the power and status implications of the helping interaction between them.

Power and Helping: Concluding Comments

The Threat to Self-Esteem model of receiving help and the model of Intergroup Helping as Status Relations share common elements. Both aver that a key element in determining how status considerations will shape interpersonal and intergroup helping relations is the set of expectations held by the recipient and the helper in the helping scenario. If recipients expect to become dependent on the assistance of their helpers, and helpers view themselves as obliged to care for recipients, then helping relations will be relatively frictionless. One party gives and the other is expected to appreciatively receive. These are relations within a secure hierarchy that is reinforced by the unidirectional flow of assistance. The extension or receipt of help conforms to expectations and is a behavioral affirmation that the unequal hierarchy is not only "the way things are and will be" (i.e., stable) but also "how they ought to be" (i.e., legitimate). Under such conditions the strong gives patronage to the weak, who reciprocates in submission and loyalty. On interpersonal and intergroup levels, such a helping relationship justifies the existing social system.

What precipitates the expectation that one is chronically dependent on others? From an interpersonal perspective this may be the result of personal disposition such as low self-esteem. At the intergroup level, cultural values and social norms constitute the source of such expectations. When dependency is viewed as chronic, low self-esteem individuals or members of low-status groups run the danger of overutilizing existing sources of help. This prevents them from achieving self-reliance and feeds back into the vicious cycle of a legitimate inequality. Changes in the perceived "justice" and "inevitability" (i.e., legitimacy and stability, respectively) of this inequality bring about immediate changes in helping relations. At the interpersonal level this can occur because the person has gained self-confidence or has learned the important distinction between things she can accomplish on her own and those she cannot. At the intergroup level such changes are likely to be the outcome of changes in social values and societal beliefs.

An important aspect of these helping dynamics is the nature of the help provided. Some forms of help reinforce the recipient's belief that he is not chronically dependent. On the interpersonal and intergroup levels the giving of autonomy-oriented help feeds the perception that one can control one's fate and regain self-reliance. Such help, which highlights the transient nature of dependency, is likely to instigate a positive cycle of expectations. It will encourage the recipient to view himself as able to become independent, lead him to invest in self-help efforts to regain independence, and, if successful, this will translate into deeper and more enduring perceptions of positive self-worth.

Finally, helping relations can take the form of unilateral action carried out by the helper or of a joint project that is first negotiated by the helper and the recipient. The preceding discussion suggests that the status concerns that are inherent in interpersonal and intergroup helping will be lower when the interactants adopt the second approach. A joint discussion of this kind may also promote a common in-group identity representation of the relationship between the helper and the recipient, which further reduces the negative aspects that can potentially impair helping relations.

I want to conclude by noting that this analysis does not hold that helping relations need to be looked at only through the prism of power and status. As decades of research indicate, people often extend help because they feel empathy in the face of the suffering of other human beings and not because they seek to assert their dominance. Also, people help out-group members not only because they aim to defend against threats to in-group status. When people view out-group members as sharing a common human essence with the in-group they perceive them as relatively similar to the in-group and this facilitates empathy-based helping (Stürmer, Snyder, Kropp, & Siem, 2006; Stürmer & Snyder, Chapter 2 in the present volume). The present chapter suggests that in order to better understand the complex social phenomenon of helping relations we need to view helping as a dynamic of social relationships rather than as a behavior that is straightforward and incontrovertibly beneficent. Appreciating the complex nature of the relationships between helpers and recipients of help will enable us to construct helping relations in a way that promotes equality and respect for all the involved parties.

15

Beyond Help
A Social Psychology of Collective Solidarity and Social Cohesion

Stephen Reicher and S. Alexander Haslam

Introduction: Beyond Help

Our focus in this chapter is both narrower and broader than the topic of helping. It is narrower in the sense that we are interested in just one of the many ways in which people act to secure benefit for others – often at considerable costs to themselves. That is, our specific concern is with *in-group* helping (which, for reasons that we shall explain in due course, we will term social solidarity). It is broader in the sense that solidarity, we argue, is but one (albeit crucial) link in a cycle of processes which shape the creation and cohesion of social groups in our society. In this sense, we regard the topic of helping as integral to issues that are of foundational importance not only to the well-being of particular individuals (or groups) but also to the very possibility of society, and not only for the discipline of psychology but also for the social sciences in general. Indeed, it represents a domain where psychologists can engage with other social sciences and where we can demonstrate how and why a psychological level of analysis is essential to any overall understanding of social life.

There is some irony in claiming broad social relevance through treating helping as a collective phenomenon. After all there is a strong and general tendency in social psychology to view group phenomena as fundamentally asocial: in the group we lose our sense of social responsibility and social constraints upon our behavior no longer apply (Le Bon, 1895/1947; Zimbardo, 1969; for a critique, see Reicher, 2001). This tendency is well reflected in the helping literature through the classic work on bystander intervention (or, rather, bystander *non*-intervention). Building on the iconic murder of Kitty Genovese in which, we are told, 38 witnesses watched a young woman being attacked and murdered and did absolutely nothing, Latané and Darley's "bystander effect" suggests that company inhibits helping and that, the larger the group, the lower the probability that anyone will intervene (Latané & Darley, 1970; Latané & Nida, 1981).

From this perspective, the way to promote helping is to individuate people and the explanation of when and why particular people offer help must lie in their distinctive individuality. The more extreme the situation is, the more helping depends upon personal heroism. Thus, a number of authors have sought to distil the qualities which led certain remarkable individuals to risk their own lives in order to save others from the Nazi Holocaust (Baron, 1985/6; Oliner & Oliner, 1992; Tec, 1986). As the Oliners have put it, their aim is to isolate the "altruistic personality."

Yet the seemingly secure story of Kitty Genovese – which can be recited by almost any first year psychology student – is built on foundations of sand. Close analysis of primary sources (as opposed to media reports weeks after the event) reveals that no one saw Kitty Genovese as she was murdered, few saw her being attacked, and of those who did, several did try to alert the police (Manning, Levine, & Collins, 2007). As for the experimental evidence, it is much more mixed than is usually assumed. Certainly, there are cases where more bystanders means less intervention. But not always. Sometimes people intervene as much or even more in company than when alone (Bryan & Test, 1967; Darley, Lewis, & Teger, 1973; Horowitz, 1971; Rutkowski, Gruder, & Romer, 1983; Levine & Cassidy, Chapter 11 this volume).

In order to explain this variability, it seems important to make a distinction between a *physical* group – a set of people who are physically co-present – and a *psychological* group – a set of people who share a common sense of "we-ness" or social identity (Turner, 1982, 1991; Turner, Hogg, Oakes, Reicher, & Wetherell, 1987). Psychological group membership transforms the relationship between people such that what matters is no longer who people are as individuals but rather which category they belong to – notably "us" or "them." It equally transforms the bases upon which they behave. People do not lose constraint in such groups, rather they are constrained by collective norms rather than personal values.

In subsequent sections, we will discuss in more detail the *ways* in which psychological group membership links to helping behavior including the role of norms in helping. For now, we simply want to note that the mere fact of such a link changes the nature, the scope, and the significance of the phenomenon. First, while literature at the individual level is highly diverse, there is often an emphasis on

15 | Beyond Help 291

helping as direct intervention at the moment of need. Open most major social psychology textbooks and, if they don't start with the Genovese story, they will preface their reviews of helping with an anecdote about strangers going out of their way to assist a stranded passenger (Baron, Byrne, & Branscombe, 2006), or helping an unknown mother by calming her frightened child (Baron & Byrne, 2004), or else the heroic individuals who lost their lives while guiding others to safety from the Twin Towers during 9/11 (Aronson, Wilson, & Akert, 2005). At a collective level, however, the paradigm tends to have a different emphasis. On the one hand, it centers less on helpers giving succor to sufferers in a context of asymmetrical need. It focuses more on fellow group members in a context of mutual need. On the other hand, it centers less on directly addressing a witnessed need and more on indirectly addressing a generalized need. Collective helping has more to do with participating in a campaign against homophobia than stepping in to defend a gay person from a racist attack; with objecting to racist government policies rather than sheltering an asylum seeker from deportation. The actions are often less dramatic, but, by that very token, far more frequent and widespread. They are the stuff of everyday life.

Second, then, although, at the collective level, the interventions of any given person may be much more banal than at the individual level, their combined effect is likely to be far greater. However heroic individual Holocaust rescuers might have been, in the end they made little difference to the "final solution." By contrast, mass mobilizations – an aggregation of many smaller contributions – largely stopped deportations to the death camps in a number of countries: Denmark, Finland, and Bulgaria (Ben-Yakov, 1990; Cohen & Assa, 1977; Gilbert, 1985; see also Reicher, Cassidy, Wolpert, Hopkins, & Levine, 2006).

If we want to understand rescue, then, we may do better to turn our gaze from the heroic but sporadic to the (relatively) mundane. The same is true of less extreme circumstances. The nature of the society we live in has little to do with whether people occasionally make great sacrifices for others. It is more to do with the presence or absence of countless small, often unnoticed acts of civility.

Third, this combination of banality at the level of the single actor and consequentiality at the aggregated collective level suggests that we may be getting at something of basic significance in the relationship between the individual and society. In the same way that Billig (1995) argues that the real importance of nationalism and the conditions of national being are not to be found in their occasional passionate manifestations but rather in the everyday manner that we presuppose a national framework for talking about everything from wars to the weather, so we suggest that our very ability to cohere in any form of social organization arises out of the thousand little acts of support – whether it be giving space to oncoming pedestrians or paying our taxes – that we perform every day.

Let us be more concrete. At the moment, one of us (Reicher) is involved in the study of the Magh Mela in Allahabad (also known as Prayag), North India. It is a Hindu festival that takes place at the confluence of the Ganges and Yamuna rivers for a month at the start of every year. In many ways it is the most exotic of events. With its legions of holy men, its processions of gurus protected by babu nagas who have renounced the world and live naked coated in ash, it fulfils almost every orientalist fantasy (Said, 1988). Yet perhaps even more remarkable is the fact that this vast city suddenly comes into being for the month and that it works as a largely harmonious and cohesive community. Certainly, this has much to do with the year-round organization by the Mela authorities, local government and police. But it has just as much to do with the ordinary courtesies that people show to each other, to the fact that they support each other if ill or lost, to the fact that as they wait they do so without pushing – sometimes for many hours – to reach the holy bathing sites (Cassidy, Hopkins, Levine, Pandey, Reicher, & Singh, 2007). If we want to understand how this vast peripatetic city can exist we need to understand how these acts come about and, in turn, what further consequences they bring about.

It is in order to emphasize our interest in these multiple, additive, reciprocal acts of support – often singly banal but socially consequential in combination – that we use the term "solidarity" rather than helping. There is, of course, a danger that we have leapt from one terminological frying pan into another terminological fire by using a term which has so many diverse meanings and resonances across the social sciences and the world of politics. Nonetheless, we consider this danger to be outweighed by the advantages of a language that necessarily engages psychology with the wider context and which requires us to address the societal implications of action. We also consider that the danger is diminished not only by specifying, as above, what we mean by "solidarity," but also by specifying its antecedents and its consequences. That is, what are the psychological roots of solidarity and how does solidarity fit into the way in which social categories are produced and reproduced? These are the questions we will now try to address.

Social Identity, Collective Solidarity, and Co-Action

We have already provided a partial answer to the first question: solidarity is rooted in psychological group membership. As promised, however, we now need to explain exactly how the two are related. In order to do so we will draw on research which has also been alluded to above: that which examines the rescue of Bulgarian Jewry (Reicher et al., 2006). Of all the interventions against the Holocaust, this is possibly the most remarkable. It was the sole example, in an area under Axis control, where a population stopped Nazi deportations dead in their tracks.

When we examined the key texts which were used to mobilize the Bulgarian population to contribute to this rescue, three core arguments could be found. The first was normative. National leaders and key opinion makers repeatedly asserted that Bulgarian identity is centered on opposition to oppression. According to the accounts that these people promulgated, the nation arose by throwing off the Turkish yoke and hence it was asserted that Bulgarians have an inherent disposition to fight off oppressors whoever they are and whoever their victims might be.

The effectiveness of such arguments is corroborated by a range of evidence which shows the importance of social identity content for the ways in which group members behave (see Reicher & Hopkins, 2001; Turner, 1991). Indeed, far from group members being generically predisposed to treat out-groups negatively, where in-group norms are prosocial, groups may actually compete to act more positively towards the other (Jetten, Spears, & Manstead, 1996). This idea is expressed somewhat more poetically by Martin Luther King in his famous 1968 sermon on the "drum major instinct." In this, King notes that groups strive to be best and that, often, this can result in conflict and war. But then, drawing on the Southern Baptist ideology that informed both his identity as a clergyman and as a civil rights leader, he asked:

> [Jesus] said in substance, "Oh, I see, you want to be first. You want to be great. You want to be important. You want to be significant. Well, you ought to be. If you're going to be my disciple, you must be." But he reordered priorities. And he said, "Yes, don't give up this instinct. It's a good instinct if you use it right. It's a good instinct if you don't distort it and pervert it. Don't give it up. Keep feeling the need for

being important. Keep feeling the need for being first. But I want you to be first in love. I want you to be first in moral excellence. I want you to be first in generosity. That is what I want you to do." (from www.stanford.edu/group/King/publications/sermons/ 680204.000_Drum_Major_Instinct.html)

Moving on, the second argument in the Bulgarian texts was based on reputational concerns. That is, it was argued that a failure to challenge the deportations would reflect badly on Bulgarians and undermine their claims to be part of the family of (civilized) nations in the postwar period. Not surprisingly, this argument was more central in stopping the second attempt by the Germans to send Jews to the death camps. This took place in 1943 (the first attempt was in 1941) when the tide of the war was turning against the Nazis.

Further experimental research has shed light on the way in which reputational concerns can influence solidarity in more everyday circumstances. Thus Hopkins, Reicher, Harrison, Cassidy, Bull, and Levine (2007) have shown that, when it is made salient to Scots that the English consider them to be mean, they increase the level of support they give to members of a *third* out-group (the Welsh) rather than to in-group members. It appears that they do this because supporting in-group members is not diagnostic of generosity (it might be just a matter of helping one's own) whereas supporting out-group members is.

If normative processes can lead to support for in-group *and* out-group members, and if reputational processes can lead to support for out-group members *more than* in-group members, the Bulgarian example points to a third set of social identity processes that affect support for in-group members *rather than* out-group members. Indeed, it suggests that in-group inclusion may, in and of itself, increase support. Thus, one of the most remarkable features of the texts that relate to this period in history is that they only very rarely referred to the Jewish population as such but rather referred to them as a "national minority" or by some other term which stressed their Bulgarian identity. Indeed, even where the term "Jew" was used, it was in order to make explicit just how Bulgarian these people were. For instance, in one particularly poetic speech, Todor Polakov (a Communist parliamentarian) declared in the National Assembly:

> Bulgaria's Jews ... speak and think in Bulgarian, have fashioned their style of thinking and their feelings after Botev, Vazov, Pencho, Slaveikov, Yavorov, etc. They sing Bulgarian songs and tell Bulgarian stories. Their private selves are modelled on ours – in the street, on our playing fields,

at school, in the barracks, in workshops and factories, in the mountains and the fields, our sufferings are their sufferings, our joys their joys too. (Quoted in Todorov, 2001)

The significance of these processes is again underlined by further experimental evidence (Levine, Prosser, Evans, & Reicher, 2005). Supporters of Manchester United football team had their team's identity made salient and then witnessed someone wearing either a Manchester United shirt, a Liverpool shirt (a rival team), or a non-football shirt fall over and hurt themselves. They intervened to help the first of these people but generally ignored the other two. In a second condition, also involving Manchester United supporters, participants had their identity as football fans made salient. Again they saw someone wearing one of the three different shirts take a tumble. This time there was helping when the victim wore either the Manchester United or the Liverpool shirt, but not when the ordinary shirt was worn.

This study makes two important points that accord well with the general body of theorizing informed by social identity and self-categorization theories (e.g., Tajfel & Turner, 1979; Turner et al., 1987, 1994; see also Oakes, Haslam, & Turner, 1994). First, there is a general tendency for people to be concerned for the welfare of fellow in-group members and hence to support them. That is, insofar as others form part of a common "we" then a benefit to them is a benefit to one's (collective) self. Second, though, the boundaries of our in-groups are flexible and the wider the boundaries are the more people we will help. Indeed, the very same people, who are ignored under one condition, are supported under another more inclusive definition of the in-group.

There is by now a range of work which makes a similar point: we generally help people to the extent that they are incorporated in the in-group (Cialdini, Brown, Lewis, Luce, & Neuberg, 1997; Dovidio, Gaertner, Validizic, Matoka, Johnson, & Frazier, 1997; Dovidio, Piliavin, Gaertner, Schroeder, & Clark, 1991; Levine, Cassidy, Brazier, & Reicher, 2002; Piliavin, Dovidio, Gaertner, & Clark, 1981; Piliavin, Rodin, & Piliavin, 1969). This is not to say that they will always do so – there may, for instance, be specific instances of groups whose norms specify that group members should stand on their own two feet and be self-reliant (although it is arguable that, in such cases, group members do still wish to help each other but believe that is best done by *non*-intervention). Equally, we do not suggest that in-group members will always be helped *more* than out-group members. Indeed, we have already given an example from our own research where reputational considerations lead to out-group members being helped more than in-group members (Hopkins et al., 2007; see also Dutton & Lake, 1973). What we do suggest, however, in common with several others in this volume, is that there are differences in the processes that underlie in-group and out-group helping, and moreover that these differences render support for the in-group (but not the out-group) as the default case. Thus, we are generically concerned for and empathize with fellow group members, and, unless there are specific and explicit norms to the contrary, will provide them with support. However, when it comes to out-group members, there is no such generic concern, and for help to occur we have either to be specifically attracted to particular others (Stürmer, Snyder, & Omoto, 2005), to have particular strategic reasons for wishing to be seen to help others (Hopkins et al., 2007), or else to have specific and explicit norms for helping them (Reicher et al., 2005). In sum, we help in-group members unless there are exceptional reasons for not doing so; we only help out-group members where there are situated reasons for doing so.

However, if we only look to the helping literature for evidence of the ways in which group membership impacts on the support we give to others, we only scratch the surface of a much wider phenomenon. Indeed, mutual support takes us to the very core of what it means to be a social group. As such, it involves a whole series of processes which, conventionally, have not been seen as linked with each other or with matters of helping/solidarity.

We can approach these matters by comparing how we might respond to the two questions: "Should we support them?" and "Should we support us?" The former is clearly a meaningful enquiry. Sometimes we might respond in the affirmative and sometimes we might answer in the negative. However, the second question appears somewhat bizarre. It seems superfluous even to ask, for giving and receiving support from each other would seem to be part-and-parcel of the very nature of being "us." This intuition is expressed more formally in the core claim of self-categorization theory that social identity is the psychological mechanism that makes group behavior possible (Turner, 1982; Turner et al., 1987).

There are two ways of interpreting this statement, and the difference between them is important. One is to suggest that the salience of a given social identity (say, being a conservative) leads people to activate a common set of category-based representations ("I value tradition and order") which in turns leads to shared thoughts and actions. This approach, we believe, is a simplistic misreading of self-categorization theory. It gives rise to a somewhat mechanical view of the group in which there is little space for individual deliberation or discussion between people (see Postmes & Jetten, 2006). Indeed, at the extreme, it seems to suggest that group members are akin to monads in a strange silent universe who may become aligned through a coincidence of internal processes, but who never talk to each other, never argue with each other, and never try to persuade each other (see Condor, 1996).

The other approach is to argue that the salience of social identity invokes a set of processes which impact upon intra- and interpersonal phenomena in such a way as to produce the conditions of coordinated joint action. Thus the group should not be counterposed to the individual, nor should a focus on group behavior mean taking the focus off interpersonal interactions. Quite the opposite in fact: group processes work through their impact on individuals and hence we discover these processes by looking at what individuals do. Or rather, to be more precise, we discover these processes by investigating the different ways that people act singly and jointly as a function of whether or not social identity is salient. A key aspect of these processes, and a key condition of joint action, concerns the several ways in which salient social identities transform strangers into intimates and thereby lead them to support each other. It is through an analysis of this transformation that the integral link between shared social identification and mutual solidarity becomes apparent.

Even at the most basic level, that of physical intimacy, social identity exerts a powerful effect. By way of illustration, think first of the experience of being in a crowded place – say a train compartment – where, psychologically, people think and experience events as individuals. Here, the greater the density the worse the experience; the smells of others and the feelings as they brush up against you are something deeply aversive. Now contrast this with another crowd – say at a football match – where people are fellow group members. Here, a sparse crowd is a source of disappointment, and when a goal is scored one is prone to embrace and dance with complete (and often unsavory) strangers. Thus, where others are in-group members we both desire greater physical proximity and overcome the feelings of sensual disgust which normally keep us apart.

As concerns the former claim concerning proximity preferences, we (Reicher) are currently conducting studies which simply divide people into two groups on minimal grounds (e.g., overestimating or underestimating the number of dots in a complex pattern; after Tajfel, Billig, Bundy, & Flament, 1971), then tell them that they will be talking either to an in-group member or an out-group member and that they should arrange the chairs so that they feel comfortable. In these experiments the out-group member tends to be placed about 20 percent further away than the in-group member (Novelli, Drury, Reicher, & Fenn, 2007).

As concerns the latter claim about disgust, there is ample anthropological evidence to show that aversion derives from the intrusion of the out-group "other" into our own sensual space (for a white racist, say, a black waiter's thumb in the soup). Historically, psychologists have also been aware of the fact that intergroup relations are bound up with, and may even be regulated by, feelings of disgust (e.g., Allport, 1954a). It is striking, for instance, how often the racist will complain about "their smell" or "the stench of their food." However, in recent times, the focus on this embodied dimension of group processes has fallen away and there is little or no systematic research into the way that disgust for the touch or odor of others may be moderated by shared social identification. This is certainly an area crying out for investigation.

There has, however, been a wealth of research on other dimensions of our relations with others which are transformed when others become included as "we." Take, for instance, the work of Haslam, Turner, and colleagues on the way in which consensus is formed in groups (e.g., Haslam, Turner, Oakes, McGarty, & Reynolds, 1998). As this shows, when we see ourselves and others as members of a common group, we have an expectation that we will agree on issues of relevance to the group (see also Abrams, Wetherell, Cochrane, Hogg, & Turner, 1990; Turner, 1991). This leads us to pick up on points of accord in our conversations with other members such that, if they say some things on which we concur and others on which we do not, we will base our response on the former rather than the latter. That is to say, social identification leads people to support the views of other group members and this leads to a progressive convergence of views. Such is the process of *consensualization*. Without shared group membership there is no expectation of agreement, no tendency to prioritize accord over discord, no tendency to support for the views of others, no necessary convergence – in short, no progress towards consensus.

The expectation of agreement is of importance in more respects than actual agreement alone. If we feel that we will share core beliefs and values with others, we are more likely to respect them and also to trust them. It also makes us more able to cooperate with them since we can be confident that our efforts will be devoted to bringing about the same ends (for reviews of the relevant literature, see Haslam, 2001;

Hogg & Terry, 2001; Tyler & Blader, 2000). In these various ways, then, social identity creates spontaneous forms of mutual social support and social organization. However, there is one further factor which raises this to another level: leadership.

Over recent years, leadership research – relatively neglected in social psychology as opposed to organizational and management disciplines – has been reinvigorated by a social identity approach (for overviews, see Haslam, Reicher, & Platow, in press; Hogg, 2001; Reicher, Haslam, & Hopkins, 2005; Reicher, Haslam, & Platow, 2007; Turner & Haslam, 2001; van Knippenberg & Hogg, 2004). The core argument here is that leadership does not center around the personality of individuals and it is not founded on an interpersonal relationship between leaders and led. Rather, it is a social relationship between leaders and led which is premised on a joint group membership. We heed a leader because he or she can represent what "we" believe in. Hence leaders, however great their skills, need to be firmly seen as "one of us" so that we can be confident that they will apply those skills in order to achieve what we consider valuable – in technical terms, leaders need to reflect the group prototype.

This has been the focus of much of the work in this area: when someone is seen as prototypical, we will be more likely to endorse them as leader, more likely to approve of their ideas, more likely to put effort into supporting their plans and more likely to support each other in realizing these plans (e.g., Haslam & Platow, 2001; Hogg, 2001; Platow, Hoar, Reid, Harley, & Morrison, 1997). Yet it is important to take the argument back a step: in order to represent the group prototype, there has to be a group; in order to be "one of us," there has to be an "us" in the first place. That is, the very possibility of leadership depends upon the development of a common social identity (Haslam & Reicher, 2007).

So, on the one hand, social identity is the precondition for people to support a leader. On the other hand, a leader is then in a position to structure the ways in which group members support each other in working for a common goal. These various dynamics were dramatically brought home to us in a large field study we conducted into intergroup relations – the BBC Prison study (for overviews of the study, see Haslam & Reicher, 2005; Reicher & Haslam, 2006; for a discussion of the relationship between social identity and organizational issues in the study, see Haslam & Reicher, 2006a).

In this study we randomly divided participants into Prisoners and Guards within a simulated prison setting with the aim of investigating the ways in which people respond to intergroup inequalities and the conditions under which subordinate group members – the Prisoners – might join together to challenge their position. As we expected, under conditions where the Prisoners developed shared identification, they were indeed able to work as an effective unit against the Guards. At any given point, a single Prisoner felt confident to take them on, trusting completely that others would back them up. To take but one of many examples, the first major confrontation between the two groups started when one of the Prisoners threw his plate to the ground and refused to eat the food. As the Guards surrounded him, his cellmates initiated other complaints – about their rights to smoke cigarettes, about blistering caused by the prison footwear – which drew other Guards away and divided their forces. Such spontaneous support was complemented by the willingness of the prisoners to endorse a leader who could then plan and direct their joint efforts (for details, see Haslam & Reicher, 2007; Reicher, Haslam, & Hopkins, 2005).

Even more interesting in many ways was the contrast between the Prisoners and the Guards. The latter never developed a common group identity and hence were never able to develop even the most rudimentary forms of social organization let alone agree on a leader. For instance, we had suggested to the Guards that, since their duties extended throughout the day, they should devise a shift system with people taking turns to work and rest. But to do that, those who were off duty would have had to trust those who were on duty to act in ways they found acceptable. But the lack of shared social identification, and hence the lack of shared values and norms, meant that the Guards could never trust each other in this way. Accordingly, all the Guards stayed on duty all of the time in order to keep an eye on each other. They certainly could not agree on a leader to represent them or to make decisions on behalf of all. If ever a decision had to be made about how to treat the Prisoners – say how to deal with a rule violation – the Guards would compete to intervene quickly in order to pre-empt what they feared would be the wrong response of their fellows. In this way, not only was there a failure to support each other, but Guards actively impeded each other. As we will discuss presently, their numbers became a source of weakness rather than strength.

Overall, the contrast in social functioning between these groups could not have been clearer. For the Prisoners, shared identification led to shared values which enabled the development of trust, respect, and leadership, and hence to mutual support among group members. This in turn formed the basis of organized action. For the Guards, however, lack of identification impeded the development of shared values and this in turn fomented distrust, lack of respect, an absence

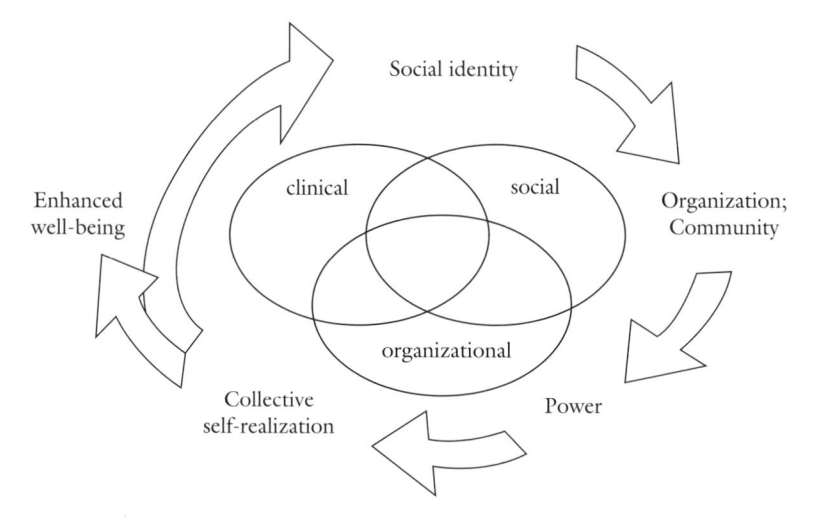

Figure 15.1 Steps in the cycle of social identification (from Reicher & Haslam, 2006). Reproduced with permission.

of leadership, and hence mutual undermining between individuals. The outcome was disorganized action. To put it slightly differently, and returning to the point with which we started this section, the study reveals the chain of processes through which social identification makes coordinated group action possible – and demonstrates that solidarity (in the sense defined above of multiple, reciprocal, and additive acts of support) lies at the very heart of these processes.

Solidarity in Context

Thus far, we have used the notion of solidarity to broaden the way in which we think about helping and about its social significance. We have also argued that solidarity should not be seen as just one in a long list of consequences of social identification. Instead, it represents the culmination of a series of transformations in social relations which are brought about when people think of others as "we" rather than "you and I."

It is time to broaden the focus still further. The links between social identification, solidarity, and coordinated group action are, we suggest, a key step in the wider processes governing the creation and consolidation of cohesive groups in society. We refer to these processes as "the virtuous circle of social identification." This is illustrated in Figure 15.1.

As can be seen from this figure, our discussion thus far has served to flesh out the first step – from social identity to organization and community through the medium of solidarity. In this section, we will consider how this links in to the other steps of the cycle. Before we do so, however, it is necessary to make a general point about the way in which we conceptualize social identity: the starting and the finishing point of our analysis (for fuller accounts, see Reicher, Haslam, & Hopkins, 2005; Reicher & Hopkins, 2001).

A central tenet of self-categorization theory is that the way we use social categories to describe self and other relates to the organization of social reality (Turner, 1982; Turner et al., 1987). In exploring this idea, much of the research emphasis has involved showing how social identities reflect existing relations between self and other in context (e.g., Oakes, Haslam, & Turner, 1994). However, it is equally important to stress that self-categories relate to how we aim to organize social reality in the *future*. In other words, they are prospective, not simply descriptive. They are as much projects aimed at shaping collective action to create new worlds as perceptions of the existing world. An obvious example of this lies in the dynamics of national categories. On the one hand, we describe ourselves in national terms because we live in a world structured into nations, but on the other, nationalism is a force that mobilizes people to create nation-states – which is why much of the work on the prospective construction of social identities addresses the topic of nationhood (e.g., Reicher & Hopkins, 2001).

Overall, then, a social identity may not always match the world as it currently is, but where a disjunction exists temporarily, there must at least be the prospect of creating a new world in the image of one's identity. Social identities, that is, don't always have to be veridical but they do have to be practical. An identity that has no possibility of forming a basis for organizing the world is not "false." It is something worse. It is useless and will therefore be rejected as such. With this understanding in mind, we can now proceed round the cycle of social identification.

From Organization to Power

The link between organization and power was implicit in the description we gave above of the BBC Prison study. That is, for group members who, due to shared social identity, are able to coordinate their actions and work together to reach a common goal (e.g., the Prisoners), the effects of their separate efforts become fully additive. Greater numbers thereby increase the power of the group to overcome obstacles (constituted either by the physical environment or by the countervailing actions of other groups) to reach their goal. Conversely, for group members who, due to a lack of shared identity, are unable to coordinate their actions or agree on a shared goal (e.g., the Guards), the effects of their shared efforts are liable to cancel each other out. Greater numbers do not therefore increase the power of the group to overcome obstacles. In fact, they may even diminish it. The overall consequence of these dynamics, in our study, was that power gradually shifted from the divided Guards to the united Prisoners and, ultimately, the Prisoners were able to usurp the Guards and destroy the original prison system (Reicher & Haslam, 2006).

Once again we suggest that the issue of power is not incidental to the social identity approach but rather lies at the very heart of the tradition. Turner (2005) has recently drawn out this relationship. He argues that, in contrast to traditional models which see control over resources as leading to power which in turn leads to influence and group formation, psychological group formation (based on shared identity) represents the start of the process. This then leads to mutual influence (to which we would add "and mutual support") which then leads to power and hence control over resources. Power, in this sense, is not the power of certain individuals (those with resources) *over* others. In the case of leadership, as discussed above, it is a matter of gaining power *through* others: leader power consists of mobilizing people to achieve goals by defining these goals as consistent with group-based norms and values. That is to say, effective leaders help members to determine what they want to do, they don't instruct members what they must do. Even without leadership, though, group members gain power *through* each other. Mutual influence and mutual support is what gives groups – large groups in particular – so much power and makes them so feared by the guardians of the status quo (Reicher, 1987, 2001).

Somewhat more controversially, it can be argued that, at least implicitly, social identity theory was initially generated by a concern with power. Whereas the theory is often (mis)represented as oriented to the question of intergroup discrimination (as generated by a desire for positive group-based esteem which can only be achieved by denigrating the out-group), Tajfel himself saw the dynamics surrounding the quest for positive self-esteem as merely a starting point for asking the question "What do we do, then, if, in our unequal world, we find ourselves ascribed to negatively valued groups: black people in a racist society, women in a sexist society, gays and lesbians in a homophobic society . . . ?" (Tajfel, 1982; Tajfel & Turner, 1979; see also

Reicher, 2004). This question was answered by considering the conditions under which people shift from trying to distance themselves from the group in order to progress within the unequal world (a strategy of social mobility) to acting collectively in order to dismantle the system of inequalities (a strategy of social change). The critical point here is that it is presupposed that only by identifying as a group and by acting collectively do people gain the power to change society. In this sense, then, social identity theory is more properly seen as a theory of group power rather than a theory of group discrimination.

From Power to Collective Self-Realization (CSR)

Psychology has long had a tendency to counterpose power to reason at a group level. In Le Bon's (1895/1947) classic formulation, immersion in a group – "submergence," as he termed it – simultaneously removes our sense of personal identity and personal responsibility while providing us with a sense of invincible might. Hence power without responsibility is the characteristic condition of collective life. This assumption has fed into modern social psychology not so much in the form of deindividuation theory (which oddly enough, stresses the loss of responsibility while neglecting the importance of power; e.g., see Zimbardo, 1969) but more in a general approach to the study of group process, and group influence in particular, which asserts that members will follow the powerful in their midst irrespective of what they propose (see Moscovici, 1976; Turner, 2005). Group members will do anything if they are enjoined to by those with authority (e.g., see Milgram, 1974). In particular, they are prone to extremes of negativity and destruction which, alone, they would abhor. Groups, as Brown (1999) has put it, are generally portrayed as bad for you.

From a social identity perspective, however, the exercise of group power is framed by group beliefs, norms, and values. In particular, power allows in-group members to enact those aspects of their identity which, otherwise, would be repressed by the out-group (Haslam & Reicher, in prep; Reicher & Levine, 1994a, 1994b). As a consequence, the more the relative power of in-groups over out-groups, the more likely it is that their actions will accurately reflect their social identities. Thus, in complete opposition to Le Bon's claim, crowds present a privileged site in which to discover how the groups that constitute them see their world. To paraphrase Lefebvre's famous study of crowds in the French revolution, perhaps it is only in the crowd that people shake off their petty day-to-day concerns and act as the subjects of history (Lefebvre, 1954, see also Reicher, 1987, 2001).

But there is more to it than this. It is not simply that groups seek to act on the basis of their identities. It is also that groups seek to structure social reality according to social identity. Group members aspire to objectify their subjective beliefs and values as real-world structures and policies (Drury & Reicher, 2005; Drury, Reicher, & Stott, 2003). Their success in achieving this is what we have more recently termed "collective self-realization" (CSR) (Reicher & Haslam, 2006). Indeed, as we made clear above, we view identities as projects oriented specifically towards the (re)organization of the social world. Hence, we are once again dealing with the core logic of social identification – as opposed to an incidental epiphenomenon – in arguing that group power is aimed at CSR.

The importance of CSR is reflected in the reactions that ensue when it is (or isn't) achieved. As we have found in a variety of settings from environmental protests, to political demonstrations, to religious festivals in India, the opportunity to achieve group goals or to live a life according to group precepts – especially when that is achieved against the odds through considerable sacrifice or else against strong out-group opposition – is experienced with great positivity (Drury & Reicher, 1999, 2000; Prayag Magh Mela Research Group, 2007). This has elements of excitement captured by Durkheim's concept of "effervescence" (Durkheim, 1912/2001), but also it has elements of an intense, even blissful, contentment and "flow" which is captured by the Indian concept of "paramanand" (which, literally, means the merging of the self into the divine – see Yogananda, 1996). By contrast, the failure to achieve CSR, and more particularly, the sense that one's ability to live by one's social identity is being blocked by an out-group, can lead to intense resentment against those seen to be responsible for the impediment. Indeed, it is precisely by arguing that an out-group is stopping us realizing our identity that anger can be mobilized against it (Reicher, Haslam, & Rath, 2008; Reicher, Hopkins, Levine, & Rath, 2005).

From Collective Self-Realization to Well-Being and Enhanced Social Identification

One of the more interesting developments of recent years is the use of social identity concepts to bring together the domains of social and clinical psychology. The argument that collective self-realization leads to a strong sense of positivity already points in this direction. There is further indication from work in progress conducted by Reicher and others (collectively referred to as the Allahabad Magh Mela Research

Group) at a multi-million strong religious festival – the Magh Mela – in India, that collective participation and CSR, in the sense of being able to live a good Hindu life in the Mela, leads to enhanced mental and even physical well-being (Cassidy et al., 2007).

However, to date, the best evidence of the link between identification and well-being (and the ways in which it is mediated by constructs such as support and CSR) is provided by research on stress. For instance, Haslam, Jetten, and colleagues have shown that identification acts as a prophylactic against stress for those with demanding and even dangerous occupations (bomb disposal experts and, more prosaically, bar-tenders) as well as those undergoing threatening life transitions (e.g., recovering from heart surgery or stroke; Haslam, Holme, Haslam, Iyer, Jetten, & Williams, 2008; Haslam, O'Brien, Jetten, Vormedal, & Penna, 2005; Jetten, Haslam, Iyer, & Haslam, Chapter 7 this volume). In line with arguments outlined above, this research indicates that social support is contingent upon identification but also that this impacts upon both cognition and action.

Haslam and Reicher (2006b) have incorporated these ideas within an Integrated Social Identity model of Stress (ISIS; see also Jetten et al., Chapter 7 this volume). They argue that, where people fail to identify or to act collectively, they will either attempt to avoid or to deny the nature of the stressors they confront. In either case this means adapting to existing stressors and accepting the social reality that gives rise to them. However, where group members are able to act collectively and where they can remold social reality in the group interest, then they are also able to resist stressors and thereby reduce the levels of stress they experience.

In changing social reality, of course, group members do far more than change the levels of stress that they experience. They validate the group in the double sense of showing it to be effective, creating group pride which is a powerful antecedent of identification (Haslam, 2001) and of showing the group perspective to be valid. That is, members now have a social identity which matches social reality retrospectively as well as prospectively. To borrow from Gramsci's redolent term, such social identities have "practical adequacy" (Gramsci, 1987; see also Sayer, 1983). As such, they provide a useful and truthful basis for defining one's place in the world. In this way, the virtuous circle of social identification is completed.

At this point, it is necessary to make an important clarification to our argument. While we are arguing that there are links between identification, support/organization, power, collective self-realization, and enhanced identification, we are not suggesting that the link is automatic and inevitable or that each step necessarily leads to the next. Such a position would be mechanical and implausible. It would suggest that group identities can only ever get stronger and stronger and that wherever there is identification, groups will always succeed in molding the world to their wishes. This is plainly not the case. Many groups fail to overcome their adversaries, to fulfill their aims, and many groups weaken and disappear. Quite evidently, at each step of the cycle the links are general tendencies rather than rigid determinations and they are moderated by various factors – many of which are structural not just psychological.

Thus, for instance, to take the first step from identification to support and organization, we argued that one of the consequences of shared social identity is an expectation of agreement with in-group members and that this leads to a process of consensualization which produces agreement between group members. However, there is another side to this. That is, where people cannot agree on something that is seen as critical to the group, the implication is that they cannot be members of the same group. Under these conditions, a process which generally produces consensus can produce schismatic tendencies (Sani & Reicher, 1999, 2000).

Equally, to take the later step from support/organization to power to collective self-realization, it may be true that an organized group of mutually supportive members is *relatively* more powerful than one which is not, but this does not mean that it will necessarily have sufficient power to overcome impediments in the social or physical environment. History teaches us that resistance is rarely entirely futile, but that it is often unsuccessful (Haslam & Reicher, in prep). Equally, while organization and support may provide potential power, their effectiveness will depend upon how this potential is directed against such impediments. Notably, the skill of leadership is not limited to uniting and mobilizing followers, it also involves strategic and tactical awareness in directing mobilizations to act where resistance is most vulnerable (Reicher, Haslam, & Hopkins, 2005).

Such variability, far from undermining the overall argument, provides further evidence for our model. Indeed, perhaps the most powerful evidence we have for the link from CSR to identification comes from our BBC Prison experiment (Haslam & Reicher, 2005; Reicher & Haslam, 2006). Here, after the Prisoner–Guard system collapsed, participants formed a Commune with which most members identified very strongly. Initially this led to sustained effort and mutual help in making the system work. Members had considerable potential power. The problem they faced was an unwillingness to wield it against those who were opposed to the Commune. As a result, the system began to fall apart, members lost faith in it and they began to become more accepting of the precise opposite – a rigid, unequal, and authoritarian regime. However much they identified with and believed in a Communal identity, a Communal system could not be realized, the identity proved useless to them and so it was discarded. As we would predict, then, if CSR fails to occur, identification will be attenuated, and a vicious circle of social atomization can ensue (Reicher & Haslam, 2006).

Conclusion

The purpose of this chapter has been to argue that helping (as solidarity) has a wider significance than is routinely addressed in the helping literature. What makes the phenomena that fall within this broader compass interesting and important is not their spectacular nature – the occasional acts of heroism whereby people make great sacrifices to save others from perdition. Rather, it is the fact that we are dealing with the building blocks of everyday life. We have gradually widened our focus in order to make that point. In so doing we may have seemed to stray a long way from the point – and from the topic of this book. It is therefore worth concluding by restating why we believe it is so important to bring these wider issues into a chapter in a volume on helping.

There are two stages to our argument. The first involves the relationship between group processes and helping. This involves reconceptualizing both sides of the relationship. On the one hand, we argue that group processes – and, more specifically, social identity processes – should be understood in terms of the ways that the interactions between people are transformed when they conceptualize themselves as members of a common social category in such a way as to produce organized co-action. On the other hand, we argue that the focus of helping research should lie more on the multiple little acts of mutual support that occur routinely between group members. Once these reconceptualizations are made, it is possible to adduce a wide range of evidence to support the case that helping/solidarity is a key consequence of social identification and an integral part of the way in which social identification makes group behavior possible. To make the same point with a slightly different emphasis, placing helping in the context of group process has important implications for our understanding of helping (as we have previously argued; see Levine et al.,

2005; Reicher et al., 2006), but it has equally important implications for our understanding of group process.

The second stage of our argument concerns the place of helping/solidarity in the wider processes which govern the ways in which people identify with and consolidate social categories in the world. At this stage also, an important reconceptualization is involved – this time of the very concept of social identification. Here we emphasize the practical and experiential dimensions of identification in addition to the cognitive and representational. That is, social identities are about the creation as well as the contemplation of the social world. Once again, this act of reconceptualization in itself goes a long way towards teasing out the wider significance of helping/solidarity. For it allows us to see how such solidarity is critical to the success of social groups in being able to shape society and hence consolidate the group itself. That said, it needs to be acknowledged that the notion of a "cycle of social identification" is, at present, a work in progress. We have had to bring together research from a wide variety of sources to give prima facie plausibility to our model. But it is clear that it is more a tool to generate further research than a record of research completed.

We therefore finish, as we started, by emphasizing the importance of such work. Helping, seen as solidarity, and solidarity, seen as a key link in the chain relating social understanding to the making of social reality, goes to the heart of what Allport (1954b) once called the "master problem" of social psychology. It is high time we reclaim our rightful place at the core of the discipline.

16

Cross-Group Helping
Perspectives on Why and Why Not

Stephen C. Wright and
Norann T. Richard

Introduction

For more than forty years (Campbell, 1965), when groups are considered in discussions of helping – which is itself relatively rare – it is usually to describe the importance of shared group membership. Helping, it seems, has been conceptualized primarily as an intragroup phenomenon. When intergroup helping is considered, the usual focus is on the absence or deficiencies in helping across group lines, and research from this perspective has shown that people not only tend to show higher rates of actual aid to in-group members than out-group members (e.g., Dovidio, Gaertner, Validzic, Matoka, Johnson, & Frazier, 1997; Levine, Prosser, Evans, & Reicher, 2005; Piliavin, Rodin, & Piliavin, 1969; Saucier, Miller, & Doucet, 2005), but that they are also, at times, well aware of their biases and will report a greater probability of helping an in-group member than an out-group member (e.g., Levine, Cassidy, Brazier, & Reicher, 2002). In fact, psychology offers a plethora of theoretical explanations for why we should avoid providing assistance to out-groups and their members, including evolutionary and genetic predispositions, basic cognitive and motivational processes, justice principles and political ideology, and even existential angst and fear of death. In fact, some have even forwarded the view that shared group membership is the primary basis for altruistic behavior (see Campbell, 1965).

Yet, this simply cannot be the entire (or even the bulk of the) story. Assistance and kindness across groups is basic to daily life; it is common, even expected. It would probably be fair to say that most of us are the frequent recipients of help from someone who is clearly recognizable (even at the time) as an out-group member. In fact, we take notice and are dismayed when members of an out-group fail to perform customary acts of assistance and courtesy. In addition, cross-group altruism can be much more significant and memorable. Travelers often return home with stories of extraordinary hospitality and altruism. One of the authors is reminded of an old man in Turkey who walked, leaning heavily on his cane, for more than half an hour to show an obvious foreigner the way to the bus station and then disappeared back across the square before even an adequate "thank you" could be provided. In his book *The Kindness of Strangers*, Don George (2003), writer and editor for *The Lonely Planet* series, provides a collection of stories of kindness and assistance provided to travelers who were clearly recognized by their helper as outsiders. In their analysis of sex differences in heroism, Eagly and Becker (2005) consider five groups of heroes: Carnegie medalists, Righteous among the Nations (non-Jews who risked their lives in order to save Jews during the Nazi Holocaust), living kidney donors, Peace Corps Volunteers, and Doctors of the World. It is interesting to note that while it seems that kidney donations to out-group members are rare (most are to relatives), and we are unable to determine the number of Carnegie medalists who saved out-group members, the other three groups are all involved explicitly in cross-group helping.

Yet, the dominant theme in social psychology is that a lack of shared group membership makes helping unlikely. This theme seems especially strong when the potential helper belongs to a higher-status advantaged group and the potential recipient is a member of a lower-status disadvantaged group. In these cases, even when theories recognize acts of helping and sharing across groups, there remains a decided air of cynicism. Advantaged-group helping ends up described as a strategic effort to maintain or strengthen in-group superiority (see Nadler, 2002; Nadler & Halabi, 2006), to improve the in-group's image (Hopkins, Reicher, Harrison, Cassidy, Bull, & Levine, 2007), to manage other threats to the in-group's identity (van Leeuwen, 2007), or to relieve collective guilt resulting from the in-group's previous misdeeds (see Doosje, Branscombe, Spears, & Manstead, 1998; Reid, Gunter, & Smith, 2005). Others have theorized that advantaged group helping is limited to types of help which will not threaten the material position of the in-group (e.g., Jackson & Esses, 2000). It is perhaps not surprising then that suggestions for increasing cross-group helping often involve strategies that attempt to hide or remove group distinctions by encouraging perceptions of similarity (e.g., Cuddy, Rock, & Norton, 2007) or focusing attention on a shared superordinate category that "turns 'us' and 'them' into 'we'" (e.g., Dovidio et al., 1997; Dovidio, Gaertner, Hodson, Houlette, & Johnson, 2005; Nier,

Gaertner, Dovidio, Banker, Ward, & Rust, 2001) – including at times an extremely high-level categorization, that of our shared humanity.

We do not doubt the validity of these claims or the evidence provided for them, and accept with certainty that intergroup helping is constrained by intrapersonal and intragroup concerns, by negative stereotypes and prejudices towards the out-group, and by the state of relations between the groups. However, this need not mean that intergroup helping can never be as freely given and as sincere as interpersonal helping, which is itself constrained by concerns for personal safety, status, and well-being, and is dependent on past experience with the other and the current interpersonal relationship (see Dovidio, Paliavin, Schroeder, & Penner, 2006). Of course, when helping is understood to involve social identities, the factors that constrain helping may now be experienced at the collective or intergroup level (Turner, Hogg, Oakes, Reicher, & Wetherell, 1987), and while there may be reasons that interactions at this level of identity face additional barriers to compassion and helping, it seems premature to conclude that these barriers are insurmountable.

Intergroup Relations: Beyond Intergroup Comparisons

It is our contention that social psychology's lack of attention to and tantamount denial of cross-group helping that is not motivated by in-group interests results in part from a lingering perception of groups as the source of negative, less human, behavior (see Oakes, 2001; see also Wright & Taylor, 2003), which has at times lead to the near equating of intergroup relations with intergroup conflict. However, we also contend that this tendency to see intergroup relations as primarily negative has been strengthened by the heavy emphasis on the role of social comparison found in the dominant theories of intergroup relations (e.g., Relative Deprivation, Social Identity Theory). While it is certainly true that out-groups provide the basis for determining the value and position of the in-group within the broader social hierarchy, there are other intergroup relationships that do not describe the two groups in terms of their relative status along some comparative dimension. Groups can be allies or enemies. Their relationship can be intimate or superficial. There can be cooperation as well as competition. They can be helper and helped, and help can be reciprocated. By focusing heavily on the out-group's role as a source of comparison to determine in-group status and worth, social psychology may have under-represented the degree to which out-groups fill other relational roles with the in-group.[1]

For example, the intergroup relationship between adults and children has relatively little to do with social comparison. Of course, members of the two groups engage in intergroup comparisons, but this is a woefully inadequate description of the relationship. The relationship is much more about the clearly understood obligation for the members of the more powerful group to protect, nurture, educate, and even sacrifice themselves for members of the other group. These relational obligations have little to do with social comparison, and structure the relationship such that the dominant emotions and evaluation associated with the out-group are very positive. There are also rules about out-group respect and obedience for members of the lower power group. Adults, for the most part, love, adore, and care for children, and children admire, respect, and trust adults. Similarly, the relationship between students and teachers is more about the complementary goals of educating and learning than about relative status comparisons. Nation-states can struggle against each other for superiority, but they can also establish alliances that include a list of relationship rules designed to undermine the basis for competitive social comparison and which structure the relationship to produce mutual assistance and support. All of these relationships (and many others) involve at their core, and are defined by, cross-group helping, especially by the more advantaged group. Woven into the fabric of these relationships is the requirement that cross-group assistance be provided and that it be provided in a spirit of civility, respect, and/or compassion.

Thus, it appears to us that a more complete analysis of the social psychology of intergroup relations broadly, and cross-group helping specifically, needs to consider the broad array of relational roles that out-groups can play. In this regard, we might take a cue from the study of interpersonal relations, which, of course, includes a large literature on social comparison, social competition, and self-serving biases, and provides ample evidence that behavior at the interpersonal level can be selfish, competitive, aggressive, hostile, and violent. However, it also examines interpersonal relationships that are less concerned with social comparisons to determine one's relative worth. The result is that the social psychology of interpersonal relations also considers at length the ways that interpersonal relations can be cooperative, warm, caring, kind, and even loving.

With this perspective as the background, the current chapter is really a story of two distinct lines of research and theorizing, which are connected by the general idea that intergroup relations can be more positive than they are usually portrayed. The first section of the chapter describes theorizing and work on self-expansion motives and the inclusion of out-groups in the self. These processes provide one explanation for why cross-group helping may be similar in its motivation impetus, and just as willingly provided, as intragroup helping. The second part of the chapter describes an explanation for failure to provide help across groups, which, although prevalent, is far less malignant than many of the explanations provided in the literature.

Genuine Cross-Group Helping: One Explanation for When and Why

In collaboration with Art Aron and other colleagues, we have considered a number of ways in which Aron and Aron's (1986) *self-expansion model* and the idea of *including-others-in-the-self*, a perspective that emerged initially from the study of interpersonal closeness, might also shed light on the more positive side of intergroup relations (e.g., Brody, Wright, Aron, & McLaughlin-Volpe, 2008; McLaughlin, Aron, Wright, & Lewandowski, 2006; Wright, Aron, & Tropp, 2002). The general thesis of the self-expansion model is that people actively seek opportunities to enhance their potential efficacy by expanding the self to include material and social resources, perspectives, and identities that might facilitate achievement of future goals and the meeting of future challenges (see Aron & Aron, 1996). Self-expansion, in the pursuit of increased general self-efficacy, is described as a central human motivation. One way to achieve self-expansion is by forming and maintaining close relations with others. Aron and colleagues have demonstrated in a wide variety of ways (for a review, see Aron, McLaughlin-Volpe, Mashek, Lewandowski, Wright, & Aron, 2004) that in close interpersonal relations, partners "included the other in the self." That is, they come to experience a strong and genuine sense that "what's yours is mine" (and what's mine is yours). The resources, perspectives, and identities of the partner become, to some extent, one's own. Thus, the development of friendships and romantic relationships are seen to be motivated, at least in part, by a need for self-expansion, and meeting this need through the successful inclusion of the other in the self (as a relationship develops) results in strong positive feelings. Further, the outcome of the inclusion in the self is not only feeling of warmth and closeness with the other, but also that the friend or partner is treated increasingly as one treats oneself. Thus, positive bias in attribution usually reserved for self is extended to the other; one feels pain at their troubles; one takes genuine pride in their successes; resources are generously shared, and so on.

In addition, this model proposes that because self-expansion is a basic motive, the satisfaction of this motive is in and of itself pleasurable. Thus, some of the positive emotions one experiences when forming new relationships result from the associated satisfaction of self-expansion needs. The model leads to the additional novel claim that rather than seeking only similarity in our interpersonal relations, we also seek difference. If forming relationships is in service of self-expansion, others who have numerous resources, perspectives, and identities that we do not have should be particularly attractive to us. Thus, the model proposes that we are actually most attracted to those who provide the greatest opportunity for self-expansion – those who are most different from us. However, this appetite for difference is constrained by the recognition that similarity greatly increases the likelihood that closeness will be obtained. Thus, the strong preference for similarity, commonly shown in research on interpersonal relationships, is a response to the recognition that it is unlikely we will be able to easily and quickly form a close relationship with a highly different other. However, there is evidence that when there is a fairly clear message that a friendship is likely, this similarity/attraction effect is replaced with a dissimilarity/attraction effect (Aron, Steele, Kashdan, & Perez, 2006; Aronson & Worchel, 1966; Jones, Bell, & Aronson, 1972; Zhou, Wright, & Moretti, 2008).

We have extended this model of interpersonal closeness to consider ideas in the domain of group processes and intergroup relations, hypothesizing that self-expansion motives can also be met through the inclusion of *groups* in the self (see Wright et al., 2002). We propose that self-expansion is one of a number of motivations that lead to identification with groups. Like self-enhancement motives (Tajfel & Turner, 1979), inclusion and distinctiveness motives (Brewer, 1991), and uncertainty reduction motives (Hogg, 2001b), self-expansion motives lead people to psychologically connect themselves to larger social entities. However, unlike other models of identification that focus on why we join and identify with *in-groups*, self-expansion theory allows for the possibility that we can include *out-groups* in the self. Although it is probably more common that the target of self-expansion is a group that we can actually join, this model proposes that even groups where actual membership is impossible can be included in the self. In fact, due to their clear difference from the current self, out-groups may represent especially exciting possibilities. Put another way, working against the many reasons for fearing and avoiding out-groups may be an appetitive orientation towards out-groups resulting from self-expansion needs (see Wright et al., 2002). The critical novel idea is that self-expansion provides a basis by which people become psychologically tied to an out-group such that this group now receives the positive regard and treatment that is usually reserved for aspects of the self. Thus, acting on behalf of this out-group and its members becomes very much like acting on behalf of one's in-group, or close others who are included in the self, or acting on behalf of the self. In this case, cross-group helping is as automatic and "selfless" as intragroup, interpersonal, or even self-help.

To elaborate the concept of *inclusion of the out-group in the self* it may be useful to briefly consider the underlying theoretical assumptions about the nature of the self. First, our perspective shares with other theoretical accounts based in the social identity approach the idea that the self includes both personal and collective self-aspects. That is, the self-concept is defined not only by attributes and characteristics that make one unique and independent of others, but also by identities one shares with others through membership in social groups. Similarly, our representation of others can be in terms of their individual character or in terms of their group memberships.

However, our perspective differs from many conceptions of social identity that imply an inevitable symmetry in the level of categorization of the self and other. It may be that when a collective self-categorization is salient, it is most likely that target others will also be perceived in terms of their collective identities. Similarly, when one's individual personal self is salient, it may be likely that others will also be perceived as unique individuals. Nevertheless, just because this symmetry in the level of categorization of self and others may be most common, it need not always be so. At times, groups of people may have a distinct and meaningful relationship with a single individual. When this relationship is the focus of attention, the salient self-representation of group members may be depersonalized and collective, while the perception of the other may be highly personalized. When a group of angry workers confront the company owner, their beef may be with "the company," but it might also be with the particular individual owner who is thought to be making unilateral, independent decisions that harm the in-group (the workers). Similarly, and most relevant to our argument here, the other asymmetry is also possible. An individual self-categorized in terms of his or her own personal identity can have a meaningful relationship with a group that he or she represents as a unitary entity. That is, our perspective focuses on the possibility that when an individual perceived herself to have a meaningful relationship with a group, self-categorization at the level of the individual does not preclude the possibility that others are categorized at the level of their group membership.

With this perspective as background, we propose that when an individual perceives a group as a distinct entity and believes that he or she has a meaningful positive relationship with that entity, that group will be included in the self. When the group is one that the individual can or does belong to, this is a case of in-group identification (anticipated or actual). However, if the group is one that the individual knows that he or she cannot join, the outcome is the inclusion of the out-group in the self. This process of including the out-group in the self then leads to positive attitudes and a supportive helping orientation towards the out-group and its members.

This claim is consistent with findings showing that majority group members involved in cross-group helping may be more willing to help when reminded of their personal identity than when reminded of their collective identity. For example, Simon, Stürmer, and Steffens (2000) found that among heterosexual AIDS volunteers willingness to provide generalized help to the AIDS community (an out-group) and its members was positively related to their strength of identification as a unique individual and negatively related to their strength of identification with their heterosexual in-group. From our perspective, this makes perfect sense. Identification with the heterosexual in-group should make salient the general lack of interest in helping AIDS victims that is thought to be the norm for heterosexuals. Identification as a unique individual should remind the heterosexual volunteer of their unique personal relationship with the community of AIDS victims, thus making them more likely to help members of the community.

This raises an important distinction. The attentive reader may have noticed that we have consistently used the term *cross-group* helping rather than *intergroup* helping to describe the outcome of inclusion of the in-group in the self. We believe the term intergroup helping should be reserved for situations where the helper is self-categorized at the level of a collective identity and is also considering out-group members at the collective level. Thus intergroup helping involves supportive actions offered an out-group member by those acting as representatives of their in-group. Cross-group helping, on the other hand, is the kind we have been describing here: involving an individual who is focused on his or her individual identity, but is well aware that the targets of help are members of an out-group and his or her "special relationship" with that out-group makes them worthy of help. There is a second situation that might also be referred to as cross-group helping, but which is less interesting from the perspective of intergroup relations. In this case, an individual assists another individual when the helper's understanding of the interaction is entirely interpersonal even though the targets happen to be members of different groups. So, when a woman helps a man, at some "objective" level this could be described as cross-group helping. However, if gender differences are not salient at all to the helper and thus are not relevant to the decision to help or the helping behavior, describing this as cross-group helping may be objectively true, but psychologically this would not be the case.

Cross-Group Contact and Including Others (and their Group) in the Self

So, how might it happen that an out-group could be included in the self? Our explorations of this idea began with research on intergroup contact. The intergroup contact hypothesis (Allport, 1954a), one of the most enduring and important contributions to the psychological study of intergroup relations, holds that contact between members of different groups can, under the right conditions, lead to improvements in intergroup attitudes (e.g., Dovidio, Gaertner, & Kawakami, 2003; Pettigrew & Tropp, 2006; Wright, Brody, & Aron, 2005). Given its roots in the close relations literature, the self-expansion perspective seemed most applicable to an intergroup phenomenon that has as an essential component interactions between individuals. Also, there is growing research literature showing that friendship is the type of cross-group contact most likely to inspire meaningful intergroup attitude change (e.g., Brown & Hewstone, 2005; Pettigrew, 1998). Thus, a model of interpersonal closeness might well have something to offer an analysis of the mechanisms underlying intergroup contact effects.

We have proposed that the concept of inclusion of other in self provides a novel perspective on one of the key issues for the contact hypothesis – how and why the positive feelings generated toward the single contact partner can be generalized to the partner's group as a whole. As is the case in all close interpersonal relationships, as the individual makes friends with a member of another group, she or he increasingly includes aspects of that other person in the self. The important difference in the case of a cross-group friendship is that one element of the friendship partner's identity is his or her out-group membership. Thus, as friendship grows and circumstances inevitably make the friend's group membership salient, this aspect of the friend's identity, like everything else about him or her, becomes a candidate for inclusion in the self. Thus, with increasing interpersonal closeness, there is an increasing inclusion of the friend's group identity in the self. Sometimes, cross-group relationship can give us real entrée into some of our partner's social groups (e.g., their friendship groups, clubs, even their family), and in this case, what was previously an out-group actually becomes an in-group. In other cases, actual membership in the out-group is unlikely or even impossible (e.g., ethnic, national, or occupational groups). Nonetheless, these groups can be included in the self despite the person's keen awareness that he or she is not actually included in the group. Here, the self/out-group connection is exclusively psychological. Nevertheless, this connection can be strong and the out-group and its members can be experienced as personally meaningful. Events that affect the out-group are experienced as though they are happening to oneself, and the friend's group is now accorded some of the positive regard and generous treatment usually reserved for the self.

Data from cross-sectional and experimental studies have provided support for critical parts of this model. Surveys of members of a variety of ethnic groups in the US and in Canada have shown that the degree of interpersonal closeness and perceptions of self/other overlap (a measure of inclusion of the other in the self) with a cross-ethnic friend predicted more positive attitudes towards the out-group (for reviews, see Aron et al., 2004; Wright, Comeau, & Aron, 2007; Wright et al., 2005). Consistently we find that feelings of closeness and/or the perception that the close other is included in the self are stronger predictors of positive intergroup attitudes than the number of cross-group contacts. Moreover, in several studies, we have found that the quantity of cross-group contact actually interacts with feelings of closeness to the contact partner, such that when contact involves feelings of closeness and inclusion of the other in the self, more contact produces more positive feelings towards the out-group, but when contact with the out-group lacks these feelings of closeness and inclusion, more cross-contact can be associated with more negative attitudes towards the out-group (McLaughlin-Volpe, Aron, Wright, & Reis, 2007).

We have also gathered experimental data that supports and strengthens the results of these cross-sectional studies. In our first experiment (Wright & Van Der Zande, 1999), participants were randomly assigned to cross-ethnic or same-ethnic friendship partners and then participated in a series of closeness-building activities. Not only did those who made a cross-group friend later report more positive intergroup attitudes, but the strength of this effect was predicted by the felt closeness of the relationship (see Wright et al., 2005). In a replication of this study, we measured interpersonal closeness using a measure specifically tapping inclusion of the other in the self (see Aron, Aron, & Smollan, 1992), and this measure also predicted the degree to which making a cross-group friend produced more positive attitudes towards the out-group.

In short, it appears that feelings of closeness with a member of the out-group and the resulting inclusion of that out-group member in the self can produce a more positive orientation towards the out-group on a variety of measures. There is also evidence that part of what is included in the self is the out-group itself, and that this inclusion of the group in the self accounts, at least in part, for the generalization of positive orientation from the close other to the group as a whole. More importantly, there also appears to be evidence that this positive orientation towards the out-group also results in increased helping of the out-group and its members. Included in the studies mentioned above are a number of measures that could be appropriately interpreted as measures of willingness to help the out-group. For example, one of our experimental studies was carried out in California around the time that a set of three highly publicized propositions had been included on state ballots, all of which had important implications for minority groups. They included a proposition to end affirmative action in government organizations (including universities), another to end bilingual education in public schools, and a third to clamp down on illegal immigrants (including requiring public employees including teachers and health care providers to inform on people who they suspected of being illegal). Incidentally, all three propositions passed. Affirmative action is explicitly designed to assist ethnic minorities and women, bilingual education was primarily utilized by Latino children, and the primary target of efforts against illegal immigration are Mexicans, other Latinos, and people from Asia. Thus, all of these policies could be seen as directly targeting minority groups, and opposition to these policies was clearly associated with a desire to retain programs thought to assist members of these groups. To the degree that these measures tapped participants' willingness to openly oppose these policies and to vote against them, our findings that forming cross-group friendships and the inclusion of the other in the self produced stronger opposition to all three of these propositions can be interpreted as evidence of a greater willingness to help.

Also, in several experimental studies, we have included a non-obvious behavioral measure (Haddock, Zanna, & Esses, 1993, *budget-cutting* task) on which participants are asked (ostensibly by the university administration) to distribute budget cuts among 15 student organizations. Participants are led to believe that their responses will directly influence the decisions of the committee that will be making these cuts. Compared to those who made in-group friends, Whites who made friends with a Latina made significantly smaller cuts to the budget of the "Latino/Chicano Student Association," and those with a new Asian American friend cut less from the "Asian & Pacific Islander Student Alliance." This effort to reduce the harm of budget cuts on an out-group organization seems a clear example of aid provided to the out-group resulting from newly acquired cross-group closeness.

Finally, in a recent survey investigating the impact of cross-ethnic friendships (Wright et al., 2007), one dependent measure tapped supporting behavior and included items like willingness to intervene on behalf of a member of the out-group who was being mistreated. Scores on this measure were also predicted by the quality of reported cross-group friendships and correlated with a measure of inclusion of the out-group in the self. Thus, there is evidence that one of the positive effects of interpersonal closeness with an out-group member can be the inclusion of the out-group in the self, which leads not only to more positive attitudes towards that group, but also to effortful opposition to policies or practices that might harm the out-group and a willingness to aid out-group members who are being mistreated.

Genuine Out-Group Help: Summary and Conclusions

We began this chapter with the contention that social psychology has underestimated the prevalence and likelihood of genuine cross-group helping. We also proposed that a good place to start would be to expand our focus beyond the out-group's role as a source of social comparison to more carefully explore the range of relationships that can exist between social groups. In addition, we provided evidence from our work on cross-group contact that the development of close interpersonal relationships across groups can lead to the inclusion of the out-group in the self. This direct connection of the personal self to the out-group can then lead to genuine acts of support and help to the out-group and its members.

Our use of the term *genuine* out-group help need not be equated with the concept of altruism. Others have debated the issue of whether helping that results from inclusion of the other in the self should be considered true altruism (see Batson, 1997; Batson, Sager, Garst, Kang, Rubchinsky, & Dawson, 1997; Cialdini, Brown, Lewis, Luce, & Neuberg, 1997; Neuberg, Cialdini, Brown, Luce, Sagarin, & Lewis, 1997). We believe that the inclusion of the other (or a group) in the self obscures the distinction between other-focused and self-focused helping. The other (the group) is part of the self, and helping the other (the out-group) is, therefore, helping an aspect of the self. The merging or overlapping of the self with the other entity makes help given to that entity like self-help. Whether this meets the criteria for altruism depends on the definition of altruism. However, we believe that help provided to others (or groups of others) that is psychologically equivalent to help given to the self qualifies as "genuine" help.

Intergroup Helping, Why Not? Ambiguity in Cross-Group Helping Decisions

As we mentioned earlier in this chapter, it is certainly true that negative intergroup attitudes, competitive intergroup relations, biases in favor of one's in-group, and self-interest in general can lead members of advantaged groups to ignore the plight of those who are disadvantaged. It is also true that even when cross-group support is provided, there can be ulterior motives that make these benevolent acts more about serving the in-group (e.g., Nadler, 2002). However, we would also like to draw attention to an addition explanation for the apparent reluctance to engage in cross-group helping, which, although effective, involves a much less malignant orientation towards the out-group. This explanation revolves around the concept of uncertainty and the power of ambiguity to undermine prosocial action.

We focus here on the case of members of advantaged groups helping a more disadvantaged out-group because this form of helping seems particularly important for improving social justice. First, it is likely that advantaged group members have access to the means necessary to genuinely help disadvantaged group members, and the procedures designed to resolve social inequality are often dependent upon support from at least some members of the advantaged group (see Beaton & Deveau, 2005). Second, advantaged group help can encourage more assertive actions by members of the disadvantaged groups. For example, Cihangir, Barreto, and Ellemers (2007) showed that even expressions of verbal disapproval of discrimination (a very mild form of help indeed) were enough to increase the likelihood that members of the low-status group would take action against the injustice. Thus, while we believe that ambiguity plays an important role in all cases of cross-group helping, our attention will be focused on the case of advantaged group support for the disadvantaged group.

Ambiguity in Helping Decisions

A classic study by Frey and Gaertner (1986), though framed in terms of underlying prejudice, also appears to provide evidence of the impact of ambiguity on cross-group helping. These researchers found that cross-group helping (White Americans helping Black Americans) was substantially more likely when the norms for providing help were clear. When norms about providing help were more ambiguous, participants were more likely to help members of their own group (Whites) than the out-group (Blacks). Massar and Moffat (2006) expanded on this idea, examining heterosexual men's helping behavior towards homosexual men. Men low in homophobia did not distinguish between in-group and out-group members when offering help. However, the ambiguity of norms regarding helping did impact on the behaviors of men high in homophobia. When helping norms were ambiguous, they offered less help to an out-group member than to an in-group member. However, when a third party clarified that norms supported cross-group helping, the homosexual man received high levels of helping even from those high in homophobia. These two studies appear to demonstrate that situational ambiguity can reduce tendencies for cross-group helping, and suggest that clarifying information (clearer social norms, in this instance) may be all that is needed to reduce the disparity between in-group and out-group support.

The idea that ambiguity plays a role in undermining helping has a long and convincing history in social psychological research. Latané and Darley's (1970) highly cited *decision model of bystander intervention* clearly proposes a role for ambiguity in determining when help will be provided. Both the first (noticing that something is wrong) and the second (defining it as an emergency) steps in the decision model recognize the importance of situational clarity in determining when help will be provided. The findings of some of the first studies on the bystander effect – that people are less likely to intervene in an emergency when other people are around as compared to when they are alone (Darley & Latané, 1968) – were interpreted in part as the result of situational ambiguity. People look to other bystanders to help ascertain whether the situation is really one in which helping is needed and, if so, to determine the norms for helping in this situation. When (if) no one reacts, it is assumed that help is unnecessary or inappropriate.

Research has shown that this bystander effect may be even stronger in the case of cross-group helping (e.g., Mason & Allen, 1976). Gaertner, Dovidio, and Johnson (1982) found that when White students were alone (and thus in the non-ambiguous situation), they were equally quick to offer help to an out-group member (a Black confederate) as to an in-group member (a White confederate) who appeared to have suffered an injury. In contrast, when there were other passive bystanders (creating situational ambiguity), not only were participants slower to respond generally, they were slower to provide help to the out-group member than the in-group member. Although this effect can, and has, been interpreted as evidence of subtle prejudice that emerges only when there is an excuse not to help, it is also possible that cross-group helping may involve greater inherent ambiguity than in-group helping, and thus the impact of the bystander manipulation was compounded for cross-group helping.

Even more generally, this idea is based on the claim that most cross-group interactions involve greater uncertainty than the same interactions with in-group members and helping should be no exception. In addition to a general unfamiliarity with out-group behavior, norms, and expectations, it may be that the needs of others who are different from oneself are less obvious than the needs of those with whom we are more familiar (Reykowski, 2002). Advantaged group members may be less able to confidently determine the needs of out-group members. Of course, this may ring with the tones of privilege and ignorance, reminiscent perhaps of the famous phrase "let them eat cake" thought to symbolize the sheer ignorance of the privileged about the suffering of those with less. However, in addition to the ignorance of out-group need that is born out of privilege, we are referring to a more general type of "ignorance" that comes from a lack of experience with out-group members. Thus, members of disadvantaged groups might also be less able to confidently recognize that an advantaged group member is in need of their help.

In addition to ignorance resulting from a lack of experience, research and theorizing about intergroup anxiety also provides evidence of the uncertainty inherent in cross-group interactions. Recent discussions of intergroup anxiety have proposed that we are anxious when interacting with out-group members not only because of underlying fear or distrust of the out-group, but also because we are simply uncertain about how exactly to behave, leading us to be worried about our own performance (e.g., Jauernig, Wright, Lubensky, & Tropp, 2006;

Vorauer & Turpie, 2004). These kinds of concerns about whether our actions will be appropriate and performed correctly should be particularly important in cases of helping. Thus, the anxiety surrounding cross-group interactions generally should also heighten feelings of uncertainty when the situation calls for prosocial action.

It is, of course, certain that prejudice plays a role in reducing cross-group helping. Saucier, Miller, & Doucet (2005), for example, in a meta-analysis of research on Whites helping Whites compared to Blacks, provide convincing evidence of the role of subtle forms of racism in helping behavior. However, we think it wise to allow for the possibility that in some cases cross-group helping can be influenced by the same factors as in-group helping, but just more so. Helping of both in-group and out-group members is undermined by situational ambiguity, but this effect is compounded when the person in need is an out-group member. If this is the case, procedures designed to reduce ambiguity will improve the chances of both kinds of helping, but will have a more powerful impact on cross-group helping. Thus, out-group helping may be particularly susceptible to situational influences and cues that clarify the appropriateness of help.

There is some indirect evidence to support this claim. First, if situational ambiguity is particularly relevant to cross-group helping decisions, these decisions should be highly susceptible to the influence of framing. Research by Karacanta and Fitness (2006) appears to bear this out. They had heterosexual university students watch a video of a homosexual student recounting negative treatment on the basis of his sexual orientation. Participants were instructed to either focus on themselves, on the experiences of the person in the video, or to remain objective. When instructed to be other-focused, straight participants showed greater willingness to volunteer for a gay and lesbian anti-violence program than in the other conditions. This suggests that the same appeal from an out-group member can result in different levels of helping depending on the framing.

In addition, consistent with the more general argument that ambiguity reduction can be an effective tool in improving the orientation towards the out-group, it has been argued that clarifications that demonstrate the illegitimacy of policies that discriminate against the out-group can increase feelings of injustice, make perceptions of a disadvantaged out-group more positive, and increase feelings of collective guilt (Powell, Branscombe, & Schmitt, 2005). All of these are feelings that may help to motivate prosocial behavior by the advantaged group (see Veilleux & Tougas, 1989). Thus, it appears that messages that disambiguate the illegitimacy of the disadvantaged group's conditions can be effective tools in motivating efforts to support the disadvantaged group and its members.

The Case of Tokenism

Our own research on advantaged group support for a disadvantaged out-group has focused specifically on the context of tokenism. Tokenism is defined as "an intergroup context in which boundaries between the advantaged and disadvantaged groups are not entirely closed, but where there are severe restrictions on access to advantaged positions of the basis of group membership" (Wright, 2001). In other words, tokenism occurs when very few qualified members of a disadvantaged out-group are granted access to a more privileged in-group.

There exists a considerable volume of research on the negative effects of tokenism on individual tokens. Token status in organizational settings can result in reduced task performance (Sekaquaptewa & Thompson, 2002) and job satisfaction (Niemann & Dovidio, 1998), as well as increased psychological symptoms (Jackson, Thoits, & Taylor, 1995). These negative outcomes can result from the extra scrutiny and unfair treatment received by tokens (McDonald, Toussaint, & Schweiger, 2004), but also from the internal stress resulting from feeling overly exposed and vulnerable when token status makes one's category membership especially salient (e.g., Lord & Saenz, 1985).

Another line of research focuses on the impact of tokenism on the reactions of other disadvantaged group members. Initial research by Wright and colleagues (Wright, Taylor, & Moghaddam, 1990) contrasted tokenism with conditions where all members of the disadvantaged group were excluded (a completely closed system) and another where all qualified members of the disadvantaged group were admitted (an open/meritocratic system). While complete exclusion evoked strong endorsement of disruptive forms of collective actions from members of the disadvantaged group, the tokenism condition in which only 2 percent of the qualified members of their group gained access to the advantaged positions led to low endorsement of collective action at levels equivalent to those in the open condition. These findings, which have been replicated a number of times (e.g., Lalonde & Silverman, 1994; Reynolds, Oakes, Haslam, Nolan, & Dolnik, 2000; Vanbeselaere, Boen, & Smeesters, 2003; Wright, 1997; Wright & Taylor, 1998), lead to the conclusion that tokenism not only has negative effects on the tokens themselves, but also can effectively reduce the forms of action most likely to increase intergroup equality and improve the status of the disadvantaged group as a whole.

Ambiguity in Tokenism

In our original paper on the topic (Wright et al., 1990), we proposed a number of mechanisms that might account for this somewhat surprising tokenism effect. However, after a number of replications (e.g., Wright & Taylor, 1998), the most persuasive explanation for the effect appears to involve the unique ambiguity inherent in tokenism (see Wright, 1997, 2001). Whereas a system that does not allow any members of a particular group access to advantaged positions is clearly illegitimate, and an open, meritocratic process is widely considered to be just, tokenism falls between these two poles. Under tokenism, both group membership (as in a closed system) and individual performance (as in an open system) are overt criteria for success, and the resulting uncertainty about the legitimacy of the system also may lead to uncertainty about whether others would support a collective response. If this ambiguity was to be resolved, disadvantaged group members may respond to tokenism in a more collective (and assertive) manner. This is precisely what was found (Wright, 1997). When another member of the disadvantaged group overtly labeled tokenism as "discrimination" and/or expressed anger, participants were more likely to engage in collective action. This suggests that when the ambiguity in the interpretation of tokenism is reduced, participants are more likely to react in a manner more consistent with being the targets of a closed, and therefore discriminatory, system.

Advantaged Group Members

Although some researchers have theorized about advantaged group members' reactions to tokenism (e.g., Laws, 1975; Wright, 2001), there has been little empirical research on this topic. This seems somewhat surprising given the powerful role that members of this group play in determining the policy and the general treatment of out-group members. Does a policy of tokenism lead to the same sense of ambiguity among advantaged group members that it appears to among members of the disadvantaged group? Does this ambiguity lead advantaged group members to be unsure about whether the policy should be described as just or unjust, and does it reduce their support for members of the disadvantaged group who are negatively impacted by the policy? Finally, and most importantly perhaps, can this uncertainty about tokenism, should it exist, be clarified in such a way that advantaged group members are willing to take action to help the disadvantaged group? Past research has suggested that when advantaged group members recognize clear illegitimacy in the treatment of a disadvantaged group, they are more likely to offer help through tactics such as taking political action and supporting policies that promote group equality (e.g., Iyer, Leach, & Crosby, 2003; Leach, Iyer, & Pederson, 2006; Veilleux & Tougas, 1989). Thus, it might be interesting to determine whether messages that focus attention on the negative impacts of tokenism on the disadvantaged group might also serve to reduce the ambiguity of this context and lead advantaged group members to be less supportive of this policy and to act in ways that would aid the out-group. It may be particularly important to determine under what conditions advantaged group members are likely to recognize tokenism as discriminatory and offer help, both because of the direct positive effects of that help, but also because this support may serve to disambiguate the system for disadvantaged group members. Given that a primary problem with tokenism is its ability to reduce collective action by the disadvantaged group, recognition of the injustice by advantaged group members may be particularly influential in increasing collective efforts by the disadvantaged group as well (Cihangir et al., 2007).

Initial Research Evidence

In an initial study (Richard & Wright, 2008) we sought, first, to examine how advantaged groups would respond to a policy of tokenism compared to policies that produced an open/meritocratic and an entirely closed system. How would they evaluate these three policies in terms of justice, would they be willing to speak out against the policies, and, most importantly, would they provide different amounts of instrumental support for disadvantaged group members negatively affected by these policies? Second, if our hypothesis that ambiguity is a key element of tokenism and that this ambiguity plays a critical role in determining the responses to it, advantaged group members evaluating a policy of tokenism should be particularly influenced by manipulations that focus their attention in ways that reduce this ambiguity. This same manipulation was not expected to impact on advantaged group members' evaluations and actions of the relatively unambiguous closed and open policies. Thus, similar to the work described earlier by Karacanta and Fitness (2006; see also Powell et al., 2005), we utilized a focus of attention manipulation. Advantaged group members received mild encouragement to consider the policy while thinking about members of their own group or members of the disadvantaged group.

Also noteworthy, the current study differs from much of previous intergroup relations research, which tends to focus on opinions and evaluations of an out-group or a policy. However, in the current study, although participants answer questions about their reactions to the policy, they believe their responses are going to be given to the relevant policymakers and that they will directly influence the future of the policy. Thus, their answers can be interpreted as a form directly speaking out for or against the policy. Furthermore, we also employed a second unusual dependent variable involving the opportunity to provide a monetary donation to directly assist the disadvantaged group, a direct form of helping.

In summary, it was predicted that advantaged group members would respond differently to the closed, tokenism, and open conditions. A closed system should be recognized as unjust, changes should be demanded, and the disadvantaged out-group should be offered meaningful assistance in this condition. An open system should be seen as just and appropriate, should lead to little or no demands for change, and little assistance should be provided to the disadvantaged group. In addition, responses in these two conditions should be unaffected by manipulations of focus of attention. However, the inherent ambiguity of the tokenism system should make advantaged group members particularly likely to be influenced by the focus of attention manipulation. When considering the policy with the in-group in mind they should respond similarly to those who believe the system is open. That is, tokenism will be seen as just, there will be little call for change, and little out-group help. However, when considering the policy with the out-group in mind, they should respond in a manner more consistent with the closed condition. They should express feelings of injustice, demand change, and offer more out-group help.

During regular class sessions, undergraduate students from the University of California at Santa Cruz (UCSC) were told that the university administration was seeking student opinions on a number of university policies that were currently being reviewed. They were told their class was being asked to evaluate the university's policies related to admission of students from underdeveloped countries and received a description of UCSC's policy for acceptance of students from the two little-known African nations of Guinea Bissau and Namibia. The first paragraph set the stage for out-group disadvantage by describing problems with these two nations' educational systems, and some initiatives undertaken by Californian universities in these two nations. The second paragraph provided the policy manipulation. In the open condition, the university policy was to admit all students from these two nations who met minimum academic and English language requirements. In the closed condition, the policy was to not admit any students from these two countries. In the tokenism condition, the policy was to admit only 2 percent of those who met English language and academic requirements. Finally, the final sentence in the handout contained the focus of attention manipulation. Participants were asked either to consider the implications of the policy for the developing nations or California and US residents.

As predicted, when asked to rate the justice of the policy, students who read that the system was open rated the policy as more just than those who read that the system was closed and these ratings were not influenced by which group was the focus of their attention. It appears that the illegitimacy (or legitimacy) of these two policies was sufficiently clear to undermine the influence of an effort to focus attention on one group or the other. What are now fundamental norms of non-discrimination make a complete ban of disadvantaged group members seem unfair even if one is thinking about the implications of the ban for one's own group. Similarly, the strength of North American beliefs in a meritocratic system makes a policy consistent with merit-based selection seem fair even when focusing on the effects of the policy for the in-group.

In contrast, perceptions of the policy of tokenism were highly affected by the focus of attention instructions. On one hand, when their attention was focused on the disadvantaged out-group, members of the advantaged group recognized the severe restrictions imposed by the policy of tokenism were unjust, rating the policy similar to the closed condition. Including only 2 percent of the qualified members of the out-group seemed extremely unfair when they thought about the implications of the policy for the out-group. On the other hand, when attention was focused on their in-group, members of the advantaged group described the policy of tokenism as equivalent to the open condition. Now when thinking about their in-group, advantaged group members described the inclusion of only 2 percent of the qualified members of the disadvantaged out-group as quite fair.

Virtually identical effects emerged on a measure of negative emotions (i.e., anger and frustration), and more importantly for the current discussion, participants' demands for policy change were consistent. Again, the demands for change to the policy were stronger in the closed condition that in the open condition and were unaffected by focus of attention. Whether students focused on the disadvantaged group or their own in-group influenced their demands for change only when the current policy was one of tokenism.

The degree to which the perceptions of justice, emotional responses, and demands for change in response to a policy of tokenism can be influenced by a single simple statement encouraging participants to think about one group or the other illustrates the ambiguity that this policy engenders. This uncertainty means that advantaged group members' evaluations and their desire to see change that would increase support to the disadvantaged group will be influenced by situational factors and external cues that help to clarify the appropriate responses to tokenism.

But what about direct instrumental aid? Participants in this study were also given the opportunity to provide monetary donations to the disadvantaged group. After participants had provided their evaluations and recommendations to the university administration, a representative of a student organization that was advocated for international students asked the students for donations to support their efforts. She indicated that she had been given permission to approach students after they had been made aware of the university policy. Participants were thus given an opportunity to provide direct help (money) to the disadvantaged group. The outcome of this measure showed a similar effect for the closed and open conditions, with much more money being donated when all members of the disadvantaged group were excluded than when all qualified members of the disadvantaged group were included. However, on this measure the tokenism condition did not appear to show the strong effect of focus of attention. Those who believed that university policy was to accept only 2 percent of the qualified members of the disadvantaged group gave an amount of money that fell directly between those in the closed and open conditions, and was unaffected by the statement encouraging them to focus on the in-group or the out-group.

It is noteworthy, and not particularly surprising, that the monetary donations did not produce data that are as clean as the questionnaire data. For example, the data were highly skewed and the variance in donations ranged considerably. This resulted in difficulties with the power of statistical tests (there was evidence of some inconclusive but interesting trends). However, there are also reasons to believe that this lack of effect of focus of attention in the tokenism condition for this measure (despite strong effects for the other measures) may be meaningful. Others have found real differences between people's willingness to report dissatisfaction with a current situation, their indication of an intention to act, and actual direct actions to change the system. For example, Beaton and Deveau (2005) found substantial discrepancies between advantaged group members' self-reports of levels of willingness to participate in a collective action on behalf of the out-group and their actual participation. In fact, fewer than half of those who stated their intention to help actually completed the task. In addition, the personal sacrifice and the focus on "money" involved in donating to charity may invoke additional psychological barriers to helping like a focus on self-sufficiency (see Vohs, Mead, & Goode, 2006) or simple self-interest (Holmes, Miller, & Lerner, 2002). These additional normative pressures may undermine the influence of the focus of attention manipulation but provide an alternative clarification in the tokenism condition.

Summary and Conclusions

Overall, we believe this study represents an interesting specific example of how ambiguity can influence advantaged group members' decisions to speak out in support of the disadvantaged group. The ambiguity, in this case, came in the form of a policy of tokenism, one that restricted access to a valued position for members of the disadvantaged group. The ambiguity inherent in tokenism (see Wright, 1997, 2001) reduced the degree to which participants could make a clear decision to help the out-group or not. Thus, they were more receptive to the influence of a focus of attention manipulation. Encouraging thoughts about the in-group versus the out-group effectively changed the perceived legitimacy of the tokenism policy and thus the willingness to demand changes that would help the out-group. When the policy was clearly inconsistent (complete exclusion) or consistent (meritocratic inclusion) with existing norms of meritocracy and non-discrimination, responses to the policy were not influenced by focus of attention. In addition, there is some evidence that the ambiguity of tokenism also played a role in direct monetary helping as well, as the tokenism policy elicited levels of helping that fell directly between the complete exclusion and the meritocratic inclusion policies.

From this data, we can conclude that when there is clear discrimination against an out-group, advantaged groups will help. When reading about a policy that completely excluded members of a clearly disadvantaged out-group, students indicated strong feelings of injustice, and made strong calls for change. In addition, many gave money in an effort to advocate on behalf of the out-group. It should be noted that these actions could have meaningful impacts on resources for the in-group. UCSC is a publicly funded institution with limited access even to very talented Californian and US students. Opening more places to students from African nations would only divert resources away from the in-group and increase restrictions on in-group access to these valued positions. Nonetheless, a manipulation encouraging a focus on the in-group had no impact on helping in this unambiguously exclusionary situation. So, there is evidence in this study of a strong and genuine interest in helping the out-group even when there are potential costs to one's own group. However, as importantly, the results for those responding to a policy of tokenism provide support for our general contention that ambiguity plays a key role in intergroup helping and that clarifying messages may play a strong role in determining whether helping will bias towards in-group over out-group members.

General Conclusions

We end this chapter where we began, with a call for a more balanced look at intergroup helping. While not denying the important impediments to help across group boundaries – such a denial would simply be foolish, as the evidence for these numerous obstacles is strong – we are seeking a psychology that (a) recognizes that even with these impediments, acts of assistance and helping across groups are commonplace, and (b) can explain more fully genuine and meaningful cross-group prosocial acts. We believe that a greater attention to intergroup relations that are defined primarily by an interdependent or supportive relationship (caregivers, allies, partners, etc.), rather than social comparison, might be one place to start.

We also provided the theoretical basis and some research evidence for a process that can produce cross-group helping that is as genuine and selfless as intragroup helping. The inclusion of the out-group in the self, which can result from building a close personal relationship with an out-group member, can lead to strong support for out-group interests and genuine assistance to out-group members. We believe that this process and the self-expansion theory on which it is built provide an important addition to the literature. They propose what may be a basic underlying process through which out-groups and their members can be seen as attractive possibilities for self-expansion. Thus, self-expansion motives and inclusion of the out-group in the self may represent antagonistic processes to the many other psychological processes that lead us to avoid and fear out-groups. Thus, while the many discussions of basic processes that "push us away" from out-groups provide abundant explanations for the apparent failure to help across group boundaries, self-expansion motives and the inclusion of the out-group in the self provide one explanation for why out-group helping can and does occur.

In addition, we presented an alternative, less malevolent explanation for the failure to help across group lines. We proposed that situational ambiguity creates uncertainty that can lead to inertia and tendency not to help, and that this uncertainty is likely to be much greater in cases of cross-group helping. We presented research from our work on tokenism showing that not only will advantaged group members at times provide support and assistance to the disadvantaged out-group when the situation is clearly discriminatory, but they will also provide greater support when the ambiguity of a tokenism context is reduced. When simply encouraged to think about the disadvantaged group, advantaged group members described a policy of tokenism as unjust and made clear demands for change. However, when encouraged to focus on their in-group, advantaged group members no longer perceived tokenism as unjust and were unlikely to make demands for change. It appears that while situational ambiguity can effectively undermine cross-group helping, it is also possible that contextual variables that clarify the situation can be particularly effective in increasing out-group assistance and support. In short, we see our work as part of a growing effort to paint a more positive image of human psychology and, in this case, a more optimistic view of cross-group helping.

NOTE

1 This idea initially emerged at a meeting of a Dutch Research Council funded Expert Meeting – *The Role of Outgroups in Self-Conception and Group Behavior*. Thus, credit for the general idea of an expanded "relational" role for the out-group is shared equally with Marilyn Brewer, Michael Hogg, Amélie Mummendey, Dan van Knippenberg, and Esther van Leeuwen.

17

Helping Disadvantaged Out-Groups Challenge Unjust Inequality
The Role of Group-Based Emotions

Aarti Iyer and Colin Wayne Leach

Introduction

Most theory and research on the psychology of helping has taken an individual-level perspective (for a review, see Penner, Dovidio, Piliavin, & Schroeder, 2005). For example, classic empirical studies investigated when and why individuals were willing to help another individual to complete a task (e.g., Weiner, 1980) or obtain treatment after an injury (e.g., Piliavin, Dovidio, Gaertner, & Clark, 1981). More recent work has considered individuals' willingness to help individual members of in-groups and out-groups who are suffering from relatively minor injuries (e.g., Levine, Prosser, Evans, & Reicher, 2005) or serious illnesses (e.g., Stürmer, Snyder, & Omoto, 2005). Although these studies take group membership into account, the dependent variable of interest is still help provided to an individual.

In the present chapter we move away from the individual level to consider when and why people choose to help out-groups as a whole. More specifically, we focus on help to out-groups who suffer unjust treatment or who unjustly occupy low-status positions. Such injustice is often challenged in deliberate acts of resistance, which illustrate what some social psychologists term "collective action" (Wright, Taylor, & Moghaddam, 1990). Collective action may be undertaken by an individual acting alone (e.g., displaying a political button), or by many people in concert (e.g., participating in a demonstration), as long as the goal is to improve the status of an entire group, rather than one or a few individuals (Wright, 2001).

It is important to understand how advantaged groups come to help disadvantaged out-groups, because their involvement can be crucial to the achievement of justice. The advantaged collectively wield a great deal of political, economic, and social power within society (Jackman,

1994; Kimmel & Ferber, 2001), and thus are able to provide valuable resources to social movements that seek to combat injustice (Goodman, 2001; Marx & Useem, 1971). Members of advantaged groups can also add momentum to social justice efforts because their participation can encourage others to join the endeavor, thus increasing the critical mass needed to effect change (Goodman, 2001). For example, the involvement of European American anti-racist activists attracted national attention to the US civil rights movement in the mid-1960s, bringing many new sympathizers and activists to the struggle (Thompson, 2001).

It is important to note, however, that help from the advantaged is not a panacea for all social problems. No matter how well intentioned it may be, involvement from the advantaged can often create as many (or more) difficulties than it solves. Members of advantaged groups can stand in the way of a movement's success by assuming (rather than earning) dominant and intrusive roles based on the group-based advantages they have become accustomed to. Such paternalistic helping (see Nadler, 2002) can re-create structural inequalities within the organization, thus reinforcing the very power structures that the movement is trying to dismantle (hooks, 1989; Marx & Useem, 1971).

In this chapter, we consider how members of advantaged groups come to help disadvantaged out-groups by participating in efforts to achieve social justice. The first section reviews approaches to collective action, which offer a fairly limited account of participation by advantaged groups. In the second section, we present a framework of group-based emotions to better explain advantaged groups' involvement in collective action.

Current Approaches to Collective Action

Established frameworks of participation in collective action have developed primarily from literatures in sociology and social psychology. Although these approaches are quite diverse in the variables and factors they emphasize, they share in common a tendency to downplay the role of the advantaged group in efforts to achieve social justice. More specifically, frameworks of collective action tend to (1) focus exclusively on disadvantaged groups' collective action; or (2) focus on the self-interest of advantaged groups; or (3) downplay the distinct psychological experiences of the advantaged group. Recently developed frameworks of helping have given more attention to the role of the advantaged. However, these approaches (4) tend to emphasize self-relevance as an explanation for out-group helping. These four perspectives are described in more detail below.

(1) Exclusive Focus on the Disadvantaged

Many frameworks of collective action make little mention of the (potential or actual) involvement by advantaged groups in efforts to achieve social justice. Rather, they aim to explain only how members of *disadvantaged* groups come to participate in collective action. For instance, the standard widely used definition of collective action (Wright et al., 1990) states that "a group member engages in collective action strategies any time that she or he is acting as a representative of the group and the action is directed at improving the conditions of the entire group" (p. 995). Collective action here is explicitly theorized as aiming to improve the status of the *in-group*, suggesting that only those who are disadvantaged by a system of inequality would seek to change it (for a review, see Kelly, 1996).

The emphasis within this definition on the disadvantaged reflects the limited scope of some classic theories of collective action. For instance, relative deprivation theory posits that only when individuals perceive their situation as relatively deprived will they experience dissatisfaction and anger, and seek to improve their lot (Pettigrew, 1967; Runciman, 1966; for a review, see Walker & Smith, 2002). By definition, this framework focuses exclusively on how disadvantaged groups experience, and respond to, their own low-status position. There is little mention of how members of advantaged groups might perceive an out-group's disadvantage or, indeed, the in-group's own high-status position.

Similarly, early formulations of social identity theory (Tajfel, 1978b; Tajfel & Turner, 1979) emphasized the experience of low-status groups, whose members seek to improve their (relative) status position either through individual-level strategies (e.g., individual mobility into a higher-status group) or group-level strategies (e.g., collective action). Little was said about high-status groups, except that their members should feel satisfied with the status quo. Recent development of the social identity model has continued this view of the advantaged group (e.g., Kawakami & Dion, 1995; Wright, 2001). For instance, Wright (2001) proposed that positive personal and social identities (based on favorable interpersonal or intergroup comparisons, respectively) are associated with *inaction* for those in advantaged positions. This model implies that the advantaged are automatically satisfied with their group's high-status position, regardless of the socio-structural characteristics (e.g., legitimacy and stability) of the intergroup inequality.

Empirical research testing the predictions of relative deprivation theory (e.g., Guimond & Dubé-Simard, 1983; Martin, Brickman, & Murray, 1984; Olson, Roese, Meen, & Robertson, 1995) and social identity theory (e.g., Boen & Vanbeselaere, 2000; Wright et al., 1990) has also paid little attention to advantaged groups. These studies typically recruit (or experimentally create) members of disadvantaged groups and investigate the predictors of their collective action intentions to improve the in-group's position. For instance, research on the role of identification with a group in predicting collective action intentions has only surveyed members of disadvantaged occupation groups (e.g., Klandermans, Sabucedo, Rodriguez, & de Weerd, 2002), trade union organizations (e.g., Veenstra & Haslam, 2000), and low-status demographic groups based on race (e.g., Berman & Wittig, 2004) and sexual orientation (e.g., Simon et al., 1998; Stürmer & Simon, 2004). As a result, this work says little about how members of advantaged groups become willing to work for social justice.

In this way, some theoretical and empirical work on collective action can be narrowly focused on the disadvantaged. In our view, this implies a crucial (theoretical and political) assumption: that participation in efforts to achieve social justice is irrelevant to the relatively advantaged. In other words, members of advantaged groups take no action against injustice because they do not notice it or because they do not care about it. This perspective is consistent with work showing that when a group enjoys a secure high-status position, its members are more likely to think of themselves as individuals than as group members (Mullen, 1991) and are thus less likely to notice that they are benefiting from group-based inequality (for a review, see Leach, Snider, & Iyer, 2002). It is also consistent with the view that collective action is motivated by self-interest, a point we discuss in more detail below.

(2) Exclusive Focus on the Self-Interest of the Advantaged

Some approaches do address collective action by members of advantaged groups, but the focus of these investigations has been quite narrow. More specifically, these frameworks only consider the advantaged group's participation in collective action to protect in-group advantage. This follows from the general relative deprivation argument that individuals take action to further their group's collective interest (e.g., Grant & Brown, 1995; Walker & Mann, 1987), as well as their own individual interests (e.g., Tropp & Brown, 2004).

Indeed, research has shown that members of high-status groups often work to legitimize inequality and defend their group's position (for reviews, see Brewer, 1986; Leach et al., 2002). However, frameworks that focus exclusively on self-interested collective action by the advantaged do not contribute to an understanding of how the advantaged may help further the interests of low-status out-groups.

An illustration of this approach can be found in some formulations of social identity theory. According to this analysis, members of a high-status group that occupies an insecure status position will work to strengthen their group's position against threats to the status quo (Tajfel, 1978c; Tajfel & Turner, 1986). In a review of how perceptions of the intergroup context influence responses to inequality, Ellemers' (1993) brief discussion of advantaged groups focuses solely on strategies of status protection in the face of perceived threats. Within this approach, members of low-status groups might engage in individual or group-level attempts to change the inequality, whereas members of groups that are advantaged by the inequality strive to protect the status quo. Indeed, some of the empirical studies reviewed in this paper do not provide participants in (or assigned to) the high-status group with an opportunity to engage in collective action to achieve equality. Rather, they are only given the possibility of protecting the in-group's position (e.g., Ellemers & Bos, 1998), whereas members of the low-status group are offered the option of improving the status of the in-group or pursuing individual mobility (e.g., Ellemers, van Knippenberg, & Wilke, 1990). Not allowing the advantaged group the choice to take action on behalf of an out-group's interest makes it impossible to test the implied assumption that they will always refuse to take such action.

Another approach that emphasizes self-interest is Simon and Klandermans' (2001) framework of politicized collective identity as a precursor to collective action. They propose that politicized collective identity involves (1) a salient collective identity as a group member, which (2) occurs in the context of that group's active power struggle with another group, within (3) a larger social context which includes the general public (as well as additional groups) who are not directly involved. In this framework, both advantaged groups and disadvantaged groups can develop politicized collective identities on behalf of their own group's interests: "As for all groups, the first step to politicized collective identity is awareness of shared grievances, which, for high-status groups, most likely means awareness that their status and the associated privileges are threatened" (pp. 326–327). Although Simon and Klandermans do point out that third-party groups (which may include other powerful or advantaged groups) may be enlisted to support the interests of one of the antagonistic groups, their conceptual analysis emphasizes the antecedents and implications of self-interested politicized identities, rather than politicized identities on behalf of an out-group. Understandably, then, they do not provide a detailed discussion of how the advantaged may come to help disadvantaged out-groups.

(3) Downplaying the Psychology of the Advantaged

A final set of collective action frameworks focuses on how people who are sympathetic to a social cause become actively involved in a social movement (typically marked by sustained organized activity by a fairly large group of people; Klandermans & Oegema, 1987). Theories of social movement participation recognize that those who become active in the movement do not necessarily have to belong to the social categories that would benefit from the achievement of the movement's goals (Klandermans & Oegema, 1987; McCarthy & Zald, 1977). For example, resource mobilization theory proposes that the success of a social movement is determined by the power and resources that a social movement organization has at its disposal (Gurney & Tierney, 1982; McCarthy & Zald, 1977). As such, it recognizes the important role that the advantaged can play in a social movement, given their access to resources (such as money and volunteers) and power (McCarthy & Zald, 1977).

The expectancy-value model of social movement participation also explicitly includes members of advantaged and disadvantaged groups in its analysis (Klandermans & Oegema, 1987; Oegema & Klandermans, 1994). This framework outlines four steps to social movement participation: (1) becoming sympathetic to the cause represented by the social movement; (2) becoming persuaded to become active by the activist organization (Klandermans & Oegema, 1987); (3) becoming motivated to get involved in the movement (as determined by perceived costs and benefits; Klandermans, 1984); and (4) overcoming concrete barriers to participation, such as lack of time or resources (Klandermans & Oegema, 1987; Oegema & Klandermans, 1994). These four steps outline a path to active participation that can be followed by the advantaged as well as the disadvantaged, making the expectancy-value model applicable to members of both groups.

The clear strength of resource mobilization theory and the expectancy-value model is that they present broad frameworks of the social psychological processes underlying (presumably all) people's pathways to collective action. However, this breadth of analysis can also present a limitation: neither framework outlines the specific factors or processes that might differentiate the advantaged group's psychological experience of inequality from the disadvantaged group's experience. The structural position of the advantaged means that they have unique concerns when facing injustice suffered by others, and, by extension, unique obstacles to overcome in the pathway to collective action. Not addressing these issues limits these frameworks' ability to provide a full account of collective action by advantaged groups.

For instance, members of advantaged groups have to come to terms with systems of inequality that have accorded them their high-status position. Advantaged groups define the mainstream culture and establish the dominant ideology through institutional structures, systems, and practices (Goodman, 2001). Systems of inequality are created and maintained in ways that confer privileges to the high-status group (Lipsitz, 1998; Memmi, 1965). When the advantaged recognize the illegitimacy of an inequality, they must often recognize their group's illegitimate privileges (Goodman, 2001). This means that the advantaged have to change their perception of a cultural system that has favored their group (Katz, 1978; cf. Thompson, 2001). In deciding to help dismantle social inequality and injustice, the advantaged have to work against their group's collective interest (Lipsitz, 1998), a concern that members of disadvantaged groups do not face.

Second, members of advantaged groups may have to face their group's responsibility for creating and/or maintaining the system of inequality. When an advantaged group creates a system of privilege for itself or actively harms other groups, its members must (attempt to) come to terms with their group's actions (Barkan, 2000). Perceiving that one's group is responsible for an inequality poses a threat to the value of the group (Branscombe, Ellemers, Spears, & Doosje, 1999; Leach et al., 2002), and can lead to feelings of guilt, shame, and/or anger (e.g., Doosje, Branscombe, Spears, & Manstead, 1998; Iyer, Leach, & Crosby, 2003; Iyer, Schmader, & Lickel, 2007; Leach, Iyer, & Pedersen, 2006). This sense of collective responsibility for the inequality is unique to the experience of the advantaged because the disadvantaged are by definition not attached to the group that is causing the harm. By glossing over these specific experiences and focusing instead on broad motivations, resource mobilization theory and the expectancy-value model may be limited in their ability to provide a comprehensive account of why advantaged groups participate in social justice efforts.

(4) Emphasis on Self-Relevance as an Explanation of Out-Group Helping

Recent theoretical work has focused more attention on the role of out-groups in helping those who are in low-status positions. Broadly speaking, these frameworks emphasize the process by which members of an advantaged group interpret and understand the experiences of a disadvantaged group. Runciman (1966) foreshadowed this approach in suggesting that advantaged groups may experience "relative deprivation on behalf of the other" when faced with a disadvantaged group, which should increase willingness to help the out-group (see also Beaton & Deveau, 2005). This implies that the advantaged will help when the plight of a disadvantaged out-group becomes self-relevant – when they are able to vicariously experience its perspective and interests.

The emphasis on self-relevance is more directly endorsed by work on perspective taking and helping: students who were experimentally induced to take the perspective of a heroin addict recommended a higher allocation of their Student Union budget to be donated to an agency that helps drug addicts, compared to participants in the control condition (Batson, Chang, Orr, & Rowland, 2002). Batson et al. (2002) propose that the underlying mediating process is altruistic motivation, where the ultimate goal is to improve another's situation rather than to serve one's own interests. However, this altruism is conceptualized as being based in feelings of empathy, which allow an individual to vicariously experience the thoughts and emotions (and, by extension, the interests and motivations) of others. In this way, empathy arguably increases the self-relevance of the out-group's experiences.

The social identity model of helping (e.g., Reicher, Cassidy, Wolpert, Hopkins, & Levine, 2006) also suggests that self-relevance plays a role in explaining help given to an out-group. Reicher et al. (2006) propose that individuals are more likely to help an out-group when the help (1) serves category (in-group) goals and (2) is consistent with (in-group) norms. Help is also likely when (3) the out-group and in-group can be recast as part of a shared common in-group whose interests will be harmed by the injustice. In our view, the emphasis on in-group goals and norms, as well as on recategorization processes, implies that out-groups are helped when their interests and goals are made more self-relevant to members of an in-group.

Taken together, these frameworks suggest that the processes of perspective taking, empathy, and recategorization can increase the self-relevance of an out-group's experience and thus serve as important routes to out-group helping. However, these are not necessarily the only predictors of intergroup helping. Frameworks that narrowly highlight the advantaged group's understanding of the disadvantaged group's experiences and interests do not consider other motivations or processes that lead to collective action. For instance, advantaged groups may wish to help a disadvantaged out-group after considering the role that their in-group, or a third-party agent, has played in perpetuating the injustice (see Iyer et al., 2007; Leach et al., 2006). As a result, current frameworks of intergroup helping do not necessarily provide a comprehensive view of the various reasons underlying advantaged groups' willingness to help disadvantaged out-groups.

Group-Based Emotions and Participation in Collective Action

For various reasons, traditional frameworks of collective action have paid relatively little attention to the range of specific psychological processes and motivations that could underlie advantaged groups' willingness to help achieve social justice. Recent theoretical and empirical work on group-based emotions has aimed to fill this gap, in offering an account of various ways in which advantaged groups may interpret, (emotionally) experience, and respond to, injustice faced by an out-group.

Accounting for Various Experiences of Inequality and Injustice

Drawing from the social identity theory perspective (Tajfel & Turner, 1979, 1986), the group-based emotions framework posits that people can experience emotions on the basis of their self-categorization as group members (see Iyer & Leach, 2008a; Smith, 1993). Group-based emotions are conceptualized as based in people's interpretations of intergroup contexts, just as individual-level emotions are based in interpretations of interpersonal contexts. They are thus one indicator of how people experience intergroup relations (Smith, 1993; Tiedens & Leach, 2004).

According to appraisal theories, distinct emotions are based in particular interpretations of events, situations, and relationships (Frijda, 1986; Ortony, Clore, & Collins, 1988). Research on individual-level emotions has linked specific combinations of appraisals to specific emotional experiences (Roseman, Spindel, & Jose, 1990). While some appraisal researchers question whether appraisals are necessary causes of emotions (see Frijda & Zeelenberg, 2001), they agree that patterns of appraisals at least covary with emotions, and thus can serve to differentiate between different emotional experiences (Scherer, 2001).

Theoretical frameworks of group-based emotions also link specific emotions with specific patterns of appraisal (see Smith, 1993; Leach et al., 2002). Several empirical studies have found support for the idea that patterns of appraisal differentiate between group-based emotions such as fear, anger, guilt, and sympathy (e.g., Iyer et al., 2003; Iyer et al., 2007; Mackie, Devos, & Smith, 2000). This approach is more precise than are traditional frameworks of prejudice or general attitude, which characterize the general valence of people's orientations towards the out-group, but do not further differentiate between various reactions of the same valence, such as fear and anger (see Smith, 1993).

The language of group-based emotions also provides a meaningful interpretation of people's various appraisals of intergroup relations. For example, knowing that people assess the legitimacy and stability of an inequality does not tell us much about their experience of the inequality. What does it *mean* to believe that an inequality is unstable and illegitimate? Group-based emotions provide a specific vocabulary to describe the different combinations of these perceptions of inequality, thus differentiating between these experiences of inequality in a meaningful way (Tiedens & Leach, 2004).

We (Leach et al., 2002) recently proposed a typology of emotional responses to relative advantage, differentiated along four key dimensions: *self-other focus* (i.e., whether attention is directed at the in-group or an out-group); *perceived legitimacy* (i.e., whether the status differential is deserved or unfair); *perceived stability* (i.e., whether the status differential is changeable or fixed); and *perceived control* (i.e., internal or external attributions for having obtained the high-status position). By accounting for a fuller range of responses to group inequality, the typology incorporates the various perspectives offered by previous frameworks. First, it acknowledges that when inequality is perceived to be legitimate and stable, it is not likely to be noticed by members of the advantaged group. This response is consistent with the view that the advantaged do not participate in social justice efforts.

Second, the typology includes a range of responses to inequality that is perceived to be legitimate, but less than fully stable. These responses would include the status protection strategies outlined in approaches that focus on the advantaged group's self-interested view of inequality. From a self-focused view, for instance, the advantaged should feel proud of their in-group's status position when the inequality is perceived to be legitimate, (a little bit) unstable, with high control (i.e., internal attributions of responsibility) for the group's success. In contrast, an other-focused view of the inequality should elicit emotions directed at the disadvantaged group from a position of legitimate superiority: disdain, pity, and indignation (anger).

The typology also extends previous frameworks of collective action by outlining various specific interpretations and emotions underlying the advantaged group's willingness to help achieve social justice. We propose that illegitimate inequality can be experienced in self-focused ways (i.e., emphasizing the in-group's position and responsibility for inequality), as well as other-focused ways (i.e., emphasizing the out-group's unearned low-status). Thus, distinct emotions (e.g., anger, sympathy, and guilt) that reflect distinct self-focused and other-focused experiences of inequality can motivate willingness to help disadvantaged out-groups improve their status position. This provides a broader range of motivations for collective action than perspective taking and common in-group identity.

Accounting for Multiple Responses to Inequality and Injustice

Affect has long been conceptualized as an important determinant of participation in collective action (Grant & Brown, 1995; Guimond & Dubé-Simard, 1983; Kawakami & Dion, 1995). Appraisal theorists add more precision to this general claim, arguing that each emotion is associated with specific action tendencies that lead to distinct responses to the situation or target (Frijda, 1986; Frijda, Kuipers, & ter Shure, 1989; Roseman, Wiest, & Swartz, 1994). Particular group-based emotions should thus lead to particular intergroup actions (Iyer et al., 2007; Leach et al., 2006; Mackie et al., 2000; Smith, 1993). Outlining specific emotional responses to inequality can help us understand why members of advantaged groups respond to the same inequality in very different ways, based on their different subjective appraisals of the structural conditions (Iyer et al., 2003; Leach et al., 2002; Montada & Schneider, 1989; Smith, 1993).

The group-based emotions framework is especially useful in explaining efforts to improve the status of disadvantaged out-groups, because such help can take different forms. Social justice efforts often reflect specific political strategies and ideologies (South End Press Collective,

1998). For example, some activists work to *confront or challenge the people or institutions responsible* for causing or perpetuating the inequality or injustice (Goodman, 2001). Others have concentrated on seeking *restitution for victims* of inequality (Barkan, 2000). Still others attempt to *help increase opportunities* for the disadvantaged group (Pratkanis & Turner, 1999). Collective action and political participation thus rarely occur in a strategic vacuum: people often choose to support a particular justice strategy in their political involvement (see Thompson, 2001). As such, the group-based emotions framework is well-positioned to explain the basis (or bases) of participation in different strategies.

Investigations of the implications of emotion have included a range of outcome variables, each with distinct implications for action. To our knowledge, almost no empirical research has included direct measures of *actual behavior* (for an exception, see Batson et al., 2002). A number of studies have assessed the *willingness to take concrete actions* (e.g., Iyer et al., 2007; Iyer & Leach, 2008a; Leach & Iyer, 2008; Leach et al., 2006), which should be the best predictor of future behavior. Such measures typically ask participants to indicate how willing they would be to engage in a range of political actions (e.g., sign a petition, or participate in a demonstration) to advocate a specific response strategy.

Most research assesses the link between felt emotion and *action tendencies*, which reflect a general readiness to engage or disengage in a particular fashion (see Frijda et al., 1989; Roseman et al., 1994). Illustrative measures of action tendencies include van Zomeren, Spears, Fischer, and Leach's (2004) measure of collective action (sample item: *I would participate in a demonstration against this proposal*) and Mackie et al.'s (2000) measure of offensive action tendencies (items: *confront them, oppose them, argue with them*). These measures differ from the willingness for concrete action because they refer only to the readiness to engage in quite general and abstract behavior, without actual intention or specification of how this behavior would be enacted (Leach et al., 2006).

Most research also measures support for *"motivational" goals* (Roseman et al., 1994), which reflect generalized motives (e.g., wanting to hurt someone, or wanting to make amends) rather than specific (actual or intended) actions. Iyer and Leach's (2008a) measure of support for "abstract goals" would fit in this category (e.g., "I want to make amends for the harm done by race relations at [the university]"). A number of studies (e.g., Iyer et al., 2003; McGarty, Pedersen, Leach, Mansell, Waller, & Bliuc, 2005; Swim & Miller, 1999) assess support for specific government and social policy (e.g., government apology or compensative affirmative action). Support for such policies should reflect support for the general goals they encompass (e.g., restitution). However, such support does not necessarily say much about the concrete action that people are willing to take to pursue these goals.

Helping by confronting those responsible for wrong-doing
Anger has been conceptualized as a high-arousal emotion that often motivates individuals to action (Lazarus, 1991). Thus, it is not surprising that empirical work has found anger to be the most action-oriented among the emotions investigated in group and intergroup contexts. People who feel angry typically want to move against the target of their anger in a confrontational way. For instance, Mackie et al. (2000) found that opinion-group members' anger towards the opposing out-group predicted a desire to confront, oppose, and argue with them. Similarly, British football fans' anger about the result of a match predicted an increased desire to "confront the opposition's fans" and "argue with the opposition's fans" (Crisp, Heuston, Farr, & Turner, 2007). Another set of studies has shown that anger about intergroup harm is associated with wanting the abstract goal of taking offensive action against the cause of the harm (Gordijn, Yzerbyt, Wigboldus, & Dumont, 2006; Yzerbyt, Dumont, Wigboldus, & Gordijn, 2003).

Most relevant to the question at hand are two studies we have conducted to investigate members of advantaged groups' support for the goal of confronting those responsible for racial discrimination (Iyer & Leach, 2008a; Leach & Iyer, 2008). In both studies, we presented European American students with an ostensible report detailing their in-group's discrimination against African Americans. Participants' anger about their in-group's responsibility for this discrimination was moderately associated with wanting to confront those responsible. Feelings of group-based anger about the in-group's own discrimination also moderately predicted a willingness to take concrete action with a student political group to confront those responsible for the injustice.

The link between anger and willingness for confrontation action has also been demonstrated in other studies. Van Zomeren et al. (2004, Study 1) demonstrated that individuals' anger about an out-group's unfair treatment by an authority moderately predicted intentions to participate in collective action (e.g., participate in a demonstration, sign a petition) to challenge this authority ($\hat{a}$ = .40). Interestingly, Van Zomeren et al. (2004) showed that the link between anger and the willingness for confrontational action was just as strong in response to the unfair treatment of an out-group as it was for the unjust treatment of the in-group. Similarly, German citizens' moral outrage about social and economic inequality was the strongest independent predictor of readiness to take various political actions to challenge inequality, such as donating money, participating in a demonstration, and joining an activity group (Montada & Schneider, 1989). And, a final study showed British people's anger at the American government regarding the occupation of Iraq to uniquely predict willingness for concrete political action to confront the government (Iyer et al., 2007, Study 2). In some of these studies, the predictive effect of anger remained robust after controlling for other emotions such as guilt (Iyer & Leach, 2008a; Iyer et al., 2007; Leach & Iyer, 2008; Montada & Schneider, 1989) and sympathy (Montada & Schneider, 1989).

Helping by providing restitution
Guilt. Research has shown individuals' "vicarious guilt" about another's wrong-doing to be associated with an approach motivation to repair the wrong-doing and "make it better" (Lickel, Schmader, Curtis, Scarnier, & Ames, 2005; Schmader & Lickel, 2006). In a minimal group context, Doosje et al. (1998, Study 1) found that guilt about an in-group's past wrong-doing against an out-group predicted agreement with the goal of compensation (e.g., "I think [in-group members] owe something to [out-group members] because of the things [in-group members] have done"). And, in Iyer and Leach (2008), European Americans' guilt about their in-group's racial discrimination increased their support for the goal of restitution (e.g., "I want to make amends for the harm done by race relations at [the university]").

The link between guilt and restitution has also been demonstrated in the context of government policies. Non-Aboriginal Australians' guilt about racial advantage predicted their support for a federal apology to Aboriginal Australians (McGarty et al., 2005, Study 1). Dutch guilt about their country's colonization of Indonesia predicted support for government compensation to the former colony (Doosje et al., 1998, Study 2). In the context of contemporary racial inequality, European Americans' (Iyer et al., 2003; Swim & Miller, 1999) and non-Aboriginal Australians' (Leach et al., 2006, Study 3) group-based guilt was moderately associated with increased support for policies offering material compensation to the disadvantaged to make up for the harm done by racial discrimination.

Given guilt's strong association with the abstract goal of restitution, it seems reasonable to expect that it should also predict individuals' intentions and willingness to take concrete action to bring about restitution. However, various studies have demonstrated that this predictive relationship does not exist after controlling for the effect of other emotions and related constructs (e.g., Harth, Kessler, & Leach, 2008). For instance, European Americans' guilt about racial discrimination did not predict willingness to take political action to bring about restitution, after controlling for feelings of anger (Iyer & Leach, 2008a; Leach & Iyer, 2008). Similarly, non-Aboriginal Australians' guilt about racial advantage did not predict willingness to take action to bring about systemic compensation, after controlling for prejudice and feelings of anger (Leach et al., 2006, Study 3). Lastly, American (Study 1) and British (Study 2) citizens' guilt about their countries' occupation of Iraq did not predict willingness to take action to advocate compensation to the Iraqi people, after controlling for feelings of anger and shame (Iyer et al., 2007). Leach, Iyer, and their colleagues have argued that the low arousal and narrow self-focus of guilt makes it a more likely predictor of the abstract goal of compensation than a willingness for concrete action. The willingness for concrete action should be best predicted by emotions, such as anger, that are characterized by higher levels of arousal and activity than guilt (Leach et al., 2002, 2006).

Anger directed at the in-group. Given that anger can be based in appraised in-group responsibility for a wrong-doing, it could also predict support for, and action intentions to advocate, the goal of restitution. Indeed, research has demonstrated that European Americans' anger about racial discrimination was a predictor of support for the goal of restitution to African American victims (Iyer & Leach, 2008a; Leach & Iyer, 2008). This predictive effect of anger was robust after accounting for feelings of guilt. Anger about racial inequality also predicted a willingness to take action to bring about systemic compensation among non-Aboriginal Australians (Leach et al., 2006, Study 3) and European Americans (Iyer & Leach, 2008a; Leach & Iyer, 2008). Similarly, British citizens' anger *at the in-group* (British people) regarding the occupation of Iraq was uniquely associated with willingness for political action to bring about compensation for those harmed by the occupation (Iyer et al., 2007, Study 2).

An alternative interpretation of these results is that anger predicted these outcomes simply because it is associated with other relevant variables, such as feelings of guilt or prejudice. However, each of the afore-mentioned studies included these related constructs in their analyses, thus demonstrating the independent role of anger in predicting willingness for compensation action. Thus, the predictive effects of anger remained reliable after controlling for the effects of guilt (Iyer & Leach, 2008a; Iyer et al., 2007; Leach & Iyer, 2006; Leach et al., 2006), anger at an out-group (Iyer et al., 2007), and prejudice (Leach et al., 2006).

Helping by increasing opportunities
Sympathy has been conceptualized as a prosocial emotion, as it is typically associated with a positive orientation towards those who are suffering. Research in group and intergroup contexts has found evidence for this claim in a number of ways. Sympathy for the disadvantaged is associated with support for social policies that will help the group. Iyer et al. (2003, Study 2) found that European Americans' feelings of sympathy about racial discrimination predicted their support for a racial policy that sought to increase opportunities for African Americans who had been disadvantaged by this inequality. Unlike guilt, sympathy was here based in a view that the out-group suffered from discrimination rather than a view that the in-group was the perpetrator of the discrimination (see also Harth et al., 2008). This focus on the out-group's suffering is central to sympathy and to its relatively strong association to helping (for a review, see Leach et al., 2002).

Pagano and Huo (2007) found that Americans' feelings of sympathy about the war in Iraq predicted support for four different policy responses: humanitarian action to help the Iraqi people obtain food and shelter, reparative action to compensate the Iraqi people for the harm they have suffered, preventative action to reduce future political abuses against Iraqi people, and retributive action to punish Saddam Hussein and his collaborators. Sympathy was the strongest predictor of the humanitarian and reparative policies, which most clearly and directly offer help to the out-group.

Sympathy for the disadvantaged has also been shown to increase helping behavior (e.g., Harth et al., 2008). Students who were experimentally induced to feel more sympathetic towards a heroin addict recommended a higher allocation of their Student Union budget to be donated to an agency that helps drug addicts, compared to participants in the control condition (Batson et al., 2002). This help was clearly directed at the group, as the experimental materials specified that the agency could not help the individual for whom the sympathy is felt. However, sympathy does not appear to motivate more direct political action: German citizens' sympathy for disadvantaged groups was not a strong predictor of their readiness to engage in political acts on these group's behalf, such as participating in a demonstration or signing a petition (Montada & Schneider, 1989).

Conclusions

Due to unfair inequality, and other forms of social injustice, low-status groups suffer in their societies. Under many circumstances, the disadvantaged recognize their illegitimate position and do what they can to improve their individual status or take collective action to improve the status of the group as a whole. Although history suggests that such efforts by the disadvantaged may achieve social justice on their own, it seems clear that help from groups advantaged by their high-status position can advance such aims.

For a number of reasons that we outlined above, prevailing approaches to social movements and other collective action tend to either ignore the advantaged or presume that they are uninterested in, or necessarily opposed to, efforts at social justice that would threaten their advantage. While acknowledging this reality, we sought to highlight some of the many other ways in which members of advantaged groups react to the unjust treatment of others. By using the framework of group-based emotion, we could identify several specific feelings that lead members of high-status groups to want to help out-groups suffering social injustice. These include guilt, sympathy, and anger.

The group-based emotions approach is also able to explain why members of advantaged groups pursue different strategies to help disadvantaged out-groups. Our review of recent research suggests that sympathy is a key predictor of the willingness to provide help to the disadvantaged out-group. In addition, anger (directed at different targets) predicted the willingness to provide restitution to victims of unjust inequality, as well as a willingness to challenge those responsible for creating the inequality. Thus, anger emerged as especially important to explaining advantaged groups' concrete willingness and intentions to engage in the personal and political action necessary to achieve social justice.

Bibliography

Aberson, C. L., & Haig, S. C. (2007). Contact, perspective taking, and anxiety as predictors of stereotype endorsement, explicit attitudes, and implicit attitudes. *Group Processes and Intergroup Relations, 10,* 179–201.

Abrams, D., Ando, K., & Hinkle, S. (1998). Psychological attachment to the group: Cross-cultural differences in organizational identification and subjective norms as predictors of workers' turnover intentions. *Personality and Social Psychology Bulletin, 24,* 1027–1039.

Abrams, D., & Hogg, M. A. (1990). Social identification, self-categorization and social influence. In W. Stroebe & M. Hewstone (Eds.), *European review of social psychology* (Vol. 1, pp. 195–228). Chichester: Wiley.

Abrams, D., Wetherell, M. S., Cochrane, S., Hogg, M. A., & Turner, J. C. (1990). Knowing what to think by knowing who you are: A social identity approach to norm formation, conformity and group polarization. *British Journal of Social Psychology, 29,* 97–119.

Ajzen, I., & Fishbein, M. (2005). The influence of attitudes on behavior. In D. Albarracin, B. T. Johnson, & M. P. Zanna (Eds.), *The handbook of attitudes* (pp. 173–221). Mahwah, NJ: Erlbaum.

Alcock, J. (2004). *Animal behavior.* Sunderland, MA: Sinauer.

Alexander, R. D. (1987). *The biology of moral systems.* London: Aldine.

Allen, N. J. (1996). Affective reactions to the group and the organization. In M. A. West (Ed.), *The handbook of work group psychology* (pp. 371–396). Chichester: Wiley.

Allen, N. J., & Meyer, J. P. (1990). The measurement and antecedents of affective, continuance and normative commitment to the organization. *Journal of Occupational Psychology, 63,* 1–18.

Allik, J., & Realo, A. (2004). Individualism-collectivism and social capital. *Journal of Cross-Cultural Psychology, 35,* 29–49.

Allport, G. W. (1954a). *The nature of prejudice.* Reading, MA: Addison Wesley.

Allport, G. W. (1954b). The historical background of modern social psychology. In G. Lindzey (Ed.), *Handbook of Social Psychology* (Vol. 1). Cambridge, MA: Addison Wesley.

356 Bibliography

Ames, D. R. (2004). Inside the mind reader's tool kit: Projection and stereotyping in mental state inference. *Journal of Personality and Social Psychology, 87,* 340–353.

amfAR, The Foundation for AIDS Research. (2008, March 31). *Stigma clings stubbornly to women living with HIV/AIDS.* Retrieved April 1, 2008 from www.sciencedaily.com/releases/2008/03/080331084115.htm.

Anastasio, P., Bachman, B., Gaertner, S. L., & Dovidio, J. F. (1997). Categorization, recategorization, and common ingroup identity. In R. Spears, P. J. Oakes, N. Ellemers, & S. A. Haslam (Eds.), *The social psychology of stereotyping and group life* (pp. 236–256). Malden, MA: Blackwell.

Anderson, L. R., Mellor, J. M., & Milyo, J. (2004). *Social capital and contributions in a public goods experiment.* Unpublished manuscript, College of William and Mary, Williamsburg, VA.

Archer, R. L., Diaz-Loving, R., Gollwitzer, P. M., Davis, M. H., & Foushee, H. C. (1981). The role of dispositional empathy and social evaluation in the empathic mediation of helping. *Journal of Personality and Social Psychology, 46,* 786–796.

Aron, A., & Aron, E. N. (1986). *Love and the expansion of self: Understanding attraction and satisfaction.* New York: Hemisphere.

Aron, A., & Aron, E. N. (1996). Love and the expansion of the self: The state of the model. *Personal Relationships, 3,* 45–58.

Aron, A., Aron, E. N., & Smollan, D. (1992). Inclusion of other in the self scale and the structure of interpersonal closeness. *Journal of Personality and Social Psychology, 63,* 596–612.

Aron, A., McLaughlin-Volpe, T., Mashek, D., Lewandowski, G., Wright, S. C., & Aron, E. N. (2004). Including others in the self. In W. Stroebe & M. Hewstone (Eds.), *European review of social psychology* (Vol. 15, pp. 101–132). Hove: Psychology Press.

Aron, A., Steele, J., Kashdan, T., & Perez, M. (2006). When similars do not attract: Tests of a prediction from the self-expansion model. *Personal Relationships, 13,* 387–396.

Aronson, E., Blaney, N., Stephan, C., Sikes, J., & Snapp, M. (1978). *The jigsaw classroom.* Beverly Hills, CA: Sage.

Aronson, E., Wilson, T. D., & Akert, R. M. (2005). *Social psychology.* Upper Saddle River, NJ: Prentice-Hall.

Aronson, E., & Worchel, P. (1966). Similarity vs. liking as determinants of interpersonal attractiveness. *Psychological Science, 5,* 157–158.

Arthur, W., Doverspike, D., & Fuentes, R. (1992). Recipients' affective responses to affirmative action interventions: A cross-cultural perspective. *Behavioral Science and the Law, 10,* 229–243.

Ashforth, B. E. (2001). Which hat to wear? The relative salience of multiple identities in organizational contexts. In M. A. Hogg & D. J. Terry (Eds.), *Social identity processes in organizational contexts* (pp. 31–48). Philadelphia, PA: Psychology Press.

Ashforth, B. E., & Mael, F. (1989). Social identity theory and the organization. *Academy of Management Review, 14,* 20–39.

Asser, E. S. (1978). Social class and help-seeking behavior. *American Journal of Community Psychology, 6,* 465–474.
Associated Press. (2005). Kanye West rips Bush at telethon. *FOXNews.com,* September 5. Retrieved from www.foxnews.com/story/0,2933,168387,00.html.
Astin, A. W., & Sax, L. J. (1998). How undergraduates are affected by service participation. *Journal of College Student Development, 39,* 251–262.
Avdeyeva, T. V., Burgetova, K., & Welch, I. D. (2006). To help or not to help? Factors that determined helping responses to Katrina victims. *Analyses of Social Issues and Public Policy, 6,* 159–173.
Baard, P. P., Deci, E. L., & Ryan, R. M. (2004). Intrinsic need satisfaction: A motivational basis of performance and well-being in two work settings. *Journal of Applied Social Psychology, 34,* 2045–2068.
Bargh, J. A. (1997). The automaticity of everyday life. In R. Wyer, Jr. (Ed.), *The automaticity of everyday life: Advances in social cognition* (Vol. 10, pp. 1–61). Mahwah, NJ: Erlbaum.
Bargh, J. A., Chen, M., & Burrows, L. (1996). Automaticity of social behavior: Direct effects of trait construct and stereotype activation on action. *Journal of Personality and Social Psychology, 71,* 230–244.
Barkan, E. (2000). *The guilt of nations: Restitution and negotiating historical injustices.* New York: W. W. Norton.
Barker, R. G., & Gump, P. V. (1964). *Big school, small school: High school size and student behavior.* Stanford, CA: Stanford University Press.
Baron, L. (1985/6). The Holocaust and human decency: a review of research on the rescue of Jews in occupied Europe. *Humboldt Journal of Social Relations, 13,* 239–240.
Baron, R. A., & Byrne, D. (2004). *Social psychology* (10th ed.). Boston: Pearson.
Baron, R. A., Byrne, D., & Branscombe, N. (2006). *Social psychology* (11th ed.). Boston: Pearson.
Baron, R. M., & Kenny, D. A. (1986). The moderator-mediator variable distinction in social psychological research: Conceptual, strategic, and statistical considerations. *Journal of Personality and Social Psychology, 51,* 1173–1182.
Barsness, Z. I., Tenbrunsel, A. E., Michael, J. H., & Lawson, L. (2002). Why am I here? The influence of group and relational attributes on member-initiated team selection. In H. Sondak (Ed.), *Toward phenomenology of groups and group membership* (Vol. 4, pp. 141–171). Amsterdam: JAI Press.
Bar-Zohar, M. (1998). *Beyond Hitler's grasp: The heroic rescue of Bulgaria's Jews.* Avon, MA: Adams Media.
Batson, C. D. (1991). *The altruism question: Toward a social psychological answer.* Hillsdale, NJ: Erlbaum.
Batson, C. D. (1994). Prosocial motivation: Why do we help others? In A. Tesser (Ed.), *Advanced social psychology* (pp. 333–381). Boston: McGraw-Hill.
Batson, C. D. (1997). Self-other merging and the empathy-altruism hypothesis: Reply to Neuberg et al. (1997). *Journal of Personality and Social Psychology, 73,* 517–522.

Batson, C. D., & Ahmad, N. (2001). Empathy-induced altruism in a prisoner's dilemma II: What if the target of empathy has defected? *European Journal of Social Psychology, 31*, 25–36.

Batson, C. D., Chang, J., Orr, R., & Rowland, J. (2002). Empathy, attitudes, and action: Can feeling for a member of a stigmatized group motivate one to help the group? *Personality and Social Psychology Bulletin, 28*, 1656–1666.

Batson, C. D., Duncan, B. D., Ackerman, P., Buckley, T., & Birch, K. (1981). Is empathic emotion a source of altruistic motivation? *Journal of Personality and Social Psychology, 40*, 290–302.

Batson, C. D., Early, S., & Salvarani, G. (1997). Perspective taking: Imagining how another feels versus imagining how you would feel. *Personality and Social Psychology Bulletin, 23*, 751–758.

Batson, C. D., Pate, S., Lawless, H., Sparkman, P., Lambert, S., & Worman, B. (1979). Helping under conditions of common threat: Increased "we-feeling" or ensuring reciprocity. *Social Psychology Quarterly, 42*, 410–414.

Batson, C. D., Polycarpou, M. P., Harmon-Jones, E., Imhoff, H. J., Mitchener, E. C., Bednar, L. L., Klein, T. R., & Highberger, L. (1997). Empathy and attitudes: Can feeling for a member of a stigmatized group improve feelings toward the group? *Journal of Personality and Social Psychology, 72*, 105–118.

Batson, C. D., Sager, K., Garst, E., Kang, M., Rubchinsky, K., & Dawson, K. (1997). Is empathy-induced helping due to self-other merging? *Journal of Personality and Social Psychology, 73*, 495–509.

Batson, C. D., & Shaw, L. L. (1991). Evidence for altruism: Toward a pluralism of prosocial motives. *Psychological Inquiry, 2*, 107–116.

Batson, C. D., Turk, C. L., Shaw, L. L., & Klein, T. R. (1995). Information function of empathic emotion: Learning that we value the other's welfare. *Journal of Personality and Social Psychology, 68*, 300–313.

Baumeister, R. F., & Leary, M. R. (1995). The need to belong: Desire for interpersonal attachments as a fundamental human motivation. *Psychological Bulletin, 117*, 497–529.

Baumeister, R. F., & Sommer, K. L. (1997). What do men want? Gender differences and two spheres of belongingness: Comment on Cross & Madson (1997). *Psychological Bulletin, 122*, 38–44.

Beal, D. J., O'Neal, E. C., Ong, J., & Ruscher, J. B. (2000). The ways and means of interracial aggression: Modern racists' use of covert retaliation. *Personality and Social Psychology Bulletin, 26*, 1225–1238.

Beaton, A. M., & Deveau, M. (2005). Helping the less fortunate: A predictive model of collective action. *Journal of Applied Social Psychology, 35*, 1609–1629.

Becker, S. W., & Eagly, A. H. (2004). The heroism of women and men. *American Psychologist, 59*, 163–178.

Begley, T. M., & Czajka, J. M. (1993). Panel analysis of the moderating effect of commitment on job satisfaction, intent to quit and health following organizational change. *Journal of Applied Psychology, 78*, 552–556.

Belloni, R. (2001). Civil society and peacebuilding in Bosnia and Herzegovina. *Journal of Peace Research*, *38*, 163–180.
Benedict, R. (1967). *The chrysanthemum and the sword*. Cleveland: World. (Original work published 1946)
Benson, P. L., Karabenick, S. A., & Lerner, R. M. (1976). Pretty pleases: The effects of physical attractiveness, race, and sex on receiving help. *Journal of Experimental Social Psychology*, *12*, 409–415.
Bentler, P. M., & Wu, E. J. W. (2004). *EQS 6.1 for Windows*. Multivariate Software, Inc.
Ben-Yakov, A. (1990). Bulgaria. In I. Gutman (Ed.), *Encyclopedia of the Holocaust* (Vol. 2). New York: Macmillan.
Berman, S. L., & Wittig, M. A. (2004). An intergroup theories approach to direct political action among African Americans. *Group Processes and Intergroup Relations*, *7*, 19–34.
Bessenoff, G. R., & Sherman, J. W. (2000). Automatic and controlled components of prejudice toward fat people: Evaluation versus stereotype activation. *Social Cognition*, *18*, 329–353.
Betancourt, H. (1990). An attribution-empathy model of helping behavior: Behavioral intentions and judgments of help-giving. *Personality and Social Psychology Bulletin*, *16*, 573–591.
Bickman, L., & Kamzan, M. (1973). The effect of race and need on helping behavior. *Journal of Social Psychology*, *89*, 73–77.
Biernat, M., & Dovidio, J. (2000). Stigma and stereotypes. In T. F. Heatherton, R. E. Kleck, M. R. Hebl, & J. G. Hull (Eds.), *The social psychology of stigma* (pp. 88–125). New York: Guilford Press.
Billig, M. (1987). *Arguing and thinking: A rhetorical approach to social psychology*. Cambridge: Cambridge University Press.
Billig, M. (1995). *Banal nationalism*. Cambridge: Cambridge University Press.
Blascovich, J., Mendes, W. B., Hunter, S. B., Lickel, B., & Kowai-Bell, N. (2001). Perceiver threat in social interactions with stigmatized others. *Journal of Personality and Social Psychology*, *80*, 253–267.
Blau, P. M., & Schwartz, J. E. (1984). *Crosscutting social circles: Testing a macro-structural theory of intergroup relations*. Orlando, FL: Academic Press.
Boen, F., & Vanbeselaere, N. (2000). Responding to membership of a low-status group: The effects of stability, permeability, and individual ability. *Group Processes and Intergroup Relations*, *3*, 41–62.
Boezeman, E. J., & Ellemers, N. (2007). Volunteering for charity: Pride, respect, and the commitment of volunteers. *Journal of Applied Psychology*, *92*, 771–785.
Boezeman, E. J., & Ellemers, N. (2008a). Pride and respect in volunteers' organizational commitment. *European Journal of Social Psychology*, *38*, 159–172.
Boezeman, E. J., & Ellemers, N. (2008b). Volunteer recruitment: The role of organizational support and anticipated respect in non-volunteers' attraction to charitable volunteer organizations. *Journal of Applied Psychology*, *93*, 1013–1026.

Boezeman, E. J., Ellemers, N., & Duijnhoven, P. H. M. (2007). Satisfaction with the volunteer job and its predictors: The relevance (and irrelevance) of status evaluations concerning the volunteer organization and being a volunteer within the volunteer organization to the work satisfaction of volunteers. Manuscript in preparation.

Boone, J. L. (1998). The evolution of magnanimity: When is it better to give than to receive? *Human Nature, 9,* 1–22.

Bourdieu, P. (1990). *The logic of practice.* Cambridge: Polity.

Bourhis, R. Y., Moïse, L. C., & Perrault, S. (1997). Towards an interactive acculturation model: A social psychological approach. *International Journal of Psychology, 32,* 369–386.

Boyadjieff, C. (1989). *Saving the Bulgarian Jews in World War II.* Singer Island: Free Bulgarian Center.

Boyte, H. C., & Kari, N. N. (1996). *Building America: The democratic promise of public work.* Philadelphia, PA: Temple University Press.

Brammer, L. M. (1992). Coping with life transitions. *International Journal for the Advancement of Counselling, 15,* 239–253.

Branscombe, N. R., Ellemers, N., Spears, R., & Doosje, B. (1999). The context and content of social identity threat. In N. Ellemers, R. Spears, & B. Doosje (Eds.), *Social identity: Context, commitment, content* (pp. 35–58). Oxford: Blackwell.

Branscombe, N. R., Spears, R., Ellemers, N., & Doosje, B. (2002). Intragroup and intergroup evaluation effects on group behavior. *Personality and Social Psychology Bulletin, 28,* 744–753.

Branscombe, N. R., & Wann, D. L. (1991). The positive social and self-concept consequences of sports team identification. *Journal of Sport and Social Issues, 15,* 115–127.

Branscombe, N. R., & Wann, D. L. (1994). Collective self-esteem consequences of outgroup derogation when a valued social identity is on trial. *European Journal of Social Psychology, 24,* 641–657.

Brener, L., von Hippel, W., & Kippax, S. (2007). Prejudice among health care workers toward injecting drug users with hepatitis C: Does greater contact lead to less prejudice? *International Journal of Drug Policy, 18,* 381–387.

Brewer, M. B. (1979). In-group bias in the minimal intergroup situation: A cognitive-motivational analysis. *Psychological Bulletin, 86,* 307–324.

Brewer, M. B. (1986). The role of ethnocentrism in intergroup conflict. In S. Worchel & W. G. Austin (Eds.), *Psychology of intergroup relations* (pp. 88–102). Chicago: Nelson-Hall.

Brewer, M. B. (1991). The social self: On being the same and different at the same time. *Personality and Social Psychology Bulletin, 17,* 475–482.

Brewer, M. B. (1999). The psychology of prejudice: Ingroup love or outgroup hate? *Journal of Social Issues, 55,* 429–444.

Brewer, M. B., & Brown, R. J. (1998). Intergroup relations. In D. T. Gilbert, S. T. Fiske, & G. Lindzey (Eds.), *The handbook of social psychology* (pp. 554–594). New York: McGraw-Hill.

Brewer, M. B., & Campbell, D. T. (1976). *Ethnocentrism and intergroup attitudes: East African evidence*. New York: Sage.

Brewer, M. B., & Caporael, L. (2006). An evolutionary perspective on social identity: Revisiting groups. In M. Schaller, J. A. Simpson, & D. T. Kenrick (Eds.), *Evolution and social psychology* (pp. 143–161). New York: Psychology Press.

Brewer, M. B., Dull, V., & Lui, L. (1981). Perceptions of the elderly: Stereotypes as prototypes. *Journal of Personality and Social Psychology, 41*, 656–670.

Brickman, P., Rabinowitz, V. C., Karuza, J., Jr., Coates, D., Cohn, E., & Kidder, L. (1982). Models of helping and coping. *American Psychologist, 37*, 368–384.

Brief, A. P. (1998). *Attitudes in and around organizations*. London: Sage.

Brigham, J. C. (1993). College students' racial attitudes. *Journal of Applied Social Psychology, 23*, 1933–1967.

Brissette, I., Scheier, M. F., & Carver, C. S. (2002). The role of optimism in social network development, coping, and psychological adjustment during a life transition. *Journal of Personality and Social Psychology, 82*, 102–111.

Broadbent, D. E., Cooper, P. F., FitzGerald, P., & Parkes, K. R. (1982). The Cognitive Failures Questionnaire (CFQ) and its correlates. *British Journal of Clinical Psychology, 21*, 1–16.

Brodsky, A. E. (1996). Resilient single mothers in risky neighborhoods: Negative psychological sense of community. *Journal of Community Psychology, 24*, 347–363.

Brodsky, A. E., O'Campo, P. J., & Aronson, R. E. (1999). PSOC in community context: Multi-level correlates of a measure of psychological sense of community in low-income, urban neighbourhoods. *Journal of Community Psychology, 27*, 659–679.

Brody, S. M., Wright, S. C., Aron, A., & McLaughlin-Volpe, T. (2008). Compassionate love for individuals outside one's social group. In L. Underwood, S. Sprecher, & B. Fehr (Eds.), *The science of compassionate love: Research, theory, and applications* (pp. 283–308). Malden, MA: Wiley-Blackwell.

Brown, J. D., & Smart, S. A. (1991). The self and social conduct: Linking self-representations to prosocial behavior. *Journal of Personality and Social Psychology, 60*, 368–375.

Brown, L., Macintyre, K., & Trujillo, L. (2003). Interventions to reduce HIV/AIDS stigma: What have we learned? *AIDS Education and Prevention, 15*, 49–69.

Brown, R. (1999). *Group processes*. Oxford: Blackwell.

Brown, R. (2000). Social identity theory: Past achievements, current problems and future challenges. *European Journal of Social Psychology, 30*, 745–778.

Brown, R., & Gaertner, S. L. (Eds.). (2001). *Blackwell handbook of social psychology: Intergroup processes*. Oxford: Blackwell.

Brown, R., & Hewstone, M. (2005). An integrative theory of intergroup contact. In M. Zanna (Ed.), *Advances in experimental social psychology* (Vol. 37, pp. 255–343). San Diego: Elsevier Academic Press.

Bryan, J. H., & Test, M. A. (1967). Models and helping: Naturalistic studies in aiding behaviour. *Journal of Personality and Social Psychology*, 6, 400–407.

Burnstein, E., Crandall, C., & Kitayama, S. (1994). Some neo-Darwinian decision rules for altruism: Weighing cues for inclusive fitness as a function of the biological importance of the decision. *Journal of Personality and Social Psychology*, 67, 773–789.

Buss, D. M. (1999). *Evolutionary psychology*. London: Allyn & Bacon.

Buss, D. M. (2005). *Handbook of evolutionary psychology*. Hoboken, NJ: Wiley.

Buss, D. M., & Schmitt, D. P. (1993). Sexual strategies theory: An evolutionary perspective on human mating. *Psychological Review*, 100, 204–232.

Butler, R., & Neuman, O. (1995). Effects of task and ego achievement goals on help-seeking behaviors and attitudes. *Journal of Educational Psychology*, 87, 261–271.

Byrne, S. (2001). Consociational and civic society approaches to peace-building in Northern Ireland. *Journal of Peace Research*, 38, 327–352.

Cable, D. M., & Turban, D. B. (2003). The value of organizational reputation in the recruitment context: A brand-equity perspective. *Journal of Applied Social Psychology*, 33, 2244–2266.

Cacioppo, J. T., Gardner, W. L., & Berntson, G. G. (1999). The affect system has parallel and integrative processing components: Form follows function. *Journal of Personality and Social Psychology*, 76, 839–855.

Campbell, D. T. (1958). Common fate, similarity and other indices of the status of aggregates of persons as social entities. *Behavioral Science*, 3, 14–25.

Campbell, D. T. (1965). Ethnocentric and other altruistic motives. In D. Levine (Ed.), *Nebraska symposium on motivation* (pp. 283–311). Lincoln: University of Nebraska Press.

Carlo, G., Okun, M. A., Knight, G. P., & De Guzman, M. R. T. (2005). The interplay of traits and motives on volunteering: Agreeableness, extraversion, and prosocial value motivation. *Personality and Individual Differences*, 38, 1293–1305.

Cassidy, C., Hopkins, N., Levine, M., Pandey, J., Reicher, S., & Singh, P. (2007). Social identity and collective behaviour: Some lessons from Indian research at the Magh Mela at Prayag. *Psychological Studies*, 52 (Special Issue on the Social Psychology of Collectivity), 286–292.

CBS/Associated Press. (2005). Race an issue in Katrina response. *CBSNews.com*, September 3. Retrieved from www.cbsnews.com/stories/2005/09/03/katrina/.

Chagnon, N. A. (1988). Life histories, blood revenge, and warfare in a tribal population. *Science*, 239, 985–992.

Chaiken, S., & Trope, Y. (1999). *Dual-process theories in social psychology*. New York: Guilford Press.

Chai-Tcherniak, L., & Nadler, A. (2008). *The effects of seeking autonomy- and dependency-oriented help on perceptions of the help seeker*. Unpublished manuscript, Tel Aviv University.

Chamberlin, J. (1997). A working definition of empowerment. *Psychiatric Rehabilitation Journal, 20,* 43–46.

Chavis, D. M., & Wandersman, A. (1990). Sense of community in the urban environment: A catalyst for participation and community development. *American Journal of Community Psychology, 18,* 55–81.

Chryssochoou, X. (2000). Membership in a superordinate level: Re-thinking European Union as a multi-national society. *Journal of Community and Applied Social Psychology, 10,* 403–420.

Cialdini, R. B., Borden, R. J., Thorne, A., Walker, M. R., Freeman, S., & Sloan, L. R. (1976). Basking in reflected glory: Three (football) field studies. *Journal of Personality and Social Psychology, 34,* 366–375.

Cialdini, R. B., Brown, S. L., Lewis, B. P., Luce, C., & Neuberg, S. L. (1997). Reinterpreting the empathy-altruism relationship: When one into one equals oneness. *Journal of Personality and Social Psychology, 73,* 481–494.

Cialdini, R. B., Kenrick, D. T., & Baumann, D. J. (1982). Effects of mood on prosocial behavior in children and adults. In N. Eisenberg (Ed.), *The development of prosocial behavior* (pp. 339–359). New York: Academic Press.

Cialdini, R. B., Schaller, M., Houlihan, D., Arps, K., Fultz, J., & Beaman, A. L. (1987). Empathy-based helping: It is selflessly or selfishly motivated? *Journal of Personality and Social Psychology, 52,* 749–758.

Cihangir, S., Barreto, M., & Ellemers, N. (2007, January). *When "they" help more than "us": The impact of ingroup and outgroup opinions on self-views, performance, and protest within a subtle discrimination context.* Poster presented at the 8th Annual Meeting of the Society for Personality and Social Psychology, Memphis, TN, United States.

Clark, M. S., Mills, J., & Corcoran, D. M. (1989). Keeping track of needs and inputs of friends and strangers. *Personality and Social Psychology Bulletin, 15,* 533–542.

Clark, R. D. (1974). Effects of sex and race on helping behavior in a nonreactive setting. *Representative Research in Social Psychology, 5,* 1–6.

Clary, E. G. (1987). Social support as a unifying concept in voluntary action. *Journal of Voluntary Action Research, 16,* 58–68.

Clary, E. G., & Snyder, M. (2002). Opportunities and challenges in socializing adults to participate in society. *Journal of Social Issues, 58,* 581–591.

Clary, E. G., Snyder, M., Ridge, R. D., Copeland, J., Stukas, A. A., Haugen, J., & Miene, P. (1998). Understanding and assessing the motivations of volunteers: A functional approach. *Journal of Personality and Social Psychology, 74,* 1516–1530.

Cnaan, R. A., & Cascio, T. A. (1999). Performance and commitment: Issues in management of volunteers in human service organizations. *Journal of Social Service Research, 24,* 1–37.

Cnaan, R. A., & Goldberg-Glen, R. S. (1991). Measuring motivation to volunteer in human services. *Journal of Applied Behavioral Science, 27,* 269–284.

Cohen, A., & Assa, A. (1977). *Saving the Jews in Bulgaria: 1941–1944.* Sofia: State Publishing House "Septemvri."

Coleman, J. S. (1990). *Foundations of social theory.* Cambridge, MA: Harvard University Press.

Condor, S. (1996). Social identity and time. In P. Robinson (Ed.), *Social groups and identities: Developing the legacy of Henri Tajfel* (pp. 285–316). Oxford: Butterworth-Heinemann.

Connors, J., & Heaven, P. C. (1990). Belief in a just world and attitudes toward AIDS sufferers. *Journal of Social Psychology, 130,* 559–60.

Cooper, C. L. (1990). Coping strategies to minimize the stress of transitions. In S. Fisher & C. L. Cooper (Eds.), *On the move: The psychology of change and transition* (pp. 315–327). Chichester: Wiley.

Cooper, C. L. (1995, February 24). Your place in the stress league. *Sunday Times.*

Corrigan, P. W., Faber, D., Rashid, F., & Leary, M. (1999). The construct validity of empowerment among consumers of mental health services. *Schizophrenia Research, 38,* 77–84.

Corrigan, P. W., Markowitz, F. E., Watson, A., Rowan, D., & Kubiak, M. A. (2003). An attribution model of public discrimination towards persons with mental illness. *Journal of Health and Social Behavior, 44,* 162–179.

Corrigan, P. W., & Watson, A. C. (2004). At issue: Stop the stigma: Call mental illness a brain disease. *Schizophrenia Bulletin, 30,* 477–479.

Corrigan, P. W., Watson, A. C., & Barr, L. (2006). The self-stigma of mental illness: Implications for self-esteem and self-efficacy. *Journal of Social and Clinical Psychology, 25,* 875–884.

Corrigan, P. W., Watson, A. C., Garcia, G., Slopen, N., Rasinski, K., & Hall, L. L. (2005). Newspaper stories as measures of structural stigma. *Psychiatric Services, 56,* 551–556.

Corrigan, P. W., Watson, A. C., & Miller, F. E. (2006). Blame, shame, and contamination: The impact of mental illness and drug dependence stigma on family members. *Journal of Family Psychology, 20,* 239–246.

Cosmides, L., & Tooby, J. (1992). Cognitive adaptions for social exchange. In J. H. Barkow & L. Cosmides (Eds.), *The adapted mind: Evolutionary psychology and the generaltion of culture* (pp. 163–228). Oxford: Oxford University Press.

Cottrell, C. A., & Neuberg, S. L. (2005). Different emotional reactions to different groups: A sociofunctional threat-based approach to "prejudice." *Journal of Personality and Social Psychology, 88,* 770–789.

Crain, A. L., Snyder, M., & Omoto, A. M. (2000, May). *Volunteers make a difference: Relationship quality, active coping, and functioning among PWAs with volunteer buddies.* Paper presented at the annual meetings of the Midwestern Psychological Association, Chicago, IL.

Crandall, C. S. (1994). Prejudice against fat people: Ideology and self-interest. *Journal of Personality and Social Psychology, 66,* 882–894.

Crandall, C. S., D'Anello, S., Sakalli, N., Lazarus, E., Wieczorkowska, G., & Feather, N. T. (2001). An attribution-value model of prejudice:

Anti-fat attitudes in six nations. *Personality and Social Psychology Bulletin, 27,* 30–37.

Crandall, C. S., & Eshleman, A. (2003). A justification-suppression model of the expression and experience of prejudice. *Psychological Bulletin, 129,* 414–446.

Crandall, C. S., Eshleman, A., & O'Brien, L. (2002). Social norms and the expression and suppression of prejudice: The struggle for internalization. *Journal of Personality and Social Psychology, 82,* 359–378.

Crandall, C. S., & Moriarty, D. (1995). Physical illness stigma and social rejection. *British Journal of Social Psychology, 34,* 67–83.

Crisp, R. J., Heuston, S., Farr, M. J., & Turner, R. N. (2007). Seeing red or feeling blue: Differentiated intergroup emotions and ingroup identification in soccer fans. *Group Processes and Intergroup Relations, 10,* 9–25.

Crisp, R. J., Stone, C. H., & Hall, N. R. (2006). Recategorization and subgroup identification: Predicting and preventing threats from common ingroups. *Personality and Social Psychology Bulletin, 32,* 230–243.

Crisp, R. J., Walsh, J., & Hewstone, M. (2006). Crossed categorization in common ingroup contexts. *Personality and Social Psychology Bulletin, 32,* 1204–1218.

Crocker, J., & Luhtanen, R. (1990). Collective self-esteem and ingroup bias. *Journal of Personality and Social Psychology, 58,* 60–67.

Crocker, J., Major, B., & Steele, C. (1998). Social stigma. In D. T. Gilbert, S. T. Fiske, & G. Lindzey (Eds.), *The handbook of social psychology* (pp. 504–553). Boston: McGraw-Hill.

Crosby, F., Bromley, S., & Saxe, L. (1980). Recent unobtrusive studies of Black and White discrimination and prejudice: A literature review. *Psychological Bulletin, 87,* 546–563.

Cuddy, A. J. C., Rock, M. S., & Norton, M. I. (2007). Aid in the aftermath of Hurricane Katrina: Inferences of secondary emotions and intergroup helping. *Group Processes and Intergroup Relations, 10,* 107–118.

Cunningham, M. R. (1986). Levites and brother's keepers: A sociobiological perspective on prosocial behavior. *Humboldt Journal of Social Relations, 13,* 35–67.

Curtis, J. E., Grabb, E., & Baer, D. (1992). Voluntary association membership in fifteen countries: A comparative analysis. *American Sociological Review, 57,* 139–152.

Czopp, A. M., & Monteith, M. J. (2006). Thinking well of African Americans: Measuring complimentary stereotypes and negative prejudice. *Basic and Applied Social Psychology, 28,* 233–250.

Dailey, R. C. (1986). Understanding organizational commitment for volunteers: Empirical and managerial implications. *Journal of Voluntary Action Research, 15,* 19–31.

Daly, M., & Wilson, M. (1988). *Homicide.* Hawthorne, NY: De Gruyter.

Darley, J. M., & Batson, C. D. (1973). "From Jerusalem to Jericho": The study of situational and dispositional variables in helping behavior. *Journal of Personality and Social Psychology, 27*, 100–108.

Darley, J. M., & Latané, B. (1968). Bystander intervention in emergencies: Diffusion of responsibility. *Journal of Personality and Social Psychology, 8*, 377–383.

Darley, J. M., Lewis, L. D., & Teger, A. (1973). Do groups always inhibit individuals' response to potential emergencies? *Journal of Personality and Social Psychology, 26*, 395–400.

Darwin, C. (1871). *The descent of man, and selection in relation to sex.* London: Murray.

Davidson, W. B., & Cotter, P. R. (1989). Sense of community and political participation. *Journal of Community Psychology, 17*, 119–125.

Davidson, W. B., & Cotter, P. R. (1991). The relationship between sense of community and subjective well-being: A first look. *Journal of Community Psychology, 19*, 246–253.

Davis, M. H. (1983a). Measuring individual differences in empathy: Evidence for a multidimensional approach. *Journal of Personality and Social Psychology, 44*, 113–126.

Davis, M. H. (1983b). The effects of dispositional empathy on emotional reactions and helping: A multidimensional approach. *Journal of Personality, 51*, 167–184.

Davis, M. H. (1994). *Empathy: A social psychological approach.* Madison, WI: Brown & Benchmark.

Davis, M. H., Conklin, L., Smith, A., & Luce, C. (1996). Effect of perspective taking on the cognitive representation of persons: A merging of self and other. *Journal of Personality and Social Psychology, 70*, 713–726.

Davis, M. H., Hall, J. A., & Meyer, M. (2003). The first year: Influences on the satisfaction, involvement, and persistence of new community volunteers. *Personality and Social Psychology Bulletin, 29*, 248–260.

Davis, M. H., Soderlund, T., Cole, J., Gadol, E., Kute, M., Myers, M., & Weihing, J. (2004). Cognitions associated with attempts to empathize: How *do* we imagine the perspective of another? *Personality and Social Psychology Bulletin, 30*, 1625–1635.

Dawkins, R. (1976). *The selfish gene.* Oxford: Oxford University Press.

Dawley, D. D., Stephens, R. D., & Stephens, D. B. (2005). Dimensionality of organizational commitment in volunteer workers: Chamber of commerce board members and role fulfillment. *Journal of Vocational Behavior, 67*, 511–525.

Deci, E. L., La Guardia, J. G., Moller, A. C., Scheiner, M. J., & Ryan, R. M. (2006). On the benefits of giving as well as receiving autonomy support: Mutuality in close friendships. *Personality and Social Psychology Bulletin, 32*, 313–327.

De Cremer, D., & van Vugt, M. (1999). Social identification effects in social dilemmas: A transformation of motives. *European Journal of Social Psychology, 29*, 871–893.

Deelstra, J. T., Peeters, M. C. W., Schaufeli, W. B., Stroebe, W., Zijlstra, F. R. H., & van Doornen, L. P. (2003). Receiving instrumental support at work: When help is not welcome. *Journal of Applied Psychology*, *88*, 324–331.

DeJong, W. (1993). Obesity as a characterological stigma: The issue of responsibility and judgments of task performance. *Psychological Reports*, *73*, 963–970.

De Liver, Y., van der Pligt, J., & Wigboldus, D. (2007). Positive and negative associations underlying ambivalent attitudes. *Journal of Experimental Social Psychology*, *43*, 319–326.

De Waal, F. (2006). *Our inner ape*. London: Granta Books.

Des Jarlais, D. C., Galea, S., Tracy, M., Tross, M., & Vlahov, D. (2006). Stigmatization of newly emerging infectious diseases: AIDS and SARS. *American Journal of Public Health*, *96*, 561–567.

Devine, P. G. (1989). Stereotypes and prejudice: Their automatic and controlled components. *Journal of Personality and Social Psychology*, *56*, 5–18.

Devine, P. G., Plant, E. A., Amodio, D. M., Harmon-Jones, E., & Vance, S. L. (2002). The regulation of explicit and implicit race bias: The role of motivations to respond without prejudice. *Journal of Personality and Social Psychology*, *82*, 835–848.

Dietrich, S., Beck, M., Bujantugs, B., Kenzine, D., Matschinger, H., & Angermeyer, M. C. (2004). The relationship between public causal beliefs and social distance toward mentally ill people. *Australian and New Zealand Journal of Psychiatry*, *38*, 348–354.

Dijker, A. J. (1987). Emotional reactions to ethnic minorities. *European Journal of Social Psychology*, *17*, 305–325.

Dijker, A. J., & Koomen, W. (2003). Extending Weiner's attribution-emotion model of stigmatization of ill persons. *Basic and Applied Social Psychology*, *25*, 51–68.

Dijker, A. J., & Koomen, W. (2007). *Stigmatization, tolerance and repair: An integrative psychological analysis of responses to deviance*. Cambridge: Cambridge University Press.

Dixon, J. A., Durrheim, K., & Tredoux, C. (2005). Beyond the optimal strategy: A "reality check" for the contact hypothesis. *American Psychologist*, *60*, 697–711.

Doosje, B., Branscombe, N. R., Spears, R., & Manstead, A. S. R. (1998). Guilty by association: When one's group has a negative history. *Journal of Personality and Social Psychology*, *75*, 872–886.

Doosje, B., Ellemers, N., & Spears, R. (1995). Perceived intragroup variability as a function of group status and identification. *Journal of Experimental Social Psychology*, *31*, 410–436.

Doosje, B., Spears, R., & Ellemers, N. (2002). Social identity as both cause and effect: The development of group identification in response to anticipated and actual changes in the intergroup status hierarchy. *British Journal of Social Psychology*, *41*, 57–76.

Dovidio, J. F. (1984). Helping behavior and altruism: An empirical and conceptual overview. *Advances in Experimental Social Psychology, 17,* 361–427.

Dovidio, J. F., Allen, J. L., & Schroeder, D. A. (1990). The specificity of empathy-induced helping: Evidence for altruism. *Journal of Personality and Social Psychology, 59,* 249–260.

Dovidio, J. F., Brigham, J. C., Johnson, B. T., & Gaertner, S. L. (1996). Stereotyping, prejudice, and discrimination: Another look. In C. N. Macrae, C. Stangor, & M. Hewstone (Eds.), *Stereotypes and stereotyping* (pp. 276–319). New York: Guilford Press.

Dovidio, J. F., & Gaertner, S. L. (1981). The effects of race, status, and ability on helping behavior. *Social Psychology Quarterly, 44,* 192–203.

Dovidio, J. F., & Gaertner, S. L. (1991). Changes in the expression of racial prejudice. In H. J. Knopke, R. J. Norrell, & R. W. Rogers (Eds.), *Opening doors: Perspectives on race relations in contemporary America* (pp. 119–148). Tuscaloosa: University of Alabama Press.

Dovidio, J. F., & Gaertner, S. L. (2000). Aversive racism and selection decisions: 1989 and 1999. *Psychological Science, 11,* 319–323.

Dovidio, J. F., & Gaertner, S. L. (2004). Aversive racism. In M. P. Zanna (Ed.), *Advances in experimental social psychology* (Vol. 36, pp. 1–51). San Diego: Academic Press.

Dovidio, J. F., Gaertner, S. L., Hodson, G., Houlette, M. A., & Johnson, K. M. (2005). Social inclusion and exclusion: Recategorization and perception of intergroup boundaries. In D. Abrams, M. A. Hogg, & J. M. Marques (Eds.), *The social psychology of inclusion and exclusion* (pp. 245–264). New York: Psychology Press.

Dovidio, J. F., Gaertner, S. L., & Johnson, J. D. (1999). *New directions in prejudice and prejudice reduction: The role of cognitive representations and affect.* Symposium paper presented at the annual meeting of the Society for Experimental Social Psychology, St. Louis, MO.

Dovidio, J. F., Gaertner, S. L., & Kafati, G. (2000). Group identity and intergroup relations: The Common Ingroup Identity Model. In S. R. Thye, E. Lawler, M. W. Macy, & H. A. Walker (Eds.), *Advances in group processes* (Vol. 17, pp. 1–34). Stamford, CT: JAI Press.

Dovidio, J., Gaertner, S., & Kawakami, K. (2003). Intergroup contact: The past, present, and the future. *Group Processes and Intergroup Relations, 6,* 5–20.

Dovidio, J. F., Gaertner, S. L., Kawakami, K., & Hodson, G. (2002). Why can't we just get along? Interpersonal biases and interracial distrust. *Cultural Diversity and Ethnic Minority Psychology, 8,* 88–102.

Dovidio, J. F., Gaertner, S. L., & Saguy, T. (2007). Another view of "we": Majority and minority group perspectives on a Common Ingroup Identity. In W. Stroebe & M. Hewstone (Eds.), *European review of social psychology* (Vol. 18, pp. 296–330). New York: Psychology Press.

Dovidio, J. F., Gaertner, S. L., Validzic, A., Matoka, K., Johnson, B., & Frazier,

S. (1997). Extending the benefits of recategorization: Evaluations, self-disclosure, and helping. *Journal of Experimental Social Psychology, 33,* 401–420.

Dovidio, J. F., Kawakami, K., Johnson, C., Johnson, B., & Howard, A. (1997). On the nature of prejudice: Automatic and controlled processes. *Journal of Experimental Social Psychology, 33,* 510–540.

Dovidio, J. F., Piliavin, J. A., Gaertner, S. L., Schroeder, D. A., & Clark, R. D., III. (1991). The arousal: Cost-reward model and the process of intervention: A review of the evidence. In M. S. Clark (Ed.), *Prosocial behavior* (pp. 86–118). Newbury Park, CA: Sage.

Dovidio, J. F., Piliavin, J. A., Schroeder, D. A., & Penner, L. (2006). *The social psychology of prosocial behavior.* Mahwah, NJ: Erlbaum.

Dovidio, J. F., ten Vergert, M., Stewart, T. L., Gaertner, S. L., Johnson, J. D., Esses, V. M., Riek, B. M., & Pearson, A. R. (2004). Perspective and prejudice: Antecedents and mediating mechanisms. *Personality and Social Psychology Bulletin, 30,* 1537–1549.

Drury, J. (2004). No need to panic. *The Psychologist, 17,* 118–119.

Drury, J., Cocking, C., & Reicher, S. (2006, January). *Every man for himself – or for the group? How crowd solidarity can arise in an emergency: An interview study of disaster survivors.* Paper presented at the Group and Intergroup Relations pre-conference, Society for Personality and Social Psychology 7th Annual Meeting, Palm Springs, CA.

Drury, J., & Reicher, S. D. (1999). The intergroup dynamics of collective empowerment: Substantiating the social identity model of crowd behaviour. *Group Processes and Intergroup Relations, 2,* 381–402.

Drury, J., & Reicher, S. D. (2000). Collective action and social change: The emergence of new social identities. *British Journal of Social Psychology, 39,* 579–604.

Drury, J., & Reicher, S. D. (2005). Explaining enduring empowerment: A comparative study of collective action and psychological outcomes. *European Journal of Social Psychology, 35,* 35–58.

Drury, J., Reicher, S. D., & Stott, C. (2003). Transforming the boundaries of collective identity: From the "local" anti-road campaign to "global" resistance. *Social Movement Studies, 2,* 191–212.

Dugatkin, L. A. (1997). *Cooperation among animals: An evolutionary perspective.* New York: Oxford University Press.

Dunham, H. W. (1986). The community today: Place or process? *Journal of Community Psychology, 14,* 399–404.

Dunton, B. C., & Fazio, R. H. (1997). An individual difference measure of motivation to control prejudiced reactions. *Personality and Social Psychology Bulletin, 23,* 316–326.

Durkheim, E. (1951). *Suicide* (J. Spalding & G. Simpson, Trans.). New York: Free Press. (Original work published 1898)

Durkheim, E. (2001). *The elementary forms of religious life.* Oxford: Oxford Paperbacks. (Original work published 1912)

Dutton, D. G., & Lake, R. A. (1973). Threat of own prejudice and reverse discrimination in interracial situations. *Journal of Personality and Social Psychology*, 28, 94–100.

Eagly, A., & Becker, S. (2005). Comparing the heroism of women and men. *American Psychologist*, 60, 343–344.

Eagly, A. H., & Wood, W. (1999). The origins of sex differences in human behavior: Evolved dispositions versus social roles. *American Psychologist*, 54, 408–423.

Eder, D., & Hallinan, M. T. (1978). Sex differences in children's friendships. *American Sociological Review*, 43, 237–250.

Eggins, R. A., Haslam, S. A., & Reynolds, K. J. (2002). Social identity and negotiation: Subgroup representation and superordinate consensus. *Personality and Social Psychology Bulletin*, 28, 887–899.

Eggins, R. A., O'Brien, A. T., Reynolds, K. J., Haslam, S. A., & Crocker, A. S. (2008). Refocusing the focus group: AIRing as a basis for effective workplace planning. *British Journal of Management*, 19, 277–293.

Ehrhart, K. H., & Ziegert, J. C. (2005). Why are individuals attracted to organizations? *Journal of Management*, 31, 901–919.

Eisenberg, N., & Fabes, R. A. (1991). Prosocial behavior and empathy: A multimethod development perspective. In M. S. Clark (Ed.), *Review of personality and social psychology: Prosocial behavior* (Vol. 12, pp. 34–61). Newbury Park, CA: Sage.

Eisenberg, N., & Strayer, J. (1987). Critical issues in the study of empathy. In N. Eisenberg & J. Strayer (Eds.), *Empathy and its development* (pp. 3–13). Cambridge: Cambridge University Press.

Eisenberger, R., Armeli, S., Rexwinkel, B., Lynch, P. D., & Rhoades, L. (2001). Reciprocation of perceived organizational support. *Journal of Applied Psychology*, 86, 42–51.

Ellemers, N. (1993). The influence of socio-structural variables on identity management strategies. In W. Stroebe & M. Hewstone (Eds.), *European review of social psychology* (Vol. 3, pp. 27–57). Chichester: Wiley.

Ellemers, N. (2003). Identity, culture, and change in organizations: A social identity analysis and three illustrative cases. In S. A. Haslam, D. van Knippenberg, M. J. Platow, & N. Ellemers (Eds.), *Social identity at work: Developing theory for organizational practice* (pp. 191–203). New York: Psychology Press.

Ellemers, N., & Bos, A. E. R. (1998). Social identity, relative deprivation, and coping with the threat of position loss: A field study among native shopkeepers in Amsterdam. *Journal of Applied Social Psychology*, 28, 1987–2006.

Ellemers, N., De Gilder, D., & Haslam, S. A. (2004). Motivating individuals and groups at work: A social identity perspective on leadership and group performance. *Academy of Management Review*, 29, 459–478.

Ellemers, N., Spears, R., & Doosje, B. (1997). Sticking together or falling apart: In-group identification as a psychological determinant of group commitment versus individual mobility. *Journal of Personality and Social Psychology, 72,* 617–626.

Ellemers, N., Spears, R., & Doosje, B. (Eds.). (1999). *Social identity: Context, commitment, content.* Oxford: Blackwell.

Ellemers, N., van Knippenberg, A., & Wilke, H. A. (1990). The influence of permeability of group boundaries and stability of group status on strategies of individual mobility and social change. *British Journal of Social Psychology, 29,* 233–246.

Ellemers, N., & van Rijswijk, W. (1997). Identity needs versus social opportunities: The use of group-level and individual-level identity management strategies. *Social Psychology Quarterly, 60,* 52–65.

Ellemers, N., van Rijswijk, W., Bruins, J., & De Gilder, D. (1998). Group commitment as a moderator of attributional and behavioural responses to power use. *European Journal of Social Psychology, 28,* 555–573.

Ellemers, N., Wilke, H., & van Knippenberg, A. (1993). Effects of the legitimacy of low group or individual status on individual and collective identity enhancement strategies. *Journal of Personality and Social Psychology, 64,* 766–778.

Elliott, G. C., Colangelo, M. F., & Gelles, R. J. (2005). Mattering and suicide ideation: Establishing and elaborating a relationship. *Social Psychology Quarterly, 68,* 223–238.

Elliott, G. C., Kao, S., & Grant, A.-M. (2004). Mattering: Empirical validation of a social-psychological concept. *Self and Identity, 3,* 339–354.

Engaging Youth in Lifelong Service: Findings and Recommendations for Encouraging a Tradition of Voluntary Action Among America's Youth. (2002). Independent Sector. Summary on the web at www.independentsector.org/programs/research/engagingyouth.html.

Epley, N., Keysar, B., Van Boven, L., & Gilovich, T. (2004). Perspective taking as egocentric anchoring and adjustment. *Journal of Personality and Social Psychology, 87,* 327–349.

Farmer, S. M., & Fedor, D. B. (1999). Volunteer participation and withdrawal: A psychological contract perspective on the role of expectations and organizational support. *Nonprofit Management and Leadership, 9,* 349–367.

Farmer, S. M., & Fedor, D. B. (2001). Changing the focus on volunteering: An investigation of volunteers' multiple contributions to a charitable organization. *Journal of Management, 27,* 191–211.

Fazio, R. H., & Hilden, L. E. (2001). Emotional reactions to a seemingly prejudiced response: The role of automatically activated racial attitudes and motivation to control prejudiced reactions. *Personality and Social Psychology Bulletin, 27,* 538–549.

Fazio, R. H., Jackson, J. R., Dunton, B. C., & Williams, C. J. (1995). Variability in automatic activation as an unobtrusive measure of racial attitudes: A bona fide pipeline? *Journal of Personality and Social Psychology, 69,* 1013–1027.

Fazio, R. H., & Olson, M. A. (2003). Implicit measures in social cognition research: Their meaning and use. *Annual Review of Psychology, 54,* 297–327.
Fehr, E., & Gächter, S. (2002). Altruistic punishment in humans. *Nature, 415,* 137–140.
Feldman, D. B., & Crandall, C. S. (2007). Dimensions of mental illness stigma: What about mental illness causes social rejection? *Journal of Social and Clinical Psychology, 26,* 137–154.
Felton, B., & Shinn, M. (1992). Social integration and social support: Moving "social support" beyond the individual level. *Journal of Community Psychology, 20,* 103–115.
Finlay, K. A., & Stephan, W. G. (2000). Improving intergroup relations: The effects of empathy on racial attitudes. *Journal of Applied Social Psychology, 30,* 1720–1737.
Fischer, E. H., Winer, D., & Abramowitz, S. I. (1983). Seeking professional help for psychological problems. In A. Nadler, J. D. Fisher, & B. M. DePaulo (Eds.), *New directions in helping: Applied perspectives on help seeking and receiving* (pp. 163–189). New York: Academic Press.
Fisher, J. D., Cornman, D. H., Norton, D. W., & Fisher, W. A. (2006). Involving behavioral scientists, health care providers and HIV-infected patients as collaborators in theory-based HIV prevention and antiretroviral adherence interventions. *Journal of Acquired Immune Deficiency Syndrome, 43,* 10–17.
Fisher, J. D., Nadler, A., Little, J. S., & Saguy, T. (2008). Help as a vehicle to reconciliation, with particular reference to help for extreme health needs. In A. Nadler, T. Malloy, & J. D. Fisher (Eds.), *Social psychology of intergroup reconciliation* (pp. 447–471). New York: Oxford University Press.
Fisher, J. D., Nadler, A., & Whitcher-Alagna, S. J. (1983). Recipient reactions to aid. *Psychological Bulletin, 91,* 27–54.
Fisher, R. J., & Ackerman, D. (1998). The effects of recognition and group need on volunteerism: A social norm perspective. *Journal of Consumer Research, 25,* 262–275.
Fiske, S. T. (2002). What we now know about bias and intergroup conflict, the problem of the century. *Current Directions in Psychological Science, 11,* 123–128.
Fiske, S. T., Cuddy, A. J. C., & Glick, P. (2006). Universal dimensions of social cognition: Warmth and competence. *Trends in Cognitive Sciences, 11,* 77–83.
Fiske, S. T., Cuddy, A. J. C., Glick, P., & Xu, J. (2002). A model of (often mixed) stereotype content: Competence and warmth respectively follow from perceived status and competition. *Journal of Personality and Social Psychology, 82,* 878–902.
Fiske, S. T., Lin, M., & Neuberg, S. L. (1999). The continuum model: Ten years later. In S. Chaiken & Y. Trope (Eds.), *Dual-process theories in social psychology* (pp. 231–254). New York: Guilford Press.
Fiske, S. T., & Taylor, S. E. (1991). *Social cognition.* New York: McGraw-Hill.

Folkman, S., Chesney, M., McKusick, L., Ironson, G., Johnson, D., & Coates, T. (1991). Translating coping theory into an intervention. In J. Eckenrode (Ed.), *The social context of coping* (pp. 239–260). New York: Plenum.

Frey, D. L., & Gaertner, S. L. (1986). Helping and the avoidance of inappropriate interracial behavior: A strategy that perpetuates a nonprejudiced self-image. *Journal of Personality and Social Psychology, 50*, 1083–1090.

Friedland, R. P., Fritsch, T., Smyth, K. A., Koss, E., Lerner, A. J., Chen, C. H., Petot, G. J., & Debanne, S. M. (2001). Patients with Alzheimer's Disease have reduced activities in midlife compared with healthy control-group members. *Proceedings of the National Academy of Sciences, 98*, 3440–3445.

Friedman, M. D., & Rosenman, R. H. (1974). *Type A behaviour and your heart.* New York: Knopf.

Frijda, N. H. (1986). *The emotions.* Cambridge: Cambridge University Press.

Frijda, N. H., Kuipers, P., & ter Shure, E. (1989). Relations among emotion, appraisal, and emotional action readiness. *Journal of Personality and Social Psychology, 57*, 212–289.

Frijda, N. H., & Zeelenberg, M. (2001). Appraisal: What is the dependent? In K. A. Scherer, A. Schorr, & T. Johnstone (Eds.), *Appraisal processes in emotion: Theory, methods, research* (pp. 141–155). New York: Oxford University Press.

Fuller, J. B., Hester, K., Barnett, T., Frey, L., Relyea, C., & Beu, D. (2006). Perceived external prestige and internal respect: New insights into the organizational identification process. *Human Relations, 59*, 815–846.

Furnham, A. (1990). Expatriate stress: The problems of living abroad. In S. Fisher & C. L. Cooper (Eds.), *On the move: The psychology of change and transition* (pp. 275–301). Chichester: Wiley.

Gabriel, S., & Gardner, W. L. (1999). Are there his and hers types of interdependence? The implications of gender differences in collective versus relational interdependence for affect, behavior and cognition. *Journal of Personality and Social Psychology, 77*, 642–655.

Gade, P., Segal, D., & Johnson, E. (1996). The experience of foreign militaries. In G. M. Herek, J. J. Jobe, & R. Carney (Eds.), *Out in force: Sexual orientation and the military* (pp. 106–130). Chicago: University of Chicago Press.

Gaertner, S. L., & Bickman, L. (1971). Effects of race on the elicitation of helping behavior: The wrong number technique. *Journal of Personality and Social Psychology, 20*, 218–222.

Gaertner, S. L., & Dovidio, J. F. (1977). The subtlety of white racism, arousal, and helping behavior. *Journal of Personality and Social Psychology, 35*, 691–707.

Gaertner, S. L., & Dovidio, J. F. (1986). The aversive form of racism. In J. F. Dovidio & S. L. Gaertner (Eds.), *Prejudice, discrimination, and racism* (pp. 61–90). Orlando, FL: Academic Press.

Gaertner, S. L., & Dovidio, J. F. (2000). *Reducing intergroup bias: The Common Ingroup Identity Model.* New York: Psychology Press.

Gaertner, S. L., & Dovidio, J. F. (2007). Reducing contemporary racism: The Common Ingroup Identity Model. In C. W. Esqueda (Ed.), *Nebraska symposium on motivation: Motivational aspects of prejudice and racism* (pp. 111–133). New York: Springer.

Gaertner, S. L., Dovidio, J. F., & Johnson, G. (1982). Race of victim, non-responsive bystanders, and helping behavior. *Journal of Social Psychology, 117,* 69–77.

Gaertner, S. L., Dovidio, J. F., Rust, M. C., Nier, J. A., Banker, B. S., Ward, C. M., Mottola, G. R., & Houlette, M. (1999). Reducing intergroup bias: Elements of intergroup cooperation. *Journal of Personality and Social Psychology, 76,* 388–402.

Gaertner, S. L., Mann, J. A., Murrell, A. J., & Dovidio, J. F. (1989). Reduction of intergroup bias: The benefits of recategorization. *Journal of Personality and Social Psychology, 57,* 239–249.

Galindo-Kuhn, R., & Guzley, R. M. (2001). The volunteer satisfaction index: Construct definition, measurement, development, and validation. *Journal of Social Service Research, 28,* 45–68.

Galinsky, A. D., & Ku, G. (2004). The effects of perspective-taking on prejudice: The moderating role of self-evaluation. *Personality and Social Psychology Bulletin, 30,* 594–604.

Galinsky, A. D., & Moskowitz, G. B. (2000). Perspective-taking: Decreasing stereotype expression, stereotype accessibility, and in-group favoritism. *Journal of Personality and Social Psychology, 78,* 708–724.

Gallup, Inc. (2009). *Homosexual relations.* Retrieved on March 23, 2009 from www.gallup.com/poll/1651/Homosexual-Relations.aspx.

Galper, R. E. (1976). Turning observers into actors: Differential causal attributions as a function of "empathy." *Journal of Research in Personality, 10,* 328–335.

Gamson, W. A. (1992). The social psychology of collective action. In A. D. Morris & C. M. Mueller (Eds.), *Frontiers in social movement theory* (pp. 53–76). New Haven, CT: Yale University Press.

Gawronski, B., & Bodenhausen, G. V. (2006). Associative and propositional processes in evaluation: An integrative review of implicit and explicit attitude change. *Psychological Bulletin, 132,* 692–731.

Geller, D., Ellis, S., & Nadler, A. (2008). *Functional diversity, social networks and team performance: The mediating role of help-seeking behaviors.* Unpublished manuscript, Tel Aviv University.

George, D. (Ed.). (2003). *The kindness of strangers: Travellers' tales of trouble and salvation around the globe.* Oakland, CA: Lonely Planet.

Gerard, H. B., & Hoyt, M. F. (1974). Distinctiveness of social categorization and attitude toward ingroup members. *Journal of Personality and Social Psychology, 29,* 836–842.

Gibbons, F. X., & Gerrard, M. (1989). Effects of upward and downward social comparison on mood states. *Journal of Social and Clinical Psychology, 8,* 14–31.

Gidron, B. (1983). Sources of job satisfaction among service volunteers. *Journal of Voluntary Action Research*, 12, 20–35.
Gilbert, D., & Hixon, J. G. (1991). The trouble with thinking: Activation and application of stereotypic beliefs. *Journal of Personality and Social Psychology*, 60, 509–517.
Gilbert, D. T., & Silvera, D. H. (1999). Overhelping. *Journal of Personality and Social Psychology*, 70, 678–690.
Gilbert, M. (1985). *The Holocaust*. London: Holt, Rinehart, & Winston.
Goffman, E. (1963). *Stigma: Notes on the management of spoiled identity*. Englewood Cliffs, NJ: Prentice-Hall.
Goldstein, J. (2003). *War and gender*. Cambridge: Cambridge University Press.
Goodall, J. (1986). *The chimpanzees of Gombe: Patterns of behavior*. Cambridge, MA: Harvard University Press.
Goodman, D. J. (2001). *Promoting diversity and social justice: Educating people from privileged groups*. Thousand Oaks, CA: Sage.
Gordijn, E. H., Yzerbyt, V., Wigboldus, D., & Dumont, M. (2006). Emotional reactions to harmful intergroup behaviour. *European Journal of Social Psychology*, 36, 15–30.
Gramsci, A. (1987). *Prison notebooks: Selections*. London: Lawrence & Wishart.
Grandfield, T. A., Thomson, A., & Turpin, G. (2005). An attitudinal study of responses to a range of dermatological conditions using the Implicit Association Test. *Journal of Health Psychology*, 10, 821–829.
Grant, P. R., & Brown, R. (1995). From ethnocentrism to collective protest: Responses to relative deprivation and threats to social identity. *Social Psychology Quarterly*, 58, 195–211.
Greenwald, A. G., & Banaji, M. R. (1995). Implicit social cognition: Attitudes, self-esteem, and stereotypes. *Psychological Review*, 102, 4–27.
Greenwald, A. G., Banaji, M. R., Rudman, L. A., Farnham, S. D., Nosek, B. A., & Mellott, D. S. (2002). A unified theory of implicit attitudes, stereotypes, self-esteem, and self-concept. *Psychological Review*, 109, 3–25.
Greenwald, A. G., McGhee, D. E., & Schwartz, J. L. K. (1998). Measuring individual differences in implicit cognition: The implicit association test. *Journal of Personality and Social Psychology*, 74, 1464–1480.
Grube, J. A., & Piliavin, J. A. (2000). Role identity, organizational experiences and volunteer performance. *Personality and Social Psychology Bulletin*, 26, 1108–1119.
Guerra, R., Rebelo, M., Monteiro, M. B., Riek, B. M., Mania, E. W., Gaertner, S. L., & Dovidio, J. F. (2007). *How should intergroup contact be structured to facilitate generalization among majority and minority group members?* Manuscript submitted for publication.
Guimond, S., & Dubé-Simard, L. (1983). Relative deprivation and the Quebec nationalist movement: The cognition-emotion distinction and the personal-group deprivation issue. *Journal of Personality and Social Psychology*, 44, 526–535.

Gurney, J. N., & Tierney, K. J. (1982). Relative deprivation and social movements: A critical look at 20 years of theory and research. *Sociological Quarterly, 23,* 33–47.

Gustavo, C., Eisenberg, N., Troyer, D., Switzer, G., & Speer, A. L. (1991). The altruistic personality: In what contexts is it apparent? *Journal of Personality and Social Psychology, 61,* 450–458.

Haddock, G., Zanna, M. P., & Esses, V. M. (1993). Assessing the structure of prejudicial attitudes: The case of attitudes towards homosexuals. *Journal of Personality and Social Psychology, 65,* 1105–1118.

Haidt, J. (2001). The emotional dog and its rational tail: A social intuitionist approach to moral judgment. *Psychological Review, 108,* 814–834.

Halabi, S., Dovidio, J. F., & Nadler, A. (2008). When and how high-status groups offer help: Effects of social dominance orientation and status threat. *Political Psychology, 29,* 841–858.

Halabi, S., Nadler A., & Dovidio, J. F. (2008). *Reactions to receiving assumptive help: The moderating effects of group membership and perceived need for help.* Paper submitted for publication.

Halabi, S., Nadler, A., & Saguy, T. (2008). [Different interpretations of help offered by a high- to low-status group]. Unpublished data.

Hamilton, W. D. (1964). The genetical evolution of social behaviour. *Journal of Theoretical Biology, 7,* 1–52.

Handy, C. (1988). *Understanding voluntary organizations.* London: Penguin.

Handy, F., Cnaan, R. A., Brudney, J. L., Ascoli, U., Meijs, L. C. M. P., & Ranade, S. (2000). Public perception of "Who is a volunteer": An examination of the net-cost approach from a cross-cultural perspective. *Voluntas: International Journal of Voluntary and Nonprofit Organizations, 11,* 45–65.

Harber, K. D. (1998). Feedback to minorities: Evidence of a positive bias. *Journal of Personality and Social Psychology, 74,* 622–628.

Hardy, C., & van Vugt, M. (2006). Nice guys finish first: The competitive altruism hypothesis. *Personality and Social Psychology Bulletin, 32,* 1402–1413.

Harpaz-Gorodeisky, G. (2008). *Habitual patterns of seeking autonomy- or dependency-oriented help: A validation study.* Unpublished manuscript, Tel Aviv University.

Harris, M. (2001). This charity business: Who cares? *Nonprofit Management and Leadership, 12,* 95–109.

Harth, N. S., Kessler, T., & Leach, C. W. (2008). Advantaged group's emotional reactions to inter-group inequality: The dynamics of pride, guilt, and sympathy. *Personality and Social Psychology Bulletin, 34,* 115–129.

Haslam, C., Holme, A., Haslam, S. A., Iyer, A., Jetten, J., & Williams, W. H. (2008). Maintaining group memberships: Social identity predicts well-being after stroke. *Neuropsychological Rehabilitation, 18,* 671–691.

Haslam, C., Jetten, J., Haslam, S. A., & Yates, P. (2007). [Mapping identity change: A case study of change in the centrality, exclusivity, and compatibility of social identities after stroke]. Unpublished data.

Haslam, N., & Bain, P. (2007). Humanizing the self: Moderators of the attribution of lesser humanness to others. *Personality and Social Psychology Bulletin, 33*, 57–68.

Haslam, S. A. (2001). *Psychology in organizations: The social identity approach.* London: Sage.

Haslam, S. A. (2004). *Psychology in organizations: The social identity approach* (2nd ed.). London: Sage.

Haslam, S. A., & Ellemers, N. (2005). Social identity in industrial and organizational psychology. *International Review of Industrial and Organizational Psychology, 20*, 39–118.

Haslam, S. A., Jetten, J., O'Brien, A., & Jacobs, E. (2004). Social identity, social influence, and reactions to potentially stressful tasks: Support for the self-categorization model of stress. *Stress and Health, 20*, 3–9.

Haslam, S. A., O'Brien, A., Jetten, J., Vormedal, K., & Penna, S. (2005). Taking the strain: Social identity, social support and the experience of stress. *British Journal of Social Psychology, 44*, 355–370.

Haslam, S. A., & Platow, M. J. (2001). The link between leadership and followership: How affirming social identity translates vision into action. *Personality and Social Psychology Bulletin, 27*, 1469–1479.

Haslam, S. A., & Reicher, S. D. (2005). The psychology of tyranny. *Scientific American Mind, 16*, 44–51.

Haslam, S. A., & Reicher, S. D. (2006a). Social identity and the dynamics of organizational life: Insights from the BBC Prison Study. In C. Bartel, S. Blader, & A. Wrzesniewski (Eds.), *Identity and the modern organization* (pp. 135–166). New York: Erlbaum.

Haslam, S. A., & Reicher, S. (2006b). Stressing the group: Social identity and the unfolding dynamics of responding to stress. *Journal of Applied Psychology, 91*, 1037–1052.

Haslam, S. A., & Reicher, S. D. (2007). Identity entrepreneurship and the consequences of identity failure: The dynamics of leadership in the BBC Prison Study. *Social Psychology Quarterly, 70*, 125–147.

Haslam, S. A., & Reicher, S. D. (in prep.). *The social psychology of resistance: Prison studies and the case for a more expansive theoretical imagination.* Unpublished manuscript, Universities of Exeter and St. Andrews.

Haslam, S. A., Reicher, S. D., & Platow, M. (in press). *The new psychology of leadership.* Hove: Psychology Press.

Haslam, S. A., & Turner, J. C. (1992). Context-dependent variation in social stereotyping 2: The relationship between frame of reference, self-categorization and accentuation. *European Journal of Social Psychology, 22*, 251–277.

Haslam, S. A., Turner, J. C., Oakes, P. J., McGarty, C., & Reynolds, K. J. (1998). The group as a basis for emergent stereotype consensus. In

W. Stroebe & M. Hewstone (Eds.), *European review of social psychology* (Vol. 8, pp. 203–239). Hoboken, NJ: Wiley.

Hebl, M. R., Foster, J. B., Mannix, L. M., & Dovidio, J. F. (2002). Formal and interpersonal discrimination: A field study of bias toward homosexual applicants. *Personality and Social Psychology Bulletin, 28,* 815–825.

Hebl, M. R., & Kleck, R. E. (2000). The social consequences of physical disability. In T. Heatherton, R. Kleck, M. Hebl, & J. Hull (Eds.), *The social psychology of stigma* (pp. 419–439). New York: Guilford Press.

Hebl, M. R., & Mannix, L. M. (2003). The weight of obesity in evaluating others: A mere proximity effect. *Personality and Social Psychology Bulletin, 29,* 28–38.

Hedges, S. J. (2005). Navy ship nearby underused. *Chicago Tribune,* September 4. Retrieved from www.chicagotribune.com/news/nationworld/chi-0509040369sep04,1,4144825.story?coll=chi-news-hed&ctrack=3&cset=true.

Heilman, M. E. (1996). Affirmative action's contradictory consequences. *Journal of Social Issues, 52,* 105–110.

Henderson, J. G., Pollard, C. A., Jacobi, K. A., & Merkel, W. T. (1992). Help-seeking patterns of community residents with depressive symptoms. *Journal of Affective Disorders, 26,* 157–162.

Henkel, K. E., Dovidio, J. F., & Gaertner, S. L. (2006). Institutional discrimination, individual racism, and Hurricane Katrina. *Analyses of Social Issues and Public Policy, 6,* 99–124.

Herek, G. M. (1991). Myths about sexual orientation: A lawyer's guide to social science research. *Law and Sexuality, 1,* 133–172.

Herek, G. M. (2002). Gender gaps in public opinion about lesbians and gay men. *Public Opinion Quarterly, 66,* 40–66.

Herek, G. M. (2009). Sexual prejudice. In T. Nelson (Ed.), *Handbook of prejudice, stereotyping, and discrimination* (pp. 439–465). New York: Psychology Press.

Herek, G. M., & Capitanio, J. P. (1995). Black heterosexuals' attitudes toward lesbians and gay men in the United States. *Journal of Sex Research, 32,* 95–105.

Herek, G. M., Capitanio, J. P., & Widaman, K. F. (2002). HIV-related stigma and knowledge in the United States: Prevalence and trends, 1991–1999. *American Journal of Public Health, 92,* 371–377.

Hewstone, M. (1996). Contact and categorization: Social psychological interventions to change intergroup relations. In C. N. Macrae, C. Stangor, & M. Hewstone (Eds.), *Stereotypes and stereotyping* (pp. 323–368). New York: Guilford Press.

Hewstone, M., Rubin, M., & Willis, H. (2002). Intergroup bias. *Annual Review of Psychology, 53,* 575–604.

Hexmoor, H. (2002). A model of absolute autonomy and power: Toward group effects. *Connection Science, 14,* 323–333.

Hilberg, R. (1993). *Perpetrators, victims, bystanders: Jewish catastrophe 1933–1945.* London: Lime Tree.

Hill, J. L. (1996). Psychological sense of community: Suggestions for future research. *Journal of Community Psychology, 24,* 431–438.
Hodgson, S. A., Hornstein, H. A., & LaKind, E. (1972). Socially mediated Zeigarnik effects as a function of sentiment, valence and desire for goal attainment. *Journal of Experimental Social Psychology, 28,* 191–218.
Hoffman, M. L. (1981). Is altruism part of human nature? *Journal of Personality and Social Psychology, 40,* 121–137.
Hofmann, W., Gschwendner, T., Nosek, B. A., & Schmitt, M. (2005). What moderates implicit-explicit consistency? In W. Stroebe & M. Hewstone (Eds.), *European review of social psychology* (Vol. 16, pp. 335–390). Hove: Psychology Press.
Hoge, C. W., Castro, C. A., Messer, S. C., McGurk, D., Cotting, D. I., & Koffman, R. L. (2004). Combat duty in Iraq and Afghanistan, mental health problems, and barriers to care. *New England Journal of Medicine, 351,* 13–22.
Hogg, M. A. (2001a). A social identity theory of leadership. *Personality and Social Psychology Review, 5,* 184–200.
Hogg, M. A. (2001b). Subjective uncertainty reduction through self-categorization: A motivational theory of social identity processes. In W. Stroebe & M. Hewstone (Eds.), *European review of social psychology* (Vol. 11, pp. 223–255). Chichester: Wiley.
Hogg, M. A., & Abrams, D. (2001). *Intergroup relations: Essential readings.* Philadelphia, PA: Psychology Press.
Hogg, M. A., & Terry, D. J. (2000). Social identity and self-categorization processes in organizational contexts. *Academy of Management Review, 25,* 121–140.
Hogg, M. A., & Terry, D. J. (Eds.). (2001). *Social identity processes in organizational contexts.* Philadelphia, PA: Psychology Press.
Holmes, J. G., Miller, D. T., & Lerner, M. J. (2002). Committing altruism under the cloak of self-interest: The exchange fiction. *Journal of Experimental Social Psychology, 38,* 144–151.
Holmes, T. H., & Rahe, R. H. (1967). The social readjustment scale. *Journal of Psychomatic Research, 11,* 213–218.
hooks, b. (1989). *Talking back: Thinking feminist, thinking black.* Boston: South End Press.
Hopkins, N., Reicher, S., Harrison, K., Cassidy, C., Bull, R., & Levine, M. (2007). Helping to improve the group stereotype: On the strategic dimension of prosocial behavior. *Personality and Social Psychology Bulletin, 33,* 776–788.
Hornsey, M. J. (2005). Why being right is not enough: Predicting defensiveness in the face of group criticism. In W. Stroebe & M. Hewstone (Eds.), *European review of social psychology* (Vol. 16, pp. 301–334). Hove: Psychology Press.
Hornsey, M. J., Dwyer, L., & Oei, T. P. S. (2007). Beyond cohesiveness: Reconceptualizing the link between group processes and outcomes in group psychotherapy. *Small Group Research, 38,* 567–592.

Hornsey, M. J., & Hogg, M. A. (2000). Subgroup relations: A comparison of mutual intergroup differentiation and common ingroup identity models of prejudice reduction. *Personality and Social Psychology Bulletin*, *26*, 242–256.

Hornstein, H. A. (1972). Promotive tension and prosocial behavior: The basis of prosocial behavior from a Lewinian perspective. *Journal of Social Issues*, *28*, 191–218.

Hornstein, H. A. (1976). *Cruelty and kindness: A new look at aggression and altruism.* Englewood Cliffs, NJ: Prentice-Hall.

Hornstein, H. A., Masor, H. N., Sole, K., & Heilman, M. (1971). Effects of sentiment and completion of a helping act on observer helping: A case for socially mediated Zeigarnik effects. *Journal of Personality and Social Psychology Bulletin*, *17*, 107–112.

Horowitz, I. A. (1971). The effect of group norms on bystander intervention. *Journal of Social Psychology*, *83*, 265–273.

House, J. S. (1995). *Americans' changing lives: Waves I and II, 1986 and 1989.* Ann Arbor, MI: Interuniversity Consortium for Political and Social Research.

Hoyt, D. R., Conger, R. D., Valde, J. G., & Weihs, K. (1997). Psychological distress and help seeking in rural America. *American Journal of Community Psychology*, *25*, 449–470.

Hughey, J., Speer, P. W., & Peterson, N. A. (1999). Sense of community in community organizations: Structure and evidence in validity. *Journal of Community Psychology*, *27*, 97–113.

Hulin, C. L. (1991). Adaptation, persistence, and commitment in organizations. In M. D. Dunnette & L. M. Hough (Eds.), *Handbook of industrial and organizational psychology* (pp. 445–505). Palo Alto, CA: Consulting Psychologists Press.

Independent Sector. (2001). *Giving and volunteering in the United States: Findings from a national survey.* Washington, DC: Independent Sector. Summary on the web at www.independentsector.org/programs/research/GV01main.html.

Insko, C. A., & Schopler, J. (1998). Differential distrust of groups and individuals. In C. Sedikikides, J. Schopler, & C. A. Insko (Eds.), *Intergroup cognition and intergroup behavior* (pp. 75–107). Hillsdale, NJ: Erlbaum.

Insko, C. A., Schopler, J., Gaertner, L., Wildschut, T., Kozar, R., Pinter, B., Finkel, E. J., Brazil, D. M., Cecil, C. L., & Montoya, M. R. (2001). Interindividual-intergroup discontinuity reduction through the anticipation of future interaction. *Journal of Personality and Social Psychology*, *80*, 95–111.

Insko, C. A., Schopler, J., Graetz, K. A., Drigotas, S. M., Currey, D. P., Smith, S. L., Brazil, D., & Bornstein, G. (1994). Interindividual-intergroup discontinuity in the prisoner's dilemma game. *Journal of Conflict Resolution*, *38*, 87–116.

Insko, C. A., Schopler, J., Hoyle, R. H., Dardis, G. J., & Graetz, K. A. (1990). Individual-group discontinuity as a function of fear and greed. *Journal of Personality and Social Psychology*, *58*, 68–79.

Iyer, A., Jetten, J., & Tsivrikos, D. (2008). Torn between identities: Predictors of adjustment to identity change. In F. Sani (Ed.), *Self-continuity: Individual and collective perspectives* (pp. 187–197). New York: Psychology Press.

Iyer, A., Jetten, J., Tsivrikos, D., Postmes, T., & Haslam, S. A. (in press). The more (and the more compatible) the merrier: Multiple group memberships and identity compatibility as predictors of adjustment after life transitions. *British Journal of Social Psychology.*

Iyer, A., & Leach, C. W. (2008a). Emotion in inter-group relations. In W. Stroebe & M. Hewstone (Eds.), *European review of social psychology* (Vol. 19, pp. 86–125). Hove: Psychology Press.

Iyer, A., & Leach, C. W. (2008b). *Predicting European Americans' willingness to challenge systemic discrimination: The limits of group-based guilt.* Manuscript submitted for publication.

Iyer, A., Leach, C. W., & Crosby, F. J. (2003). White guilt and racial compensation: The benefits and limits of self-focus. *Personality and Social Psychology Bulletin, 29,* 117–129.

Iyer, A., Schmader, T., & Lickel, B. (2007). Why individuals protest the perceived transgressions of their country: The role of anger, shame, and guilt. *Personality and Social Psychology Bulletin, 33,* 572–587.

Jackman, M. R. (1994). *The velvet glove: Paternalism and conflict in gender, class, and race relations.* Berkeley: University of California Press.

Jackson, L. A., & Sullivan, L. A. (1989). Cognition and affect in evaluations of stereotyped group members. *Journal of Social Psychology, 129,* 659–672.

Jackson, L. M., & Esses, V. M. (1997). Of scripture and ascription: The relation between religious fundamentalism and intergroup helping. *Personality and Social Psychology Bulletin, 23,* 893–906.

Jackson, L. M., & Esses, V. M. (2000). Effects of perceived economic competition on people's willingness to help empower immigrants. *Group Processes and Intergroup Relationships, 3,* 419–435.

Jackson, P. B., Thoits, P. A., & Taylor, H. F. (1995). Composition of the workplace and psychological well-being: The effects of tokenism on America's Black elite. *Social Forces, 74,* 543–557.

Jauernig, N. J., Wright, S. C., Lubensky, M. E., & Tropp, L. R. (2006, February). *Stereotype threat and social relations: Implications for intergroup relations.* Paper presented at the meeting of the Society for Personality and Social Psychology, Palm Springs, CA.

Jellison, W. A., McConnell, A. R., & Gabriel, S. (2004). Implicit and explicit measures of sexual orientation attitudes: Ingroup preferences and related behaviors and beliefs among gay and straight men. *Personality and Social Psychology Bulletin, 30,* 629–642.

Jenner, J. R. (1981). Volunteerism as an aspect of women's work lives. *Journal of Vocational Behavior, 19,* 302–314.

Jetten, J., Branscombe, N. R., Schmitt, M. T., & Spears, R. (2001). Rebels with a cause: Group identification as a response to perceived discrimination from the mainstream. *Personality and Social Psychology Bulletin, 27,* 1204–1213.

Jetten, J., Duck, J., Terry, D. J., & O'Brien, A. (2002). Being attuned to intergroup differences in mergers: The role of aligned leaders for low-status groups. *Personality and Social Psychology Bulletin, 28*, 1194–1201.

Jetten, J., & Haslam, S. A. (2005). [Who says it isn't stressful? Social identification with a source is a moderator of the impact of informational support]. Unpublished data.

Jetten, J., & Haslam, S. A. (2006). [Care workers' stress appraisals: Evidence that feedback from ingroup members enhances social identification]. Unpublished data.

Jetten, J., Iyer, A., Tsivrikos, T., & Young, B. M. (2008). When is individual mobility costly? The role of economic and social identity factors. *European Journal of Social Psychology, 38*, 866–879.

Jetten, J., O'Brien, A., & Trindall, N. (2002). Changing identity: Predicting adjustment to organisational restructure as a function of subgroup and superordinate identification. *British Journal of Social Psychology, 41*, 281–297.

Jetten, J., Schmitt, M. T., Branscombe, N. R., & McKimmie, B. M. (2005). Suppressing the negative effect of devaluation on group identification: The role of intergroup differentiation and intragroup respect. *Journal of Experimental Social Psychology, 41*, 208–215.

Jetten, J., Spears, R., & Manstead, A. S. R. (1996). Ingroup norms and intergroup discrimination: Distinctive self-categorization and social identity effects. *Journal of Personality and Social Psychology, 71*, 1222–1233.

Jetten, J., Spears, R., & Manstead, A. S. R. (1997). Distinctiveness threat and prototypicality: Combined effects on intergroup discrimination and collective self-esteem. *European Journal of Social Psychology, 27*, 635–657.

Johnson, D. D. P., McDermott, R., Barrett, E. S., Crowden, J., Wrangham, R., McIntyre, M. H., & Rosen, S. P. (2006). Overconfidence in war games: Experimental evidence on expectations, aggression, gender and testosterone. *Proceedings of the Royal Society B, 273*, 2513–2520.

Jonas, E., Schimel, J., Greenberg, J., & Pyszczynski, T. (2002). The Scrooge effect: Evidence that mortality salience increases prosocial attitudes and behavior. *Personality and Social Psychology Bulletin, 28*, 1342–1353.

Jones, E. E., Bell, L., & Aronson, E. (1972). The reciprocation of attraction from similar and dissimilar others: A study in person perception and evaluation. In C. G. McClintock (Ed.), *Experimental social psychology* (pp. 142–179). New York: Holt, Rinehart.

Jones, E. E., Farina, A., Hastorf, A., Markus, H., Miller, D. T., Scott, R., & French, R. (1984). *Social stigma: The psychology of marked relationships.* New York: W. H. Freeman.

Jones, J. M. (1997). *Prejudice and racism.* New York: McGraw-Hill.

Jost, J. T., Banaji, M. R., & Nosek, B. A. (2004). A decade of system justification theory: Accumulated evidence of conscious and unconscious bolstering of the status quo. *Political Psychology, 25*, 881–919.

Judd, C. M., & Park, B. (1988). Outgroup homogeneity: Judgments of variability at the individual and group levels. *Journal of Personality and Social Psychology, 54*, 778–788.

Kampmeier, C., & Simon, B. (2001). Individuality and group formation: The role of independence and differentiation. *Journal of Personality and Social Psychology, 81,* 448–462.

Kang, N., & Kwak, N. (2003). A multilevel approach to civic participation: Individual length of residence, neighborhood residential stability, and their interactive effects with media use. *Communication Research, 30,* 80–106.

Karabenick, S. A. (1998). *Strategic help seeking: Implications for learning and teaching.* Mahwah, NJ: Erlbaum.

Karacanta, A., & Fitness, J. (2006). Majority support for minority outgroups: The roles of compassion and guilt. *Journal of Applied Psychology, 36,* 2730–2749.

Kasarda, J., & Janowitz, M. (1974). Community attachment in mass society. *American Sociological Review, 39,* 328–339.

Katz, I. (1981). *Stigma: A social psychological analysis.* Hillsdale, NJ: Erlbaum.

Katz, I., Cohen, S., & Glass, D. (1975). Some determinants of cross-racial helping behavior. *Journal of Personality and Social Psychology, 32,* 964–970.

Katz, I., & Hass, R. G. (1988). Racial ambivalence and American value conflict: Correlational and priming studies of dual cognitive structures. *Journal of Personality and Social Psychology, 55,* 893–905.

Katz, J. H. (1978). *White awareness: Handbook for anti-racism training.* Norman: University of Oklahoma Press.

Kawachi, I., Kennedy, B. P., & Lochner, K. (1997). Social capital, income inequality, and mortality. *American Journal of Public Health, 87,* 1491–1498.

Kawakami, K., & Dion, K. L. (1995). Social identity and affect as determinants of collective action: Toward an integration of relative deprivation and social identity theories. *Theory and Psychology, 5,* 551–577.

Kawakami, K., Phills, C. E., Steele, J. R., & Dovidio, J. F. (2007). (Close) distance makes the heart grow fonder: Improving implicit racial attitudes and interracial interactions through approach behaviors. *Journal of Personality and Social Psychology, 92,* 957–971.

Keegan, J. (1994). *A history of warfare.* New York: Random House.

Keeley, L. (1996). *War before civilization.* New York: Oxford University Press.

Keller, J. (2005). In genes we trust: The biological component of psychological essentialism and its relationship to mechanisms of motivated social cognition. *Journal of Personality and Social Psychology, 88,* 686–702.

Kelly, C. (1996). *The social psychology of collective action: Identity, injustice, gender.* London: Taylor & Francis.

Kenrick, D. T., Li, N. P., & Butner, J. (2003). Dynamical evolutionary psychology: Individual decision rules and emergent social norms. *Psychological Review, 110,* 3–28.

Keridis, D. (2006). Earthquakes, diplomacy, and new thinking in foreign policy. *Fletcher Forum of World Affairs, 30,* 207–214.

Keyes, C. L. M. (1995). *Social functioning and social well-being: Studies of the social nature of personal wellness.* Unpublished doctoral dissertation, University of Wisconsin-Madison.

Kimmel, M. S., & Ferber, A. L. (Eds.). (2001). *Privilege: A reader*. Boulder, CO: Westview Press.

Kingston, S., Mitchell, R., Forin, P., & Stevenson, J. (1999). Sense of community in neighborhoods as a multi-level construct. *Journal of Community Psychology, 27*, 384–394.

Kiviniemi, M. T., Snyder, M., & Omoto, A. M. (2002). Too many of a good thing? The effects of multiple motivations on task fulfillment, satisfaction, and cost. *Personality and Social Psychology Bulletin, 28*, 732–743.

Klandermans, B. (1984). Mobilization and participation: Social-psychological expansions of resource mobilization theory. *American Sociological Review, 49*, 583–600.

Klandermans, B., & Oegema, K. (1987). Potentials, networks, motivations, and barriers: Steps toward participation in social movements. *American Sociological Review, 52*, 519–531.

Klandermans, B., Sabucedo, J. M., Rodriguez, M., & de Weerd, M. (2002). Identity processes in collective action participation: Farmers' identity and farmers' protest in the Netherlands and Spain. *Political Psychology, 23*, 235–251.

Kleck, R. E. (1969). Physical stigma and task-oriented interactions. *Human Relations, 22*, 53–60.

Kleck, R. E., Ono, H., & Hastorf, A. H. (1966). The effects of physical deviance upon face-to-face interaction. *Human Relations, 19*, 425–436.

Klein, O., & Azzi, A. E. (2001). The strategic confirmation of meta-stereotypes: How group members attempt to tailor an out-group's representation of themselves. *British Journal of Social Psychology, 40*, 279–293.

Komorita, S. S., & Parks, C. D. (1995). Interpersonal relations: Mixed-motive interaction. *Annual Review of Psychology, 46*, 183–207.

Kramer, R. M. (1999). Trust and distrust in organizations: Emerging perspectives, enduring questions. *Annual Review of Psychology, 50*, 569–598.

Kramer, R. M., & Brewer, M. B. (1984). Effects of group identity on resource utilization in a simulated commons dilemma. *Journal of Personality and Social Psychology, 46*, 1044–1057.

Krebs, D. (1975). Empathy and altruism. *Journal of Personality and Social Psychology, 32*, 1134–1146.

Krebs, D. (1987). The challenge of altruism in biology and psychology. In C. Crawford, M. Smith, & D. Krebs (Eds.), *Sociobiology and psychology: Ideas, issues, and applications* (pp. 81–118). Hillsdale, NJ: Erlbaum.

Kuppuswamy, B. (1978). Concept of begging in ancient thought. *Indian Journal of Social Work, 39*, 187–192.

Kurzban, R., & Leary, M. R. (2001). Evolutionary origins of stigmatization: The functions of social exclusion. *Psychological Bulletin, 127*, 187–208.

Kurzban, R., & Neuberg, S. (2005). Managing ingroup and outgroup relationships. In D. M. Buss (Ed.), *The handbook of evolutionary psychology* (pp. 653–675). Hoboken, NJ: Wiley.

Kurzban, R., Tooby, J., & Cosmides, L. (2001). Can race be erased? Coalitional computation and social categorization. *Proceedings of the National Academy of Sciences, 98*, 15387–15392.

Kymlicka, W., & Norman, W. (1994). Return of the citizen: A survey of recent work on citizen theory. *Ethics, 104*, 352–381.

Lalonde, R. N., & Silverman, R. A. (1994). Behavioral preferences in response to social injustice: The effects of group permeability and social identity salience. *Journal of Personality and Social Psychology, 66*, 78–85.

Lambda Legal HIV Project. (2007, February). The state of HIV stigma and discrimination 2007: An evidence-based report. Retrieved November 1, 2007 from www.lambdalegal.org/assets/pdf/page.jsp?itemID=34429384.

LaPiere, R. T. (1934). Attitudes vs. action. *Social Forces, 13*, 230–237.

Latané, B., & Darley, J. M. (1970). *The unresponsive bystander: Why doesn't he help?* New York: Appleton Century Crofts.

Latané, B., & Nida, S. (1981). Ten years of research on group size and helping. *Psychological Bulletin, 89*, 308–324.

Laws, J. L. (1975). The psychology of tokenism: An analysis. *Sex Roles, 1*, 51–67.

Lazarus, R. S. (1966). *Psychological stress and the coping process.* New York: McGraw-Hill.

Lazarus, R. S. (1991). *Emotion and adaptation.* New York: Oxford University Press.

Lazarus, R. S., & Folkman, S. (1984). *Stress, appraisal, and coping.* New York: Springer.

Le Bon, G. (1947). *The crowd: A study of the popular mind.* London: Ernest Benn. (Original work published 1895)

Leach, C. W., & Iyer, A. (2008). *Rage against the machine? Perceived responsibility for injustice against an out-group and willingness for political action.* Manuscript under review.

Leach, C. W., Iyer, A., & Pedersen, A. (2006). Anger and guilt about ingroup advantage explain the willingness for political action. *Personality and Social Psychology Bulletin, 32*, 1232–1245.

Leach, C. W., Snider, N., & Iyer, A. (2002). "Poisoning the consciences of the fortunate": The experience of relative advantage and support for social equality. In I. Walker & H. J. Smith (Eds.), *Relative deprivation: Specification, development, and integration* (pp. 136–163). New York: Cambridge University Press.

Leach, C. W., Spears, R., Branscombe, N. R., & Doosje, B. (2003). Malicious pleasure: Schadenfreude at the suffering of another group. *Journal of Personality and Social Psychology, 84*, 932–943.

Lederach, J. P. (1997). *Building peace: Sustainable reconciliation in divided societies.* Washington, DC: US Institute of Peace.

Lefebvre, G. (1954). *Etudes sur la Révolution française.* Paris: PUF.

Lerner, M. J., & Miller, D. T. (1978). Just world research and the attribution process: Looking back and ahead. *Psychological Bulletin, 85*, 1030–1051.

Lerner, M. J., & Simmons, C. (1966). Observer's reaction to the "innocent victim": Compassion or rejection? *Journal of Personality and Social Psychology, 4*, 203–210.

Lerner, R. M., & Frank, P. (1974). Relation of race and sex to supermarket helping behavior. *Journal of Social Psychology, 94*, 201–203.

Lever, J. (1976). Sex differences in the games children play. *Social Problems,* 23, 478–487.

Levine, M., Cassidy, C., Brazier, G., & Reicher, S. (2002). Self-categorization and bystander non-intervention: Two experimental studies. *Journal of Applied Social Psychology,* 32, 1452–1463.

Levine, M., Prosser, A., Evans, D., & Reicher, S. (2005). Identity and emergency intervention: How social group membership and inclusiveness of group boundaries shape helping behavior. *Personality and Social Psychology Bulletin,* 31, 443–453.

Levine, R. M. (1999). Identity and illness: The effects of identity salience and frame of reference on evaluation of illness and injury. *British Journal of Health Psychology,* 4, 63–80.

Levine, R. M., & Reicher, S. D. (1996). Making sense of symptoms: Self-categorisation and the meaning of illness and injury. *British Journal of Social Psychology,* 35, 245–256.

Levine, R. V., Norenzayan, A., & Philbrick, K. (2001). Cross-cultural differences in helping strangers. *Journal of Cross-Cultural Psychology,* 32, 543–560.

Levy, S. R., Freitas, A. L., & Salovey, P. (2002). Construing action abstractly and blurring social distinctions: Implications for perceiving homogeneity among, but also empathizing with and helping, others. *Journal of Personality and Social Psychology,* 83, 1224–1238.

Lewin, K. (1948). *Field theory in social science.* New York: Harper & Row.

Leyens, J.-P., Cortes, B., Demoulin, S., Dovidio, J. F., Fiske, S. T., Gaunt, R., Paladino, M.-P., Rodriguez-Perez, A., Rodriguez-Torres, R., & Vaes, J. (2003). Emotional prejudice, essentialism, and nationalism: The 2002 Tajfel Lecture. *European Journal of Social Psychology,* 33, 703–717.

Leyens, J.-P., Paladino, P. M., Rodriguez-Torres, R., Vaes, J., Demoulin, S., Rodriguez-Perez, A., & Gaunt, R. (2000). The emotional side of prejudice: The attribution of secondary emotions to ingroups and outgroups. *Personality and Social Psychology Review,* 4, 186–197.

Leyens, J.-P., Rodriguez-Perez, A., Rodriguez-Torres, R., Gaunt, R., Paladino, M. P., Vaes, J., & Demoulin, S. (2001). Psychological essentialism and the differential attribution of uniquely human emotions to ingroups and outgroups. *European Journal of Social Psychology,* 31, 395–411.

Liao-Troth, M. A. (2001). Attitude differences between paid workers and volunteers. *Nonprofit Management and Leadership,* 11, 423–442.

Lickel, B., Schmader, T., Curtis, M., Scarnier, M., & Ames, D. R. (2005). Vicarious shame and guilt. *Group Processes and Intergroup Relations,* 8, 145–157.

Lieberman, M. D., Gaunt, R., Gilbert, D. T., & Trope, Y. (2002). Reflexion and reflection: A social cognitive neuroscience approach to attributional inference. In M. P. Zanna (Ed.), *Advances in experimental social psychology* (Vol. 34, pp. 199–249). San Diego: Academic Press.

Lindsay, J. J., Snyder, M., & Omoto, A. M. (2003, May-June). *Volunteers' impact on psychological and physical functioning of persons living with HIV.*

Paper presented at the annual meeting of the American Psychological Society, Atlanta, GA.

Lindsay, J. J., Snyder, M., & Omoto, A. M. (2006, May). *Antecedents and consequences of psychological sense of community.* Paper presented at the annual meeting of the Midwestern Psychological Association, Chicago, IL.

Link, B. G., Cullen, F. T., Struening, E. L., Shrout, P. E, & Dohrenwend, B. P. (1989). A modified labeling theory approach to mental disorders: An empirical assessment. *American Sociological Review, 54,* 400–423.

Link, B. G., Phelan, J. C., Bresnahan, M., Stueve, A., & Pescosolido, B. A. (1999). Public conceptions of mental illness: Labels, causes, dangerousness, and social distance. *American Journal of Public Health, 89,* 1328–1333.

Linville, P. W. (1985). Self-complexity and affective extremity: Don't put all of your eggs in one cognitive basket. *Social Cognition, 3,* 94–120.

Linville, P. W. (1987). Self-complexity as a cognitive buffer against stress-related illness and depression. *Journals of Personality and Social Psychology, 52,* 663–676.

Lipsitz, G. (1998). *The possessive investment in Whiteness: How White people profit from identity politics.* Philadelphia, PA: Temple University Press.

Living with Stigma. (April 7, 2008). Retrieved May 19, 2008 from www. revolutionhealth.com/stories/stories/show/352f5d77a9d64963ace8a36c8a9 498bf.

Lord, C., & Saenz, D. (1985). Memory deficits and memory surfeits: Differential cognitive consequences of tokenism for tokens and observers. *Journal of Personality and Social Psychology, 49,* 918–926.

Luoh, M.-C., & Herzog, A. R. (2002). Individual consequences of volunteer and paid work in old age: Health and mortality. *Journal of Health and Social Behavior, 43,* 490–509.

Lyons, R. F., Mickelson, K. D., Sullivan, M. J., & Coyne, J. C. (1998). Coping as a communal process. *Journal of Social and Personal Relationships, 15,* 579–605.

Mackie, D. M., Devos, T., & Smith, E. R. (2000). Intergroup emotions: Explaining offensive action tendencies in an intergroup context. *Journal of Personality and Social Psychology, 79,* 602–616.

Mackie, D. M., Maitner, A. T., & Smith, E. R. (2009). Intergroup emotions theory. In T. D. Nelson (Ed.), *Handbook of prejudice, stereotyping, and discrimination* (pp. 285–306). New York: Psychology Press.

Macrae, C. N., Milne, A. B., & Bodenhausen, G. V. (1994). Stereotypes as energy-saving devices: A peek inside the cognitive toolbox. *Journal of Personality and Social Psychology, 66,* 37–47.

Malsch, A. M. (2005). *Prosocial behavior beyond borders: Understanding a psychological sense of global community.* Unpublished doctoral dissertation, Claremont Graduate University, Claremont, CA.

Maner, J. K., & Gailliot, M. T. (2007). Altruism and egoism: Prosocial motivations for helping depend on relationship context. *European Journal of Social Psychology, 37,* 347–358.

Maner, J. K., Kenrick, D. T., Becker, D. V., Robertson, T. E., Hofer, B., Neuberg, S. L., Delton, A. W., Butner, J., & Schaller, M. (2005). Functional projection: How fundamental social motives can bias interpersonal perception. *Journal of Personality and Social Psychology, 88*, 63–78.

Maner, J. K., Luce, C. L., Neuberg, S. L., Cialdini, R. B., Brown, S., & Sagarin, B. J. (2002). The effects of perspective taking on motivations for helping: Still no evidence for altruism. *Personality and Social Psychology Bulletin, 28*, 1601–1610.

Manis, M., Nelson, T. E., & Shedler, J. (1988). Stereotypes and social judgment: Extremity, assimilation, and contrast. *Journal of Personality and Social Psychology, 55*, 28–36.

Manning, R., Levine, M., & Collins, A. (2007). The Kitty Genovese murder and the social psychology of helping: The parable of the 38 witnesses. *American Psychologist, 62*, 555–562.

Manucia, G. K., Baumann, D. J., & Cialdini, R. B. (1984). Mood influences in helping: Direct effects or side effects? *Journal of Personality and Social Psychology, 46*, 357–364.

Marcus-Newhall, A., Blake, L. P., & Baumann, J. (2002). Perceptions of hate crime perpetrators and victims as influenced by race, political orientation, and peer group. *American Behavioral Scientist, 46*, 108–135.

Marks, S. R. (1977). Multiple roles and role strain: Some notes on human energy, time and commitment. *American Sociological Review, 42*, 921–936.

Marques, J. M., Yzerbyt, V. Y., & Leyens, J.-P. (1988). The "black sheep effect": Extremity of judgments towards ingroup members as a function of group identification. *European Journal of Social Psychology, 18*, 1–16.

Martin, J., Brickman, P., & Murray, A. (1984). Moral outrage and pragmatism: Explanations for collective action. *Journal of Experimental Social Psychology, 20*, 484–496.

Martin, J., Pescosolido, B., Olafsdottir, S., & Mcleod, J. (2007). The construction of fear: Americans' preferences for social distance from children and adolescents with mental health problems. *Journal of Health and Social Behavior, 48*, 50–67.

Marx, G. T., & Useem, M. (1971). Majority involvement in minority movements: Civil rights, abolition, untouchability. *Journal of Social Issues, 27*, 81–104.

Mason, D., & Allen, B. P. (1976). The bystander effect as a function of ambiguity and emergency character. *Journal of Social Psychology, 100*, 145–146.

Massar, B., & Moffat, K. B. (2006). With friends like these . . . : The role of prejudice and situational norms on discriminatory helping behavior. *Journal of Homosexuality, 51*, 121–138.

Mauss, M. (1957). *The gift: Forms and functions of exchange in archaic societies.* Glencoe, IL: Free Press. (Original work published 1907)

McCall, G. J., & Simmons, J. L. (1978). *Identities and interactions.* New York: Free Press.

McCarthy, J. D., & Zald, M. N. (1977). Resource mobilization and social movements: A partial theory. *American Journal of Sociology, 82*, 1212–1241.

McConahay, J. B. (1986). Modern racism, ambivalence, and the modern racism scale. In J. F. Dovidio & S. L. Gaertner (Eds.), *Prejudice, discrimination, and racism* (pp. 91–125). San Diego: Academic Press.

McConnell, A. R., Rydell, R. J., Strain, L. M., & Mackie, D. M. (2008). Forming implicit and explicit attitudes toward individuals: Social group association cues. *Journal of Personality and Social Psychology, 94*, 792–807.

McDonald, T. W., Toussaint, L. L., & Schweiger, J. A. (2004). The influence of social status on token women leaders' expectations about leading male-dominated groups. *Sex Roles, 50*, 401–409.

McDougall, W. (1908). *An introduction to social psychology*. London: Methuen.

McGarty, C., Pedersen, A., Leach, C. W., Mansell, T., Waller, J., & Bliuc, A.-M. (2005). Group-based guilt as a predictor of commitment to apology. *British Journal of Social Psychology, 44*, 659–680.

McGregor, J. (1993). Effectiveness of role playing and antiracist teaching in reducing student prejudice. *Journal of Educational Research, 86*, 215–226.

McLaughlin-Volpe, T., Aron, A., Wright, S. C., & Lewandowski, G. W., Jr. (2006). Inclusion of the self by close others and by groups: Implications of the self-expansion model. In D. Abrams, J. Marques, & M. Hogg (Eds.), *Social inclusion and exclusion, diversity and deviance* (pp. 114–134). New York: Psychology Press.

McLaughlin-Volpe, T., Aron, A., Wright, S. C., & Reis, H. T. (2007). *Intergroup social interactions and intergroup prejudice: Quantity versus quality*. Unpublished manuscript.

McManus, J. L., & Saucier, D. A. (in prep.). *The role of financial cost in helping*.

McMillan, D. W. (1996). Sense of community. *Journal of Community Psychology, 24*, 315–325.

McMillan, D. W., & Chavis, D. M. (1986). Sense of community: A definition of theory. *Journal of Community Psychology, 14*, 6–23.

Medin, D. L., & Ortony, A. (1989). Psychological essentialism. In S. Vosniadou & A. Ortony (Eds.), *Similarity and analogical reasoning* (pp. 179–195). New York: Cambridge University Press.

Mehta, S. I., Farina, A. (1988). Associative stigma: Perceptions of the difficulties of college-aged children of stigmatized fathers. *Journal of Social and Clinical Psychology, 7*, 192–202.

Memmi, A. (1965). *The colonizer and the colonized*. Boston: Beacon.

Meyer, J. P., Stanley, D. J., Herscovitch, L., & Topolnytsky, L. (2002). Affective, continuance, and normative commitment to the organization: A meta-analysis of antecedents, correlates, and consequences. *Journal of Vocational Behavior, 61*, 20–52.

Milgram, S. (1974). *Obedience to authority: An experimental view*. New York: Harper & Row.

Miller, C. T., & Kaiser, C. R. (2001). A theoretical perspective on coping with stigma. *Journal of Social Issues, 57*, 73–92.

Miller, L. E., Powell, G. N., & Seltzer, J. (1990). Determinants of turnover among volunteers. *Human Relations, 43*, 901–917.

Miller, N. (2002). Personalization and the promise of contact theory. *Journal of Social Issues, 58*, 387–410.

Mirowsky, J., & Ross, C. E. (1986). Social patterns of distress. In R. H. Turner & J. F. Short (Eds.), *Annual review of sociology* (Vol. 12, pp. 23–45). Palo Alto, CA: Annual Reviews.

Moen, P., Dempster-McClain, D., & Williams, R. M., Jr. (1989). Social integration and longevity. *American Sociological Review, 54*, 635–647.

Moen, P., Dempster-McClain, D., & Williams, R. M., Jr. (1992). Successful aging: A life-course perspective on women's multiple roles and health. *American Journal of Sociology, 97*, 1612–1638.

Moller, A. C., Deci, E. L., & Ryan, R. M. (2006). Choice and ego-depletion: The moderating role of autonomy. *Personality and Social Psychology Bulletin, 32*, 1024–1036.

Monroe, K. R. (1996). *The heart of altruism*. Princeton, NJ: Princeton University Press.

Montada, L., & Schneider, A. (1989). Justice and emotional reactions to the disadvantaged. *Social Justice Research, 3*, 313–334.

Monteith, M. J. (1993). Self-regulation of prejudiced responses: Implications for progress in prejudice-reduction efforts. *Journal of Personality and Social Psychology, 65*, 469–485.

Monteith, M. J., Deneen, N. E., & Tooman, G. D. (1996). The effect of social norm activation on the expression of opinions concerning gay men and Blacks. *Basic and Applied Social Psychology, 18*, 267–288.

Monteith, M. J., Sherman, J. W., & Devine, P. G. (1998). Suppression as a stereotype control strategy. *Personality and Social Psychology Review, 2*, 63–82.

Montjabi, R., Olfson, M., & Mechanic, D. (2002). Perceived need and help-seeking in adults with mood, anxiety, or substance use disorders. *Archives of General Psychiatry, 59*, 77–84.

Morrison, E. W. (1993). Newcomer information seeking: Exploring types, modes, sources, and outcomes. *Academy of Management Journal, 36*, 557–589.

Moscovici, S. (1976). *Social influence and social change*. London: Academic Press.

Moss, M. K., & Page, R. A. (1972). Reinforcement and helping behavior. *Journal of Applied Social Psychology, 2*, 360–371.

Mullen, B. (1991). Group composition, salience, and cognitive representations: The phenomenology of being in a group. *Journal of Experimental Social Psychology, 27*, 1–27.

Mummendey, A., & Wenzel, M. (1999). Social discrimination and tolerance in intergroup relations: Reactions to intergroup difference. *Personality and Social Psychology Review, 3*, 158–174.

Musick, M. W., Herzog, A. R., & House, J. S. (1999). Volunteering and mortality among older adults: Findings from a national sample. *Journals of Gerontology: Psychological Sciences and Social Sciences, 54B*, 173–180.

Musick, M. W., & Wilson, J. (2003). Volunteering and depression: The role of psychological and social resources in different age groups. *Social Science and Medicine, 56*, 259–269.

Nadler, A. (1986). Self-esteem and help-seeking and receiving: Empirical and theoretical perspectives. In B. A. Maher & W. Maher (Eds.), *Progress in experimental personality research* (Vol. 14, pp. 115–165). New York: Academic Press.

Nadler, A. (1987). Determinants of help-seeking behavior: The effects of helper's similarity, task centrality and recipient's self esteem. *European Journal of Social Psychology, 17*, 57–67.

Nadler, A. (1997). Autonomous and dependent help seeking: Personality characteristics and the seeking of help. In B. Sarason, I. Sarason, & R. G. Pierce (Eds.), *Handbook of personality and social support* (pp. 258–302). New York: Plenum.

Nadler, A. (1998). Relationship, esteem and achievement perspectives on autonomous and dependent help seeking. In S. A. Karabenick (Ed.), *Strategic help seeking: Implications for learning and teaching* (pp. 61–95). Mahwah, NJ: Erlbaum.

Nadler, A. (2002). Inter-group helping relations as power relations: Maintaining or challenging social dominance between groups through helping. *Journal of Social Issues, 58*, 487–502.

Nadler, A., Ellis, S., & Bar, R. (2003). To seek or not to seek: The relationship between help seeking and job performance as affected by task-relevant expertise. *Journal of Applied Social Psychology, 33*, 91–110.

Nadler, A., & Fisher, J. D. (1986). The role of threat to self-esteem and perceived control in recipient reactions to aid: Theory development and empirical validation. In L. Berkowitz (Ed.), *Advances in experimental social psychology* (Vol. 19, pp. 81–123). New York: Academic Press.

Nadler, A., Fisher, J. D., & Ben-Itzhak, S. (1983). With a little help from my friend: Effects of single or multiple act aid as a function of donor and task characteristics. *Journal of Personality and Social Psychology, 44*, 310–321.

Nadler, A., & Halabi, S. (2006). Intergroup helping as status relations: Effects of status stability, identification, and type of help on receptivity to high status group's help. *Journal of Personality and Social Psychology, 91*, 97–110.

Nadler, A., Halabi, S., & Harpaz-Gorodeisky, G. (2008). Helping relations as status maintenance mechanisms. In S. Demoulin, J.-P. Leyens, & J. F. Dovidio (Eds.), *Intergroup misunderstanding: Impact of divergent social realities*. Psychology Press: Washington, DC.

Nadler, A., Halabi, S., & Harpaz-Gorodeisky, G. (2009). Intergroup helping as status organizing processes: Creating, maintaining and challenging status relations through giving, seeking and receiving help. In S. Demoulin, J.-P. Leyens, & J. F. Dovidio (Eds.), *Intergroup misunderstanding: Impact of divergent social realities* (pp. 313–327). Washington, DC: Psychology Press.

Nadler, A., & Harpaz-Gorodeisky, G. (2006). *Coping with threat to social identity by helping the source of threat: Effects of in-group identification and threat to social identity.* Unpublished manuscript, Tel Aviv University.

Nadler, A., Harpaz-Gorodeisky, G., & Ben-David, Y. (2008). *Defensive helping: Threat to group identity, ingroup identification, status stability and common group identity as determinants of intergroup help-giving.* Unpublished manuscript, Tel Aviv University.

Nadler, A., & Saguy, T. (2004). Trust building and reconciliation between adversarial groups: A social psychological perspective. In H. Langholtz & C. E. Stout (Eds.), *The psychology of diplomacy* (pp. 29–46). New York: Praeger.

Napier, J. L., Mandisodza, A. N., Andersen, S. M., & Jost, J. T. (2006). System justification in responding to the poor and displaced in the aftermath of Hurricane Katrina. *Analyses of Social Issues and Public Policy, 6,* 57–73.

Neuberg, S., Cialdini, R., Brown, S., Luce, C., Sagarin, B., & Lewis, B. (1997). Does empathy lead to anything more than superficial helping? Comment on Batson et al. (1997). *Journal of Personality and Social Psychology, 73,* 510–516.

Neuberg, S. L., & Cottrell, C. A. (2006). Evolutionary bases of prejudice. In M. Schaller, J. A. Simpson, & D. T. Kenrick (Eds.), *Evolution and social psychology* (pp. 163–187). New York: Psychology Press.

Neuberg, S. L., Smith, D. M., Hoffman, J. C., & Russell, F. J. (1994). When we observe stigmatized and "normal" individuals interacting: Stigma by association. *Personality and Social Psychology Bulletin, 20,* 196–209.

Neumann, R., Hulsenbeck, K., & Seibt, B. (2004). Attitudes towards people with AIDS and avoidance behavior: Automatic and reflective bases of behavior. *Journal of Experimental Social Psychology, 40,* 543–550.

Neumann, R., & Strack, F. (2000). Approach and avoidance: The influence of proprioceptive and exteroceptive cues on encoding of affective information. *Journal of Personality and Social Psychology, 79,* 39–48.

Newman, S., Vasudev, J., & Onawola, R. (1985). Older volunteers' perceptions of impacts of volunteering on their psychological well-being. *Journal of Applied Gerontology, 4,* 123–127.

Nickerson, R. S. (1999). How we know – and sometimes misjudge – what others know: Imputing one's own knowledge to others. *Psychological Bulletin, 125,* 737–759.

Niemann, Y. F., & Dovidio, J. F. (1998). Relationship of solo status, academic rank, and perceived distinctiveness to job satisfaction of racial/ethnic minorities. *Journal of Applied Psychology, 83,* 55–71.

Nier, J. A., Gaertner, S. L., Dovidio, J. F., Banker, B. S., Ward, C. M., & Rust, M. C. (2001). Changing interracial evaluations and behaviour: The effects of a common group identity. *Group Processes and Intergroup Relations, 4,* 299–316.

Nishi, T. (2004, March). *The humiliating gift: Discontent in response to international help.* Paper presented at the annual meeting of the International Studies Association, Montreal, Quebec, Canada.

Nosek, B. A. (2007). Implicit-explicit relations. *Current Directions in Psychological Science, 16,* 65–69.

Novelli, D., Drury, J., Reicher, S. D., & Fenn, C. (2007, September). *"Personal space" as a function of self-categorization: Behavioural and experiential dimensions.* Paper presented to the Social Section of the British Psychological Society, Kent, UK.

Oakes, P. (2001). The root of all evil in intergroup relations? Unearthing the categorization process. In R. Brown & S. Gaertner (Eds.), *Blackwell handbook of social psychology: Intergroup processes* (Vol. 4, pp. 3–21). Oxford: Blackwell.

Oakes, P. J., Haslam, S. A., & Turner, J. C. (1994). *Stereotyping and social reality.* Oxford: Blackwell.

O'Brien, K., & Bender, B. (2005). Chronology of errors: How a disaster spread. *Boston Globe,* September 11. Retrieved from www.boston.com/news/weather/articles/2005/09/11/chronology_of_errors_how_a_disaster_spread/.

O'Brien, L. T., Crain, A. L., Omoto, A. M., & Snyder, M. (2000, May). *Matching motivations to outcomes: Implications for persistence in service.* Presentation at the annual meetings of the Midwestern Psychological Association, Chicago, IL.

Oegema, D., & Klandermans, B. (1994). Why social movement sympathizers don't participate: Erosion and non-conversion of support. *American Sociological Review, 59,* 703–722.

Oishi, S., Rothman, A. J., Snyder, M., Su, J., Zehm, K., Hertel, A., Gonzales, M. H., & Sherman, G. D. (2007). The social-ecological model of pro-community action: The benefits of residential stability. *Journal of Personality and Social Psychology, 93,* 831–844.

Oliner, P., & Oliner, S. (1988). *The altruistic personality: Rescuers of Jews in Nazi Europe.* New York: Free Press.

Oliner, S. P., & Oliner, P. M. (1992). *The altruistic personality – Rescuers of Jews in Nazi Europe: What led ordinary men and women to risk their lives on behalf of others?* New York: Free Press.

Olson, J. M., Roese, N. J., Meen, J., & Robertson, D. J. (1995). The preconditions and consequences of relative deprivation: Two field studies. *Journal of Applied Social Psychology, 25,* 944–964.

Olson, K. R., Dunham, Y., Dweck, C. S., Spelke, E. S., & Banaji, M. R. (2008). Judgments of the lucky across development and culture. *Journal of Personality and Social Psychology, 94,* 757–776.

Oman, D., Thoresen, C. E., & McMahon, K. (1999). Volunteerism and mortality among the community-dwelling elderly. *Journal of Health Psychology, 4,* 301–316.

Omoto, A. M. (Ed.). (2005). *Processes of community change and social action*. Mahwah, NJ: Erlbaum.

Omoto, A. M., & Crain, A. L. (1995). AIDS volunteerism: Lesbian and gay community-based responses to HIV. In G. M. Herek & B. Greene (Eds.), *Contemporary perspectives on lesbian and gay issues. Vol. 2: AIDS, identity, and community* (pp. 187–209). Thousand Oaks, CA: Sage.

Omoto, A. M., Gunn, D. G., & Crain, A. L. (1998). Helping in hard times: Relationship closeness and the AIDS volunteer experience. In V. J. Derlega & A. P. Barbee (Eds.), *HIV infection and social interaction* (pp. 106–128). Thousand Oaks, CA: Sage.

Omoto, A. M., & Malsch, A. (2005). Psychological sense of community: Conceptual issues and connections to volunteerism-related activism. In A. M. Omoto (Ed.), *Processes of community change and social action* (pp. 83–102). Mahwah, NJ: Erlbaum.

Omoto, A. M., & Snyder, M. (1990). Basic research in action: Volunteerism and society's response to AIDS. *Personality and Social Psychology Bulletin, 16*, 152–165.

Omoto, A. M., & Snyder, M. (1993). AIDS volunteers and their motivations: Theoretical issues and practical concerns. *Nonprofit Management and Leadership, 4*, 157–176.

Omoto, A. M., & Snyder, M. (1995). Sustained helping without obligation: Motivation, longevity of service, and perceived attitude change among AIDS volunteers. *Journal of Personality and Social Psychology, 68*, 671–686.

Omoto, A. M., & Snyder, M. (2002). Considerations of community: The context and process of volunteerism. *American Behavioral Scientist, 45*, 846–867.

Omoto, A. M., Snyder, M., & Berghuis, J. P. (1993). The psychology of volunteerism: A conceptual analysis and a program of action research. In J. B. Pryor & G. D. Reeder (Eds.), *The social psychology of HIV infection* (pp. 333–356). Hillsdale, NJ: Erlbaum.

Omoto, A. M., Snyder, M., Chang, W., & Lee, D. H. (2001, August). *Knowledge and attitude change among volunteers and their associates.* Paper presented at the annual meetings of the American Psychological Association, San Francisco, CA.

Omoto, A. M., Snyder, M., & Martino, S. C. (2000). Volunteerism and the life course: Investigating age-related agendas for action. *Basic and Applied Social Psychology, 22*, 181–198.

Ortony, A., Clore, G. L., & Collins, A. (1988). *The cognitive structure of emotions*. Cambridge: Cambridge University Press.

Oskamp, S. (2000). A sustainable future for humanity? How can psychology help? *American Psychologist, 55*, 496–508.

Ostman, M., & Kjellin, L. (2002). Stigma by association: Psychological factors in relatives of people with mental illness. *British Journal of Psychiatry, 181*, 494–498.

Ostroff, C. (1992). The relationship between satisfaction, attitudes, and performance: An organizational level analysis. *Journal of Applied Psychology, 77*, 963–974.

Otten, S., & Moskowitz, G. B. (2000). Evidence for implicit evaluative in-group bias: Affect-based spontaneous trait inference in a minimal group paradigm. *Journal of Experimental Social Psychology*, 36, 77–89.

Pachankis, J. E. (2007). The psychological implications of concealing a stigma: A cognitive-affective-behavioral model. *Psychological Bulletin*, 133, 328–345.

Pagano, S. J., & Huo, Y. J. (2007). The role of moral emotions in predicting support for political actions in post-war Iraq. *Political Psychology*, 28, 227–255.

Palmer, C. T., & Tilley, C. F. (1995). Sexual access to females as a motivation for joining gangs: An evolutionary approach. *Journal of Sex Research*, 32, 213–217.

Park, J., Felix, K., & Lee, G. (2007). Implicit attitudes towards Arab-Muslims and the moderating effects of social information. *Basic and Applied Social Psychology*, 29, 35–45.

Park, J. H., & Schaller, M. (2005). Does attitude similarity serve as a heuristic cue for kinship? Evidence of an implicit cognitive association. *Evaluation and Human Behavior*, 26, 158–170.

Payne, B. K., Cheng, C. M., Govorun, O., & Stewart, B. D. (2005). An inkblot for attitudes: Affect misattribution as implicit measurement. *Journal of Personality and Social Psychology*, 89, 277–293.

Pearce, J. L. (1993). *Volunteers: The organizational behavior of unpaid workers*. London and New York: Routledge.

Pemberton, M. B., Insko, C. A., & Schopler, J. (1996). Memory for and experience of differential competitive behavior of individuals and groups. *Journal of Personality and Social Psychology*, 71, 953–966.

Penner, L. A., Dovidio, J. F., Piliavin, J. A., & Schroeder, D. A. (2005). Prosocial behavior: Multilevel perspectives. *Annual Review of Psychology*, 56, 365–392.

Penner, L. A., & Finkelstein, M. A. (1998). Dispositional and structural determinants of volunteerism. *Journal of Personality and Social Psychology*, 74, 525–537.

Perkins, D. D., & Long, D. A. (2002). Neighborhood sense of community and social capital: A multi-level analysis. In A. Fisher, C. Sonn, & B. Bishop (Eds.), *Psychological sense of community: Research, application, and implications* (pp. 291–318). New York: Kluwer.

Pettigrew, T. F. (1967). Social evaluation theory: Convergences and applications. In D. Levine (Ed.), *Nebraska symposium on motivation* (Vol. 15, pp. 241–311). Lincoln: University of Nebraska Press.

Pettigrew, T. F. (1998). Intergroup contact theory. *Annual Review of Psychology*, 49, 65–85.

Pettigrew, T. F., & Meertens, R. W. (1995). Subtle and blatant prejudice in Western Europe. *European Journal of Social Psychology*, 25, 57–75.

Pettigrew, T. F., & Tropp, L. (2006). A meta-analytic test of intergroup contact theory. *Journal of Personality and Social Psychology*, 90, 751–783.

Pew Research Center. (2006). *Pragmatic Americans liberal and conservative on social issues most want middle ground on abortion*. Retrieved February 2, 2008 from people-press.org/reports/display.php3?ReportID=283.

Pew Research Center. (2007). *Trends in political values and core attitudes: 1987–2007*. Retrieved February 2, 2008 from people-press.org/reports/pdf/312.pdf.

Piliavin, I. M., Piliavin, J. A., & Rodin, J. (1975). Costs, diffusion, and the stigmatized victim. *Journal of Personality and Social Psychology, 32*, 429–438.

Piliavin, I. M., Rodin, J., & Piliavin, J. A. (1969). Good Samaritanism: An underground phenomenon? *Journal of Personality and Social Psychology, 13*, 289–299.

Piliavin, J. A. (2003). Doing well by doing good: Benefits for the benefactor. In C. L. M. Keyes & J. Haidt (Eds.), *Flourishing: The positive personality and the life well lived* (pp. 227–247). Washington, DC: American Psychological Association.

Piliavin, J. A., & Charng, H. (1990). Altruism: A review of recent theory and research. *Annual Review of Sociology, 16*, 27–65.

Piliavin, J. A., Dovidio, J. F., Gaertner, S. L., & Clark, R. D., III (1981). *Emergency intervention*. New York: Academic Press.

Piliavin, J. A., & Siegl, E. (2007). Health benefits of volunteering in the Wisconsin Longitudinal Study. *Journal of Health and Social Behavior, 48*, 450–464.

Piontkowski, U., Rohmann, A., & Florack, A. (2002). Concordance of acculturation attitudes and perceived threat. *Group Processes and Intergroup Relations, 5*, 221–232.

Plant, A. E., & Devine, P. G. (1998). Internal and external motivation to respond without prejudice. *Journal of Personality and Social Psychology, 75*, 811–832.

Platow, M. J., Hoar, S., Reid, S., Harley, K., & Morrison, D. (1997). Endorsement of distributively fair or unfair leaders in interpersonal and intergroup situations. *European Journal of Social Psychology, 27*, 465–494.

Portes, A. (1998). Social capital: Its origins and applications in modern sociology. *Annual Review of Sociology, 24*, 1–24.

Postmes, T., & Jetten, J. (Eds.). (2006). *Individuality and the group: Advances in social identity*. London: Sage.

Powell, A. A., Branscombe, N. R., & Schmitt, M. T. (2005). Inequality as ingroup privilege: The impact of group focus on collective guilt and interracial attitudes. *Personality and Social Psychology Bulletin, 31*, 508–521.

Pratkanis, A. R., & Turner, M. E. (1999). The significance of affirmative action for the souls of White folk: Further implications of a helping model. *Journal of Social Issues, 55*, 787–815.

Pratto, F., & Shih, M. (2000). Social dominance orientation and group context in implicit group prejudice. *Psychological Science, 11*, 515–518.

Pratto, F., Sidanius, J., Stallworth, L. M., & Malle, B. F. (1994). Social dominance orientation: A personality variable predicting social and political attitudes. *Journal of Personality and Social Psychology, 67*, 741–763.

Pratto, F., & Walker, A. (2001). Dominance in disguise: Power, beneficence and exploitation in personal relationships. In A. Y. Lee-Chai & J. A. Bargh

(Eds.), *The use and abuse of power: Multiple perspectives on the causes of corruption* (pp. 93–112). Washington, DC: Psychology Press.

Prayag Magh Mela Research Group. (2007). Living the Magh Mela at Prayag: Collective identity, collective experience and the impact of participation in a mass event. *Psychological Studies, 52* (Special Issue on the Social Psychology of Collectivity), 293–301.

Pruett, S., & Chan, F. (2006). The development and psychometric validation of the Disability Attitude Implicit Association Test. *Rehabilitation Psychology, 51,* 202–213.

Pryor, J. B. (2007, May). *The stigma of lung cancer.* Paper presented at the meetings of the Association for Psychological Science, Washington, DC.

Pryor, J. B., Reeder, G. D., & Landau, S. (1999). A social psychological analysis of HIV-related stigma: A two-factor theory. *American Behavioral Scientist, 42,* 1193–1211.

Pryor, J. B., Reeder, G. D., Wesselmann, E. D., Williams, K. D., & Wirth, J. (2007). *They played a game: Reactions to obesity stigma in a Cyberball game.* Paper presented at the Society for Personality and Social Psychology meetings, Memphis, TN.

Pryor, J. B., Reeder, G. D., Yeadon, C., & Hesson-McInnis, M. (2004). A dual-process model of reactions to perceived stigma. *Journal of Personality and Social Psychology, 87,* 436–452.

Putnam, R. D. (1993). *Making democracy work: Civic traditions in modern Italy.* Princeton, NJ: Princeton University Press.

Putnam, R. D. (1995). Bowling alone: America's declining social capital. *Journal of Democracy, 6,* 65–78.

Putnam, R. D. (2000). *Bowling alone: The collapse and revival of American community.* New York: Simon & Schuster.

Rafaeli-Mor, E., & Steinberg, J. (2002). Self-complexity and well-being: A review and research synthesis. *Personality and Social Psychology Review, 6,* 31–58.

Reay, D. (2005). Beyond consciousness? The psychic landscape of social class. *Sociology, 39,* 911–928.

Rebelo, M., Guerra, R., & Monteiro, M. B. (2005, July). *Generalizing positive intergroup relations in realistic settings: A comparison among recategorization, decategorization and dual identity models.* Paper presented at the General Meeting of the European Association of Experimental Social Psychology, Würzburg, Germany.

Reed, A., II, & Aquino, K. F. (2003). Moral identity and the expanding circle of moral regard toward out-groups. *Journal of Personality and Social Psychology, 84,* 1270–1286.

Reeder, G. D., & Pryor, J. B. (2000). Attitudes toward persons with HIV/AIDS: Linking a functional approach with underlying process. In G. Maio & J. Olson (Eds.), *Why we evaluate: Functions of attitudes* (pp. 295–323). Hillsdale, NJ: Erlbaum.

Regan, D. T. (1971). Effect of a favor on liking and compliance. *Journal of Experimental Social Psychology, 7,* 627–639.

Regan, D. T., & Totten, J. (1975). Empathy and attribution: Turning observers into actors. *Journal of Personality and Social Psychology, 32*, 850–856.

Reicher, S. D. (1987). Crowd behaviour as social action. In J. C. Turner, M. A. Hogg, P. J. Oakes, S. D. Reicher, & M. S. Wetherell, *Rediscovering the social group: A self-categorization theory* (pp. 171–202). Oxford: Blackwell.

Reicher, S. D. (1996). Social identity and social change: Rethinking the context of social psychology. In P. Robinson (Ed.), *Social groups and identities: Developing the legacy of Henri Tajfel* (pp. 317–336). Oxford: Butterworth-Heinemann.

Reicher, S. D. (2001). The psychology of crowd dynamics. In M. Hogg & S. Tindale (Eds.), *Blackwell handbook of social psychology: Group processes* (pp. 182–207). Oxford: Blackwell.

Reicher, S. D. (2004). The context of social identity: Domination, resistance and change. *Political Psychology, 25*, 921–946.

Reicher, S. D., Cassidy, C., Wolpert, I., Hopkins, N., & Levine, M. (2006). Saving Bulgaria's Jews: An analysis of social identity and the mobilisation of social solidarity. *European Journal of Social Psychology, 36*, 49–72.

Reicher, S. D., & Haslam, S. A. (2006). Tyranny revisited: Groups, psychological well-being and the health of societies. *The Psychologist, 19*, 46–50.

Reicher, S. D., Haslam, S. A., & Hopkins, N. (2005). Social identity and the dynamics of leadership: Leaders and followers as collaborative agents in the transformation of social reality. *Leadership Quarterly, 16*, 547–568.

Reicher, S. D., Haslam, S. A., & Platow, M. (2007). The new psychology of leadership. *Scientific American Mind, 18*, 22–29.

Reicher, S. D., Haslam, S. A., & Rath, R. (2008). Making a virtue of evil: A five-step model of the development of collective hate. *Social and Personality Psychology Compass, 2*, 1313–1344.

Reicher, S. D., & Hopkins, N. (2001). *Self and nation: Categorization, contestation and mobilisation*. London: Sage.

Reicher, S., Hopkins, N., Levine, M., & Rath, R. (2005). Entrepreneurs of hate and entrepreneurs of solidarity: Social identity as a basis for mass communications. *International Review of the Red Cross, 87*, 621–637.

Reicher, S. D., & Levine, M. (1994a). Deindividuation, power relations between groups and the expression of social identity: The effects of visibility to the out-group. *British Journal of Social Psychology, 33*, 145–163.

Reicher, S. D., & Levine, M. (1994b). On the consequences of deindividuation manipulations for the strategic communication of self: Identifiability and the presentation of social identity. *European Journal of Social Psychology, 24*, 511–524.

Reid, S. A., Gunter, H. N., & Smith, J. R. (2005). Aboriginal self-determination in Australia: The effects of majority-minority frames and target universalism on majority collective guilt and compensation attitudes. *Human Communication Research, 31*, 189–211.

Reykowski, J. (2002). The justice motive and altruistic helping: The rescuer of Jews in Nazi-occupied Europe. In M. Ross (Ed.), *The justice motive in everyday life* (pp. 251–270). Cambridge: Cambridge University Press.

Reynolds, K. J., Oakes, P. J., Haslam, S. A., Nolan, M. A., & Dolnik, L. (2000). Responses to powerlessness: Stereotyping as an instrument of social conflict. *Group Dynamics: Theory, Research, and Practice, 4,* 275–290.

Richard, N., & Wright, S. C. (2008). *Advantaged group members' reactions to tokenism.* Manuscript submitted for publication.

Richerson, P., & Boyd, R. (2005). *Not by genes alone: How culture transformed human evolution.* Chicago: University of Chicago Press.

Riek, B. M., Mania, E. W., & Gaertner, S. L. (2006). Intergroup threat and outgroup attitudes: A meta-analytic review. *Personality and Social Psychology Review, 10,* 336–353.

Roccas, S. (2003). The effects of status on identification with multiple groups. *European Journal of Social Psychology, 33,* 297–440.

Rogers, E. S., Chamberlin, J., Ellison, M. L., & Crean, T. (1997). A consumer-constructed scale to measure empowerment among users of mental health services. *Psychiatric Services, 48,* 1042–1047.

Rogers, R. W., & Prentice-Dunn, S. (1981). Deindividuation and anger-mediated interracial aggression: Unmasking regressive racism. *Journal of Personality and Social Psychology, 41,* 63–67.

Roseman, I. J., Spindel, M. S., & Jose, P. E. (1990). Appraisals of emotion-eliciting events: Testing a theory of discrete emotions. *Journal of Personality and Social Psychology, 59,* 899–915.

Roseman, I. J., Wiest, C., & Swartz, T. S. (1994). Phenomenology, behaviors, and goals differentiate discrete emotions. *Journal of Personality and Social Psychology, 67,* 206–221.

Rosenberg, M., & McCullogh, B. C. (1981). Mattering: Inferred significance and mental health among adolescents. *Research in Community and Mental Health, 2,* 163–182.

Rosenbrock, R., & Wright, M. T. (Eds.). (2000). *Partnership and pragmatism: Germany's response to AIDS prevention and care.* London: Routledge.

Rosenthal, A. M. (1999). *Thirty-eight witnesses: The Kitty Genovese case.* Berkeley: University of California Press. (Original work published 1964)

Rothbart, M., & Taylor, M. (1992). Category labels and social reality: Do we view social categories as natural kinds? In G. R. Semin & K. Fiedler (Eds.), *Language, interaction and social cognition* (pp. 11–36). Thousand Oaks, CA: Sage.

Rozin, P., Haidt, J., McCauley, C., Dunlop, L., & Ashmore, M. (1999). Individual differences in disgust sensitivity: Comparisons and evaluations of paper-and-pencil versus behavioral measures. *Journal of Research in Personality, 33,* 330–351.

Rozin, P., Lowery, L., & Ebert, R. (1994). Varieties of disgust faces and the structure of disgust. *Journal of Personality and Social Psychology, 66,* 870–881.

Rozin, P., Markwith, M., & McCauley, C. (1994). Sensitivity to indirect contacts with other persons: AIDS aversion as a composite of aversion to strangers, infection, moral taint, and misfortune. *Journal of Abnormal Psychology, 103,* 495–505.

Rozin, P., Markwith, M., & Nemeroff, C. (1992). Magical contagion beliefs and fear of AIDS. *Journal of Applied Social Psychology, 22,* 1081–1092.

Rozin, P., Millman, L., & Nemeroff, C. (1986). Operation of the laws of sympathetic magic in disgust and other domains. *Journal of Personality and Social Psychology, 50,* 703–712.

Rubin, Z., & Peplau, L. A. (1975). Who believes in a just world? *Journal of Social Issues, 31,* 65–90.

Runciman, W. G. (1966). *Relative deprivation and social justice: A study of attitudes to social inequality in twentieth-century England.* Berkeley: University of California Press.

Rutkowski, G. K., Gruder, C. L., & Romer, D. (1983). Group cohesiveness, social norms, and bystander intervention. *Journal of Personality and Social Psychology, 44,* 545–552.

Ryan, R. M., & Deci, E. L. (2001). On happiness and human potentials: A review of research on hedonic and eudaimonic well-being. *Annual Review of Psychology, 52,* 141–166.

Ryan, R. M., & Deci, E. L. (2006). Self-regulation and the problem of human autonomy: Does psychology need choice, self-determination, and will? *Journal of Personality, 74,* 1557–1585.

Ryff, C. D. (1989). *The parental experience in midlife.* Chicago: University of Chicago Press.

Ryff, C. D., & Keyes, C. L. M. (1995). The structure of psychological well-being revisited. *Journal of Personality and Social Psychology, 69,* 719–727.

Rynes, R. L. (1991). Recruitment, job-choice, and post-hire consequences. In M. D. Dunnette (Ed.), *Handbook of industrial and organizational psychology* (2nd ed., pp. 399–344). Palo Alto, CA: Consulting Psychologists Press.

Sachdev, I., & Bourhis, R. (1984). Minimal majorities and minorities. *European Journal of Social Psychology, 14,* 35–52.

Saegert, S., Winkel, G., & Swartz, C. (2002). Social capital and crime in New York City's low-income housing. *Housing Policy Debate, 13,* 189–226.

Sahlins, M. (1972). *Stone age economics.* Chicago: Aldine.

Said, E. (1988). *Orientalism.* New York: Vintage.

Sampson, R. J., Raudenbush, S. W., & Earls, F. (1997). Neighborhoods and violent crime: A multilevel study of collective efficacy. *Science, 277,* 918–927.

Sani, F. (2008). *Self-continuity: Individual and collective perspectives.* New York: Psychology Press.

Sani, F., & Reicher, S. D. (1999). Identity, argument and schism: Two longitudinal studies of the split in the Church of England over the ordination of women. *Group Processes and Intergroup Relations, 2,* 279–300.

Sani, F., & Reicher, S. D. (2000). Contested identities and schisms: Opposing the ordination of women as priests in the Church of England. *British Journal of Social Psychology, 39*, 95–112.

Sarason, S. B. (1974). *The psychological sense of community: Prospects for a community psychology.* San Francisco: Jossey-Bass.

Saucier, D. A., Hockett, J. M., & Wallenberg, A. S. (2008). The impact of racial slurs and racism on the perceptions and punishment of violent crime. *Journal on Interpersonal Violence, 23*, 685–701.

Saucier, D. A., & Miller, C. T. (2001). Effects of helping on the racist attitudes of the helpers. *Representative Research in Social Psychology, 25*, 43–54.

Saucier, D. A., & Miller, C. T. (2003). The persuasiveness of racial arguments as a subtle measure of racism. *Personality and Social Psychology Bulletin, 29*, 1303–1315.

Saucier, D. A., Miller, C. T., & Doucet, N. (2005). Differences in helping Whites and Blacks: A meta-analysis. *Personality and Social Psychology Review, 9*, 2–16.

Saucier, D. A., Smith, S. J., & McManus, J. L. (2007). The possible role of discrimination in the rescue response after Hurricane Katrina. *Journal of Race and Policy, 3*, 113–121.

Saucier, D. A., Smith, S. J., & McManus, J. L. (in prep.). *Perceptions of the victims, situational characteristics, and helping response following Hurricane Katrina.*

Sayer, D. (1983). *Marx's method.* Brighton: Harvester Wheatsheaf.

Schaller, M. (2003). Ancestral environments and motivated social perception: Goal-like blasts from the evolutionary past. In S. J. Spencer, S. Fein, M. P. Zanna, & J. M. Olson (Eds.), *Motivated social perception: The Ontario symposium* (pp. 215–231). Mahwah, NJ: Erlbaum.

Schaller, M., & Abeysinghe, A. M. N. D. (2006). Geographical frame of reference and dangerous intergroup attitudes: A double-minority study in Sri Lanka. *Political Psychology, 27*, 615–631.

Schaller, M., & Cialdini, R. B. (1988). The economics of empathic helping: Support for a mood management motive. *Journal of Experimental Social Psychology, 24*, 163–181.

Schaller, M., & Duncan, L. A. (2007). The behavioral immune system: Its evolution and social psychological implications. In J. P. Forgas, M. G. Haselton, & W. von Hippel (Eds.), *Evolution and the social mind: Evolutionary psychology and social cognition* (pp. 293–307). New York: Psychology Press.

Schaller, M., & Neuberg, S. L. (2008). Intergroup prejudices and intergroup conflicts. In C. Crawford & D. L. Krebs (Eds.), *Foundations of evolutionary psychology: Ideas, issues, and applications* (pp. 399–412). Mahwah, NJ: Erlbaum.

Schaller, M., Park, J. H., & Faulkner, J. (2003). Prehistoric dangers and contemporary prejudices. In W. Stroebe & M. Hewstone (Eds.), *European review of social psychology* (Vol. 14, pp. 105–137). Hove: Psychology Press.

Schaller, M., Park, J. H., & Kenrick, D. T. (2007). Human evolution and social cognition. In R. I. M. Dunbar & L. Barrett (Eds.), *Oxford handbook of evolutionary psychology* (pp. 491–504). Oxford: Oxford University Press.

Schaller, M., Park, J. H., & Mueller, A. (2003). Fear of the dark: Interactive effects of beliefs about danger and ambient darkness on ethnic stereotypes. *Personality and Social Psychology Bulletin, 29,* 637–649.

Scheider, M. E., Major, B., Luhtanen, R., & Crocker, J. (1996). Social stigma and the potential costs of assumptive help. *Personality and Social Psychology Bulletin, 22,* 201–209.

Scherer, K. R. (2001). The nature and study of appraisal: A review of the issues. In K. A. Sherer, A. Schorr, & T. Johnstone (Eds.), *Appraisal processes in emotion: Theory, methods, research* (pp. 369–391). New York: Oxford University Press.

Schlenker, B. R., & Britt, T. W. (2001). Strategically controlling information to help friends: Effects of empathy and friendship on beneficial impression management. *Journal of Experimental Social Psychology, 37,* 357–372.

Schmader, T., & Lickel, B. (2006). The approach and avoidance function of guilt and shame emotions: Comparing reactions to self-caused and other-caused wrongdoing. *Motivation and Emotion, 30,* 43–56.

Schneider, M. E., Major, B., Luhtanen, R., & Crocker, J. (1996). Social stigma and the potential costs of assumptive help. *Personality and Social Psychology Bulletin, 22,* 201–209.

Schreiber, P., & van Vugt, M. (2008). *I love the man in the uniform: Why women prefer male warriors.* Unpublished manuscript, University of Kent.

Schwartz, S. H., & Gottlieb, A. (1976). Bystanders' reaction to violent theft: A crime in Jerusalem. *Journal of Personality and Social Psychology, 36,* 1188–1199.

Seacat, J. D., Hirschman, R., & Mickelson, K. D. (2007). Attributions of HIV onset controllability, emotional reactions, and helping intentions: Implicit effects of victim sexual orientation. *Journal of Applied Social Psychology, 37,* 1442–1461.

Sears, D. O. (1988). Symbolic racism. In P. Katz & D. Taylor (Eds.), *Eliminating racism: Profiles and controversy* (pp. 53–84). New York: Plenum.

Seeman, M. (1959). On the meaning of alienation. *American Sociological Review, 24,* 783–791.

Sekaquaptewa, D., & Thompson, M. (2002). The differential effects of solo status on members of high- and low-status groups. *Personality and Social Psychology Bulletin, 28,* 694–707.

Sewell, W. H., Hauser, R. M., Springer, K. W., & Hauser, T. S. (2004). As we age: The Wisconsin longitudinal study, 1957–2001. In K. T. Leicht (Ed.), *Research in social stratification and mobility* (pp. 3–111). Greenwich, CT: JAI Press.

Sherif, M. (1966). *Group conflict and cooperation: Their social psychology.* London: Routledge & Kegan Paul.

Sherif, M., Harvey, O. J., White, B. J., Hood, W. R., & Sherif, C. W. (1961). *Intergroup conflict and cooperation: The Robbers Cave experiment.* Norman: University of Oklahoma Book Exchange.

Sherman, D. K., Kinias, Z., Major, B., Kim, H. S., & Prenovost, M. (2007). The group as a resource: Reducing biased attributions for group success and failure via group affirmation. *Personality and Social Psychology Bulletin, 33,* 1100–1112.

Shlomniuk, E., Nadler, A., & Halabi, S. (2008). *Effects of perceived legitimacy on the kind of help preferred.* Unpublished manuscript, Tel Aviv University.

Shotland, R. L., & Straw, M. K. (1976). Bystander response to an assault: When a man attacks a woman. *Journal of Personality and Social Psychology, 34,* 990–999.

Sibicky, M. E., Schroeder, D. A., & Dovidio, J. F. (1995). Empathy and helping: Considering the consequences of intervention. *Basic and Applied Social Psychology, 16,* 435–453.

Sidanius, J., Feshbach, S., Levin, S., & Pratto, F. (1997). The interface between ethnic and national attachment: Ethnic pluralism or ethnic dominance? *Public Opinion Quarterly, 61,* 103–133.

Sidanius, J., & Pratto, F. (1999). *Social dominance: An intergroup theory of social hierarchy and oppression.* New York: Cambridge University Press.

Sidanius, J., Pratto, F., & Bobo, L. (1996). Racism, conservatism, affirmative action, and intellectual sophistication: A matter of principled conservatism or group dominance? *Journal of Personality and Social Psychology, 70,* 476–490.

Sieber, S. D. (1974). Toward a theory of role accumulation. *American Sociological Review, 39,* 567–578.

Siem, B. (2008). *Prosoziale Emotionen und interkulturelles Helfen [Prosocial emotions and intercultural helping].* Unpublished doctoral dissertation, FernUniversität Hagen.

Siem, B., & Stürmer, S. (2008). *The subtle differences in intercultural helping: Intercultural (dis)similarity, empathy, and interpersonal attraction.* Manuscript submitted for publication.

Simon, B. (1998). Individuals, groups, and social change: On the relationship between individual and collective self-interpretations and collective action. In C. Sedikides, J. Schopler, & C. A. Insko (Eds.), *Intergroup cognition and intergroup behavior* (pp. 257–282). Mahwah, NJ: Erlbaum.

Simon, B. (2004). *Identity in modern society: A social psychological perspective.* Oxford: Blackwell.

Simon, B., & Klandermans, B. (2001). Politicized collective identity: A social psychological analysis. *American Psychologist, 56,* 319–331.

Simon, B., Loewy, M., Stürmer, S., Weber, U., Freytag, P., Habig, C., Kampmeier, C., & Spahlinger, P. (1998). Collective identification and social movement participation. *Journal of Personality and Social Psychology, 74,* 646–658.

Simon, B., & Stürmer, S. (2003). Respect for group members: Intragroup determinants of collective identification and group-serving behavior. *Personality and Social Psychology Bulletin, 29,* 183–193.

Simon, B., Stürmer, S., & Steffens, K. (2000). Helping individuals or group members? The role of individual and collective identification in AIDS volunteerism. *Personality and Social Psychology Bulletin, 4,* 497–506.

Sleebos, E., Ellemers, N., & De Gilder, D. (2006). The carrot and the stick: Affective commitment and acceptance anxiety as motives for discretionary group efforts by respected and disrespected group members. *Personality and Social Psychology Bulletin, 32,* 244–255.

Sloman, S. A. (1996). The empirical case for two systems of reasoning. *Psychological Bulletin, 119,* 3–22.

Smith, A. (1976). *The theory of moral sentiments.* Oxford: Clarendon Press. (Original work published 1759)

Smith, E. R. (1993). Social identity and social emotions: Toward a new conceptualization of prejudice. In D. M. Mackie & D. L. Hamilton (Eds.), *Affect, cognition, and stereotyping* (pp. 297–315). San Diego: Academic Press.

Smith, E. R., & DeCoster, J. (2000). Dual-process models in social and cognitive psychology: Conceptual integration and links to underlying memory systems. *Personality and Social Psychology Review, 4,* 108–131.

Smith, P. C., Kendall, L. M., & Hulin, C. L. (1969). *The measurement of satisfaction in work and retirement: A strategy for the study of attitudes.* Chicago: Rand McNally.

Smolej, M., & Kivivuori, J. (2006). The relation between crime news and fear of violence. *Journal of Scandinavian Studies in Criminology and Crime Prevention, 7,* 211–227.

Snyder, M. (1984). When beliefs create reality. In M. Zanna (Ed.), *Advances in experimental social psychology* (Vol. 18, pp. 247–305). New York: Academic Press.

Snyder, M., Clary, E. G., & Stukas, A. A. (2000). The functional approach to volunteerism. In J. M. Olson & G. R. Maio (Eds.), *Why we evaluate: Functions of attitudes* (pp. 365–393). Mahwah, NJ: Erlbaum.

Snyder, M., & Omoto, A. M. (1992a). Volunteerism and society's response to the HIV epidemic. *Current Directions in Psychological Science, 1,* 113–116.

Snyder, M., & Omoto, A. M. (1992b). Who helps and why? The psychology of AIDS volunteerism. In S. Spacapan & S. Oskamp (Eds.), *Helping and being helped: Naturalistic studies* (pp. 213–239). Newbury Park, CA: Sage.

Snyder, M., & Omoto, A. M. (2000). Doing good for self and society: Volunteerism and the psychology of citizen participation. In M. van Vugt, M. Snyder, T. Tyler, & A. Biel (Eds.), *Collective helping in modern society: Dilemmas and solutions* (pp. 127–141). London: Routledge.

Snyder, M., & Omoto, A. M. (2001). Basic research and practical problems: Volunteerism and the psychology of individual and collective action. In

W. Wosinska, R. Cialdini, & D. Barrett (Eds.), *The practice of social influence in multiple cultures* (pp. 287–307). Mahwah, NJ: Erlbaum.

Snyder, M., & Omoto, A. M. (2007). Social action. In A. W. Kruglanski & E. T. Higgins (Eds.), *Social psychology: A handbook of basic principles* (2nd ed., pp. 940–961). New York: Guilford Press.

Snyder, M., & Omoto, A. M. (2008). Volunteerism: Social issues perspectives and social policy implications. *Social Issues and Policy Review, 2*, 1–36.

Snyder, M., Omoto, A. M., & Crain, A. L. (1999). Punished for their good deeds: Stigmatization of AIDS volunteers. *American Behavioral Scientist, 42*, 1175–1192.

Snyder, M., Omoto, A. M., & Smith, D. M. (2009). The role of persuasion strategies in motivating individual and collective action. In E. Borgida, C. Federico, & J. Sullivan (Eds.), *The political psychology of democratic citizenship* (pp. 125–150). New York: Oxford University Press.

Sonn, C. C., & Fischer, A. T. (1998). Sense of community: Community-resilient responses to oppression and change. *Journal of Community Psychology, 26*, 457–472.

South End Press Collective. (Eds.). (1998). *Talking about a revolution: Interviews with Manning Marable, Winona LaDuke, Michael Albert, Howard Zinn, bell hooks, Urvashi Vaid, Peter Kwong, Noam Chomsky, and Barbara Ehrenreich*. Cambridge, MA: South End Press.

Spears, R., Doosje, B., & Ellemers, N. (1997). Self-stereotyping in the face of threats to group status and distinctiveness: The role of group identification. *Personality and Social Psychology Bulletin, 23*, 538–553.

Spector, P. (1996). *Industrial and organizational psychology: Research and practice*. New York: Wiley.

Spence, M. (1973). Job market signalling. *Quarterly Journal of Economics, 87*, 355–374.

Stephan, W. G., & Finlay, K. A. (2000). Improving intergroup relations: The effects of empathy and racial attitudes. *Journal of Applied Social Psychology, 30*, 1720–1737.

Stephan, W. G., & Stephan, C. W. (1985). Intergroup anxiety. *Journal of Social Issues, 41*, 157–175.

Stephens, R. D., Dawley, D. D., & Stephens, D. B. (2004). Commitment on the board: A model of volunteer directors' levels of organizational commitment and self-reported performance. *Journal of Managerial Issues, 16*, 483–504.

Stone, V. E., Cosmides, L., Tooby, J., Kroll, N., & Knight, R. T. (2002). Selective impairment of reasoning about social exchange in a patient with bilateral limbic system damage. *Proceeding of the National Academy of USA, 99*, 11531–11536.

Stotland, E. (1969). Exploratory investigations of empathy. In L. Berkowitz (Ed.), *Advances in experimental social psychology* (Vol. 4, pp. 271–314). New York: Academic Press.

Strack, F., & Deutsch, R. (2004). Reflective and impulsive determinants of social behavior. *Personality and Social Psychology Review, 8*, 220–247.

Stryker, S. (1980). *Symbolic interactionism: A social structural version.* Menlo Park, CA: Benjamin/Cummings.

Stukas, A. A., Daly, M., & Cowling, M. J. (2005). Volunteerism and the creation of social capital: A functional approach. *Australian Journal of Volunteering, 10*, 35–44.

Stürmer, S., & Kampmeier, C. (2003). Active citizenship: The role of community identification in community volunteerism and local participation. *Psychologica Belgica, 43*, 103–122.

Stürmer, S., & Simon, B. (2004). The role of collective identification in social movement participation: A panel study in the context of the German gay movement. *Personality and Social Psychology Bulletin, 30*, 263–277.

Stürmer, S., Simon, B., & Loewy, M. I. (2008). Intraorganizational respect and organizational participation: The mediating role of collective identity. *Group Processes and Intergroup Relations, 11*, 5–20.

Stürmer, S., Snyder, M., Kropp, A., & Siem, B. (2006). Empathy-motivated helping: The moderating role of group membership. *Personality and Social Psychology Bulletin, 32*, 943–956.

Stürmer, S., Snyder, M., & Omoto, A. M. (2005). Prosocial emotions and helping: The moderating role of group membership. *Journal of Personality and Social Psychology, 88*, 532–546.

Suedfeld, P. (1997). The social psychology of "Invictus": Conceptual and methodological approaches to indomitability. In C. McGarty & S. A. Haslam (Eds.), *The message of social psychology: Perspectives on mind in society* (pp. 328–341). Oxford: Blackwell.

Suls, J., & Wills, T. A. (Eds.). (1990). *Social comparison: Contemporary theory and research.* Hillsdale, NJ: Erlbaum.

Swim, J. K., & Miller, D. L. (1999). White guilt: Its antecedents and consequences for attitudes toward affirmative action. *Personality and Social Psychology Bulletin, 25*, 500–514.

Tajfel, H. (1970). Experiments in intergroup discrimination. *Scientific American, 223*, 96–102.

Tajfel, H. (1978a). *Differentiation between social groups.* London: Academic Press.

Tajfel, H. (1978b). Social categorization, social identity, and social comparison. In H. Tajfel (Ed.), *Differentiation between social groups: Studies in the social psychology of intergroup relations* (pp. 61–76). London: Academic Press.

Tajfel, H. (1978c). The achievement of group differentiation. In H. Tajfel (Ed.), *Differentiation between social groups: Studies in the social psychology of intergroup relations* (pp. 77–98). London: Academic Press.

Tajfel, H. (1982). *Social identity and intergroup relations.* Cambridge: Cambridge University Press.

Tajfel, H., Billig, M. G., Bundy, R. P., & Flament, C. (1971). Social categorization and intergroup behaviour. *European Journal of Social Psychology, 1*, 149–178.

Tajfel, H., & Turner, J. C. (1979). An integrative theory of intergroup conflict. In W. G. Austin & S. Worchel (Eds.), *The social psychology of intergroup relations* (pp. 33–47). Monterey, CA: Brooks/Cole.

Tajfel, H., & Turner, J. C. (1986). The social identity theory of intergroup behavior. In S. Worchel & W. G. Austin (Eds.), *Psychology of intergroup relations* (pp. 7–24). Chicago: Nelson-Hall.

Täuber, S., & van Leeuwen, E. (2007). *Seeking out-group help under public or private conditions: The burden of a good reputation.* Manuscript submitted for publication.

Taylor, S. E., Klein, L. C., Lewis, B. P., & Gruenewald, R. A. R. (2000). Biobehavioral responses to stress in females: Tend-and-befriend not fight-or-flight. *Psychological Review, 107*, 413–429.

Teachman, B. A., & Brownell, K. D. (2001). Implicit anti-fat bias among health professionals: Is anyone immune? *International Journal of Obesity, 25*, 1525–1531.

Teachman, B. A., Gapinski, K., Brownell, K. D., Rawlins, M., & Jeyaram, S. (2003). Demonstrations of implicit anti-fat bias: The impact of providing causal information and evoking empathy. *Health Psychology, 22*, 68–78.

Teachman, B. A., Wilson, J. G., & Komarovskaya, I. (2006). Implicit and explicit stigma of mental illness in diagnosed and healthy samples. *Journal of Social and Clinical Psychology, 25*, 75–95.

Tec, N. (1986). *When light shines in the darkness.* Oxford: Oxford University Press.

Terry, D. J., Callan, V. J., & Sartori, G. (1996). Employee adjustment to an organizational merger: Stress, coping and intergroup differences. *Stress Medicine, 12*, 105–122.

Tesser, A. (1988). Toward a self-evaluation maintenance model of social behavior. In L. Berkowitz (Ed.), *Advances in experimental social psychology* (Vol. 21, pp. 181–227). San Diego: Academic Press.

Tett, R. P., & Meyer, J. P. (1993). Job satisfaction, organizational commitment, turnover intentions, and turnover: Path analyses based on meta-analytic findings. *Personnel Psychology, 46*, 259–293.

Thoits, P. A. (1986). Social support and psychological well-being: Theoretical possibilities. In I. G. Sarason & B. R. Sarason (Eds.), *Social support: Theory, research, and application* (pp. 51–72). Dordrecht: Martinus Nijhoff.

Thoits, P. A. (1992). Multiple identities: Examining gender and marital status differences in distress. *Social Psychology Quarterly, 55*, 236–256.

Thoits, P. A. (1995). Identity-relevant events and psychological symptoms: A cautionary tale. *Journal of Health and Social Behavior, 36*, 72–82.

Thoits, P. A. (2003). Personal agency in the accumulation of multiple role-identities. In P. J. Burke, T. J. Owens, R. T. Serpe, & P. A. Thoits (Eds.), *Advances in identity theory and research* (pp. 179–194). New York: Kluwer Academic/Plenum.

Thoits, P. A., & Hewitt, L. N. (2001). Volunteer work and well-being. *Journal of Health and Social Behavior, 42*, 115–131.

Thomas, E. (2005). Katrina: How Bush blew it. *Newsweek*, September 19. Retrieved from www.msnbc.msn.com/id/9287434/site/newsweek/.
Thompson, B. (2001). *A promise and a way of life: White antiracist activism*. Minneapolis: University of Minnesota Press.
Tidwell, M. V. (2005). A social identity model of prosocial behaviors within nonprofit organizations. *Nonprofit Management and Leadership, 15*, 449–467.
Tiedens, L. Z., & Leach, C. W. (Eds.). (2004). *The social life of emotion*. New York: Cambridge University Press.
Tocqueville, A. de (1956). *Democracy in America*. In R. D. Heffner (Ed.), *Democracy in America: Mentor book edition*. New York: New American Library. (Original work published 1853)
Todorov, T. (2001). *The fragility of goodness*. London: Weidenfeld & Nicolson.
Toi, M., & Batson, C. D. (1982). More evidence that empathy is a source of altruistic motivation. *Journal of Personality and Social Psychology, 43*, 281–292.
Tooby, J., & Cosmides, L. (1988). *The evolution of war and its cognitive foundations* (Institute for Evolutionary Studies Tech. Rep. No. 88–1). Palo Alto, CA: Institute for Evolutionary Studies.
Trivers, R. L. (1971). The evolution of reciprocal altruism. *Quarterly Review of Biology, 46*, 35–57.
Tropp, L. R., & Brown, A. C. (2004). What benefits the group can also benefit the individual: Group-enhancing and individual-enhancing motives for collective action. *Group Processes and Intergroup Relations, 7*, 267–282.
Turban, D. B., & Cable, D. M. (2003). Firm reputation and applicant pool characteristics. *Journal of Organizational Behaviour, 24*, 733–751.
Turban, D. B., & Greening, D. W. (1996). Corporate social performance and organizational attractiveness to prospective employees. *Academy of Management Journal, 40*, 658–672.
Turner, J. C. (1982). Towards a cognitive redefinition of the social group. In H. Tajfel (Ed.), *Social identity and intergroup relations* (pp. 15–40). Cambridge: Cambridge University Press.
Turner, J. C. (1991). *Social influence*. Milton Keynes: Open University Press.
Turner, J. C. (2005). Explaining the nature of power: A three-process theory. *European Journal of Social Psychology, 35*, 1–22.
Turner, J. C., & Brown, R. (1978). Social status, cognitive alternatives and intergroup relations. In H. Tajfel (Ed.), *Differentiation between social groups: Studies in the social psychology of intergroup relations* (pp. 201–234). London: Academic Press.
Turner, J. C., & Haslam, S. A. (2001). Social identity, organizations and leadership. In M. E. Turner (Ed.), *Groups at work: Advances in theory and research* (pp. 25–65). Hillsdale, NJ: Erlbaum.

Turner, J. C., Hogg, M. A., Oakes, P. J., Reicher, S. D., & Wetherell, M. S. (1987). *Rediscovering the social group: A self-categorization theory*. Oxford: Blackwell.

Turner, J. C., Oakes, P. J., Haslam, S. A., & McGarty, C. A. (1994). Self and collective: Cognition and social context. *Personality and Social Psychology Bulletin, 20*, 454–463.

Turner, J. C., & Reynolds, K. J. (2001). The social identity perspective in intergroup relations: Theories, themes and controversies. In R. Brown, & S. L. Gaertner (Eds.), *Blackwell handbook of social psychology: Intergroup processes* (pp. 133–153). Oxford: Blackwell.

Tyler, T. R. (1999). Why people cooperate with organizations: An identity-based perspective. In R. I. Sutton & B. M. Staw (Eds.), *Research in organizational behavior: An annual series of analytical essays and critical reviews* (pp. 210–246). Stanford, CA: JAI Press.

Tyler, T. R., & Blader, S. (2000). *Co-operation in groups: Procedural justice, social identity and behavioral engagement*. Philadelphia, PA: Psychology Press.

Tyler, T. R., & Blader, S. L. (2001). Identity and cooperative behavior in groups. *Group Processes and Intergroup Relations, 4*, 207–226.

Tyler, T. R., & Blader, S. L. (2002). Autonomous vs. comparative status: Must we be better than others to feel good about ourselves? *Organizational Behavior and Human Decision Processes, 89*, 813–838.

Uggen, C., & Janikula, J. (1999). Volunteerism and arrest in the transition to adulthood. *Social Forces, 78*, 331–362.

Uhlmann, E., Dasgupta, N., Elgueta, A., Greenwald, A. G., & Swanson, J. (2002). Subgroup prejudice based on skin color among Hispanics in the United States and Latin America. *Social Cognition, 20*, 198–226.

Underwood, P. W. (2000). Social support: The promise and reality. In B. H. Rice (Ed.), *Handbook of stress, coping and health* (pp. 367–391). Newbury Park, CA: Sage.

United States Department of Labor. (2008). Volunteering in the United States, 2007. Washington, DC: Bureau of Labor Statistics. Retrieved July 25, 2008 from www.bls.gov/news.release/pdf/volun.pdf.

Utman, C. H. (1997). Performance effects of motivational state: A meta-analysis. *Personality and Social Psychology Review, 1*, 170–182.

Vanbeselaere, N., Boen, F., & Smeesters, D. (2003). Tokenism also works with groups as tokens: The impact of group openness and group qualification on reactions to membership in a low-status group. *Group Dynamics: Theory, Research, and Practice, 7*, 104–121.

van Knippenberg, D., & Hogg, M. A. (2004). *Leadership and power: Identity processes in groups and organizations*. London: Sage.

van Leeuwen, E. (2007). Restoring identity through outgroup helping: Beliefs about international aid in response to the December 2004 tsunami. *European Journal of Social Psychology, 37*, 661–671.

van Leeuwen, E., & Oostenbrink, J. (2005, July). *The effects of meta-stereotypes and audience on intergroup helping*. Paper presented at the

14th General Meeting of the European Association for Experimental Social Psychology, Würzburg, Germany.
van Leeuwen, E., & Täuber, S. (in prep.). *Helping the out-group benefits the in-group: Offering and providing help as an attempt to improve low group status.* Manuscript in preparation.
van Leeuwen, E., Täuber, S., & Sassenberg, K. (2006). *Knocking on the out-group's door: The instrumental gains and psychological costs of seeking out-group help.* Manuscript submitted for publication.
van Vugt, M., & Chang, K. (2008). *Group reactions to loyal and disloyal members: The moderating role of member criticality.* Unpublished manuscript, University of Kent.
van Vugt, M., & De Cremer, D. (1999). Helping the group or helping yourself? Social motives and group identity in resource dilemmas. *Journal of Personality and Social Psychology, 76*, 587–599.
van Vugt, M., De Cremer, D., & Janssen, D. P. (2007). Gender differences in cooperation and competition: The male-warrior hypothesis. *Psychological Science, 18*, 19–23.
van Vugt, M., & Hart, C. M. (2004). Social identity as social glue: The origins of group loyalty. *Journal of Personality and Social Psychology, 86*, 585–598.
van Vugt, M., Roberts, G., & Hardy, C. (2007). Competitive altruism: Reputation-based cooperation in groups. In R. Dunbar & L. Barrett (Eds.), *Handbook of evolutionary psychology* (pp. 531–540). Oxford: Oxford University Press.
van Vugt, M., & Schaller, M. (2008). Evolutionary perspectives on group dynamics: An introduction. *Group Dynamics, 12*, 1–6.
van Vugt, M., & Snyder, M. (2002). Cooperation in society: Fostering community action and civic participation. *American Behavioral Scientist, 45*, 765–768.
van Vugt, M., Snyder, M., Tyler, T. R., & Biel, A. (Eds.). (2000). *Cooperation in modern society: Promoting the welfare of communities, states and organizations.* New York: Routledge.
van Vugt, M., & van Lange, P. A. M. (2006). Psychological adaptations for prosocial behavior: The altruism puzzle. In M. Schaller, J. A. Simpson, & D. T. Kenrick (Eds.), *Evolution and social psychology* (pp. 237–261). New York: Psychology Press.
van Willigen, M. (2000). Differential benefits of volunteering across the life course. *Journal of Gerontology: Social Sciences, 55*, 1–11.
van Zomeren, M., Spears, R., Fischer, A. H., & Leach, C. W. (2004). Put your money where your mouth is! Explaining collective action tendencies through group-based anger and group efficacy. *Journal of Personality and Social Psychology, 84*, 649–664.
Veenstra, K., & Haslam, S. A. (2000). Willingness to participate in industrial protest: Exploring social identification in context. *British Journal of Social Psychology, 39*, 153–172.

Veilleux, F., & Tougas, F. (1989). Male acceptance of affirmative action programs for women: The results of altruistic or egotistical motives? *International Journal of Psychology, 24,* 485–496.

Verba, S., Schlozman, K. L., & Brady, H. E. (1995). *Voice and equality: Civic voluntarism in American politics.* Cambridge, MA: Harvard University Press.

Verkuyten, M. (2006). Multicultural recognition and ethnic minority rights: A social identity perspective. In W. Stroebe & M. Hewstone (Eds.), *European review of social psychology* (Vol. 17, pp. 148–184). New York: Psychology Press.

Vescio, T. K., Sechrist, G. B., & Paolucci, M. P. (2003). Perspective taking and prejudice reduction: The mediational role of empathy arousal and situational attributions. *European Journal of Social Psychology, 33,* 455–472.

Voci, A. (2006). The link between identification and in-group favouritism: Effects of threat to social identity and trust-related emotions. *British Journal of Social Psychology, 45,* 265–284.

Vogel, D. L., Wade, N. G., & Hackler, A. H. (2007). Perceived public stigma and the willingness to seek counseling: The mediating roles of self-stigma and attitudes toward counseling. *Journal of Counseling Psychology, 54,* 40–50.

Vohs, K., Mead, N., & Goode, M. (2006). The psychological consequences of money. *Science, 314,* 1154–1156.

von Hippel, W., Sekaquaptewa, D., & Vargas, P. (1997). The linguistic intergroup bias as an implicit indicator of prejudice. *Journal of Experimental Social Psychology, 33,* 490–509.

Vorauer, J. D., Hunter, A. J., Main, K. J., & Roy, S. A. (2000). Meta-stereotype activation: Evidence from indirect measures for specific evaluative concerns experienced by members of dominant groups in intergroup interaction. *Journal of Personality and Social Psychology, 78,* 690–707.

Vorauer, J. D., Main, K. J., & O'Connell, G. B. (1998). How do individuals expect to be viewed by members of lower-status groups? Content and implications of meta-stereotypes. *Journal of Personality and Social Psychology, 75,* 917–937.

Vorauer, J. D., & Turpie, C. A. (2004). Disruptive effects of vigilance on dominant group members' treatment of outgroup members: Choking versus shining under pressure. *Journal of Personality and Social Psychology, 87,* 384–399.

Walker, I., & Mann, L. (1987). Unemployment, relative deprivation, and social protest. *Personality and Social Psychology Bulletin, 13,* 275–283.

Walker, I., & Smith, H. J. (Eds.). (2002). *Relative deprivation: Specification, development, and integration.* New York: Cambridge University Press.

Walther, E., Nagengast, B., & Trasselli, C. (2005). Evaluative conditioning in social psychology: Facts and speculations. *Cognition and Emotion, 19,* 175–196.

Wandersman, A. (1980). Community and individual difference characteristics as influences on initial participation. *American Journal of Community Psychology, 8,* 217–228.

Wandersman, A., Florin, P., Friedmann, R. R., & Meier, R. B. (1987). Who participates and who does not, and why? An analysis of voluntary neighborhood organizations in the United States and Israel. *Sociological Forum, 2,* 534–555.

Wang, S. S., Brownell, K. D., & Wadden, T. A. (2004). The influence of the stigma of obesity on overweight individuals. *International Journal of Obesity, 28,* 1333–1337.

Weiner, B. (1980). A cognitive (attribution)-emotion-action model of motivated behavior: An analysis of judgments of help-giving. *Journal of Personality and Social Psychology, 34,* 112–124.

Weiner, B. (1995). *Judgments of responsibility: A foundation for a theory of social conduct.* New York: Guilford Press.

Weiner, B., Perry, R. B., & Magnussen, J. (1988). An attributional analysis of reactions to stigmas. *Journal of Personality and Social Psychology, 55,* 738–748.

Weiss, D. J., Dawis, R. V., Lofquist, L. H., & England, G. W. (1966). *Instrumentation for the theory of work adjustment.* Minneapolis: University of Minnesota Press.

Weiss, H. M., & Knight, P. A. (1980). The utility of humility: Self-esteem, information search and problem-solving efficiency. *Organizational Behavior and Human Performance, 25,* 216–223.

West, S. G., Whitney, G., & Schnedler, R. (1975). Helping of a motorist in distress: The effects of sex, race, and neighborhood. *Journal of Personality and Social Psychology, 31,* 691–698.

Whatley, M. A., Webster, J. M., Smith, R. H., & Rhodes, A. (1999). The effect of a favor on public and private compliance: How internalized is the norm of reciprocity? *Basic and Applied Social Psychology, 21,* 251–259.

Wilder, D. A. (1981). Perceiving persons as a group: Categorization and intergroup relations. In D. L. Hamilton (Ed.), *Cognitive processes in stereotyping and intergroup behavior* (pp. 213–257). Hillsdale, NJ: Erlbaum.

Wilder, D. A. (1986). Social comparison: Implications for creation and reduction of intergroup bias. In L. Berkowitz (Ed.), *Advances in experimental social psychology* (Vol. 19, pp. 291–355). New York: Academic Press.

Wildschut, T., Pinter, B., Vevea, J. L., Insko, C. A., & Schopler, J. (2003). Beyond the group mind: A quantitative review of the interindividual-intergroup discontinuity effect. *Psychological Bulletin, 129,* 698–722.

Williamson, G. M., & Clark, M. S. (1989). Providing help and desired relationship type as determinants of changes in moods and self-evaluations. *Journal of Personality and Social Psychology, 56,* 722–734.

Wilson, D. S., van Vugt, M., & O'Gorman, R. (2008). Multilevel selection theory and its implications for psychological science. *Current Directions in Psychological Science, 17,* 6–9.

Wilson, E. O. (1975). *Sociobiology: The new synthesis.* Cambridge, MA: Harvard University Press.
Wilson, J. (2000). Volunteering. *Annual Review of Sociology, 26,* 215–240.
Wilson, T. D., Lindsey, S., & Schooler, T. Y. (2000). A model of dual attitudes. *Psychological Review, 107,* 101–126.
Wispé, L. G., & Freshley, H. B. (1971). Race, sex, and sympathetic helping behavior: The broken bag caper. *Journal of Personality and Social Psychology, 17,* 59–65.
Wit, A. P., & Kerr, N. L. (2002). "Me versus just us versus us all" categorization and cooperation in nested social dilemmas. *Journal of Personality and Social Psychology, 83,* 616–637.
Witte, D. R., Bots, M. L., Hoes, A. W., & Grobbee, D. E. (2000). Cardiovascular mortality in Dutch men during the 1996 European Championship: Longitudinal population study. *British Medical Journal, 321,* 1552–1554.
Wolf, S. T., Insko, C. A., Kirchner, J. L., & Wildschut, T. (2008). Interindividual-intergroup discontinuity in the domain of correspondent outcomes: The roles of relativistic concern, perceived categorization, and the doctrine of mutual assured destruction. *Journal of Personality and Social Psychology, 94,* 479–494.
Wolsko, C., Park, B., & Judd, C. M. (2000). Framing interethnic ideology: Effects of multicultural and color-blind perspectives on judgments of groups and individuals. *Journal of Personality and Social Psychology, 78,* 635–654.
Wolsko, C., Park, B., & Judd, C. M. (2006). Considering the Tower of Babel: Correlates of assimilation and multiculturalism among ethnic minority and majority groups in the United States. *Social Justice Research, 19,* 277–306.
Worchel, S. W. (1984). The dark side of helping: The social dynamics of helping and cooperation. In E. Staub, D. Bar-Tal, J. Karylowski, & J. Reykowski (Eds.), *Development and maintenance of prosocial behavior* (pp. 379–395). New York: Plenum.
Worchel, S. W., Wong, F. Y., & Scheltema, K. E. (1989). Improving intergroup relations: Comparative effects of anticipated cooperation and helping on attraction for an aid-giver. *Social Psychology Quarterly, 52,* 213–219.
Wrangham, R. W., & Peterson, D. (1996). *Demonic males: Apes and the origins of human violence.* Boston: Houghton Mifflin.
Wright, S. C. (1997). Ambiguity, social influence, and collective action: Generating collective protest in response to tokenism. *Personality and Social Psychology Bulletin, 23,* 1277–1290.
Wright, S. C. (2001). Restricted ingroup boundaries: Tokenism, ambiguity, and the tolerance of injustice. In J. T. Jost & B. Major (Eds.), *The psychology of legitimacy: Emerging perspectives on ideology, justice, and intergroup relations* (pp. 223–254). New York: Cambridge University Press.

Wright, S. C. (2001). Strategic collective action: Social psychology and social change. In R. Brown & S. Gaertner (Eds.), *Blackwell handbook of social psychology: Intergroup processes* (Vol. 4, pp. 409–430). Oxford: Blackwell.

Wright, S. C., Aron, A., & Tropp, L. R. (2002). Including others (and groups) in the self: Self-expansion and intergroup relations. In J. P. Forgas & K. D. Williams (Eds.), *The social self: Cognitive, interpersonal and intergroup perspectives* (pp. 343–363). Philadelphia, PA: Psychology Press.

Wright, S. C., Brody, S. M., & Aron, A. (2005). Intergroup contact: Still our best hope for improving intergroup relations. In C. S. Crandall & M. Schaller (Eds.), *Social psychology of prejudice: Historical and contemporary issues* (pp. 115–142). Seattle, WA: Lewinian Press.

Wright, S. C., Comeau, J., & Aron, A. (2007, July). *Direct and extended contact in a multi-ethnic context.* Paper presented at the annual meeting of the International Society of Political Psychology, Portland, OR.

Wright, S. C., & Taylor, D. M. (1998). Responding to tokenism: Individual action in the face of collective injustice. *European Journal of Social Psychology, 28,* 647–667.

Wright, S. C., & Taylor, D. M. (2003). The social psychology of cultural diversity: Social stereotyping, prejudice and discrimination. In M. A. Hogg & J. Cooper (Eds.), *Sage handbook of social psychology* (pp. 432–457). London: Sage.

Wright, S. C., Taylor, D. M., & Moghaddam, F. M. (1990). Responding to membership in a disadvantaged group: From acceptance to collective protest. *Journal of Personality and Social Psychology, 58,* 994–1003.

Wright, S. C., & Van Der Zande, C. C. (1999, October). *Bicultural friends: When cross-group friendships cause improved intergroup attitudes.* Paper presented at the annual convention of the Society for Experimental Social Psychology, St. Louis, MO.

Yogananda, P. (1996). *God talks with Arjuna: The Bhagavad Gita.* Los Angeles: Self-Realization Fellowship.

Young, F. W., & Glasgow, N. (1998). Voluntary social participation and health. *Research on Aging, 20,* 339–362.

Yzerbyt, V., Dumont, M., Wigboldus, D., & Gordijn, E. (2003). I feel for us: The impact of categorization and identification on emotions and action tendencies. *British Journal of Social Psychology, 42,* 533–549.

Zdaniuk, B., & Levine, J. M. (2001). Group loyalty: Impact of members' identification and contributions. *Journal of Experimental Social Psychology, 37,* 502–509.

Zhou, S. C., Wright, S. C., & Moretti, M. M. (2008, April). *Directed self-expansion: Ideal self and individual differences in self-expansion motives.* Poster presented at the Western Psychological Association annual conference, Irvine, CA.

Zimbardo, P. (1969). The human choice: Individuation, reason and order versus deindividuation, impulse and chaos. In W. J. Arnold & D. Levine (Eds.), *Nebraska symposium on motivation* (Vol. 17, pp. 237–307). Lincoln: University of Nebraska Press.

Zimbardo, P. (1971). The power and pathology of imprisonment. *Congressional Record*. (Serial No. 15, 1971-10-25).

Zimmerman, M. A., Israel, B. A., Schulz, A. J., & Checkoway, B. (1992). Further explorations in empowerment theory: An empirical analysis of psychological empowerment. *American Journal of Community Psychology, 20*, 707–727.

Zimmerman, M. A., & Rappaport, J. (1988). Citizen participation, perceived control and psychological empowerment. *American Journal of Community Psychology, 16*, 725–750.

Author Index

Aberson, C. L. 179, 188
Abeysinghe, A. M. N. D. 21–22
Abramowitz, S. I. 275
Abrams, D. 4, 15, 16, 298
Ackerman, D. 245, 250, 259
Ackerman, P. 4, 182
Ahmad, N. 176
Ajzen, I. 201
Akert, R. M. 291
Alcock, J. 30
Alexander, R. D. 19, 20
Allahabad Magh Mela Research Group 305–306
Allen, B. P. 325
Allen, J. L. 201
Allen, N. J. 151, 255
Allik, J. 223
Allport, G. W. 6, 56, 57, 298, 309
Ames, D. R. 179, 350
amFAR 62
Amodio, D. M. 70
Anastasio, P. 283
Andersen, S. M. 114
Anderson, L. R. 242
Ando, K. 16
Angermeyer, M. C. 67
Aquino, K. F. 180
Archer, R. L. 106
Armeli, S. 81
Aron, A. 178, 315, 316, 319, 320, 321

Aron, E. N. 178, 315, 321
Aronson, E. 17, 188, 291, 316
Aronson, R. E. 241
Arps, K. 107
Arthur, W. 281
Ascoli, U. 260
Ashforth, B. E. 150, 151, 247
Ashmore, M. 75
Assa, A. 291
Asser, E. S. 283
Associated Press 114
Astin, A. W. 158
Avdeyeva, T. V. 114
Azzi, A. E. 89

Baard, P. P. 85
Bachman, B. 283
Baer, D. 223
Bain, P. 188
Banaji, M. R. 64, 78, 113, 135
Banker, B. S. 195, 204, 313
Bar, R. 275, 276
Bargh, J. A. 73, 113
Barkan, E. 343, 348
Barker, R. G. 164
Barnett, T. 248
Baron, L. 290
Baron, R. A. 291
Baron, R. M. 53
Barr, L. 78
Barreto, M. 323
Barsness, Z. I. 259

Author Index

Bar-Zohar, M. 216
Batson, C. D. 4, 14, 35, 36, 37, 38–39, 42, 57, 69, 81, 176, 182, 184, 185, 187, 188, 189, 201, 214, 269, 323, 344, 348, 352
Baumann, D. J. 106
Baumann, J. 105
Baumeister, R. F. 29, 63
Beal, D. J. 105
Beaman, A. L. 107
Beaton, A. M. 323, 333, 344
Beck, M. 67
Becker, S. 28, 312
Begley, T. M. 151
Bell, L. 316
Belloni, R. 282
Ben-David, Y. 133, 271, 274, 281, 284
Bender, B. 113
Benedict, R. 270–271
Ben-Itzhak, S. 271
Benson, P. L. 33, 106
Bentler, P. M. 251, 252, 257, 262
Ben-Yakov, A. 216, 291
Berghuis, J. P. 224
Berman, S. L. 340
Berntson, G. G. 73
Bessenoff, G. R. 60
Betancourt, H. 177
Beu, D. 248
Bickman, L. 33, 106, 212
Biel, A. 5, 223, 224
Biernat, M. 71
Billig, M. 209, 291
Billig, M. G. 41, 212, 297
Birch, K. 4, 182
Blader, S. 245, 246, 247, 248, 249, 299
Blake, L. P. 105
Blaney, N. 17, 188
Blascovich, J. 71
Blau, P. M. 56
Bliuc, A.-M. 348
Bobo, L. 63

Bodenhausen, G. V. 70, 113
Boen, F. 327, 340
Boezeman, E. J. 9, 250, 251, 252, 254, 256, 257, 260, 262
Boone, J. L. 271
Borden, R. J. 230
Bos, A. E. R. 341
Bots, M. L. 17
Bourdieu, P. 122
Bourhis, R. 137, 197
Boyadjieff, C. 216
Boyd, R. 25
Boyte, H. C. 223
Brady, H. E. 224
Brammer, L. M. 140
Branscombe, N. R. 16, 123, 127, 132, 145, 248, 291, 312, 326, 343
Brazier, G. 95, 213, 311
Brener, L. 60
Bresnahan, M. 62
Brewer, M. B. 6, 15, 16, 17, 19, 33, 40, 44, 57, 106, 120, 189, 195, 316, 341
Brickman, P. 273, 340
Brief, A. P. 251
Brigham, J. C. 191, 199
Brissette, I. 140
Britt, T. W. 183, 184
Broadbent, D. E. 152
Brodsky, A. E. 241
Brody, S. M. 315, 319
Bromley, S. 105
Brown, A. C. 340
Brown, J. D. 271
Brown, L. 77
Brown, R. 33, 123, 125, 135, 304, 319, 340, 347
Brown, R. J. 15, 17
Brown, S. L. 14, 37, 107, 178, 180, 295, 323
Brownell, K. D. 60, 71
Brudney, J. L. 260
Bruins, J. 255
Bryan, J. H. 290

Buckley, T. 4, 182
Bujantugs, B. 67
Bull, R. 43, 81, 218, 294, 312
Bundy, R. P. 41, 212, 297
Burgetova, K. 114
Burnstein, E. 16, 37, 39
Burrows, L. 113
Buss, D. M. 14, 15, 22, 27
Butler, R. 275
Butner, J. 14
Byrne, D. 291
Byrne, S. 282

Cable, D. M. 259
Cacioppo, J. T. 73
Callan, V. J. 148
Campbell, D. T. 19, 192, 311
Capitanio, J. P. 62, 65
Caporael, L. 19
Carlo, G. 246
Carver, C. S. 140
Cascio, T. A. 247, 253, 256
Cassidy, C. 9, 43, 81, 95, 213, 216, 218, 290, 291, 292, 294, 306, 311, 312, 344
Castro, C. A. 77
CBS/Associated Press 114
Chagnon, N. A. 20, 22, 24
Chaiken, S. 70
Chai-Tcherniak, L. 274
Chamberlin, J. 230
Chan, F. 60
Chang, J. 69, 184, 344
Chang, K. 16
Chang, W. 226
Chavis, D. M. 228, 241
Checkoway, B. 230
Chen, M. 113
Cheng, C. M. 60
Chesney, M. 141
Chryssochoou, X. 137
Cialdini, R. B. 14, 37, 39, 47, 106, 107, 178, 180, 181, 230, 295, 323
Cihangir, S. 323, 329
Clark, M. S. 4, 55, 106

Clark, R. D., III 4, 36, 103, 107, 182, 192, 295, 337
Clary, E. G. 53, 81, 82, 162, 163, 246, 247, 248, 253, 261, 262, 264
Clore, G. L. 345
Cnaan, R. A. 246, 247, 253, 256, 260
Coates, D. 273
Coates, T. 141
Cochrane, S. 298
Cocking, C. 219
Cohen, A. 291
Cohen, S. 107
Cohn, E. 273
Colangelo, M. F. 162
Coleman, J. S. 224
Collins, A. 210, 290, 345
Comeau, J. 320
Condor, S. 141, 297
Conger, R. D. 275
Conklin, L. 177
Connors, J. 67
Cooper, C. L. 140, 144
Cooper, P. F. 152
Corcoran, D. M. 4, 55
Cornman, D. H. 282
Corrigan, P. W. 64, 67, 71, 78, 230
Cosmides, L. 14, 19, 20, 23, 39
Cotter, P. R. 241
Cotting, D. I. 77
Cottrell, C. A. 22
Cowling, M. J. 234
Coyne, J. C. 230
Crain, A. L. 43, 226, 229, 231
Crandall, C. S. 16, 65, 66, 68, 103, 104, 108, 110
Crean, T. 230
Crisp, R. J. 189, 196, 349
Crocker, A. S. 149
Crocker, J. 59, 84, 107, 124, 230, 252, 274
Crosby, F. 105, 109, 329, 343
Cuddy, A. J. C. 88, 312
Cullen, F. T. 78

Cunningham, M. R. 39, 41
Curtis, J. E. 223, 243
Curtis, M. 350
Czajka, J. M. 151
Czopp, A. M. 104

Dailey, R. C. 255
Daly, M. 17, 234
D'Anello, S. 66
Dardis, G. J. 17
Darley, J. M. 108, 209, 210, 211, 214, 290, 324
Darwin, C. 13, 24
Dasgupta, N. 61
Davidson, W. B. 241
Davis, M. H. 4, 8, 37, 106, 115, 177–178, 182, 188, 245
Dawis, R. V. 251
Dawkins, R. 30
Dawley, D. D. 256
Dawson, K. 184, 323
Deci, E. L. 84, 85, 161
DeCoster, J. 70, 113
De Cremer, D. 19, 23, 27, 271
Deelstra, J. T. 84, 98
De Gilder, D. 247, 248, 255
De Guzman, M. R. T. 246
DeJong, W. 67
De Liver, Y. 79
Dempster-McClain, D. 159
Deneen, N. E. 104
Des Jarlais, D. C. 67
Deutsch, R. 70, 71
Deveau, M. 323, 333, 344
Devine, P. G. 70, 72, 104, 105, 113
Devos, T. 346
De Waal, F. 17, 22, 24–25
de Weerd, M. 340
Diaz-Loving, R. 106
Dietrich, S. 67
Dijker, A. J. 42, 67, 79
Dion, K. L. 339, 347
Dixon, J. A. 191
Dohrenwend, B. P. 78
Dolnik, L. 327

Doosje, B. 16, 123, 127, 128, 132, 248, 312, 343, 350
Doucet, N. 34, 81, 110, 212, 311, 326
Doverspike, D. 281
Dovidio, J. F. 4, 6, 9, 15, 31, 34, 35, 36, 37, 45, 55, 60, 71, 76, 95, 103, 104, 105, 106, 110, 114, 122, 124, 132, 179, 181, 182, 186, 188, 191, 192, 193, 194, 195, 196, 197, 198, 201, 202, 204, 206, 207, 212, 222, 245, 269, 283, 284, 295, 311, 312, 313, 319, 325, 327, 337
Drury, J. 219, 298, 305
Dubé-Simard, L. 340, 347
Duck, J. 148
Dugatkin, L. A. 39
Duijnhoven, P. H. M. 252, 254
Dull, V. 44
Dumont, M. 349
Duncan, B. D. 4, 182
Duncan, L. A. 63, 71
Dunham, H. W. 227
Dunham, Y. 64
Dunlop, L. 75
Dunton, B. C. 70, 104, 105
Durkheim, E. 160, 169, 171, 305
Durrheim, K. 191
Dutton, D. G. 34, 212, 296
Dweck, C. S. 64
Dwyer, L. 146

Eagly, A. 28, 30, 312
Earls, F. 241
Early, S. 182
Ebert, R. 71
Eder, D. 29
Eggins, R. A. 99, 149
Ehrhart, K. H. 259
Eisenberg, N. 36, 107, 182
Eisenberger, R. 81
Elgueta, A. 61
Ellemers, N. 9, 93, 123, 125, 127, 128, 129, 132, 147, 247, 248, 250, 251, 252, 254, 255,

256, 257, 260, 262, 323, 341, 343
Elliott, G. C. 161, 162, 163, 171
Ellis, S. 275, 276
Ellison, M. L. 230
England, G. W. 251
Epley, N. 179
Eshleman, A. 68, 103, 104, 108, 110
Esses, V. M. 95, 312, 321
Evans, D. 81, 181, 215, 295, 311, 337

Faber, D. 230
Fabes, R. A. 36
Farina, A. 64
Farmer, S. M. 247, 258, 266
Farnham, S. D. 78
Farr, M. J. 349
Faulkner, J. 20, 21, 23, 31
Fazio, R. H. 60, 70, 72, 104, 105, 113
Feather, N. T. 66
Fedor, D. B. 247, 258, 266
Fehr, E. 16
Feldman, D. B. 65
Felix, K. 60
Fenn, C. 298
Ferber, A. L. 338
Feshbach, S. 205
Finkelstein, M. A. 42, 46, 56
Finlay, K. A. 179, 190
Fischer, A. H. 348
Fischer, A. T. 227
Fischer, E. H. 275
Fishbein, M. 201
Fisher, J. D. 121, 122, 123, 269, 271, 272, 278, 282
Fisher, R. J. 245, 250, 259
Fisher, W. A. 282
Fiske, S. T. 31, 44, 88, 192
Fitness, J. 326, 329
FitzGerald, P. 152
Flament, C. 41, 212, 297
Florack, A. 197
Florin, P. 241

Folkman, S. 141, 142, 143
Forin, P. 241
Foster, J. B. 105
Foushee, H. C. 106
Frank, P. 106
Frazier, S. 45, 95, 181, 194, 212, 284, 295, 311
Freeman, S. 230
Freitas, A. L. 184
Freshley, H. B. 33
Frey, D. L. 324
Frey, L. 248
Friedland, R. P. 159–160
Friedman, D. 140
Friedmann, R. 241
Frijda, N. H. 345, 346, 347, 348
Fuentes, R. 281
Fuller, J. B. 248, 252, 253
Fultz, J. 107
Furnham, A. 140

Gabriel, S. 29, 60
Gächter, S. 16
Gade, P. 63
Gaertner, S. L. 4, 9, 31, 33, 34, 36, 45, 55, 95, 96, 103, 104, 105, 106, 110, 114, 129, 181, 182, 186, 191, 192, 193, 194, 195, 197, 198, 201, 204, 206, 212, 283, 284, 295, 311, 312, 313, 319, 324, 325, 337
Gailliot, M. T. 39, 183
Galea, S. 67
Galindo-Kuhn, R. 252, 253, 261, 262
Galinsky, A. D. 178, 179, 189
Gallup Poll 63
Galper, R. E. 176
Gamson, W. A. 6
Gapinski, K. 60
Garcia, G. 71
Gardner, W. L. 29, 73
Garst, E. 184, 323
Gaunt, R. 70
Gawronski, B. 70

Geller, D. 275, 276, 277
Gelles, R. J. 162
George, D. 312
Gerard, H. B. 23
Gerrard, M. 230
Gibbons, F. X. 230
Gide, A. 139
Gidron, B. 262
Gilbert, D. T. 70, 84, 93, 113
Gilbert, M. 291
Gilovich, T. 179
Glasgow, N. 159
Glass, D. 107
Glick, P. 88
Goffman, E. 59, 60
Goldberg-Glen, R. S. 246
Goldstein, J. 17, 25
Gollwitzer, P. M. 106
Goodall, J. 18, 22, 25
Goode, M. 333
Goodman, D. J. 338, 343, 348
Gordijn, E. H. 349
Gottlieb, A. 211
Govorun, O. 60
Grabb, E. 223
Graetz, K. A. 17
Gramsci, A. 306
Grandfield, T. A. 60
Grant, A.-M. 161, 171
Grant, P. R. 340, 347
Greenberg, J. 87
Greening, D. W. 259
Greenwald, A. G. 60, 61, 72, 78, 113
Grobbee, D. E. 17
Grube, J. A. 163, 248
Gruder, C. L. 211, 290
Gruenewald, R. A. R. 22
Gschwendner, T. 61
Guerra, R. 206
Guimond, S. 340, 347
Gump, P. V. 164
Gunn, D. G. 226
Gunter, H. N. 312
Gurney, J. N. 342
Gustavo, C. 107

Guzley, R. M. 252, 253, 261, 262

Hackler, A. H. 78
Haddock, G. 321
Haidt, J. 68, 75
Haig, S. C. 179, 188
Halabi, S. 8, 17, 32, 43, 55, 81, 83, 85, 96, 122, 124, 128, 129, 130, 131, 132, 133, 137, 207, 253, 270, 271, 279, 280, 281, 312
Hall, J. A. 245
Hall, L. L. 71
Hall, N. R. 189
Hallinan, M. T. 29
Hamilton, W. D. 24, 39
Handy, C. 250
Handy, F. 260
Harber, K. D. 119
Hardy, C. 17, 24, 32, 81, 271
Harley, K. 299
Harmon-Jones, E. 70
Harpaz-Gorodeisky, G. 84, 133, 137, 271, 274, 277, 280, 281, 284
Harris, M. 250
Harrison, K. 43, 81, 218, 294, 312
Hart, C. M. 16
Harth, N. S. 351, 352
Harvey, O. J. 133
Haslam, C. 8, 148, 149, 151, 306
Haslam, N. 188
Haslam, S. A. 8, 10, 50, 99, 141, 142, 143, 144, 145, 148, 149, 151, 152, 156, 213, 247, 255, 295, 298, 299, 300, 301, 302, 303, 304, 305, 306, 307, 308, 327, 340
Hass, R. G. 104, 116
Hastorf, A. H. 70
Hauser, R. M. 163
Hauser, T. S. 163
Heaven, P. C. 67
Hebl, M. R. 64, 70, 105

Hedges, S. J.   113
Heilman, M.   212
Heilman, M. E.   281
Henderson, J. G.   275
Henkel, K. F.   114
Herek, G. M.   62, 65, 77
Herscovitch, L.   255
Herzog, A. R.   160
Hesson-McInnis, M.   70
Hester, K.   248
Heuston, S.   349
Hewitt, L. N.   159
Hewstone, M.   15, 196, 319
Hexmoor, H.   84
Hilberg, R.   216
Hilden, L. E.   105
Hill, J. L.   227
Hinkle, S.   16
Hirschman, R.   67
Hixon, J. G.   113
Hoar, S.   299
Hockett, J. M.   105
Hodgson, S. A.   212
Hodson, G.   197, 312
Hoes, A. W.   17
Hoffman, J. C.   64
Hoffman, M. L.   35, 36
Hoffmann, W.   61
Hoge, C. W.   77
Hogg, M. A.   4, 15, 89, 123, 142, 186, 192, 196, 211, 230, 247, 290, 298, 299, 313, 316
Holme, A.   151, 152, 306
Holmes, J. G.   333
Holmes, T. H.   144, 146
Hood, W. R.   133
hooks, b.   338
Hopkins, N.   43, 55, 81, 89, 90, 97, 213, 216, 218, 291, 292, 293, 294, 296, 299, 300, 302, 305, 307, 312, 344
Hornsey, M. J.   143, 146, 196
Hornstein, H. A.   4, 37, 212
Horowitz, I. A.   290
Houlette, M. A.   312
Houlihan, D.   107

House, J. S.   159, 160
Howard, A.   76
Hoyle, R. H.   17
Hoyt, D. R.   275
Hoyt, M. F.   23
Hughey, J.   227, 230
Hulin, C. L.   251
Hulsenbeck, K.   60
Hunter, A. J.   90, 189
Hunter, S. B.   71
Huo, Y. J.   352

Independent Sector   224
Insko, C. A.   17, 26, 99, 133, 192
Ironson, G.   141
Israel, B. A.   230
Iyer, A.   8, 10, 147, 149, 151, 152, 154, 155, 306, 329, 340, 343, 345, 346, 347, 348, 349, 350, 351, 352

Jackman, M. R.   136, 338
Jackson, J. R.   70, 104
Jackson, L. A.   42
Jackson, L. M.   95, 312
Jackson, P. B.   327
Jacobi, K. A.   275
Jacobs, E.   141
Janikula, J.   158
Janowitz, M.   241
Janssen, D. P.   19, 23
Jauernig, N. J.   325
Jellison, W. A.   60
Jenner, J. R.   255
Jetten, J.   8, 128, 141, 142, 143, 144, 145, 147, 148, 149, 150, 151, 152, 155, 196, 218, 293, 297, 306
Jeyaram, S.   60
Johnson, B.   76, 95, 181, 194, 212, 284, 295, 311
Johnson, B. T.   191
Johnson, C.   76
Johnson, D.   141
Johnson, D. D. P.   17, 23
Johnson, E.   63

Johnson, G. 95, 325
Johnson, J. 9
Johnson, J. D. 198
Johnson, K. M. 312
Jonas, E. 87
Jones, E. E. 63, 316
Jones, J. M. 104
Jose, P. E. 346
Jost, J. T. 114, 135
Judd, C. M. 16, 197, 207

Kafati, G. 197
Kaiser, C. R. 145
Kampmeier, C. 150, 234
Kamzan, M. 33, 106, 212
Kang, M. 184, 323
Kang, N. 241
Kao, S. 161, 171
Karabenick, S. A. 33, 106
Karacanta, A. 326, 329
Kari, N. N. 223
Karuza, J., Jr. 273
Kasarda, J. 241
Kashdan, T. 316
Katz, I. 70, 79, 104, 107, 116
Katz, J. H. 343
Kawachi, I. 242
Kawakami, K. 60, 72, 76, 197, 319, 339, 347
Keegan, J. 22, 24, 25–26, 32
Keeley, L. 17, 20
Keller, J. 39, 41
Kelly, C. 339
Kendall, L. M. 251
Kennedy, B. P. 242
Kenny, D. A. 53
Kenrick, D. T. 14, 106
Kenzine, D. 67
Keridis, D. 284
Kerr, N. L. 195
Kessler, T. 351
Keyes, C. L. M. 161
Keysar, B. 179
Kidder, L. 273
Kim, H. S. 146
Kimmel, M. S. 338

Kingston, S. 241
Kinias, Z. 146
Kippax, S. 60
Kirchner, J. L. 99
Kitayama, S. 16
Kiviniemi, M. T. 226
Kivivuori, J. 31
Kjellin, L. 64
Klandermans, B. 340, 341, 342
Kleck, R. E. 70
Klein, L. C. 22
Klein, O. 89
Klein, T. R. 37
Knight, G. P. 246
Knight, P. A. 276
Knight, R. T. 39
Koffman, R. L. 77
Komarovskaya, I. 60
Komorita, S. S. 86
Koomen, W. 67, 79
Kowai-Bell, N. 71
Kramer, R. M. 41, 195
Krebs, D. 35, 37, 39
Kroll, N. 39
Kropp, A. 16, 79, 81, 183, 286
Ku, G. 179
Kubiak, M. 67
Kuipers, P. 347
Kuppuswamy, B. 270
Kurzban, R. 14, 18, 19, 20, 31, 43, 63, 70
Kwak, N. 241
Kymlicka, W. 224

La Guardia, J. G. 85
Lake, R. A. 34, 212, 296
LaKind, E. 212
Lalonde, R. N. 327
Lambda Legal HIV Project 77
Lambert, S. 38–39
Landau, S. 70
LaPierre, R. T. 105
Latané, B. 108, 209, 210, 222, 290, 324
Lawless, H. 38–39
Laws, J. L. 328

Lawson, L. 259
Lazarus, E. 66, 143
Lazarus, R. S. 141, 142, 145, 349
Leach, C. W. 10, 16, 329, 340, 341, 343, 345, 346, 347, 348, 349, 350, 351, 352
Leary, M. 230
Leary, M. R. 19, 20, 43, 63, 70
Le Bon, G. 289, 304
Lederach, J. P. 281
Lee, D. H. 226
Lee, G. 60
Lefebvre, G. 304
Lerner, M. J. 67, 187, 333
Lerner, R. M. 33, 106
Lever, J. 29
Levin, S. 205
Levine, J. M. 16
Levine, M. 9, 43, 81, 91, 95, 96, 97, 120, 181, 188, 210, 213, 215, 217, 218, 290, 291, 292, 294, 295, 304, 305, 308, 311, 312, 337, 344
Levine, R. M. 142, 145
Levine, R. V. 65
Levy, S. R. 184, 185, 187, 188
Lewandowski, G. 315
Lewin, K. 139, 147
Lewis, B. P. 14, 22, 37, 180, 295, 323
Lewis, L. D. 211, 290
Leyens, J.-P. 16, 17, 41, 188, 192
Li, N. P. 14
Liao-Troth, M. A. 256
Lickel, B. 71, 343, 350
Lieberman, M. D. 70, 72
Lin, M. 44
Lindsay, J. J. 226
Lindsey, S. 113
Link, B. G. 62, 78
Linville, P. W. 149, 153
Lipsitz, G. 343
Little, J. S. 282
Lochner, K. 242
Loewy, M. 246

Lofquist, L. H. 251
Long, D. A. 241
Lord, C. 327
Lowery, L. 71
Lubensky, M. E. 325
Luce, C. 14, 37, 107, 177, 178, 180, 295, 323
Luhtanen, R. 84, 107, 124, 230, 252, 274
Lui, L. 44
Luoh, M.-C. 160
Lynch, P. D. 81
Lyons, R. F. 230

Macintyre, K. 77
Mackie, D. M. 61, 186, 346, 347, 348, 349
Macrae, C. N. 113
Mael, F. 151, 247
Magnussen, J. 66
Main, K. J. 89, 90, 189
Maitner, A. T. 8, 186
Major, B. 59, 84, 107, 124, 146, 274
Malle, B. F. 28, 116
Malsch, A. M. 224, 234
Mandisodza, A. N. 114
Maner, J. K. 26, 27, 39, 107, 178, 180, 183
Mania, E. W. 129
Manis, M. 44
Mann, J. A. 194
Mann, L. 340
Manning, R. 210, 290
Mannix, L. M. 64, 105
Mansell, T. 348
Manstead, A. S. R. 128, 196, 218, 293, 312, 343
Manucia, G. K. 106
Marcus-Newhall, A. 105
Markowitz, F. E. 67
Marks, S. R. 161
Markwith, M. 64
Marques, J. M. 16
Martin, J. 62, 340
Martino, S. C. 225

Marx, G. T. 338
Mashek, D. 315
Mason, D. 325
Masor, H. N. 212
Massar, B. 324
Matoka, K. 45, 95, 181, 194, 212, 284, 295, 311
Matschinger, H. 67
Mauss, M. 270
McCall, G. J. 161
McCarthy, J. D. 342
McCauley, C. 64, 75
McConahay, J. B. 104
McConnell, A. R. 60, 61
McCullogh, B. C. 161, 171
McDonald, T. W. 327
McDougall, W. 35
McGarty, C. 141, 298, 348, 350
McGhee, D. E. 60
McGregor, J. 190
McGurk, D. 77
McKimmie, B. M. 145
McKusick, L. 141
McLaughlin-Volpe, T. 315, 320
McLeod, J. 62
McMahon, K. 159
McManus, J. L. 8, 115, 118
McMillan, D. W. 228
Mead, N. 333
Mechanic, D. 275
Medin, D. L. 39, 41
Meen, J. 340
Meertens, R. W. 104
Mehta, S. I. 64
Meier, R. B. 241
Meijs, L. C. M. P. 260
Mellor, J. M. 242
Mellott, D. S. 78
Memmi, A. 343
Mendes, W. B. 71
Merkel, W. T. 275
Messer, S. C. 77
Meyer, J. P. 251, 255
Meyer, M. 245
Michael, J. H. 259
Mickelson, K. 67, 230

Milgram, S. 304
Miller, C. T. 34, 81, 107, 110, 116, 118, 119, 145, 212, 311, 326
Miller, D. L. 348, 350
Miller, D. T. 67, 333
Miller, F. E. 64
Miller, L. E. 255
Miller, N. 193
Millman, L. 64
Mills, J. 4, 55
Milne, A. B. 113
Milyo, J. 242
Mirowsky, J. 160
Mitchell, R. 241
Moen, P. 159
Moffat, K. B. 324
Moghaddam, F. M. 327, 337
Moïse, L. C. 197
Moller, A. C. 85
Monroe, A. E. 7
Monroe, K. R. 216
Montada, L. 347, 350, 352
Monteiro, M. B. 206
Monteith, M. J. 104, 105, 113
Montjabi, R. 275
Moretti, M. M. 316
Moriarty, D. 65
Morrison, D. 299
Morrison, E. W. 275
Moscovici, S. 304
Moskowitz, G. B. 178, 179, 189, 192
Moss, M. K. 106
Mueller, A. 21
Mullen, B. 340
Mummendey, A. 205
Murray, A. 340
Murrell, A. J. 194
Musick, M. W. 160

Nadler, A. 8, 10, 17, 32, 43, 55, 81, 83, 84, 85, 91, 94, 96, 121, 122, 123, 124, 126, 128, 129, 130, 131, 132, 133, 134, 137, 207, 253, 269, 270, 271,

272, 274, 275, 276, 277, 278, 279, 280, 281, 282, 284, 312, 323, 338
Nagengast, B. 63
Napier, J. L. 114
Nelson, T. E. 44
Nemeroff, C. 64
Neuberg, S. L. 14, 18, 22, 37, 44, 64, 107, 178, 180, 295, 323
Neuman, O. 275
Neumann, R. 60, 72, 73
Newman, S. 158
Nickerson, R. S. 179
Nida, S. 209, 222, 290
Niemann, Y. F. 327
Nier, J. A. 195, 204, 312
Nishi, T. 122
Nolan, M. A. 327
Norenzayan, A. 65
Norman, W. 224
Norton, D. W. 282
Norton, M. I. 312
Nosek, B. A. 61, 78, 135
Novelli, D. 298

Oakes, P. J. 4, 89, 123, 141, 142, 186, 192, 211, 213, 230, 290, 295, 298, 302, 313, 327
O'Brien, A. 141, 142, 148, 149, 306
O'Brien, K. 113
O'Brien, L. 68, 104
O'Brien, L. T. 226
O'Campo, P. J. 241
O'Connell, G. B. 89
Oegema, K. 342
Oei, T. P . S. 146
O'Gorman, R. 24
Oishi, S. 240, 241
Okun, M. A. 246
Olafsdottir, S. 62
Olfson, M. 275
Oliner, P. M. 216, 290
Oliner, S. P. 216, 290
Olson, J. M. 340

Olson, K. R. 64
Olson, M. O. 60
Oman, D. 159, 160
Omoto, A. M. 9, 16, 43, 46, 79, 81, 183, 223, 224, 225, 226, 227, 229, 231, 232, 234, 240, 243, 245, 246, 247, 248, 296, 337
Onawola, R. 158
O'Neal, E. C. 105
Ong, J. 105
Ono, H. 70
Oostenbrink, J. 90, 98
Orr, R. 69, 184, 344
Ortony, A. 39, 41, 345
Oskamp, S. 223
Ostman, M. 64
Ostroff, C. 251
Otten, S. 192

Pachankis, J. E. 77
Pagano, S. J. 352
Page, R. A. 106
Palmer, C. T. 24
Pandey, J. 292
Paolucci, M. P. 176
Park, B. 16, 197, 207
Park, J. H. 7, 14, 20, 21, 23, 31, 37, 39, 40, 60
Parkes, K. R. 152
Parks, C. D. 86
Pate, S. 38–39
Patel, A. 7
Payne, B. K. 60
Pearce, J. L. 245, 246, 247, 250, 253, 258
Pedersen, A. 329, 343, 348
Peeters, M. C. W. 84
Pemberton, M. B. 26
Penna, S. 141, 306
Penner, L. 6, 15, 35, 36, 42, 46, 56, 76, 106, 122, 245, 246, 265, 269, 313, 337
Peplau, A. 115
Perez, M. 316
Perkins, D. D. 241

Perrault, S. 197
Perry, R. B. 66
Pescosolido, B. 62
Peterson, D. 18, 25
Peterson, N. A. 227
Pettigrew, T. F. 104, 191, 319, 339
Pew Research Center 62, 63
Phelan, J. C. 62
Philbrick, K. 65
Phills, C. E. 60
Piliavin, I. M. 4, 106, 295, 311, 313
Piliavin, J. A. 4, 6, 8, 15, 35, 36, 76, 103, 106, 110, 122, 163, 182, 192, 245, 248, 269, 295, 311, 337
Pinter, B. 26
Piontkowski, U. 197
Plant, A. E. 105
Plant, E. A. 70
Platow, M. 299
Pollard, C. A. 275
Polycarpou, M. P. 69, 184
Portes, A. 224
Postmes, T. 149, 152, 297
Powell, A. A. 326, 329
Powell, G. N. 255
Pratkanis, A. R. 348
Pratto, F. 19, 23, 28, 63, 116, 131, 132, 136, 205
Prayag Magh Mela Research Group 305
Prenovost, M. 146
Prentice-Dunn, S. 104
Prosser, A. 81, 181, 215, 295, 311, 337
Pruett, S. 60
Pryor, J. B. 7, 60, 70, 72, 73, 76, 77
Putnam, R. D. 153, 224, 243
Pyszczynski, T. 87

Rabinowitz, V. C. 273
Rafaeli-Mor, E. 149
Rahe, R. H. 144, 146

Ranade, S. 260
Rappaport, J. 230
Rashid, F. 230
Rasinski, K. 71
Rath, R. 218, 305
Raudenbush, S. W. 241
Rawlins, M. 60
Realo, A. 223
Reay, D. 154
Rebelo, M. 206
Reed, A. II 180
Reeder, G. D. 7, 70, 76
Regan, D. T. 106, 176
Reicher, S. 4, 10, 43, 81, 89, 95, 123, 141, 142, 181, 186, 192, 211, 213, 215, 216, 218, 219, 230, 289, 290, 291, 292, 293, 294, 295, 296, 297, 298, 299, 300, 301, 302, 303, 304, 305, 306, 307, 308, 309, 311, 312, 313, 337, 344
Reid, S. 299
Reid, S. A. 312
Reis, H. T. 320
Relyea, C. 248
Rexwinkel, B. 81
Reykowski, J. 325
Reynolds, K. J. 99, 122, 149, 278, 298, 327
Rhoades, L. 81
Rhodes, A. 106
Richard, N. T. 10, 329
Richardson, P. 25
Rick, B. M. 129
Roberts, G. 24
Robertson, D. J. 340
Roccas, S. 150
Rock, M. S. 312
Rodin, J. 4, 106, 295, 311
Rodriguez, M. 340
Roese, N. J. 340
Rogers, E. S. 230
Rogers, R. W. 104
Rohmann, A. 197
Romer, D. 211, 290
Roseman, I. J. 346, 347, 348

Rosenberg, M. 161, 171
Rosenbrock, R. 5
Rosenman, R. H. 140
Rosenthal, A. M. 210
Ross, C. E. 160
Rothbart, M. 39, 41
Rowan, D. 67
Rowland, J. 69, 184, 344
Roy, S. A. 90, 189
Rozin, P. 64, 71, 75
Rubchinsky, K. 184, 323
Rubin, M. 15
Rubin, Z. 115
Rudman, L. A. 78
Runciman, W. G. 339, 344
Ruscher, J. B. 105
Russell, F. J. 64
Rust, M. C. 195, 204, 313
Rutkowski, G. K. 211, 290
Ryan, R. M. 84, 85, 161
Rydell, R. J. 61
Ryff, C. D. 163
Rynes, R. L. 259

Sabucedo, J. M. 340
Sachdev, I. 137
Saegert, S. 242
Saenz, D. 327
Sagarin, B. J. 107, 178, 323
Sager, K. 184, 187, 188, 189, 323
Saguy, T. 9, 121, 133, 197, 282
Sahlins, M. 121, 122
Said, E. 292
Sakalli, N. 66
Salovey, P. 184
Salvarani, G. 182
Sampson, R. J. 241
Sani, F. 151, 307
Sarason, S. B. 228
Sartori, G. 148
Sassenberg, K. 85
Saucier, D. A. 8, 34, 57, 81, 105, 107, 110, 111, 112, 113, 115, 116, 118, 119, 212, 311, 326
Sax, L. J. 158

Saxe, L. 105
Sayer, D. 306
Scarnier, M. 350
Schaller, M. 14, 20, 21–22, 23, 31, 37, 39, 40, 63, 71, 107
Schaufeli, W. B. 84
Scheier, M. F. 140
Scheiner, M. J. 85
Scheltema, K. E. 87, 271
Scherer, K. R. 346
Schimel, J. 87
Schlenker, B. R. 183, 184
Schlozman, K. L. 224
Schmader, T. 343, 350
Schmitt, D. P. 22
Schmitt, M. 61
Schmitt, M. T. 145, 326
Schnedler, R. 106
Schneider, A. 347, 350, 352
Schneider, M. E. 84, 93, 98, 107, 124, 274
Schooler, T. Y. 113
Schopler, J. 17, 26, 133
Schreiber, P. 24
Schroeder, D. A. 4, 6, 15, 35, 36, 37, 76, 106, 122, 182, 201, 245, 269, 295, 313, 337
Schulz, A. J. 230
Schwartz, J. E. 56
Schwartz, S. H. 211
Schwartz, S. L. K. 60
Schweiger, J. A. 327
Seacat, J. D. 67
Sears, D. O. 104
Sechrist, G. B. 176
Seeman, M. 160
Segal, D. 63
Seibt, B. 60
Sekaquaptewa, D. 119, 327
Seltzer, J. 255
Sewell, W. H. 163
Shaw, L. L. 35, 36, 37
Shedler, J. 44
Sherif, C. W. 133
Sherif, M. 56, 133, 193
Sherman, D. K. 146

Sherman, J. W. 60, 113
Shih, M. 132
Shlomniuk, E. 130, 135
Shnabel, N. 9
Shotland, R. L. 211
Shrout, P. E. 78
Sibicky, M. E. 37, 57
Sidanius, J. 19, 23, 28, 63, 116, 131, 132, 205
Sieber, S. D. 161
Siegl, E. 163
Siem, B. 16, 51, 57, 79, 81, 183, 286
Sikes, J. 17, 188
Silvera, D. H. 84, 93
Silverman, R. A. 327
Simmons, C. 187
Simmons, J. L. 161
Simon, B. 43, 45, 150, 230, 246, 248, 318, 340, 341
Singh, P. 292
Sleebos, E. 248
Sloan, L. R. 230
Sloman, S. A. 70, 72
Slopen, N. 71
Smart, S. A. 271
Smeesters, D. 327
Smith, A. 35, 177
Smith, D. M. 64, 225, 243
Smith, E. R. 70, 113, 186, 345, 346, 347
Smith, H. J. 339
Smith, J. R. 312
Smith, P. C. 251
Smith, R. H. 106
Smith, S. J. 8, 115
Smolej, M. 31
Smollan, D. 178, 321
Snapp, M. 17, 188
Snider, N. 340
Snyder, M. 5, 7, 9, 16, 17, 43, 46, 79, 81, 82, 183, 223, 224, 225, 226, 227, 229, 231, 232, 234, 240, 243, 245, 246, 247, 248, 286, 296, 337
Sole, K. 212

Sommer, K. L. 29
Sonn, C. C. 227
South End Press Collective 347
Sparkman, P. 38–39
Spears, R. 16, 123, 127, 128, 132, 145, 196, 218, 248, 293, 312, 343, 348
Spector, P. 251
Speer, A. L. 107
Speer, P. W. 227
Spelke, E. S. 64
Spence, M. 259
Spindel, M. S. 346
Springer, K. W. 163
Stallworth, L. M. 28, 116
Stanley, D. J. 255
Steele, C. 59
Steele, J. 316
Steele, J. R. 60
Steffens, K. 43, 246, 318
Steinberg, J. 149
Stephan, C. 17, 188
Stephan, C. W. 40, 42
Stephan, W. G. 40, 42, 179, 190
Stephens, D. B. 256
Stephens, R. D. 256
Stevenson, J. 241
Stewart, B. D. 60
Stone, C. H. 189
Stone, V. E. 39
Stotland, E. 35, 37
Stott, C. 305
Strack, F. 70, 71, 73
Strain, L. M. 61
Straw, M. K. 211
Strayer, J. 182
Stroebe, W. 84
Struening, E. L. 78
Stryker, S. 161
Stueve, A. 62
Stukas, A. A. 82, 234
Stürmer, S. 7, 16, 43, 45, 47, 51, 56, 57, 79, 81, 96, 120, 183, 234, 246, 248, 286, 296, 318, 337, 340
Suedfeld, P. 141

Sullivan, L. A. 42
Sullivan, M. J. 230
Suls, J. 230
Swanson, J. 61
Swartz, C. 242
Swartz, T. S. 347
Swim, J. K. 348, 350
Switzer, G. 107

Tajfel, H. 16, 18, 41, 49, 82, 89, 123, 124, 125, 128, 133, 139, 141, 161, 192, 193, 196, 211, 212, 230, 245, 246, 247, 295, 297, 303, 316, 339, 341, 345
Täuber, S. 8, 85, 92, 94
Taylor, D. M. 313, 327, 328, 337
Taylor, H. F. 327
Taylor, M. 39, 41
Taylor, S. E. 22, 192
Teachman, B. A. 60, 67, 71
Tec, N. 290
Teger, A. 211, 290
Tenbrunsel, A. E. 259
Terry, D. J. 148, 247, 299
ter Shure, E. 347
Tesser, A. 230
Test, M. A. 290
Tett, R. P. 251
Thoits, P. A. 151, 159, 161, 327
Thomas, E. 113
Thompson, B. 338, 343, 348
Thompson, M. 327
Thomson, A. 60
Thoresen, C. E. 159
Thorne, A. 230
Tidwell, M. V. 247
Tiedens, L. Z. 345, 346
Tierney, K. J. 342
Tilley, C. F. 24
Tocqueville, A. de 135–136, 270
Todorov, T. 216, 295
Toi, M. 182
Tooby, J. 14, 19, 20, 23, 39
Tooman, G. D. 104
Topolnytsky, L. 255
Totten, J. 176

Tougas, F. 326, 329
Toussaint, L. L. 327
Tracy, M. 67
Trasselli, C. 63
Tredoux, C. 191
Trindall, N. 142
Trivers, R. L. 19, 39, 55
Trope, Y. 70
Tropp, L. 191, 319
Tropp, L. R. 315, 325, 340
Tross, M. 67
Troyer, D. 107
Trujillo, L. 77
Tsivrikos, D. 147, 149, 152
Tsivrikos, T. 155
Turban, D. B. 259
Turk, C. L. 37
Turner, J. C. 4, 16, 18, 19, 40, 50, 82, 89, 122, 123, 124, 125, 128, 133, 135, 139, 141, 142, 143, 161, 186, 192, 193, 196, 211, 213, 230, 245, 246, 247, 278, 290, 293, 295, 296, 298, 299, 302, 303, 304, 313, 316, 339, 341, 345
Turner, M. E. 348
Turner, R. N. 349
Turpie, C. A. 189, 326
Turpin, G. 60
Tyler, T. R. 5, 223, 224, 245, 246, 247, 248, 249, 299

Uggen, C. 158
Uhlmann, E. 60
Underwood, P. W. 155
United States Department of Labor 224, 232
Useem, M. 338
Utman, C. H. 85

Valde, J. G. 275
Validzic, A. 45, 95, 181, 194, 212, 284, 295, 311
Vanbeselaere, N. 327, 340
Van Boven, L. 179
Vance, S. L. 70

Author Index

van der Pligt, J. 79
Van Der Zande, C. C. 320
van Doornen, L. P. 84
van Knippenberg, A. 93, 125, 248
van Knippenberg, D. 299, 341
van Lange, P. A. M. 15
van Leeuwen, E. 8, 32, 55, 85, 87, 90, 92, 94, 98, 218, 312
Van Rijswijk, W. 255
van Vugt, M. 5, 7, 14, 15, 16, 17, 19, 23, 24, 27, 28, 32, 81, 223, 224, 271
Van Willigen, M. 160
van Zomeren, M. 348, 349
Vargas, P. 119
Vasudev, J. 158
Veenstra, K. 340
Veilleux, F. 326, 329
Verba, S. 224
Verkuyten, M. 197
Vescio, T. K. 176, 179, 188
Vevea, J. L. 26
Vlahov, D. 67
Vogel, D. L. 78
Vohs, K. 333
von Hippel, W. 60, 119
Vorauer, J. D. 89, 90, 189, 326
Vormedal, K. 141, 306

Wadden, T. A. 60
Wade, N. G. 78
Walker, A. 136
Walker, I. 339, 340
Walker, M. R. 230
Wallenberg, A. S. 105
Waller, J. 348
Walsh, J. 196
Walther, E. 63, 71
Wandersman, A. 241
Wang, S. S. 60
Wann, D. L. 16, 132
Ward, C. M. 195, 204, 313
Watson, A. C. 64, 67, 71, 78
Webster, J. M. 106
Weihs, K. 275

Weiner, B. 66–67, 68, 69, 72, 337
Weiss, D. J. 251
Weiss, H. M. 276
Welch, I. D. 114
Wenzel, M. 205
Wesselmann, E. D. 76
West, S. G. 106
Wetherell, M. S. 4, 89, 123, 142, 186, 192, 211, 230, 290, 298, 313
Whatley, M. A. 106
Whitcher-Alagna, S. J. 122
White, B. J. 133
Whitney, G. 106
Widaman, K. F. 62
Wieczorkowska, G. 66
Wiest, C. 347
Wigboldus, D. 79, 349
Wilder, D. A. 40, 41, 193
Wildschut, T. 99
Wilke, H. 93, 125, 248, 341
Williams, C. J. 104
Williams, J. C. 70
Williams, K. D. 76
Williams, R. M., Jr. 159
Williams, W. H. 151, 152, 306
Williamson, G. M. 106
Willis, H. 15
Wills, T. A. 230
Wilschut, T. 26
Wilson, D. S. 24
Wilson, E. O. 13
Wilson, J. 158, 160, 246
Wilson, J. G. 60
Wilson, M. 17
Wilson, T. D. 113, 291
Winer, D. 275
Winkel, G. 242
Wirth, J. 76
Wispé, L. G. 33
Wit, A. P. 195
Witte, D. R. 17
Wittig, M. A. 340
Wolf, S. T. 99
Wolpert, I. 216, 291, 344

Wolsko, C. 197, 207
Wong, F. Y. 87, 271
Wood, W. 30
Worchel, P. 316
Worchel, S. W. 87, 121, 271
Worman, B. 38–39
Wrangham, R. W. 18, 25
Wright, M. T. 5
Wright, S. C. 10, 313, 315, 316, 317, 319, 320, 321, 322, 325, 327, 328, 329, 333, 337, 339, 340
Wu, E. J. W. 251, 252, 257, 262

Xu, J. 88

Yates, P. 148
Yeadon, C. 70
Yogananda, P. 305
Young, B. M. 155
Young, F. W. 159
Yzerbyt, V. Y. 16, 349

Zald, M. N. 342
Zanna, M. P. 321
Zdaniuk, B. 16
Zeelenberg, M. 346
Zhou, S. C. 316
Ziegert, J. C. 259
Zijlstra, F. R. H. 84
Zimbardo, P. 23, 211, 289, 304
Zimmerman, M. A. 230

Subject Index

Note: page numbers in *italics* denote figures or tables

acculturation   197–198, 206–207
adaptations   14–15, 18–20
adjustment
  social identity theory   146–150, *152*
  university students   152–155, 178
adults/children relations   314
advantaged group members
  helping out-groups   325, 337–338
  high-status   94, 340
  open/closed systems   328, 330–331
  paternalism   338
  self-relevance   344–345
  social injustice   343
  status assertion   312
  tokenism   328–333
  see also in-groups
affect
  collective action   347
  intergroup conflict   26
  stigma   59, 60, 63–64
  see also emotion
Affective Misattribution Procedure   60
affirmative action   281, 321
Afghanistan   26
Africa   282–283
aggression   17, 22, 23–24, 25, 105

AIDS community   242–243
  buddy programs   5, 232
  implicit attitudes   62, 72
  in-group/out-group members   79
  responsibility for   66, 69
  stigma   60, 229
  volunteers   6, 42, 46–47, 229, 318
  see also HIV/AIDS
AIDS service organization   232, 235, 238
alienation   160–161
altruism
  competitive   17, 24
  cross-group   312
  existence of   107
  helping   36–37, 183–184
  including-others-in-the-self   322–323
  inequality   271
  motivation   35–37
  personality   290
  reciprocity   63, 71
  shared group membershp   311
  social psychological theory   33
Americans' Changing Lives dataset   159
anger   27, 331–332, 343, 349–350, 351–352, 353

Subject Index

anti-fat attitudes 66, 76
  see also obesity
anti-racist activists 338
anti-stigma interventions 67
appraisal theorists 347
approach and avoidance motor tendencies 71–72
arousal 110–111, 182
assimilation 197, 200–201, 204, 206–207
attachments 16, 20, 255
attention deficit hyperactivity disorder 62
Attitudes toward Blacks Scale 198–199, 201
attractiveness
  buddy volunteers 52
  helping 45, 46, 51, 56, 57
  in-groups 46–47
  out-groups 44, 46–47, 57
attribution-emotion-action theory 66
attribution/stigma 65–70, 72, 176–177
Australia
  non-Aboriginals 350, 351
  Queenslanders 145–146
autonomy 83, 84–87
autonomy-oriented help 129–131, 272–275
  empowerment 83, 91–92, 126, 253
  Intergroup Helping as Status Relations 134–135
  Israeli Jews 132–133
  knowledge quiz 86
  university students 276–277
aversion 36, 60–65, 298
aversive racism theory 103, 110, 111–113

BBC Prison study
  Commune 307–308
  organization/power 302–303
  Prisoners/Guards 299–303
belongingness 29, 63, 230

Bennett, Arnold 146
bias 22–23, 33, 188, 191–193, 212
bias reduction/recategorization 191, 193–194, 205–206
bilingual education ending 321
Black Americans
  assumptive help 124
  Colgate study 198–202
  discriminatory behavior 191
  dual identity 199–201
  IAT 72
  seen as threat 71
  students getting help 84–85
  unemployment 104
  and White Americans 60, 176–177, 179, 195–196, 324
Black children, Portugal 206
black sheep effect 16
blaming the victim 68–69
Blanco, Kathleen 113
blind people 68
bravery 27–28
  see also heroism
Britain
  anger at US invasion of Iraq 350
  university students study 152–153, 154
  welfare state 220
  see also football fans; Scots example
buddy volunteers 5, 51–52, 232
budget-cutting task 321–322
Bulgaria 216–217, 291, 293, 294
Bureau of Statistics 144
burns patients volunteering 254
Bush, George W. 113, 114
bystander effect
  cross-group helping 325
  groups 209–210, 211, 213–214, 290
  social identity theory 211, 221–222
bystander intervention 9, 209, 289–290, 324–325

Subject Index

California minority groups
    legislation 321
Canadian studies 21, 23
cancer cure volunteers 251
change
    coping with 150–153, 155
    identity 147, 153–155
    organizations 150–151
    resistance to 147
    see also adjustment; life changes; social change
Child Rights Information Network 220–221
chimpanzee studies 18, 25
Christians/Muslims 60
civic participation 230–231, 243
coalitions 22, 23–24, 25, 31
cognitive misers 192
Colgate University study 198–202
collective action 337
    affect 347
    participation 345–352
    self-interest 340–342
    social identity 293–301
    social (in)justice 10, 338–345
Collective Self-Realization 304–308
color preferences study 29
commitment 127, 131–133, 255–258
Common In-Group Identity Model
    applicability 195
    bias 192
    Colgate study 198–202
    dual identity 197
    intergroup helping 193–194, 283–285
    recategorization 186–187, 191, 206
commonalities 55, 97
    see also identity, common
community 235, 237
    connectedness 236, 237
    identification 235–236, 237, 241
    individuals 242
    involvement 224
    legacy of 236–237, 240
    as place/process 227–228
    psychological 228–231, 234–240
    self-esteem 229–230
    social action 237, 240–242
    social capital 241–242
    successful 236, 237
    volunteering 5, 9, 226–228, 231–234
community building 238, 239–240
compensation 36, 350
competence in helping 91–95
competition
    intergroup relations 17, 24, 95
    for resources 19
    social 86
    sports 26
complexity, cognitive models of 149
conflict resolution 190
Congressional Black Caucus 114
connectedness 38–39, 236, 237
consensualization 298, 307
cooperation
    common threat 219–220
    jigsaw classroom example 17
    knowledge quiz 86
    shared goals 99
    social identity-based model 245
    trust 281, 282
    volunteerism 5
coping 140–142, 150–153, 155, 230
cost-reward model 103, 182
courtesy, everyday 292
cross-group helping 315–319
    altruism 312
    ambiguity 324–327
    bystander effect 325
    everyday occurrences 334
    as exception 6
    friendships 319–320

Subject Index 437

including-others-in-the-self 319–322
intergroup helping 318–319
motivation 34
personal/collective identity 318
reciprocity 32
reluctance 323–324
similarity 312–313
cultural similarity 48–49, 50–53
culture shock 140
Current Population Survey 157, 232
customer service behaviors 105
Cyberball study 77

danger, beliefs about 32, 62–63
decategorizing process 99, 193, 194, 207
deindividuation theory 304
Delaware, University of 195–196
deliberative processes 72–75, 78
Denmark 291
dependency
 chronic 274–275, 279–281, 285–286
 relations 87, 271
 transient 274–275, 281, 286
dependency-oriented help 129–131, 272–275
 disempowering 91–92, 126
 Intergroup Helping as Status Relations 127, 134–135
 Israeli Jews 132–133
 knowledge quiz 86
 recipients 253
 refusal of 85
 university students 276–277
Descent of Man (Darwin) 13
developing countries 257, 330–331
developmental differences 29
diabetes research volunteers 256
dialysis patient example 178
disabilities, people with 60, 65, 70

disadvantaged out-groups 10, 327–328, 329, 337–338, 352
 see also low-status groups
discrimination
 emergencies 111–113
 financial cost of helping 117–119
 helping 35, 103, 274
 homosexuality 65
 Hurricane Katrina 113–116
 intergroup 19, 33
 justifying 120
 motivation 106
 out-groups 8, 54–55
 reverse 34
 social acceptance of 68
 social categorization 193
 tokenism 328
 verbal disapproval 323–324
 see also racial discrimination
disgust 71, 75, 297, 298
disloyalty, punished 16
dissociation model of prejudice 104
distancing 65, 178
distress 36, 141, 182, 183
dominance: *see* social dominance
domination, symbolic 122
drug abuse 60, 68, 69
drug addict study 184, 344, 352
dual identity
 assimilation 206
 Black Americans 199–201
 common identity 202–204
 process 189, 196–198
 recategorization 205
dual-process model of stigma 7, 59, 70–76
Dutch entries: *see* Netherlands

earthquake diplomacy 284–285
effervescence (Durkheim) 305
emergency situations
 dependency-oriented help 273
 discrimination 111–113
 groups 211

emergency situations (*cont'd*)
  intervention   209
  out-groups   57, 103
  shared groups   9
  social identity   214–215
emotion
  appraisal theorists   347
  group-based   345–352, 353
  perspective-taking   182–185
  self-categorization   345–346
  stigma   75
empathy
  AIDS volunteerism   42
  attachments   16
  with drug abusers   69
  group-level perspective   49
  helping   14–15, 36–37, 46, 47–50, 81
  in-group/out-group distinctions   47–50
  in-groups   79
  kin   79
  out-group helping   42, 183–185
  perspective-taking   182
  self-relevance   344–345
  similarity   41–42, 52
empathy–altruism hypothesis   36, 37–38
esteem enhancement   162
ethnic groups   320–321
eudaimonia   161–162, 169
European Union   137
eustress   141
evolutionary biology   14, 30
evolutionary cost-benefit analysis   21
evolutionary psychology   30, 63–65
evolutionary social psychology   13, 14–15

facial disfigurement   60, 71
Federal Emergency Management Agency (FEMA)   113, 116
feeling good about oneself   162
female warriors   25

fight-or-flight   19
Finland   291
focus of attention manipulation   329–330, 331, 333
football fans example   96–97, 181–182, 214–216, 295, 349
forced compliance paradigm   107
free-rider problem   24
French Revolution   304–305
friendships   29, 315–316, 319–320, 322
functional projection   26–27

Gallup Organization   63, 157
game-playing behavior   76
gay men: *see* homosexual men
gender differences
  belongingness   29
  biases, intergroup   22–23
  developmental   29
  discontinuity effect   26
  intergroup relations   17, 18
  scholastic achievement   130–131, 135
  selection pressures   30
  sex appeal   24
  social identity processes   28–29
  socialization   25
  status relations   130
  stress   143
  warfare   25–26
gender-role theories   30
Genovese, Kitty   209, 210, 219, 221, 289–290
Germany
  Chinese enterprises example   94
  disadvagtaged groups   352
  inequalities study   350
  Nazism   216
  Turks study   48–49, 50–53
Gide, André   139
giving, unreciprocated   121–122
Good Samaritan study   214–215
Greece   137, 284–285
group conflict theory   19

group membership
  adaptations 14
  belongingness 63
  bystanders 209–210, 211, 213–214, 290
  consensualization 298, 307
  emergency intervention 211
  emotion 345–352, 353
  helping 4, 7, 37–40, 83–84, 308–309
  individuals 127, 131–133
  leadership 299
  multi-perspectives 7
  multiple memberships 151, 152–153
  norms 218
  physical/psychological 289–290
  prosocial behavior 3, 4, 33
  for protection 20
  recategorization 9
  resource allocation 41
  self-reliance 295–296
  shared membership 9, 311
  social identity 290, 293–294, 303–304, 345–347
  sociality 6
  stress 142, 145
  structural factors 5–6
  survival 24
  trust 40–41
  volunteering 252
  see also social groups
group-level perspectives 6, 41, 49, 57–58
guilt 343, 350–351, 352
Guinea Bissau 330–331

health issues 153, 165–171
hedonism 161–162
help
  assumptive 124, 274–275, 280, 281
  deciding not to 31, 71, 108, 110, 111–113, 324–327
  deciding to 107–108
  offering 93
  rejected 121
  stigma 77–78
  as threat 121–122, 129, 136–137
  under-/overutilization 275, 276–277
  unsolicited 98
  withholding of 34
  see also autonomy-oriented help; dependency-oriented help
helping
  altruism 36–37, 183–184
  ambivalence 70, 133
  attractiveness 45, 46, 51, 56, 57
  and attribution 66–67
  competence 91–95
  costs/benefits 14–15, 44, 182
  discrimination 35, 103, 274
  empathy 14–15, 36–37, 46, 47–50, 81
  group level 4, 7, 37–40, 83–84, 308–309
  in-group 10, 27, 192, 289
  in-group/out-group distinctions 16, 33, 40–44, 45–50, 56, 57
  interpersonal contact 4, 8, 109–110, 136, 269–270
  motivation 34–35, 36–40, 55, 106–107
  natural disasters 38–39
  out-groups 7, 33–34, 43–44, 55, 56–57, 81–84, 103, 192, 217–219, 222, 296, 337–338
  power inequalities 121, 280
  prejudice 198–205
  race 8, 34, 326
  racial discrimination 109–113, 119–120
  social identity 82, 212–213, 217–219
  solidarity 309
  status assertion 32, 87, 122, 280–281
  sustained 4–5, 9
  transaction costs 42–43, 44

helping (cont'd)
    types of 87–89, 124, 218, 349–351
    warmth 89–91, 98
    see also cross-group helping; intergroup helping; recipients of helping
helping relations 279, 283
help-seeking behavior 86, 273–274, 275, 276–277, 283
heroin addict study 344, 352
heroism 27–28, 290, 308
heterosexual men studies 324, 326
high-status groups: see Intergroup Helping as Status Relations model (IHSR)
Hinduism 270, 292, 306
Hispanics/skin color 60
HIV/AIDS
    Africa 282–283
    buddy programs 5, 232
    contamination fear 61–62, 64
    homosexuality 67
    responsibility for 66, 69
    stigma 34, 77
    volunteerism 228, 232–233
    see also AIDS community
Holocaust 216, 290, 291, 293, 294
homosexual men 60, 62–63, 65–66, 67, 324, 326
humanness 188, 192, 285, 313
Hurricane Katrina
    discrimination in helping 113–116
    financial cost of helping 118
    victims' perceptions 103, 115–117

IAT: see Implicit Associations Test
ICM/Guardian survey 26
identification
    collective 219–220, 248
    community 235–236, 237, 241
    group 28–29, 95, 153
    in-group 131–133, 300–301
    well-being 306
    see also social identification
identity
    common 194–196, 197, 202–204, 219–220, 285
    differentiation 149–150
    group-based 7, 83–84, 87–88, 147–148, 213, 222, 247
    multiple 150–155
    national 98
    personal/collective 318, 341–342
    roles 248
    self-categorization theory 123
    sense of self 148, 156
    shifting 147, 148, 153–155
    social change 139–140
    social group membership 139
    superordinate 151, 182, 198
    volunteering 165
    work-group 148–149
    see also dual identity
identity loss 140–142, 147
IHSR: see Intergroup Helping as Status Relations
illegal immigrants legislation 321
Implicit Associations Test (IAT) 60, 72, 78
impression formation 84, 88–95, 198–199
inbreeding, avoidance of 24–25
including-others-in-the-self 315, 317–318, 319–323, 334–335
Inclusion of Other in Self (IOS) scale 178
Independent Sector 157, 224
individuals
    assimilation 200–201
    community 242
    helping 290
    society 291–292
    submergence 304
Indonesia 350
inequalities
    collective responsibility 343
    experiences of 345–347

Subject Index   441

illegitimate   341, 347
intergroup relations   299–303
multiple responses to   347–352
outrage   350
perceptions of   346–347
power   121, 123–124, 280
recipients   270
restitution   348
social   83, 84, 269, 270–271, 280–283
social identity theory   303–304
in-group/out-group distinctions   4
  AIDS patients   79
  commonalities   97
  cultural backgrounds   48–49
  empathy   47–50
  helping   16, 33, 40–44, 45–50, 56, 57
  helping studies   105–106
  humanness, levels of   192
  intergroup helping   17, 44, 311–312
  intervention   213–214
  motivation   40–44
  perspective-taking   175–176
  recategorization   186–187
  Sterna antillarum (least tern)   175, 190
  tribalism   6
  warfare   13
in-groups
  anger   351–352
  attractiveness   46–47
  bias   33, 212
  commitment   127
  dominance   32
  empathy   79
  helping   10, 27, 192, 289
  identification   131–133, 300–301
  self-similarity   50
  social identity   8
  status-maintenance   17
  stereotyping   89
  well-being of   57

in-group-serving functions
  helping out-groups   83–84
  impression management   88–95
  meaning and existence   87–88
Integrated Social Identity model of Stress (ISIS)   141–142, 147, 155, 306
intergroup conflict   17, 19–20, 26, 30–31
intergroup contact hypothesis   319–322
intergroup helping
  Common In-Group Identity model   193–194, 283–285
  constraints   313
  cross-group helping   318–319
  in-group/out-group distinctions   17, 44, 311–312
  minority groups   207
  motives not to   323
  overcoming inequality   283–285
  power dynamics   10, 121, 137–138
  real-world helping   280–283
  recategorization   195
  reciprocity   56
  social tension   133
  status relations   125, 278–285
Intergroup Helping as Status Relations model (IHSR)   122, 123–124, 270, 278–285
  autonomy/dependency-oriented help   126
  Common In-Group Identity model   284–285
  determinants   124–127
  HIV in Africa   282–283
  intergroup tensions   134–135
  motivations   132–133
  real-world   280–283
  supporting data for   127–133
  Threat to Self-Esteem model   285–287
  types of help   129–131, 134–135

442 Subject Index

intergroup psychology 13, 14–15, 325–326
intergroup relations 3–4, 15–18, 313–315
  cognition and behavior 25–26
  Common In-Group Identity Model 193–194
  competition 17, 24, 95
  discrimination 19, 33
  gender differences 17, 18
  inequalities 299–303
  interpersonal closeness 320–321
  Prisoners/Guards 299–303
  social identity 191
  social identity theory 82, 341
Internet 243
interpersonal closeness 315, 320–321
interpersonal contexts
  helping 4, 8, 109–110, 136, 269–270
  oneness 37
  stigma 76
interracial relationships 34
Iraq 350, 351, 352
Iraqi participants, Canadian study 23
ISIS model: *see* Integrated Social Identity model of Stress
Israel
  Arabs/Jews 17, 124, 128–129, 131, 132, 133, 135
  female warriors 25
  high school experiment 130, 135
  Oslo Agreement 121, 282
  Palestinian Territories 121, 188, 282

Jackson, Jesse 114
Japanese/Koreans 60
Jewish people 216–217
  see also Holocaust; Israel
Jewish religion 270
jigsaw classroom example 17, 188, 190

jogging accident study 181–182, 215–216, 295
justification-suppression model 68, 103, 104, 108, 110, 111

"Katie Banks" story example 181, 184–185
kidney donation 312
Kindness of Strangers, The (George) 312
King, Martin Luther 293–294
kinship 24, 39–40, 79
knowledge quiz example 85–86, 92, 94
Koran 270
Koreans/Japanese 60

leadership 299, 300
life changes 141, 144, 146–147, 148–149, 156
Liverpool Football Club fans 215–216, 295
lost letter paradigm 212
Louisiana hurricane emergency: *see* Hurricane Katrina
low-status groups
  competence 92
  defensive behavior 131
  dependence issues 126
  exploiting high-status group 134
  help as threat 124, 136–137
  psychological losses 94
  social identity 129
  social identity theory 339–340
  social injustice 353

macro-level analysis 5, 9–10, 76–78
Magh Mela, Allahabad 292, 306
Major League Baseball 241
male warrior hypothesis 15, 23–25
  bravery/heroism 27–28
  evidence for 25–29

Subject Index   443

gender differences   22–23
mating opportunities   22, 23, 24
natural selection   30
out-group threats   27
social identity processes   28–29
social play activities   29
tribal instinct hypothesis   25–29
Manchester United fans   215–216, 295
mating opportunities   22, 23, 24
mattering in society   161–162
mental illness
  combat veterans   77
  as label   71
  stigma   60, 65, 66, 67, 275
  violence   62
  volunteering   158–159
meso-level analysis   5, 76–78
meta-stereotypes   89, 90, 189
micro-communities, stability   241
micro-level analysis   5, 76–78
minority groups   21, 107, 116, 191, 207, 321
monetary donation   330, 332, 333–334
moral regard, circle of   180
Moseley, Winston   210
motivation
  altruistic   35–37
  cross-group   34
  discrimination   106
  egoistic   35–37
  goals   348–349
  helping   34–35, 36–40, 106–107
  in-group/out-group distinctions   40–44
  out-group helping   81–83, 286–287
  perspective-taking   188
  prejudice   105
multiculturalism   197, 204, 206–207
multi-level selection theory   24
Muslims/Christians   60

Namibia   330–331
nationalism   302
nation-states   121–122, 302, 314
natural disasters   38–39, 218, 284–285
natural selection   13, 30
Nazi Germany   216
  see also Holocaust
Netherlands
  cancer cure volunteers   251
  diabetes research volunteers   256
  guilt over Indonesia   350
  Ministry of Social Affairs   260
  soccer fans study   17
  tsunami disaster   87–88, 218
  university study   90–91
  volunteer organizations   257
New York Times   210
non-verbal behavior   76, 105

obesity   60, 66, 67, 71
occupations
  disadvantaged groups   340
  stress   145, 306
on, Japan   270–271
oneness, feeling of   37, 180–181
organizations
  BBC Prison study   302–303
  change   150–151
  commitment   255
  volunteering   5, 246–247
Oslo Agreement   121, 282
out-group helping
  by advantaged groups   325, 337–338
  benefits   55
  bystanders   325
  costs of   43–44
  empathy   56–57, 183–185
  genuine   322–323
  and in-groups   33–34
  meaning and existence   87–88
  motivation   81–83, 286–287
  perspective-taking   176–177, 180–182, 183–185, 186–189
  reputation   296

out-group helping (*cont'd*)
  self-relevance 344–345
  social identity 217–219
  see also recipients of help
out-group members in self 315
out-groups
  aggression against 17
  anger-perception 27
  attractiveness 44, 46–47, 57
  avoidance of 31, 334–335
  bias 191, 192
  dependence 84
  discrimination 8, 54–55
  disliked/feared 187–188
  emergency help 57, 103
  empathy for 42
  evaluation potential 90–91
  female 27
  help from 122, 311–312
  perspective-taking 186–190
  proximation 298
  and self 315
  socialization to help 43
  stigmatized 7, 185
  threat 21
overhelping 84
over-/under-estimators experiment 128, 181, 194–195, 297–298

paid work/volunteering
  comparisons 247, 251–252, 255–256
Palestinian Territories 121, 188, 282
Paramanand 305
participation
  civic 230–231
  collective action 345–352
  health and well-being 165–171
  non-volunteers 262–263
  recruitment to volunteering 164–165
  social 163–165
paternalism 107, 136, 282, 338
patriarchal society 279
patrilocal groups 24–25

peace-building projects 281–282
peacemakers 17, 22
peer counseling position 104
Pericles 156
personal responsibility 65, 66–69, 73
perspective-taking
  attribution 176–177
  bias 188
  drug addict 184, 344
  effectiveness of 185–190
  emotional response 182–185
  empathy 182
  in-group/out-group distinctions 175–176
  interracial 179
  motivation 188
  oneness 181
  out-group helping 176–177, 180–182, 183–185, 186–190
  prejudice 179
  projection 179
  self-relevance 344–345
  stereotypes 179
pity 72
Polakov, Todor 294–295
political correctness 61
population density 19
Portugal 206
Potlach 270
power inequalities 121, 123–124, 280
power relations 10, 83, 84–87, 127
prejudice
  avoidance of 110, 212–213
  control of 78–79
  dissociation model of 104
  genuine 68, 108
  helping 198–205
  justification-suppression model 104
  non-reactive 212
  perspective-taking 179
  racial 103–105, 191, 198–199, 326

Subject Index

social sanctions 104–105, 110
Sri Lanka 22
stigma 72
suppression of 104, 113
tribalism 21
pride
 anticipated 258–260, 261–263
 volunteer organization 9, 248, 250–251, 253
 volunteers 252, 253–255, 257, 263–265
primates studies 39
 see also chimpanzee studies
prisoner's dilemma games 17
projection 179, 205
prosocial behavior
 collective 9–10
 common identity 194–196
 groups 3, 4, 33
 long-term benefits 160–162
 stigma 59, 76–78
 tradition of 243
Protagoras 210
proximity preferences 297, 298
public goods 242
public policy 220

Queenslanders study 145–146

race
 attitudes 60, 76
 coalitions 31
 helping 8, 34, 326
 scholarships 118–119
 superordinate category 195
 unemployment 104
 US 192, 206
 wage levels 104
 see also Black Americans; White Americans
Racial Argument Scale 118
racial discrimination
 Colgate Study 198–202
 employment 104
 guilt 350, 352

helping situations 109–113, 119–120
Hurricane Katrina 113–116
racial prejudice 103–105, 191, 198–199, 326
racism 104, 114–115, 326
rape 27, 209
real-world helping 280–283
recategorization
 assimilation 204
 bias reduction 191, 193–194, 205–206
 Common In-Group Identity Model 186–187, 191, 206
 dual identity 197, 205
 groups 9
 in-group/out-group distinctions 186–187
 intergroup helping 195
 multiculturalism 204
 self-relevance 344–345
 superordinate group 189, 191, 205, 216
recipients of help
 inequality 270
 paradox 277–278
 reluctance 280–281
 self-esteem 121, 123, 271–272, 275
 stress 99
 Threat to Self-Esteem model 269–270, 271–272, 277–278
 volunteering 232–233, 253
 see also help-seeking behavior
reciprocal altruism 39, 71
reciprocity
 altruism 63, 71
 cross-group 32
 food-sharing 19
 helping 81
 intergroup helping 56
 self–other 38–39, 40
 social 55
recruitment to volunteering 164–165, 245, 246–247, 258–259, 264–265

Relative Deprivation 313, 340
reputation 294, 295–296
rescue 216–217, 291–292
resource allocation 14, 41, 342
respect
  anticipated 258–260, 261–263
  volunteer organizations 248, 250–251, 253
  volunteers 9, 253–255, 257, 263–265
responsibility
  AIDS/HIV 66, 69
  anger 349
  collective 343
  diffusion of 209
  internal attributions 347
  personal 65, 66–69, 73
restitution 350–351, 353
reverse discrimination 34
Richardson, Bill 113
risk contract theory 23
role accumulation approach 161
role identity 248
romantic relationships 315–316
rule-based processes 72–75

sacrifice 27, 308
schizophrenia 60, 62
scholastic achievement 130–131, 135
Scots example
  and English 218–219
  reputation 294
  stereotypes 89–90, 97
selection pressures 22, 30
self-categorization 123, 193, 278–279
  bystanders 211
  collective 317–318
  emotions 345–346
  identity 123
  social identity 295, 296–297, 302
self-esteem
  collective 122, 131, 230, 248
  community 229–230

competence-based 98
enhancement 162
getting help 78, 84–85
minority groups 107
recipients of help 121, 123, 271–272, 275
social change 93
social identity theory 161–162
volunteerism 82
self-expansion 315, 316, 319, 334–335
self-focused emotions 37
self-interest 106–107, 340–342
self-other representations 7, 37–40, 54, 177–179
self-relevance 344–345
self-reliance 273, 278, 295–296
self-stigma 77–78
Serbs/Croats 188
sex differences: *see* gender differences
Shia/Sunni Muslims 188
similarity
  cross-group helping 312–313
  cultural 48–49, 50–53
  intergroup 41, 51, 54
  preferred 316
  self–other 40, 50, 51–52, 54
Sinhalese 21–22
SIT: *see* social identity theory
smell, sense of 298
smokers, stigmatized 60
social action 223–224, 237, 240–242
social capital 224, 234, 241–242
social categorization 192–193
social change 10, 93, 139–140, 280–283
social class 154–155
social dominance 28, 83, 127, 131–133, 134
social groups 139, 151–152, 296
social identification
  collective self-realization 305–308
  cycle of *301*, 309

Subject Index 447

enhanced 144–145
virtuous circle of 301–306
social identity
  co-action 293–301
  cooperation 245
  emergency situations 214–215
  groups 290, 293–294, 303–304, 345–347
  helping 82, 212–213, 217–219
  in-groups 8
  intergroup contact 191
  intervention, practical 31
  leadership 299
  low-status groups 129
  processes 8, 28–29, 246, 247–249
  public places 219
  public policy 220
  self-categorization 295, 296–297, 302
  self-relevance 344
  social reality 305
  solidarity 293–301
  stress 141, 142–146
  support 299
  threat 134
  volunteer organizations 249–251
Social Identity Model of Adjustment to Identity Change 146–150
social identity theory (SIT)
  adjustment 146–150, *152*
  bystander effect 211, 221–222
  groups 209, 293–294, 303–304, 345–347
  intergroup relations 82, 341
  low-status groups 129, 339–340
  power inequality 123–124
  relative deprivation 313
  self-esteem 161–162
  social categorization 192–193
  status relations 135, 247
  stereotypes 89
  volunteering 245, 259

social inequality 83, 84, 269, 270–271, 280–283
social injustice 10, 338–347, 353
social integration 160–161, 169, 255, 264
social justice 10, 337–345, 347–348, 353
social mobility 155, 304
social movements 338, 342–343
social play activities 29
social psychological theory 33, 171, 269
social reality 305, 306
sociality 6, 14, 19
socialization 25, 30, 43
society/individuals 291–292
solidarity
  in context 301–306
  helping 309
  intragroup 6
  psychology of 292
  reputation 294
  social 10, 289
  social identity 293–301
Sri Lanka 21–22
Stanford Prison Experiment 22–23
status assertion 32, 122, 270–271, 312
status relations
  gender relations 130
  intergroup helping *125*, 278–285
  maintaining 17
  security of 124–126, 128–129, 136
  social identity theory 135, 247
  volunteer organization 245, 252–253, 259–260
  see also Intergroup Helping as Status Relations model (IHSR)
stereotypes
  danger-relevant 21–22, 31
  in-groups 89
  mental illness 62
  perspective-taking 179

stereotypes (*cont'd*)
  Scots example 89–90, 97, 218–219
  social identity theory 89
  stigma 59, 61–63, 64–65
  warmth/competence 88–89
Sterna antillarum (least tern) 175, 190
stigma
  abominations of body 59, 60, 71
  affective response 59, 60, 63–64
  AIDS community 60, 229
  anger 72
  attribution 65–70, 72, 176–177
  aversion 61, 63–65, 71, 72
  contamination 64
  as cue 42
  delayed response to 72–73
  deliberative process 78
  dual-process model 7, 59, 70–76
  emotion 75
  help, asking for 77–78
  HIV/AIDS patients 34, 77
  hospital patients study 73–75
  illness 65, 66
  instinctual 70–72, 79
  mental illness 65, 275
  moral character flaws 59, 60
  personal responsibility 66–69, 73
  prejudice 72
  prosocial behavior 59, 76–78
  reflexive processes 70–72
  self 77–78
  stereotyping 59, 61–63, 64–65
  tribal 59, 60
  uncontrollable 66, 73, 75
  Weiner's model 66–70
stigmatization 185, 229
stigmatized groups 5, 7, 34, 60–65, 78
street gang members 24

stress
  and coping 140–142
  gender differences 143
  groups 142, 145
  identity loss 147
  occupations 145, 306
  social identity 141, 142–146
  transitions 140, 146
  video testing 143
strokes 148–149, 151–152, 306
students: *see* university students
superordinate category
  football fans example 216
  helping 312–313
  identity 151, 182, 198
  race 195
  recategorization 186–187, 189, 191, 194–196, 205
support 296, 299, 300
support groups 146
Sweden 220–221
sympathy 69, 352

Tamils 21–22
task performance, reduced 327
terns example 175, 190
Thatcher, Margaret 220
Thomas, Oliver 114
threat
  in common 38
  cooperation 219–220
  deviance 42
  out-groups 21
  social identity 134
  stigma 71
Threat to Self-Esteem model
  dependency 273, 275–278
  Intergroup Helping as Status Relations 279, 285–288
  recipients 269–270, 271–272, 277–278
tokenism
  advantaged group members 328–333
  ambiguity 328, 333

disadvantaged out-groups 10,
    327–328
discrimination 108
job satisfaction 327
reduced task performance 327
transaction costs 42–43, 44
travelers' tales 312
tribal instinct hypothesis 15
    Allport 57
    evolutionary origins 18–20
    intergroup psychology 29–30
    male warrior hypothesis 25–29
    specific groups 20–22
tribal psychology 19, 23–25
tribalism 6, 13, 15, 18
trust 40–41, 281, 282
tsunami disaster 87–88, 97–98
Turkish earthquake 284–285

uncertainty reduction motives
    316
under-manning theory 164
unemployment 104
United States of America
    Foreign Services 77
    homosexuality in military 63
    invasion of Iraq 350
    race relations 192, 206, 352
    see also Black Americans; White
        Americans
University of California at Santa
    Cruz 330–334
university policies study (UCSC)
    330–334
university students
    adjustment 152–155, 178
    Black 84–85
    conceptions of elderly 178–179
    reluctance to seek help 275
    seeking help 276–277
    social class 154–155
    teachers 314

victim-blaming 68–69
victims' perceptions 115–117
violence 31, 62, 220–221

volunteer organizations
    empowering 265–266
    engagement with 249
    human resources 258–259
    Netherlands 257
    pride 9, 164–165, 248,
        250–251, 253
    recruitment 245, 246–247,
        258–259, 264–265
    respect 248, 250–251, 253
    social identity 249–251
    status evaluation 245, 252–253,
        259–260
    successfulness/recruitment
        259–260
Volunteer Process Model
    224–226, 231–234
volunteering 4–5
    benefits 82, 157–160, 166–169,
        223
    community 5, 9, 226–228,
        231–234
    developing countries 257
    effectiveness 234
    formal/informal 224
    group status 252
    identity 165
    motivation 162, 169
    optimum amounts 159–160,
        167
    organizational problem
        246–247
    public policy 171–172
    recipients 232–233, 253
    self-esteem 82
    social identity theory 245, 259
    social participation 163–165
volunteers
    age of 157, 158–159, 163, 164
    AIDS community 6, 42,
        46–47, 228–229, 232–233,
        318
    attachment 255
    co-workers 264
    pride 252, 253–255, 257,
        258–260, 263–265

volunteers (*cont'd*)
  respect 9, 253–255, 257, 263–265
  retention of 255–258
  satisfaction 53, 226, 251–255
  social integration 255, 264
  support for 253–254, 261–263, 265–266
  well-being 8, 158–159, 170–171, 172

wage levels 104
war heroes 24
warfare 13, 23, 25–26, 27
welfare state 220
well-being
  collective self-realization 305–308
  identification 306
  in-groups 57
  life changes 156
  participation 165–171
  psychological 8, 165–171
  social/psychological 161
  volunteering 158–159, 170–171, 172
West, Kanye 114
Westchester State University 195–196
White Americans
  and Black Americans 60, 176–177, 179, 195–196, 324
  Black dual identity 199–201
  Colgate University study 198–202
  discriminatory behavior 191
  prejudice avoidance 212–213
  racial discrimination 352
  students giving help 84–85
Wisconsin Longitudinal Study 162–163
work motivation 247–249
  see also paid work/volunteering comparisons

Yanomamo tribe 20, 24